MODERN POETRY

Modern Poetry

AMERICAN

AND

BRITISH

EDITED BY

KIMON FRIAR

AND

JOHN MALCOLM BRINNIN

New York

APPLETON-CENTURY-CROFTS, Inc.

ACKNOWLEDGMENTS

LÉONIE ADAMS for her poem "The Runner with the Lots."

GEORGE ALLEN & UNWIN, LTD. for "The Jungle" from *Ha! Ha! Among the Trumpets* by Alun Lewis.

DJUNA BARNES for selections from *Nightwood*.

R. P. BLACKMUR for his poem "The Dead Ride Fast."

BRANDT & BRANDT for "Winter for a moment takes the mind" and "Rimbaud and Verlaine, precious pair" from *Preludes for Memnon*, published by CHARLES SCRIBNER'S SONS, copyright, 1930, 1931 by Conrad Aiken; "what if a much of a which of a wind" and "no man, if men are gods" from *One Times One*, published by HENRY HOLT & COMPANY, copyright, 1944, by E. E. Cummings, "somewhere i have never traveled" from *Viva*, published by HORACE LIVERIGHT, INC., copyright, 1931, by E. E. Cummings; "The Return" from *Wine from These Grapes*, published by HARPER & BROTHERS, copyright, 1934, by Edna St. Vincent Millay, "Only the diamond and the diamond's dust" and "Here lies, and none to mourn him" from *Wine from These Grapes*, published by HARPER & BROTHERS, copyright, 1928, by Edna St. Vincent Millay.

JOHN MALCOLM BRINNIN for his poem "The Worm in the Whirling Cross."

CHATTO & WINDUS for "Strange Meeting" from *The Poems of Wilfred Owen*; and "God," "A Worm Fed on the Heart of Corinth," "Midsummer Frost," "My Soul Is Robbed," and "Dead Man's Dump" from *The Collected Works of Isaac Rosenberg*.

THE CLARENDON PRESS for "The Storm is Over," "Nightingales" and "Poor Poll" from Robert Bridges' *Poetical Works*: by permission of The Clarendon Press, Oxford.

CREATIVE AGE PRESS, INC. for "Milk at the Bottom of the Sea" by Oscar Williams, reprinted by permission of the author and *Tomorrow* magazine.

THE CUMMINGTON PRESS for "Seasons of the Soul" from *The Winter Sea* by Allen Tate; and "Burning the Christmas Greens," "The Clouds," and "The Monstrous Marriage" from *The Wedge* by William Carlos Williams.

CURTIS BROWN, LTD. for "Reading Time: 1 Minute 26 Seconds" and "Rotten Lake Elegy" from *Turning Wind*, copyright, 1939 by Muriel Rukeyser, reprinted by permission of the author.

THE JOHN DAY COMPANY for "Country Summer" reprinted from *The High Falcon* by Léonie Adams, by permission of the John Day Company, copyright by Léonie Adams, October 10, 1929.

DIAL PRESS, INC. for "First Cycle of Love Poems" reprinted from *Love Poems* by George Barker by permission of Dial Press, Inc., copyright, 1947 by Dial Press, Inc.; and "A Pilot from the Carrier" and "The Snow Leopard" reprinted from *Little Friend, Little Friend* by Randall Jarrell by permission of Dial Press, Inc., copyright, 1945 by Dial Press, Inc.

DOUBLEDAY & COMPANY, INC. for "The Lost Son" from *The Lost Son and Other Poems* by Theodore Roethke, copyright, 1948 by Theodore Roethke, reprinted by permission of Doubleday & Company, Inc.

DUELL, SLOAN AND PEARCE, INC. for "my father moved through dooms of love" and "anyone lived in a pretty how town" from *Fifty Poems*, reprinted by permission of the Publishers, Duell, Sloan and Pearce, Inc., copyright, 1940 by E. E. Cummings.

EDITIONS POETRY LONDON for "The Fall," "Desire" and "Love Poem" from *Stone and Flower* by Kathleen Raine and "An Autumn Park"; and "Jardin du Palais Royal" from *Poems, 1937-1942* by David Gascoyne.

FABER AND FABER, LTD. for "To Argos," "At Epidaurus," and "Conon in Alexandria" from *A Private Country* by Lawrence Durrell; "The Grove" and "The Recurrence" from *The Narrow Place* by Edwin Muir; "A Mile from Eden" and "For a Christening" from *The Nine Bright Shiners* by Anne Ridler; and "The Mummy" and "The Sunbather" from *The Ballad of the Mari Lwyd* by Vernon Watkins.

HORACE GREGORY for his poem "The Woman Who Disapproved of Music at the Bar" which first appeared in *The Harvard Advocate*.

HARCOURT, BRACE AND COMPANY, INC. for "Burnt Norton," "Ash Wednesday," "The Waste Land," and "Gerontion" from *Collected Poems, 1909-1935* by T. S. Eliot, copyright, 1936, by Harcourt, Brace and Company, Inc.; "Missing Dates," "Four Legs, Two Legs, Three Legs," and "Fighting for Duck" from *Collected Poems,* copyright, 1935, 1940, 1949, by William Empson, reprinted by permission of Harcourt, Brace and Company, Inc.; "90 North" from *Blood for a Stranger* by Randall Jarrell, copyright, 1942, by Harcourt, Brace and Company, Inc.; "The Drunken Fisherman," "Mr. Edwards and the Spider," and "The Quaker Graveyard in Nantucket" from *Lord Weary's Castle,* copyright, 1944, 1945, by Robert Lowell, reprinted by permission of Harcourt, Brace and Company, Inc.; "Waterwall Blues" and "Around the Fish: After Paul Klee" from *The Wound and the Weather,* copyright, 1946, by Howard Moss, reprinted by permission of Harcourt, Brace and Company, Inc.; "A World Within a War" from *A World Within a War* by Herbert Read, copyright, 1945, by Harcourt, Brace and Company, Inc.; "The People Will Live On" from *The People, Yes* by Carl Sandburg, copyright, 1936, by Harcourt, Brace and Company, Inc.; "Haircut," "Elegy Written on a Frontporch," and "The Dome of Sunday" from *Person, Place and Thing,* copyright, 1942, by Karl Jay Shapiro, reprinted by permission of Harcourt, Brace and Company, Inc.; "Terror," "Pursuit," and "Revelation" from *Selected Poems, 1923-1943,* by Robert Penn Warren, copyright, 1944, by Harcourt, Brace and Company, Inc.; "O" from *The Beautiful Changes,* copyright, 1947, by Richard Wilbur, reprinted by permission of Harcourt, Brace and Company, Inc.; "The White Rat" and "Noah's Ark" from *Moderate Fable,* copyright, 1944, by Marguerite Young, reprinted by permission of Harcourt, Brace and Company, Inc.

HARPER & BROTHERS for "Wonder Is Not Precisely Knowing," "Until the Desert Knows," and "Dying, To Be Afraid of Thee" from *Bolts of Melody: New Poems of Emily Dickinson,* edited by Mabel Loomis Todd and Millicent Todd Bingham, copyright, 1945, by Millicent Todd Bingham.

THE HOGARTH PRESS, LTD. for "The Plains" from *A Lost Season* by Roy Fuller and "November 1941" from *The Middle of a War* by Roy Fuller; and "In Heaven, I Suppose, Lie Down Together" from *Transitional Poem* by C. Day Lewis.

HENRY HOLT AND COMPANY, INC. for "The Old Summerhouse," "The Bottle," and "The Listeners" from *Collected Poems* by Walter de la Mare, reprinted by permission of Henry Holt and Company, Inc., copyright, 1941, by Walter de la Mare; "The Silken Tent," "A Soldier," "The Most of It," "To Earthward," "After Apple-Picking," "Happiness Makes Up in Height," and "All Revelation" from *Complete Poems of Robert Frost,* 1949, copyright, 1928, 1930, 1942, 1949, by Henry Holt and Company, Inc.; "The Opponent Charm Sustained," "The Philosophic Apology," "Essence," "Tusks of Blood," and "To Dear Daniel" from *Poems by Samuel Greenberg,* edited by Harold Holden and Jack McManis, reprinted by permission of Henry Holt and Company, Inc., copyright, 1947, by Harold Holden and Jack McManis; "The Night Is Freezing Fast," "Smooth Between Sea and Land," and "Tell Me Not Here" from *The Collected Poems of A. E. Housman,* copyright, 1922, 1949, by Henry Holt and Company, Inc., copyright, 1936, by Barclays Bank, Ltd.; "The Anti-Symbolist" and "Were I to Mount Beyond the Field" from *The Collected Poems of Sidney Keyes,* edited by Michael Meyer, copyright, 1947, by Henry Holt and Company, Inc.; "The Tower," "This Amber Sunstream," "Young Woman at a Window," and "Axel Song" from *Collected Poems* by Mark Van Doren, reprinted by permission of Henry Holt and Company, Inc., copyright, 1939, by Mark Van Doren.

HOUGHTON MIFFLIN COMPANY for "The Monument" and "The Weed" by Elizabeth Bishop from *North and South,* copyright, 1946, by Elizabeth Bishop; and "Einstein" by Archibald MacLeish from *Streets in the Moon,* copyright, 1926, by Archibald MacLeish.

ALFRED A. KNOPF, INC. for "Two in August," "The Equilibrists," "Painted Head," "Prelude to an Evening," and "Judith of Bethulia" reprinted from *Selected Poems* by John Crowe Ransom, by permission of Alfred A. Knopf, Inc., copyright, 1924, 1927, 1945 by Alfred A. Knopf, Inc.; "The Poems of Our Climate," "The Glass of Water," "The Sense of the Sleight-of-Hand Man," "Mrs. Alfred Uruguay," and "Connoisseur of Chaos" reprinted from *Parts of a World* by Wallace Stevens, by permission of Alfred A. Knopf, Inc., copyright, 1942, by Wallace Stevens, "Evening without Angels," "Academic Discourse at Havana," "Sailing after Lunch," "The Idea of Order in Key West" reprinted from *Ideas of Order* by Wallace Stevens, by permission of Alfred A. Knopf, Inc., copyright, 1935, 1936 by Wallace Stevens, "The Emperor of Ice Cream" reprinted from *Harmonium* by Wallace Stevens, by permission of Alfred A. Knopf, Inc., copyright, 1923, 1931 by Alfred A. Knopf, Inc., "Notes Toward a Supreme Fiction" reprinted from *Transport to Summer* by Wallace Stevens, by permission of Alfred A. Knopf, Inc., copyright, 1942, 1947 by Wallace Stevens; "Hymn to Earth," and "O Virtuous Light" reprinted from *Collected Poems* by Elinor Wylie, by permission of Alfred A. Knopf, Inc., copyright, 1929, 1932 by Alfred A. Knopf, Inc.

THE KENYON REVIEW for "The Starlight's Intuitions Pierced the Twelve" by Delmore Schwartz with the permission of the author.

LITTLE, BROWN & COMPANY for "That After Horror That Was Us," "After Great Pain a Formal Feeling Comes," "Two Lengths Has Every Day," "After a Hundred Years," "It Was Not Death, For I Stood Up," "No Rack Can Torture Me," "Because I Could Not Stop for Death," "Safe in Their Alabaster Chambers," "Of Bronze and Blaze," and "There's a Certain Slant of Light" from *The Poems of Emily Dickinson* edited by Martha Dickinson Bianchi and Alfred Leete Hampson, by permission of Little, Brown & Company, copyright, 1914, by Martha Dickinson Bianchi.

LIVERIGHT PUBLISHING CORPORATION for "To Brooklyn Bridge," "Ave Maria," "The Harbor Dawn," and "Atlantis" from *The Bridge* and "O Carib Isle!" "The Broken Tower," "And yet this great wink of eternity," "Infinite consanguinity it bears," and "Meticulous, past midnight in clear rime" from *Voyages* from *The Collected Poems of Hart Crane* published by Liveright Publishing Corporation; "Not Honey" from *The Collected Poems of H. D.* by permission of Liveright Publishing Corporation.

THE MACMILLAN COMPANY for "Summer Idyll" from George Barker, *Selected Poems*, copyright, 1941 by The Macmillan Company and used with their permission; "The Convergence of the Twain," "ΑΓΝΩΣΤΩι ΘΕΩι," "Channel Firing," "Nature's Questioning," "An Ancient to Ancients," and "Darkling Thrush" from Thomas Hardy, *Collected Poems*, copyright, 1925, by The Macmillan Company and used with their permission; "General William Booth Enters into Heaven" from Vachel Lindsay, *General William Booth Enters Into Heaven*, copyright, 1913, by The Macmillan Company and used with their permission; "The Passing Strange" from John Masefield, *Enslaved*, copyright, 1920, 1948 by John Masefield and used with the permission of The Macmillan Company, "Night on the Downland" from John Masefield, *Lollingdon Downs*, copyright, 1917, 1945 by John Masefield and used with the permission of The Macmillan Company; "What Are Years," from Marianne Moore, *What Are Years*, copyright, 1941, by Marianne Moore and used with the permission of The Macmillan Company, "A Grave," "The Jerboa," and "Steeple-Jack" from Marianne Moore, *Selected Poems*, copyright, 1935, by Marianne Moore and used with the permission of The Macmillan Company, "The Mind Is an Enchanting Thing" from Marianne Moore, *Nevertheless*, copyright, 1944, by Marianne Moore and used with the permission of The Macmillan Company; "Eros Turannos" and "Ben Jonson Entertains a Man from Stratford" from Edwin Arlington Robinson, *Man Against the Sky*, copyright, 1916, 1944, by Edwin Arlington Robinson and used with the permission of The Macmillan Company; "The Progress of Photography" and "All the Farewells" from Byron Vazakas, *Transfigured Night*, copyright, 1943, 1944, by Byron Vazakas and used with the permission of The Macmillan Company; "News for the Delphic Oracle" and "Lapis Lazuli" from William Butler Yeats, *Last Poems and Plays*, copyright, 1940, by Georgie Yeats and used with the permission of The Macmillan Company, "Two Songs from a Play," "Sailing to Byzantium," "Nineteen Hundred and Nineteen" and "The Tower" from William Butler Yeats, *The Tower*, copyright, 1928, by The Macmillan Company and used with their permission, "Byzantium" from William Butler Yeats, *Winding Stair*, copyright, 1933, by The Macmillan Company and used with their permission. Also "The Jungle" from *Ha! Ha! Among the Trumpets* by Alun Lewis.

EDGAR LEE MASTERS for his poems "The Lost Orchard," "Thomas Trevelyan" and "Scholfield Huxley."

HAROLD MATSON for "Departure in the Dark," "In the Heart of Contemplation," and "O Dreams, O Destinations" by C. Day Lewis.

ROBERT M. McBRIDE & COMPANY for "Medusa" from *Body of This Death* by Louise Bogan.

JAMES MERRILL for his poems "The Black Swan" (also The Icaros Publishing Company, Athens) and "Foliage of Vision" (also *The Quarterly Review of Literature*.)

NEW DIRECTIONS for "Holy Poems I, II, III" and "Sacred Elegy V" from *Sacred and Secular Elegies* by George Barker, copyright, 1943 by New Directions; "Song of the Demented Priest" from *Poems* by John Berryman, copyright, 1942, by John Berryman; "Mysticism Has Not the Patience" from *Poems New and Selected* by Richard Eberhart, copyright, 1944, by New Directions; "Souls Lake" and "Colorado" from *A Wreath for the Sea* by Robert Fitzgerald, copyright, 1943, by New Directions; "The Clovers" and "The Circle" by Jean Garrigue, from *Five Young American Poets*, 1944, copyright, 1944, by New Directions; Cantos XIV, XXI, XXIX, XLVII from *Cantos*, copyright, 1937, by Ezra Pound, Cantos XV, XVI, XX from *A Draft of XXX Cantos* by Ezra Pound, copyright, 1937, by New Directions, Canto XLV from *The Fifth Decad of Cantos*, copyright, 1937, by New Directions, "Hugh Selwyn Mauberley," "Mauberley," "The Return," and "The River-Merchant's Wife: A Letter" from *Personae*, copyright, 1926, by Ezra Pound; "The Heavy Bear Who Goes With Me" from *In Dreams Begin Responsibilities* by Delmore Schwartz, copyright, 1938, by New Directions; "A Refusal to Mourn the Death," "Among Those Killed in the Dawn Raid," "Ceremony After a Fire Raid," "Fern Hill," and "Vision and Prayer" from *Selected Writings of Dylan Thomas*, copyright, 1946, by New Directions, "In Memory of Ann Jones," "The Hand that Signed the Paper," and "The Force that through the Green Fuse" from *Selected Writings of Dylan Thomas*, copyright, 1939, by New Directions; "Ave Eva" and "Train Ride" from *Selected Poems* by John Wheelwright, copyright, 1941, by New Directions; "The Yachts," from *Complete Collected Poems, 1906-1938* by William Carlos Williams, copyright, 1938, by New Directions, "St. Francis Einstein of the Daffodils" from *Selected Poems* by William Carlos Williams, copyright, 1936, by Ronald Lane Latimer.

OXFORD UNIVERSITY PRESS, LONDON for "The Caged Skylark," "Spring and Fall" and "Spelt from Sybil's Leaves" from Gerard Manley Hopkins, *Collected Poems*, by permission of Oxford University Press and the poet's family.

OXFORD UNIVERSITY PRESS, NEW YORK for "The Windover," "The Terrible Sonnets I, II, III," "That Nature Is a Heraclitean Fire and of the Nature of the Resurrection," "The Blessed Virgin Compared to the Air We Breathe," "Felix Randal," "Hurrahing in Harvest," "God's Grandeur" from Gerard Manley Hopkins, *The Poems of Gerard Manley Hopkins*, by permission of Oxford University Press, New York; "There Is a Spell for Instance" by H. D., *The Walls Do Not Fall*, by permission of Oxford University Press, New York; "Dwarf of Disintegration" from Oscar Williams, *The Man Coming Toward You*, by permission of Oxford University Press, New York; for "The Goal of Intellectual Man" and "I Walked Out to the Graveyard," from *Song and Idea*, and "The Groundhog," from *Reading the Spirit*, by Richard Eberhart, by permission of the Oxford University Press, New York.

RANDOM HOUSE, INC. for "At the Grave of Henry James," "Alonso to Ferdinand," "Musée des Beaux Arts," "Lay Your Sleeping Head, My Love," "As He Is," "Let the Florid Music Praise," "Casino," "Petition," and "Perhaps" from W. H. Auden, *Collected Poems*, copyright, 1945, by W. H. Auden, reprinted by permission of Random House, Inc., lines from "Commentary" from W. H. Auden, *Journey to a War*, copyright, 1939, by W. H. Auden and Christopher Isherwood, reprinted by permission of Random House, Inc.; "Winter and Summer," "Port Bou," "An Elementary School Classroom in a Slum" and "Polar Exploration" from Stephen Spender, *Ruins and Visions*, copyright, 1942, by Stephen Spender, reprinted by permission of Random House, Inc., "What I Expected Was" from Stephen Spender *Poems*, copyright, 1934, by Random House, Inc. and reprinted with their permission; "Stylite," "June Thunder," "The Sunlight on the Garden," and "Eclogue for Christmas" from Louis MacNeice, *Collected Poems*, copyright, 1937, 1939, 1940, by Louis MacNeice, reprinted by permission of Random House, Inc.; "Night," "Post Mortem," by Robinson Jeffers, copyright, 1935, by the Modern Library, reprinted by permission of Random House, Inc., "November Surf" by Robinson Jeffers, copyright, 1932, by Robinson Jeffers, reprinted by permission of Random House, Inc.; "What Happened: A Five-Act Play" from Gertrude Stein, *Selected Writings of Gertrude Stein*, copyright, 1946, by Random House, Inc., and used with their permission.

RINEHART & COMPANY for "The Task" and "Final Poem" from *The Task* by Robert Bhain Campbell, copyright, 1945, by Rinehart & Company, Inc., and reprinted with their permission.

CHARLES SCRIBNER'S SONS for "A Frieze," "The Return," "Colloquy with a King-Crab," and "Ode" reprinted from *The Collected Poems of John Peale Bishop*, copyright, 1933, 1941, 1948, by Charles Scribner's Sons, used by permission of the publishers; "The Mark" reprinted from *Dark Summer* by Louise Bogan, copyright, 1929, by Charles Scribner's Sons, used by permission of the publishers, "Henceforth from the Mind" reprinted from *The Sleeping Fury* by Louise Bogan, copyright, 1937, by Charles Scribner's Sons, used by permission of the publishers; "Ode to the Confederate Dead" and "Aeneas at Washington" reprinted from *Poems, 1922-1947* by Allen Tate, copyright, 1932, 1937, 1948, by Charles Scribner's Sons, used by permission of the publishers; "Luke Havergal" from Edwin Arlington Robinson, *Children of the Night*.

SIMON AND SCHUSTER, INC. for "Largo" from *Poems* by Dunstan Thompson, copyright, 1943, by Dunstan Thompson, reprinted by permission of Simon and Schuster, Publishers.

WILLIAM SLOANE ASSOCIATES, INC. for "Canto Amor" from John Berryman's *The Dispossessed*, copyright, 1948, by John Berryman.

THE VIKING PRESS, INC. for selections from *Finnegans Wake* by James Joyce, copyright, 1939, by James Joyce, reprinted by permission of The Viking Press, New York; "Song of a Man Who Has Come Through" and "Snake" from *Collected Poems* by D. H.

Lawrence, copyright, 1929, by Jonathan Cape & Harrison Smith, Inc., reprinted by permission of The Viking Press, Inc., New York.

ANN WATKINS, INC. for "Heart and Mind" by Edith Sitwell from *Green Song*, copyright, 1946, View, Inc., "An Old Woman," "Tears," "Street Song," and "Still Falls the Rain" by Edith Sitwell from *Street Song*, copyright, 1942, by Edith Sitwell.

A. P. WATT & SON for "To Juan at the Winter Solstice," "The Worms of History," "Sea Side," and "Pure Death" from Robert Graves, *Collected Poems* with the permission of Robert Graves.

RICHARD WILBUR for his poem, "Still, Citizen Sparrow."

PREFACE

THIS BOOK is a selection of poetry in the modern idiom as it has developed in England and America during the past hundred years or so. Changes in poetry during these years show a great deviation from the representative poetry of the nineteenth century, yet the modern idiom is itself elusive of definition and difficult to disentangle from its spurious imitations and the many influences bearing upon it. Most of the poems we have chosen may be described as stemming from the "metaphysical" and "symbolist" schools of the earlier periods which, in our opinion, have given to the modern idiom its most true and salient characteristics. The reader is referred to *Myth and Metaphysics: An Introduction to Modern Poetry*, which prefaces the appendix to this book, for an analysis of some central problems of modern poetry and a more thorough explanation of the basis of our selection. In the Appendix will also be found notes to many representative poems of our time; we hope these may help the reader to overcome his prejudice against much of modern poetry and to understand better the causes of its notorious "difficulty" and "obscurity."

In all cases we have chosen works which, we feel, belong to the highest effort of each poet. Consequently we have had to omit poems in a lighter mood, occasional poems, and those which struck us as *tours de force*, even though many of these beguiled or charmed us; and we have reluctantly omitted folk poetry. A number of poems, deservedly famous, and for that reason overanthologized, have been replaced by poems which we felt were as good and often better but not so well known. In many cases we hope that our selections may lead to a revaluation of a poet's work. Over a period of several years we have thoughtfully considered some two thousand volumes, so that our inclusion or omission of a poet or an example of his work is in the nature of a criticism. On the other hand, cost and lack of space have forced us reluctantly to omit several poets we should have liked to see represented. Our taste, inevitably, has been influenced by personal as well as catholic elements, and we hope we may be granted that margin of individual selection which no editor can nor should avoid.

Only Edith Sitwell, by not granting us permission to publish some of her earlier poetry, would not allow us to make a completely free choice. We are sorry that Laura Riding has refused to publish any more of her poetry, work which she now considers to be a labor performed in vain, for we wanted to give an emphasis to her poetry hitherto denied it. We should have liked to have included more poems of Marianne Moore, and many more of Yeats, but their publisher has withheld permission; in other cases, as in that of Eliot, or Wallace Stevens' "Notes Toward a Supreme Fiction," the cost of fees has prevented us from adding more. Again, as in the selections from Ezra Pound, the choice of a long poem, "Hugh Selwyn Mauberley," and an attempt to make an adequate compilation from the *Cantos* (central to the thesis of this anthology) may give a false impression of undue representation. For many reasons, therefore, our evaluation of a poet is not to be measured only by the number of pages allotted him. Few readers will question the inclusion of *Finnegans Wake* in an anthology of poetry, but many may argue against the inclusion of selections from Djuna Barnes' novel, *Nightwood*. Passages from this work need only be spaced as free verse in order for the concentrated use of the rhythms, allusions and tropes of modern poetry to become apparent. Selections from other "prose" work might have been included but, with the admission of Djuna Barnes, we are content to make the slow beginnings of what we hope will be a widening recognition of the breakdown between poetry and prose in modern times, and of the similarity between poetry and imaginative prose of the first order.

We have included a few poets who, primarily on technical consideration, do not belong to the main stream of metaphysical and symbolist tradition, although good cases could be made out for several of them, since there is no clean division anywhere. We have included them because they do have a place in an anthology of modern poetry, because of their historical importance, and for contrast.

As we present our considered choice, we should like to think that we have compiled works which represent a distillation of the finest poetry in a period as rich as any in our history.

Although we have made use of many libraries in the general procuring of books, we should like especially to thank Mr. John Sweeney of the Poetry Room at the Lamont Library of Harvard who obtained for us many rare and English editions. To Miss Agnes Eisenberger we are indebted for the typing and checking of manuscript. And we are deeply grateful to Mr. Allen Tate for his kind encouragement and advice.

KIMON FRIAR
JOHN MALCOLM BRINNIN

CONTENTS

PAGE

MODERN POETRY

EMILY DICKINSON
1830-1886

❦

"Wonder Is Not Precisely Knowing"

Wonder is not precisely knowing,
And not precisely knowing not,
A beautiful but bleak condition
He has not lived who has not felt.

Suspense is his maturer sister;
Whether adult delight is pain
Or of itself a new misgiving—
This is the gnat that mangles men.

"Until the Desert Knows"

Until the desert knows
· That water grows
His sands suffice;
But let him once suspect
· That Caspian fact,
Sahara dies.

Utmost is relative,
Have not or have
Adjacent sums;
Enough, the first abode
On the familiar road
Galloped in dreams.

"Dying! To Be Afraid of Thee"

Dying! To be afraid of thee
One must to thine artillery
Have left exposed a friend.
Than thine old arrow is a shot
Delivered straighter to the heart,
The leaving love behind.

Not for itself the dust is shy,
But, enemy, belovèd be
  Thy batteries' divorce.
Fight sternly in a dying eye
Two armies, love and certainty,
  And love and the reverse.

"That After Horror That Was Us"

That after horror that was Us—
That passed the mouldering pier
Just as the granite crumb let go,
Our savior by a hair—

A second more had dropped too deep
For fisherman to plumb—
The very profile of the thought
Puts recollection numb!

The possibility to pass,
Without a moment's bell,
Into Conjecture's presence—
Is like a face of steel

That suddenly looks into ours
With a metallic grin,—
The cordiality of Death
Who drills his welcome in.

"After Great Pain a Formal Feeling Comes"

After great pain a formal feeling comes—
The nerves sit ceremonious like tombs;
The stiff Heart questions—was it He that bore?
And yesterday—or centuries before?

The feet mechanical
Go round a wooden way
Of ground or air or Ought, regardless grown,
A quartz contentment like a stone.

This is the hour of lead
Remembered if outlived,
As freezing persons recollect the snow—
First chill, then stupor, then the letting go.

"Two Lengths Has Every Day"

Two lengths has every day,
Its absolute extent—
And area superior
By hope or heaven lent.
Eternity will be
Velocity, or pause,
At fundamental signals
From fundamental laws.
To die, is not to go—
On doom's consummate chart
No territory new is staked,
Remain thou as thou art.

"After a Hundred Years"

After a hundred years
Nobody knows the place,—
Agony, that enacted there,
Motionless as peace.

Weeds triumphant ranged,
Strangers strolled and spelled
At the lone orthography
Of the elder dead.

Winds of summer fields
Recollect the way,—
Instinct picking up the key
Dropped by memory.

"It Was Not Death, for I Stood Up"

It was not death, for I stood up,
And all the dead lie down;
It was not night, for all the bells
Put out their tongues, for noon.

It was not frost, for on my flesh
I felt siroccos crawl,—
Nor fire, for just my marble feet
Could keep a chancel cool.

And yet it tasted like them all;
The figures I have seen
Set orderly, for burial,
Reminded me of mine,

As if my life were shaven
And fitted to a frame,
And could not breathe without a key;
And 'twas like midnight, some,

When everything that ticked has stopped,
And space stares, all around,
Or grisly frosts, first autumn morns,
Repeal the beating ground.

But most like chaos,—stopless, cool,—
Without a chance or spar,
Or even a report of land
To justify despair.

"No Rack Can Torture Me"

No rack can torture me,
My soul's at liberty,
Behind this mortal bone
There knits a bolder one

You cannot prick with saw,
Nor rend with scimitar.
Two bodies therefore be;
Bind one, and one will flee.

The eagle of his nest
No easier divest
And gain the sky,
Than mayest thou,

Except thyself may be
Thine enemy;
Captivity is consciousness,
So's liberty.

"Because I Could Not Stop for Death"

Because I could not stop for Death,
He kindly stopped for me;
The carriage held but just ourselves
And Immortality.

We slowly drove, he knew no haste,
And I had put away
My labor, and my leisure too,
For his civility.

We passed the school where children played
At wrestling in a ring;
We passed the fields of gazing grain,
We passed the setting sun.

We paused before a house that seemed
A swelling of the ground;
The roof was scarcely visible,
The cornice but a mound.

Since then 'tis centuries; but each
Feels shorter than the day
I first surmised the horses' heads
Were toward eternity.

"Safe in Their Alabaster Chambers"

Safe in their alabaster chambers,
Untouched by morning and untouched by noon,
Sleep the meek members of the resurrection,
Rafter of satin, and roof of stone.

Light laughs the breeze in her castle of sunshine;
Babbles the bee in a stolid ear;
Pipe the sweet birds in ignorant cadence,—
Ah, what sagacity perished here!

Grand go the years in the crescent above them;
Worlds scoop their arcs, and firmaments row,
Diadems drop and Doges surrender,
Soundless as dots on a disk of snow.

"Of Bronze and Blaze"

Of bronze and blaze
  The north, to-night!
  So adequate its forms,
So preconcerted with itself,
  So distant to alarms,—
An unconcern so sovereign
  To universe, or me,

It paints my simple spirit
  With tints of majesty,
Till I take vaster attitudes,
  And strut upon my stem,
Disdaining men and oxygen,
  For arrogance of them.

My splendors are menagerie;
  But their competeless show
Will entertain the centuries
  When I am, long ago,
An island in dishonored grass,
  Whom none but daisies know.

"There's a Certain Slant of Light"

There's a certain slant of light,
On winter afternoons,
That oppresses, like the weight
Of cathedral tunes.

Heavenly hurt it gives us;
We can find no scar,
But internal difference
Where the meanings are.

None may teach it anything,
'Tis the seal, despair,—
An imperial affliction
Sent us of the air.

When it comes, the landscape listens,
Shadows hold their breath;
When it goes, 'tis like the distance
On the look of death.

THOMAS HARDY
1840-1928

The Convergence of the Twain

LINES ON THE LOSS OF THE "TITANIC"

I

In a solitude of the sea
Deep from human vanity,
And the Pride of Life that planned her, stilly couches she.

II

Steel chambers, late the pyres
Of her salamandrine fires,
Cold currents thrid, and turn to rhythmic tidal lyres.

III

Over the mirrors meant
To glass the opulent
The sea-worm crawls—grotesque, slimed, dumb, indifferent.

IV

Jewels in joy designed
To ravish the sensuous mind
Lie lightless, all their sparkles bleared and black and blind.

V

Dim moon-eyed fishes near
Gaze at the gilded gear
And query: "What does this vaingloriousness down here?" . . .

VI

Well: while was fashioning
This creature of cleaving wing,
The Immanent Will that stirs and urges everything

VII

Prepared a sinister mate
For her—so gaily great—
A Shape of Ice, for the time far and dissociate.

VIII

And as the smart ship grew
In stature, grace, and hue,
In shadowy silent distance grew the Iceberg too.

IX

Alien they seemed to be:
No mortal eye could see
The intimate welding of their later history,

X

Or signs that they were bent
By paths coincident
On being anon twin halves of one august event,

XI

Till the Spinner of the Years
Said "Now!" And each one hears,
And consummation comes, and jars two hemispheres.

Channel Firing

That night your great guns, unawares,
Shook all our coffins as we lay,
And broke the chancel window-squares,
We thought it was the Judgment-day

And sat upright. While drearisome
Arose the howl of wakened hounds:
The mouse let fall the altar-crumb,
The worms drew back into the mounds,

The glebe cow drooled. Till God called, "No;
It's gunnery practice out at sea
Just as before you went below;
The world is as it used to be:

"All nations striving strong to make
Red war yet redder. Mad as hatters
They do no more for Christés sake
Than you who are helpless in such matters.

"That this is not the judgment-hour
For some of them's a blessed thing,
For if it were they'd have to scour
Hell's floor for so much threatening. . . .

"Ha, ha. It will be warmer when
I blow the trumpet (if indeed
I ever do; for you are men,
And rest eternal sorely need)."

So down we lay again. "I wonder,
Will the world ever saner be,"
Said one, "than when He sent us under
In our indifferent century!"

And many a skeleton shook his head.
"Instead of preaching forty year,"
My neighbour Parson Thirdly said,
"I wish I had stuck to pipes and beer."

Again the guns disturbed the hour,
Roaring their readiness to avenge,
As far inland as Stourton Tower,
And Camelot, and starlit Stonehenge.

April 1914

ΑΓΝΩΣΤΩι ΘΕΩι

Long have I framed weak phantasies of Thee,
        O Willer masked and dumb!
        Who makes Life become,—
As though by labouring all-unknowingly,
        Like one whom reveries numb.

How much of consciousness informs Thy will,
        Thy biddings, as if blind,
        Of death-inducing kind,
Nought shows to us ephemeral ones who fill
        But moments in Thy mind.

Perhaps Thy ancient rote-restricted ways
Thy ripening rule transcends;
That listless effort tends
To grow percipient with advance of days,
And with percipience mends.

For, in unwonted purlieus, far and nigh,
At whiles or short or long,
May be discerned a wrong
Dying as of self-slaughter; whereat I
Would raise my voice in song.

Nature's Questioning

When I look forth at dawning, pool,
Field, flock, and lonely tree,
All seem to gaze at me
Like chastened children sitting silent in a school;

Their faces dulled, constrained, and worn,
As though the master's ways
Through the long teaching days
Had cowed them till their early zest was overborne.

Upon them stirs in lippings mere
(As if once clear in call,
But now scarce breathed at all)—
"We wonder, ever wonder, why we find us here!

"Has some Vast Imbecility,
Mighty to build and blend,
But impotent to tend,
Framed us in jest, and let us now to hazardry?

"Or come we of an Automaton
Unconscious of our pains? . . .
Or are we live remains
Of Godhead dying downwards, brain and eye now gone?

"Or is it that some high Plan betides,
As yet not understood,
Of Evil stormed by Good,
We the Forlorn Hope over which Achievement strides?"

Thus things around. No answerer I . . .
Meanwhile the winds, and rains,
And Earth's old glooms and pains
Are still the same, and Life and Death are neighbours nigh.

An Ancient to Ancients

Where once we danced, where once we sang,
        Gentlemen,
The floors are sunken, cobwebs hang,
And cracks creep; worms have fed upon
The doors. Yea, sprightlier times were then
Than now, with harps and tabrets gone,
        Gentlemen!

Where once we rowed, where once we sailed,
        Gentlemen,
And damsels took the tiller, veiled
Against too strong a stare (God wot
Their fancy, then or anywhen!)
Upon that shore we are clean forgot,
        Gentlemen!

We have lost somewhat, afar and near,
        Gentlemen,
The thinning of our ranks each year
Affords a hint we are nigh undone,
That we shall not be ever again
The marked of many, loved of one,
        Gentlemen.

In dance the polka hit our wish,
        Gentlemen,
The paced quadrille, the spry schottische,
"Sir Roger."—And in opera spheres
The "Girl" (the famed "Bohemian"),
And "Trovatore," held the ears,
        Gentlemen.

This season's paintings do not please,
        Gentlemen,
Like Etty, Mulready, Maclise;
Throbbing romance has waned and wanned;
No wizard wields the witching pen
Of Bulwer, Scott, Dumas, and Sand,
        Gentlemen.

The bower we shrined to Tennyson,
            Gentlemen,
Is roof-wrecked; damps there drip upon
Sagged seats, the creeper-nails are rust,
The spider is sole denizen;
Even she who voiced those rhymes is dust,
            Gentlemen!

We who met sunrise sanguine-souled,
            Gentlemen,
Are wearing weary. We are old;
These younger press; we feel our rout
Is imminent to Aides' den,—
That evening shades are stretching out,
            Gentlemen!

And yet, though ours be failing frames,
            Gentlemen,
So were some others' history names,
Who trode their track light-limbed and fast
As these youth, and not alien
From enterprise, to their long last,
            Gentlemen.

Sophocles, Plato, Socrates,
            Gentlemen,
Pythagoras, Thucydides,
Herodotus, and Homer,—yea,
Clement, Augustin, Origen,
Burnt brightlier towards their setting-day,
            Gentlemen.

And ye, red-lipped and smooth-browed; list,
            Gentlemen;
Much is there waits you we have missed;
Much lore we leave you worth the knowing,
Much, much has lain outside our ken:
Nay, rush not: time serves: we are going,
            Gentlemen.

The Darkling Thrush

I leant upon a coppice gate
  When Frost was spectre-gray,
And Winter's dregs made desolate
  The weakening eye of day.
The tangled bine-stems scored the sky
  Like strings of broken lyres,
And all mankind that haunted nigh
  Had sought their household fires.

The land's sharp features seemed to be
  The Century's corpse outleant,
His crypt the cloudy canopy,
  The wind his death-lament.
The ancient pulse of germ and birth
  Was shrunken hard and dry,
And every spirit upon earth
  Seemed fervorless as I.

At once a voice arose among
  The bleak twigs overhead
In a full-hearted evensong
  Of joy illimited;
An aged thrush, frail, gaunt, and small,
  In blast-beruffled plume,
Had chosen thus to fling his soul
  Upon the growing gloom.

So little cause for carolings
  Of such ecstatic sound
Was written on terrestrial things
  Afar or nigh around,
That I could think there trembled through
  His happy good-night air
Some blessèd Hope, whereof he knew
  And I was unaware.

GERARD MANLEY HOPKINS
1844-1889

That Nature Is a Heraclitean Fire and of the Comfort of the Resurrection

Cloud-puffball, torn tufts, tossed pillows flaunt forth, then chevy on an air-
built thoroughfare: heaven-roysterers, in gay-gangs they throng;
they glitter in marches.
Down roughcast, down dazzling whitewash, wherever an elm arches,
Shivelights and shadowtackle in long lashes lace, lance, and pair.
Delightfully the bright wind boisterous ropes, wrestles, beats earth bare
Of yestertempest's creases; in pool and rut peel parches
Squandering ooze to squeezed dough, crust, dust; stanches, starches
Squadroned masks and manmarks treadmire toil there
Footfretted in it. Million-fuelèd, nature's bonfire burns on.
But quench her bonniest, dearest to her, her clearest-selvèd spark
Man, how fast his firedint, his mark on mind, is gone!
Both are in an unfathomable, all is in an enormous dark
Drowned. O pity and indignation! Manshape, that shone
Sheer off, disseveral, a star, death blots black out; nor mark
        Is any of him at all so stark
But vastness blurs and time beats level. Enough! the Resurrection,
A heart's-clarion! Away grief's gasping, joyless days, dejection.
        Across my foundering deck shone
A beacon, an eternal beam. Flesh fade, and mortal trash
Fall to the residuary worm; world's wildfire, leave but ash:
        In a flash, at a trumpet crash,
I am all at once what Christ is, since he was what I am, and
This Jack, joke, poor potsherd, patch, matchwood, immortal diamond,
        Is immortal diamond.

The Terrible Sonnets

I

Not, I'll not, carrion comfort, Despair, not feast on thee;
Not untwist—slack they may be—these last strands of man
In me ór, most weary, cry *I can no more.* I can;
Can something, hope, wish day come, not choose not to be.

But ah, but O thou terrible, why wouldst thou rude on me
Thy wring-world right foot rock? lay a lionlimb against me? scan
With darksome devouring eyes my bruisèd bones? and fan,
O in turns of tempest, me heaped there; me frantic to avoid thee
    and flee?

  Why? That my chaff might fly; my grain lie, sheer and clear.
Nay in all that toil, that coil, since (seems) I kissed the rod,
Hand rather, my heart lo! lapped strength, stole joy, would laugh,
    chéer.
Cheer whom though? the hero whose heaven-handling flung me,
    fóot tród
Me? or me that fought him? O which one? is it each one? That
    night, that year
Of now done darkness I wretch lay wrestling with (my God!) my
    God.

II

No worst, there is none. Pitched past pitch of grief,
More pangs will, schooled at forepangs, wilder wring.
Comforter, where, where is your comforting?
Mary, mother of us, where is your relief?
My cries heave, herds-long; huddle in a main, a chief
Woe, world-sorrow; on an age-old anvil wince and sing—
Then lull, then leave off. Fury had shrieked 'No ling-
ering! Let me be fell: force I must be brief.'

O the mind, mind has mountains; cliffs of fall
Frightful, sheer, no-man-fathomed. Hold them cheap
May who ne'er hung there. Nor does long our small
Durance deal with that steep or deep. Here! creep,
Wretch, under a comfort serves in a whirlwind: all
Life death does end and each day dies with sleep.

III

I wake and feel the fell of dark, not day.
What hours, O what black hoürs we have spent
This night! what sights you, heart, saw; ways you went!
And more must, in yet longer light's delay.
  With witness I speak this. But where I say
Hours I mean years, mean life. And my lament
Is cries countless, cries like dead letters sent
To dearest him that lives alas! away.

  I am gall, I am heartburn. God's most deep decree
Bitter would have me taste: my taste was me;

Bones built in me, flesh filled, blood brimmed the curse.
 Selfyeast of spirit a dull dough sours. I see
The lost are like this, and their scourge to be
As I am mine, their sweating selves; but worse.

The Blessed Virgin Compared
to the Air We Breathe

Wild air, world-mothering air,
Nestling me everywhere,
That each eyelash or hair
Girdles; goes home betwixt
The fleeciest, frailest-flixed
Snowflake; that's fairly mixed
With, riddles, and is rife
In every least thing's life;
This needful, never spent,
And nursing element;
My more than meat and drink,
My meal at every wink;
This air, which, by life's law,
My lung must draw and draw
Now but to breathe its praise,
Minds me in many ways
Of her who not only
Gave God's infinity
Dwindled to infancy
Welcome in womb and breast,
Birth, milk, and all the rest
But mothers each new grace
That does now reach our race—
Mary Immaculate,
Merely a woman, yet
Whose presence, power is
Great as no goddess's
Was deemèd, dreamèd; who
This one work has to do—
Let all God's glory through,
God's glory which would go
Through her and from her flow
Off, and no way but so.

I say that we are wound
With mercy round and round

As if with air: the same
Is Mary, more by name.
She, wild web, wondrous robe,
Mantles the guilty globe,
Since God has let dispense
Her prayers his providence:
Nay, more than almoner,
The sweet alms' self is her
And men are meant to share
Her life as life does air.
    If I have understood,
She holds high motherhood
Towards all our ghostly good
And plays in grace her part
About man's beating heart,
Laying, like air's fine flood,
The deathdance in his blood;
Yet no part but what will
Be Christ our Saviour still.
Of her flesh he took flesh:
He does take fresh and fresh,
Though much the mystery how,
Not flesh but spirit now
And makes, O marvellous!
New Nazareths in us,
Where she shall yet conceive
Him, morning, noon, and eve;
New Bethlems, and he born
There, evening, noon, and morn—
Bethlem or Nazareth,
Men here may draw like breath
More Christ and baffle death;
Who, born so, comes to be
New self and nobler me
In each one and each one
More makes, when all is done,
Both God's and Mary's Son.
    Again, look overhead
How air is azurèd;
O how! nay do but stand
Where you can lift your hand
Skywards: rich, rich it laps
Round the four fingergaps.
Yet such a sapphire-shot,
Charged, steepèd sky will not
Stain light. Yea, mark you this:

It does no prejudice.
The glass-blue days are those
When every colour glows,
Each shape and shadow shows.
Blue be it: this blue heaven
The seven or seven times seven
Hued sunbeam will transmit
Perfect, not alter it.
Of if there does some soft,
On things aloof, aloft,
Bloom breathe, that one breath more
Earth is the fairer for.
Whereas did air not make
This bath of blue and slake
His fire, the sun would shake,
A blear and blinding ball
With blackness bound, and all
The thick stars round him roll
Flashing like flecks of coal,
Quartz-fret, or sparks of salt,
In grimy vasty vault.
       So God was god of old:
A mother came to mould
Those limbs like ours which are
What must make our daystar
Much dearer to mankind;
Whose glory bare would blind
Or less would win man's mind.
Through her we may see him
Made sweeter, not made dim,
And her hand leaves his light
Sifted to suit our sight.
       Be thou then, O thou dear
Mother, my atmosphere;
My happier world, wherein
To wend and meet no sin;
Above me, round me lie
Fronting my froward eye
With sweet and scarless sky;
Stir in my ears, speak there
Of God's love, O live air,
Of patience, penance, prayer:
World-mothering air, air wild,
Wound with thee, in thee isled,
Fold home, fast fold thy child.

Spelt from Sibyl's Leaves

Earnest, earthless, equal, attuneable, | vaulty, voluminous, . . stu-
pendous

Evening strains to be tíme's vást, | womb-of-all, home-of-all, hearse-
of-all night.

Her fond yellow hornlight wound to the west, | her wild hollow
hoarlight hung to the height

Waste; her earliest stars, earl-stars, | stárs principal, overbend us,

Fíre-féaturing heaven. For earth | her being has unbound, her dap-
ple is at an end, as-

tray or aswarm, all throughther, in throngs; | self ín self steepèd
and páshed—qúite

Disremembering, dísmémbering | áll now. Heart, you round me
right

With: Óur évening is over us; óur night | whélms, whélms, ánd will
end us.

Only the beak-leaved boughs dragonish | damask the tool-smooth
bleak light; black

Ever so black on it. Óur tale, O óur oracle! | Lét life, wáned, ah
lét life wind

Off hér once skéined stained véined varíety | upon, áll on twó spools;
párt, pen, páck

Now her áll in twó flocks, twó folds—black, white; | right, wrong;
reckon but, reck but, mind

But thése two; wáre of a wórld where bút these | twó tell, each off
the óther; of a rack

Where, selfwrung, selfstrung, sheathe- and shelterless, | thóughts
agaínst thoughts ín groans grínd.

Spring and Fall

TO A YOUNG CHILD

Márgarét, are you gríeving
Over Goldengrove unleaving?
Leáves, líke the things of man, you
With your fresh thoughts care for, can you?
Áh! ás the heart grows older
It will come to such sights colder
By and by, nor spare a sigh
Though worlds of wanwood leafmeal lie;
And yet you wíll weep and know why.
Now no matter, child, the name:

Sórrow's springs áre the same.
Nor mouth had, no nor mind, expressed
What heart heard of, ghost guessed:
It ís the blight man was born for,
It is Margaret you mourn for.

Felix Randal

Felix Randal the farrier, O he is dead then? my duty all ended,
Who have watched his mould of man, big-boned and hardy-hand-
some
Pining, pining, till time when reason rambled in it and some
Fatal four disorders, fleshed there, all contended?

Sickness broke him. Impatient he cursed at first, but mended
Being anointed and all; though a heavenlier heart began some
Months earlier, since I had our sweet reprieve and ransom
Tendered to him. Ah well, God rest him all road ever he offended!

This seeing the sick endears them to us, us too it endears.
My tongue had taught thee comfort, touch had quenched thy tears,
Thy tears that touched my heart, child, Felix, poor Felix Randal;

How far from then forethought of, all thy more boisterous years,
When thou at the random grim forge, powerful amidst peers,
Didst fettle for the great grey drayhorse his bright and battering
sandal!

The Caged Skylark

As a dare-gale skylark scanted in a dull cage
    Man's mounting spirit in his bone-house, mean house, dwells—
    That bird beyond the remembering his free fells;
This in drudgery, day-labouring-out life's age.

Though aloft on turf or perch or poor low stage,
    Both sing sometimes the sweetest, sweetest spells,
    Yet both droop deadly sómetimes in their cells
Or wring their barriers in bursts of fear or rage.

Not that the sweet-fowl, song-fowl, needs no rest—
Why, hear him, hear him babble and drop down to his nest,
    But his own nest, wild nest, no prison.

Man's spirit will be flesh-bound when found at best,
But uncumbered: meadow-down is not distressed
For a rainbow footing it nor he for his bónes rísen.

Hurrahing in Harvest

Summer ends now; now, barbarous in beauty, the stooks arise
  Around; up above, what wind-walks! what lovely behaviour
  Of silk-sack clouds! has wilder, wilful-wavier
Meal-drift moulded ever and melted across skies?

I walk, I lift up, I lift up heart, eyes,
  Down all that glory in the heavens to glean our Saviour;
  And, éyes, heárt, what looks, what lips yet gave you a
Rapturous love's greeting of realer, of rounder replies?

And the azurous hung hills are his world-wielding shoulder
  Majestic—as a stallion stalwart, very-violet-sweet!—
These things, these things were here and but the beholder
  Wanting; which two when they once meet,
The heart rears wings bold and bolder
  And hurls for him, O half hurls earth for him off under his feet.

The Windhover

TO CHRIST OUR LORD

I caught this morning morning's minion, king-
  dom of daylight's dauphin, dapple-dawn-drawn Falcon, in his riding
  Of the rolling level underneath him steady air, and striding
High there, how he rung upon the rein of a wimpling wing
In his ecstacy! then off, off forth on swing,
  As a skate's heel sweeps smooth on a bow-bend: the hurl and
    gliding
  Rebuffed the big wind. My heart in hiding
Stirred for a bird,—the achieve of, the mastery of the thing!

Brute beauty and valour and act, oh, air, pride, plume, here
  Buckle! AND the fire that breaks from thee then, a billion
Times told lovelier, more dangerous, O my chevalier!
  No wonder of it: shéer plód makes plough down sillion
Shine, and blue-bleak embers, ah my dear,
  Fall, gall themselves, and gash gold-vermilion.

God's Grandeur

The world is charged with the grandeur of God.
It will flame out, like shining from shook foil;
It gathers to a greatness, like the ooze of oil
Crushed. Why do men then now not reck his rod?
Generations have trod, have trod, have trod;
And all is seared with trade; bleared, smeared with toil;
And wears man's smudge and shares man's smell: the soil
Is bare now, nor can foot feel, being shod.

And for all this, nature is never spent;
There lives the dearest freshness deep down things;
And though the last lights off the black West went
Oh, morning, at the brown brink eastward, springs—
Because the Holy Ghost over the bent
World broods with warm breast and with ah! bright wings.

ROBERT BRIDGES
1844-1930

Poor Poll

I saw it all, Polly, how when you had call'd for sop
and your good friend the cook came & fill'd up your pan
you yerk'd it out deftly by beakfuls scattering it
away far as you might upon the sunny lawn
then summon'd with loud cry the little garden birds
to take their feast. Quickly came they flustering around
Ruddock & Merle & Finch squabbling among themselves
nor gave you thanks nor heed while you sat silently
watching, and I beside you in perplexity
lost in the maze of all mystery and all knowledge
felt how deep lieth the fount of man's benevolence
if a bird can share it & take pleasure in it.
     If you, my bird, I thought, had a philosophy
it might be a sounder scheme than what our moralists
propound: because thou, Poll, livest in the darkness
which human Reason searching from outside would pierce,
but, being of so feeble a candle-power, can only
show up to view the cloud that it illuminates.
Thus reason'd I: then marvell'd how you can adapt

your wild bird-mood to endure your tame environment
the domesticities of English household life
and your small brass-wire cabin, who sh^{dst} live on wing
harrying the tropical branch-flowering wilderness:
Yet Nature gave you a gift of easy mimicry
whereby you have come to win uncanny sympathies
and morsell'd utterance of our Germanic talk
as schoolmasters in Greek will flaunt their hackney'd tags
φωνᾶντα συνετοῖσιν and κτῆμα ἐς ἀεὶ,
ἡ γλῶσσ' ὁμώμοχ', ἡ δὲ φρὴν ἀνώμοτος
tho' you with a better ear copy ús more perfectly
nor without connotation as when you call'd for sop
all with that stumpy wooden tongue & vicious beak
that dry whistling shrieking tearing cutting pincer
now eagerly subservient to your cautious claws
exploring all varieties of attitude
in irrepressible blind groping for escape
—a very figure & image of man's soul on earth
the almighty cosmic Will fidgeting in a trap—
in your quenchless unknown desire for the unknown life
of which some homely British sailor robb'd you, alas!
'Tis all that doth your silly thoughts so busy keep
the while you sit moping like Patience on a perch
—Wie viele Tag' und Nächte bist du geblieben!
La possa delle gambe posta in tregue—
the impeccable spruceness of your grey-feather'd poll
a model in hairdressing for the dandiest old Duke
enough to qualify you for the House of Lords
or the Athenaeum Club, to poke among the nobs
great intellectual nobs and literary nobs
scientific nobs and Bishops ex officio:
nor lack you simulation of profoundest wisdom
such as men's features oft acquire in very old age
by mere cooling of passion & decay of muscle
by faint renunciation even of untold regrets;
who seeing themselves a picture of that wh: man should-be
learn almost what it were to be what they are-not.
But you can never have cherish'd a determined hope
consciously to renounce or lose it, you will live
your threescore years & ten idle and puzzle-headed
as any mumping monk in his unfurnish'd cell
in peace that, poor Polly, passeth Understanding—
merely because you lack what we men understand
by Understanding. Well! well! that's the difference
C'est la seule différence, mais c'est important.
Ah! your pale sedentary life! but would you change?

exchange it for one crowded hour of glorious life,
one blind furious tussle with a madden'd monkey
who would throttle you and throw your crude fragments away
shreds unintelligible of an unmeaning act
dans la profonde horreur de l'éternelle nuit?
Why ask? You cannot know. 'Twas by no choice of yours
that you mischanged for monkeys' man's society,
'twas that British sailor drove you from Paradise—
Εἴθ' ὤφελ' Ἀργοῦς μὴ διαπτάσθαι σκάφος!
I'd hold embargoes on such ghastly traffic.

    I am writing verses to you & grieve that you sh^d be
absolument incapable de les comprendre,
Tu, Polle, nescis ista nec potes scire:—
Alas! Iambic, scazon and alexandrine,
spondee or choriamb, all is alike to you—
my well-continued fanciful experiment
wherein so many strange verses amalgamate
on the secure bedrock of Milton's prosody:
not but that when I speak you will incline an ear
in critical attention lest by chánce I míght
póssibly say sómething that was worth repeating:
I am adding (do you think?) pages to literature
that gouty excrement of human intellect
accumulating slowly & everlastingly
depositing, like guano on the Peruvian shore,
to be perhaps exhumed in some remotest age
(*piis secunda, vate me, detur fuga*)
to fertilize the scanty dwarf'd intelligence
of a new race of beings the unhallow'd offspring
of them who shall have quite dismember'd & destroy'd
our temple of Christian faith & fair Hellenic art
just as that monkey would, poor Polly, have done for you.

Nightingales

    Beautiful must be the mountains whence ye come,
  And bright in the fruitful valleys the streams, wherefrom
        Ye learn your song:
Where are those starry woods? O might I wander there,
  Among the flowers, which in that heavenly air
        Bloom the year long!

    Nay, barren are those mountains and spent the streams:
  Our song is the voice of desire, that haunts our dreams,
        A throe of the heart,

Whose pining visions dim, forbidden hopes profound,
No dying cadence nor long sigh can sound,
    For all our art.

Alone, aloud in the raptured ear of men
We pour our dark nocturnal secret; and then,
    As night is withdrawn
From these sweet-springing meads and bursting boughs of May,
Dream, while the innumerable choir of day
    Welcome the dawn.

"The Storm Is Over"

The storm is over, the land hushes to rest:
The tyrannous wind, its strength fordone,
Is fallen back in the west
To couch with the sinking sun.
The last clouds fare
With fainting speed, and their thin streamers fly
In melting drifts of the sky.
Already the birds in the air
Appear again; the rooks return to their haunt,
And one by one,
Proclaiming aloud their care,
Renew their peaceful chant.

Torn and shattered the trees their branches again reset,
They trim afresh the fair
Few green and golden leaves withheld from the storm,
And awhile will be handsome yet.
To-morrow's sun shall caress
Their remnant of loveliness:
In quiet days for a time
Sad Autumn lingering warm
Shall humour their faded prime.

But ah! the leaves of summer that lie on the ground!
What havoc! The laughing timbrels of June,
That curtained the birds' cradles, and screened their song,
That sheltered the cooing doves at noon,
Of airy fans the delicate throng,—
Torn and scattered around:
Far out afield they lie,
In the watery furrows die,
In grassy pools of the flood they sink and drown,

Green-golden, orange, vermilion, golden and brown,
The high year's flaunting crown
Shattered and trampled down.

The day is done: the tired land looks for night:
She prays to the night to keep
In peace her nerves of delight:
While silver mist upstealeth silently,
And the broad cloud-driving moon in the clear sky
Lifts o'er the firs her shining shield,
And in her tranquil light
Sleep falls on forest and field.
Sée! sléep hath fallen: the trees are asleep:
The night is come. The land is wrapt in sleep.

A. E. HOUSMAN
1859-1936

"Smooth Between Sea and Land"

Smooth between sea and land
Is laid the yellow sand,
And here through summer days
The seed of Adam plays.

Here the child comes to found
His unremaining mound,
And the grown lad to score
Two names upon the shore.

Here, on the level sand,
Between the sea and land,
What shall I build or write
Against the fall of night?

Tell me of runes to grave
That hold the bursting wave,
Or bastions to design
For longer date than mine.

Shall it be Troy or Rome
I fence against the foam,

Or my own name, to stay
When I depart for aye?

Nothing: too near at hand,
Planing the figured sand,
Effacing clean and fast
Cities not built to last
And charms devised in vain,
Pours the confounding main.

"The Night Is Freezing Fast"

The night is freezing fast,
   To-morrow comes December;
      And winterfalls of old
Are with me from the past;
      And chiefly I remember
         How Dick would hate the cold.

Fall, winter, fall; for he,
   Prompt hand and headpiece clever,
      Has woven a winter robe,
And made of earth and sea
      His overcoat for ever,
         And wears the turning globe.

"Tell Me Not Here"

Tell me not here, it needs not saying,
   What tune the enchantress plays
In aftermaths of soft September
   Or under blanching mays,
For she and I were long acquainted
   And I knew all her ways.

On russet floors, by waters idle,
   The pine lets fall its cone;
The cuckoo shouts all day at nothing
   In leafy dells alone;
And traveller's joy beguiles in autumn
   Hearts that have lost their own.

On acres of the seeded grasses
   The changing burnish heaves;

Or marshalled under moons of harvest
    Stand still all night the sheaves;
Or beeches strip in storms for winter
    And stain the wind with leaves.

Possess, as I possessed a season,
    The countries I resign,
Where over elmy plains the highway
    Would mount the hills and shine,
And full of shade the pillared forest
    Would murmur and be mine.

For nature, heartless, witless nature,
    Will neither care nor know
What stranger's feet may find the meadow
    And trespass there and go,
Nor ask amid the dews of morning
    If they are mine or no.

WILLIAM BUTLER YEATS
1865-1939

News for the Delphic Oracle

I

There all the golden codgers lay,
There the silver dew,
And the great water sighed for love,
And the wind sighed too.
Man-picker Niamh leant and sighed
By Oisin on the grass;
There sighed amid his choir of love
Tall Pythagoras.
Plotinus came and looked about,
The salt-flakes on his breast,
And having stretched and yawned awhile
Lay sighing like the rest.

II

Straddling each a dolphin's back
And steadied by a fin,

Those Innocents re-live their death,
Their wounds open again.
The ecstatic waters laugh because
Their cries are sweet and strange,
Through their ancestral patterns dance,
And the brute dolphins plunge
Until, in some cliff-sheltered bay
Where wades the choir of love
Proffering its sacred laurel crowns,
They pitch their burdens off.

III

Slim adolescence that a nymph has stripped,
Peleus on Thetis stares.
Her limbs are delicate as an eyelid,
Love has blinded him with tears;
But Thetis' belly listens.
Down the mountain walls
From where Pan's cavern is
Intolerable music falls.
Foul goat-head, brutal arm appear,
Belly, shoulder, bum,
Flash fishlike; nymphs and satyrs
Copulate in the foam.

Lapis Lazuli

FOR HARRY CLIFTON

I have heard that hysterical women say
They are sick of the palette and fiddle-bow,
Of poets that are always gay,
For everybody knows or else should know
That if nothing drastic is done
Aeroplane and Zeppelin will come out,
Pitch like King Billy bomb-balls in
Until the town lie beaten flat.

All perform their tragic play,
There struts Hamlet, there is Lear,
That's Ophelia, that Cordelia;
Yet they, should the last scene be there,
The great stage curtain about to drop,
If worthy their prominent part in the play,

Do not break up their lines to weep.
They know that Hamlet and Lear are gay;
Gaiety transfiguring all that dread.
All men have aimed at, found and lost;
Black out; Heaven blazing into the head:
Tragedy wrought to its uttermost.
Though Hamlet rambles and Lear rages,
And all the drop-scenes drop at once
Upon a hundred thousand stages,
It cannot grow by an inch or an ounce.

On their own feet they came, or on shipboard,
Camel-back, horse-back, ass-back, mule-back,
Old civilisations put to the sword.
Then they and their wisdom went to rack:
No handiwork of Callimachus,
Who handled marble as if it were bronze,
Made draperies that seemed to rise
When sea-wind swept the corner, stands;
His long lamp-chimney shaped like the stem
Of a slender palm, stood but a day;
All things fall and are built again,
And those that build them again are gay.

Two Chinamen, behind them a third,
Are carved in Lapis Lazuli,
Over them flies a long-legged bird,
A symbol of longevity;
The third, doubtless a serving-man,
Carries a musical instrument.

Every discolouration of the stone,
Every accidental crack or dent,
Seems a water-course or an avalanche,
Or lofty slope where it still snows
Though doubtless plum or cherry-branch
Sweetens the little half-way house
Those Chinamen climb towards, and I
Delight to imagine them seated there;
There, on the mountain and the sky,
On all the tragic scene they stare.
One asks for mournful melodies;
Accomplished fingers begin to play.
Their eyes mid many wrinkles, their eyes,
Their ancient, glittering eyes, are gay.

Byzantium

The unpurged images of day recede;
The Emperor's drunken soldiery are abed;
Night resonance recedes, night-walkers' song
After great cathedral gong;
A starlit or a moonlit dome disdains
All that man is,
All mere complexities,
The fury and the mire of human veins.

Before me floats an image, man or shade,
Shade more than man, more image than a shade;
For Hades' bobbin bound in mummy-cloth
May unwind the winding path;
A mouth that has no moisture and no breath
Breathless mouths may summon;
I hail the superhuman;
I call it death-in-life and life-in-death.

Miracle, bird or golden handiwork,
More miracle than bird or handiwork,
Planted on the star-lit golden bough,
Can like the cocks of Hades crow,
Or, by the moon embittered, scorn aloud
In glory of changeless metal
Common bird or petal
And all complexities of mire or blood.

At midnight on the Emperor's pavement flit
Flames that no faggot feeds, nor steel has lit,
Nor storm disturbs, flames begotten of flame,
Where blood-begotten spirits come
And all complexities of fury leave,
Dying into a dance,
An agony of trance,
An agony of flame that cannot singe a sleeve.

Astraddle on the dolphin's mire and blood,
Spirit after spirit! The smithies break the flood,
The golden smithies of the Emperor!
Marbles of the dancing floor
Break bitter furies of complexity,
Those images that yet
Fresh images beget,
That dolphin-torn, that gong-tormented sea.

1930

Sailing to Byzantium

I

That is no country for old men. The young
In one another's arms, birds in the trees,
—Those dying generations—at their song,
The salmon-falls, the mackerel-crowded seas,
Fish, flesh, or fowl, commend all summer long
Whatever is begotten, born, and dies.
Caught in that sensual music all neglect
Monuments of unageing intellect.

II

An aged man is but a paltry thing,
A tattered coat upon a stick, unless
Soul clap its hands and sing, and louder sing
For every tatter in its mortal dress,
Nor is there singing school but studying
Monuments of its own magnificence;
And therefore I have sailed the seas and come
To the holy city of Byzantium.

III

O sages standing in God's holy fire
As in the gold mosaic of a wall,
Come from the holy fire, perne in a gyre,
And be the singing-masters of my soul.
Consume my heart away; sick with desire
And fastened to a dying animal
It knows not what it is; and gather me
Into the artifice of eternity.

IV

Once out of nature I shall never take
My bodily form from any natural thing,
But such a form as Grecian goldsmiths make
Of hammered gold and gold enamelling
To keep a drowsy Emperor awake;
Or set upon a golden bough to sing
To lords and ladies of Byzantium
Of what is past, or passing, or to come.

1927

Two Songs from a Play

I

I saw a staring virgin stand
Where holy Dionysus died,
And tear the heart out of his side,
And lay the heart upon her hand
And bear that beating heart away;
And then did all the Muses sing
Of Magnus Annus at the spring,
As though God's death were but a play.

Another Troy must rise and set,
Another lineage feed the crow,
Another Argo's painted prow
Drive to a flashier bauble yet.
The Roman Empire stood appalled:
It dropped the reins of peace and war
When that fierce virgin and her Star
Out of the fabulous darkness called.

II

In pity for man's darkening thought
He walked that room and issued thence
In Galilean turbulence;
The Babylonian starlight brought
A fabulous, formless darkness in;
Odour of blood when Christ was slain
Made all Platonic tolerance vain
And vain all Doric discipline.

Everything that man esteems
Endures a moment or a day.
Love's pleasure drives his love away,
The painter's brush consumes his dreams;
The herald's cry, the soldier's tread
Exhaust his glory and his might:
Whatever flames upon the night
Man's own resinous heart has fed.

The Tower

I

What shall I do with this absurdity—
O heart, O troubled heart—this caricature,
Decrepit age that has been tied to me
As to a dog's tail?
                              Never had I more
Excited, passionate, fantastical
Imagination, nor an ear and eye
That more expected the impossible—
No, not in boyhood when with rod and fly,
Or the humbler worm, I climbed Ben Bulben's back
And had the livelong summer day to spend.
It seems that I must bid the Muse go pack,
Choose Plato and Plotinus for a friend
Until imagination, ear and eye,
Can be content with argument and deal
In abstract things; or be derided by
A sort of battered kettle at the heel.

II

I pace upon the battlements and stare
On the foundations of a house, or where
Tree, like a sooty finger, starts from the earth;
And send imagination forth
Under the day's declining beam, and call
Images and memories
From ruin or from ancient trees,
For I would ask a question of them all.

Beyond that ridge lived Mrs. French, and once
When every silver candlestick or sconce
Lit up the dark mahogany and the wine,
A serving-man, that could divine
That most respected lady's every wish,
Ran and with the garden shears
Clipped an insolent farmer's ears
And brought them in a little covered dish.

Some few remembered still when I was young
A peasant girl commended by a song,
Who'd lived somewhere upon that rocky place,
And praised the colour of her face,

And had the greater joy in praising her,
Remembering that, if walked she there,
Farmers jostled at the fair
So great a glory did the song confer.

And certain men, being maddened by those rhymes,
Or else by toasting her a score of times,
Rose from the table and declared it right
To test their fancy by their sight;
But they mistook the brightness of the moon
For the prosaic light of day—
Music had driven their wits astray—
And one was drowned in the great bog of Cloone.

Strange, but the man who made the song was blind;
Yet, now I have considered it, I find
That nothing strange; the tragedy began
With Homer that was a blind man,
And Helen has all living hearts betrayed.
O may the moon and sunlight seem
One inextricable beam,
For if I triumph I must make men mad.

And I myself created Hanrahan
And drove him drunk or sober through the dawn
From somewhere in the neighbouring cottages.
Caught by an old man's juggleries
He stumbled, tumbled, fumbled to and fro
And had but broken knees for hire
And horrible splendour of desire;
I thought it all out twenty years ago:

Good fellows shuffled cards in an old bawn;
And when that ancient ruffian's turn was on
He so bewitched the cards under his thumb
That all but the one card became
A pack of hounds and not a pack of cards,
And that he changed into a hare.
Hanrahan rose in frenzy there
And followed up those baying creatures towards—

O towards I have forgotten what—enough!
I must recall a man that neither love
Nor music nor an enemy's clipped ear
Could, he was so harried, cheer;
A figure that has grown so fabulous

There's not a neighbour left to say
When he finished his dog's day;
An ancient bankrupt master of this house.

Before that ruin came, for centuries,
Rough men-at-arms, cross-gartered to the knees
Or shod in iron, climbed the narrow stairs,
And certain men-at-arms there were
Whose images, in the Great Memory stored,
Come with loud cry and panting breast
To break upon a sleeper's rest
While their great wooden dice beat on the board.

As I would question all, come all who can;
Come old, necessitous, half-mounted man;
And bring beauty's blind rambling celebrant;
The red man the juggler sent
Through God-forsaken meadows; Mrs. French,
Gifted with so fine an ear;
The man drowned in a bog's mire,
When mocking muses chose the country wench.

Did all old men and women, rich and poor,
Who trod upon these rocks or passed this door,
Whether in public or in secret rage
As I do now against old age?
But I have found an answer in those eyes
That are impatient to be gone;
Go therefore; but leave Hanrahan,
For I need all his mighty memories.

Old lecher with a love on every wind,
Bring up out of that deep considering mind
All that you have discovered in the grave,
For it is certain that you have
Reckoned up every unforeknown, unseeing
Plunge, lured by a softening eye,
Or by a touch or a sigh,
Into the labyrinth of another's being;

Does the imagination dwell the most
Upon a woman won or woman lost?
If on the lost, admit you turned aside
From a great labyrinth out of pride,
Cowardice, some silly over-subtle thought
Or anything called conscience once;

And that if memory recur, the sun's
Under eclipse and the day blotted out.

III

It is time that I wrote my will;
I choose upstanding men
That climb the streams until
The fountain leap, and at dawn
Drop their cast at the side
Of dripping stone; I declare
They shall inherit my pride,
The pride of people that were
Bound neither to Cause nor to State,
Neither to slaves that were spat on,
Nor to the tyrants that spat,
The people of Burke and Grattan
That gave, though free to refuse—
Pride, like that of the morn,
When the headlong light is loose,
Or that of the fabulous horn,
Or that of the sudden shower
When all streams are dry,
Or that of the hour
When the swan must fix his eye
Upon a fading gleam,
Float out upon a long
Last reach of glittering stream
And there sing his last song.
And I declare my faith:
I mock Plotinus' thought
And cry in Plato's teeth,
Death and life were not
Till man made up the whole,
Made lock, stock and barrel
Out of his bitter soul,
Aye, sun and moon and star, all,
And further add to that
That, being dead, we rise,
Dream and so create
Translunar Paradise.
I have prepared my peace
With learned Italian things
And the proud stones of Greece,
Poet's imaginings
And memories of love,

Memories of the words of women,
All those things whereof
Man makes a superhuman
Mirror-resembling dream.

As at the loophole there
The daws chatter and scream,
And drop twigs layer upon layer.
When they have mounted up,
The mother bird will rest
On their hollow top,
And so warm her wild nest.

I leave both faith and pride
To young upstanding men
Climbing the mountain side,
That under bursting dawn
They may drop a fly;
Being of that metal made
Till it was broken by
This sedentary trade.

Now shall I make my soul,
Compelling it to study
In a learned school
Till the wreck of body,
Slow decay of blood,
Testy delirium
Or dull decrepitude,
Or what worse evil come—
The death of friends, or death
Of every brilliant eye
That made a catch in the breath—
Seem but the clouds of the sky
When the horizon fades;
Or a bird's sleepy cry
Among the deepening shades.

                                    1926

Nineteen Hundred and Nineteen

I

Many ingenious lovely things are gone
That seemed sheer miracle to the multitude,
Protected from the circle of the moon
That pitches common things about. There stood
Amid the ornamental bronze and stone
An ancient image made of olive wood—
And gone are Phidias' famous ivories
And all the golden grasshoppers and bees.

We too had many pretty toys when young;
A law indifferent to blame or praise,
To bribe or threat; habits that made old wrong
Melt down, as it were wax in the sun's rays;
Public opinion ripening for so long
We thought it would outlive all future days.
O what fine thought we had because we thought
That the worst rogues and rascals had died out.

All teeth were drawn, all ancient tricks unlearned,
And a great army but a showy thing;
What matter that no cannon had been turned
Into a ploughshare? Parliament and king
Thought that unless a little powder burned
The trumpeters might burst with trumpeting
And yet it lack all glory; and perchance
The guardsmen's drowsy chargers would not prance.

Now days are dragon-ridden, the nightmare
Rides upon sleep: a drunken soldiery
Can leave the mother, murdered at her door,
To crawl in her own blood, and go scot-free;
The night can sweat with terror as before
We pieced our thoughts into philosophy,
And planned to bring the world under a rule,
Who are but weasels fighting in a hole.

He who can read the signs nor sink unmanned
Into the half-deceit of some intoxicant
From shallow wits; who knows no work can stand,
Whether health, wealth or peace of mind were spent
On master-work of intellect or hand,
No honour leave its mighty monument,

Has but one comfort left: all triumph would
But break upon his ghostly solitude.

But is there any comfort to be found?
Man is in love and loves what vanishes,
What more is there to say? That country round
None dared admit, if such a thought were his,
Incendiary or bigot could be found
To burn that stump on the Acropolis,
Or break in bits the famous ivories
Or traffic in the grasshoppers or bees.

II

When Loie Fuller's Chinese dancers enwound
A shining web, a floating ribbon of cloth,
It seemed that a dragon of air
Had fallen among dancers, had whirled them round
Or hurried them off on its own furious path;
So the Platonic Year
Whirls out new right and wrong,
Whirls in the old instead;
All men are dancers and their tread
Goes to the barbarous clangour of a gong.

III

Some moralist or mythological poet
Compares the solitary soul to a swan;
I am satisfied with that,
Satisfied if a troubled mirror show it,
Before that brief gleam of its life be gone,
An image of its state;
The wings half spread for flight,
The breast thrust out in pride
Whether to play, or to ride
Those winds that clamour of approaching night.

A man in his own secret meditation
Is lost amid the labyrinth that he has made
In art or politics;
Some Platonist affirms that in the station
Where we should cast off body and trade
The ancient habit sticks,
And that if our works could
But vanish with our breath

That were a lucky death,
For triumph can but mar our solitude.

The swan has leaped into the desolate heaven:
That image can bring wildness, bring a rage
To end all things, to end
What my laborious life imagined, even
The half-imagined, the half-written page;
O but we dreamed to mend
What ever mischief seemed
To afflict mankind, but now
That winds of winter blow
Learn that we were crack-pated when we dreamed.

IV

We, who seven years ago
Talked of honour and of truth,
Shriek with pleasure if we show
The weasel's twist, the weasel's tooth.

V

Come let us mock at the great
That had such burdens on the mind
And toiled so hard and late
To leave some monument behind,
Nor thought of the levelling wind.

Come let us mock at the wise;
With all those calendars whereon
They fixed old aching eyes,
They never saw how seasons run,
And now but gape at the sun.

Come let us mock at the good
That fancied goodness might be gay,
And sick of solitude
Might proclaim a holiday:
Wind shrieked—and where are they?

Mock mockers after that
That would not lift a hand maybe
To help good, wise or great
To bar that foul storm out, for we
Traffic in mockery.

VI

Violence upon the roads: violence of horses;
Some few have handsome riders, are garlanded
On delicate sensitive ear or tossing mane,
But wearied running round and round in their courses
All break and vanish, and evil gathers head:
Herodias' daughters have returned again,
A sudden blast of dusty wind and after
Thunder of feet, tumult of images,
Their purpose in the labyrinth of the wind;
And should some crazy hand dare touch a daughter
All turn with amorous cries, or angry cries,
According to the wind, for all are blind.
But now wind drops, dust settles; thereupon
There lurches past, his great eyes without thought
Under the shadow of stupid straw-pale locks,
That insolent fiend Robert Artisson
To whom the love-lorn Lady Kyteler brought
Bronzed peacock feathers, red combs of her cocks.

1919

EDGAR LEE MASTERS

1869-1950

The Lost Orchard

Loves and sorrows of those who lose an orchard
Are less seen than the shadow shells
Of butterflies whose wings are tortured
In the perilous escape of rainy dells,
In the ecstatic flight of blinding Junes.
Save for the breath dirge of the wind-rung harebells
They have no words that ever shall be known,
Neither have they speech or tone,
Save the tones when the sun with gold galloons
Trims the blue edges of the air;
And save the quiet which quells
The music of the water drop in the well's
Water far down, where vision swoons.

These are the voices and these alone
Of the lost orchard, and its vague despair.

Branches may gnarl with scale and lift their bare
Paralysis, or the withered crone
Of loneliness breed water sprouts; or frost
Heap the dull turf over the strawberry vines;
Or rust unhinge the gates; or the fallen pear
Waste like the Cretan gold of ruined shrines
In tangled grasses; or the broken share
Be sunk in leaf mould—these are noonday signs
Of the deserted, but not of the orchard that is lost.
Silver secrets speak of the lost orchard, as the shells
Of butterflies escaped whisper the vanished wings;
Or as light shaken from the field of clover tells
Of the zephyr's irised wanderings.

A lost orchard is the memory of a friend
Wronged by life to death, who lies
Lifelike, but with unseeing eyes.
It is music made a ghost, because the end
Of life has come which made the music mean
Eyes that look and lips that thrill.
Music is no breast where wounded souls may lean,
If played when hands it signified are still.
A lost orchard is the road on which we passed
Where a house was with a candle in the night;
And we must go that way still, but at last
The house is by the roadside, but no light.

Over a lost orchard I have strayed
In March when down the wooded ravine
The behemoth wind bellowed to the glade
By the sky-blue water before the rushes were green.
While yet the acorn cups crushed under feet
Against the moss mould, yellow as smoke;
And the lanterns of wild cucumbers quenched by sleet,
And gusts of winter hung by the leafless oak;
When the crow's nest was a splotch of sticks on the sky,
And burnt out torches of feast the sumach cone.
And I have climbed till the wind was naught but a sigh
Over the stairs of stone and the seat of stone.
And there I have seen the orchard, the apple trees
Patient in loneliness, and forgotten care;
And the grass as heavy as the Sargasso Sea's
Around the trunks, grown like a dead man's hair.
And I have returned in Spring when the nebulae
Of early blossoms whitened before it was June;
And I have seen them merge in their leafy sky

Till they became the light of the full moon.
Warm is the orchard as the stalls of the sun
At midnight, when each budded stem is dewed
With a firefly and the whispering zephyrs run
From leaf to leaf, awaking the dreams that brood
Before the gray woolens of the shadows fall
From the sleeping earth, and the lights of the orchard are wooed
From sea gray to sea green in a carnival
Change of flame, in a dawning many hued.
Till the long winds come, blowing from woodlands over
The glistening water, and meadows beyond the citrine
Sand of the hill that walls the field of clover
Nod their blossoms amid a tide of green.

Angles are never in caverns, nor presences
That speak the will to leave it lingering
About the orchard lost. Nor does the chrysalis
Lie thick in paths of the arisen wing;
Nor butterflies haunt the grasses like innocent
Desires defeated; not the coverts mourn
With doves; nor are the wild bees rent
From habitations in old trees; nor the forlorn
Grass grow rich bespeaking humble hopes;
Nor corners of giant heliotropes
Droop so memorially; nor the stair of stone
Hold the silence that follows a footfall; nor the sky
Above the stone seat by its emptiness alone
Tell of a face and of a wondering eye;
Nor are flowers without the fruit so richly grown.

The house of the lost orchard is loneliness to the uttermost:
The chimney in the top of the elm tree,
Like the open mouth of a musing ghost
Has nothing but the void of the sky,
And the sequestered flight of the passing cloud,
Though the expectant breeze goes by
To gather smoke from the hearth long disavowed.
And under a brick of the porch the key to the fastened door
Glints out of rust and waits
For those who won the orchard to explore
The rooms and find the unveiled Fates.
Out of the lost orchard is life that needs the orchard no more,
The fence has broken places, and the gates
Swing to the passing wind. But butterflies soar
Over the treetops to predestined mates.

                                        1935

Thomas Trevelyan

Reading in Ovid the sorrowful story of Itys,
Son of the love of Tereus and Procne, slain
For the guilty passions of Tereus for Philomela,
The flesh of him served to Tereus by Procne,
And the wrath of Tereus, the murderess pursuing
Till the gods made Philomela a nightingale,
Lute of the rising moon, and Procne a swallow!
Oh livers and artists of Hellas a century gone,
Sealing in little thuribles dreams and wisdom,
Incense beyond all price, forever fragrant,
A breath whereof makes clear the eyes of the soul!
How I inhaled its sweetness here in Spoon River!
The thurible opening when I had lived and learned
How all of us kill the children of love, and all of us,
Knowing not what we do, devour their flesh;
And all of us change to singers, although it be
But once in our lives, or change—alas!—to swallows,
To twitter amid cold winds and falling leaves!

Scholfield Huxley

God! ask me not to record your wonders,
I admit the stars and the suns
And the countless worlds.
But I have measured their distances
And weighed them and discovered their substances.
I have devised wings for the air,
And keels for water,
And horses of iron for the earth.
I have lengthened the vision you gave me a million times,
And the hearing you gave me a million times,
I have leaped over space with speech,
And taken fire for light out of the air.
I have built great cities and bored through the hills,
And bridged majestic waters.
I have written the *Iliad* and *Hamlet*;
And I have explored your mysteries,
And searched for you without ceasing,
And found you again after losing you
In hours of weariness—
And I ask you:
How would you like to create a sun

And the next day have the worms
Slipping in and out between your fingers?
1916

EDWIN ARLINGTON ROBINSON
1869-1935

Luke Havergal

Go to the western gate, Luke Havergal,
There where the vines cling crimson on the wall,
And in the twilight wait for what will come.
The leaves will whisper there of her, and some,
Like flying words, will strike you as they fall;
But go, and if you listen, she will call.
Go to the western gate, Luke Havergal—
Luke Havergal.

No, there is not a dawn in eastern skies
To rift the fiery night that's in your eyes;
But there, where western glooms are gathering,
The dark will end the dark, if anything:
God slays himself with every leaf that flies,
And hell is more than half of paradise.
No, there is not a dawn in eastern skies—
In eastern skies.

Out of a grave I come to tell you this,
Out of a grave I come to quench the kiss
That flames upon your forehead with a glow
That blinds you to the way that you must go.
Yes, there is yet one way to where she is,
Bitter, but one that faith may never miss.
Out of a grave I come to tell you this—
To tell you this.

There is the western gate, Luke Havergal,
There are the crimson leaves upon the wall.
Go, for the winds are tearing them away,—
Nor think to riddle the dead words they say,
Nor any more to feel them as they fall;
But go, and if you trust her she will call.
There is the western gate, Luke Havergal—
Luke Havergal.

Eros Turannos

She fears him, and will always ask
  What fated her to chose him;
She meets in his engaging mask
  All reasons to refuse him;
But what she meets and what she fears
Are less than are the downward years,
Drawn slowly to the foamless weirs
  Of age, were she to lose him.

Between a blurred sagacity
  That once had power to sound him,
And Love, that will not let him be
  The Judas that she found him,
Her pride assuages her almost,
As if it were alone the cost.
He sees that he will not be lost,
  And waits and looks around him.

A sense of ocean and old trees
  Envelops and allures him;
Tradition, touching all he sees,
  Beguiles and reassures him;
And all her doubts of what he says
Are dimmed with what she knows of days—
Till even prejudice delays
  And fades, and she secures him.

The falling leaf inaugurates
  The reign of her confusion;
The pounding wave reverberates
  The dirge of her illusion;
And home, where passion lived and died,
Becomes a place where she can hide,
While all the town and harbor-side
  Vibrate with her seclusion.

We tell you, tapping on our brows,
  The story as it should be,
As if the story of a house
  Were told, or ever could be;
We'll have no kindly veil between
Her visions and those we have seen,—
As if we guessed what hers have been,
  Or what they are or would be.

Meanwhile we do no harm; for they
  That with a god have striven,
Not hearing much of what we say,
  Take what the god has given;
Though like waves breaking it may be,
Or like a changed familiar tree,
Or like a stairway to the sea
  Where down the blind are driven.

Ben Jonson Entertains a Man from Stratford

You are the friend then, as I make it out,
Of our man Shakespeare, who alone of us
Will put an ass's head in Fairyland
As he would add a shilling to more shillings,
All most harmonious,—and out of his
Miraculous inviolable increase
Fills Ilion, Rome, or any town you like
Of olden time with timeless Englishmen;
And I must wonder what you think of him—
All you down there where your small Avon flows
By Stratford, and where you're an Alderman.
Some, for a guess, would have him riding back
To be a farrier there, or say a dyer;
Or maybe one of your adept surveyors;
Or like enough the wizard of all tanners.
Not you—no fear of that; for I discern
In you a kindling of the flame that saves—
The nimble element, the true caloric;
I see it, and was told of it, moreover,
By our discriminate friend himself, no other.
Had you been one of the sad average,
As he would have it,—meaning, as I take it,
The sinew and the solvent of our Island,
You'd not be buying beer for this Terpander's
Approved and estimated friend Ben Jonson;
He'd never foist it as a part of his
Contingent entertainment of a townsman
While he goes off rehearsing, as he must,
If he shall ever be the Duke of Stratford.
And my words are no shadow on your town—
Far from it; for one town's as like another
As all are unlike London. Oh, he knows it,—
And there's the Stratford in him; he denies it.
And there's the Shakespeare in him. So, God help him!

I tell him he needs Greek; but neither God
Nor Greek will help him. Nothing will help that man.
You see the fates have given him so much,
He must have all or perish,—or look out
Of London, where he sees too many lords.
They're part of half what ails him: I suppose
There's nothing fouler down among the demons
Than what it is he feels when he remembers
The dust and sweat and ointment of his calling
With his lords looking on and laughing at him.
King as he is, he can't be king *de facto,*
And that's as well, because he wouldn't like it;
He'd frame a lower rating of men then
Than he has now; and after that would come
An abdication or an apoplexy.
He can't be king, not even king of Stratford,—
Though half the world, if not the whole of it,
May crown him with a crown that fits no king
Save Lord Apollo's homesick emissary:
Not there on Avon, or on any stream
Where Naiads and their white arms are no more,
Shall he find home again. It's all too bad.
But there's a comfort, for he'll have that House—
The best you ever saw; and he'll be there
Anon, as you're an Alderman. Good God!
He makes me lie awake o'night and laugh.

And you have known him from his origin,
You tell me; and a most uncommon urchin
He must have been to the few seeing ones—
A trifle terrifying, I dare say,
Discovering a world with his man's eyes,
Quite as another lad might see some finches,
If he looked hard and had an eye for nature.
But this one had his eyes and their foretelling,
And he had you to fare with, and what else?
He must have had a father and a mother—
In fact I've heard him say so—and a dog,
As a boy should, I venture; and the dog,
Most likely, was the only man who knew him.
A dog, for all I know, is what he needs
As much as anything right here to-day,
To counsel him about his disillusions,
Old aches, and parturitions of what's coming,—
A dog of orders, an emeritus,
To wag his tail at him when he comes home,

And then to put his paws up on his knees
And say, "For God's sake, what's it all about?"

I don't know whether he needs a dog or not—
Or what he needs. I tell him he needs Greek;
I'll talk of rules and Aristotle with him,
And if his tongue's at home, he'll say to that,
"I have your word that Aristotle knows,
And you mine that I don't know Aristotle."
He's all at odds with all the unities,
And what's yet worse, it doesn't seem to matter;
He treads along through Time's old wilderness
As if the tramp of all the centuries
Had left no roads—and there are none, for him;
He doesn't see them, even with those eyes,—
And that's a pity, or I say it is.
Accordingly we have him as we have him—
Going his way, the way that he goes best,
A pleasant animal with no great noise
Or nonsense anywhere to set him off—
Save only divers and inclement devils
Have made of late his heart their dwelling place.
A flame half ready to fly out sometimes
At some annoyance may be fanned up in him,
But soon it falls, and when it falls goes out;
He knows how little room there is in there
For crude and futile animosities,
And how much for the joy of being whole,
And how much for long sorrow and old pain.
On our side there are some who may be given
To grow old wondering what he thinks of us
And some above us, who are, in his eyes,
Above himself,—and that's quite right and English.
Yet here we smile, or disappoint the gods
Who made it so: the gods have always eyes
To see men scratch; and they see one down here
Who itches, manor-bitten to the bone,
Albeit he knows himself—yes, yes, he knows—
The lord of more than England and of more
Than all the seas of England in all time
Shall ever wash. D'ye wonder that I laugh?
He sees me, and he doesn't seem to care;
And why the devil should he? I can't tell you.

I'll meet him out alone of a bright Sunday,
Trim, rather spruce, and quite a gentleman.

"What ho, my lord!" say I. He doesn't hear me;
Wherefore I have to pause and look at him.
He's not enormous, but one looks at him.
A little on the round if you insist,
For now, God save the mark, he's growing old;
He's five and forty, and to hear him talk
These days you'd call him eighty; then you'd add
More years to that. He's old enough to be
The father of the world, and so he is.
"Ben, you're a scholar, what's the time of day?"
Says he; and there shines out of him again
An aged light that has no age or station—
The mystery that's his—a mischievous
Half-mad serenity that laughs at fame
For being won so easy, and at friends
Who laugh at him for what he wants the most,
And for his dukedom down in Warwickshire;—
By which you see we're all a little jealous. . . .
Poor Greene! I fear the color of his name
Was even as that of his ascending soul;
And he was one where there are many others,—
Some scrivening to the end against their fate,
Their puppets all in ink and all to die there;
And some with hands that once would shade an eye
That scanned Euripides and Aeschylus
Will reach by this time for a pot-house mop
To slush their first and last of royalties.
Poor devils! and they all play to his hand;
For so it was in Athens and old Rome.
But that's not here or there; I've wandered off.
Greene does it, or I'm careful. Where's that boy?

Yes, he'll go back to Stratford. And we'll miss him?
Dear sir, there'll be no London here without him.
We'll all be riding, one of these fine days,
Down there to see him—and his wife won't like us;
And then we'll think of what he never said
Of women—which, if taken all in all
With what he did say, would buy many houses.
Though nowadays he's not so much for women:
"So few of them," he says, "are worth the guessing."
But there's a worm at work when he says that,
And while he says it one feels in the air
A deal of circumambient hocus-pocus.
They've had him dancing till his toes were tender,
And he can feel 'em now, come chilly rains.

There's no long cry for going into it,
However, and we don't know much about it.
But you in Stratford, like most here in London,
Have more now in the *Sonnets* than you paid for;
He's put one there with all her poison on,
To make a singing fiction of a shadow
That's in his life a fact, and always will be.
But she's no care of ours, though Time, I fear,
Will have a more reverberant ado
About her than about another one
Who seems to have decoyed him, married him,
And sent him scuttling on his way to London,—
With much already learned, and more to learn,
And more to follow. Lord! how I see him now,
Pretending, maybe trying, to be like us.
Whatever he may have meant, we never had him;
He failed us, or escaped, or what you will,—
And there was that about him (God knows what,—
We'd flayed another had he tried it on us)
That made as many of us as had wits
More fond of all his easy distances
Than one another's noise and clap-your-shoulder.
But think you not, my friend, he'd never talk!
Talk? He was eldritch at it; and we listened—
Thereby acquiring much we knew before
About ourselves, and hitherto had held
Irrelevant, or not prime to the purpose.
And there were some, of course, and there be now,
Disordered and reduced amazedly
To resignation by the mystic seal
Of young finality the gods had laid
On everything that made him a young demon;
And one or two shot looks at him already
As he had been their executioner;
And once or twice he was, not knowing it,—
Or knowing, being sorry for poor clay
And saying nothing. . . . Yet, for all his engines,
You'll meet a thousand of an afternoon
Who strut and sun themselves and see around 'em
A world made out of more that has a reason
Than his, I swear, that he sees here today;
Though he may scarcely give a Fool an exit
But we mark how he sees in everything
A law that, given that we flout it once too often,
Brings fire and iron down on our naked heads.
To me it looks as if the power that made him,

For fear of giving all things to one creature,
Left out the first,—faith, innocence, illusion,
Whatever 'tis that keeps us out o' Bedlam,—
And thereby, for his too consuming vision,
Empowered him out of nature; though to see him
You'd never guess what's going on inside him.
He'll break out some day like a keg of ale
With too much independent frenzy in it;
And all for cellaring what he knows won't keep,
And what he'd best forget—but that he can't.
You'll have it, and have more than I'm foretelling;
And there'll be such a roaring at the Globe
As never stunned the bleeding gladiators.
He'll have to change the color of his hair
A bit, for now he calls it Cleopatra.
Black hair would never do for Cleopatra.
But you and I are not yet two old women,
And you're a man of office. What he does
Is more to you than how it is he does it,—
And that's what the Lord God has never told him.
They work together, and the Devil helps 'em;
They do it of a morning, or if not,
They do it of a night; in which event
He's peevish of a morning. He seems old;
He's not the proper stomach or the sleep—
And they're two sovran agents to conserve him
Against the fiery art that has no mercy
But what's in that prodigious grand new House.
I gather something happening in his boyhood
Fulfilled him with a boy's determination
To make all Stratford 'ware of him. Well, well,
I hope at last he'll have his joy of it,
And all his pigs and sheep and bellowing beeves,
And frogs and owls and unicorns, moreover,
Be less than hell to his attendant ears.
Oh, past a doubt we'll all go down to see him.

He may be wise. With London two days off,
Down there some wind of heaven may yet revive him.
But there's no quickening breath from anywhere
Shall make of him again the poised young faun
From Warwickshire, who'd made, it seems, already
A legend of himself before I came
To blink before the last of his first lightning.
Whatever there be, there'll be no more of that;
The coming on of his old monster Time

Has made him a still man; and he has dreams
Were fair to think on once, and all found hollow.
He knows how much of what men paint themselves
Would blister in the light of what they are;
He sees how much of what was great now shares
An eminence transformed and ordinary;
He knows too much of what the world has hushed
In others, to be loud now for himself;
He knows now at what height low enemies
May reach his heart, and high friends let him fall;
But what not even such as he may know
Bedevils him the worst: his lark may sing
At heaven's gate how he will, and for as long
As joy may listen, but *he* sees no gate,
Save one whereat the spent clay waits a little
Before the churchyard has it, and the worm.
Not long ago, late in an afternoon,
I came on him unseen down Lambeth way,
And on my life I was afear'd of him:
He gloomed and mumbled like a soul from Tophet,
His hands behind him and his head bent solemn.
"What is it now," said I,—"another woman?"
That made him sorry for me, and he smiled.
"No, Ben," he mused; "it's Nothing. It's all Nothing.
We come, we go; and when we're done, we're done.
Spiders and flies—we're mostly one or t'other—
We come, we go; and when we're done, we're done."
"By God, you sing that song as if you knew it!"
Said I, by way of cheering him: "what ails ye?"
"I think I must have come down here to think,"
Says he to that, and pulls his little beard;
"Your fly will serve as well as anybody,
And what's his hour? He flies, and flies, and flies,
And in his fly's mind has a brave appearance;
And then your spider gets him in her net,
And eats him out, and hangs him up to dry.
That's Nature, the kind mother of us all.
And then your slattern housemaid swings her broom,
And where's your spider? And that's Nature, also.
It's Nature, and it's Nothing. It's all Nothing.
It's all a world where bugs and emperors
Go singularly back to the same dust,
Each in his time; and the old, ordered stars
That sang together, Ben, will sing the same
Old stave to-morrow."

When he talks like that,
There's nothing for a human man to do
But lead him to some grateful nook like this
Where we be now, and there to make him drink.
He'll drink, for love of me, and then be sick;
A sad sign always in a man of parts,
And always very ominous. The great
Should be as large in liquor as in love,—
And our great friend is not so large in either:
One disaffects him, and the other fails him;
Whatso he drinks that has an antic in it,
He's wondering what's to pay in his insides;
And while his eyes are on the Cyprian
He's fribbling all the time with that damned House.
We laugh here at his thrift, but after all
It may be thrift that saves him from the devil;
God gave it, anyhow,—and we'll suppose
He knew the compound of his handiwork.
To-day the clouds are with him, but anon
He'll out of 'em enough to shake the tree
Of life itself and bring down fruit unheard-of,—
And, throwing in the bruised and whole together,
Prepare a wine to make us drunk with wonder;
And if he live, there'll be a sunset spell
Thrown over him as over a glassed lake
That yesterday was all a black wild water.

God send he live to give us, if no more,
What now's a-rampage in him, and exhibit,
With a decent half-allegiance to the ages
An earnest of at least a casual eye
Turned once on what he owes to Gutenberg,
And to the fealty of more centuries
Than are as yet a picture in our vision.
"There's time enough,—I'll do it when I'm old,
And we're immortal men," he says to that;
And then he says to me, "Ben, what's 'immortal'?
Think you by any force of ordination
It may be nothing of a sort more noisy
Than a small oblivion of component ashes
That of a dream-addicted world was once
A moving atomy much like your friend here?"
Nothing will help that man. To make him laugh,
I said then he was a mad mountebank,—
And by the Lord I nearer made him cry.
I could have eat an eft then, on my knees,

Tail, claws, and all of him; for I had stung
The king of men, who had no sting for me,
And I had hurt him in his memories;
And I say now, as I shall say again,
I love the man this side idolatry.

He'll do it when he's old, he says. I wonder.
He may not be so ancient as all that.
For such as he, the thing that is to do
Will do itself,—but there's a reckoning;
The sessions that are now too much his own,
The roiling inward of a stilled outside,
The churning out of all those blood-fed lines,
The nights of many schemes and little sleep,
The full brain hammered hot with too much thinking,
The vexed heart over-worn with too much aching,—
This weary jangling of conjoined affairs
Made out of elements that have no end.
And all confused at once, I understand,
Is not what makes a man to live forever.
O no, not now! He'll not be going now:
There'll be time yet for God knows what explosions
Before he goes. He'll stay awhile. Just wait:
Just wait a year or two for Cleopatra,
For she's to be a balsam and a comfort;
And that's not all a jape of mine now, either.
For granted once the old way of Apollo
Sings in a man, he may then, if he's able,
Strike unafraid whatever strings he will
Upon the last and wildest of new lyres;
Nor out of his new magic, though it hymn
The shrieks of dungeoned hell, shall he create
A madness or a gloom to shut quite out
A cleaving daylight, and a last great calm
Triumphant over shipwreck and all storms.
He might have given Aristotle creeps,
But surely would have given him his *katharsis*.

He'll not be going yet. There's too much yet
Unsung within the man. But when he goes,
I'd stake ye coin o' the realm his only care
For a phantom world he sounded and found wanting
Will be a portion here, a portion there,
Of this or that thing or some other thing
That has a patent and intrinsical
Equivalence in those egregious shillings.

And yet he knows, God help him! Tell me, now,
If ever there was anything let loose
On earth by gods or devils heretofore
Like this mad, careful, proud, indifferent Shakespeare!
Where was it, if it ever was? By heaven,
'Twas never yet in Rhodes or Pergamon—
In Thebes or Ninevah, a thing like this!
No thing like this was ever out of England;
And that he knows. I wonder if he cares.
Perhaps he does . . . O Lord, that House in Stratford!

WALTER DE LA MARE

1873-

The Old Summerhouse

This blue-washed, old, thatched summerhouse—
Paint scaling, and fading from its walls—
How often from its hingeless door
I have watched—dead leaf, like the ghost of a mouse,
Rasping the worn brick floor—
The snows of the weir descending below,
And their thunderous waterfall.

Fall—fall: dark, garrulous rumour,
Until I could listen no more.
Could listen no more—for beauty with sorrow
Is a burden hard to be borne:
The evening light on the foam, and the swans, there;
That music, remote, forlorn.

The Bottle

Of green and hexagonal glass,
    With sharp, fluted sides—
Vaguely transparent these walls,
    Wherein motionless hides
A simple so potent it can
    To oblivion lull
The weary, the racked, the bereaved,
    The miserable.

Flowers in silent desire
      Their life-breath exhale—
Self-heal, hellebore, aconite,
      Chamomile, dwale:
Sharing the same gentle heavens,
      The sun's heat and light,
And, in the dust at their roots,
      The same shallow night.

Each its own livelihood hath,
      Shape, pattern, hue;
Age on to age unto these
      Keeping steadfastly true;
And, musing amid them, there moves
      A stranger, named Man,
Who of their ichor distils
      What virtue he can;

Plucks them ere seed-time to blazon
His house with their radiant dyes;
Prisons their attar in wax;
Candies their petals; denies
Them freedom to breed in their wont;
Buds, fecundates, grafts them at will;
And with cunningest leechcraft compels
      Their good to his ill.

Intrigue fantastic as this
      Where shall we find?
Mute in their beauty they serve him,
      Body and mind.
And one—but a weed in his wheat—
Is the poppy—frail, pallid, whose juice
With its saplike and opiate fume
      Strange dreams will induce

Of wonder and horror. And none
      Can silence the soul,
Wearied of self and of life,
      Earth's darkness and dole,
More secretly, deeply. But finally?—
      Waste not thy breath;
The words that are scrawled on this phial
      Have for synonym, death—

Wicket out into the dark
      That swings but one way;

Infinite hush in an ocean of silence
    Aeons away—
Thou forsaken!—even thou!—
    The dread good-bye;
The abandoned, the thronged, the watched, the unshared—
    Awaiting me—I!

The Listeners

"Is there anybody there?" said the Traveller,
    Knocking on the moonlit door;
And his horse in the silence champed the grasses
    Of the forest's ferny floor:
And a bird flew up out of the turret,
    Above the Traveller's head:
And he smote upon the door again a second time;
    "Is there anybody there?" he said.
But no one descended to the Traveller;
    No head from the leaf-fringed sill
Leaned over and looked into his grey eyes,
    Where he stood perplexed and still.
But only a host of phantom listeners
    That dwelt in the lone house then
Stood listening in the quiet of the moonlight
    To that voice from the world of men:
Stood thronging the faint moonbeams on the dark stair,
    That goes down to the empty hall,
Hearkening in an air stirred and shaken
    By the lonely Traveller's call.
And he felt in his heart their strangeness,
    Their stillness answering his cry,
While his horse moved, cropping the dark turf,
    'Neath the starred and leafy sky;
For he suddenly smote on the door, even
    Louder, and lifted his head:—
"Tell them I came, and no one answered,
    That I kept my word," he said.
Never the least stir made the listeners,
    Though every word he spake
Fell echoing through the shadowiness of the still house
    From the one man left awake:
Ay, they heard his foot upon the stirrup,
    And the sound of iron on stone,
And how the silence surged softly backward,
    When the plunging hoofs were gone.

GERTRUDE STEIN
1874-1946

What Happened

A FIVE-ACT PLAY

ACT ONE

(*One*)

Loud and no cataract. Not any nuisance is depressing.

(*Five*)

A single sum four and five together and one, not any sun a clear signal and an exchange.

Silence is in blessing and chasing and coincidences being ripe. A simple melancholy clearly precious and on the surface and surrounded and mixed strangely. A vegetable window and clearly most clearly an exchange in parts and complete.

A tiger a rapt and surrounded overcoat securely arranged with spots old enough to be thought useful and witty quite witty in a secret and in a blinding flurry.

Length what is length when silence is so windowful. What is the use of a sore if there is no joint and no toady and no tag and not even an eraser. What is the commonest exchange between more laughing and most. Carelessness is carelessness and a cake well a cake is a powder, it is very likely to be powder, it is very likely to be much worse.

A shutter and only shutter and Christmas, quite Christmas, an only shutter and a target a whole color in every center and shooting real shooting and what can hear, that can hear that which makes such an establishment provided with what is provisionary.

(*Two*)

Urgent action is not in graciousness it is not in clocks it is not in water wheels. It is the same so essentially, it is a worry a real worry.

A silence a whole waste of a desert spoon, a whole waste of any little shaving, a whole waste altogether open.

(*Two*)

Paralysis why is paralysis a syllable why is it not more lively.

A special sense a very special sense is ludicrous.

(*Three*)

Suggesting a sage brush with a turkey and also something abominable is not the only pain there is in so much provoking. There is even more. To begin a lecture is a strange way of taking dirty apple blossoms and is there more use in water, certainly there is if there is going to be fishing, enough water would make desert and even prunes, it would make nothing throw any shade because after all is there not more practical humor in a series of photographs and also in a treacherous sculpture.

Any hurry and little hurry has so much subsistence, it has and choosing, it has.

ACT TWO

(Three)

Four and nobody wounded, five and nobody flourishing, six and nobody talkative, eight and nobody sensible.

One and a left hand lift that is so heavy that there is no way of pronouncing perfectly.

A point of accuracy, a point of a strange stove, a point that is so sober that the reason left is all the chance of swelling.

(The same three)

A wide oak a wide enough oak, a very wide cake, a lightning cooky, a single wide open and exchanged box filled with the same little sac that shines.

The best the only better and more left footed stranger.

The very kindness there is in all lemons oranges apples pears and potatoes.

(The same three)

A same frame a sadder portal, a singular gate and a bracketed mischance.

A rich market where there is no memory of more moon than there is everywhere and yet where strangely there is apparel and a whole set.

A connection, a clam cup connection, a survey, a ticket and a return to laying over.

ACT THREE

(Two)

A cut, a cut is not a slice, what is the occasion for representing a cut and a slice. What is the occasion for all that.

A cut is a slice, a cut is the same slice. The reason that a cut is a slice is that if there is no hurry any time is just as useful.

(Four)

A cut and a slice is there any question when a cut and a slice are just the same.

A cut and a slice has no particular exchange it has such a strange exception to all that which is different.

A cut and only slice, only a cut and only a slice, the remains of a taste may remain and tasting is accurate.

A cut and an occasion, a slice and a substitute a single hurry and a circumstance that shows that, all this is so reasonable when every thing is clear.

(One)

All alone with the best reception, all alone with more than the best reception, all alone with a paragraph and something that is worth something, worth almost anything, worth the best example there is of a little occasional archbishop. This which is so clean is precious little when there is no bath water. A long time a very long time there is no use in an obstacle that is original and has a source.

ACT FOUR

(Four and four more)

A birthday, what is a birthday, a birthday is a speech, it is a second time when there is tobacco, it is only one time when there is poison. It is more than one time when the occasion which shows an occasional sharp separation is unanimous.

A blanket, what is a blanket, a blanket is so speedy that heat much heat is hotter and cooler, very much cooler almost more nearly cooler than at any other time often.

A blame what is a blame, a blame is what arises and cautions each one to be calm and an ocean and a masterpiece.

A clever saucer, what is a clever saucer, a clever saucer is very likely practiced and even has toes, it has tiny things to shake and really if it were not for a delicate blue color would there be any reason for every one to differ.

The objection and the perfect central table, the sorrow in borrowing and the hurry in a nervous feeling, the question is it really a plague, is it really an oleander, is it really saffron in color, the surmountable appetite which shows inclination to be warmer, the safety in a match and the safety in a little piece of splinter, the real reason why cocoa is cheaper, the same use for bread as for any breathing that is softer, the lecture and the surrounding large white soft unequal and spread out sale of more and still less is no better, all this makes one regard in a season, one hat in a curtain that in rising higher, one landing and many many more, and many more many more many many more.

ACT FIVE

(Two)

A regret a single regret makes a door way. What is a door way, a door way is a photograph.

What is a photograph a photograph is a sight and a sight is always a sight of something. Very likely there is a photograph that gives color if there is then there is that color that does not change any more than it did when there was much more use for photography.

ROBERT FROST
1875-

The Silken Tent

She is as in a field a silken tent
At midday when a sunny summer breeze
Has dried the dew and all its ropes relent,
So that in guys it gently sways at ease,
And its supporting central cedar pole,
That is its pinnacle to heavenward
And signifies the sureness of the soul,
Seems to owe naught to any single cord,
But strictly held by none, is loosely bound
By countless silken ties of love and thought
To everything on earth the compass round,
And only by one's going slightly taut
In the capriciousness of summer air
Is of the slightest bondage made aware.

A Soldier

He is that fallen lance that lies as hurled,
That lies unlifted now, come dew, come rust,
But still lies pointed as it plowed the dust.
If we who sight along it round the world,
See nothing worthy to have been its mark,
It is because like men we look too near,
Forgetting that as fitted to the sphere,
Our missiles always make too short an arc.
They fall, they rip the grass, they intersect
The curve of earth, and striking, break their own;
They make us cringe for metal-point on stone.
But this we know, the obstacle that checked
And tripped the body, shot the spirit on
Further than target ever showed or shone.

The Most of It

He thought he kept the universe alone;
For all the voice in answer he could wake
Was but the mocking echo of his own
From some tree-hidden cliff across the lake.
Some morning from the boulder-broken beach
He would cry out on life, that what it wants
Is not its own love back in copy speech,
But counter-love, original response.
And nothing ever came of what he cried
Unless it was the embodiment that crashed
In the cliff's talus on the other side,
And then in the far distant water splashed,
But after a time allowed for it to swim,
Instead of proving human when it neared
And someone else additional to him,
As a great buck it powerfully appeared,
Pushing the crumpled water up ahead,
And landed pouring like a waterfall,
And stumbled through the rocks with horny **tread,**
And forced the underbrush—and that was all.

To Earthward

Love at the lips was touch
As sweet as I could bear;
And once that seemed too much;
I lived on air

That crossed me from sweet things,
The flow of—was it musk
From hidden grapevine springs
Down hill at dusk?

I had the swirl and ache
From sprays of honeysuckle
That when they're gathered shake
Dew on the knuckle.

I craved strong sweets, but those
Seemed strong when I was young;
The petal of the rose
It was that stung.

Now no joy but lacks salt
That is not dashed with pain
And weariness and fault;
I crave the stain .

Of tears, the aftermark
Of almost too much love,
The sweet of bitter bark
And burning clove.

When stiff and sore and scarred
I take away my hand
From leaning on it hard
In grass and sand,

The hurt is not enough:
I long for weight and strength
To feel the earth as rough
To all my length.

After Apple-Picking

My long two-pointed ladder's sticking through a tree
Toward heaven still,
And there's a barrel that I didn't fill
Beside it, and there may be two or three
Apples I didn't pick upon some bough.
But I am done with apple-picking now.
Essence of winter sleep is on the night,
The scent of apples: I am drowsing off.
I cannot rub the strangeness from my sight
I got from looking through a pane of glass
I skimmed this morning from the drinking trough
And held against the world of hoary grass.
It melted, and I let it fall and break.
But I was well
Upon my way to sleep before it fell,
And I could tell
What form my dreaming was about to take.
Magnified apples appear and disappear,
Stem end and blossom end,
And every fleck of russet showing clear.
My instep arch not only keeps the ache,
It keeps the pressure of a ladder-round.
I feel the ladder sway as the boughs bend.

And I keep hearing from the cellar bin
The rumbling sound
Of load on load of apples coming in.
For I have had too much
Of apple-picking: I am overtired
Of the great harvest I myself desired.
There were ten thousand thousand fruit to touch,
Cherish in hand, lift down, and not let fall.
For all
That struck the earth,
No matter if not bruised or spiked with stubble,
Went surely to the cider-apple heap
As of no worth.
One can see what will trouble
This sleep of mine, whatever sleep it is.
Were he not gone,
The woodchuck could say whether it's like his
Long sleep, as I describe its coming on,
Or just some human sleep.

Happiness Makes Up in Height
for What It Lacks in Length

Oh, stormy stormy world,
The days you were not swirled
Around with mist and cloud,
Or wrapped as in a shroud,
And the sun's brilliant ball
Was not in part or all
Obscured from mortal view—
Were days so very few
I can but wonder whence
I get the lasting sense
Of so much warmth and light.
If my mistrust is right
It may be altogether
From one day's perfect weather,
When starting clear at dawn,
The day swept clearly on
To finish clear at eve.
I verily believe
My fair impression may
Be all from that one day
No shadow crossed but ours

As through its blazing flowers
We went from house to wood
For change of solitude.

All Revelation

A head thrusts in as for the view,
But where it is it thrusts in from
Or what it is it thrusts into
By that Cyb'laean avenue,
And what can of its coming come,

And whither it will be withdrawn,
And what take hence or leave behind,
These things the mind has pondered on
A moment and still asking gone.
Strange apparition of the mind!

But the impervious geode
Was entered, and its inner crust
Of crystals with a ray cathode
At every point and facet glowed
In answer to the mental thrust.

Eyes seeking the response of eyes
Bring out the stars, bring out the flowers,
Thus concentrating earth and skies
So none need be afraid of size.
All revelation has been ours.

CARL SANDBURG
1878-

"The People Will Live On"

The people will live on.
The learning and blundering people will live on.
They will be tricked and sold and again sold
And go back to the nourishing earth for rootholds,
The people so peculiar in renewal and comeback,
You can't laugh off their capacity to take it.
The mammoth rests between his cyclonic dramas.

The people so often sleepy, weary, enigmatic,
is a vast huddle with many units saying:
    "I earn my living
    I make enough to get by
    and it takes all my time.
    If I had more time
    I could do more for myself
    and maybe for others.
    I could read and study
    and talk things over
    and find out about things.
    It takes time.
    I wish I had the time."

The people is a tragic and comic two-face:
hero and hoodlum: phantom and gorilla twisting to moan with a gargoyle mouth: "They
buy me and sell me . . . it's a game . . .
sometime I'll break loose . . ."

    Once having marched
    Over the margins of animal necessity,
    Over the grim line of sheer subsistence
      Then man came
    To the deeper rituals of his bones,
    To the lights lighter than any bones,
    To the time for thinking things over,
    To the dance, the song, the story,
    Or the hours given over to dreaming,
      Once having so marched.

Between the finite limitations of the five senses
and the endless yearnings of man for the beyond
the people hold to the humdrum bidding of work **and food**
while reaching out when it comes their way
for lights beyond the prison of the five senses,
for keepsakes lasting beyond any hunger or death.
    This reaching is alive.
The panderers and liars have violated and smutted **it.**
    Yet this reaching is alive yet
    for lights and keepsakes.

    The people know the salt of the sea
    and the strength of the winds
    lashing the corners of the earth.
    The people take the earth

as a tomb of rest and a cradle of hope.
Who else speaks for the Family of Man?
They are in tune and step
with constellations of universal law.

The people is a polychrome,
a spectrum and a prism
held in a moving monolith,
a console organ of changing themes,
a clavilux of color poems
wherein the sea offers fog
and the fog moves off in rain
and the labrador sunset shortens
to a nocturne of clear stars
serene over the shot spray
of northern lights.

The steel mill sky is alive.
The fire breaks white and zigzag
shot on a gun-metal gloaming.
Man is a long time coming.
Man will yet win.
Brother may yet line up with brother:

This old anvil laughs at many broken hammers.
        There are men who can't be bought.
        The fireborn are at home in fire.
        The stars make no noise.
        You can't hinder the wind from blowing.
        Time is a great teacher.
        Who can live without hope?

In the darkness with a great bundle of grief
        the people march.
In the night, and overhead a shovel of stars for
        keeps, the people march:
                            "Where to? What next?"

JOHN MASEFIELD
1878-

Night on the Downland

Night is on the downland, on the lonely moorland,
On the hills where the wind goes over sheep-bitten turf,
Where the bent grass beats upon the unplowed poorland
And the pine-woods roar like the surf.

Here the Roman lived on the wind-barren lonely,
Dark now and haunted by the moorland fowl;
None comes here now but the peewit only,
And moth-like death in the owl.

Beauty was here on this beetle-droning downland;
The thought of a Caesar in the purple came
From the palace by the Tiber in the Roman townland
To this wind-swept hill with no name.

Lonely Beauty came here and was here in sadness,
Brave as a thought on the frontier of the mind,
In the camp of the wild upon the march of madness,
The bright-eyed Queen of the Blind.

Now where Beauty was are the wind-withered gorses,
Moaning like old men in the hill-wind's blast;
The flying sky is dark with running horses,
And the night is full of the past.

The Passing Strange

Out of the earth to rest or range
Perpetual in perpetual change,
The unknown passing through the strange.

Water and saltness held together
To tread the dust and stand the weather,
And plow the field and stretch the tether,

To pass the wine-cup and be witty,
Water the sands and build the city,
Slaughter like devils and have pity,

Be red with rage and pale with lust,
Make beauty come, make peace, make trust,
Water and saltness mixed with dust;

Drive over earth, swim under sea,
Fly in the eagle's secrecy,
Guess where the hidden comets be;

Know all the deathy seeds that still
Queen Helen's beauty, Caesar's will,
And slay them even as they kill;

Fashion an altar for a rood,
Defile a continent with blood,
And watch a brother starve for food:

Love like a madman, shaking, blind,
Till self is burnt into a kind
Possession of another mind;

Brood upon beauty, till the grace
Of beauty with the holy face
Brings peace into the bitter place;

Probe in the lifeless granites, scan
The stars for hope, for guide, for plan;
Live as a woman or a man;

Fasten to lover or to friend,
Until the heart break at the end
The break of death that cannot mend:

Then to lie useless, helpless, still,
Down in the earth, in dark, to fill
The roots of grass or daffodil.

Down in the earth, in dark, alone,
A mockery of the ghost in bone,
The strangeness, passing the unknown.

Time will go by, that outlasts clocks,
Dawn in the thorps will rouse the cocks,
Sunset be glory on the rocks:

But it, the thing, will never heed
Even the rootling from the seed
Thrusting to suck it for its need.

*

Since moons decay and suns decline,
How else should end this life of mine?
Water and saltness are not wine.

But in the darkest hour of night,
When even the foxes peer for sight,
The byre-cock crows; he feels the light.

So, in this water mixed with dust,
The byre-cock spirit crows from trust
That death will change because it must;

For all things change, the darkness changes,
The wandering spirits change their ranges,
The corn is gathered to the granges.

The corn is sown again, it grows;
The stars burn out, the darkness goes;
The rhythms change, they do not close.

They change, and we, who pass like foam,
Like dust blown through the streets of Rome,
Change ever, too; we have no home,

Only a beauty, only a power,
Sad in the fruit, bright in the flower,
Endlessly erring for its hour,

But gathering as we stray, a sense
Of Life, so lovely and intense,
It lingers when we wander hence,

That those who follow feel behind
Their backs, when all before is blind,
Our joy, a rampart to the mind.

VACHEL LINDSAY

1879-1931

General William Booth Enters into Heaven

TO BE SUNG TO THE TUNE OF "THE BLOOD OF
THE LAMB" WITH INDICATED INSTRUMENT

I

(Bass drum beaten loudly)
Booth led boldly with his big bass drum—
(Are you washed in the blood of the Lamb?)
The Saints smiled gravely and they said: "He's come."
(Are you washed in the blood of the Lamb?)
Walking lepers followed, rank on rank,
Lurching bravos from the ditches dank,
Drabs from the alleyways and drug fiends pale—
Minds still passion-ridden, soul-powers frail:—
Vermin-eaten saints with moldy breath,
Unwashed legions with the ways of Death—
(Are you washed in the blood of the Lamb?)

 (Banjos)
Every slum had sent its half-a-score
The round world over. (Booth had groaned for more.)
Every banner that the wide world flies
Bloomed with glory and transcendent dyes.
Big-voiced lasses made their banjos bang,
Tranced, fanatical they shrieked and sang:—
"Are you washed in the blood of the Lamb?"
Hallelujah! It was queer to see
Bull-necked convicts with that land make free.
Loons with trumpets blowed a blare, blare, blare
On, on upward thro' the golden air!
(Are you washed in the blood of the Lamb?)

II

 (Bass drum slower and softer)
Booth died blind and still by faith he trod,
Eyes still dazzled by the ways of God.
Booth led boldly, and he look the chief

Eagle countenance in sharp relief,
Beard a-flying, air of high command
Unabated in that holy land.

(Sweet flute music)
Jesus came from out the court-house door,
Stretched his hands above the passing poor.
Booth saw not, but led his queer ones there
Round and round the mighty court-house square.
Then, in an instant all that blear review
Marched on spotless, clad in raiment new.
The lame were straightened, withered limbs uncurled
And blind eyes opened on a new, sweet world.

(Bass drum louder)
Drabs and vixens in a flash made whole!
Gone was the weasel-head, the snout, the jowl!
Sages and sibyls now, and athletes clean,
Rulers of empires, and of forest green!

*(Grand chorus of all instruments. Tambourines to the
    foreground)*
The hosts were sandalled, and their wings were fire!
(Are you washed in the blood of the Lamb?)
But their noise played havoc with the angel-choir.
(Are you washed in the blood of the Lamb?)
Oh, shout Salvation! It was good to see
Kings and Princes by the Lamb set free.
The banjos rattled and the tambourines
Jing-jing-jingled in the hands of Queens.

(Reverently sung, no instruments)
And when Booth halted by the curb for prayer
He saw his Master thro' the flag-filled air.
Christ came gently with a robe and crown
For Booth the soldier, while the throng knelt down.
He saw King Jesus. They were face to face,
And he knelt a-weeping in that holy place.
Are you washed in the blood of the Lamb?

WALLACE STEVENS
1879-

from
Notes Toward a Supreme Fiction

II

It is the celestial ennui of apartments
That sends us back to the first idea, the quick
Of this invention; and yet so poisonous

Are the ravishments of truth, so fatal to
The truth itself, the first idea becomes
The hermit in a poet's metaphors,

Who comes and goes and comes and goes all day.
May there be an ennui of the first idea?
What else, prodigious scholar, should there be?

The monastic man is an artist. The philosopher
Appoints man's place in music, say, today.
But the priest desires. The philosopher desires.

And not to have is the beginning of desire.
To have what is not is its ancient cycle.
It is desire at the end of winter, when

It observes the effortless weather turning blue
And sees the myosotis on its bush.
Being virile, it hears the calendar hymn.

It knows that what it has is what is not
And throws it away like a thing of another time,
As morning throws off stale moonlight and shabby sleep.

V

The lion roars at the enraging desert,
Reddens the sand with his red-colored noise,
Defies red emptiness to evolve his match,

Master by foot and jaws and by the mane,
Most supple challenger. The elephant
Breaches the darkness of Ceylon with blares,

The glitter-goes on surfaces of tanks,
Shattering velvetest far-away. The bear,
The ponderous cinnamon, snarls in his mountain

At summer thunder and sleeps through winter snow.
But you, ephebe, look from your attic window,
Your mansard with a rented piano. You lie

In silence upon your bed. You clutch the corner
Of the pillow in your hand. You writhe and press
A bitter utterance from your writhing, dumb,

Yet voluble of dumb violence. You look
Across the roofs as sigil and as ward
And in your centre mark them and are cowed . . .

These are the heroic children whom time breeds
Against the first idea—to lash the lion,
Caparison elephants, teach bears to juggle.

VII

It feels good as it is without the giant,
A thinker of the first idea. Perhaps
The truth depends on a walk around a lake,

A composing as the body tires, a stop
To see hepatica, a stop to watch
A definition growing certain and

A wait within that certainty, a rest
In the swags of pine-trees bordering the lake.
Perhaps there are times of inherent excellence,

As when the cock crows on the left and all
Is well, incalculable balances,
At which a kind of Swiss perfection comes

And a familiar music of the machine
Sets up its Schwärmerei, not balances
That we achieve but balances that happen,

As a man and woman meet and love forthwith.
Perhaps there are moments of awakening,
Extreme, fortuitous, personal, in which

We more than awaken, sit on the edge of sleep,
As on an elevation, and behold
The academies like structures in a mist.

XVI

Bethou me, said sparrow, to the crackled blade,
And you, and you, bethou me as you blow,
When in my coppice you behold me be.

Ah, ké! the bloody wren, the felon jay,
Ké-ké, the jug-throated robin pouring out,
Bethou, bethou, bethou me in my glade.

There was such idiot minstrelsy in rain,
So many clappers going without bells,
That these bethous compose a heavenly gong.

One voice repeating, one tireless chorister,
The phrases of a single phrase, ké-ké,
A single text, granite monotony,

One sole face, like a photograph of fate,
Glass-blower's destiny, bloodless episcopus,
Eye without lid, mind without any dream—

These are of minstrels lacking minstrelsy,
Of an earth in which the first leaf is the tale
Of leaves, in which the sparrow is a bird

Of stone, that never changes. Bethou him, you
And you, bethou him and bethou. It is
A sound like any other. It will end.

Mrs. Alfred Uruguay

So what said the others and the sun went down
And, in the brown blues of evening, the lady said,
In the donkey's ear, "I fear that elegance
Must struggle like the rest." She climbed until
The moonlight in her lap, mewing her velvet,

And her dress were one and she said, "I have said no
To everything, in order to get at myself.
I have wiped away moonlight like mud. Your innocent ear
And I, if I rode naked, are what remain."

The moonlight crumbled to degenerate forms,
While she approached the real, upon her mountain,
With lofty darkness. The donkey was there to ride,
To hold by the ear, even though it wished for a bell,
Wished faithfully for a falsifying bell.
Neither the moonlight could change it. And for her,
To be, regardless of velvet, could never be more
Than to be, she could never differently be,
Her no and no made yes impossible.

Who was it passed her there on a horse all will,
What figure of capable imagination?
Whose horse clattered on the road on which she rose,
As it descended, blind to her velvet and
The moonlight? Was it a rider intent on the sun,
A youth, a lover with phosphorescent hair,
Dressed poorly, arrogant of his streaming forces,
Lost in an integration of the martyrs' bones,
Rushing from what was real; and capable?

The villages slept as the capable man went down,
Time swished on the village clocks and dreams were alive,
The enormous gongs gave edges to their sounds,
As the rider, no chevalere and poorly dressed,
Impatient of the bells and midnight forms,
Rode over the picket rocks, rode down the road,
And, capable, created in his mind,
Eventual victor, out of the martyrs' bones,
The ultimate elegance: the imagined land.

The Sense of the Sleight-of-Hand Man

One's grand flights, one's Sunday baths,
One's tootings at the weddings of the soul
Occur as they occur. So bluish clouds
Occurred above the empty house and the leaves
Of the rhododendrons rattled their gold,
As if someone lived there. Such floods of white

Came bursting from the clouds. So the wind
Threw its contorted strength around the sky.

Could you have said the bluejay suddenly
Would swoop to earth? It is a wheel, the rays
Around the sun. The wheel survives the myths.
The fire eye in the clouds survives the gods.

To think of a dove with an eye of grenadine
And pines that are cornets, so it occurs,
And a little island full of geese and stars:
It may be that the ignorant man, alone,
Has any chance to mate his life with life
That is the sensual, pearly spouse, the life
That is fluent in even the wintriest bronze.

Connoisseur of Chaos

I

A. A violent order is disorder; and
B. A great disorder is an order. These
Two things are one. (Pages of illustrations.)

II

If all the green of spring was blue, and it is;
If the flowers of South Africa were bright
On the tables of Connecticut, and they are;
If Englishmen lived without tea in Ceylon, and they do;
And if it all went on in an orderly way,
And it does; a law of inherent opposites,
Of essential unity, is as pleasant as port,
As pleasant as the brush-strokes of a bough,
An upper, particular bough in, say, Marchand.

III

After all the pretty contrast of life and death
Proves that these opposite things partake of one,
At least that was the theory, when bishops' books•
Resolved the world. We cannot go back to that.
The squirming facts exceed the squamous mind,
If one may say so. And yet relation appears,
A small relation expanding like the shade
Of a cloud on sand, a shape on the side of a hill.

IV

A. Well, an old order is a violent one.
This proves nothing. Just one more truth, one more
Element in the immense disorder of truths.
B. It is April as I write. The wind
Is blowing after days of constant rain.
All this, of course, will come to summer soon.
But suppose the disorder of truths should ever come
To an order, most Plantagenet, most fixed. . .
A great disorder is an order. Now, A
And B are not like statuary, posed
For a vista in the Louvre. They are things chalked
On the sidewalk so that the pensive man may see.

V

The pensive man. . . He sees that eagle float
For which the intricate Alps are a single nest.

The Glass of Water

That the glass would melt in heat,
That the water would freeze in cold,
Shows that this object is merely a state,
One of many, between two poles. So,
In the metaphysical, there are these poles.

Here in the centre stands the glass. Light
Is the lion that comes down to drink. There
And in that state, the glass is a pool.
Ruddy are his eyes and ruddy are his claws
When light comes down to wet his frothy jaws

And in the water winding weeds move round.
And there and in another state—the refractions,
The *metaphysica*, the plastic parts of poems
Crash in the mind—But, fat Jocundus, worrying
About what stands here in the centre, not the glass,

But in the centre of our lives, this time, this day,
It is a state, this spring among the politicians
Playing cards. In a village of the indigenes,
One would have still to discover. Among the dogs and dung,
One would continue to contend with one's ideas.

The Poems of Our Climate

I

Clear water in a brilliant bowl,
Pink and white carnations. The light
In the room more like a snowy air,
Reflecting snow. A newly-fallen snow
At the end of winter when afternoons return.
Pink and white carnations—one desires
So much more than that. The day itself
Is simplified: a bowl of white,
Cold, a cold porcelain, low and round,
With nothing more than the carnations there.

II

Say even that this complete simplicity
Stripped one of all one's torments, concealed
The evilly compounded, vital I
And made it fresh in a world of white,
A world of clear water, brilliant-edged,
Still one would want more, one would need more,
More than a world of white and snowy scents.

III

There would still remain the never-resting mind,
So that one would want to escape, come back
To what had been so long composed.
The imperfect is our paradise.
Note that, in this bitterness, delight,
Since the imperfect is so hot in us,
Lies in flawed words and stubborn sounds.

Academic Discourse at Havana

I

Canaries in the morning, orchestras
In the afternoon, balloons at night. That is
A difference, at least, from nightingales,
Jehovah and the great sea-worm. The air
Is not so elemental nor the earth
So near.
          But the sustenance of the wilderness
Does not sustain us in the metropoles.

II

Life is an old casino in a park.
The bills of the swans are flat upon the ground.
A most desolate wind has chilled Rouge-Fatima
And a grand decadence settles down like cold.

III

The swans . . . Before the bills of the swans fell flat
Upon the ground, and before the chronicle
Of affected homaged foxed so many books,
They warded the blank waters of the lakes
And island canopies which were entailed
To that casino. Long before the rain
Swept through its boarded windows and the leaves
Filled its encrusted fountains, they arrayed
The twilights of the mythy goober khan.
The centuries of excellence to be
Rose out of promise and became the sooth
Of trombones floating in the trees.

                              The toil
Of thought evoked a peace eccentric to
The eye and tinkling to the ear. Gruff drums
Could beat, yet not alarm the populace.
The indolent progressions of the swans
Made earth come right; a peanut parody
For peanut people.

                    And serener myth
Conceiving from its perfect plenitude,
Lusty as June, more fruitful than the weeks
Of ripest summer, always lingering
To touch again the hottest bloom, to strike
Once more the longest resonance, to cap
The clearest woman with apt weed, to mount
The thickest man on thickest stallion-back,
This urgent, competent, serener myth
Passed like a circus.

                    Politic man ordained
Imagination as the fateful sin.
Grandmother and her basketful of pears
Must be the crux for our compendia.
That's world enough, and more, if one includes

Her daughters to the peached and ivory wench
For whom the towers are built. The burgher's breast,
And not a delicate ether star-impaled,
Must be the place for prodigy, unless
Prodigious things are tricks. The world is not
The bauble of the sleepless nor a word
That should import a universal pith
To Cuba. Jot these milky matters down.
They nourish Jupiters. Their casual pap
Will drop like sweetness in the empty nights
When too great rhapsody is left annulled
And liquorish prayer provokes new sweats: so, so:
Life is an old casino in a wood.

IV

Is the function of the poet here mere sound,
Subtler than the ornatest phophecy,
To stuff the ear? It causes him to make
His infinite repetition and alloys
Of pick of ebon, pick of halcyon.
It weights him with nice logic for the prim.
As part of nature he is part of us.
His rarities are ours: may they be fit
And reconcile us to our selves in those
True reconcilings, dark, pacific words,
And the adroiter harmonies of their fall.
Close the cantina. Hood the chandelier.
The moonlight is not yellow but a white
That silences the ever-faithful town.
How pale and how possessed a night it is,
How full of exhalations of the sea . . .
All this is older than its oldest hymn,
Has no more meaning than tomorrow's bread.
But let the poet on his balcony
Speak and the sleepers in their sleep shall move,
Waken, and watch the moonlight on their floors.
This may be benediction, sepulcher,
And epitaph. It may, however, be
An incantation that the moon defines
By mere example opulently clear.
And the old casino likewise may define
An infinite incantation of our selves
In the grand decadence of the perished swans.

Evening Without Angels

the great interests of man:
air and light, the joy of
having a body, the volup-
tuousness of looking.
       MARIO ROSSI

Why seraphim like lutanists arranged
Above the trees? And why the poet as
Eternal *chef d'orchestre?*

                Air is air.
Its vacancy glitters round us everywhere.
Its sounds are not angelic syllables
But our unfashioned spirits realized
More sharply in more furious selves.

                And light
That fosters seraphim and is to them
Coiffeur of haloes, fecund jeweller—
Was the sun concoct for angels or for men?
Sad men made angels of the sun, and of
The moon they made their own attendant ghosts,
Which led them back to angels, after death.

Let this be clear that we are men of sun
And men of day and never of pointed night,
Men that repeat antiquest sounds of air
In an accord of repetitions. Yet,
If we repeat, it is because the wind
Encircling us, speaks always with our speech.

Light, too, encrusts us making visible
The motions of the mind and giving form
To moodiest nothings, as, desire for day
Accomplished in the immensely flashing East,
Desire for rest, in that descending sea
Of dark, which in its very darkening
Is rest and silence spreading into sleep.

. . . Evening, when the measure skips a beat
And then another, one by one, and all
To a seething minor swiftly modulate.
Bare night is best. Bare earth is best. Bare, bare,
Except for our own houses, huddled low

Beneath the arches and their spangled air,
Beneath the rhapsodies of fire and fire,
Where the voice that is in us makes a true response,
Where the voice that is great within us rises up,
As we stand gazing at the rounded moon.

The Idea of Order in Key West

She sang beyond the genius of the sea.
The water never formed to mind or voice,
Like a body wholly body, fluttering
Its empty sleeves; and yet its mimic motion
Made constant cry, caused constantly a cry,
That was not ours although we understood,
Inhuman, of the veritable ocean.

The sea was not a mask. No more was she.
The song and water were not medleyed sound,
Even if what she sang was what she heard,
Since what she sang she uttered word by word.
It may be that in all her phrases stirred
The grinding water and the gasping wind;
But it was she and not the sea we heard.

For she was the maker of the song she sang.
The ever-hooded, tragic-gestured sea
Was merely a place by which she walked to sing.
Whose spirit is this? we said, because we knew
It was the spirit that we sought and knew
That we should ask this often as she sang.

If it was only the dark voice of the sea
That rose, or even colored by many waves;
If it was only the outer voice of sky
And cloud, of the sunken coral water-walled,
However clear, it would have been deep air,
The heaving speech of air, a summer sound
Repeated in a summer without end
And sound alone. But it was more than that,
More even than her voice, and ours, among
The meaningless plungings of water and the wind,
Theatrical distances, bronze shadows heaped
On high horizons, mountainous atmospheres
Of sky and sea.

It was her voice that made
The sky acutest at its vanishing.
She measured to the hour its solitude.
She was the single artificer of the world
In which she sang. And when she sang, the sea,
Whatever self it had, became the self
That was her song, for she was maker. Then we,
As we beheld her striding there alone,
Knew that there never was a world for her
Except the one she sang and, singing, made.

Ramon Fernandez, tell me, if you know,
Why, when the singing ended and we turned
Toward the town, tell why the glassy lights,
The lights in the fishing boats at anchor there,
As the night descended, tilting in the air,
Mastered the night and portioned out the sea,
Fixing emblazoned zones and fiery poles,
Arranging, deepening, enchanting night.

Oh! Blessed rage for order, pale Ramon,
The maker's rage to order words of the sea,
Words of the fragrant portals, dimly-starred,
And of ourselves and of our origins,
In ghostlier demarcations, keener sounds.

Sailing After Lunch

It is the word *pejorative* that hurts.
My old boat goes round on a crutch
And doesn't get under way.
It's the time of the year
And the time of the day.

Perhaps it's the lunch that we had
Or the lunch that we should have had.
But I am, in any case,
A most inappropriate man
In a most unpropitious place.

Mon Dieu, hear the poet's prayer.
The romantic should be here.
The romantic should be there.
It ought to be everywhere.
But the romantic must never remain,

Mon Dieu, and must never again return.
This heavy historical sail
Through the mustiest blue of the lake
In a really vertiginous boat
Is wholly the vapidist fake. . . .

It is least what one ever sees.
It is only the way one feels, to say
Where my spirit is I am,
To say the light wind worries the sail,
To say the water is swift today,

To expunge all people and be a pupil
Of the gorgeous wheel and so to give
That slight transcendence to the dirty sail,
By light, the way one feels, sharp white,
And then rush brightly through the summer air.

The Emperor of Ice-Cream

Call the roller of big cigars,
The muscular one, and bid him whip
In kitchen cups concupiscent curds.
Let the wenches dawdle in such dress
As they are used to wear, and let the boys
Bring flowers in last month's newspapers.
Let be be finale of seem.
The only emperor is the emperor of ice-cream.

Take from the dresser of deal,
Lacking the three glass knobs, that sheet
On which she embroidered fantails once
And spread it so as to cover her face.
If her horny feet protrude, they come
To show how cold she is, and dumb.
Let the lamp affix its beam.
The only emperor is the emperor of ice-cream.

JAMES JOYCE
1882-1941

from Part I
Finnegans Wake

Well, you know or don't you kennet or haven't I told you every
telling has a taling and that's the he and the she of it. Look, look,
the dusk is growing! My branches lofty are taking root. And my
cold cher's gone ashley. Fieluhr? Filou! What age is at? It saon
5 is late. 'Tis endless now senne eye or erewone last saw Waterhouse's
clogh. They took it asunder, I hurd thum sigh. When will they reassemble it? O, my back, my back, my bach! I'd want to go to
Aches-les-Pains. Pingpong! There's the Belle for Sexaloitez! And
Concepta de Send-us-pray! Pang! Wring out the clothes! Wring
10 in the dew! Godavari, vert the showers! And grant thaya grace!
Aman. Will we spread them here now? Ay, we will. Flip! Spread
on your bank and I'll spread mine on mine. Flep! It's what I'm
doing. Spread! It's churning chill. Der went is rising. I'll lay a
few stones on the hostel sheets. A man and his bride embraced
15 between them. Else I'd have sprinkled and folded them only. And
I'll tie my butcher's apron here. It's suety yet. The strollers will
pass it by. Six shifts, ten kerchiefs, nine to hold to the fire and
this for the code, the convent napkins, twelve, one baby's shawl.
Good mother Jossiph knows, she said. Whose head? Mutter snores?
20 Deataceas! Wharnow are alle her childer, say? In kingdome gone
or power to come or gloria be to them farther? Allalivial, allalluvial!
Some here, more no more, more again lost alla stranger. I've heard
tell that same brooch of the Shannons was married into a family in
Spain. And all the Dunders de Dunnes in Markland's Vineland
25 beyond Brendan's herring pool takes number nine in yangsee's hats.
And one of Biddy's beads went bobbing till she rounded up lost
histereve with a marigold and a cobbler's candle in a side strain
of a main drain of a manzinahurries off Bachelor's Walk. But all
that's left to the last of the Meaghers in the loup of the years pre-
30 fixed and between is one kneebuckle and two hooks in the front.
Do you tell me that now? I do in troth. Orara por Orbe and poor
Las Animas! Ussa, Ulla, we're umbas all! Mezha, didn't you hear
it a deluge of times, ufer and ufer, respund to spond? You deed,
you deed! I need, I need! It's that irrawaddyng I've stoke in my
35 aars. It all but husheth the lethest zswound. Oronoko! What's

your trouble? Is that the great Finnleader himself in his joakimono on his statue riding the high horse there forehengist? Father of Otters, it is himself! Yonne there! Isset that? On Fallareen Common? You're thinking of Astley's Amphitheayter where the bobby restrained you making sugarstuck pouts to the ghostwhite horse of the Peppers. Throw the cobwebs from your eyes, woman, and spread your washing proper! It's well I know your sort of slop. Flap! Ireland sober is Ireland stiff. Lord help you, Maria, full of grease, the load is with me! Your prayers. I sonht zo! Madammangut! Were you lifting your elbow, tell us, glazy cheeks, in Conway's Carrigacurra canteen? Was I what, hobbledyhips? Flop! Your rere gait's creakorheuman bitts your butts disagrees. Amn't I up since the damp dawn, marthared mary allacook, with Corrigan's pulse and varicoarse veins, my pramaxle smashed, Alice Jane in decline and my oneeyed mongrel twice run over, soaking and bleaching boiler rags, and sweating cold, a widow like me, for to deck my tennis champion son, the laundryman with the lavandier flannels? You won your limpopo limp fron the husky hussars when Collars and Cuffs was heir to the town and your slur gave the stink to Carlow. Holy Scamander, I sar it again! Near the golden falls. Icis on us! Seints of light! Zezere! Subdue your noise, you hamble creature! What is it but a blackburry growth or the dwyergray ass them four old codgers owns. Are you meanam Tarpey and Lyons and Gregory? I meyne now, thank all, the four of them, and the roar of them, that draves that stray in the mist and old Johnny MacDougal along with them. Is that the Poolbeg flasher beyant, pharphar, or a fireboat coasting nyar the Kishtna or a glow I behold within a hedge or my Garry come back from the Indes? Wait till the honeying of the lune, love! Die eve, little eve, die! We see that wonder in your eye. We'll meet again, we'll part once more. The spot I'll seek if the hour you'll find. My chart shines high where the blue milk's upset. Forgivemequick, I'm going! Bubye! And you, pluck your watch, forgetmenot. Your evenlode. So save to jurna's end! My sights are swimming thicker on me by the shadows to this place. I sow home slowly now by own way, moy-valley way. Towy I too, rathmine.

Ah, but she was the queer old skeowsha anyhow, Anna Livia, trinkettoes! And sure he was the quare old buntz too, Dear Dirty Dumpling, foostherfather of fingalls and dottergills. Gammer and gaffer we're all their gangsters. Hadn't he seven dams to wive him? And every dam had her seven crutches. And every crutch had its seven hues. And each hue had a differing cry. Sudds for me and supper for you and the doctor's bill for Joe John. Befor! Bifur! He married his markets, cheap by foul, I know, like any Etrurian Catholic Heathen, in their pinky limony creamy birnies and their turkiss indienne mauves. But at milkidmass who was the spouse?

Then all that was was fair. Tys Elvenland! Teems of times and happy returns. The seim anew. Ordovico or viricordo. Anna was, Livia is, Plurabelle's to be. Northmen's thing made southfolk's
85 place but howmulty plurators made eachone in person? Latin me that, my trinity scholard, out of eure sanscreed into oure eryan! *Hircus Civis Eblanensis!* He had buckgoat paps on him, soft ones for orphans. Ho, Lord! Twins of his bosom. Lord save us! And ho! Hey? What all men. Hot? His tittering daughters of. Whawk?
90 Can't hear with the waters of. The chittering waters of. Flittering bats, fieldmice bawk talk. Ho! Are you not gone ahome? What Thom Malone? Can't hear with bawk of bats, all thim liffeying waters of. Ho, talk save us! My foos won't moos. I feel as old as yonder elm. A tale told of Shaun or Shem? All Livia's daughter-
95 sons. Dark hawks hear us. Night! Night! My ho head halls. I feel as heavy as yonder stone. Tell me of John or Shaun? Who were Shem and Shaun the living sons or daughters of? Night now! Tell me, tell me, tell me, elm! Night night! Telmetale of stem or stone. Beside the rivering waters of, hitherandthithering waters
100 of. Night!

from Part IV

Soft morning, city! Lsp! I am leafy speafing. Lpf! Folty and folty all the nights have fallen on to long my hair. Not a sound, falling. Lispn! No wind no word. Only a leaf, just a leaf and then leaves. The woods are fond always. As were we their babes in.
105 And robins in crews so. It is for me goolden wending. Unless? Away! Rise up, man of the hooths, you have slept so long! Or is it only so mesleems? On your pondered palm. Reclined from cape to pede. With pipe on bowl. Terce for a fiddler, sixt for makmerriers, none for a Cole. Rise up now and aruse! Norvena's over.
110 I am leafy, your goolden, so you called me, may me life, yea your goolden, silve me solve, exsogerraider! You did so drool. I was so sharm. But there's a great poet in you too. Stout Stokes would take you offly. So has he as bored me to slump. But am good and rested. Taks to you, toddy, tan ye! Yawhawaw. Helpunto min,
115 helpas vin. Here is your shirt, the day one, come back. The stock, your collar. Also your double brogues. A comforter as well. And here your iverol and everthelest your umbr. And stand up tall! Straight. I want to see you looking fine for me. With your brand-new big green belt and all. Blooming in the very lotust and second
120 to nill, Budd! When you're in the buckly shuit Rosensharonals near did for you. Fiftyseven and three, cosh, with the bulge. Proudpurse Alby with his pooraroon Eireen, they'll. Pride, comfytousness, enevy! You make me think of a wonderdecker I once. Or somebalt thet sailder, the man megallant, with the bangled ears.

Or an earl was he, at Lucan? Or, no, it's the Iren duke's I mean. 125
Or somebrey erse from the Dark Countries. Come and let us!
We always said we'd. And go abroad. Rathgreany way perhaps.
The childher are still fast. There is no school today. Them boys
is so contrariy. The Head does be worrying himself. Heel trouble
and heal travel. Galliver and Gellover. Unless they changes by 130
mistake. I seen the likes in the twinngling of an aye. Som. So oft.
Sim. Time after time. The sehm asnuh. Two bredder as doffered
as nors in soun. When one of him sighs or one of him cries 'tis
you all over. No peace at all. Maybe it's those two old crony
aunts held them out to the water front. Queer Mrs Quickenough 135
and odd Miss Doddpebble. And when them two has had a good
few there isn't much more dirty clothes to publish. From the
Laundersdale Minssions. One chap googling the holyboy's thing-
abib and this lad wetting his widdle. You were pleased as Punch,
recitating war exploits and pearse orations to them jackeen 140
gapers. But that night after, all you were wanton! Bidding me do
this and that and the other. And blowing off to me, hugly Judsys,
what wouldn't you give to have a girl! Your wish was mewill. And,
lo, out of a sky! The way I too. But her, you wait. Eager to
choose is left to her shade. If she had only more matcher's wit. 145
Findlings makes runaways, runaways a stray. She's as merry as the
gricks still. 'Twould be sore should ledden sorrow. I'll wait. And
I'll wait. And then if all goes. What will be is. Is is. But let
them. Slops hospodch and the slusky slut too. He's for thee what
she's for me. Dogging you round cove and haven and teaching 150
me the perts of speech. If you spun your yarns to him on the
swishbarque waves I was spelling my yearns to her over cottage
cake. We'll not disturb their sleeping duties. Let besomes be
bosuns. It's Phoenix, dear. And the flame is, hear! Let's our
journee saintomichael make it. Since the lausafire has lost and the 155
book of the depth is. Closed. Come! Step out of your shell! Hold
up you free fing! Yes. We've light enough. I won't take our
laddy's lampern. For them four old windbags of Gustsofairy to be
blowing at. Not you your rucksunck. To bring all the dannymans
out after you on the hike. Send Arctur guiddus! Isma! Sft! It is 160
the softest morning that ever I can ever remember me. But she
won't rain showerly, our Ilma. Yet. Until it's the time. And me
and you have made our. The sons of bursters won in the games.
Still I'll take me owld Finvara for my shawlders. The trout will be
so fine at brookfisht. With a taste of roly polony from Blugpuddels 165
after. To bring out the tang of the tay. Is't you fain for a roost
brood? Oaxmealturn, all out of the woolpalls! And then all the
chippy young cuppinjars cluttering round us, clottering for their
creams. Crying, me, grownup sister! Are me not truly? Lst! Only
but, theres a but, you must buy me a fine new girdle too, nolly. 170

When next you go to Market Norwall. They're all saying I need it since the one from Isaacsen's slooped its line. Mrknrk? Fy arthou! Come! Give me your great bearspaw, padder avilky, fol a miny tiny. Dola. Mineninecy handsy, in the languo of flows.
175 That's Jorgen Jargonsen. But you understood, nodst? I always know by your brights and shades. Reach down. A lil mo. So. Draw back your glave. Hot and hairy, hugon, is your hand! Here's where the falskin begins. Smoos as an infams. One time you told you'd been burnt in ice. And one time it was chemicalled after you
180 taking a lifeness. Maybe that's why you hold your hodd as if. And people thinks you missed the scaffold. Of fell design. I'll close me eyes. So not to see. Or see only a youth in his florizel, a boy in innocence, peeling a twig, a child beside a weenywhite steed. The child we all love to place our hope in for ever. All men has
185 done something. Be the time they've come to the weight of old fletch. We'll lave it. So. We will take our walk before in the timpul they ring the earthly bells. In the church by the hearseyard. Pax Goodmens will. Or the birds start their treestirm shindy. Look, there are yours off, high on high! And cooshes, sweet good
190 luck they're cawing you, Coole! You see, they're as white as the riven snae. For us. Next peaters poll you will be elicted or I'm not your elicitous bribe. The Kinsella woman's man will never reduce me. A MacGarath O'Cullagh O'Muirk MacFewney sookadoodling and sweepacheeping round the lodge of Fjorn na Galla of the
195 Trumpets! It's like potting the po to shambe on the dresser or tamming Uncle Tim's Caubeen on to the brows of a Viker Eagle. Not such big strides, huddy foddy! You'll crush me antilopes I saved so long for. They're Penisole's. And the two goodiest shoeshoes. It is hardly a Knut's mile or seven, possumbotts. It is very
200 good for the health of a morning. With Buahbuah. A gentle motion all around. As leisure paces. And the helpyourselftoastrool cure's easy. It seems so long since, ages since. As if you had been long far away. Afartodays, afeartonights, and me as with you in thadark. You will tell me some time if I can believe its all. You
205 know where I am bringing you? You remember? When I ran berrying after hucks and haws. With you drawing out great aims to hazel me from the hummock with your sling. Our cries. I could lead you there and I still by you in bed. Les go dutc to Danegreven, nos? Not a soul but ourselves. Time? We have loads
210 on our hangs. Till Gilligan and Halligan call again to hooligan. And the rest of the guns. Sullygan eight, from left to right. Olobobo, ye foxy theagues! The moskors thought to ball you out. Or the Wald Unicorns Master, Bugley Captain, from the Naul, drawls up by the door with the Honourable Whilp and the Reverend
215 Poynter and the two Lady Pagets of Tallyhaugh, Ballyhuntus, in their riddletight raiding hats for to lift a hereshealth to their robost,

the Stag, evers the Carlton hart. And you needn't host out with
your duck and your duty, capapole, while they reach him the glass
he never starts to finish. Clap this wis on your poll and stick this
in your ear, wiggly! Beauties don't answer and the rich never pays.   220
If you were the enlarged they'd hue in cry you, Heathtown, Har-
bourstown, Snowtown, Four Knocks, Flemingtown, Bodingtown to
the Ford of Fyne on Delvin. How they housed to house you after
the Platonic garlens! And all because, loosed in her reflexes, she
seem she seen Ericoricori coricome huntsome with his three poach   225
dogs aleashing him. But you came safe through. Enough of that
horner corner! And old mutther-goosip! We might call on the Old
Lord, what do you say? There's something tells me. He is a fine
sport. Like the score and a moighty went before him. And a proper
old promnentory. His door always open. For a newera's day. Much   230
as your own is. You invoiced him last Eatster so he ought to give
us hockockles and everything. Remember to take off your white
hat, ech? When we come in the presence. And say hoothoothoo,
ithmuthisthy! His is house of laws. And I'll drop my graciast
kertssey too. If the Ming Tung no go bo to me homage me hamage   235
kow bow tow to the Mong Tang. Ceremonialness to stand lowest
place be! Saying: What'll you take to link to light a pike on
porpoise, plaise? He might knight you an Armor elsor daub you
the first cheap magyerstrape. Remember Bomthomanew vim vam
vom Hungerig. Hoteform, chain and epolettes, botherbumbose.   240
And I'll be your aural eyeness. But we vain. Plain fancies. It's in
the castles air. My current bread's full of sillymottocraft. Aloof is
anoof. We can take or leave. He's reading his ruffs. You'll know
our way from there surely. Flura's way. Where once we led so
many car couples have follied since. Clatchka! Giving Shaugh-   245
nessy's mare the hillymount of her life. With her strulldeburgghers!
Hnmn hnmn! The rollcky road adondering. We can sit us down on
the heathery benn, me on you, in quolm unconsciounce. To scand
the arising. Out from Drumleek. It was there Evora told me I had
best. If I ever. When the moon of mourning is set and gone.   250
Over Glinaduna. Lonu nula. Ourselves, oursouls alone. At the
site of salvocean. And watch would the letter you're wanting be
coming may be. And cast ashore. That I prays for be mains of me
draims. Scratching it and patching at with a prompt from a primer.
And what scrips of nutsnolleges I pecked up me meself. Every   255
letter is a hard but yours sure is the hardest crux ever. Hack an
axe, hook an oxe, hath an an, heth hith ences. But omce done,
dealt and delivered, tattat, you're on the map. Rased on traumscrapt from Maston, Boss. After rounding his world of ancient
days. Carried in a caddy or screwed and corked. On his mugisstosst   260
surface. With a bob, bob, bottledby. Blob. When the waves give
up yours the soil may for me. Sometime then, somewhere there,

I wrote me hopes and buried the page when. I heard Thy voice,
ruddery dunner, so loud that none but, and left it to lie till a
265 kissmiss coming. So content me now. Lss. Unbuild and be buildn
our bankaloan cottage there and we'll cohabit respectable. The
Gowans, ser, for Medem, me. With acute bubel runtoer for to
pippup and gopeep where the sterres be. Just to see would we hear
how Jove and the peers talk. Amid the soleness. Tilltop, bigmaster!
270 Scale the summit! You're not so giddy any more. All your ground-
plotting and the little it brought! Humps, when you hised us
and dumps, when you doused us! But sarra one of me cares a
brambling ram, pomp porteryark! On limpidy marge I've made me
hoom. Park and a pub for me. Only don't start your stunts of
275 Donachie's yeards agoad again. I could guessp to her name who
tuckt you that one, tufnut! Bold bet backwords. For the loves of
sinfintins! Before the naked universe. And the bailby pleasemarm
rincing his eye! One of these fine days, lewdy culler, you must
redoform again. Blessed shield Martin! Softly so. I am so exquisitely
280 pleased about the loveleavest dress I have. You will always call me
Leafiest, won't you, dowling? Wordherfhull Ohldhbhoy! And you
won't urbjunk to me parafume, oiled of kolooney, with a spot of
marashy. Sm! It's Alpine Smile from Yesthers late Yhesters. I'm
in everywince nasturtls. Even in Houlth's nose. Medeurscodeignus!
285 Astale of astoun. Grand owld marauder! If I knew who you are!
When that hark from the air said it was Captain Finsen makes
cumhulments and was mayit pressing for his suit I said are you
there here's nobody here only me. But I near fell off the pile of
samples. As if your tinger winged ting to me hear. Is that right
290 what your brothermilk in Bray bes telling the district you were
bragged up by Brostal because your parents would be always tumbling into his foulplace and losing her pentacosts after drinking
their pledges? Howsomendeavor, you done me fine! The only man
was ever known could eat the crushts of lobsters. Our native night
295 when you twicetook me for some Marienne Sherry and then your
Jermyn cousin who signs hers with exes and the beardwig I found
in your Clarksome bag. Pharaops you'll play you're the king of
Aeships. You certainly make the most royal of noises. I will tell
you all sorts of makeup things, strangerous. And show you to every
300 simple storyplace we pass. *Cadmillersfolly, Bellevenue, Wellcrom,
Quid Superabit,* villities valleties. Change the plates for the next
course of murphies! Spendlove's still there and the canon going
strong and so is Claffey's habits endurtaking and our parish pomp's
a great warrent. But you'll have to ask that same four that named
305 them is always snugging in your barsalooner, saying they're the best
relics of Conal O'Daniel and writing *Finglas since the Flood.*
That'll be some kingly work in progress. But it's by this route he'll
come some morrow. And I can signal you all flint and fern are

rasstling as we go by. And you'll sing thumb a bit and then wise
your selmon on it. It is all so often and still the same to me. Snf? 310
Only turf, wick dear! Clane turf. You've never forgodden batt on
tarf, have you, at broin burroow, what? Mch? Why, them's the
muchrooms, come up during the night. Look, agres of roofs in
parshes. Dom on dam, dim in dym. And a capital part for olympics
to ply at. Steadyon, Cooloosus! Mind your stride or you'll knock. 315
While I'm dodging the dustbins. Lood what I found! A lintil pea.
And look at here! This cara weeseed. Pretty mites, my sweetthings,
was they poorloves abandoned by wholawidey world? Neighboulotts
for newtown. The Eblanamagna you behazyheld loomening up out
of the dumblynass. But the still sama sitta. I've lapped so long. 320
As you said. It fair takes. If I lose my breath for a minute or two
don't speak, remember! Once it happened, so it may again. Why
I'm all these years within years in soffran, allbeleaved. To hide
away the tear, the parted. It's thinking of all. The brave that
gave their. The fair that wore. All them that's gunne. I'll begin 325
again in a jiffey. The nik of a nad. How glad you'll be I waked
you! My! How well you'll feel! For ever after. First we turn by
the vagurin here and then it's gooder. So side by side, turn agate,
weddingtown, laud men of Londub! I only hope whole the heavens
sees us. For I feel I could near to faint away. Into the deeps. 330
Annamores leep. Let me lean, just a lea, if you le, bowldstrong
bigtider. Allgearls is wea. At times. So. While you're adamant
evar. Wrhps, that wind as if out of norewere! As on the night of
the Apophanypes. Jumpst shootst throbbst into me mouth like a
bogue and arrohs! Ludegude of the Lashlanns, how he whips me 335
cheeks! Sea, sea! Here, weir, reach, island, bridge. Where you
meet I. The day. Remember! Why there that moment and us
two only? I was but teen a tiler's dot. The swankysuits was boost-
ing always, sure him, he was like to me fad. But the swaggerest
swell off Shackvulle Strutt. And the fiercest freaky ever followed 340
a pining child round the sluppery table with a forkful of fat.
But a king of whistlers. Scieoula! When he'd prop me atlas against
his goose and light our two candles for our singers duohs on the
sewingmachine. I'm sure he squirted juice in his eyes to make
them flash for flightening me. Still and all he was awful fond 345
to me. Who'll search for *Find Me Colours* now on the hillydroops
of Vikloefells? But I read in Tobecontinued's tale that while blubles
blows there'll still be sealskers. There'll be others but non so for
me. Yed he never knew we seen us before. Night after night. So
that I longed to go to. And still with all. One time you'd stand 350
fornenst me, fairly laughing, in your bark and tan billows of
branches for to fan me coolly. And I'd lie as quiet as a moss. And
one time you'd rush upon me, darkly roaring, like a great black
shadow with a sheeny stare to perce me rawly. And I'd frozen up

355 and pray for thawe. Three times in all. I was the pet of everyone
then. A princeable girl. And you were the pantymammy's Vulking
Corsergoth. The invision of Indelond. And, by Thorror, you looked
it! My lips went livid for from the joy of fear. Like almost now.
How? How you said how you'd give me the keys of me heart. And
360 we'd be married till delth to uspart. And though dev do espart.
O mine! Only, no, now it's me who's got to give. As duv herself
div. Inn this linn. And can it be it's nnow fforvell? Illas! I wisht
I had better glances to peer to you through this baylight's growing.
But you're changing, acoolsha, you're changing from me, I can feel.
365 Or is it me is? I'm getting mixed. Brightening up and tightening
down. Yes, you're changing, sonhusband, and you're turning, I can
feel you, for a daughterwife from the hills again. Imlamaya. And
she is coming. Swimming in my hindmoist. Diveltaking on me
tail. Just a whisk brisk sly spry spink spank sprint of a thing
370 theresomere, saultering. Saltarella come to her own. I pity your
oldself I was used to. Now a younger's there. Try not to part!
Be happy, dear ones! May I be wrong! For she'll be sweet for you
as I was sweet when I came down out of me mother. My great
blue bedroom, the air so quiet, scarce a cloud. In peace and silence.
375 I could have stayed up there for always only. It's something fails
us. First we feel. Then we fall. And let her rain now if she likes.
Gently or strongly as she likes. Anyway let her rain for my time
is come. I done me best when I was let. Thinking always if I go
all goes. A hundred cares, a tithe of troubles and is there one who
380 understands me? One in a thousand of years of the nights? All me
life I have been lived among them but now they are becoming
lothed to me. And I am lothing their little warm tricks. And lothing
their mean cosy turns. And all the greedy gushes out through their
small souls. And all the lazy leaks down over their brash bodies.
385 How small it's all! And me letting on to meself always. And lilting
on all the time. I thought you were all glittering with the noblest
of carriage. You're only a bumpkin. I thought you the great in all
things, in guilt and in glory. You're but a puny. Home! My people
were not their sort out beyond there so far as I can. For all the
390 bold and bad and bleary they are blamed, the seahags. No! Nor
for all our wild dances in all their wild din. I can see meself among
them, allaniuvia pulchrabelled. How she was handsome, the wild
Amazia, when she would seize to my other breast! And what is
she weird, haughty Niluna, that she will snatch from my ownest
395 hair! For 'tis they are the stormies. Ho hang! Hang ho! And the
clash of our cries till we spring to be free. Auravoles, they says,
never heed of your name! But I'm loothing them that's here and all
I lothe. Loonely in me loneness. For all their faults. I am passing
out. O bitter ending! I'll slip away before they're up. They'll never
400 see. Nor know. Nor miss me. And it's old and old it's sad and

old it's sad and weary I go back to you, my cold father, my cold mad father, my cold mad feary father, till the near sight of the mere size of him, the moyles and moyles of it, moananoaning, makes me seasilt saltsick and I rush, my only, into your arms. I see them rising! Save me from those therrble prongs! Two more. Onetwo 405 moremens more. So. Avelaval. My leaves have drifted from me. All. But one clings still. I'll bear it on me. To remind me of. Lff! So soft this morning, ours. Yes. Carry me along, taddy, like you done through the toy fair! If I seen him bearing down on me now under whitespread wings like he'd come from Arkangels, I sink 410 I'd die down over his feet, humbly dumbly, only to washup. Yes, tid. There's where. First. We pass through grass behush the bush to. Whish! A gull. Gulls. Far calls. Coming, far! End here. Us then. Finn, again! Take. Bussoftlhee, mememormee! Till thousendsthee. Lps. The keys to. Given! A way a lone a last a 415 loved a long the

WILLIAM CARLOS WILLIAMS

1883-

The Clouds

I

Filling the mind
upon the rim of the overarching sky, the horses of
the dawn charge from south to north, gigantic beasts
rearing flame-edged above the pit,
a rank confusion of the imagination still uncured,
a rule, piebald under the streetlamps, reluctant
to be torn from its hold.

           Their flanks still
caught among low blocking forms their fore-parts
rise lucid beyond this smell of a swamp, a mud
livid with decay and life! turtles
that burrowing among the white roots lift their green
red-striped faces startled before the dawn.

A black flag, writhing and whipping at the staff-head
mounts the sepulcher of the empty bank, fights
to be free.

South to north! the direction
unmistakable, they move distinct beyond the unclear
edge of the world, clouds! like statues
before which we are drawn—in darkness, thinking of
our dead, unable, knowing no place
where else rightly to lodge them.

Tragic outlines
and the bodies of horses, mindfilling—but
visible! against the invisible; actual against
the imagined and the concocted; unspoiled by hands
and unshaped also by them but caressed by sight only,
moving among them, not that that propels
the eyes from under, while it blinds:

—upon whose backs the dead ride, high!
undirtied by the putridity we fasten upon them—
South to north, for this moment distinct and undeformed,
into the no-knowledge of their nameless destiny.

II

Where are the good minds of past days, the unshorn?
Villon, to be sure, with his
saw-toothed will and testament? Erasmus
who praised folly and

Shakespeare who wrote so that
no schoolman or churchman could sanction him without
revealing his own imbecility? Aristotle,
shrewd and alone, an herb peddler?

They all, like Aristophanes, knew the clouds and
said next to nothing of the soul's flight
but kept their heads and died—
like Socrates, Plato's better self, unmoved.

Where? They live today in their old state because
of the pace they kept that keeps
them now fresh in our thoughts, their
relics, ourselves: Toulouse Lautrec, the

deformed who lived in a brothel and painted
the beauty of whores. These were
the truth-tellers of who we are the sole heirs
beneath the clouds that bring

shadow and darkness full of thought deepened
by rain against the clatter
of an empty sky. But anything to escape humanity!
Now it's spiritualism—again,

as if the certainty of a future life
were any solution to our dilemma: how to get
published not what we write but what we would write were
it not for the laws against libelous truth.

The poor brain unwilling to own the obtrusive body
would crawl from it like a crab and
because it succeeds, at times, in doffing that,
by its wiles of drugs or other "ecstasies," thinks

at last that it is quite free—exulted, scurrying to
some slightly larger shell some snail
has lost (where will it live). And so, thinking,
pretends a mystery! an unbodied

thing that would still be a brain—but no body,
something that does not eat but flies by the propulsions
of pure—what? into the sun itself, illimitedly
and exists so forever, blest, washed, purged

and at ease in non-representational bursts
of shapeless flame, sentient (naturally!)—and keeps
touch with the earth (by former works) at least.
The intellect leads, leads still! Beyond the clouds.

III

I came upon a priest once at St. Andrew's
in Amalfi in crimson and gold brocade riding
the clouds of his belief.

It happened that we tourists had intervened
at some mid-moment of the ritual—
tipped the sacristan or whatever it was.

No one else was there—porphyry and alabaster,
the light flooding in scented
with sandalwood—but this holy man

jiggling upon his buttocks to the litany
chanted, in response, by two kneeling altar boys!
I was amazed and stared in such a manner

that he, caught half off the earth
in his ecstasy—though without losing a beat—
turned and grinned at me from his cloud.

IV

With each, dies a piece of the old life, which he carries,
a precious burden, beyond! Thus each
is valued by which he carries and that is his soul—
diminishing the bins by that much
unless replenished.

            It is that which is the brotherhood:
the old life, treasured. But if they live?
What then?

            The clouds remain
—the disordered heavens, ragged, ripped by winds
or dormant, a calligraphy of scaly dragons and bright moths,

of straining thought, bulbous and smooth,
ornate, the flesh itself (in which
the poet foretells his own death); convoluted, lunging upon
a pismire, a conflagration, a . . . .

The Monstrous Marriage

She who with innocent and tender hands
reached up to take the wounded
pigeon from the branch found it turn

into a fury as it bled. Maddened she clung
to it stabbed by its pain and the blood
of her hands and the bird's blood

mingled while she stilled it for the moment
and wrapped it in her thought's
clean white handkerchief. After that

she adopted a hawk's life as her own.
For it looked up and said, You are
my wife for this. Then she released him.

But he came back shortly. Certainly,
since we are married, she said to him, no
one will accept it. Time passed.

I try to imitate you, he said while she
cried a little in smiling. Mostly,
he confided, my head is clouded

except for hunting. But for parts of
a day it's clear as any man's—by
your love. No, she would

answer him pitifully, what clearer than
a hawk's eye and reasonably the
mind also must be so. He turned his

head and seeing his profile in her
mirror ruffled his feathers and gave
a hawk's cry, desolately.

Nestling upon her as was his wont he
hid his talons from her soft flesh
fluttering his wings against her sides

until her mind, always astonished at
his assumptions, agonized, heard
footsteps and hurried him to

the open window whence he made off.
After that she had a leather belt made
upon which he perched to enjoy her.

Burning the Christmas Greens

Their time past, pulled down
cracked and flung to the fire
—go up in a roar

All recognition lost, burnt clean
clean in the flame, the green
dispersed, a living red,
flame red, red as blood' wakes
on the ash—

and ebbs to a steady burning
the rekindled bed become
a landscape of flame

At the winter's midnight
we went to the trees, the coarse
holly, the balsam and
the hemlock for their green

At the thick of the dark
the moment of the cold's
deepest plunge we brought branches
cut from the green trees

to fill our need, and over
doorways, about paper Christmas
bells covered with tinfoil
and fastened by red ribbons

we stuck the green prongs
in the windows hung
woven wreaths and above pictures
the living green. On the

mantel we built a green forest
and among those hemlock
sprays put a herd of small
white deer as if they

were walking there. All this!
and it seemed gentle and good
to us. Their time past,
relief! The room bare. We

stuffed the dead grate
with them upon the half burntout
log's smouldering eye, opening
red and closing under them

and we stood there looking down.
Green is a solace
a promise of peace, a fort
against the cold (though we

did not say so) a challenge
above the snow's
hard shell. Green (we might
have said) that, where

small birds hide and dodge
and lift their plaintiff

rallying cries, blocks for them
and knocks down

the unseeing bullets of
the storm. Green spruce boughs
pulled down by a weight of
snow—Transformed!

Violence leaped and appeared.
Recreant! roared to life
as the flame rose through and
our eyes recoiled from it.

In the jagged flames green
to red, instant and alive. Green!
those sure abutments. Gone!
lost to mind

and quick in the contracting
tunnel of the grate
appeared a world! Black
mountains, black and red—as

yet uncolored—and ash white,
an infant landscape shimmering
ash and flame and we, in
that instant, lost,

breathless to be witnesses,
as if we stood
ourselves refreshed among
the shining fauna of that fire.

St. Francis Einstein of the Daffodils

ON THE FIRST VISIT OF PROFESSOR EINSTEIN

TO THE UNITED STATES IN THE

SPRING OF 1921

"Sweet land"
at last!
out of the sea—
the Venusremembering wavelets
rippling with laughter—
freedom

for the daffodils!
—in a tearing wind
that shakes
the tufted orchards—
Einstein, tall as a violet
in the lattice-arbor corner
is tall as
a blossomy peartree

O Samos, Samos
dead and buried. Lesbia
a black cat in the freshturned
garden. All dead.
All flesh they sung
is rotten
Sing of it no longer—
Side by side young and old
take the sun together—
maples, green and red
yellowbells
and the vermilion quinceflower
together—

The peartree
with foetid blossoms
sways its high topbranches
with contrary motions
and there are both pinkflowered
and coralflowered peachtrees
in the bare chickenyard
of the old negro
with white hair who hides
poisoned fish-heads
here and there
where stray cats find them—
find them

Spring days
swift and mutable
winds blowing four ways
hot and cold
shaking the flowers—
Now the northeast wind
moving in fogs leaves the grass
cold and dripping. The night
is dark. But in the night

the southeast wind approaches.
The owner of the orchard
lies in bed
with open windows
and throws off his covers
one by one

The Yachts

contend in a sea which the land partly encloses
shielding them from the too heavy blows
of an ungoverned ocean which when it chooses

tortures the biggest hulls, the best man knows
to pit against its beatings, and sinks them pitilessly.
Mothlike in mists, scintillant in the minute

brilliance of cloudless days, with broad bellying sails
they glide to the wind tossing green water
from their sharp prows while over them the crew crawls

ant like, solicitously grooming them, releasing,
making fast as they turn, lean far over and having
caught the wind again, side by side, head for the mark.

In a well guarded arena of open water surrounded by
lesser and greater craft which, sycophant, lumbering
and flittering follow them, they appear youthful, rare

as the light of a happy eye, live with the grace
of all that in the mind is feckless, free and
naturally to be desired. Now the sea which holds them

is moody, lapping their glossy sides, as if feeling
for some slightest flaw but fails completely.
Today no race. Then the wind comes again. The yachts

move, jockeying for a start, the signal is set and they
are off. Now the waves strike at them but they are too
well made, they slip through, though they take in canvas.

Arms with hands grasping seek to clutch at the prows.
Bodies thrown recklessly in the way are cut aside.
It is a sea of faces about them in agony, in despair

until the horror of the race dawns staggering the mind,
the whole sea become an entanglement of watery bodies
lost to the world bearing what they cannot hold. Broken,

beaten, desolate, reaching from the dead to be taken up
they cry out, failing, failing! their cries rising
in waves still as the skillful yachts pass over.

ELINOR WYLIE
1885-1928

Hymn to Earth

Farewell, incomparable element,
Whence man arose, where he shall not return;
And hail, imperfect urn
Of his last ashes, and his firstborn fruit;
Farewell, the long pursuit,
And all the adventures of his discontent;
The voyages which sent
His heart averse from home:
Metal of clay, permit him that he come
To thy slow-burning fire as to a hearth;
Accept him as a particle of earth.

Fire, being divided from the other three,
It lives removed, or secret at the core;
Most subtle of the four,
When air flies not, nor water flows,
It disembodied goes,
Being light, elixir of the first degree,
More volatile than he;
With strength and power to pass
Through space, where never his least atom was:
He has no part in it, save as his eyes
Have drawn its emanation from the skies.

A wingless creature heavier than air,
He is rejected of its quintessence;
Coming and going hence,
In the twin minutes of his birth and death,
He may inhale as breath,

As breath relinquish heaven's atmosphere,
Yet in it have no share,
Nor can survive therein
Where its outer edge is filtered pure and thin:
It doth but lend its crystal to his lungs
For his early crying, and his final songs.

The element of water has denied
Its child; it is no more his element;
It never will relent;
Its silver harvests are more sparsely given
Than the rewards of heaven,
And he shall drink cold comfort at its side:
The water is too wide:
The seamew and the gull
Feather a nest made soft and pitiful
Upon its foam; he has not any part
In the long swell of sorrow at its heart.

Hail and farewell, beloved element,
Whence he departed, and his parent once;
See where thy spirit runs
Which for so long hath had the moon to wife;
Shall this support his life
Until the arches of the waves be bent
And grow shallow and spent?
Wisely it cast him forth
With his dead weight of burdens nothing worth,
Leaving him, for the universal years,
A little seawater to make his tears.

Hail, element of earth, receive thy own,
And cherish, at thy charitable breast,
This man, this mongrel beast:
He ploughs the sand, and, at his hardest need,
He sows himself for seed;
He ploughs the furrow, and in this lies down
Before the corn is grown;
Between the apple bloom
And the ripe apple is sufficient room
In time, and matter, to consume his love
And make him parcel of a cypress grove.

Receive him as thy lover for an hour
Who will not weary, by a longer stay,
The kind embrace of clay;

Even within thine arms he is dispersed
To nothing, as at first;
The air flings downward from its four-quartered tower
Him whom the flames devour;
At the full tide, at the flood,
The sea is mingled with his salty blood:
The traveller dust, although the dust be vile,
Sleeps as thy lover for a little while.

O Virtuous Light

A private madness has prevailed
Over the pure and valiant mind;
The instrument of reason failed
And the star-gazing eyes struck blind.

Sudden excess of light has wrought
Confusion in the secret place
Where the slow miracles of thought
Take shape through patience into grace.

Mysterious as steel and flint
The birth of this destructive spark
Whose inward growth has power to print
Strange suns upon the natural dark.

O break the walls of sense in half
And make the spirit fugitive!
This light begotten of itself
Is not a light by which to live!

The fire of farthing tallow dips
Dispels the menace of the skies
So it illuminate the lips
And enter the discerning eyes.

O virtuous light, if thou be man's
Or matter of the meteor stone,
Prevail against this radiance
Which is engendered of its own!

D. H. LAWRENCE
1885-1930

Song of a Man Who Has Come Through

Not I, not I, but the wind that blows through me!
A fine wind is blowing the new direction of Time.
If only I let it bear me, carry me, if only it carry me!
If only I am sensitive, subtle, oh, delicate, a winged gift!
If only, most lovely of all, I yield myself and am borrowed
By the fine, fine wind that takes its course through the chaos of
    the world
Like a fine, an exquisite chisel, a wedge-blade inserted;
If only I am keen and hard like the sheer tip of a wedge
Driven by invisible blows,
The rock will split, we shall come at the wonder, we shall find
    the Hesperides.

Oh, for the wonder that bubbles into my soul,
I would be a good fountain, a good well-head,
Would blur no whisper, spoil no expression.

What is the knocking?
What is the knocking at the door in the night?
It is somebody wants to do us harm.

No, no, it is the three strange angels.
Admit them, admit them.

Snake

A snake came to my water-trough
On a hot, hot day, and I in pyjamas for the heat,
To drink there.

In the deep, strange-scented shade of the great dark carob-tree
I came down the steps with my pitcher
And must wait, must stand and wait, for there he was at the trough
    before me.

He reached down from a fissure in the earth-wall in the gloom
And trailed his yellow-brown slackness soft-bellied down, over
    the edge of the stone trough

And rested his throat upon the stone bottom,
And where the water had dripped from the tap, in a small
    clearness,
He sipped with his straight mouth,
Softly drank through his straight gums, into his slack long body,
Silently.

Someone was before me at my water-trough,
And I, like a second-comer, waiting.

He lifted his head from his drinking, as cattle do,
And looked at me vaguely, as drinking cattle do,
And flickered his two-forked tongue from his lips, and mused a
    moment,
And stooped and drank a little more,
Being earth-brown, earth-golden from the burning bowels of the
    earth
On the day of Sicilian July, with Etna smoking.

The voice of my education said to me
He must be killed,
For in Sicily the black, black snakes are innocent, the gold are
    venomous.

And voices in me said, If you were a man
You would take a stick and break him now, and finish him off.

But must I confess how I liked him,
How glad I was he had come like a guest in quiet, to drink at
    my water-trough
And depart peaceful, pacified, and thankless,
Into the burning bowels of this earth?

Was it cowardice, that I dared not kill him?
Was it perversity, that I longed to talk to him?
Was it humility, to feel so honoured?
I felt so honoured.

And yet those voices:
If you were not afraid, you would kill him!

And truly I was afraid, I was most afraid,
But even so, honoured still more
That he should seek my hospitality
From out the dark door of the secret earth.

He drank enough
And lifted his head, dreamily, as one who has drunken,
And flickered his tongue like a forked night on the air, so black,
Seeming to lick his lips,
And looked around like a god, unseeing, into the air,
And slowly turned his head,
And slowly, very slowly, as if thrice adream,
Proceeded to draw his slow length curving round
And climb again the broken bank of my wall-face.

And as he put his head into that dreadful hole,
And as he slowly drew up, snake-easing his shoulders, and entered
    further,
A sort of horror, a sort of protest against his withdrawing into that
    horrid black hole,
Deliberately going into the blackness, and slowly drawing himself
    after,
Overcame me now his back was turned.

I looked round, I put down my pitcher,
I picked up a clumsy log
And threw it at the water-trough with a clatter.

I think it did not hit him,
But suddenly that part of him that was left behind convulsed in
    undignified haste,
Writhed like lightning, and was gone
Into the black hole, the earth-lipped fissure in the wall-front,
At which, in the intense still noon, I stared with fascination.

And immediately I regretted it.
I thought how paltry, how vulgar, what a mean act!
I despised myself and the voices of my accursed human education.

And I thought of the albatross,
And I wished he would come back, my snake.

For he seemed to me again like a king,
Like a king in exile, uncrowned in the underworld,
Now due to be crowned again.

And so, I missed my chance with one of the lords
Of life.
And I have something to expiate:
A pettiness.

                                    Taormina.

EZRA POUND

1885-

The Cantos

from

CANTO XVI

And before hell mouth; dry plain
    and two mountains;
On the one mountain, a running form,
    and another
In the turn of the hill; in hard steel
The road like a slow screw's thread,
The angle almost imperceptible,
    so that the circuit seemed hardly to rise;
And the running form, naked, Blake,
Shouting, whirling his arms, the swift limbs,
Howling against the evil,
    his eyes rolling,
Whirling like flaming cart-wheels,
    and his head held backward to gaze on the evil
As he ran from it,
    to be hid by the steel mountain,
And when he showed again from the north side;
    his eyes blazing toward hell mouth,
His neck forward,
    and like him Peire Cardinal.
And in the west mountain, Il Fiorentino,
Seeing hell in his mirror,
    and lo Sordels
Looking on it in his shield;
And Augustine, gazing toward the invisible.

And past them, the criminal
    lying in blue lakes of acid,
The road between the two hills, upward
    slowly,
The flames patterned in lacquer, crimen est actio,
The limbo of chopped ice and saw-dust,
And I bathed myself with the acid to free myself
    of the hell ticks,

Scales, fallen louse eggs.
      Palux Laerna,
the lake of bodies, aqua morta,
of limbs fluid, and mingled, like fish heaped in a bin,
and here an arm upward, clutching a fragment of marble,
And the embryos, in flux,
      new inflow, submerging,
Here an arm upward, trout, submerged by the eels;
      and from the bank, the stiff herbage
the dry nobbled path, saw many known, and unknown,
for an instant;
      submerging,
The face gone, generation.

      Then light air, under saplings,
the blue banded lake under æther,
      an oasis, the stones, the calm field,
the grass quiet,
      and passing the tree of the bough
The grey stone posts,
      and the stair of gray stone,
the passage clean-squared in granite:
      descending,
and I through this, and into the earth,
      patet terra,
entered the quiet air
      the new sky,
the light as after a sun-set,
      and by their fountains, the heroes,
Sigismundo, and Malatesta Novello,
      and founders, gazing at the mounts of their cities.

The plain, distance, and in fount-pools
      the nymphs of that water
rising, spreading their garlands,
      weaving their water reeds with the boughs,
In the quiet,
      and now one man rose from his fountain
and went off into the plain.

     *   *   *

And because that son of a bitch,
      Franz Josef of Austria......
And because that son of a bitch Napoléon Barbiche...
They put him on Hill 70, in a trench
      dug through corpses

With a lot of kids of sixteen,
Howling and crying for their mamas,
And he sent a chit back to his major:
          I can hold out for ten minutes
With my sergeant and a machine-gun.
          And they rebuked him for levity.
And Henri Gaudier went to it,
          and they killed him,
And killed a good deal of sculpture,
And ole T.E.H. he went to it,
With a lot of books from the library,
London Library, and a shell buried 'em in a dug-out,
And the Library expressed its annoyance.
          And a bullet hit him on the elbow
. . . gone through the fellow in front of him,
And he read Kant in the Hospital, in Wimbledon,
in the original,
And the hospital staff didn't like it.

And Maxy Larmann went to it,
With a heavy bit of artillery,
          and the airmen came by with a mitrailleuse,
And cleaned out most of his company,
          and a shell lit on his tin hut,
While he was out in the privy,
          and he was all there was left of that outfit.

Barham Vanderberg went to it,
          and he was out in the Ægæan,
And down in the hold of his ship
          pumping gas into a sausage,
And the boatswain looked over the rail,
          down into amidships, and he said:
          Gees! look a' the Kept'n,
The Kept'n's a-gettin' 'er up.

And Ole Captain Corcoran went to it,
          with his legs full of rheumatics,
So much so he couldn't run,
          so he was six months in hospital,
Observing the mentality of the patients.

And Bimmy was 19 when he went to it,
And his major went mad in the control pit,
          about midnight, and started throwing the 'phone about

And he had to keep him quiet
        till about six in the morning,
And direct that bunch of artillery.

And Cyril Hammerton went to it,
        too much in a hurry,
And they buried him for four days.

from
CANTO XIV

And the betrayers of language
        . . . n and the press gang
And those who had lied for hire;
the perverts, the perverters of language,
        the perverts, who have set money-lust
Before the pleasures of the senses;
howling, as of a hen-yard in a printing-house,
        the clatter of presses,
the blowing of dry dust and stray paper,
fœtor, sweat, the stench of stale oranges,
dung, last cess-pool of the universe,
mysterium, acid of sulphur,
the pusillanimous, raging;
plunging jewels in mud,
        and howling to find them unstained;
sadic mothers driving their daughters to bed with decrepitude,
sows eating their litters,
here the placard ΕΙΚΩΝ ΓΗΣ,
        and here: THE PERSONNEL CHANGES,

        *   *   *

The slough of unamiable liars,
        bog of stupidities,
malevolent stupidities, and stupidities,
the soil living pus, full of vermin,
dead maggots begetting live maggots,
        slum owners,
usurers squeezing crab-lice, pandars to authority,
pets-de-loup, sitting on piles of stone books,
obscuring the texts with philology,
        hiding them under their persons,
the air without refuge of silence,
        the drift of lice, teething,
and above it the mouthing of orators,
        the arse-belching of preachers.
        And Invidia,

the corruptio, fœtor, fungus,
liquid animals, melted ossifications,
slow rot, fœtid combustion,
          chewed cigar-butts, without dignity, without tragedy,
. . . . . m Episcopus, waving a condom full of black-beetles,
monopolists, obstructors of knowledge,
          obstructors of distribution.

from
CANTO XV

skin-flakes, repetitions, erosions,
endless rain from the arse-hairs,
as the earth moves, the centre
          passes over all parts in succession,
a continual bum-belch
          distributing its productions.
Andiamo!
          One's feet sunk,
the welsh of mud gripped one, no hand-rail,
the bog-suck like a whirl-pool,
and he said:
          Close the pores of your feet!
And my eyes clung to the horizon,
          oil mixing with soot;
and again Plotinus:
          To the door,
Keep your eyes on the mirror!
Prayed we to the Medusa,
          petrifying the soil by the shield,
Holding it downward
          he hardened the track
Inch before us, by inch,
          the matter resisting,
The heads rose from the shield,
          hissing, held downwards.
Devouring maggots,
          the face only half potent,
The serpents' tongues
          grazing the swill top,
Hammering the souse into hardness,
          the narrow rast,
Half the width of a sword's edge.
          By this through the dern evil,
now sinking, now clinging,
          Holding the unsinkable shield.

Oblivion,
   forget how long,
sleep, fainting nausea.
   "Whether in Naishapur or Babylon"
I heard in the dream.
   Plotinus gone,
And the shield tied under me, woke;
The gate swung on its hinges;
Panting like a sick dog, staggered,
Bathed in alkali, and in acid.
'Ηέλιον τ' 'Ηέλιον
   blind with the sunlight,
Swollen-eyed, rested,
   lids sinking, darkness unconscious.

from
CANTO XX

        Jungle:
Glaze green and red feathers, jungle,
Basis of renewal, renewals;
Rising over the soul, green virid, of the jungle,
Lozenge of the pavement, clear shapes,
Broken, disrupted, body eternal,
Wilderness of renewals, confusion
Basis of renewals, subsistence,
Glazed green of the jungle;
Zoe, Marozia, Zothar,
       loud over the banners,
Glazed grape, and the crimson,
HO BIOS,
     cosi Elena vedi,
In the sunlight, gate cut by the shadow;
And then the faceted air:
Floating. Below, sea churning shingle,
Floating, each on invisible raft,
On the high current, invisible fluid,
Borne over the plain, recumbent,
The right arm cast back,
    the right wrist for a pillow,
The left hand like a calyx,
Thumb held against finger, the third,
The first fingers petal'd up, the hand as a lamp,
A calyx.
   From toe to head
The purple, blue-pale smoke, as of incense;

Wrapped each in burnous, smoke as the olibanum's,
Swift, as if joyous.
Wrapped, floating; and the blue-pale smoke of the incense
Swift to rise, then lazily in the wind
            as Aeolus over bean-field,
As hay in the sun, the olibanum, saffron,
As myrrh without styrax;
Each man in his cloth, as on raft, on
        The high invisible current;
On toward the fall of water;
And then over that cataract,
In air, strong, the bright flames, V shaped;
            Nel fuoco
D'amore mi mise, nel fuoco d'amore mi mise. . .
Yellow, bright saffron, croceo;
And as the olibanum bursts into flame,
The bodies so flamed in the air, took flame,
            ". . .Mi mise, il mio sposo novello."
Shot from stream into spiral,

Or followed the water. Or looked back to the flowing;
Others approaching that cataract,
As to dawn out of shadow, the swathed cloths
Now purple and orange,
And the blue water dusky beneath them,
            pouring there into the cataract,
With noise of sea over shingle,
                striking with:
                hah hah ahah thmm, thunb, ah
                woh woh araha thumm, bhaaa.
And from the floating bodies, the incense
            blue-pale, purple above them.
Shelf of the lotophagoi,
Aerial, cut in the æther.
                        Reclining,
With the silver spilla,
The ball as of melted amber, coiled, caught up, and turned.
Lotophagoi of the suave nails, quiet, scornful,
Voce-profondo:
            "Feared neither death nor pain for this beauty;
If harm, harm to ourselves."
And beneath: the clear bones, far down,
Thousand on thousand.
            "What gain with Odysseus,
"They that died in the whirlpool
"And after many vain labours,

"Living by stolen meat, chained to the rowingbench,
"That he should have a great fame
            "And lie by night with the goddess?
"Their names are not written in bronze
            "Nor their rowing sticks set with Elpenor's;
"Nor have they mound by sea-bord.
            "That saw never the olives under Sparta
"With the leaves green and then not green,
            "The click of light in their branches;
"That saw not the bronze hall nor the ingle
"Nor lay there with the queen's waiting maids,
"Nor had they Circe to couch-mate, Circe Titania,
"Nor had they meats of Kalüpso
"Or her silk skirts brushing their thighs.
"Give! What were they given?
                        Ear-wax.
"Poison and ear-wax,
                        and a salt grave by the bull-field,
"*neson amumona,* their heads like sea cows in the foam,
"Black splotches, sea-weed under lightning;
"Canned beef of Apollo, ten cans for a boat load."
Ligur' aoide.

And from the plain whence the water-shoot,
Across, back, to the right, the roads, a way in the grass,
The Khan's hunting leopard, and young Salustio
And Ixotta; the suave turf
Ac ferae familiares, and the cars slowly,
And the panthers, soft-footed.
Plain, as the plain of Somnus,
            the heavy cars, as a triumph,
Gilded, heavy on wheel,
            and the panthers chained to the cars,
Over suave turf, the form wrapped,
Rose, crimson, deep crimson,
And, in the blue dusk, a colour as of rust in the sunlight,
Out of white cloud, moving over the plain,
Head in arm's curve, reclining;
The road, back and away, till cut along the face of the rock,
And the cliff folds in like a curtain,
The road cut in under the rock,
Square groove in the cliff's face, as chiostri,
The columns crystal, with peacocks cut in the capitals,
The soft pad of beasts dragging the cars;
Cars, slow, without creak,

And at windows in inner roadside:
     le donne e i cavalieri
     smooth face under hennin,
The sleeves embroidered with flowers,
Great thistle of gold, or an amaranth,
Acorns of gold, or of scarlet,
Cramoisi and diaspre
     slashed white into velvet;
Crystal columns, acanthus, sirens in the pillar heads;
And at last, between gilded barocco,
Two columns coiled and fluted,
Vanoka, leaning half naked,
     waste hall there behind her.
"Peace!
     Borso. . . , Borso!"

from
CANTO XXI

And there was grass on the floor of the temple,
Or where the floor of it might have been;
     Gold fades in the gloom,
     Under the blue-black roof, Placidia's,
Of the exarchate; and we sit here
By the arena, *les gradins* . . .
And the palazzo, baseless, hangs there in the dawn
With low mist over the tide-mark;
And floats there nel tramonto
With gold mist over the tide-mark.
The tesserae of the floor, and the patterns.
Fools making new shambles;
     night over green ocean,
And the dry black of the night.
     Night of the golden tiger,
And the dry flame in the air,
     Voices of the procession,
Faint now, from below us,
And the sea with tin flash in the sun-dazzle,
     Like dark wine in the shadows.
"Wind between the sea and the mountains"
The tree-spheres half dark against sea
     half clear against sunset,
The sun's keel freighted with cloud,
And after that hour, dry darkness
Floating flame in the air, gonads in organdy,
Dry flamelet, a petal borne in the wind.

Gignetei kalon.
Impenetrable as the ignorance of old women.
In the dawn, as the fleet coming in after Actium,
Shore to the eastward, and altered,
And the old man sweeping leaves:
   "Damned to you Midas, Midas lacking a Pan!"
And now in the valley,
Valley under the day's edge:
   "Grow with the Pines of Ise;
"As the Nile swells with Inopos.
   "As the Nile falls with Inopos."
Phoibos, turris eburnea,
   ivory against cobalt,
And the boughs cut on the air,
The leaves cut on the air,
The hounds on the green slope by the hill,
   water still black in the shadow.
In the crisp air,
   the discontinuous gods;
Pallas, young owl in the cup of her hand,
And, by night, the stag runs, and the leopard,
Owl-eye amid pine boughs.
Moon on the palm-leaf,
      confusion;
Confusion, source of renewals;
Yellow wing, pale in the moon shaft,
Green wing, pale in the moon shaft,
Pomegranate, pale in the moon shaft,
White horn, pale in the moon shaft, and Titania
By the drinking hole,
   steps, cut in the basalt.
Danced there Athame, danced, and there Phæthusa
With color in the vein,
Strong as with blood-drink, once,
With colour in the vein,
Red in the smoke-faint throat. Dis caught her up.

And the old man went on there
   beating his mule with an asphodel.

from
CANTO XXIX

She is submarine, she is an octopus, she is
A biological process,
So Arnaut turned there

Above him the wave pattern cut in the stone
Spire-top alevel the well-curb
And the tower with cut stone above that, saying:
     "I am afraid of the life after death."
and after a pause:
"Now, at last. I have shocked him."
And another day or evening toward sundown by the arena
(les gradins)
A little lace at the wrist
And not very clean lace either. . .
And I, "But this beats me,
"Beats me, I mean that I do not understand it;
"This love of death that is in them."
     Let us consider the osmosis of persons
nondum orto jubare;
The tower, ivory, the clear sky
Ivory rigid in sunlight
And the pale clear of the heaven
Phoibus of narrow thighs,
The cut cool of the air,
Blossom cut on the wind, by Helios
Lord of the Light's edge, and April
Blown round the feet of the God,
Beauty on an ass-cart
Sitting on five sacks of laundry
That wd have been the road by Perugia
That leads out to San Piero. Eyes brown topaz,
Brookwater over brown sand,
The white hounds on the slope,
Glide of water, lights and the prore,
Silver beaks out of night,
Stone, bough over bough,
     lamps fluid in water,
Pine by the black trunk of its shadow
And on hill black trunks of the shadow
The trees melted in air.

CANTO XLVII

Who even dead, yet hath his mind entire!
This sound came in the dark
First must thou go the road
        to hell
And to the bower of Ceres' daughter Proserpine,
Through overhanging dark, to see Tiresias,
Eyeless that was, a shade, that is in hell

So full of knowing that the beefy men know less than he,
Ere thou come to thy road's end.
        Knowledge the shade of a shade,
Yet must thou sail after knowledge
Knowing less than drugged beasts. *phtheggometha*
thasson
φθεγγώμεθα θᾶσσου
        The small lamps drift in the bay
And the sea's claw gathers them.
Neptunus drinks after neap-tide.
Tamuz! Tamuz!!
The red flame going seaward.
        By this gate art thou measured.
From the long boats they have set lights in the water,
The sea's claw gathers them outward.
Scilla's dogs snarl at the cliff's base,
The white teeth gnaw in under the crag,
But in the pale night the small lamps float seaward
               Τυ Διώνα,
            TU DIONA

Καὶ Μοῖραι' "Αδονιν
KAI MOIRAI' ADONIN
The sea is streaked red with Adonis,
The lights flicker red in small jars.
Wheat shoots rise new by the altar,
        flower from the swift seed.
Two span, two span to a woman,
Beyond that she believes not. Nothing is of any importance.
To that is she bent, her intention
To that art thou called ever turning intention,
Whether by night the owl-call, whether by sap in shoot,
Never idle, by no means by no wiles intermittent
Moth is called over mountain
The bull runs blind on the sword, *naturans*
To the cave art thou called, Odysseus,
By Molü hast thou respite for a little,
By Molü art thou freed from the one bed
        that thou may'st return to another
The stars are not in her counting,
        To her they are but wandering holes.
Begin thy plowing
When the Pleiades go down to the rest,
Begin they plowing
40 days are they under seabord,
Thus do in fields by seabord
And in valleys winding down toward the sea.

When the cranes fly high
                think of plowing.
By this gate art thou measured
Thy day is between a door and a door
Two oxen are yoked for plowing
Or six in the hill field
White bulk under olives, a score for drawing down stone,
Here the mules are gabled with slate on the hill road.
Thus was it in time.
And the small stars now fall from the olive branch,
Forked shadow falls dark on the terrace
More black than the floating martin
                that has no care for your presence,
His wing-print is black on the roof tiles
And the print is gone with his cry.
So light is thy weight on Tellus
Thy notch no deeper indented
Thy weight less than the shadow
Yet hast thou gnawed through the mountain,
                Scylla's white teeth less sharp.
Hast thou found a nest softer than cunnus
Or hast thou found better rest
Hast'ou a deeper planting, doth thy death year
Bring swifter shoot?
Hast thou entered more deeply the mountain?

The light has entered the cave. Io! Io!
The light has gone down into the cave,
Splendour on splendour!
By prong have I entered these hills:
That the grass grow from my body,
That I hear the roots speaking together,
The air is new on my leaf,
The forked boughs shake with the wind.
Is Zephyrus more light on the bough, Apeliota
more light on the almond branch?
By this door have I entered the hill.
Falleth,
Adonis falleth.
Fruit cometh after. The small lights drift out with the tide,
sea's claw has gathered them outward,
Four banners to every flower
The sea's claw draws the lamps outward.
Think thus of thy plowing
When the seven stars go down to their rest
Forty days for their rest, by seabord

And in valleys that wind down toward the sea
                Καὶ Μοῖραι᾽ ῎Αδονιν
                KAI MOIRAI᾽ ADONIN
When the almond bough puts forth its flame,
When the new shoots are brought to the altar,
                Τυ Διώνα, Καὶ Μοῖραι᾽
                TU DIONA, KAI MOIRAI
Καὶ Μοῖραι᾽ ῎Αδονιν
KAI MOIRAI᾽ ADONIN
                that hath the gift of healing,
that hath the power over wild beasts.

CANTO XLV

With *Usura*
With usura hath no man a house of good stone
each block cut smooth and well fitting
that design might cover their face,
with usura
hath no man a painted paradise on his church wall
harpes et luthes
or where virgin receiveth message
and halo projects from incision,
with usura
seeth no man Gonzaga his heirs and his concubines
no picture is made to endure nor to live with
but it is made to sell and sell quickly
with usura, sin against nature,
is thy bread ever more of stale rags
is thy bread dry as paper,
with no mountain wheat, no strong flour
with usura the line grows thick
with usura is no clear demarcation
and no man can find site for his dwelling.
Stone cutter is kept from his stone
weaver is kept from his loom
WITH USURA
wool comes not to market
sheep bringeth no gain with usura
Usura is a murrain, usura
blunteth the needle in the maid's hand
and stoppeth the spinner's cunning. Pietro Lombardo
came not by usura
Duccio came not by usura
nor Pier della Francesca; Zuan Bellin' not by usura

nor was 'La Calunnia' painted.
Came not by usura Angelico; came not Ambrogio Praedis,
Came no church of cut stone signed: *Adamo me fecit.*
Not by usura St. Trophime
Not by usura Saint Hilaire,
Usura rusteth the chisel
It rusteth the craft and the craftsman
It gnaweth the thread in the loom
None learneth to weave gold in her pattern;
Azure hath a canker by usura; cramoisi is unbroidered
Emerald findeth no Memling
Usura slayeth the child in the womb
It stayeth the young man's courting
It hath brought palsey to bed, lyeth
between the young bride and her bridegroom
CONTRA NATURAM
They have brought whores for Eleusis
Corpses are set to banquet
at behest of usura.

Hugh Selwyn Mauberley

(LIFE AND CONTACTS)

'Vocat æstus in umbram'
Nemesianus, Ec. IV

I

E. P. ODE POUR L'ELECTION
DE SON SEPULCHRE

For three years, out of key with his time,
He strove to resuscitate the dead art
Of poetry; to maintain 'the sublime'
In the old sense. Wrong from the start—

No, hardly, but seeing he had been born
In a half-savage country, out of date;
Bent resolutely on wringing lilies from the acorn;
Capaneus; trout for factitious bait;

Ἴδμεν γάρ τοι πάνθ', ὅσ' ἐνὶ Τροίη
Caught in the unstopped ear;
Giving the rocks small lee-way
The chopped seas held him, therefore, that year.

His true Penelope was Flaubert,
He fished by obstinate isles;
Observed the elegance of Circe's hair
Rather than the mottoes on sundials.

Unaffected by 'the march of events,'
He passed from men's memory in *l'an trentiesme,*
De son eage; the case presents
No adjunct to the Muses' diadem.

II

The age demanded an image
Of its accelerated grimace,
Something for the modern stage,
Not, at any rate, an Attic grace;

Not, not certainly, the obscure reveries
Of the inward gaze;
Better mendacities
Than the classics in paraphrase!

The 'age demanded' chiefly a mould in plaster,
Made with no loss of time,
A prose kinema, not, not assuredly, alabaster
Or the 'sculpture' of rhyme.

III

The tea-rose tea-gown, etc.
Supplants the mousseline of Cos,
The pianola 'replaces'
Sappho's barbitos.

Christ follows Dionysus,
Phallic and ambrosial
Made way for macerations;
Caliban casts out Ariel.

All things are a flowing,
Sage Heracleitus says;
But a tawdry cheapness
Shall outlast our days.

Even the Christian beauty
Defects—after Samothrace;

We see τὸ καλὸν
Decreed in the market-place.

Faun's flesh is not to us,
Nor the saint's vision.
We have the Press for wafer;
Franchise for circumcision.

All men, in law, are equals.
Free of Pisistratus,
We choose a knave or an eunuch
To rule over us.

O bright Apollo,
τίν' ἄνδρα, τίν' ἥρωα, τίνα θεὸν,
What god, man, or hero
Shall I place a tin wreath upon!

                        IV

These fought in any case,
and some believing,
                    pro domo, in any case . . .

Some quick to arm,
some for adventure,
some from fear of weakness,
some from fear of censure,
some for love of slaughter, in imagination,
learning later . . .
some in fear, learning love of slaughter;
Died some, pro patria,
                non 'dulce' non 'et decor' . . .
walked eye-deep in hell
believing in old men's lies, then unbelieving
came home, home to a lie,
home to many deceits,
home to old lies and new infamy;
usury age-old and age-thick
and liars in public places.

Daring as never before, wastage as never before.
Young blood and high blood,
fair cheeks, and fine bodies;

fortitude as never before

frankness as never before,
disillusions as never told in the old days,
hysterias, trench confessions,
laughter out of dead bellies.

V

There died a myriad,
And of the best, among them,
For an old bitch gone in the teeth,
For a botched civilization,

Charm, smiling at the good mouth,
Quick eyes gone under earth's lid,

For two gross of broken statues,
For a few thousand battered books.

VI

YEUX GLAUQUES

Gladstone was still respected,
When John Ruskin produced
'King's Treasuries'; Swinburne
And Rossetti still abused.

Fœtid Buchanan lifted up his voice
When that faun's head of hers
Became a pastime for
Painters and adulterers.

The Burne-Jones cartoons
Have preserved her eyes;
Still, at the Tate, they teach
Cophetua to rhapsodize;

Thin like brook-water,
With a vacant gaze.
The English Rubaiyat was still-born
In those days.

The thin, clear gaze, the same
Still darts out faun-like from the half-ruin'd face,
Questing and passive. . . .
'Ah, poor Jenny's case' . . .

Bewildered that a world
Shows no surprise
At her last maquero's
Adulteries.

VII

"SIENA MI FE', DISFECEMI MAREMMA"

Among the pickled fœtuses and bottled bones,
Engaged in perfecting the catalogue,
I found the last scion of the
Senatorial families of Strasbourg, Monsieur Verog.

For two hours he talked of Gallifet;
Of Dowson; of the Rhymers' Club;
Told me how Johnson (Lionel) died
By falling from a high stool in a pub . . .

But showed no trace of alcohol
At the autopsy, privately performed—
Tissue preserved—the pure mind
Arose toward Newman as the whisky warmed.

Dowson found harlots cheaper than hotels;
Headlam for uplift; Image impartially imbued
With raptures for Bacchus, Terpsichore and the Church.
So spoke the author of 'The Dorian Mood,'

M. Verog, out of step with the decade,
Detached from his contemporaries,
Neglected by the young,
Because of these reveries.

VIII

BRENNBAUM

The sky-like limpid eyes,
The circular infant's face,
The stiffness from spats to collar
Never relaxing into grace;

The heavy memories of Horeb, Sinai and the forty years,
Showed only when the daylight fell
Level across the face
Of Brennbaum 'The Impeccable.'

IX

MR. NIXON

In the cream gilded cabin of his steam yacht
Mr. Nixon advised me kindly, to advance with fewer
Dangers of delay. 'Consider
      Carefully the reviewer.

'I was as poor as you are;
When I began I got, of course,
Advance on royalties, fifty at first,' said Mr. Nixon,
'Follow me, and take a column,
Even if you have to work free.

'Butter reviewers. From fifty to three hundred
I rose in eighteen months;
The hardest nut I had to crack
Was Dr. Dundas.

'I never mentioned a man but with the view
Of selling my own works.
The tip's a good one, as for literature
It gives no man a sinecure.

'And no one knows, at sight, a masterpiece.
And give up verse, my boy,
There's nothing in it.'

     . . . . . .

Likewise a friend of Bloughram's once advised me:
Don't kick against the pricks,
Accept opinion. The 'Nineties' tried your game
And died, there's nothing in it.

X

Beneath the sagging roof
The stylist has taken shelter,
Unpaid, uncelebrated,
At last from the world's welter

Nature receives him;
With a placid and uneducated mistress

He exercises his talents
And the soil meets his distress.

The haven from sophistications and contentions
Leaks through its thatch;
He offers succulent cooking;
The door has a creaking latch.

XI

'Conservatrix of Milésien'
Habits of mind and feeling,
Possibly. But in Ealing
With the most bank-clerkly of Englishmen?

No, 'Milésien' is an exaggeration.
No instinct has survived in her
Older than those her grandmother
Told her would fit her station.

XII

'Daphne with her thighs in bark
Stretches toward me her leafy hands'—
Subjectively. In the stuffed-satin drawing-room.
I await The Lady Valentine's commands,

Knowing my coat has never been
Of precisely the fashion
To stimulate, in her,
A durable passion;

Doubtful, somewhat, of the value
Of well-gowned approbation
Of literary effort,
But never of The Lady Valentine's vocation:

Poetry, her border of ideas,
The edge, uncertain, but a means of blending
With other strata
Where the lower and higher have ending;

A hook to catch the Lady Jane's attention,
A modulation toward the theatre,
Also, in the case of revolution,
A possible friend and comforter.

. . . . . .

Conduct, on the other hand, the soul
'Which the highest cultures have nourished'
To Fleet St. where
Dr. Johnson flourished;

Beside this thoroughfare
The sale of half-hose has
Long since superseded the cultivation
Of Pierian roses.

XIII

ENVOI

1919

Go, dumb-born book,
Tell her that sang me once that song of Lawes:
Hadst thou but song
As thou hast subjects known,
Then were there cause in thee that should condone
Even my faults that heavy upon me lie,
And build her glories their longevity.

Tell her that sheds
Such treasure in the air,
Recking naught else but that her graces give
Life to the moment,
I would bid them live
As roses might, in magic amber laid,
Red overwrought with orange and all made
One substance and one colour
Braving time.

Tell her that goes
With song upon her lips
But sings not out the song, nor knows
The maker of it, some other mouth,
May be as fair as hers,
Might, in new ages, gain her worshippers,
When our two dusts with Waller's shall be laid,
Siftings on siftings in oblivion,
Till change hath broken down
All things save Beauty alone.

Mauberley

1920

Vacuos exercet aera morsus.

I

Turned from the 'eau-forte
Par Jaquemart'
To the strait head
Of Messalina:

'His true Penelope
Was Flaubert,'
And his tool
The engraver's.

Firmness,
Not the full smile,
His art, but an art
In profile;

Colourless
Pier Francesca,
Pisanello lacking the skill
To forge Achaia.

II

'Qu'est ce qu'ils savent de l'amour, et qu'est ce qu'ils peuvent comprendre?
'S'ils ne comprennent pas la poésie, s'ils ne sentent pas la musique, qu'est ce qu'ils peuvent comprendre de cette passion en camparaison avec laquelle la rose est grossière et le parfum des violettes un tonerre?'

CAID ALI

For three years, diabolus in the scale,
He drank ambrosia,
All passes, ANANGKE prevails,
Came end, at last, to that Arcadia.

He had moved amid her phantasmagoria,
Amid her galaxies,
NUKTIS 'AGALMA

. . . . .

Drifted . . . drifted precipitate,
Asking time to be rid of . . .
Of his bewilderment; to designate
His new-found orchid. . . .

To be certain . . . certain . . .
(Amid aerial flowers) . . . time for arrangements—
Drifted on
To the final estrangement;

Unable in the supervening blankness
To sift TO AGATHON from the chaff
Until he found his sieve . . .
Ultimately, his seismograph:

—Given that is his 'fundamental passion,'
This urge to convey the relation
Of eyelid and cheek-bone
By verbal manifestations;

To present the series
Of curious heads in medallion—

He had passed, inconscient, full gaze,
The wide-banded irides
And Botticellian sprays implied
In their diastasis;

Which anæsthesis, noted a year late,
And weighed, revealed his great affect,
(Orchid), mandate
Of Eros, a retrospect.

. . . . . .

Mouths biting empty air,
The still stone dogs,
Caught in metamorphosis, were
Left him as epilogues.

III

'THE AGE DEMANDED'

For this agility chance found
Him of all men, unfit
As the red-beaked steeds of
The Cytheræan for a chain bit.

The glow of porcelain
Brought no reforming sense
To his perception
Of the social inconsequence.

Thus, if her colour
Came against his gaze,
Tempered as if
It were through a perfect glaze

He made no immediate application
Of this to relation of the state
To the individual, the month was more temperate
Because this beauty had been.

>   The coral isle, the lion-coloured sand
>   Burst in upon the porcelain reverie:
>   Impetuous troubling
>   Of his imagery.

Mildness, amid the neo-Nietzschean clatter,
His sense of graduations,
Quite out of place amid
Resistance to current exacerbations,

Invitation, mere invitation to perceptivity
Gradually led him to the isolation
Which these presents place
Under a more tolerant, perhaps, examination.

By constant elimination
The manifest universe
Yielded an armour
Against utter consternation,

A Minoan undulation,
Seen, we admit, amid ambrosial circumstances,
Strengthened him against
The discouraging doctrine of chances,

And his desire for survival,
Faint in the most strenuous moods,
Became an Olympian *apathein*
In the presence of selected perceptions.

A pale gold, in the aforesaid pattern,
The unexpected palms

Destroying, certainly, the artist's urge,
Left him delighted with the imaginary
Audition of the phantasmal sea-surge,

Incapable of the least utterance or composition,
Emendation, conservation of the 'better tradition,'
Refinement of medium, elimination of superfluities,
August attraction or concentration.

Nothing, in brief, but maudlin confession,
Irresponse to human aggression,
Amid the precipitation, down-float
Of insubstantial manna,
Lifting the faint susurrus
Of his subjective hosannah.

Ultimate affronts to
Human redundancies;

Non-esteem of self-styled 'his betters'
Leading, as he well knew,
To his final
Exclusion from the world of letters.

IV

Scattered Moluccas
Not knowing, day to day,
The first day's end, in the next noon;
The placid water
Unbroken by the Simoon;

Thick foliage
Placid beneath warm suns,
Tawn foreshores
Washed in the cobalt of oblivions;

Or through dawn-mist
The grey and rose
Of the juridical
Flamingoes;

A consciousness disjunct,
Being but this overblotted
Series
Of intermittences;

Coracle of Pacific voyages,
The unforecasted beach;
Then on an oar
Read this:

'I was
And I no more exist;
Here drifted
An hedonist.'

V

MEDALLION

Luini in porcelain!
The grand piano
Utters a profane
Protest with her clear soprano.

The sleek head emerges
From the gold-yellow frock
As Anadyomene in the opening
Pages of Reinach.

Honey-red, closing the face-oval,
A basket-work of braids which seem as if they were
Spun in King Minos' hall
From metal, or intractable amber;

The face-oval beneath the glaze,
Bright in its suave bounding-line, as,
Beneath half-watt rays,
The eyes turn topaz.

The Return

See, they return; ah, see the tentative
Movements, and the slow feet,
The trouble in the pace and the uncertain
Wavering!

See, they return, one, and by one,
With fear, as half-awakened;
As if the snow should hesitate
And murmur in the wind,
                and half turn back;

These were the 'Wing'd-with-Awe,'
                    Inviolable.
Gods of the wingèd shoe!
With them the silver hounds,
                    sniffing the trace of air!

Haie! Haie!
                    These were the swift to harry;
These the keen-scented;
These were the souls of blood.

Slow on the leash,
                    pallid the leash-men!

The River-Merchant's Wife: A Letter

While my hair was still cut straight across my forehead
I played about the front gate, pulling flowers.
You came by on bamboo stilts, playing horse,
You walked about my seat, playing with blue plums.
And we went on living in the village of Chokan:
Two small people, without dislike or suspicion.

At fourteen I married My Lord you.
I never laughed, being bashful.
Lowering my head, I looked at the wall.
Called to, a thousand times, I never looked back.

At fifteen I stopped scowling,
I desired my dust to be mingled with yours
For ever and for ever and for ever.
Why should I climb the look out?

At sixteen you departed,
You went into far Ku-to-yen, by the river of swirling eddies,
And you have been gone five months.
The monkeys make sorrowful noise overhead.

You dragged your feet when you went out.
By the gate now, the moss is grown, the different mosses,
Too deep to clear them away!
The leaves fall early this autumn, in wind.
The paired butterflies are already yellow with August
Over the grass in the West garden;
They hurt me. I grow older.

If you are coming down through the narrows of the river Kiang,
Please let me know beforehand,
And I will come out to meet you
            As far as Cho-fu-Sa.
                    By Rihaku

H. D.
1886-

There Is a Spell, for Instance

There is a spell, for instance,
in every sea-shell:

continuous, the sea-thrust
is powerless against coral,

bone, stone, marble
hewn from within by that craftsman,

the shell-fish:
oyster, clam, mollusc

is master-mason planning
the stone marvel:

yet that flabby, amorphous hermit
within, like the planet

senses the finite,
it limits its orbit

of being, its house,
temple, fane, shrine:

it unlocks the portals
at stated intervals:

prompted by hunger,
it opens to the tide-flow:

but infinity? no,
of nothing-too-much:

I sense my own limit,
my shell-jaws snap shut

at invasion of the limitless,
ocean-weight; infinite water

can not crack me, egg in egg-shell;
closed in, complete, immortal

full circle, I know the pull
of the tide, the lull

as well as the moon;
the octopus darkness

is powerless against
her cold immortality;

so I in my own way know
that the whale

can not digest me:
be firm in your own small, static, limited

orbit and the shark-jaws
of outer circumstance

will spit you forth:
be indigestible, hard, ungiving,

so that, living within,
you beget, self-out-of-self,

selfless,
that pearl-of-great-price.

Not Honey

Not honey
Not the plunder of the bee
From meadow or sand-flower
Or mountain bush;
From winter-flower or shoot
Born of the later heat:
Not honey, not the sweet

Stain on the lips and teeth:
Not honey, not the deep
Plunge of the soft belly
And the clinging of the gold-edged
Pollen-dusted feet.

Not so—
Though rapture blind my eyes,
And hunger crisp
Dark and inert my mouth,
Not honey, not the south,
Not the tall stalk
Of red twin-lilies,
Nor light branch of fruit tree
Caught in flexible light branch.

Not honey, not the south;
Ah, flower of purple iris,
Flower of white,
Or of the iris, withering the grass—
For fleck of the sun's fire,
Gathers such heat and power,
That shadow-print is light,
Cast through the petals
Of the yellow iris flower.

Not iris—old desire—old passion—
Old forgetfulness—old pain—
Not this, nor any flower,
But if you turn again,
Seek strength of arm and throat,
Touch as the god:
Neglect the lyre-note;
Knowing that you shall feel,
About the frame,
No trembling of the string
But heat more passionate
Of bone and the white shell
And fiery tempered steel.

ROBINSON JEFFERS
1887-

November Surf

Some lucky day each November great waves awake and are drawn
Like smoking mountains bright from the west
And come and cover the cliff with white violent cleanness: then
suddenly
The old granite forgets half a year's filth:
The orange-peel, eggshells, papers, pieces of clothing, the clots
Of dung in corners of the rock, and used
Sheaths that make light love safe in the evenings: all the droppings
of the summer
Idlers washed off in a winter ecstasy:
I think this cumbered continent envies its cliff then. . . . But all
seasons
The earth, in her childlike prophetic sleep,
Keeps dreaming of the bath of a storm that prepares up the long
coast
Of the future to scour more than her sea-lines:
The cities gone down, the people fewer and the hawks more
numerous,
The rivers mouth to source pure; when the two-footed
Mammal, being someways one of the nobler animals, regains
The dignity of room, the value of rareness.

Post Mortem

Happy people die whole, they are all dissolved in a moment,
they have had what they wanted,
No hard gifts; the unhappy
Linger a space, but pain is a thing that is glad to be forgotten;
but one who has given
His heart to a cause or a country,
His ghost may spaniel it a while, disconsolate to watch it. I was
wondering how long the spirit
That sheds this verse will remain
When the nostrils are nipped, when the brain rots in its vault
or bubbles in the violence of fire
To be ash in metal. I was thinking

Some stalks of the wood whose roots I married to the earth of
    this place will stand five centuries;
I held the roots in my hand,
The stems of the trees between two fingers: how many remote
    generations of women
Will drink joy from men's loins,
And dragged from between the thighs of what mothers will
    giggle at my ghost when it curses the axemen,
Gray impotent voice on the sea-wind,
When the last trunk falls? The women's abundance will have
    built roofs over all this foreland;
Will have buried the rock foundations
I laid here: the women's exuberance will canker and fail in its
    time and like clouds the houses
Unframe, the granite of the prime
Stand from the heaps: come storm and wash clean: the plaster
    is all run to the sea and the steel
All rusted; the foreland resumes
The form we loved when we saw it. Though one at the end of
    the age and far off from this place
Should meet my presence in a poem,
The ghost would not care but be here, long sunset shadow in the
    seams of the granite, and forgotten
The flesh, a spirit for the stone.

Night

The ebb slips from the rock, the sunken
Tide-rocks lift streaming shoulders
Out of the slack, the slow west
Sombering its torch; a ship's light
Shows faintly, far out,
Over the weight of the prone ocean
On the low cloud.

Over the dark mountain, over the dark pinewood,
Down the long dark valley along the shrunken river,
Returns the splendor without rays, the shining shadow,
Peace-bringer, the matrix of all shining and quieter of shining.
Where the shore widens on the bay she opens dark wings
And the ocean accepts her glory. O soul worshipful of her
You, like the ocean, have grave depths where she dwells always,
And the film of waves above that takes the sun takes also
Her, with more love. The sun-lovers have a blond favorite,
A father of lights and noises, wars, weeping and laughter,

Hot labor, lust and delight and the other blemishes. Quietness
Flows from her deeper fountain; and he will die; and she is immortal.

Far off from here the slender
Flocks of the mountain forest
Move among stems like towers
Of the old redwoods to the stream,
No twig crackling; dip shy
Wild muzzles into the mountain water
Among the dark ferns.

O passionately at peace you being secure will pardon
The blasphemies of glowworms, the lamp in my tower, the fret-
    fulness
Of cities, the cressets of the planets, the pride of the stars.
This August night in a rift of cloud Antares reddens,
The great one, the ancient torch, a lord among lost children,
The earth's orbit doubled would not girdle his greatness, one fire
Globed, out of grasp of the mind enormous; but to you O Night
What? Not a spark? What flicker of a spark in the faint far glimmer
Of a lost fire dying in the desert, dim coals of a sand-pit the Bedouins
Wandered from at dawn . . . Ah singing prayer to what gulfs
    tempted
Suddenly are you more lost? To us the near-hand mountain
Be a measure of height, the tide-worn cliff at the sea-gate a
    measure of continuance.

The tide, moving the night's
Vastness with lonely voices,
Turns, the deep dark-shining
Pacific leans on the land,
Feeling his cold strength
To the outmost margins: you Night will resume
The stars in your time.

O passionately at peace when will that tide draw shoreward?
Truly the spouting fountains of light, Antares, Arcturus,
Tire of their flow, they sing one song but they think silence.
The striding winter-giant Orion shines, and dreams darkness.
And life, the flicker of men and moths and the wolf on the hill,
Though furious for continuance, passionately feeding, passionately
Remaking itself upon its mates, remembers deep inward
The calm mother, the quietness of the womb and the egg,
The primal and the latter silences: dear Night it is memory
Prophesies, prophecy that remembers, the charm of the dark.

And I and my people, we are willing to love the four-score years
Heartily; but as a sailor loves the sea, when the helm is for harbor.

Have men's minds changed,
Or the rock hidden in the deep of the waters of the soul
Broken the surface? A few centuries
Gone by, was none dared not to people
The darkness beyond the stars with harps and habitations.
But now, dear is the truth. Life is grown sweeter and lonelier,
And death is no evil.

EDWIN MUIR
1887-

The Grove

There was no road at all to that high place
But through the smothering grove,
Where as we went the shadows wove
Adulterous shapes of animal hate and love,
The idol-crowded nightmare Space,
Wood beyond wood, tree behind tree,
And every tree and empty face
Gashed by the casual lightning mark
The first great Luciferian animal
Scored on clay and leaf and bark.
This was, we knew, the heraldic ground,
And therefore now we heard our footsteps fall
With the true legendary sound,
Like secret trampling behind a wall,
As if they were saying: To be: to be.

And oh the silence, the drugged thicket dozing
Deep in its dream of fear,
The ring closing
And coming near,
The well-bred self-sufficient animals
With clean rank pelts and proud and fetid breath,
Screaming their arrogant calls,
Their moonstone eyes set straight at life and death.
Did we see or dream it? And the jungle cities—
For there were cities there and civilizations

Deep in the forest; powers and dominations
Like shapes begotten by dreaming animals,
Proud animal dreams uplifted high,
Booted and saddled on the animal's back
And staring with the arrogant animal's eye:
The golden dukes, the silver earls, and gleaming black
The curvetting knights sitting their curvetting steeds,
The sweet silk-tunicked eunuchs singing ditties,
Swaying like wandering weeds,
The scarlet cardinals,
And lions high in the air on the banner's field,
Crowns, sceptres, spears and stars and moons of blood,
And sylvan wars in bronze within the shield,
All quartered in the wide world's wood,
The smothering grove where there was place for pities.

We trod the maze like horses in a mill,
And then passed through it
As in a dream of the will.
How could it be? There was the stifling grove,
Yet here was light; what wonder led us to it?
How could the blind road go
To climb the crag and top the towering hill,
And all that splendour spread? We know
There was no road except the smothering grove.

The Recurrence

All things return, Nietzsche said,
The ancient wheel revolves again,
Rise, take up your numbered fate;
The cradle and the bridal bed,
Life and the coffin wait.
All has been that ever can be,
And this sole eternity
Cannot cancel, cannot add
One to your delights or tears,
Or a million million years
Tear the nightmare from the mad.

Have no fear then. You will miss
Achievement by the self-same inch,
When the great occasion comes
And they watch you, you will flinch,
Lose the moment, be for bliss

A footlength short. All done before.
Love's agonies, victory's drums
Cannot huddle the Cross away
Planted on its future hill,
The secret on the appointed day
Will be made known, the ship once more
Hit upon the waiting rock
Or come safely to the shore,
Careless under the deadly tree
The victim drowse, the urgent warning
Come too late, the dagger strike,
Strike and strike through eternity,
And worlds hence the prison clock
Will toll on execution morning,
What is ill be always ill,
Wretches die behind a dike,
And the happy be happy still.

But the heart makes reply:
This is only what the eye
From its tower on the turning field
Sees and sees and cannot tell why,
Quarterings on the turning shield,
The great non-stop heraldic show.
And the heart and the mind know,
What has been can never return,
What is not will surely be
In the changed unchanging reign,
Else the Actor on the Tree
Would loll at ease, miming pain,
And counterfeit mortality.

EDITH SITWELL

1887-

Heart and Mind

Said the Lion to the Lioness—'When you are amber dust,—
No more a raging fire like the heat of the Sun
(No liking but all lust)—
Remember still the flowering of the amber blood and bone
The rippling of bright muscles like a sea,

Remember the rose-prickles of bright paws
Though we shall mate no more
Till the fire of that sun the heart and the moon-cold bone are one.'

Said the Skeleton lying upon the sands of Time—
'The great gold planet that is the mourning heat of the Sun
Is greater than all gold, more powerful
Than the tawny body of a Lion that fire consumes
Like all that grows or leaps . . . so is the heart
More powerful than all dust. Once I was Hercules
Or Samson, strong as the pillars of the seas:
But the flames of the heart consumed me, and the mind
Is but a foolish wind.'

Said the Sun to the Moon—'When you are but a lonely white crone,
And I, a dead King in my golden armour somewhere in a dark wood,
Remember only this of our hopeless love
That never till Time is done
Will the fire of the heart and the fire of the mind be one.'

An Old Woman

I, an old woman in the light of the sun,
Wait for my Wanderer, and my upturned face
Has all the glory of the remembering Day
The hallowed grandeur of the primeval clay
That knew the Flood, and suffered all the dryness
Of the uncaring heaven, the sun its lover.

For the sun is the first lover of the world,
Blessing all humble creatures, all life-giving,
Blessing the end of life and the work done,
The clean and the unclean, ores in earth, and splendours
Within the heart of man, that second sun.

For when the first founts and deep waterways
Of the young light flow down and lie like peace
Upon the upturned faces of the blind
From life, it comes to bless
Eternity in its poor mortal dress,—
Shining upon young lovers and old lechers
Rising from their beds, and laying gold
Alike in the unhopeful path of beggars
And in the darkness of the miser's heart.
The crookèd has a shadow light made straight,

The shallow places gain their strength again,—
And desert hearts, waste heavens, the barren height
Forget that they are cold.
The man-made chasm between man and man
Of creeds and tongues are fill'd, the guiltless light
Remakes all men and things in holiness.

And he who blessed the fox with a golden fleece
And covered earth with ears of corn like the planets
Bearded with thick ripe gold,
For the holy bread of mankind, blessed my clay:
For the sun cares not that I am a simple woman,
To him, laughing, the veins in my arms and the wrinkles
From work on my nursing hands are sacred as branches
And furrows of harvest . . . to him, the heat of the earth
And beat of the heart are one,—
Born from the energy of the world, the love
That keeps the Golden Ones in their place above,
And hearts and blood of beasts even in motion,—
Without which comets, sun, plants, and all living beings
And warmth in the inward parts of the earth would freeze.
And the sun does not care if I live in holiness,
To him, my mortal dress
Is sacred, part of the earth, a lump of the world
With my splendours, ores, impurities, and harvest,
Over which shines my heart, that ripening sun.

Though the dust, the shining racer, overtake me,
I too was a golden woman like those that walk
In the fields of the heavens:—but am now grown old
And must sit by the fire and watch the fire grow cold,
—A country Fate whose spool is the household task.
Yet still I am loved by the sun, and still am part
Of earth. In the evenings bringing home the workers,
Bringing the wanderer home and the dead child,
The child unborn and never to be conceived,
Home to the mother's breast, I sit by the fire
Where the seed of gold drops dead and the kettle simmers
With a sweet sound like that of a hive of bees,
And I wait for my Wanderer to come home to rest—
Covered with earth as if he had been working
Among the happy gardens, the holy fields
Where the bread of mankind ripens in the stillness.
Unchanged to me by death, I shall hold to my breast
My little child in his sleep, I shall seem the consoling
Earth, the mother of corn, nurse of the unreturning.

Wise is the earth, consoling grief and glory,
The golden heroes proud as pomp of waves,—
Great is the earth embracing them, their graves,
And great is the earth's story.
For though the soundless wrinkles fall like snow
On many a golden cheek, and creeds grow old
And change,—man's heart, that sun,
Outlives all terrors shaking the old night:
The world's huge fevers burn and shine, turn cold,
Yet the heavenly bodies and young lovers burn and shine,
The golden lovers walk in the holy fields,
Where the Abraham-bearded sun, the father of all things
Is shouting of ripeness, and the whole world of dews and splendours
       are singing
To the cradles of earth, of men, beasts, harvests, swinging
In the peace of God's heart. And I, the primeval clay
That has known earth's grief and harvest's happiness,
Seeing mankind's dark seed-time, come to bless,—
Forgive and bless all men like the holy light.

Tears

TO PAVEL TCHELITCHEW

My tears were Orion's splendour with sextuple suns and the million
Flowers in the fields of the heaven, where solar systems are setting,—
The rocks of great diamonds in the midst of the clear wave
By May dews and early light ripened, more diamonds begetting.
I wept for the glories of air, for the millions of dawns
And the splendours within Man's heart with the darkness warring,
I wept for the beautiful queens of the world, like a flower-bed
       shining,—
Now gathered, some at six, some at seven, but all in Eternity's
       morning.
But now my tears have shrunk and like hours are falling:
I weep for Venus whose body has changed to a metaphysical city
Whose heart-beat is now the sound of the revolutions,—for love
       changed
To the hospital mercy, the scientists' hope for the future,
And for darkened Man, that complex multiplicity
Of air and water, plant and animal,
Hard diamond, infinite sun.

Street Song

"Love my heart for an hour, but my bone for a day—
At least the skeleton smiles, for it has a morrow:
But the hearts of the young are now the dark treasure of Death,
And summer is lonely.

Comfort the lonely light and the sun in its sorrow,
Come like the night, for terrible is the sun
As truth, and the dying light shows only the skeleton's hunger
For peace, under the flesh like the summer rose.

Come through the darkness of death, as once through the branches
Of youth you came, through the shade like the flowering door
That leads into Paradise, far from the street,— you, the unborn
City seen by the homeless, the night of the poor.

You walk in the city ways, where Man's threatening shadow
Red-edged by the sun like Cain, has a changing shape—
Elegant like the Skeleton, crouched like the Tiger,
With the age-old wisdom and aptness of the Ape.

The pulse that beats in the heart is changed to the hammer
That sounds in the Potter's Field where they build a new world
From our Bone, and the carrion-bird days' foul droppings and
      clamour—
But you are my night, and my peace,—

The holy night of conception, of rest, the consoling
Darkness when all men are equal,—the wrong and the right,
And the rich and the poor are no longer separate nations,—
They are brothers in night."

This was the song I heard; but the Bone is silent!
Who knows if the sound was that of the dead light calling,—
Of Caesar rolling onward his heart, that stone,
Or the burden of Atlas falling.

Still Falls the Rain

(THE RAIDS, 1940. NIGHT AND DAWN)

Still falls the Rain—
Dark as the world of man, black as our loss—
Blind as the nineteen hundred and forty nails
Upon the Cross.

Still falls the Rain
With a sound like the pulse of the heart that is changed to the
        hammer-beat
In the Potter's Field, and the sound of the impious feet

On the Tomb:
                    Still falls the Rain
In the Field of Blood where the small hopes breed and the human
        brain
Nurtures its greed, that worm with the brow of Cain.

Still falls the Rain
At the feet of the Starved Man hung upon the Cross.
Christ that each day, each night, nails there, have mercy on us—
On Dives and on Lazarus:
Under the Rain the sore and the gold are as one.

Still falls the Rain—
Still falls the Blood from the Starved Man's wounded Side:
He bears in His Heart all wounds,—those of the light that died,
The last faint spark
In the self-murdered heart, the wounds of the sad uncomprehending
        dark,
The wounds of the baited bear,—
The blind and weeping bear whom the keepers beat
On his helpless flesh . . . the tears of the hunted hare.

Still falls the Rain—
Then—O Ile leape up to my God: who pulles me doune—
See, see where Christ's blood streames in the firmament:
It flows from the Brow we nailed upon the tree
Deep to the dying, to the thirsting heart
That holds the fires of the world,—dark-smirched with pain
As Caesar's laurel crown.

Then sounds the voice of One who like the heart of man
Was once a child who among beasts has lain—
"Still do I love, still shed my innocent light, my Blood, for thee."

MARIANNE MOORE
1887-

The Mind Is an Enchanting Thing

Is an enchanted thing
    like the glaze on a
katydid-wing
        subdivided by sun
        till the nettings are legion.
Like Gieseking playing Scarlatti;

like the apteryx-awl
    as a beak, or the
kiwi's rain-shawl
        of haired feathers, the mind
        feeling its way as though blind,
walks along with its eyes on the ground.

It has memory's ear
    that can hear without
having to hear.
        Like the gyroscope's fall,
        truly unequivocal
because trued by regnant certainty,

it is a power of
    strong enchantment. It
is like the dove—
        neck animated by
        sun; it is memory's eye;
it's conscientious inconsistency.

It tears off the veil; tears
    the temptation, the
mist the heart wears,
        from its eyes,—if the heart
        has a face; it takes apart
dejection. It's fire in the dove-neck's

iridescence; in the
    inconsistencies
of Scarlatti.

Unconfusion submits
its confusion to proof; it's
not a Herod's oath that cannot change.

What Are Years?

What is our innocence,
what is our guilt? All are
  naked, none is safe. And whence
is courage: the unanswered question,
the resolute doubt,—
dumbly calling, deafly listening—that
in misfortune, even death,
    encourages others
    and in its defeat, stirs

  the soul to be strong? He
sees deep and is glad, who
  accedes to mortality
and in his imprisonment, rises
upon himself as
the sea in a chasm, struggling to be
free and unable to be,
    in its surrendering
    finds its continuing.

  So he who strongly feels,
behaves. The very bird,
  grown taller as he sings, steels
his form straight up. Though he is captive,
his mighty singing
says, satisfaction is a lowly
thing, how pure a thing is joy.
    This is mortality,
    this is eternity.

A Grave

Man looking into the sea,
taking the view from those who have as much right to it as you
    have to it yourself,
it is human nature to stand in the middle of a thing,
but you cannot stand in the middle of this;
the sea has nothing to give but a well excavated grave.

The firs stand in a procession, each with an emerald turkey-foot
    at the top,
reserved as their contours, saying nothing;
repression, however, is not the most obvious characteristic of the sea;
the sea is a collector, quick to return a rapacious look.
There are others besides you who have worn that look—
whose expression is no longer a protest; the fish no longer investigate
    them
for their bones have not lasted:
men lower nets, unconscious of the fact that they are desecrating
    a grave,
and row quickly away—the blades of the oars
moving together like the feet of water-spiders as if there were no
    such thing as death.
The wrinkles progress upon themselves in a phalanx—beautiful
    under networks of foam,
and fade breathlessly while the sea rustles in and out of the seaweed;
the birds swim through the air at stop speed, emitting cat-calls
    as heretofore—
the tortoise-shell scourges about the feet of the cliffs, in motion
    beneath them;
and the ocean, under the pulsation of lighthouses and noise of
    bell-buoys,
advances as usual, looking as if it were not that ocean in which
    dropped things are bound to sink—
in which if they turn and twist, it is neither with volition nor
    consciousness.

The Jerboa

TOO MUCH

A Roman hired an
artist, a freedman,
    to make a cone—pine-cone
    or fir-cone—with holes for a fountain. Placed on
        the Prison of St. Angelo, this cone
        of the Pompeys which is known

now as the Popes', passed
for art. A huge cast
    bronze, dwarfing the peacock
    statue in the garden of the Vatican,
        it looks like a work of art made to give
        to a Pompey, or native

of Thebes. Others could
build, and understood .
   making colossi and
   how to use slaves, and kept crocodiles and put
         baboons on the necks of giraffes to pick
         fruit, and used serpent magic.

They had their men tie
hippopotami
   and bring out dapple dog-
   cats to course antelopes, dikdik, and ibex;
         or used small eagles. They looked on as theirs,
         impallas and onagers,

the wild ostrich herd
with hard feet and bird
   necks rearing back in the
   dust like a serpent preparing to strike, cranes,
         storks, anoas, mongooses, and Nile geese.
         And there were gardens for these—

combining planes, dates,
limes, and pomegranates,
   in avenues—with square
   pools of pink flowers, tame fish, and small frogs. Besides
         yarns dyed with indigo, and red cotton,
         they had a flax which they spun

into fine linen
cordage for yachtsmen.
   These people liked small things;
   they gave to boys little paired playthings such as
         nests of eggs, ichneumon and snake, paddle
         and raft, badger and camel;

and made toys for them-
selves: the royal totem;
   and toilet-boxes marked
   with the contents. Lords and ladies put goose-grease
         paint in round bone boxes with pivoting
         lid incised with the duck-wing

or reverted duck-
head; kept in a buck
   or rhinoceros horn,
   the ground horn; and locust oil in stone locusts.

It was a picture with a fine distance;
of drought, and of assistance

in time, from the Nile
rising slowly, while
   the pig-tailed monkey on
   slab-hands, with arched-up slack-slung gait, and the brown
      dandy, looked at the jasmine two-leafed twig
      and bud, cactus-pads, and fig.

Dwarfs here and there, lent
to an evident
   poetry of frog grays,
   duck-egg greens, and egg-plant blues, a fantasy
      and a verisimilitude that were
      right to those with, everywhere,

power over the poor.
The bees' food is your
   food. Those who tended flower-
   beds and stables were like the king's cane in the
      form of a hand, or the folding bedroom
      made for his mother of whom

he was fond. Princes
clad in queens' dresses
   calla or petunia
   white that trembled at the edge, and queens in a
      king's underskirt of fine-twilled thread like silk-
      worm gut, as bee-man and milk-

maid, kept divine cows
and bees; limestone brows,
   and gold-foil wings. They made
   basalt serpents and portraits of beetles; the
      king gave his name to them and he was named
      for them. He feared snakes and tamed

Pharaoh's rat, the rust-
backed mongoose. No bust
   of it was made, but there
   was pleasure for the rat. Its restlessness was
      its excellence; it was praised for its wit;
      and the jerboa, like it,

a small desert rat,
and not famous, that
   lives without water, has
   happiness. Abroad seeking food, or at home
       in its burrow, the Sahara field-mouse
       has a shining silver house

of sand. O rest and
joy, the boundless sand,
   the stupendous sand-spout,
   no water, no palm-trees, no ivory bed,
       tiny cactus; but one would not be he
       who has nothing but plenty.

ABUNDANCE

Africanus meant
the conqueror sent
   from Rome. It should mean the
   untouched: the sand-brown jumping-rat—free-born; and
       the blacks, that choice race with an elegance
       ignored by one's ignorance.

Part terrestrial,
and part celestial,
   Jacob saw, cudgel staff
   in claw-hand—steps of air and air angels; his
       friends were the stones. The translucent mistake
       of the desert, does not make

hardship for one who
can rest and then do
   the opposite—launching
   as if on wings, from its match-thin hind legs, in
       day-time or at night; that departs with great
       speed, followed by, as a weight,

a double length, thin
tail furred like the skin;
   that curls round it when it
   sleeps 'round'—the nose nested in fur, a hind leg
       at each side of the head—or lies lengthwise,
       in view, when the body lies

flat. Seen by daylight
the body is white
   in front; and on the back,
    buffy-brown like the breast of the fawn-breasted
       bower-bird. It hops like the fawn-breast, but has
      chipmunk contours—perceived as

it turns its bird head—
the nap directed
   neatly back and blending
    with the ear which reiterates the slimness
       of the body. The fine hairs on the tail,
      repeating the other pale

markings, lengthen till
at the tip they fill
   out in a tuft—black and
    white; strange detail of the simplified creature,
       fish-shaped and silvered to steel by the force
      of the large desert moon. Course

the jerboa, or
plunder its food store,
   and you will be cursed. It
    honours the sand by assuming its colour;
       closed upper paws seeming one with the fur
      in its flight from a danger.

By fifths and sevenths,
in leaps of two lengths,
   like the uneven notes
    of the Bedouin flute, it stops its gleaning
       on little wheel castors, and makes fern-seed
      foot-prints with kangaroo speed.

Its leaps should be set
to the flageolet;
   pillar body erect
    on a three-cornered smooth-working Chippendale
       claw—propped on hind legs, and tail as third toe,
      between leaps to its burrow.

The Steeple-Jack

Dürer would have seen a reason for living
   in a town like this, with eight stranded whales
to look at; with the sweet sea air coming into your house
on a fine day, from water etched
   with waves as formal as the scales
on a fish.

One by one, in two's, in three's, the seagulls keep
   flying back and forth over the town clock,
or sailing around the lighthouse without moving the wings—
rising steadily with a slight
   quiver of the body—or flock
mewing where

a sea the purple of the peacock's neck is
   paled to greenish azure as Dürer changed
the pine green of the Tyrol to peacock blue and guinea
grey. You can see a twenty-five-
   pound lobster; and fishnets arranged
to dry. The

whirlwind fife-and-drum of the storm bends the salt
   marsh grass, disturbs stars in the sky and the
star on the steeple; it is a privilege to see so
much confusion. Disguised by what
   might seem austerity, the seaside flowers and

trees are favoured by the fog so that you have
   the tropics at first hand: the trumpet-vine,
fox-glove, giant snap-dragon, a salpiglossis that has
spots and stripes; morning-glories, gourds,
   or moon-vines trained on fishing-twine
at the back

door. There are no banyans, frangipani, nor
   jack-fruit trees; nor an exotic serpent
life. Ring lizard and snake-skin for the foot, or crocodile;
but here they've cats, not cobras, to
   keep down the rats. The diffident
little newt

with white pin-dots on black horizontal spaced
    out bands lives here; yet there is nothing that
ambition can buy or take away. The college student
named Ambrose sits on the hill-side
    with his not-native books and hat
and sees boats

at sea progress white and rigid as if in
    a groove. Liking an elegance of which
the source is not bravado, he knows by heart the antique
sugar-bowl-shaped summer-house of
    interlacing slats, and the pitch
of the church

spire, not true, from which a man in scarlet lets
    down a rope as a spider spins a thread;
he might be part of a novel, but on the sidewalk a
sign says C. J. Poole, Steeple Jack,
    in black and white; and one in red
and white says

Danger. The church portico has four fluted
    columns, each a single piece of stone, made
modester by white-wash. This would be a fit haven for
waifs, children, animals, prisoners,
    and presidents who have repaid
sin-driven

senators by not thinking about them. There
    are a school-house, a post-office in a
store, fish-houses, hen-houses, a three-masted schooner on
the stocks. The hero, the student,
    the steeple-jack, each in his way,
is at home.

It could not be dangerous to be living
    in a town like this, of simple people,
who have a steeple-jack placing danger signs by the church
while he is gilding the solid-
    pointed star, which on a steeple
stands for hope.

JOHN CROWE RANSOM
1888-

Painted Head

By dark severance the apparition head
Smiles from the air a capital on no
Column or a Platonic perhaps head
On a canvas sky depending from nothing;

Stirs up an old illusion of grandeur
By tickling the instinct of heads to be
Absolute and to try decapitation
And to play truant from the body bush;

But too happy and beautiful for those sorts
Of head (homekeeping heads are happiest)
Discovers maybe thirty unwidowed years
Of not dishonoring the faithful stem;

Is nameless and has authored for the evil
Historian headhunters neither book
Nor state and is therefore distinct from tart
Heads with crowns and guilty gallery heads;

So that the extravagant device of art
Unhousing by abstraction this once head
Was capital irony by a loving hand
That knew the no treason of a head like this;

Makes repentance in an unlovely head
For having vinegarly traduced the flesh
Till, the hurt flesh recusing, the hard egg
Is shrunken to its own deathlike surface;

And an image thus. The body bears the head
(So hardly one they terribly are two)
Feeds and obeys and unto please what end?
Not to the glory of tyrant head but to

The increase of body. Beauty is of body.
The flesh contouring shallowly on a head

Is a rock-garden needing body's love
And best bodiness to colorify

The big blue birds sitting and sea-shell flats
And caves, and on the iron acropolis
To spread the hyacinthine hair and rear
The olive garden for the nightingales.

Prelude to an Evening

Do not enforce the tired wolf
Dragging his infected wound homeward
To sit tonight with the warm children
Naming the pretty kings of France.

The images of the invaded mind
Being as monsters in the dreams
Of your most brief enchanted headful,
Suppose a miracle of confusion:

That dreamed and undreamt become each other
And mix the night and day of your mind;
And it does not matter your twice crying
From mouth unbeautied against the pillow

To avert the gun of the swarthy soldier,
For cry, cock-crow, or the iron bell
Can crack the sleep-sense of outrage,
Annihilate phantoms who were nothing.

But now, by our perverse supposal,
There is a drift of fog on your mornings;
You in your peignoir, dainty at your orange-cup,
Feel poising round the sunny room

Invisible evil, deprived and bold.
All day the clock will metronome
Your gallant fear; the needles clicking,
The heels detonating the stair's cavern.

Freshening the water in the blue bowls
For the buckberries with not all your love,
You shall be listening for the low wind,
The warning sibilance of pines.

You like a waning moon, and I accusing
Our too banded Eumenides,
You shall make Noes but wanderingly,
Smoothing the heads of the hungry children.

The Equilibrists

Full of her long white arms and milky skin
He had a thousand times remembered sin.
Alone in the press of people traveled he,
Minding her jacinth, and myrrh, and ivory.

Mouth he remembered: the quaint orifice
From which came heat that flamed upon the kiss,
Till cold words came down spiral from the head,
Grey doves from the officious tower illsped.

Body: it was a white field ready for love,
On her body's field, with the gaunt tower above,
The lilies grew, beseeching him to take,
If he would pluck and wear them, bruise and break.

Eyes talking: Never mind the cruel words,
Embrace my flowers, but not embrace the swords.
But what they said, the doves came straightway flying
And unsaid: Honor, Honor, they came crying.

Importunate her doves. Too pure, too wise,
Clambering on his shoulder, saying, Arise,
Leave me now, and never let us meet,
Eternal distance now command thy feet.

Predicament indeed, which thus discovers
Honor among thieves, Honor between lovers.
O such a little word is Honor, they feel!
But the grey word is between them cold as steel.

At length I saw these lovers fully were come
Into their torture of equilibrium;
Dreadfully had forsworn each other, and yet
They were bound each to each, and they did not forget.

And rigid as two painful stars, and twirled
About the clustered night their prison world,
They burned with fierce love always to come near,
But Honor beat them back and kept them clear.

Ah, the strict lovers, they are ruined now!
I cried in anger. But with puddled brow
Devising for those gibbeted and brave
Came I descanting: Man, what would you have?

For spin your period out, and draw your breath,
A kinder saeculum begins with Death.
Would you ascend to Heaven and bodiless dwell?
Or take your bodies honorless to Hell?

In Heaven you have heard no marriage is,
No white flesh tinder to your lecheries,
Your male and female issue sweetly shaped
Sublimed away, and furious blood escaped.

Great lovers lie in Hell, the stubborn ones
Infatuate of the flesh upon the bones;
Stuprate, they rend each other when they kiss,
The pieces kiss again, no end to this.

But still I watched them spinning, orbited nice.
Their flames were not more radiant than their ice.
I dug in the quiet earth and wrought the tomb
And made these lines to memorize their doom:—

EPITAPH

Equilibrists lie here; stranger, tread light;
Close, but untouching in each other's sight;
Mouldered the lips and ashy the tall skull,
Let them lie perilous and beautiful.

Two in August

Two that could not have lived their single lives
As can some husbands and wives
Did something strange: they tensed their vocal cords
And attacked each other with silences and words
Like catapulted stones and arrowed knives.

Dawn was not yet; night is for loving or sleeping,
Sweet dreams or safekeeping;
Yet he of the wide brows that were used to laurel
And she, the famed for gentleness, must quarrel,
Furious both of them, and scared, and weeping.

How sleepers groan, twitch, wake to such a mood
Is not well understood,
Nor why two entities grown almost one
Should rend and murder trying to get undone,
With individual tigers in their blood.

She in terror fled from the marriage chamber
Circuiting the dark rooms like a string of amber
Round and round and back,
And would not light one lamp against the black,
And heard the clock that clanged: Remember, Remember.

And he must tread barefooted the dim lawn,
Soon he was up and gone;
High in the trees the night-mastered birds were crying
With fear upon their tongues, no singing or flying
Which are their lovely attitudes by dawn.

Whether those bird-cries were of heaven or hell
There is no way to tell;
In the long ditch of darkness the man walked
Under the hackberry trees where the birds talked
With words too sad and strange to syllable.

Judith of Bethulia

Beautiful as the flying legend of some leopard
She had not yet chosen her great captain or prince
Depositary to her flesh, and our defense;
And a wandering beauty is a blade out of its scabbard.
You know how dangerous, gentlemen of threescore?
May you know it yet ten more.

Nor by process of veiling she grew the less fabulous.
Grey or blue veils, we were desperate to study
The invincible emanations of her white body,
And the winds at her ordered raiment were ominous.
Might she walk in the market, sit in the council of soldiers?
Only of the extreme elders.

But a rare chance was the girl's then, when the Invader
Trumpeted from the south, and rumbled from the north,
Beleaguered the city from four quarters of the earth,
Our soldiery too craven and sick to aid her—
Where were the arms could countervail this horde?
Her beauty was the sword.

She sat with the elders, and proved on their blear visage
How bright was the weapon unrusted in her keeping,
While he lay surfeiting on their harvest heaping,
Wasting the husbandry of their rarest vintage—
And dreaming of the broad-breasted dames for concubine?
These floated on his wine.

He was lapped with bay-leaves, and grass and fumiter weed,
And from under the wine-film encountered his mortal vision,
For even within his tent she accomplished his derision;
She loosed one veil and another, standing unafraid;
And he perished. Nor brushed her with even so much as a daisy?
She found his destruction easy.

The heathen are all perished. The victory was furnished,
We smote them hiding in our vineyards, barns, annexes,
And now their white bones clutter the holes of foxes,
And the chieftain's head, with grinning sockets, and varnished—
Is it hung on the sky with a hideous epitaphy?
No, the woman keeps the trophy.

May God send unto our virtuous lady her prince.
It is stated she went reluctant to that orgy,
Yet a madness fevers our young men, and not the clergy
Nor the elders have turned them unto modesty since.
Inflamed by the thought of her naked beauty with desire?
Yes, and chilled with fear and despair.

T. S. ELIOT

1888-

from

Four Quartets

BURNT NORTON

τοῦ λόγου δ' ἐόντος ξυνοῦ ζώουσιν οἱ πολλοὶ
ὡς ἰδίαν ἔχοντες φρόνησιν.

I. p. 77. Fr. 2.

ὁδὸς ἄνω κάτω μία καὶ ὠυτή.

I. p. 89, Fr. 60.

DIELS, *Die Fragmente der Vorsokratiker* (Herakleitos).

I

Time present and time past
Are both perhaps present in time future,
And time future contained in time past.
If all time is eternally present
All time is unredeemable.
What might have been is an abstraction
Remaining a perpetual possibility
Only in a world of speculation.
What might have been and what has been
Point to one end, which is always present.
Footfalls echo in the memory
Down the passage which we did not take
Towards the door we never opened
Into the rose-garden. My words echo
Thus, in your mind.
    But to what purpose
Disturbing the dust on a bowl of rose-leaves
I do not know.
    Other echoes
Inhabit the garden. Shall we follow?
Quick, said the bird, find them, find them,
Round the corner. Through the first gate,
Into our first world, shall we follow
The deception of the thrush? Into our first world.
There they were, dignified, invisible,
Moving without pressure, over the dead leaves,
In the autumn heat, through the vibrant air,
And the bird called, in response to
The unheard music hidden in the shrubbery,
And the unseen eyebeam crossed, for the roses
Had the look of flowers that are looked at.
There they were as our guests, accepted and accepting.
So we moved, and they, in a formal pattern,
Along the empty alley, into the box circle,
To look down into the drained pool.
Dry the pool, dry concrete, brown edged,
And the pool was filled with water out of sunlight,
And the lotos rose, quietly, quietly,
The surface glittered out of heart of light,
And they were behind us, reflected in the pool.
Then a cloud passed, and the pool was empty.
Go, said the bird, for the leaves were full of children,
Hidden excitedly, containing laughter.
Go, go, go, said the bird: human kind

Cannot bear very much reality.
Time past and time future
What might have been and what has been
Point to one end, which is always present.

II

Garlic and sapphires in the mud
Clot the bedded axle-tree.
The trilling wire in the blood
Sings below inveterate scars
And reconciles forgotten wars.
The dance along the artery
The circulation of the lymph
Are figured in the drift of stars
Ascend to summer in the tree
We move above the moving tree
In light upon the figured leaf
And hear upon the sodden floor
Below, the boarhound and the boar
Pursue their pattern as before
But reconciled among the stars.

At the still point of the turning world. Neither flesh nor fleshless;
Neither from nor towards; at the still point, there the dance is,
But neither arrest nor movement. And do not call it fixity,
Where past and future are gathered. Neither movement from nor
     towards,
Neither ascent nor decline. Except for the point, the still point,
There would be no dance, and there is only the dance.
I can only say, *there* we have been: but I cannot say where.
And I cannot say, how long, for that is to place it in time.

The inner freedom from the practical desire,
The release from action and suffering, release from the inner
And the outer compulsion, yet surrounded
By a grace of sense, a white light still and moving,
Erhebung without motion, concentration
Without elimination, both a new world
And the old made explicit, understood
In the completion of its partial ecstasy,
The resolution of its partial horror.
Yet the enchainment of past and future
Woven in the weakness of the changing body,
Protects mankind from heaven and damnation
Which flesh cannot endure.

Time past and time future
Allow but a little consciousness.
To be conscious is not to be in time
But only in time can the moment in the rose-garden,
The moment in the arbour where the rain beat,
The moment in the draughty church at smokefall
Be remembered; involved with past and future.
Only through time time is conquered.

III

Here is a place of disaffection
Time before and time after
In a dim light: neither daylight
Investing form with lucid stillness
Turning shadow into transient beauty
With slow rotation suggesting permanence
Nor darkness to purify the soul
Emptying the sensual with deprivation
Cleansing affection from the temporal.
Neither plenitude nor vacancy. Only a flicker
Over the strained time-ridden faces
Distracted from distraction by distraction
Filled with fancies and empty of meaning
Tumid apathy with no concentration
Men and bits of paper, whirled by the cold wind
That blows before and after time,
Wind in and out of unwholesome lungs
Time before and time after.
Eructation of unhealthy souls
Into the faded air, the torpid
Driven on the wind that sweeps the gloomy hills of London,
Hampstead and Clerkenwell, Campden and Putney,
Highgate, Primrose and Ludgate. Not here
Not here the darkness, in this twittering world.

Descend lower, descend only
Into the world of perpetual solitude,
World not world, but that which is not world,
Internal darkness, deprivation
And destitution of all property,
Desiccation of the world of sense,
Evacuation of the world of fancy,
Inoperancy of the world of spirit;
This is the one way, and the other
Is the same, not in movement

But abstention from movement; while the world moves
In appetency, on its metalled ways
Of time past and time future.

IV

Time and the bell have buried the day,
The black cloud carries the sun away.
Will the sunflower turn to us, will the clematis
Stray down, bend to us; tendril and spray
Clutch and cling?
Chill
Fingers of yew be curled
Down on us? After the kingfisher's wing
Has answered light to light, and is silent, the light is still
At the still point of the turning world.

V

Words move, music moves
Only in time; but that which is only living
Can only die. Words, after speech, reach
Into the silence. Only by the form, the pattern,
Can words or music reach
The stillness, as a Chinese jar still
Moves perpetually in its stillness.
Not the stillness of the violin, while the note lasts,
Not that only, but the co-existence,
Or say that the end precedes the beginning,
And the end and the beginning were always there
Before the beginning and after the end.
And all is always now. Words strain,
Crack and sometimes break, under the burden,
Under the tension, slip, slide, perish,
Decay with imprecision, will not stay in place,
Will not stay still. Shrieking voices
Scolding, mocking, or merely chattering,
Always assail them. The Word in the desert
Is most attacked by voices of temptation,
The crying shadow in the funeral dance,
The loud lament of the disconsolate chimera.

The detail of the pattern is movement,
As in the figure of the ten stairs.
Desire itself is movement
Not in itself desirable;

Love is itself unmoving,
Only the cause and end of movement,
Timeless, and undesiring
Except in the aspect of time
Caught in the form of limitation
Between un-being and being.
Sudden in a shaft of sunlight
Even while the dust moves
There rises the hidden laughter
Of children in the foliage
Quick now, here, now, always—
Ridiculous the waste sad time
Stretching before and after.

Ash-Wednesday

1930

I

Because I do not hope to turn again
Because I do not hope
Because I do not hope to turn
Desiring this man's gift and that man's scope
I no longer strive to strive towards such things
(Why should the agèd eagle stretch its wings?)
Why should I mourn
The vanished power of the usual reign?

Because I do not hope to know again
The infirm glory of the positive hour
Because I do not think
Because I know I shall not know
The one veritable transitory power
Because I cannot drink
There, where trees flower, and springs flow, for there is nothing
    again

Because I know that time is always time
And place is always and only place
And what is actual is actual only for one time
And only for one place
I rejoice that things are as they are and
I renounce the blessèd face
And renounce the voice
Because I cannot hope to turn again

Consequently I rejoice, having to construct something
Upon which to rejoice

And pray to God to have mercy upon us
And pray that I may forget
These matters that with myself I too much discuss
Too much explain
Because I do not hope to turn again
Let these words answer
For what is done, not to be done again
May the judgement not be too heavy upon us

Because these wings are no longer wings to fly
But merely vans to beat the air
The air which is now thoroughly small and dry
Smaller and dryer than the will
Teach us to care and not to care
Teach us to sit still.

Pray for us sinners now and at the hour of our death
Pray for us now and at the hour of our death.

II

Lady, three white leopards sat under a juniper-tree
In the cool of the day, having fed to satiety
On my legs my heart my liver and that which had been contained
In the hollow round of my skull. And God said
Shall these bones live? shall these
Bones live? And that which had been contained
In the bones (which were already dry) said chirping:
Because of the goodness of this Lady
And because of her loveliness, and because
She honours the Virgin in meditation,
We shine with brightness. And I who am here dissembled
Proffer my deeds to oblivion, and my love
To the posterity of the desert and the fruit of the gourd.
It is this which recovers
My guts the strings of my eyes and the indigestible portions
Which the leopards reject. The Lady is withdrawn
In a white gown, to contemplation, in a white gown.
Let the whiteness of bones atone to forgetfulness.
There is no life in them. As I am forgotten
And would be forgotten, so I would forget
Thus devoted, concentrated in purpose. And God said
Prophesy to the wind, to the wind only for only

The wind will listen. And the bones sang chirping
With the burden of the grasshopper, saying

Lady of silences
Calm and distressed
Torn and most whole
Rose of memory
Rose of forgetfulness
Exhausted and life-giving
Worried reposeful
The single Rose
Is now the Garden
Where all loves end
Terminate torment
Of love unsatisfied
The greater torment
Of love satisfied
End of the endless
Journey to no end
Conclusion of all that
Is inconclusible
Speech without word and
Word of no speech
Grace to the Mother
For the Garden
Where all love ends.

Under a juniper-tree the bones sang, scattered and shining
We are glad to be scattered, we did little good to each other,
Under a tree in the cool of the day, with the blessing of sand,
Forgetting themselves and each other, united
In the quiet of the desert. This is the land which ye
Shall divide by lot. And neither division nor unity
Matters. This is the land. We have our inheritance.

III

At the first turning of the second stair
I turned and saw below
The same shape twisted on the banister
Under the vapour in the fetid air
Struggling with the devil of the stairs who wears
The deceitful face of hope and of despair.

At the second turning of the second stair
I left them twisting, turning below;

There were no more faces and the stair was dark,
Damp, jaggèd, like an old man's mouth drivelling, beyond repair,
Or the toothed gullet of an agèd shark.

At the first turning of the third stair
Was a slotted window bellied like the fig's fruit
And beyond the hawthorn blossom and a pasture scene
The broadbacked figure drest in blue and green
Enchanted the maytime with an antique flute.
Blown hair is sweet, brown hair over the mouth blown,
Lilac and brown hair;
Distraction, music of the flute, stops and steps of the mind over the
        third stair,
Fading, fading; strength beyond hope and despair
Climbing the third stair.

Lord, I am not worthy
Lord, I am not worthy

            but speak the word only.

IV

Who walked between the violet and the violet
Who walked between
The various ranks of varied green
Going in white and blue, in Mary's colour,
Talking of trivial things
In ignorance and in knowledge of eternal dolour
Who moved among the others as they walked,
Who then made strong the fountains and made fresh the springs

Made cool the dry rock and made firm the sand
In blue of larkspur, blue of Mary's colour,
Sovegna vos

Here are the years that walk between, bearing
Away the fiddles and the flutes, restoring
One who moves in the time between sleep and waking, wearing

White light folded, sheathed about her, folded.
The new years walk, restoring
Through a bright cloud of tears, the years, restoring
With a new verse the ancient rhyme. Redeem
The time. Redeem

The unread vision in the higher dream
While jewelled unicorns draw by the gilded hearse.

The silent sister veiled in white and blue
Between the yews, behind the garden god,
Whose flute is breathless, bent her head and sighed but spoke no
    word

But the fountain sprang up and the bird sang down
Redeem the time, redeem the dream
The token of the word unheard, unspoken

Till the wind shake a thousand whispers from the yew

And after this our exile

V

If the lost word is lost, if the spent word is spent
If the unheard, unspoken
Word is unspoken, unheard;
Still is the unspoken word, the Word unheard,
The Word without a word, the Word within
The world and for the world;
And the light shone in darkness and
Against the Word the unstilled world still whirled
About the centre of the silent Word.

     O my people, what have I done unto thee.

Where shall the word be found, where will the word
Resound? Not here, there is not enough silence
Not on the sea or on the islands, not
On the mainland, in the desert or the rain land,
For those who walk in darkness
Both in the day time and in the night time
The right time and the right place are not here
No place of grace for those who avoid the face
No time to rejoice for those who walk among noise and deny the
    voice

Will the veiled sister pray for
Those who walk in darkness, who chose thee and oppose thee,
Those who are torn on the horn between season and season, time
    and time, between
Hour and hour, word and word, power and power, those who wait

In darkness? Will the veiled sister pray
For children at the gate
Who will not go away and cannot pray:
Pray for those who chose and oppose

     O my people, what have I done unto thee.

Will the veiled sister between the slender
Yew trees pray for those who offend her
And are terrified and cannot surrender
And affirm before the world and deny between the rocks
In the last desert between the last blue rocks
The desert in the garden the garden in the desert
Of drouth, spitting from the mouth the withered apple-seed.

     O my people.

VI

Although I do not hope to turn again
Although I do not hope
Although I do not hope to turn

Wavering between the profit and the loss
In this brief transit where the dreams cross
The dreamcrossed twilight between birth and dying
(Bless me father) though I do not wish to wish these things
From the wide window towards the granite shore
The white sails still fly seaward, seaward flying
Unbroken wings

And the lost heart stiffens and rejoices
In the lost lilac and the lost sea voices
And the weak spirit quickens to rebel
For the bent golden-rod and the lost sea smell
Quickens to recover
The cry of quail and the whirling plover
And the blind eye creates
The empty forms between the ivory gates
And smell renews the salt savour of the sandy earth

This is the time of tension between dying and birth
The place of solitude where three dreams cross
Between blue rocks
But when the voices shaken from the yew-tree drift away
Let the other yew be shaken and reply.

Blessèd sister, holy mother, spirit of the fountain, spirit of the garden,
Suffer us not to mock ourselves with falsehood
Teach us to care and not to care
Teach us to sit still
Even among these rocks,
Our peace in His will
And even among these rocks
Sister, mother
And spirit of the river, spirit of the sea,
Suffer me not to be separated

And let my cry come unto Thee.

The Waste Land

1922

> "Nam Sibyllam quidem Cumis ego ipse oculis
> meis vidi in ampulla pendere, et cum illi pueri
> dicerent: Σίβυλλα τί θέλεις; respondebat illa:
> ἀποθανεῖν θέλω."

For Ezra Pound *il miglior fabbro*

I. THE BURIAL OF THE DEAD

April is the cruellest month, breeding
Lilacs out of the dead land, mixing
Memory and desire, stirring
Dull roots with spring rain.
Winter kept us warm, covering   5
Earth in forgetful snow, feeding
A little life with dried tubers.
Summer surprised us, coming over the Starnbergersee
With a shower of rain; we stopped in the colonnade,
And went on in sunlight, into the Hofgarten,   10
And drank coffee, and talked for an hour.
Bin gar keine Russin, stamm' aus Litauen, echt deutsch.
And when we were children, staying at the archduke's,
My cousin's, he took me out on a sled,
And I was frightened. He said, Marie,   15
Marie, hold on tight. And down we went.
In the mountains, there you feel free.
I read, much of the night, and go south in the winter.

What are the roots that clutch, what branches grow
Out of this stony rubbish? Son of man,   20

You cannot say, or guess, for you know only
A heap of broken images, where the sun beats,
And the dead tree gives no shelter, the cricket no relief,
And the dry stone no sound of water. Only
25 There is shadow under this red rock,
(Come in under the shadow of this red rock),
And I will show you something different from either
Your shadow at morning striding behind you
Or your shadow at evening rising to meet you;
30 I will show you fear in a handful of dust.

> *Frisch weht der Wind*
> *Der Heimat zu*
> *Mein Irisch Kind,*
> *Wo weilest du?*

35 'You gave me hyacinths first a year ago;
'They called me the hyacinth girl.'
—Yet when we came back, late, from the Hyacinth garden.
Your arms full, and your hair wet, I could not
Speak, and my eyes failed, I was neither
40 Living nor dead, and I knew nothing,
Looking into the heart of light, the silence.
Oed' und leer das Meer.

Madame Sosostris, famous clairvoyante,
Had a bad cold, nevertheless
45 Is known to be the wisest woman in Europe,
With a wicked pack of cards. Here, said she,
Is your card, the drowned Phoenician Sailor,
(Those are pearls that were his eyes. Look!)
Here is Belladonna, the Lady of the Rocks,
50 The lady of situations.
Here is the man with three staves, and here the Wheel,
And here is the one-eyed merchant, and this card,
Which is blank, is something he carries on his back,
Which I am forbidden to see. I do not find
55 The Hanged Man. Fear death by water.
I see crowds of people, walking round in a ring.
Thank you. If you see dear Mrs. Equitone,
Tell her I bring the horoscope myself:
One must be so careful these days.

60 Unreal City,
Under the brown fog of a winter dawn,
A crowd flowed over London Bridge, so many,
I had not thought death had undone so many.
Sighs, short and infrequent, were exhaled,

And each man fixed his eyes before his feet.   65
Flowed up the hill and down King William Street,
To where Saint Mary Woolnoth kept the hours
With a dead sound on the final stroke of nine.
There I saw one I knew, and stopped him, crying: 'Stetson!
'You who were with me in the ships at Mylae!   70
'That corpse you planted last year in your garden,
'Has it begun to sprout? Will it bloom this year?
'Or has the sudden frost disturbed its bed?
'Oh keep the Dog far hence, that's friend to men,
'Or with his nails he'll dig it up again!   75
'You! hypocrite lecteur!—mon semblable,—mon frère!'

II. A GAME OF CHESS

The Chair she sat in, like a burnished throne,
Glowed on the marble, where the glass
Held up by standards wrought with fruited vines
From which a golden Cupidon peeped out   80
(Another hid his eyes behind his wing)
Doubled the flames of sevenbranched candelabra
Reflecting light upon the table as
The glitter of her jewels rose to meet it,
From satin cases poured in rich profusion;   85
In vials of ivory and coloured glass
Unstoppered, lurked her strange synthetic perfumes,
Unguent, powdered, or liquid—troubled, confused
And drowned the sense in odours; stirred by the air
That freshened from the window, these ascended   90
In fattening the prolonged candle-flames,
Flung their smoke into the laquearia,
Stirring the pattern on the coffered ceiling.
Huge sea-wood fed with copper
Burned green and orange, framed by the coloured stone,   95
In which sad light a carvèd dolphin swam.
Above the antique mantel was displayed
As though a window gave upon the sylvan scene
The change of Philomel, by the barbarous king
So rudely forced; yet there the nightingale   100
Filled all the desert with inviolable voice
And still she cried, and still the world pursues,
'Jug Jug' to dirty ears.
And other withered stumps of time
Were told upon the walls; staring forms   105
Leaned out, leaning, hushing the room enclosed.
Footsteps shuffled on the stair.

Under the firelight, under the brush, her hair
Spread out in fiery points
110 Glowed into words, then would be savagely still.

'My nerves are bad to-night. Yes, bad. Stay with me.
'Speak to me. Why do you never speak. Speak.
'What are you thinking of? What thinking? What?
'I never know what you are thinking. Think.'

115 I think we are in rats' alley
Where the dead men lost their bones.

'What is that noise?'
                    The wind under the door.
'What is that noise now? What is the wind doing?'
120   Nothing again nothing.

                                                  'Do
'You know nothing? Do you see nothing? Do you remember
'Nothing?'

        I remember
125 Those are pearls that were his eyes.
'Are you alive, or not? Is there nothing in your head?'
                                                  But

O O O O that Shakespeherian Rag—
It's so elegant
130 So intelligent
'What shall I do now? What shall I do?'
'I shall rush out as I am, and walk the street
'With my hair down, so. What shall we do tomorrow?
'What shall we ever do?'
135   The hot water at ten.
And if it rains, a closed car at four.
And we shall play a game of chess,
Pressing lidless eyes and waiting for a knock upon the door.

When Lil's husband got demobbed, I said—
140 I didn't mince my words, I said to her myself,
HURRY UP PLEASE ITS TIME
Now Albert's coming back, make yourself a bit smart,
He'll want to know what you done with that money he gave you
To get yourself some teeth. He did, I was there.
145 You have them all out, Lil, and get a nice set,
He said, I swear, I can't bear to look at you.
And no more can't I, I said, and think of poor Albert,
He's been in the army four years, he wants a good time,

And if you don't give it him, there's others will, I said.
Oh is there, she said. Something o' that, I said. 150
Then I'll know who to thank, she said, and give me a straight look.
HURRY UP PLEASE ITS TIME
If you don't like it you can get on with it, I said.
Others can pick and choose if you can't.
But if Albert makes off, it won't be for lack of telling. 155
You ought to be ashamed, I said, to look so antique.
(And her only thirty-one.)
I can't help it, she said, pulling a long face,
It's them pills I took, to bring it off, she said.
(She's had five already, and nearly died of young George.) 160
The chemist said it would be all right, but I've never been the
    same.
You *are* a proper fool, I said.
Well, if Albert won't leave you alone, there it is, I said,
What you get married for if you don't want children?
HURRY UP PLEASE ITS TIME 165
Well, that Sunday Albert was home, they had a hot gammon,
And they asked me in to dinner, to get the beauty of it hot—
HURRY UP PLEASE ITS TIME
HURRY UP PLEASE ITS TIME
Goonight Bill. Goonight Lou. Goonight May. Goonight. 170
Ta ta. Goonight. Goonight.
Good night, ladies, good night, sweet ladies, good night, good night.

III. THE FIRE SERMON

The river's tent is broken: the last fingers of leaf
Clutch and sink into the wet bank. The wind
Crosses the brown land, unheard. The nymphs are departed. 175
Sweet Thames, run softly, till I end my song.
The river bears no empty bottles, sandwich papers,
Silk handkerchiefs, cardboard boxes, cigarette ends
Or other testimony of summer nights. The nymphs are departed.
And their friends, the loitering heirs of city directors; 180
Departed, have left no addresses.
By the waters of Leman I sat down and wept. . .
Sweet Thames, run softly till I end my song,
Sweet Thames, run softly, for I speak not loud or long.
But at my back in a cold blast I hear 185
The rattle of the bones, and chuckle spread from ear to ear.
A rat crept softly through the vegetation
Dragging its slimy belly on the bank
While I was fishing in the dull canal
On a winter evening round behind the gashouse 190

Musing upon the king my brother's wreck
And on the king my father's death before him.
White bodies naked on the low damp ground
And bones cast in a little low dry garret,
195 Rattled by the rat's foot only, year to year.
But at my back from time to time I hear
The sound of horns and motors, which shall bring
Sweeney to Mrs. Porter in the spring.
O the moon shone bright on Mrs. Porter
200 And on her daughter
They wash their feet in soda water
Et Ó ces voix d'enfant, chantant dans la coupole!

Twit twit twit
Jug jug jug jug jug jug
205 So rudely forc'd.
Tereu

Unreal City
Under the brown fog of a winter noon
Mr. Eugenides, the Smyrna merchant
210 Unshaven, with a pocket full of currants
C.i.f. London: documents at sight,
Asked me in demotic French
To luncheon at the Cannon Street Hotel
Followed by a weekend at the Metropole.

215 At the violet hour, when the eyes and back
Turn upward from the desk, when the human engine waits
Like a taxi throbbing waiting,
I Tiresias, though blind, throbbing between two lives,
Old man with wrinkled female breasts, can see
220 At the violet hour, the evening hour that strives
Homeward, and brings the sailor home from sea,
The typist home at teatime, clears her breakfast, lights
Her stove, and lays out food in tins.
Out of the window perilously spread
225 Her drying combinations touched by the sun's last rays,
On the divan are piled (at night her bed)
Stockings, slippers, camisoles, and stays.
I Tiresias, old man with wrinkled dugs
Perceived the scene, and foretold the rest—
230 I too awaited the expected guest.
He, the young man carbuncular, arrives,
A small house agent's clerk, with one bold stare,
One of the low on whom assurance sits

As a silk hat on a Bradford millionaire.
The time is now propitious, as he guesses,   235
The meal is ended, she is bored and tired,
Endeavors to engage her in caresses
Which still are unreproved, if undesired.
Flushed and decided, he assaults at once;
Exploring hands encounter no defence;   240
His vanity requires no response,
And makes a welcome of indifference.
(And I Tiresias have foresuffered all
Enacted on this same divan or bed;
I who have sat by Thebes below the wall   245
And walked among the lowest of the dead.)
Bestows one final patronising kiss,
And gropes his way, finding the stairs unlit. . .

She turns and looks a moment in the glass,
Hardly aware of her departed lover;   250
Her brain allows one half-formed thought to pass:
'Well now that's done: and I'm glad it's over.'
When lovely woman stoops to folly and
Paces about her room again, alone,
She smoothes her hair with automatic hand,   255
And puts a record on the gramophone.

'This music crept by me upon the waters'
And along the Strand, up Queen Victoria Street.
O City city, I can sometimes hear
Beside a public bar in Lower Thames Street,   260
The pleasant whining of a mandoline
And a clatter and a chatter from within
Where fishmen lounge at noon: where the walls
Of Magnus Martyr hold
Inexplicable splendour of Ionian white and gold.   265

       The river sweats
       Oil and tar
       The barges drift
       With the turning tide
       Red sails   270
       Wide
       To leeward, swing on the heavy spar.
       The barges wash
       Drifting logs
       Down Greenwich reach   275
       Past the Isle of Dogs.

Weialala leia
Wallala leialala

Elizabeth and Leicester
280 Beating oars
The stern was formed
A gilded shell
Red and gold
The brisk swell
285 Rippled both shores
Southwest wind
Carried down stream
The peal of bells
White towers

Weialala leia
Wallala leialala

'Trams and dusty trees.
Highbury bore me. Richmond and Kew
Undid me. By Richmond I raised my knees
295 Supine on the floor of a narrow canoe.'

'My feet are at Moorgate, and my heart
Under my feet. After the event
He wept. He promised "a new start."
I made no comment. What should I resent?'

300 'On Margate Sands.
I can connect
Nothing with nothing.
The broken fingernails of dirty hands.
My people humble people who expect
305 Nothing.'

la la

To Carthage then I came

Burning burning burning burning
O Lord Thou pluckest me out
310 O Lord Thou pluckest

burning

IV. DEATH BY WATER

Phlebas the Phoenician, a fortnight dead,
Forgot the cry of gulls, and the deep sea swell
And the profit and loss.
                              A current under sea   315
Picked his bones in whispers. As he rose and fell
He passed the stages of his age and youth
Entering the whirlpool.
                              Gentile or Jew
O you who turn the wheel and look to windward,   320
Consider Phlebas, who was once handsome and tall as you.

V. WHAT THE THUNDER SAID

After the torchlight red on sweaty faces
After the frosty silence in the gardens
After the agony in stony places
The shouting and the crying   325
Prison and palace and reverberation
Of thunder of spring over distant mountains
He who was living is now dead
We who were living are now dying
With a little patience   330

Here is no water but only rock
Rock and no water and the sandy road
The road winding above among the mountains
Which are mountains of rock without water
If there were water we should stop and drink   335
Amongst the rock one cannot stop or think
Sweat is dry and feet are in the sand
If there were only water amongst the rock
Dead mountain mouth of carious teeth that cannot spit
Here one can neither stand nor lie nor sit   340
There is not even silence in the mountains
But dry sterile thunder without rain
There is not even solitude in the mountains
But red sullen faces sneer and snarl
From doors of mudcracked houses   345
                              If there were water
    And no rock
    If there were rock
    And also water
    And water   350
    A spring

A pool among the rock
If there were the sound of water only
Not the cicada
355 And dry grass singing
But sound of water over a rock
Where the hermit-thrush sings in the pine trees
Drip drop drip drop drop drop drop
But there is no water

360 Who is the third who walks always beside you?
When I count, there are only you and I together
But when I look ahead up the white road
There is always another one walking beside you
Gliding wrapt in a brown mantle, hooded
365 I do not know whether a man or a woman
—But who is that on the other side of you?

What is that sound high in the air
Murmur of maternal lamentation
Who are those hooded hordes swarming
370 Over endless plains, stumbling in cracked earth
Ringed by the flat horizon only
What is the city over the mountains
Cracks and reforms and bursts in the violet air
Falling towers
375 Jerusalem Athens Alexandria
Vienna London
Unreal

A woman drew her long black hair out tight
And fiddled whisper music on those strings
380 And bats with baby faces in the violet light
Whistled, and beat their wings
And crawled head downward down a blackened wall
And upside down in air were towers
Tolling reminiscent bells, that kept the hours
385 And voices singing out of empty cisterns and exhausted wells.

In this decayed hole among the mountains
In the faint moonlight, the grass is singing
Over the tumbled graves, about the chapel
There is the empty chapel, only the wind's home.
390 It has no windows, and the door swings,
Dry bones can harm no one.
Only a cock stood on the rooftree
Co co rico co co rico

In a flash of lighting. Then a damp gust
Bringing rain   395

Ganga was sunken, and the limp leaves
Waited for rain, while the black clouds
Gathered far distant, over Himavant.
The jungle crouched, humped in silence.
Then spoke the thunder   400
DA
Datta: what have we given?
My friend, blood shaking my heart
The awful daring of a moment's surrender
Which an age of prudence can never retract   405
By this, and this only, we have existed
Which is not to be found in our obituaries
Or in memories draped by the beneficient spider
Or under seals broken by the lean solicitor
In our empty rooms   410
DA
Dayadhvam: I have heard the key
Turn in the door once and turn once only
We think of the key, each in his prison
Thinking of the key, each confirms a prison   415
Only at nightfall, aethereal rumours
Revive for a moment a broken Coriolanus
DA
Damyata: The boat responded
Gaily, to the hand expert with sail and oar   420
The sea was calm, your heart would have responded
Gaily, when invited, beating obedient
To controlling hands

                                     I sat upon the shore
Fishing, with the arid plain behind me   425
Shall I at least set my lands in order?
London Bridge is falling down falling down falling down
Poi s'ascose nel foco che gli affina
Quando fiam uti chelidon—O swallow swallow
Le Prince d'Aquitaine à la tour abolie   430
These fragments I have shored against my ruins
Why then Ile fit you. Hieronymo's mad againe.
Datta. Dayadhvam. Damyata.
                    Shantih   shantih   shantih

Geronition

Thou hast nor youth nor age
But as it were an after dinner sleep
Dreaming of both.

Here I am, an old man in a dry month,
Being read to by a boy, waiting for rain.
I was neither at the hot gates
Nor fought in the warm rain
Nor knee deep in the salt marsh, heaving a cutlass,
Bitten by flies, fought.
My house is a decayed house,
And the jew squats on the window sill, the owner,
Spawned in some estaminet of Antwerp,
Blistered in Brussels, patched and peeled in London.
The goat coughs at night in the field overhead;
Rocks, moss, stonecrop, iron, merds.
The woman keeps the kitchen, makes tea,
Sneezes at evening, poking the peevish gutter.
                              I an old man,
A dull head among windy spaces.

Signs are taken for wonders. 'We would see a sign!'
The word within a word, unable to speak a word,
Swaddled with darkness. In the juvescence of the year
Came Christ the tiger
In depraved May, dogwood and chestnut, flowering judas,
To be eaten, to be divided, to be drunk
Among whispers; by Mr. Silvero
With caressing hands, at Limoges
Who walked all night in the next room;

By Hakagawa, bowing among the Titians;
By Madame de Tornquist, in the dark room
Shifting the candles; Fräulein von Kulp
Who turned in the hall, one hand on the door. Vacant shuttles
Weave the wind. I have no ghosts,
An old man in a draughty house
Under a windy knob.

After such knowledge, what forgiveness? Think now
History has many cunning passages, contrived corridors
And issues, deceives with whispering ambitions,
Guides us by vanities. Think now
She gives when our attention is distracted
And what she gives, gives with such supple confusions

That the giving famishes the craving. Gives too late
What's not believed in, or if still believed,
In memory only, reconsidered passion. Gives too soon
Into weak hands, what's thought can be dispensed with
Till the refusal propagates a fear. Think
Neither fear nor courage saves us. Unnatural vices
Are fathered by our heroism. Virtues
Are forced upon us by our impudent crimes.
These tears are shaken from the wrath-bearing tree.

The tiger springs in the new year. Us he devours.
        Think at last
We have not reached conclusions, when I
Stiffen in a rented house. Think at last
I have not made this show purposelessly
And it is not by any concitation
Of the backward devils.
I would meet you upon this honestly.
I that was near your heart was removed therefrom
To lose beauty in terror, terror in inquisition.
I have lost my passion: why should I need to keep it
Since what is kept must be adulterated?
I have lost my sight, smell, hearing, taste and touch:
How should I use them for your closer contact?

These with a thousand small deliberations
Protract the profit of their chilled delirium,
Excite the membrane, when the sense has cooled,
With pungent sauces, multiply variety
In a wilderness of mirrors. What will the spider do,
Suspend its operations, will the weevil
Delay? De Bailhache, Fresca, Mrs. Cammel, whirled
Beyond the circuit of the shuddering Bear
In fractured atoms. Gull against the wind, in the windy
        straits
Of Belle Isle, or running on the Horn,
White feathers in the snow, the Gulf claims,
And an old man driven by the Trades
To a sleepy corner.

                        Tenants of the house,
Thoughts of a dry brain in a dry season.

CONRAD AIKEN
1889-

from

Preludes for Memnon

I

Winter for a moment takes the mind; the snow
Falls past the arclight; icicles guard a wall;
The wind moans through a crack in the window;
A keen sparkle of frost is on the sill.
Only for a moment; as spring too might engage it,
With a single crocus in the loam, or a pair of birds;
Or summer with hot grass; or autumn with a yellow leaf.
Winter is there, outside, is here in me:
Drapes the planets with snow, deepens the ice on the moon,
Darkens the darkness that was already darkness.
The mind too has its snows, its slippery paths,
Walls bayonetted with ice, leaves ice-encased.
Here is the in-drawn room, to which you return
When the wind blows from Arcturus: here is the fire
At which you warm your hands and glaze your eyes;
The piano, on which you touch the cold treble;
Five notes like breaking icicles; and then silence.

The alarm-clock ticks, the pulse keeps time with it,
Night and the mind are full of sounds. I walk
From the fire-place, with its imaginary fire,
To the window, with its imaginary view.
Darkness, and snow ticking the window: silence,
And the knocking of chains on a motor-car, the tolling
Of a bronze bell, dedicated to Christ.
And then the uprush of angelic wings, the beating
Of wings demonic, from the abyss of the mind:
The darkness filled with a feathery whistling, wings
Numberless as the flakes of angelic snow,
The deep void swarming with wings and sound of wings,
The winnowing of chaos, the aliveness
Of depth and depth and depth dedicated to death.

Here are the bickerings of the inconsequential,
The chatterings of the ridiculous, the iterations

Of the meaningless. Memory, like a juggler,
Tosses its colored balls into the light, and again
Receives them into darkness. Here is the absurd,
Grinning like an idiot, and the omnivorous quotidian,
Which will have its day. A handful of coins,
Tickets, items from the news, a soiled handkerchief,
A letter to be answered, notice of a telephone call,
The petal of a flower in a volume of Shakspere,
The program of a concert. The photograph, too,
Propped on the mantel, and beneath it a dry rosebud;
The laundry bill, matches, an ash-tray, Utamaro's
Pearl-fishers. And the rug, on which are still the crumbs
Of yesterday's feast. These are the void, the night,
And the angelic wings that make it sound.

What is the flower? It is not a sigh of color,
Suspiration of purple, sibilation of saffron,
Nor aureate exhalation from the tomb.
Yet it is these because you think of these,
An emanation of emanations, fragile
As light, or glisten, or gleam, or coruscation,
Creature of brightness, and as brightness brief.
What is the frost? It is not the sparkle of death,
The flash of time's wing, seeds of eternity;
Yet it is these because you think of these.
And you, because you think of these, are both
Frost and flower, the bright ambiguous syllable
Of which the meaning is both no and yes.

Here is the tragic, the distorting mirror
In which your gesture becomes grandiose;
Tears form and fall from your magnificent eyes,
The brow is noble, and the mouth is God's.
Here is the God who seeks his mother, Chaos,—
Confusion seeking solution, and life seeking death.
Here is the rose that woos the icicle; the icicle
That woos the rose. Here is the silence of silences
Which dreams of becoming a sound, and the sound
Which will perfect itself in silence. And all
These things are only the uprush from the void,
The wings angelic and demonic, the sound of the abyss
Dedicated to death. And this is you.

LVI

Rimbaud and Verlaine, precious pair of poets,
Genius in both (but what is genius?) playing
Chess on a marble table at an inn
With chestnut blossom falling in blond beer
And on their hair and between knight and bishop—
Sunlight squared between them on the chess-board,
Cirrus in heaven, and a squeal of music
Blown from the leathern door of St. Sulpice—

Discussing, between moves, iamb and spondee
Anacoluthon and the open vowel
God the great peacock with his angel peacocks
And his dependent peacocks the bright stars:
Disputing too of fate as Plato loved it,
Or Sophocles, who hated and admired,
Or Socrates, who loved and was amused:

Verlaine puts down his pawn upon a leaf
And closes his long eyes, which are dishonest,
And says 'Rimbaud, there is one thing to do:
We must take rhetoric, and wring its neck! . . .'
Rimbaud considers gravely, moves his Queen;
And then removes himself to Timbuctoo.

And Verlaine dead,—with all his jades and mauves;
And Rimbaud dead in Marseilles with a vision,
His leg cut off, as once before his heart;
And all reported by a later lackey,
Whose virtue is his tardiness in time.

Let us describe the evening as it is:—
The stars disposed in heaven as they are:
Verlaine and Shakspere rotting, where they rot,
Rimbaud remembered, and too soon forgot;

Order in all things, logic in the dark;
Arrangement in the atom and the spark;
Time in the heart and sequence in the brain—

Such as destroyed Rimbaud and fooled Verlaine.
And let us then take godhead by the neck—

And strangle it, and with it, rhetoric.

ISAAC ROSENBERG
1890-1918

Dead Man's Dump

The plunging limbers over the shattered track
Racketed with their rusty freight,
Stuck out like many crowns of thorns,
And the rusty stakes like sceptres old
To stay the flood of brutish men
Upon our brothers dear.

The wheels lurched over sprawled dead
But pained them not, though their bones crunched,
Their shut mouths made no moan.
They lie there huddled, friend and foeman,
Man born of man, and born of woman;
And shells go crying over them
From night till night and now.

Earth has waited for them,
All the time of their growth
Fretting for their decay:
Now she has them at last!
In the strength of their strength
Suspended—stopped and held.

What fierce imaginings their dark souls lit?
Earth! Have they gone into you!
Somewhere they must have gone,
And flung on your hard back
Is their souls' sack
Emptied of God-ancestralled essences.
Who hurled them out? Who hurled?

None saw their spirits' shadow shake the grass,
Or stood aside for the half used life to pass
Out of those doomed nostrils and the doomed mouth,
When the swift iron burning bee
Drained the wild honey of their youth.

What of us who, flung on the shrieking pyre,
Walk, our usual thoughts untouched,

Our lucky limbs as on ichor fed,
Immortal seeming ever?
Perhaps when the flames beat loud on us,
A fear may choke in our veins
And the startled blood may stop.

The air is loud with death,
The dark air spurts with fire,
The explosions ceaseless are.
Timelessly now, some minutes past,
These dead strode time with vigorous life,
Till the shrapnel called 'And end!'
But not to all. In bleeding pangs
Some borne on stretchers dreamed of home,
Dear things, war-blotted from their hearts.

Maniac Earth! howling and flying, your bowel
Seared by the jagged fire, the iron love,
The impetuous storm of savage love.
Dark Earth! dark Heavens! swinging in chemic smoke,
What dead are born when you kiss each soundless soul
With lightning and thunder from your mined heart,
Which man's self dug, and his blind fingers loosed?

A man's brains splattered on
A stretcher-bearer's face;
His shook shoulders slipped their load,
But when they bent to look again
The drowning soul was sunk too deep
For human tenderness.

They left this dead with the older dead,
Stretched at the cross roads.

Burnt black by strange decay
Their sinister faces lie,
The lid over each eye,
The grass and coloured clay
More motion have than they,
Joined to the great sunk silences.

Here is one not long dead;
His dark hearing caught our far wheels,
And the choked soul stretched weak hands
To reach the living word the far wheels said,
The blood-dazed intelligence beating for light,

Crying through the suspense of the far torturing wheels
Swift for the end to break
Or the wheels to break,
Cried as the tide of the world broke over his sight.

Will they come? Will they ever come?
Even as the mixed hoofs of the mules,
The quivering-bellied mules,
And the rushing wheels all mixed
With his tortured upturned sight.
So we crashed round the bend,
We heard his weak scream,
We heard his very last sound,
And our wheels grazed his dead face.

"A Worm Fed on the Heart of Corinth"

A worm fed on the heart of Corinth,
Babylon and Rome:
Not Paris raped tall Helen,
But this incestuous worm,
Who lured her vivid beauty
To his amorphous sleep.
England! famous as Helen
Is thy betrothal sung
To him the shadowless,
More amorous than Solomon.

God

In his malodorous brain what slugs and mire,
Lanthorned in his oblique eyes, guttering burned!
His body lodged a rat where men nursed souls.
The world flashed grape-green eyes of a foiled cat
To him. On fragments of an old shrunk power,
On shy and maimed, on women wrung awry,
He lay, a bullying hulk, to crush them more.
But when one, fearless, turned and clawed like bronze,
Cringing was easy to blunt these stern paws,
And he would weigh the heavier on those after.

Who rests in God's mean flattery now? Your wealth
Is but his cunning to make death more hard.
Your iron sinews take more pain in breaking.

And he has made the market for your beauty
Too poor to buy, although you die to sell.
Only that he has never heard of sleep;
And when the cats come out the rats are sly.
Here we are safe till he slinks in at dawn.

But he has gnawed a fibre from strange roots,
And in the morning some pale wonder ceases.
Things are not strange and strange things are forgetful.
Ah! if the day were arid, somehow lost
Out of us, but it is as hair of us,
And only in the hush no wind stirs it.
And in the light vague trouble lifts and breathes,
And restlessness still shadows the lost ways.
The fingers shut on voices that pass through,
Where blind farewells are taken easily. . . .

Ah! this miasma of a rotting God!

"My Soul Is Robbed"

My soul is robbed by your most treacherous eyes
Treading its intricate infinities.
Stay there, rich robbers! what I lose is dross;
Since my life is your dungeon, where is loss?

Ah! as the sun is prisoned in the heaven,
Whose walls dissolve, of their own nature bereaven,
So do your looks, as idly, without strife,
Cover all steeps of sense, which no more pasture life.
Which no more feel, but only know you there,
In this blind trance of some white anywhere.

Come—come—that glance engendered ecstasy—
That subtle unspaced mutual intimacy
Whereby two spirits of one thought commune
Like separate instruments that play one tune,
And the whole miracle and amazement of
The unexpected flowering of love
Concentres to an instant that expands
And takes unto itself the strangest of strange lands.

Midsummer Frost

A July ghost, aghast at the strange winter,
Wonders, at burning noon (all summer seeming),
How, like a sad thought buried in light words,
Winter, an alien presence, is ambushed here.

See, from the fire-fountained noon, there creep
Lazy yellow ardours towards pale evening,
To thread dark and vain fire
Over my unsens'd heart,
Dead heart, no urgent summer can reach.
Hidden as a root from air or a star from day;
A frozen pool whereon mirth dances;
Where the shining boys would fish.

My blinded brain pierced is,
And searched by a thought, and pangful
With bitter ooze of a joyous knowledge
Of some starred time outworn.
Like blind eyes that have slinked past God,
And light, their untasked inheritance,
(Sealed eyes that trouble never the Sun)
Yet has feel of a Maytime pierced.
He heareth the Maytime dances;
Frees from their airy prison, bright voices,
To loosen them in his dark imagination,
Powered with girl revels rare
And silks and merry colours,
And all the unpeopled ghosts that walk in words.
Till wave white hands that ripple lakes of sadness,
Until the sadness vanishes and the stagnant pool remains.

Underneath this summer air can July dream
How, in night hanging forest of eating maladies,
A frozen forest of moon unquiet madness,
The moon-drunk haunted pierced soul dies;
Starved by its Babel folly, lying stark,
Unvexed by July's warm eyes.

JOHN PEALE BISHOP
1892-1944

A Frieze

Arrested like marble horses
In timeless prancing: in the heave of haunches
A pause in the prancing:
Arrested like marble horses, spurred
By impetuous riders, by furious young heels
In a tumultuous curve of haunches.
Confounding seasons,
To the despair of Apollo,
The light on the restless arrested horses, the stayed
Feet, and the beautiful impetuous riders.
Love longs for life, love looks toward ecstasy.
But though the passionate motion ceases
Desire is incensed and urges
The sport for which immortality leases
This extravagant, time's prodigal body
With thoughts that exult though the body tire
Appeased but afflicted
With a pain of dissolute longing
Saved from diluvium of timelessness. Whence comes
This rage? Dimensionless and undiminishable
Lust of the timeless prancing, pause in the proud prancing,
Spurred by the furious heels of immortal horsemen?

The Return

Night and we heard heavy and cadenced hoofbeats
Of troops departing; the last cohorts left
By the North Gate. That night some listened late
Leaning their eyelids toward Septentrion.

Morning flared and the young tore down the trophies
And warring ornaments: arches were strong
And in the sun but stone; no longer conquest
Circled our columns; all our state was down

In fragments. In the dust, old men with tufted
Eyebrows whiter than sunbaked faces gulped

As it fell. But they no more than we remembered
The old sea-fights, the soldiers' names and sculptors'.
We did not know the end was coming: nor why
It came; only that long before the end
Were many wanted to die. Then vultures starved
And sailed more slowly in the sky.

We still had taxes. Salt was high. The soldiers
Gone. Now there was much drinking and lewd
Houses all night loud with riot. But only
For a time. Soon the taverns had no roofs.

Strangely it was the young, the almost boys,
Who first abandoned hope; the old still lived
A little, at last a little lived in eyes.
It was the young whose child did not survive.

Some slept beneath the simulacra, until
The gods' faces froze. Then was fear.
Some had response in dreams, but morning restored
Interrogation. Then O then, O ruins!
Temples of Neptune invaded by the sea
And dolphins streaked like streams sportive
As sunlight rode and over the rushing floors
The sea unfurled and what was blue raced silver.

Colloquy with a King-Crab

Dwarf pines; the wild plum on the wind-grassed shore
Shaken by autumn to its naked fruit;
Visions of bright winds across the bay:
These are, perhaps, sufficient images
To say what I have sought. These I have found.
Let these suffice with seas—though honesty is this,
To know what's sought from what the sands have found.
It needs no Proteus to announce the sea
Above the proclamations of loud surf—
Only the horseshoe crab, black carapace,
Project of life, though hideous, persisting
From the primordial grasp of claws on shore.
This crab is no abstraction, yet presents
No difficulty to the abstract mind,
His head all belly and his sword a tail,
But to the imagination is suspect.
Reject him? Why? Though voiceless, yet he says

That any monster may remain forever
If he but keep eyes, mind and claws intent
On the main chance, be not afraid to skulk.
This proletarian of the sea is not,
But scuttles, noble as the crocodile,
As ancient in his lineage. His name
Is not unknown in heaven. But his shell
Affords no edifice where I can creep
Though I consent like him to go on claws.

Ode

Why will they never sleep
Those great women who sit
Peering at me with parrot eyes?
They sit with grave knees; they keep
Perpetual stare; and their hands move
As though hands could be aware—
Forward and back, to begin again—
As though on tumultuous shuttles of wind they wove
Shrouds out of air.

The three are sisters. There is one
Who sits divine in weeping stone
On a small chair of skeleton
And is most inescapable.
I have walked through many mirrors
But always accompanied.
I have been as many men, as many ghosts,
As there were days. The boy was seen
Always at rainfall, mistily, not lost.
I have tried changing shapes
But always, alone, I have heard
Her shadow coming nearer, and known
The awful grasp of striding hands
Goddess! upon
The screaming metamorphosis.

One has a face burned hard
As the red Cretan clay,
Who wears a white torso scarred
With figures like a calendar
She sits among broken shafts
Of stone; she is and still will be
Who feeds on cities, gods and men,

Weapons of bronze and curious ornaments,
Reckoning the evens as the odds.
Her least movement recalls the sea.

The last has idiot teeth
And a brow not made
For any thought but suffering.
Tired, she repeats
In idiot singing
A song shaped like a ring:
"Now is now and never Then
Dead Virgins will bear no men
And now that we speak of love, of love,
The woman's beneath
That's burdened with love
And the man's above
While the thing is done and done.
One is one and Three is three
Children may come from a spark in the sun
But One is one and never Three
And never a Virgin shall bear a Son
While the shadow lasts of the gray ashtree!"

Phantasmal marbles!

There was One who might have saved
Me from these grave dissolute stones
And parrot eyes. But He is dead,
Christ is dead. And in a grave
Dark as a sightless skull He lies
And of His bones are charnels made.

ARCHIBALD MacLEISH

1892-

Einstein

Standing between the sun and moon preserves
A certain secrecy. Or seems to keep
Something inviolate if only that
His father was an ape.

                  Sweet music makes
All of his walls sound hollow and he hears

Sighs in the paneling and underfoot
Melancholy voices. So there is a door
Behind the seamless arras and within
A living something:—but no door that will
Admit the sunlight nor no windows where
The mirror moon can penetrate his bones
With cold deflection. He is small and tight
And solidly contracted into space
Opaque and perpendicular which blots
Earth with its shadow. And he terminates
In shoes which bearing up against the sphere
Attract his concentration,

Einstein   upon   a
public   bench
Wednesday   the
ninth contemplates
finity

                    for he ends
If there why then no farther, as, beyond
Extensively the universe itself,
Or chronologically the two dates
Original and ultimate of time,

Nor could Jehovah and the million stars
Staring within their solitudes of light,
Nor all night's constellations be contained
Between his boundaries,
                    nor could the sun
Receive him nor his groping roots run down
Into the loam and steaming sink of time
Where coils the middle serpent and the ooze
Breeds maggots.
                    But it seems assured he ends
Precisely at his shoes in proof whereof
He can revolve in orbits opposite
The orbit of the earth and so refuse
All planetary converse. And he wears
Cloths that distinguish him from what is not
His own circumference, as first a coat
Shaped to his back or modeled in reverse
Of the surrounding cosmos and below
Trousers preserving his detachment from
The revolutions of the stars.

Einstein   descends
the Hartmannsweil-
ertsrasse

                    His hands
And face go naked and alone converse
With what encloses him, as rough and smooth
And sound and silence and the intervals
Or rippling ether and the swarming motes
Clouding a privy: move to them and make
Shadows that mirror them within his skull

In perpendiculars and curves and planes
And bodiless significances blurred
As figures undersea and images
Patterned from eddies of the air.
                              Which are
Perhaps not shadows but the thing itself
And may be understood.
                    Decorticate
The petals of the enfolding world and leave
A world in reason which is in himself
And has his own dimensions. Here do trees
Adorn the hillside and hillsides enrich
The hazy marches of the sky and skies
Kindle and char to ashes in the wind,
And winds blow toward him from the verge, and suns
Rise on his dawn and on his dusk go down
And moons prolong his shadow. And he moves
Here as within a garden in a close
And where he moves the bubble of the world
Takes center and there circle round his head
Like golden flies in summer the gold stars.

Einstein provisionally before a mirror accepts the hypothesis of subjective reality

. . . rejects it

Disintegrates.
              For suddenly he feels
The planet plunge beneath him, and a flare
Falls from the upper darkness to the dark
And awful shadows loom across the sky
That have no life from him and suns go out
And livid as a drowned man's face the moon
Floats to the lapsing surface of the night
And sinks discolored under.
                        So he knows
Less than a world and must communicate
Beyond his knowledge.
                    Outstretched on the earth
He plunges both his arms into the swirl
Of what surrounds him but the yielding grass
Excludes his finger tips and the soft soil
Will not endure confusion with his hands
Nor will the air receive him nor the light
Dissolve their difference but recoiling turns
Back from his touch. By which denial he can
Crawl on the earth and sense the opposing sun
But not make answer to them.
                          Put out leaves
And let the old remembering wind think through

Einstein unsuccessfully after lunch attempts to enter, essaying synthesis with what's not he, the Bernese Oberland

A green intelligence or under sea
Float out long filaments of amber in
The numb and wordless revery of tides.

In autumn the black branches dripping rain
Bruise his uncovered bones and in the spring
His swollen tips are gorged with aching blood
That bursts the laurel.
                         But although they seize
His sense he has no name for them, no word
To give them meaning and no utterance
For what they say. Feel the new summer's sun
Crawl up the warmed relaxing hide of earth
And weep for his lost youth, his childhood home
And a wide water on an inland shore!
Or to the night's mute asking in the blood
Give back a girl's name and three notes together!

He cannot think the smell of after rain
Nor close his thought around the long smooth lag
And falter of a wind, nor bring to mind
Dusk and the whippoorwill.
                       But violins
Split out of trees and strung to tone can sing
Strange nameless words that image to the ear
What has no waiting image in the brain.
She plays in darkness and the droning wood
Dissolves to reverberations of a world
Beating in waves against him till his sense
Trembles to rhythm and his naked brain
Feels without utterance in form the flesh
Of dumb and incommunicable earth,
And knows at once, and without knowledge how,
The stroke of the blunt rain, and blind receives
The sun.
                 When he a moment occupies
The hollow of himself and like an air
Pervades all other.
                 But the violin
Presses its dry insistence through the dream
That swims above it, shivering its speech
Back to a rhythm that becomes again
Music and vaguely ravels into sound.
So then there is no speech that can resolve
Their texture to clear thought and enter them.

*Einstein dissolved
in violins invades
the molecular struc-
ture of F. P. Paep-
ke's Sommergarten.
Is repulsed*

*To Einstein asking
at the gate of stone
none opens*

The Virgin of Chartres whose bleaching bones still wear
The sapphires of her glory knew a word—
That now is three round letters like the three
Round empty staring punctures in a skull.
And there were words in Rome once and one time
Words at Eleusis.

            Now there are no words
Nor names to name them and they will not speak
But grope against his groping touch and throw
The long unmeaning shadows of themselves
Across his shadow and resist his sense.
Why then if they resist destroy them. Dumb
Yet speak them in their elements. Whole,
Break them to reason.

Einstein hearing behind the wall of the Grand Hôtel du Nord the stars discovers the Back Stair

           He lies upon his bed
Exerting on Arcturus and the moon
Forces proportional inversely to
The squares of their remoteness and conceives
The universe.

           Atomic.

             He can count
Ocean in atoms and weigh out the air
In multiples of one and subdivide
Light to its numbers.

           If they will not speak
Let them be silent in their particles.
Let them be dead and he will lie among
Their dust and cipher them—undo the signs
Of their unreal identities and free
The pure and single factor of all sums—
Solve them to unity.

          Democritus
Scooped handfuls out of stones and like the sea
Let earth run through his fingers. Well, he too,
He can achieve obliquity and learn
The cold distortion of the winter's sun
That breaks the surfaces of summer.

Einstein on the terrasse of The Acacias forces the secret door

              Stands
Facing the world upon a windy slope
And with his mind relaxes the stiff forms
Of all he sees until the heavy hills
Impend like rushing water and the earth
Hangs on the steep and momentary crest
Of overflowing ruin.

          Overflow!
Sweep over into movement and dissolve

All differences in the indifferent flux!
Crumble to eddyings of dust and drown
In change the thing that changes!
                                    There begins
A vague unquiet in the fallow ground,
A seething in the grass, a bubbling swirl
Over the surface of the fields that spreads
Around him gathering until the green
Boils and under frothy loam the rocks
Ferment and simmer and like thinning smoke
The trees melt into nothing.
                                    Still he stands
Watching the vortex widen and involve
In swirling dissolution the whole earth
And circle through the skies till swaying time
Collapses crumpling into dark the stars
And motion ceases and the sifting world
Opens beneath.
                        When he shall feel infuse
His flesh with the rent body of all else
And spin within his opening brain the motes
Of suns and worlds and spaces.

                                                    Einstein enters
                        Like a foam
His flesh is withered and his shriveling
And ashy bones are scattered on the dark.
But still the dark denies him. Still withstands
The dust his penetration and flings back
Himself to answer him.
                        Which seems to keep
Something inviolate. A living something.

EDNA ST. VINCENT MILLAY
1892-1950

from

Epitaph for the Race of Man

I

Here lies, and none to mourn him but the sea,
That falls incessant on the empty shore,
Most various Man, cut down to spring no more;
Before his prime, even in his infancy
Cut down, and all the clamour that was he,
Silenced; and all the riveted pride he wore,
A rusted iron column whose tall core
The rains have tunnelled like an aspen tree.
Man, doughty Man, what power has brought you low,
That heaven itself in arms could not persuade
To lay aside the lever and the spade
And be as dust among the dusts that blow?
Whence, whence the broadside? whose the heavy blade? . . .
Strive not to speak, poor scattered mouth; I know.

II

Only the diamond and the diamond's dust
Can render up the diamond unto Man;
One and invulnerable as it began
Had it endured, but for the treacherous thrust
That laid its hard heart open, as it must,
And ground it down and fitted it to span
A turbaned brow or fret an ivory fan,
Lopped of its stature, pared of its proper crust.
So Man, by all the wheels of heaven unscored,
Man, the stout ego, the exuberant mind
No edge could cleave, no acid could consume,—
Being split along the vein by his own kind,
Gives over, rolls upon the palm abhorred,
Is set in brass on the swart thumb of Doom.

The Return

Earth does not understand her child,
  Who from the loud gregarious town
Returns, depleted and defiled,
  To the still woods, to fling him down.

Earth can not count the sons she bore:
  The wounded lynx, the wounded man
Come trailing blood unto her door;
  She shelters both as best she can.

But she is early up and out,
  To trim the year or strip its bones;
She has no time to stand about
  Talking of him in undertones

Who has no aim but to forget,
  Be left in peace, be lying thus
For days, for years, for centuries yet,
  Unshaven and anonymous;

Who, marked for failure, dulled by grief,
  Has traded in his wife and friend
For this warm ledge, this alder leaf:
  Comfort that does not comprehend.

DJUNA BARNES
1892-

Nightwood

from
WATCHMAN, WHAT OF THE NIGHT?

"Have you ever thought of the night?" the doctor inquired with a little irony; he was extremely put out, having expected some-one else, though his favourite topic, and one which he talked on whenever he had a chance, was the night.

"Yes," said Nora, and sat down on the only chair. "I've thought of it, but thinking about something you know nothing about does not help."

"Have you," said the doctor, "ever thought of the peculiar polarity of times and times; and of sleep? Sleep the slain white bull? Well, I, Dr. Matthew-Mighty-grain-of-salt-Dante-O'Connor, will tell you how the day and the night are related by their division. The very constitution of twilight is a fabulous reconstruction of fear, fear bottom-out and wrong side up. Every day is thought upon and calculated, but the night is not premeditated. The Bible lies the one way, but the night gown the other. The night, 'Beware of that dark door!' "

"I used to think," Nora said, "that people just went to sleep, or if they did not go to sleep that they were themselves, but now—" she lit a cigarette and her hands trembled—"now I see that the night does something to a person's identity, even when asleep."

"Ah!" exclaimed the doctor. "Let a man lay himself down in the Great Bed and his 'identity' is no longer his own, his 'trust' is not with him, and his 'willingness' is turned over and is of another permission. His distress is wild and anonymous. He sleeps in a Town of Darkness, member of a secret brotherhood. He neither knows himself nor his outriders; he berserks a fearful dimension and dismounts, miraculously, in bed!

"His heart is tumbling in his chest, a dark place! Though some go into the night as a spoon breaks easy water, others go head foremost against a new connivance; their horns make a dry crying, like the wings of the locust, late come to their shedding.

"Have you thought of the night, now, in other times, in foreign countries—in Paris? When the streets were gall high with things you wouldn't have done for a dare's sake, and the way it was then; with the pheasants' necks and the goslings' beaks dangling against the hocks of the gallants, and not a pavement in the place, and everything gutters for miles and miles, and a stench to it that plucked you by the nostrils and you were twenty leagues out! The criers telling the price of wine to such good effect that the dawn saw good clerks full of piss and vinegar, and blood-letting in side streets where some wild princess in a night shift of velvet howled under a leech; not to mention the palaces of Nymphenburg echoing back to Vienna with the night trip of late kings letting water into plush cans and fine woodwork! No," he said, looking at her sharply, "I can see you have not! You should, for the night has been going on for a long time."

She said, "I've never known it before—I thought I did, but it was not knowing at all."

"Exactly," said the doctor. "You thought you knew, and you hadn't even shuffled the cards—now the nights of one period are not the nights of another. Neither are the nights of one city the nights of another. Let us take Paris for an instance, and France for a fact. *Ah, mon dieu! La nuit effroyable! La nuit, qui est une*

immense plaine, et le cœur qui est une petite extrémité! Ah, good
Mother mine, *Notre Dame-de-bonne-Garde!* Intercede for me now,
while yet I explain what I'm coming to! French nights are those
which all nations seek the world over—and have you noticed that?
Ask Dr. Mighty O'Connor; the reason the doctor knows everything
is because he's been everywhere at the wrong time and has now
become anonymous."

"But," Nora said, "I never thought of the night as a life at all—
I've never lived it—why did she?"

"I'm telling you of French nights at the moment," the doctor
went on, "and why we all go into them. The night and the day are
two travels, and the French—gut-greedy and fist-tight though they
often are—alone leave testimony of the two in the dawn; we tear up
the one for the sake of the other; not so the French.

"And why is that; because they think of the two as one continually and keep it before their mind as the monks who repeat, 'Lord
Jesus Christ, Son of God, have mercy upon me!' Some twelve
thousand or more times a twenty-four hours, so that it is finally in
the head, good or bad, without saying a word. Bowing down from
the waist, the world over they go, that they may revolve about the
Great Enigma—as a relative about a cradle—and the Great Enigma
can't be thought of unless you turn the head the other way, and
come upon thinking with the eye that you fear, which is called the
back of the head; it's the one we use when looking at the beloved
in a dark place, and she is a long time coming from a great way.
We swoon with the thickness of our own tongue when we say,
'I love you,' as in the eye of a child lost a long while will be found
the contraction of that distance—a child going small in the claws
of a beast, coming furiously up the furlongs of the iris. We are
but skin about a wind, with muscles clenched against mortality.
We sleep in a long reproachful dust against ourselves. We are full
to the gorge with our own names for misery. Life, the pastures in
which the night feeds and prunes the cud that nourishes us to
despair. Life, the permission to know death. We were created
that the earth might be made sensible of her inhuman taste; and
love that the body might be so dear that even the earth should roar
with it. Yes, we who are full to the gorge with misery should look
well around, doubting everything seen, done, spoken, precisely
because we have a word for it, and not its alchemy.

"To think of the acorn it is necessary to become the tree. And
the tree of night is the hardest tree to mount, the dourest tree to
scale, the most difficult of branch, the most febrile to the touch,
and sweats a resin and drips a pitch against the palm that compu-
tation has not gambled. Gurus, who, I trust you know, are Indian
teachers, expect you to contemplate the acorn ten years at a stretch,
and if, in that time, you are no wiser about the nut, you are not very

bright, and that may be the only certainty with which you will come away, which is a post-graduate melancholy—for no man can find a greater truth than his kidney will allow. So I, Dr. Matthew Mighty O'Connor, ask you to think of the night the day long, and of the day the night through, or at some reprieve of the brain it will come upon you heavily—an engine stalling itself upon your chest, halting its wheels against your heart; unless you have made a roadway for it.

"The French have made a detour of filthiness—Oh, the good dirt! Whereas you are of a clean race, of a too eagerly washing people, and this leaves no road for you. The brawl of the Beast leaves a path for the Beast. You wash your brawl with every thought, with every gesture, with every conceivable emollient and *savon,* and expect to find your way again. A Frenchman makes a navigable hour with a tuft of hair, a wrenched *bretelle,* a rumpled bed. The tear of wine is still in his cup to catch back the quantity of its bereavement; his *cantiques* straddle two backs, night and day."

"But, what am I to do?" she said.

"Be as the Frenchman, who puts a *sou* in the poor box at night that he may have a penny to spend in the morning—he can trace himself back by his sediment, vegetable and animal, and so find himself in the odour of wine in its two travels, in and out, packed down beneath an air that has not changed its position during that strategy.

"The American, what then? He separates the two for fear of indignities, so that the mystery is cut in every cord; the design wildcats down the *charter mortalis,* and you get crime. The startled bell in the stomach begins to toll, the hair moves and drags upward, and you go far away backward by the crown, your conscience belly out and shaking.

"Our bones ache only while the flesh is on them. Stretch it as thin as the temple flesh of an ailing woman and still it serves to ache the bone and to move the bone about; and in like manner the night is a skin pulled over the head of day that the day may be in a torment. We will find no comfort until the night melts away; until the fury of the night rots out its fire."

"Then," Nora said, "it means—I'll never understand her—I'll always be miserable—just like this."

"Listen! Do things look in the ten and twelve of noon as they look in the dark? Is the hand, the face, the foot, the same face and hand and foot seen by the sun? For now the hand lies in a shadow; its beauties and its deformities are in a smoke—there is a sickle of doubt across the cheek bone thrown by the hat's brim, so there is half a face to be peered back into speculation. A leaf of darkness has fallen under the chin and lies deep upon the arches of the eyes; the eyes themselves have changed their colour. The very mother's

head you swore by in the dock is a heavier head, crowned with pon-
derable hair.

"And what of the sleep of animals? The great sleep of the elephant, and the fine thin sleep of the bird?"

Nora said: "I can't stand it. I don't know how—I am frightened.
What is it? What is it in her that is doing this?"

"Oh, for God's sake!" the doctor said, "give me the smelling salts."
She got up, looking among the debris on the stand. Inhaling, he
pushed his head back into the pillow; then he said:

"Take history at night; have you ever thought of that, now? Was
it at night that Sodom became Gomorrah? It was at night, I swear!
A city given over to the shades, and that's why it has never been
countenanced or understood to this day. Wait, I'll be coming to
that! All through the night Rome went burning. Put that in the
noontide and it loses some of its age-old significance, does it not?
Why? Because it has existed to the eye of the mind all these years
against a black sky. Burn Rome in a dream, and you reach and
claw down the true calamity. For dreams have only the pigmen-
tation of fact. A man who has to deal in no colour cannot find
his match, or, if he does, it is for a different rage. Rome was the
egg, but colour was the tread."

"Yes," said Nora.

"The dead have committed some portion of the evil of the night;
sleep and love, the other. For what is not the sleeper responsible?
What converse does he hold, and with whom? He lies down with
his Nelly and drops off into the arms of his Gretchen. Thousands
unbidden come to his bed. Yet how can one tell truth when it's
never in the company? Girls that the dreamer has not fashioned
himself to want scatter their legs about him to the blows of Mor-
pheus. So used is he to sleep that the dream that eats away its
boundaries finds even what is dreamed an easier custom with the
years, and at that banquet the voices blend and battle without
pitch. The sleeper is the proprietor of an unknown land. He goes
about another business in the dark—and we, his partners, who go to
the opera, who listen to gossip of café friends, who walk along the
boulevards, or sew a quiet seam, cannot afford an inch of it; because, though we would purchase it with blood, it has no counter
and no till. She who stands looking down upon her who lies sleeping knows the horizontal fear, the fear unbearable. For man goes
only perpendicularly against his fate. He was neither formed to
know that other nor compiled of its conspiracy."

"You beat the liver out of a goose to get a *pâté;* you pound the
muscles of a man's *cardia* to get a philosopher."

"Is that what I am to learn?" she asked bitterly.

The doctor looked at her. "For the lover, it is the night into which
his beloved goes," he said, "that destroys his heart; he wakes her

suddenly, only to look the hyena in the face that is her smile, as she leaves that company.

"When she sleeps, is she not moving her leg aside for an unknown garrison? Or in a moment, that takes but a second, murdering us with an axe? Eating our ear in a pie, pushing us aside with the back of her hand, sailing to some port with a ship full of sailors and medical men? And what of our own sleep? We go to it no better—and betray her with the very virtue of our days. We are continent a long time, but no sooner has our head touched the pillow, and our eyes left the day, than a host of merrymakers take and get. We wake from our doings in a deep sweat for that they happened in a house without an address, in a street in no town, citizened with people with no names with which to deny them. Their very lack of identity makes them ourselves. For by a street number, by a house, by a name, we cease to accuse ourselves. Sleep demands of us a guilty immunity. There is not one of us who, given an eternal incognito, a thumbprint nowhere set against our souls, would not commit rape, murder and all abominations. For if pigeons flew out of his bum, or castles sprang out of his ears, man would be troubled to know which was his fate, a house a bird or a man. Possibly that one only who shall sleep three generations will come up uninjured out of that unpeopled annihilation." The doctor turned heavily in bed.

"For the thickness of the sleep that is on the sleeper we 'forgive,' as we 'forgive' the dead for the account of the earth that lies upon them. What we do not see, we are told, we do not mourn; yet night and sleep trouble us, suspicion being the strongest dream and dread the thong. The heart of the jealous knows the best and the most satisfying love, that of the other's bed, where the rival perfects the lover's imperfections. Fancy gallops to take part in that duel, unconstrained by any certain articulation of the laws of that unseen game.

"We look to the East for a wisdom that we shall not use—and to the sleeper for the secret that we shall not find. So, I say, what of the night, the terrible night? The darkness is the closet in which your lover roosts her heart, and that night fowl that caws against her spirit and yours, dropping between you and her the awful estrangement of his bowels. The drip of your tears is his implacable pulse. Night people do not bury their dead, but on the neck of you, their beloved and waking, sling the creature, husked of its gestures. And where you go, it goes, the two of you, your living and her dead, that will not die; to daylight, to life, to grief, until both are carrion.

"Wait! I'm coming to the night of nights—the night you want to know about the most of all—for even the greatest generality has a little particular; have you thought of that? A high price is demanded of any value, for a value is in itself a detachment! We wash away our sense of sin, and what does that bath secure us? Sin, shining bright and hard. In what does a Latin bathe? True dust. We have made the literal error. We have used water, we are thus too sharply reminded. A European gets out of bed with a disorder that holds the balance. The layers of his deed can be traced back to the last leaf and the good slug be found creeping. *L'Echo de Paris* and his bed sheets were run off the same press. One may read in both the travail life has had with him—he reeks with the essential wit necessary to the 'sale' of both editions, night edition and day.

"Each race to its wrestling! Some throw the beast on the other side, with the stench of excrement, blood and flowers, the three essential oils of their plight! Man makes his history with the one hand and 'holds it up' with the other.

"Oh, God, I'm tired of this tirade. The French are dishevelled and wise; the American tries to approximate it with drink. It is his only clue to himself. He takes it when his soap has washed him too clean for identification. The Anglo-Saxon has made the literal error; using water, he has washed away his page. Misery melts him down by day, and sleep at night. His preoccupation with his business day has made his sleep insoluble."

from

GO DOWN, MATTHEW

The doctor stood up, then sat down again. "Yes, oh, God, Robin was beautiful. I don't like her, but I have to admit that much; sort of fluid blue under her skin, as if the hide of time had been stripped from her, and with it, all transactions with knowledge. A sort of first position in attention; a face that will age only under the blows of perpetual childhood. The temples like those of young beasts cutting horns, as if they were sleeping eyes. And that look on a face we follow like a witch-fire. Sorcerers know the power of horns; meet a horn where you like and you know you have been identified. You could fall over a thousand human skulls without the same trepidation. And do old duchesses know it also! Have you ever seen them go into a large assembly of any sort, be it opera or bezique, without feathers, flowers, sprigs of oat, or some other gadget nodding above their temples!"

She had not heard him. "Every hour is my last, and," she said desperately, "one can't live one's last hour all one's life!"

He brought his hands together. "Even the contemplative life is only an effort, Nora my dear, to hide the body so the feet won't stick out. Ah," he added, "to be an animal, born at the opening of the eye, going only forward, and, at the end of day, shutting out memory with the dropping of the lid."

"Time isn't long enough," she said, striking the table. "It isn't long enough to live down her nights. God," she cried, "what is love? Man seeking his own head? The human head, so rented by misery that even the teeth weigh! She couldn't tell me the truth because she had never planned it; her life was a continual accident, and how can you be prepared for that? Everything we can't bear in this world, some day we find in one person, and love it all at once. A strong sense of identity gives man an idea he can do no wrong; too little accomplishes the same. Some natures cannot appreciate, only regret. Will Robin *only* regret?" She stopped abruptly, gripping the back of the chair. "Perhaps not," she said, "for even her memory wearied her." Then she said with the violence of misery, "There's something evil in me that loves evil and degradation— purity's black backside! That loves honesty with a horrid love; or why have I always gone seeking it at the liar's door?"

"Look here," said the doctor. "Do you know what has made me the greatest liar this side of the moon, telling my stories to people like you, to take the mortal agony out of their guts, and to stop them from rolling about, and drawing up their feet, and screaming, with their eyes staring over their knuckles with misery which they are trying to keep off, saying, 'Say something, Doctor, for the love of God!' And me talking away like mad. Well, that, and nothing else, has made me the liar I am.

. . . . . .

"Love is death, come upon with passion; I know, that is why love is wisdom. I love her as one condemned to it."

"O Widow Lazarus! Arisen from your dead! O lunatic humour of the moon! Behold this fearful tree on which sits singing the drearful bird—*Turdus musicus,* or European singing thrush; sitting and singing the refrain—all in the tear-wet night—and it starts out *largo,* but it ends like *I Hear You Calling Me,* or *Kiss Me Again,* gone wild. And Diane, where is she? Diane of Ephesus in the Greek Gardens, singing and shaken in every bosom; and Rack and Ruin, the dogs of the Vatican, running up and down the papal esplanade and out into the Ramblar with roses in their tails to keep off care. Don't I know it all! Do you think that I, the Old Woman who lives in the closet, do not know that every child, no matter what its day, is born prehistorically and that even the wrong thought has caused the human mind incredible effort? Bend down the tree of knowledge and you'll unroost a strange bird. Suffering may be composed wickedly and of an inferior writhing. Rage and inaccuracy howl and blow the bone, for, contrary to all opinion, all suffering does *not* purify—begging everybody's pardon, which is called everybody's know. It moils and blathers some to perjury; the peritoneum boils and brings on common and cheap praying a great way sunk in pointless agony."

"Jenny," she said.

"It rots her sleep—Jenny is one of those who nip like a bird and void like an ox—the poor and lightly damned! That can be a torture also. None of us suffers as much as we should, or loves as much as we say. Love is the first lie; wisdom the last. Don't I know that the only way to know evil is through truth? The evil and the good know themselves only by giving up their secret face to face. The true good who meets the true evil (Holy Mother of Mercy! are there any such?) learns for the first time how to accept neither; the face of the one tells the face of the other the half of the story that both forgot.

"To be utterly innocent," he went on, "would be to be utterly unknown, particularly to oneself."

. . . . . .

"And then that day I'll remember all my life, when I said: 'It is over now'; she was asleep and I struck her awake. I saw her come awake and turn befouled before me, she who had managed in that sleep to keep whole. Matthew, for God's sake, say something, you are awful enough to say it, say something! I didn't know, I didn't know that it was to be me who was to do the terrible thing! No rot had touched her until then, and there before my eyes I saw her corrupt all at once and withering because I had struck her sleep away, and I went mad and I've been mad ever since; and there's nothing to do; nothing! You must say something, oh, God, say something!"

"Stop it! Stop it!" he cried. "Stop screaming! Put your hands down! Stop it! You were a 'good woman,' and so a bitch on a high plane, the only one able to kill yourself and Robin! Robin was outside the 'human type'—a wild thing caught in a woman's skin, monstrously alone, monstrously vain; like the paralysed man in Coney Island (take away a man's conformity and you take away his remedy) who had to lie on his back in a box, but the box was lined with velvet, his fingers jewelled with stones, and suspended over him where he could never take his eyes off, a sky-blue mounted mirror, for he wanted to enjoy his own 'difference.' Robin is not in your life, you are in her dream, you'll never get out of it. And why does Robin feel innocent? Every bed she leaves, without caring, fills her heart with peace and happiness. She has made her 'escape' again. That's why she can't 'put herself in another's place,' she herself is the only 'position'; so she resents it when you reproach her with what she had done. She knows she is innocent because she can't do anything in relation to anyone but herself. You almost caught hold of her, but she put you cleverly away by making you the Madonna. What was your patience and terror worth all these years if you couldn't keep them for her sake? Did you have to learn wisdom on her knees?

"Oh, for God's sweet sake, couldn't you stand not learning your lesson? Because the lesson we learn is always by giving death and a sword to our lover. You are full to the brim with pride, but I am an empty pot going forward, saying my prayers in a dark place; because I know no one loves, I, least of all, and that no one loves me, that's what makes most people so passionate and bright, because they want to love and be loved, when there is only a bit of lying in the ear to make the ear forget what time is compiling. So I, Doctor O'Connor, say, creep by, softly, softly, and don't learn anything because it's always learned of another person's body; take action in your heart and be careful whom you love—for a lover who dies, no matter how forgotten, will take somewhat of you to the grave. Be humble like the dust, as God intended, and crawl, and finally you'll crawl to the end of the gutter and not be missed and not much remembered."

. . . . . .

The doctor, walking with his coat-collar up, entered the *Café de la Mairie du VI*ᵉ. He stood at the bar and ordered a drink; looking at the people in the close, smoke-blue room, he said to himself, "Listen!" Nora troubled him, the life of Nora and the lives of the people in his life. "The way of a man in a fog!" he said. He hung his umbrella on the bar ledge. "To think is to be sick," he said to the barman. The barman nodded.

The people in the café waited for what the doctor would say, knowing that he was drunk and that he would talk; in great defaming sentences his betrayals came up; no one ever knew what was truth and what was not. "If you really want to know how hard a prize-fighter hits," he said, looking around, "you have got to walk into the circle of his fury and be carried out by the heels, not by the count."

Someone laughed. The doctor turned slowly. "So safe as all that?" he asked sarcastically; "so damned safe? Well, wait until you get in gaol and find yourself slapping the bottoms of your feet for misery."

He put his hand out for his drink—muttering to himself: "Matthew, you have never been in time with any man's life and you'll never be remembered at all, God save the vacancy! The finest instrument goes wrong in time—that's all, the instrument gets broken, and I must remember that when everyone is strange; it's the instrument gone flat. Lapidary, engrave that on my stone when Matthew is all over and lost in a field." He looked around, "It's the instrument, gentlemen, that has lost its G string; otherwise he'd be playing a fine tune; otherwise he'd still be passing his wind with the wind of the north—otherwise touching his billycock!

"Only the scorned and the ridiculous make good stories," he added angrily, seeing the habitués smiling, "so you can imagine when you'll get told! Life is only long enough for one trade; try that one!"

An unfrocked priest, a stout pale man with woman's hands, on which were many rings, a friend of the doctor's, called him and asked him to have a drink. The doctor came, carefully bringing his umbrella and hat. The priest said: "I've always wanted to know whether you were ever *really* married or not."

"Should I know that?" inquired the doctor. "I've *said* I was married and I gave the girl a name and had children by her, then, presto! I killed her off as lightly as the death of swans. And was I reproached for that story? I was. Because even your friends regret weeping for a myth, as if that were not practically the fate of all the tears in the world! What if the girl *was* the wife of my brother and the children my brother's children? When I laid her down her limbs were as handsome and still as two May boughs from the cutting—did he do as much for her? I imagined about her in my heart as pure as a French print, a girl all of a little bosom and a bird cage, lying back down comfortable with the sea for a background and a rope of roses to hold her. Has any man's wife been treated better than that? Who says she might not have been mine, and the children also? Who for that matter," he said with violence, "says they are not mine? Is not a brother his brother also, the one blood cut up in lengths, one called Michael and the other Matthew? Except that people get befuddled seeing them walk in different directions? Who's to say that I'm not my brother's wife's husband and that his children were not fathered in my lap? Is it not to his honour that he strikes me as myself? And when she died, did my weeping make his weeping less?"

The ex-priest said, "Well, there's something in that, still I like to know what is what."

"You do, do you?" said the doctor. "Well then, that's why you are where you are now, right down in the mud without a feather to fly with, like the ducks in Golden Gate park—the largest park in captivity—everybody with their damnable kindness having fed them all the year round to their ruin because when it comes time for their going south they are all a bitter consternation, being too fat and heavy to rise off the water, and, my God, how they flop and struggle all over the park in autumn, crying and tearing their hair out because their nature is weighed down with bread and their migration stopped by crumbs. You wring your hands to see it, and that's another illustration of love; in the end you are too heavy to move with the greediness in your stomach. And," said the doctor, "it would be the same with me if I'd let it, what with the wind at the one end and the cyclone at the other. Yet there are some that I have neglected for my spirit's sake—the old yeomen of the Guard and the beefeaters of the Tower because of their cold kidneys and gray hairs, and the kind of boy who only knows two existences—himself in a mirror—back and front." He was very drunk now. He looked about the café. He caught someone nudging someone. He looked up at the ex-priest and cursed. "What people! All queer in a terrible way. There were a couple of queer *good* people once in this world—but none of you," he said, addressing the room, "will ever know them. You think you are all studded with diamonds, don't you? Well, part the diamonds and you'll find slug's meat. My God," he said, turning around, "when I think!" He began to pound the table with his glass. "May they all be damned! The people in my life who have made my life miserable, coming to me to learn of degradation and the night. Nora, beating her head against her heart, sprung over, her mind closing her life up like a heel on a fan, rotten to the bone for love of Robin. My God, how that woman can hold on to an idea! And that old sandpiper, Jenny! Oh, it's a grand bad story, and who says I'm a betrayer? I say, tell the story of the world to the world!"

"A sad and a corrupt age," the ex-priest said.

Matthew O'Connor called for another drink. "What do they all come to me for? Why do they all tell me everything, then expect it to lie hushed in me, like a rabbit gone home to die? And that Baron Felix, hardly muttered a word in his life, and yet his silence breeds like scum on a pond; and that boy of his, Guido, by Robin, trying to see across the Danube with the tears in his eyes, Felix holding on to his hand and the boy holding on to the image of the Virgin on a darkening red ribbon, feeling its holy lift out of the metal and calling it mother; and me not even knowing which direction my end is coming from. So, when Felix said to me, 'Is the child infirm?' I said, 'Was the Mad King of Bavaria infirm?' I'm not one to cut the knot by drowning myself in any body of water, not even the print of a horse's hoof, no matter how it has been raining."

People had begun to whisper and the waiters moved closer, watching. The ex-priest was smiling to himself, but O'Connor did not seem to see or hear anything but his own heart. "Some people," he said, "take off head-first into *any* body of water and six glasses later someone in Haarlem gets typhoid from drinking their misery. God, take my hand and get me up out of this great argument—the more you go against your nature, the more you will know of it—hear me, Heaven! I've done and been everything that I didn't want to be or do—Lord, put the light out—so I stand here, beaten up and mauled and weeping, knowing I am not what I thought I was, a good man doing wrong, but the wrong man doing nothing much, and I wouldn't be telling you about it if I weren't talking to myself. I talk too much because I have been made so miserable by what you are keeping hushed. I'm an old worn-out lioness, a coward in my corner; for the sake of my bravery I've never been one thing that I am, to find out what I am! Here lies the body of Heaven. The mocking bird howls through the pillars of Paradise, O Lord! Death in Heaven lies couched on a mackerel sky, on her breast a helmet and at her feet a foal with a silent marble mane. Nocturnal sleep is heavy on her eyes."

"Funny little man," someone said. "Never stops talking—always getting everyone into trouble by excusing them because he can't excuse himself—the Squatting Beast, coming out at night—" As he broke off, the voice of the doctor was heard: "And what am I? I'm damned, and carefully public!"

He fumbled for a cigarette, found it and lit it.

"Once upon a time, I was standing listening to a quack hanky-panky of a medicine man saying: 'Now, ladies and gentlemen, before I behead the small boy, I will endeavour to entertain you with a few parlour tricks.' He had a turban cocked over his eye and a moaning in his left ventricle which was meant to be the whine of Tophet, and a loin-cloth as big as a tent and protecting about as much. Well, he began doing his tricks. He made a tree grow out of his left shoulder and dashed two rabbits out of his cuffs and balanced three eggs on his nose. A priest, standing in the crowd, began to laugh, and a priest laughing always makes me wring my hands with doubt. The other time was when Catherine the Great sent for me to bleed her. She took to the leech with rowdy Saxon abandon, saying: 'Let him drink; I've always wanted to be in two places at once!'"

"For Heaven's sake," the ex-priest said. "Remember your century at least!"

For a moment the doctor looked angry. "See here," he said, "don't interrupt me. The reason I'm so remarkable is that I remember everyone even when they are not about. It's the boys that look as innocent as the bottom of a plate that get you into trouble; not a man with a prehistoric memory."

"Women can cause trouble too," the ex-priest said lamely.

"That's another story," the doctor said. "What else has Jenny ever done, and what else has Robin ever done? And Nora, what's she done but cause it, by taking it in at night like a bird-coop? And I myself wish I'd never had a button up my middle—for what I've done and what I've not done all goes back to that—to be recognized, a gem should lie in a wide open field; but I'm all aglitter in the underbrush! If you don't want to suffer you should tear yourself apart. Were not the several parts of Caroline of Hapsburg put in three utterly obvious piles?—her heart in the Augustiner church, her intestines in St. Stefan's and what was left of the body in the vault of the Capucines? Saved by separation. But I'm all in one piece! Oh, the new moon!" he said. "When will she come riding?"

"Drunk and telling the world," someone said. The doctor heard, but he was too far gone to care, too muddled in his mind to argue, and already weeping.

"Come," the ex-priest said, "I'll take you home."

The doctor waved his arm. "Revenge is for those who have loved a little, for anything more than that justice is hardly enough. Some day I'm going to Lourdes and scramble into the front row and talk about all of you." His eyes were almost closed. He opened them and looked about him and a fury came over him. "Christ Almighty!" he said. "Why don't they let me alone, all of them?"

The ex-priest repeated, "Come, I'll take you home."

The doctor tried to rise. He was exceedingly drunk and now extremely angry all at once. His umbrella fell to the floor with the crash of a glass as he swung his arm upward against the helping hand. "Get out! Get out!" he said. "What a damnable year, what a bloody time! How did it happen, where did it come from?"

He began to scream with sobbing laughter. "Talking to me—all of them—sitting on me as heavy as a truck horse—talking! Love falling buttered side down, fate falling arse up! Why doesn't anyone know when everything is over, except me? That fool Nora, holding on by her teeth, going back to find Robin! And Felix—eternity is only just long enough for a Jew! But there's someone else—who was it, damn it all—who was it? I've known everyone," he said, "everyone!" He came down upon the table with all his weight, his arms spread, his head between them, his eyes wide open and crying, staring along the table where the ash blew and fluttered with his gasping breath. "For Christ's sweet sake!" he said, and his voice was a whisper. "Now that you have all heard what you wanted to hear, can't you let me loose now, let me go? I've not only lived my life for nothing, but I've told it for nothing—abominable among the filthy people—I know, it's all over, everything's over, and nobody knows it but me—drunk as a fiddler's bitch—lasted too long—" He tried to get to his feet and gave it up. "Now," he said, "the end—mark my words—now *nothing, but wrath and weeping!*"

WILFRED OWEN
1893-1918

Strange Meeting

It seemed that out of the battle I escaped
Down some profound dull tunnel, long since scooped
Through granites which titanic wars had groined.
Yet also there encumbered sleepers groaned,
Too fast in thought or death to be bestirred.
Then, as I probed them, one sprang up, and stared
With piteous recognition in fixed eyes,
Lifting distressful hands as if to bless.
And by his smile, I knew that sullen hall;
By his dead smile I knew I stood in Hell.
With a thousand fears that vision's face was grained;
Yet no blood reached there from the upper ground,
And no guns thumped, or down the flues made moan.
"Strange, friend," I said, "here is no cause to mourn."
"None," said the other, "save the undone years,
The hopelessness. Whatever hope is yours,
Was my life also; I went hunting wild
After the wildest beauty in the world,
Which lies not calm in eyes, or braided hair,
But mocks the steady running of the hour,
And if it grieves, grieves richlier than here.
For by my glee might many men have laughed,
And of my weeping something has been left,
Which must die now. I mean the truth untold,
The pity of war, the pity war distilled.
Now men will go content with what we spoiled,
Or, discontent, boil bloody, and be spilled.
They will be swift with swiftness of the tigress,
None will break ranks, though nations trek from progress.
Courage was mine, and I had mystery,
Wisdom was mine, and I had mastery;
To miss the march of this retreating world
Into vain citadels that are not walled.
Then when much blood had clogged their chariot-wheels
I would go up and wash them from sweet wells,
Even with truths that lie too deep for taint.
I would have poured my spirit without stint
But not through wounds; not on the cess of war.

Foreheads of men have bled where no wounds were.
I am the enemy you killed, my friend.
I knew you in this death; for so you frowned
Yesterday through me as you jabbed and killed.
I parried; but my hands were loath and cold.
Let us sleep now . . . ."

SAMUEL GREENBERG

1893-1917

The Tusks of Blood

My chant must enclose hell
And yet here leave behind
Myself of touch and vow;
My hour has come when gales—
The brief song of Greek—
Have found the inner teeth alone.
Here listen, someone is calling—
Why the ugly praise and fate?
Shall I be a joiner to this
And leave here the good hope?
Not to prank the lucky star
I'll apologize, wait until
The great way works for woe!
Woe? never, you Parsifal;
Never—and by the trait of love's
Light shell, sneering outpour.
Not to blame—wait, a travel
For an excuse; a good life lay
In the real actions, the pomped
Horn, and the pardons of a door.
What interfering, cloaked love rules
My thoughts!
Shall I write: O anger, hast thou
Not treated thy refuging forbear?
Perhaps I can walk a bit
To my truthful veins and relate
The sport of the steeds that trot
The stirring muscles of an earthly
Gait and my hearted glow.
O worm, worm-hearted soil,

Peal sad mereing folds
Where cometh a home afar;
And again a slow fainting ghost
Gliding over a path easily seen . . .
God! some voice disturbs me
From the inner room; and
Believe a she and aged she
Yet telling her moments, forbid
Another aged crankling noise
Sitting her defense of knowledge;
Knowledge, the last of God.
O no, I mean my own surprise,
Spoke the first, here left
In her virtue's returns—ended.
I catch the subject: Death!
Death, what a careless value
To such aged spirits. Again
A sad remark. Life not valued
By such retired souls, who
Should be apart to believe
Justice . . . Ah, man, not thy boast!
He was a marked lad
Who poorly helped himself.
What should this mean?
Fill your pockets—I'll let
You know the grass of a grave.
O the pillars of silk and good tea,
Confusion of women, the bare bust—
Embarrassment, carnal filth
Of its justice lacks environment;
O creaking earth, necessity; hell,
No more wise; than the next child—
What can he give?
You pallid stork, gazing—
Who gazed before you, cooled
The summer spray?
Very bad for an apartment Jew to claim
Everlasting renaissance.
What a delivery was this,
Sucked by secret gilded creatures
Who slew gold for a membrane!
O tear, sped into the basin
Of sparkling night aghast in silence,
And the pipes swift pain
Of the boiling steam shocks uplifting
You, endless wretch of silver!

Essence

The opera singer softly sang
Like the pellucid birds of Australian
Thicket. Anatomy's lace wrung
The cells of thousand feelings
And tastes, centigrade's power
Told climates revelations
The Psychologist felt the Heart
The poet's instinct slumber apart
Through the parks. The Forest
Filled the air of incense pure
The painter bent his brush
Through sensation's quest
Time weeps in patience duration
Through scepters create emotional resist.

The Philosophic Apology

I still bear in mind the picture of the globe
That palpitates in absorbed fear, in thought.
O sweltering dew, what chaos doth ruminate
Upon zone's firmament, what perfection in
Such listlessness, a rock of earth doth float;
Tempests' call to balance its fees,
Its unseen course through the infinite walls.
The virtue of the sulphur sun that shades
The night, that clears the heaven from reveries—
O Heavenly Father thou hast in plea
Mankind's thirsty juggle, to upheave its concept,
Who shares thy width of love and all
Whose palm holds the shadow of fear
That judgement soothes, thy dusty heart-speck's tear.

To Dear Daniel

There is a loud noise of death
Where I lay;
There is a loud noise of life
Far away.

From low and weary stride
Have I flown;

From low and weary pride
I have grown.

What does it matter now
To you or me?
What does it matter now
To whom it be?

Again the stain has come
To me;
Again the stain has come
For thee.

The Opponent Charm Sustained

Sweet thought—sweet model—that gloweth for all
    Attention that quivereth within heart's fluid wall,
How strange, such members seldom meet
    Like ripples in a gulf so deep

When holding hot green pebbles
    A burden that relieves the thought
'Tis genuine passion that warbles
    Where the amazing beauty is sought

How tiresome lines are beautiful
    How tiresome grace is charm
Wonderful seems the wrinkled brow
    When time—will mortal—bow,

Ah! there slumbers the ages
    Ah! there resteth thy kind
'Tis heavy burden to conceive thy corpse
    That is tinted with a cover sublime

We've been resting on thy scented spirit
    Were forcing to bind the ties
Ah! Mortals why art ye! raving
    Like the constant vanishing skies

But, now we retreat good Charm
    I feign to relate how warm
Thy Nature has cuddled me
    That pricks,—to renew its psalm.

               1913

HERBERT READ
1893-

A World within a War

L'espérance est le seul bien que le dégoût respecte.

VAUVENARGUES

I

Sixteen years ago I built this house
By an oak tree on an acre of wild land
Its walls white against the beechwood
Its roof of Norfolk reed and sedge.

The mossy turf I levelled for a lawn
But for the most part left the acre wild
Knowing I could never live
From its stony soil. My work is within
Between three stacks of books. My window
Looks out on a long line of elms.

A secular and insecure retreat—
The alien world is never far away.
Over the ridge, beyond the elms
The railway runs: a passing train
Sends a faint tremor through the ground
Enough to sever a rotted picture-cord
Or rattle the teaspoon against my cup.
A dozen times a day a red bus
Trundles down the lane: there is the screech and scuttle
Of minor traffic: voices rise
Suddenly from silent wheels.
But such dusty veins drain the land
And leave an interstitial stillness.

The hedgehog and the grass-snake
Still haunt my wood. Winter
Brings the starved wildings nearer: once
We woke to find a fox's tracks
Printed on the crisp film of snow.
It was the first year of my second war
When every night a maddened yaffle

Thrummed on the icicled thatch.
Another day a reckless kestrel
Dashed against a gable and fell
Dead at my feet: the children
Watched its dying flutter and the fiery eye
Slowly eclipsed under a dim grey lid.

For years the city like a stream of lava
Crept towards us: now its flow
Is frozen in fear. To the sere earth
The ancient ritual returns: the months
Have their heraldic labours once again.
A tractor chugs through frozen clods
And gold buds bead the gorse
In coppices where besom-heads are cut.
Hedges are trimmed again and primroses
Bunch in splendour on the open banks.
The sparring rooks pick twigs
For shockhead nests built high
In the dark tracery of the elms.
April and the nightingales will come
From an alien world. The squirrels
Chatter in the green hazel-trees.
The nuthatch inspects the oak's ribbed bark
While the robin jumps round his own domain.
The hay is mown in June. With summer
Comes all ripeness, rusty, red and gold
To die in September. The reaper
Spirals round the blanched fields
The corn diminishing until at last
The expected moment comes and rabbits
Zigzag across the glistening stubble
Pursued by yelping dogs and sudden guns.
In December the corn is thrashed:
In the frosty evening the engine's smoke
Trails slowly above the berried twigs
And meets the rising mist.

II

Sedate within this palisade
Which unforethinking I have made

Of brittle leaves and velvet flowers,
I re-indite a Book of Hours—

Would emulate the Lombard School
(Crisp as medals, bright but cool)

Talk mainly of the Human Passion
That made us in a conscious fashion

Strive to control our human fate:
But in the margins interpolate

Apes and angels playing tunes
On harpsichords or saxophones

Throughout the story thus maintain
Under a sacred melody the bass profane.

My saints were often silly men
Fond of wine and loose with women.

When they rose to holy stature
They kept the whims of human nature

Were mystics in their London gardens
Or wore instead of hairshirts burdens

Of a mild domestic sort: but so devout
That suddenly they would go out

And die for freedom in the street
Or fall like partridges before a butt

Of ambushed tyranny and hate.
Other legends will relate

The tale of men whose only love
Was simple work: whose usual lives

Were formed in mirth and music, or in words
Whose golden echoes are wild rewards

For all our suffering, unto death . . .

On the last page a colophon
Would conclude the liberal plan

Showing Man within a frame
Of trophies stolen from a dream.

III

The busy routine kills the flowers
That blossom only on the casual path.
The gift is sacrificed to gain: the gain
Is ploughed into the hungry ground.
The best of life is sparely spent
In contemplation of those laws
Illustrious in leaves, in tiny webs
Spun by the ground-spider: in snailshells
And mushroom gills: in acorns and gourds—
The design everywhere evident
The purpose still obscure.

　　　　　　　　　　In a free hour
I walk through the woods with God
When the air is calm and the midges
Hover in the netted sun and stillness.
Deep then I sink in reverie. There is rest
Above the beating heart: the body
Settles round its axis: mind simulates
The crystal in the cooling rock
The theorem in the beetle's eye—
After the day's mutations
Finds the silver node of sleep. . . .

In that peace
Mind looks into a mirror poised
Above body: sees in perspective
Guts, bones and glands: the make of a man.

Out of that labyrinth
The man emerges: becomes
What he is: by no grace
Can become other: can only seize
The pattern in the bone, in branching veins
In clever vesicles and valves
And imitate in acts that beauty.

His nature is God's nature: but torn
How torn and fretted by vain energies
The darting images of eye and ear
Veiled in the web of memory
Drifts of words that deaden
The subtle manuals of sense.

But the pattern once perceived and held
Is then viable: in good gait and going
In fine song and singular sign: in all
God's festival of perfect form.

IV

Here is my cell: here my houselings
Gentle in love, excelling hate, extending
Tokens of friendship to free hearts.

But well we know there is a world without
Of alarm and horror and extreme distress
Where pity is a bond of fear
And only the still heart has grace.

An ancient road winds through the wood
The wood is dark: a chancel where the mind
Sways in terror of the formal foe.

Their feet upon the peat and sand
Made no sound. But sounds were everywhere around
Life rustled under fallen leaves, rotted twigs
Snapped like rafters above the heads
Of those friars preachers, constant and firm,
Who in charity advanced against the Arian hate
Ambushed against them. See now
The falchion falls: the martyred limbs
Lie like trimmed branches on the ground.

     The ancient road winds through the wood
     A path obscure and frail.

     The martyr takes it and the man
     Who makes the martyr by his deed.

     Death waits on evil and on holiness
     Death waits in the leafy labyrinth.

     There is a grace to still the blood
     Of those who take the daring path:

There is a grace that fills the dying eye
With pity for the wielder of the axe.

There is a grace that nulls the pain
Of martyrs in their hour of death.

Death is no pain to desperate men.

Vision itself is desperate: the act
Is born of the ideal: the hand
Must seize the hovering grail.
Out of its stillness: a white light
Is in the hills and the thin cry
The sense of glory stirs the heart
Of a hunter's horn. We shall act: we shall build
A crystal city in the age of peace
Setting out from an island of calm
A limpid source of love.

V

The branches break. The beaters
Are moving in: lie still my loves
Like deer: let the lynx
Glide through the dappled underwoods.
Lie still: he cannot hear: he may not see.

Should the ravening death descend
We will be calm: die like the mouse
Terrified but tender. The claw
Will meet no satisfaction in our sweet flesh
And we shall have known peace

In a house beneath a beechwood
In an acre of wild land.

MARK VAN DOREN
1894-

The Tower

The greater world is water,
The lesser world is land.
Out of moving vastness
Promontories stand.
Out of undulation
Heaves the firm sand.

The flood of moments, flowing,
Bears desire away;
Returning unto wideness
Distributable clay.
But not the hill of reason,
The mind's high play.

The greater world is water;
This little world is rock.
Beneath it subterranean
Sinews interlock;
And round it, silent, silent,
Wheels the invisible flock.

Axle Song

That any thing should be—
Place, time, earth, error—
And a round eye in man to see:
That was the terror.

And a true mind to try
Cube, sphere, deep, short, and long:
That was the burden of the sky's
Hoarse axle song.

Improbable the stoat,
The mouse, toad, worm, wolf, tiger;
Unthinkable the stallion's trot,
Behemoth's swagger.

Unspeakable; yet worse—
Name, look, feel, memory, and number:
Man there with his perverse
Power not to slumber.

Let things created sleep:
Rock, beast, rain, sand, and sliding river.
So growled the earth's revolving heap;
And will forever.

This Amber Sunstream

This amber sunstream, with an hour to live,
Flows carelessly, and does not save itself;
Nor recognizes any entered room—
This room; not hears the clock upon a shelf,
Declaring the lone hour; for where it goes
All space in a great silence ever flows.

No living man may know it till this hour,
When the clear sunstream, thickening to amber,
Moves like a sea, and the sunk hulls of houses
Let it come slowly through, as divers clamber,
Feeling for gold. So now into this room
Peer the large eyes, unopen to their doom.

Another hour and nothing will be here.
Even upon themselves the eyes will close.
Nor will this bulk, withdrawing, die outdoors
In night, that from another silence flows.
No living man in any western room
But sits at amber sunset round a tomb.

Young Woman at a Window

Who so valiant to decide?
Who so prompt and proper-active?
Yet each muscle in her brain
Relaxes now; is unrestrictive;
Lets her lean upon this dark
November night wind; lets it work—

Oh, lets it ask her if she thinks,
Oh, lets it whisper if she knows

How much of time is like a stream
Down which her headless body flows;
How many answers, proudly made,
Will be like minnows overlaid

With inch on inch of glossy black,
With depth on depth of sliding water;
Lets it dare her to predict
Those floods of silence coming later;
Till she melts, and leaning long
Is only conscious of wind-song.

Who so valorous of voice?
Who so staunch upon the ground?
But wind-and-water-song at work
Stops both her ears against the sound
Of some here she used to know;
Of someone saying: It is so.

She leans and loses every word.
Her loudest wisdom well is gone.
But still the current of the night
Comes with its foaming on and on;
Pours round the sill; dissolves the hands;
And still the dreamless body stands.

E. E. CUMMINGS
1894-

"no man, if men are gods"

no man,if men are gods;but if gods must
be men,the sometimes only man is this
(most common,for each anguish is his grief;
and,for his joy is more than joy,most rare)

a fiend,if fiends speak truth;ifangels burn

by their own generous completely light,
an angel;or(as various worlds he'll spurn
rather than fail immeasurable fate)
coward,clown,traitor,idiot,dreamer,beast—

such was a poet and shall be and is

—who'll solve the depths of horror to defend
a sunbeam's architecture with his life:
and carve immortal jungles of despair
to hold a mountain's heartbeat in his hand

"what if a much of a which of a wind"

what if a much of a which of a wind
gives the truth to summer's lie;
bloodies with dizzying leaves the sun
and yanks immortal stars awry?
Blow king to beggar and queen to seem
(blow friend to fiend;blow space to time)
—when skies are hanged and oceans drowned,
the single secret will still be man

what if a keen of a lean wind flays
screaming hills with sleet and snow:
strangles valleys by ropes of thing
and stifles forests in white ago?
Blow hope to terror;blow seeing to blind
(blow pity to envy and soul to mind)
—whose hearts are mountains, roots are trees,
it's they shall cry hello to the spring

what if a dawn of a doom of a dream
bites this universe in two,
peels forever out of his grave
and sprinkles nowhere with me and you?
Blow soon to never and never to twice
(blow life to isn't:blow death to was)
—all nothing's only our hugest home;
the most who die,the more we live

"my father moved through dooms of love"

my father moved through dooms of love
through sames of am through haves of give,
singing each morning out of each night
my father moved through depths of height

this motionless forgetful where
turned at his glance to shining here;

that if (so timid air is firm)
under his eyes would stir and squirm

newly as from unburied which
floats the first who, his april touch
drove sleeping selves to swarm their fates
woke dreamers to their ghostly roots

and should some why completely weep
my father's fingers brought her sleep:
vainly no smallest voice might cry
for he could feel the mountains grow.

Lifting the valleys of the sea
my father moved through griefs of joy;
praising a forehead called the moon
singing desire into begin

joy was his song and joy so pure
a heart of star by him could steer
and pure so now and now so yes
the wrists of twilight would rejoice

keen as midsummer's keen beyond
conceiving mind of sun will stand,
so strictly (over utmost him
so hugely) stood my father's dream

his flesh was flesh his blood was blood:
no hungry man but wished him food;
no cripple wouldn't creep one mile
uphill to only see him smile.

Scorning the pomp of must and shall
my father moved through dooms of feel;
his anger was as right as rain
his pity was as green as grain

septembering arms of year extend
less humbly wealth to foe and friend
than he to foolish and to wise
offered immeasurable is

proudly and (by octobering flame
beckoned) as earth will downward climb,

so naked for immortal work
his shoulders marched against the dark

his sorrow was as true as bread:
no liar looked him in the head;
if every friend became his foe
he'd laugh and build a world with snow.

My father moved through theys of we,
singing each new leaf out of each tree
(and every child was sure that spring
danced when she heard my father sing)

then let men kill which cannot share,
let blood and flesh be mud and mire,
scheming imagine, passion willed,
freedom a drug that's bought and sold

giving to steal and cruel kind,
a heart to fear, to doubt a mind,
to differ a disease of same,
conform the pinnacle of am

though dull were all we taste as bright,
bitter all utterly things sweet,
maggoty minus and dumb death
all we inherit, all bequeath

and nothing quite so least as truth
—i say though hate were why men breathe—
because my father lived his soul
love is the whole and more than all

"anyone lived in a pretty how town"

anyone lived in a pretty how town
(with up so floating many bells down)
spring summer autumn winter
he sang his didn't he danced his did.

Women and men (both little and small)
cared for anyone not at all
they sowed their isn't they reaped their same
sun moon stars rain

children guessed (but only a few
and down they forgot as up they grew
autumn winter spring summer)
that noone loved him more by more

when by now and tree by leaf
she laughed his joy she cried his grief
bird by snow and stir by still
anyone's any was all to her

someones married their everyones
laughed their cryings and did their dance
(sleep wake hope and then) they
said their nevers they slept their dream

stars rain sun moon
(and only the snow can begin to explain
how children are apt to forget to remember
with up so floating many bells down)

one day anyone died i guess
(and noone stooped to kiss his face)
busy folk buried them side by side
little by little and was by was

all by all and deep by deep
and more by more they dream their sleep
noone and anyone earth by april
wish by spirit and if by yes.

Women and men (both dong and ding)
summer autumn winter spring
reaped their sowing and went their came
sun moon stars rain

"somewhere i have never travelled"

somewhere i have never travelled, gladly beyond
any experience, your eyes have their silence:
in your most frail gesture are things which enclose me,
or which i cannot touch because they are too near

your slightest look easily will unclose me
though i have closed myself as fingers,
you open always petal by petal myself as Spring opens
(touching skilfully, mysteriously) her first rose

or if your wish be to close me, i and
my life will shut very beautifully, suddenly,
as when the heart of this flower imagines
the snow carefully everywhere descending;

nothing which we are to perceive in this world equals
the power of your intense fragility: whose texture
compels me with the colour of its countries,
rendering death and forever with each breathing

(i do not know what it is about you that closes
and opens; only something in me understands
the voice of your eyes is deeper than all roses)
nobody, not even the rain, has such small hands

ROBERT GRAVES
1895-

To Juan at the Winter Solstice

There is one story and one story only
That will prove worth your telling,
Whether as learned bard or gifted child;
To it all lines or lesser gauds belong
That startle with their shining
Such common stories as they stray into.

Is it of trees you tell, their months and virtues,
Of strange beasts that beset you,
Of birds that croak at you the Triple will?
Or of the Zodiac and how slow it turns
Below the Boreal Crown,
Prison of all true kings that ever reigned?

Water to water, ark again to ark,
From woman back to woman:
So each new victim treads unfalteringly
The never altered circuit of his fate,
Bringing twelve peers as witness
Both to his starry rise and starry fall.

Or is it of the Virgin's silver beauty,
All fish below the thighs?

She in her left hand bears a leafy quince;
When with her right she crooks a finger, smiling,
How may the King hold back?
Royally then he barters life for love.

Or of undying snake from chaos hatched,
Whose coils contain the ocean,
Into whose chops with naked sword he springs,
Then in black water, tangled by the reeds,
Battles three days and nights,
To be spewed up beside her scalloped shore?

Much snow is falling, winds roar hollowly,
The owl hoots from the elder,
Fear in your heart cries to the loving-cup:
Sorrow to sorrow as the sparks fly upward.
The log groans and confesses
There is one story and one story only.

Dwell on her graciousness, dwell on her smiling,
Do not forget what flowers
The great boar trampled down in ivy time.
Her brow was creamy as the long ninth wave,
Her sea-blue eyes were wild
But nothing promised that is not performed.

The Worms of History

On the eighth day God died: his bearded mouth
That had been shut so long flew open.
So Adam's too in a dismay like death—
But the world still rolled on around him,
Instinct with all those lesser powers of life
That God had groaned against but not annulled.

"All-excellent," Adam had titled God,
And in his mourning now demeaned himself
As if all excellence, not God, had died;
Chose to be governed by those lesser powers,
More than inferior to excellence—
The worms astir in God's corrupt flesh.
God died, not excellence his name:
Excellence lived but only was not God.
It was those lesser powers who played at God,
Bloated with Adam's deferential sighs

Which were his mourning for divinity:
They reigned as royal monsters upon earth.

Adam grew lean, and wore perpetual black;
He made no reaching after excellence.
Eve gave him sorry comfort for his grief
With birth of sons, and mourning still he died.
Adam was buried in one grave with God
And the worms ranged and ravaged in between.

Into their white maws fell abundance
Of all things rotten. They were greedy-nosed
To smell the taint out and go scavenging,
Yet over excellence held no domain.
Excellence lives; they are already dead—
The ages of a putrefying corpse.

Sea Side

Into a gentle wildness and confusion,
Of here and there, of one and everyone,
Of windy sandhills by an unkempt sea,
Came two and two in search of symmetry,
Found symmetry of two in sea and sand,
In left foot, right foot, left hand and right hand.

The beast with two backs is a single beast,
Yet by his love of singleness increased
To two and two and two and two again,
Until, instead of sandhills, is a plain
Patterned in two and two, by two and two—
And the sea parts in horror at a view
Of rows of houses coupling, back to back,
While love smokes from the common chimney-stack
With two-four-eight-sixteenish single same
Re-registration of the duple name.

Pure Death

We looked, we loved, and therewith instantly
Death became terrible to you and me.
By love we disenthralled our natural terror
Of every comfortable philosopher

Or tall, grey doctor of divinity:
Death stood at last in his true rank and order.

It happened soon, so wild of heart were we,
Exchange of gifts grew to a malady:
Their worth rose always higher on each side
Till there seemed nothing but ungivable pride
That yet remained ungiven, and this degree
Called a conclusion not to be denied.

Then we at last bethought ourselves, made shift
And simultaneously this final gift
Gave: each with shaking hands unlocks
The sinister, long, brass-bound coffin-box,
Unwraps pure death, with such bewilderment
As greeted our love's first accomplishment.

LOUISE BOGAN

1897-

"Henceforth, from the Mind"

Henceforth, from the mind,
For your whole joy, must spring
Such joy as you may find
In any earthly thing,
And every time and place
Will take your thought for grace.

Henceforth, from the tongue,
From shallow speech alone,
Comes joy you thought, when young,
Would wring you to the bone,
Would pierce you to the heart
And spoil its stop and start.

Henceforward, from the shell,
Wherein you heard, and wondered
At oceans like a bell
So far from ocean sundered—
A smothered sound that sleeps
Long lost within lost deeps,

Will chime you change and hours,
The shadow of increase,
Will sound you flowers
Born under troubled peace—
Henceforth, henceforth
Will echo sea and earth.

The Mark

Where should he seek, to go away
That shadow will not point him down?
The spear of dark in the strong day
Beyond the upright body thrown,
Marking no epoch but its own.

Loosed only when, at noon and night,
The body is the shadow's prison.
The pivot swings into the light;
The center left, the shadow risen
To range out into time's long treason.

Stand pinned to sight, while now, unbidden,
The apple loosens, not at call,
Falls to the field, and lies there hidden,—
Another and another fall
And lie there hidden, in spite of all

The diagram of whirling shade,
The visible, that thinks to spin
Forever webs that time has made
Though momently time wears them thin
And all at length are gathered in.

Medusa

I had come to the house, in a cave of trees,
Facing a sheer sky.
Everything moved,—a bell hung ready to strike,
Sun and reflection wheeled by.

When the bare eyes were before me
And the hissing hair,
Held up at a window, seen through a door.

The stiff bald eyes, the serpents on the forehead
Formed in the air.

This is a dead scene forever now.
Nothing will ever stir.
The end will never brighten it more than this,
Nor the rain blur.

The water will always fall, and will not fall,
And the tipped bell make no sound.
The grass will always be growing for hay
Deep on the ground.

And I shall stand here like a shadow
Under the great balanced day,
My eyes on the yellow dust, that was lifted in the wind,
And does not drift away.

JOHN WHEELWRIGHT

1897-1940

Ave Eva

Wild strawberries, gooseberries, trampled;
sweet single roses torn; I hoofed to a ground
where a woman sat, weeping over a wounded bird.
"O silent woman, weeping without tears;
"O weeping woman, silent on this ground
"more withered than the barren; may I not help you heal
"the suffering of this wounded bird?" I said.

"But let your hand first mend the axle of this wheel,
"O scarlet-handed, azure-eyed," she answered.
"Let your eyes find the balance of these scales
"fashioned from two of my sons' brain-pans."

"Woman with scale and wheel and wounded bird
"more disconsolate than a child with broken toys;
"first, I beseech you, uncripple this wounded bird
"whose sufferings give to the mute universe
"measure of its own pain." With no reply
the frightened woman, more frightened, for an answer

dropped her frightened eyes to the unanswering
eyes of a third skull between her feet. Then I commanded:

"Get up. There are more skulls hid than the three
"skulls seen. Get going on your business!"
"You flaxen-faced and purple-lipped!" she cried,
"My business is to gather up my strength;
"my purpose is to mend the axle and the hub;
"and my intent, to find the balance of the scale."

"And . . . were the balance trued, were Adam's
"dust, which was your dearest flesh and blood,
"sifted over Abel's hunger-murdered eyes,—
"should the scale tip; my apposite pan
"I would then load with the bones of the warring hordes
"of goodly Abel's brothers, Cain and Seth . . .
"Leave your gray ground, Eve, go along with me."

"Satan," she said, "when my car moves I move.
"And the bird will fly. Its flight will heal its wing.
"I, and my best sons, Cain and Seth, require
"them who wish the bird healed mend my car.
"The bird cannot be healed except by flight.
"And when I move and my car mows the roses,
"let dust and bone mold and slowly close
"Abel's insatiate, unanswering eyes,—
"you azure-eyed, you flaxen-faced, purple-lipped and scarlet-handed!
"The bird will fly. Its flight will heal its wing."

Then I departed as I came, tearing roses
and trampling the gooseberries and the strawberries.

Train Ride

After rain, through afterglow, the unfolding fan
of railway landscape sidled on the pivot
of a larger arc into the green of evening;
I remembered that noon I saw a gradual bud
still white; though dead in its warm bloom;
always the enemy is the foe at home.
And I wondered what surgery could recover
our lost, long stride of indolence and leisure
which is labor in reverse; what physic recalls the smile

not of lips, but of eyes as of the sea bemused.

We, when we disperse from common sleep to several
tasks, we gather to despair; we, who assembled
once for hopes from common toil to dreams
or sickish and hurting or triumphal rapture;
always the enemy is our foe at home.

We, deafened with far scattered city rattles
to the hubbub of forest birds (never having
"had time" to grieve or to hear through vivid sleep
the sea knock on its cracked and hollow stones)
so that the stars, almost, and birds comply,
and the garden-wet; the trees retire; We are
a scared patrol, fearing the guns behind;
always the enemy is the foe at home.

What wonder that we fear our own eyes' look
and fidget to be at home alone, and pitifully
put off age by some change in brushing the hair
and stumble to our ends like smothered runners at their tape;

Then (as while the stars herd to the great trough
the blind, in the always-only-outward of their dismantled
archways, awake at the smell of warmed stone
or to the sound of reeds, lifting from the dim
into their segment of green dawn) *always
our enemy is our foe at home,* more
certainly than through spoken words or from grief-
twisted writing on paper, unblotted by tears
the thought came:

There is no physic
for the world's ill, nor surgery; it must
(hot smell of tar on wet salt air)
burn in a fever forever, an incense pierced
with arrows, whose name is Love and another name
Rebellion (the twinge, the gulf, split seconds,
the very raindrop, render, and instancy
of Love).

All Poetry to this not-to-be-looked-upon sun
of Passion is the moon's cupped light; all
Politics to this moon, a moon's reflected
cupped light, like the moon of Rome, after
the deep wells of Grecian light sank low;
always the enemy is the foe at home.

But these three are friends whose arms twine
without words; as, in a still air,
the great grove leans to wind, past and to come.

HORACE GREGORY
1898-

The Woman Who Disapproved of Music at the Bar

We heard her speaking of Chinese musicians,
And of the house she sold in Westchester;
She said that she could not live there forever
Waiting for things to happen in her mind
Until Martinis entered on a tray,
Or the door-bell rang, or footsteps on the stair
When one was sure the musicians had returned—
Better to live without doctors, lawyers, friends,
Even relatives might ask too many questions,
Better to sell everything and move away.
"If I could have said, 'Musicians are gentlemen:
They have asked permission
To rehearse *Persephone* on the front lawn,
Their viols and brasses
Are heard discreetly as the cries, the laughter,
Bird-song and weeping
Of a lonely child who wanders underground,
Her grief, the shadowy spray of maidenhair,
Her joy, the violet in April grasses,'
I could have hired them to play for guests at dinner,
Their music served with sherbets, iced Chianti,
Tinkling behind a plaster cast of Dante,
Echoes, farewells, Stravinsky quieted
Among white roses in a vase,
Trembling between the stems of stained wine glasses."

"It would have been difficult for me to prove
That they were Chinese;
They had come at night, I turned my face away
To the darkness of the wall beside my bed.
I knew that they were there, quiet as one knows
That death is in a room, or birth, or love,
Wailing and sighing;
I heard them play
Such music that is heard among the trees,
The sightless music, gong and waterfall,
And I knew that there were faces in the room,
The stone-carved smiling lips and empty eyes

Until I said like someone in a dream,
'I have locked the door: you cannot use my body
As though it were a room in a hotel—
You must let me sleep—
Even if you kill me, the police will come:
There will be blood upon the floor,
A broken chair, torn sheets and foot-prints in the garden,
And no one shall escape.' "

"If they had promised
Not to return, I would have stayed,
Have looked each neighbor in the eye and said,
'I have not lied:
There were twenty men among the hollyhocks,
Among sweet peas and oleanders,
And at twelve o'clock they came into my room,
Bare-footed, in rags and smelling of the East
As though the earth had opened where they walked.
I was careful not to let them know my name;
I am not responsible for what you may have heard.' "

When the woman left us, one could not have known
That two weeks later
She would actually disappear,
The phone disconnected, the top-flight suite for rent,
That perhaps the musicians had returned,
Even in the city:
One could not prove that they had followed her.

HART CRANE
1899-1932

The Broken Tower

The bell-rope that gathers God at dawn
Dispatches me as though I dropped down the knell
Of a spent day—to wander the cathedral lawn
From pit to crucifix, feet chill on steps from hell.

Have you not heard, have you not seen that corps
Of shadows in the tower, whose shoulders sway

Antiphonal carillons launched before
The stars are caught and hived in the sun's ray?

The bells, I say, the bells break down their tower;
And swing I know not where. Their tongues engrave
Membrane through marrow, my long-scattered score
Of broken intervals. . . . And I, their sexton slave!

Oval encyclicals in canyons heaping
The impasse high with choir. Banked voices slain!
Pagodas, campaniles with reveilles outleaping—
O terraced echoes prostrate on the plain! . . .

And so it was I entered the broken world
To trace the visionary company of love, its voice
An instant in the wind (I know not whither hurled)
But not for long to hold each desperate choice.

My word I poured. But was it cognate, scored
Of that tribunal monarch of the air
Whose thigh embronzes earth, strikes crystal Word
In wounds pledged once to hope—cleft to despair?

The steep encroachments of my blood left me
No answer (could blood hold such a lofty tower
As flings the question true?)—or is it she
Whose sweet mortality stirs latent power?—

And through whose pulse I hear, counting the strokes
My veins recall and add, revived and sure
The angelus of wars my chest evokes:
What I hold healed, original now, and pure . . .

And builds, within, a tower that is not stone
(Not stone can jacket heaven)—but slip
Of pebbles—visible wings of silence sown
In azure circles, widening as they dip

The matrix of the heart, lift down the eye
That shrines the quiet lake and swells a tower . . .
The commodious, tall decorum of that sky
Unseals her earth, and lifts love in its shower.

O Carib Isle!

The tarantula rattling at the lily's foot
Across the feet of the dead, laid in white sand
Near the coral beach—nor zigzag fiddler crabs
Side-stilting from the path (that shift, subvert
And anagrammatize your name)—No, nothing here
Below the palsy that one eucalyptus lifts
In wrinkled shadows—mourns.

                       And yet suppose
I count these nacreous frames of tropic death,
Brutal necklaces of shells around each grave
Squared off so carefully. Then

To the white sand I may speak a name, fertile
Albeit in a stranger tongue. Tree names, flower names
Deliberate, gainsay death's brittle crypt. Meanwhile
The wind that knots itself in one great death—
Coils and withdraws. So syllables want breath.

But where is the Captain of the doubloon isle
Without a turnstile? Who but catchword crabs
Patrols the dry groins of the underbrush?
What man, or What
Is Commissioner of the mildew throughout the ambushed
      senses?
His Carib mathematics web the eyes' baked lenses!

Under the poinciana, of a noon or afternoon
Let fiery blossoms clot the light, render my ghost
Sieved upward, white and black along the air
Until it meets the blue's comedian host.

Let not the pilgrim see himself again
For slow evisceration bound like those huge terrapin
Each daybreak on the wharf, their brine-caked eyes;
—Spiked, overturned; such thunder in their strain!

Slagged on the hurricane—I, cast within its flow,
Congeal by afternoons here, satin and vacant.
You have given me the shell, Satan,—carbonic amulet
Sere of the sun exploded in the sea.

from
The Bridge
TO BROOKLYN BRIDGE

How many dawns, chill from his rippling rest
The seagull's wings shall dip and pivot him,
Shedding white rings of tumult, building high
Over the chained bay waters Liberty—

Then, with inviolate curve, forsake our eyes
As apparitional as sails that cross
Some page of figures to be filed away;
—Till elevators drop us from our day . . .

I think of cinemas, panoramic sleights
With multitudes bent toward some flashing scene
Never disclosed, but hastened to again,
Foretold to other eyes on the same screen;

And Thee, across the harbor, silver-paced
As though the sun took step of thee, yet left
Some motion ever unspent in thy stride,—
Implicitly thy freedom staying thee!

Out of some subway scuttle, cell or loft
A bedlamite speeds to thy parapets,
Tilting there momently, shrill shirt ballooning,
A jest falls from the speechless caravan.

Down Wall, from girder into street noon leaks,
A rip-tooth of the sky's acetylene;
All afternoon the cloud-flown derricks turn . . .
Thy cables breathe the North Atlantic still.

And obscure as that heaven of the Jews,
Thy guerdon . . . Accolade thou dost bestow
Of anonymity time cannot raise:
Vibrant reprieve and pardon thou dost show.

O harp and altar, of the fury fused,
(How could mere toil align thy choiring strings!)
Terrific threshold of the prophet's pledge,
Prayer of pariah, and the lover's cry,—

Again the traffic lights that skim thy swift
Unfractioned idiom, immaculate sigh of stars,
Beading thy path—condense eternity:
And we have seen night lifted in thine arms.

Under thy shadow by the piers I waited;
Only in darkness is thy shadow clear.
The City's fiery parcels all undone,
Already snow submerges an iron year . . .

O Sleepless as the river under thee,
Vaulting the sea, the prairies' dreaming sod,
Unto us lowliest sometime sweep, descend
And of the curveship lend a myth to God.

AVE MARIA

Venient annis sæcula seris,
Quibus Oceanus vincula rerum
Laxet et ingens pateat tellus
Tethysque novos detegat orbes
Nec sit terris ultima Thule.
                                    SENECA

Be with me, Luis de San Angel, now—
Witness before the tides can wrest away
The word I bring, O you who reined my suit
Into the Queen's great heart that doubtful day;
For I have seen now what no perjured breath
Of clown nor sage can riddle or gainsay;—
To you, too, Juan Perez, whose counsel fear
And greed adjourned,—I bring you back Cathay!

Columbus, alone,
gazing toward
Spain, invokes the
presence of two
faithful partisans of
his quest . . .

Here waves climb into dusk on gleaming mail;
Invisible valves of the sea,—locks, tendons
Crested and creeping, troughing corridors
That fall back yawning to another plunge.
Slowly the sun's red caravel drops light
Once more behind us. . . . It is morning there—
O where our Indian emperies lie revealed,
Yet lost, all, let this keel one instant yield!

I thought of Genoa; and this truth, now proved,
That made me exile in her streets, stood me
More absolute than ever—biding the moon

Till dawn should clear that dim frontier, first seen
—The Chan's great continent. . . . Then faith, not fear
Nigh surged me witless. . . . Hearing the surf near—
I, wonder-breathing, kept the watch,—saw
The first palm chevron the first lighted hill.

And lowered. And they came out to us crying,
"The Great White Birds!" (O Madre Maria, still
One ship of these thou grantest safe returning;
Assure us through thy mantle's ageless blue!)
And record of more, floating in a cask,
Was tumbled from us under bare poles scudding;
And later hurricanes may claim more pawn. . . .
For here between two worlds, another, harsh,

This third, of water, tests the word; lo, here
Bewilderment and mutiny heap whelming
Laughter, and shadow cuts sleep from the heart
Almost as though the Moor's flung scimitar
Found more than flesh to fathom in its fall.
Yet under tempest-lash and surfeitings
Some inmost sob, half-heard, dissuades the abyss,
Merges the wind in measure to the waves,

Series on series, infinite,—till eyes
Starved wide on blackened tides, accrete—enclose
This turning rondure whole, this crescent ring
Sun-cusped and zoned with modulated fire
Like pearls that whisper through the Doge's hands
—Yet no delirium of jewels! O Fernando,
Take of that eastern shore, this western sea,
Yet yield thy God's, thy Virgin's charity!

—Rush down the plenitude, and you shall see
Isaiah counting famine on this lee!

*

An herb, a stray branch among salty teeth,
The jellied weeds that drag the shore,—perhaps
Tomorrow's moon will grant us Saltes Bar—
Palos again,—a land cleared of long war.
Some Angelus environs the cordage tree;
Dark waters onward shake the dark prow free.

*

O Thou who sleepest on Thyself, apart
Like ocean athwart lanes of death and birth,
And all the eddying breath between dost search
Cruelly with love thy parable of man,—
Inquisitor! incognizable Word
Of Eden and the enchained Sepulchre,
Into thy steep savannahs, burning blue,
Utter to loneliness the sail is true.

Who grindest oar, and arguing the mast
Subscribest holocaust of ships, O Thou
Within whose primal scan consummately
The glistening seignories of Ganges swim;—
Who sendest greeting by the corposant,
And Teneriffe's garnet—flamed it in a cloud,
Urging through night our passage to the Chan;—
Te Deum laudamus, for thy teeming span!

Of all that amplitude that time explores,
A needle in the sight, suspended north,—
Yielding by inference and discard, faith
And true appointment from the hidden shoal:
This disposition that thy night relates
From Moon to Saturn in one sapphire wheel:
The orbic wake of thy once whirling feet,
Elohim, still I hear thy sounding heel!

White toil of heaven's cordons, mustering
In holy rings all sails charged to the far
Hushed gleaming fields and pendant seething wheat
Of knowledge,—round thy brows unhooded now
—The kindled Crown! acceded of the poles
And biassed by full sails, meridians reel
Thy purpose—still one shore beyond desire!
The sea's green crying towers a-sway, Beyond

And kingdoms
                    naked in the
                              trembling heart—
        Te Deum laudamus
                              O Thou Hand of Fire

THE HARBOR DAWN

Insistently through sleep—a tide of voices—
They meet you listening midway in your dream,
The long, tired sounds, fog-insulated noises:
Gongs in white surplices, beshrouded wails,
Far strum of fog horns . . . signals dispersed in veils.

*400 years and more
. . . or is it from
the soundless shore
of sleep that time*

And then a truck will lumber past the wharves
As winch engines begin throbbing on some deck;
Or a drunken stevedore's howl and thud below
Comes echoing alley-upward through dim snow.

And if they take your sleep away sometimes
They give it back again. Soft sleeves of sound
Attend the darkling harbor, the pillowed bay;
Somewhere out there in blankness steam

Spills into steam, and wanders, washed away
—Flurried by keen fifings, eddied
Among distant chiming buoys—adrift. The sky,
Cool feathery fold, suspends, distills
This wavering slumber. . . . Slowly—
Immemorially the window, the half-covered chair,
Ask nothing but this sheath of pallid air.

And you beside me, blessèd now while sirens
Sing to us, stealthily weave us into day—
Serenely now, before day claims our eyes
Your cool arms murmurously about me lay.

*recalls you to your
love, there in a
waking dream to
merge your seed*

While myriad snowy hands are clustering at the panes—

> *your hands within my hands are deeds;*
> *my tongue upon your throat—singing*
> *arms close; eyes wide, undoubtful*
> > *dark*
> > > *drink the dawn—*
> *a forest shudders in your hair!*

The window goes blond slowly. Frostily clears.
From Cyclopean towers across Manhattan waters
—Two—three bright window-eyes aglitter, disk
The sun, released—aloft with cold gulls hither.

—with whom?

The fog leans one last moment on the sill.
Under the mistletoe of dreams, a star—
As though to join us at some distant hill—
Turns in the waking west and goes to sleep.

Who is the woman
with us in the
dawn? . . . whose
is the flesh our feet
have moved upon?

ATLANTIS

Music is then the knowledge of that which
relates to love in harmony and system.
                                          PLATO

Through the bound cable strands, the arching path
Upward, veering with light, the flight of strings,—
Taut miles of shuttling moonlight syncopate
The whispered rush, telepathy of wires.
Up the index of night, granite and steel—
Transparent meshes—fleckless the gleaming staves—
Sybilline voices flicker, waveringly stream
As though a god were issue of the strings. . . .

And through that cordage, threading with its call
One arc synoptic of all tides below—
Their labyrinthine mouths of history
Pouring reply as though all ships at sea
Complighted in one vibrant breath made cry,—
"Make thy love sure—to weave whose song we ply!"
—From black embankments, moveless soundings hailed,
So seven oceans answer from their dream.

And on, obliquely up bright carrier bars
New octaves trestle the twin monoliths
Beyond whose frosted capes the moon bequeaths
Two worlds of sleep (O arching strands of song!)—
Onward and up the crystal-flooded aisle
White tempest nets file upward, upward ring
With silver terraces the humming spars,
The loft of vision, palladium helm of stars.

Sheerly the eyes, like seagulls stung with rime—
Slit and propelled by glistening fins of light—
Pick biting way up towering looms that press
Sidelong with flight of blade on tendon blade
—Tomorrows into yesteryear—and link
What cipher-script of time no traveller reads

But who, through smoking pyres of love and death,
Searches the timeless laugh of mythic spears.

Like hails, farewells—up planet-sequined heights
Some trillion whispering hammers glimmer Tyre:
Serenely, sharply up the long anvil cry
Of inchling æons silence rivets Troy.
And you, aloft there—Jason! hesting Shout!
Still wrapping harness to the swarming air!
Silvery the rushing wake, surpassing call,
Beams yelling Æolus! splintered in the straits!

From gulfs unfolding, terrible of drums,
Tall Vision-of-the-Voyage, tensely spare—
Bridge, lifting night to cycloramic crest
Of deepest day—O Choir, translating time
Into what multitudinous Verb the suns
And synergy of waters ever fuse, recast
In myriad syllables,—Psalm of Cathay!
O Love, they white, pervasive Paradigm...!

We left the haven hanging in the night—
Sheened harbor lanterns backward fled the keel.
Pacific here at time's end, bearing corn,—
Eyes stammer through the pangs of dust and steel.
And still the circular, indubitable frieze
Of heaven's meditation, yoking wave
To kneeling wave, one song devoutly binds—
The vernal strophe chimes from deathless strings!

O Thou steeled Cognizance whose leap commits
The agile precincts of the lark's return;
Within whose lariat sweep encinctured sing
In single chrysalis the many twain,—
Of stars Thou are the stitch and stallion glow
And like an organ, Thou, with sound of doom—
Sight, sound and flesh Thou leadest from time's realm
As love strikes clear direction for the helm.

Swift peal of secular light, intrinsic Myth
Whose fell unshadow is death's utter wound,—
O River-throated—iridescently upborne
Through the bright drench and fabric of our viens;
With white escarpments swinging into light,
Sustained in tears the cities are endowed
And justified conclamant with ripe fields
Revolving through their harvests in sweet torment.

Forever Deity's glittering Pledge, O Thou
Whose canticle fresh chemistry assigns
To rapt inception and beatitude,—
Always through blinding cables, to our joy,
Of thy white seizure springs the prophecy:
Always through spiring cordage, pyramids
Of silver sequel, Deity's young name
Kinetic of white choiring wings . . . ascends.

Migrations that must needs void memory,
Inventions that cobblestone the heart,—
Unspeakable Thou Bridge to Thee, O Love.
Thy pardon for this history, whitest Flower,
O Answerer of all,—Anemone,—
Now while thy petals spend the suns about us, hold—
(O Thou whose radiance doth inherit me)
Atlantis,—hold thy floating singer late!

So to thine Everpresence, beyond time,
Like spears ensanguined of one tolling star
That bleeds infinity—the orphic strings,
Sidereal phalanxes, leap and converge:
—One Song, one Bridge of Fire! Is it Cathay,
Now pity steeps the grass and rainbows ring
The serpent with the eagle in the leaves. . . ?
Whispers antiphonal in azure swing.

from

Voyages

II

And yet this great wink of eternity,
Of rimless floods, unfettered leewardings,
Samite sheeted and processioned where
Her undinal vast belly moonward bends,
Laughing the wrapt inflections of our love;

Take this Sea, whose diapason knells
On scrolls of silver snowy sentences,
The sceptred terror of whose sessions rends
As her demeanors motion well or ill,
All but the pieties of lovers' hands.

And onward, as bells off San Salvador
Salute the crocus lustres of the stars,

In these poinsettia meadows of her tides,—
Adagios of islands, O my Prodigal,
Complete the dark confessions her veins spell.

Mark how her turning shoulders wind the hours,
And hasten while her penniless rich palms
Pass superscription of bent foam and wave,—
Hasten, while they are true,—sleep, death, desire,
Close round one instant in one floating flower.

Bind us in time, O Seasons clear, and awe.
O minstrel galleons of Carib fire,
Bequeath us to no earthly shore until
Is answered in the vortex of our grave
The seal's wide spindrift gaze toward paradise.

III

Infinite consanguinity it bears—
This tendered theme of you that light
Retrieves from sea plains where the sky
Resigns a breast that every wave enthrones;
While ribboned water lanes I wind
Are laved and scattered with no stroke
Wide from your side, whereto this hour
The sea lifts, also, reliquary hands.

And so, admitted through black swollen gates
That must arrest all distance otherwise,—
Past whirling pillars and lithe pediments,
Light wrestling there incessantly with light,
Star kissing star through wave on wave unto
Your body rocking!
                    and where death, if shed,
Presumes no carnage, but this single change,—
Upon the steep floor flung from dawn to dawn
The silken skilled transmemberment of song;

Permit me voyage, love, into your hands . . .

V

Meticulous, past midnight in clear rime,
Infrangible and lonely, smooth as though cast
Together in one merciless white blade—
The bay estuaries fleck the hard sky limits.

—As if too brittle or too clear to touch!
The cables of our sleep so swiftly filed,
Already hang, shred ends from remembered stars.
One frozen trackless smile . . . What words
Can strangle this deaf moonlight? For we

Are overtaken. Now no cry, no sword
Can fasten or deflect this tidal wedge,
Slow tyranny of moonlight, moonlight loved
And changed . . . "There's

Nothing like this in the world," you say,
Knowing I cannot touch your hand and look
Too, into that godless cleft of sky
Where nothing turns but dead sands flashing.

"—And never to quite understand!" No,
In all the argosy of your bright hair I dreamed
Nothing so flagless as this piracy.

                              But now
Draw in your head, alone and too tall here.
Your eyes already in the slant of drifting foam;
Your breath sealed by the ghosts I do not know:
Draw in your head and sleep the long way home.

ALLEN TATE

1899-

Seasons of the Soul

Allor porsi la mano un poco avante,
e colsi un ramicel da un gran pruno;
e il tronco suo gridò: Perchè mi schiante?

I. SUMMER

Summer, this is our flesh,
The body you let mature;
If now while the body is fresh
You take it, shall we give
The heart, lest heart endure
The mind's tattering

Blow of greedy claws?
Shall mind itself still live
If like a hunting king
It falls to the lion's jaws?

Under the summer's blast
The soul cannot endure
Unless by sleight or fast
It seize or deny its day
To make the eye secure.
Brothers in arms, remember
The hot wind dries and draws
With circular delay
The flesh, ash from the ember,
Into the summer's jaws.

It was a gentle sun
When, at the June solstice
Green France was overrun
With caterpillar feet.
No head knows where its rest is
Or may lie down with reason
When war's usurping claws
Shall take the heart escheat—
Green field in burning season
To stain the weevil's jaws.

The southern summer dies
Evenly in the fall:
We raise our tired eyes
Into a sky of glass
Blue, empty, and tall
Without tail or head
Where burn the equal laws
For Balaam and his ass
Above the invalid dead,
Who cannot lift their jaws.

When was it that the summer
(Daylong a liquid light)
And the child, a new-comer,
Bathed in the same green spray,
Could neither guess the night?
The summer had no reason;
Then, like a primal cause
It had its timeless day

Before it kept the season
Of time's engaging jaws.

Two men of our summer world
Descended winding hell
And when their shadows curled
They fearfully confounded
The vast concluding shell:
Stopping, they saw in the narrow
Light a centaur pause
And gaze, then his astounded
Beard, with a notched arrow,
Part back upon his jaws.

II. AUTUMN

It had an autumn smell
And that was how I knew
That I was down a well:
I was no longer young;
My lips were numb and blue,
The air was like fine sand
In a butcher's stall
Or pumice on the tongue;
And when I raised my hand
I stood in the empty hall.

The round ceiling was high
And the gray light like shale
Thin, crumbling, and dry;
No rug on the bare floor
Nor any carved detail
To which the eye could glide;
I counted along the wall
Door after closed door
Through which a shade might slide
To the cold and empty hall.

I will leave this house, I said,
There is the autumn weather—
Here, nor living nor dead;
The lights burn in the town
Where men fear together.
Then on the bare floor
But tiptoe lest I fall
I walked years down

Towards the front door
At the end of the empty hall.

The door was false—no key
Or lock, and I was caught
In the house; yet I could see
I had been born to it
For miles of running brought
Me back where I began.
I saw now in the wall
A door open a slit
And a fat grizzled man
Come out into the hall:

As in a moonlit street
Men meeting are too shy
To check their hurried feet
But raise their eyes and squint
As through a needle's eye
Into the faceless gloom,—
My father in a gray shawl
Gave me an unseeing glint
And entered another room!
I stood in the empty hall

And watched them come and go
From one room to another,
Old men, old women—slow,
Familiar; girls, boys;
I saw my downcast mother
Clad in her street-clothes,
Her blue eyes long and small,
Who had no look or voice
For him whose vision froze
Him in the empty hall.

III. WINTER

Goddess sea-born and bright,
Return into the sea
Where eddying twilight
Gathers upon your people—
Cold goddess, hear our plea!
Leave the burnt earth, Venus,
For the drying God above,
Hanged in his windy steeple,

No longer bears for us
The living wound of love.

All the sea-gods are dead.
You, Venus, come home
To your salt maidenhead,
The tossed anonymous sea
Under shuddering foam—
Shade for lovers, where
A shark swift as your dove
Shall pace our company
All night to nudge and tear
The livid wound of love.

And now the winter sea:
Within her hollow rind
What sleek facility
Of sea-conceited scop
To plumb the nether mind!
Eternal winters blow
Shivering flakes, and shove
Bodies that wheel and drop—
Cold soot upon the snow
Their livid wound of love.

Beyond the undertow
The gray sea-foliage
Transpires a phosphor glow
Into the circular miles:
In the centre of his cage
The pacing animal
Surveys the jungle cove
And slicks his slithering wiles
To turn the venereal awl
In the livid wound of love.

Beyond the undertow
The rigid madrepore
Resists the winter's flow—
Headless, unaging oak
That gives the leaf no more.
Wilfully as I stood
Within the thickest grove
I seized a branch, which broke:
I heard the speaking blood
(From the livid wound of love)

Drip down upon my toe:
"We are the men who died
Of self-inflicted woe,
Lovers whose stratagem
Led to their suicide."
I touched my sanguine hair
And felt it drip above
Their brother who, like them,
Was maimed and did not bear
The living wound of love.

IV.   SPRING

Irritable spring, infuse
Into the burning breast
Your combustible juice
That as a liquid soul
Shall be the body's guest
Who lights, but cannot stay
To comfort this unease
Which like a dying coal
Hastens the cooler day
Of the mother of silences.

Back in my native prime
I saw the orient corn
All space but no time,
Reaching for the sun
Of the land where I was born;
It was a pleasant land
Where even death could please
Us with an ancient pun—
All dying for the hand
Of the mother of silences.

In time of bloody war
Who will know the time?
Is it a new spring star
Within the timing chill,
Talking or just a mime,
That rises in the blood—
Thin Jack-and-Jilling seas
Without human will?
Its light is at the flood,
Mother of silences!

It burns us each alone
Whose burning arrogance
Burns up the rolling stone,
This earth—Platonic cave
Of vertiginous chance!
Come, tired Sisyphus,
Cover the cave's egress
Where light reveals the slave,
Who rests when sleeps with us
The mother of silences.

Come, old woman, save
Your sons who have gone down
Into the burning cave:
Come, mother, and lean
At the window with your son
And gaze through its light frame
These fifteen centuries
Upon the shirking scene
Where men, blind, go lame:
Then, mother of silences,

Speak, that we may hear;
Listen, while we confess
That we conceal our fear;
Regard us, while the eye
Discerns by sight or guess
Whether, as sheep foregather
Upon their crooked knees,
We have begun to die;
Whether your kindness, mother,
Is mother of silences.

Ode to the Confederate Dead

Row after row with strict impunity
The headstones yield their names to the element,
The wind whirrs without recollection;
In the riven troughs the splayed leaves
Pile up, of nature the casual sacrament
To the seasonal eternity of death;
Then driven by the fierce scrutiny
Of heaven to their election in the vast breath,
They sough the rumor of mortality.

Autumn is desolation in the plot
Of a thousand acres where these memories grow
From the inexhaustible bodies that are not
Dead, but feed the grass row after rich row.
Think of the autumns that have come and gone!—
Ambitious November with the humors of the year,
With a particular zeal for every slab,
Staining the uncomfortable angels that rot
On the slabs, a wing chipped here, an arm there:
The brute curiosity of an angel's stare
Turns you, like them, to stone,
Transforms the heaving air
Till plunged to a heavier world below
You shift your sea-space blindly
Heaving, turning like the blind crab.

          Dazed by the wind, only the wind
          The leaves flying, plunge

You know who have waited by the wall
The twilight certainty of an animal,
Those midnight restitutions of the blood
You know—the immitigable pines, the smoky frieze
Of the sky, the sudden call: you know the rage,
The cold pool left by the mounting flood,
Of muted Zeno and Parmenides.
You who have waited for the angry resolution
Of those desires that should be yours tomorrow,
You know the unimportant shrift of death
And praise the vision
And praise the arrogant circumstance
Of those who fall
Rank upon rank, hurried beyond decision—
Here by the sagging gate, stopped by the wall.

          Seeing, seeing only the leaves
          Flying, plunge and expire

Turn your eyes to the immoderate past,
Turn to the inscrutable infantry rising
Demons out of the earth—they will not last.
Stonewall, Stonewall, and the sunken fields of hemp,
Shiloh, Antietam, Malvern Hill, Bull Run.
Lost in that orient of the thick and fast
You will curse the setting sun.

Cursing only the leaves crying
Like an old man in a storm

You hear the shout, the crazy hemlocks point
With troubled fingers to the silence which
Smothers you, a mummy, in time.

The hound bitch
Toothless and dying, in a musty cellar
Hears the wind only.

Now that the salt of their blood
Stiffens the saltier oblivion of the sea,
Seals the malignant purity of the flood,
What shall we who count our days and bow
Our heads with a commemorial woe
In the ribboned coats of grim felicity,
What shall we say of the bones, unclean,
Whose verdurous anonymity will grow?
The ragged arms, the ragged heads and eyes
Lost in these acres of the insane green?
The gray lean spiders come, they come and go;
In a tangle of willows without light
The singular screech-owl's tight
Invisible lyric seeds the mind
With the furious murmur of their chivalry.

We shall say only the leaves
Flying, plunge and expire

We shall say only the leaves whispering
In the improbable mist of nightfall
That flies on multiple wing:
Night is the beginning and the end
And in between the ends of distraction
Waits mute speculation, the patient curse
That stones the eyes, or like the jaguar leaps
For his own image in a jungle pool, his victim.

What shall we say who have knowledge
Carried to the heart? Shall we take the act
To the grave? Shall we, more hopeful, set up the grave
In the house? The ravenous grave?

Leave now
The shut gate and the decomposing wall:
The gentle serpent, green in the mulberry bush,

Riots with his tongue through the hush—
Sentinel of the grave who counts us all!

1926-1936

Aeneas at Washington

I myself saw furious with blood
Neoptolemus, at his side the black Atridae,
Hecuba and the hundred daughters, Priam
Cut down, his filth drenching the holy fires.
In that extremity I bore me well
A true gentleman, valorous in arms,
Disinterested and honorable. Then fled:
That was a time when civilization
Run by the few fell to the many, and
Crashed to the shout of men, the clang of arms:
Cold victualing I seized, I hoisted up
The old man my father upon my back,
In the smoke made by sea for a new world
Saving little—a mind imperishable
If time is, a love of past things tenuous
As the hesitation of receding love.

(To the reduction of uncitied littorals
We brought chiefly the vigor of prophecy
Our hunger breeding calculation
And fixed triumphs)

                    The thirsty dove I saw
In the glowing fields of Troy, hemp ripening
And tawny corn, the thickening Blue Grass
All lying rich forever in the green sun.
I see all things apart, the towers that men
Contrive I too contrived long, long ago.
Now I demand little. The singular passion
Abides its object and consumes desire
In the circling shadow of its appetite.
There was a time when the young eyes were slow,
Their flame steady beyond the firstling fire,
I stood in the rain, far from home at nightfall
By the Potomac, the great Dome lit the water,
The city my blood had built I knew no more
While the screech-owl whistled his new delight
Consecutively dark.

Stuck in the wet mire
Four thousand leagues from the ninth buried city
I thought of Troy, what we had built her for.

LÉONIE ADAMS

1899-

The Runner with the Lots

We listen, wind from where,
And two have heard
The step across the field
That went from us unseen,
The word that scarcely stirred
Along the corn's stiff green,
Or in their hair who bend among the corn.

And two have understood:
Though the great sails untorn
Of high September bear,
Toward harbour earth and yield,
The amber-dwindled mood
Is come, the bronze, the blue,
And every hue entering its solitude.

And all about we seize,
Of all that summers knew
Or autumns reconciled,
Sense of some utmost thing,
Some clasp unransoming,
Proffered the destinies,
And on the face recalled to its grave love,

Piercing on each, one air
Has touched them, earth and child;
And fairest here,
Fair now, whom love has sealed;
But fair unseen there move
Before us unbeguiled
The equal feet of love,
And the blind hands bearing the luck of the year.

Country Summer

Now the rich cherry, whose sleek wood
And top with silver petals traced,
Like a strict box its gems encased,
Has spilt from out that cunning lid,
All in an innocent green round,
Those melting rubies which it hid;
With moss ripe-strawberry-encrusted,
So birds get half, and minds lapse merry
To taste that deep-red, lark's-bite berry,
And blackcap bloom is yellow-dusted.

The wren that thieved it in the eaves
A trailer of the rose could catch
To her poor droopy sloven thatch,
And side by side with the wren's brood—
O lovely time of beggar's luck—
Opens the quaint and hairy bud;
And full and golden is the yield
Of cows that never have to house,
But all night nibble under boughs,
Or cool their sides in the moist field.

Into the rooms flow meadow airs,
The warm farm baking smell's blown round,
Inside and out, and sky and ground
Are much the same, the wishing star,
Hesperus, kind and early born,
Is risen only finger-far;
All stars stand close in summer air,
And tremble, and look mild as amber,
When wicks are lighted in the chamber,
You might say, stars were settling there.

Now straightening from the flowery hay,
Down the still light the mowers look,
Or turn, because their dreaming shook,
And they waked half to other days,
When left alone in the yellow stubble
The rusty-coated mare would graze.
Yet thick the lazy dreams are born,
Another thought can come to mind,
But like the shivering of the wind,
Morning and evening in the corn.

OSCAR WILLIAMS

1900-

Milk at the Bottom of the Sea

In the bowl of buildings *alias* the back yard
The milk of snow endlessly pours, but the bowl never
Fills. The century's live inhabitant caught behind
The window pane watches the single rakish tree
Blaze forth in ponderously immaculate italics.
The snowflakes pour everywhere in a panic, dizzyingly,
Or whirl to re-organize in the mid-air and float
Undecided; the sky tilts its ominous mountain, insuring
Another waterfall of snowflakes with all feathery speed.
Such activity should be noisy, a school's-out! of sounds,
But the silence is reverberating on the window glass
Exploring the deep-sea life of waywardness.

I am the traveller in the middle of the winter
In a wood-and-glass ship on the deeps of the age.
From peril's hold I watch the white germs from heaven
And blithe nothingness, the delicate roe of purity
Splurging to fill the air with their multipleness,
Making not even the sound of rain against rock.
I am an eye, I know, frozen in an undersea facade,
And have lost my hearing in such fantastic depths
Where the pressures cave in the senses, but still
My eye kindles to all this whiteness bearing down
In a dance of spiritual blindspots on our town.

In the end the wandering snowflakes are driven
Together, foam fat in the bottom of time, and I
Assuage through the mouth of the mind my entity;
The army of my veins, blood-drops, pores, thoughts
Crowds to my bones in one supreme act of gravity,
Closer than earth to a hill, than leaves to a tree,
Till I am the very body of oneness and cannot go
Pure, cold, diffuse and wayward like the snow.

Dwarf of Disintegration

I

Who is it runs through the many-storied mansion
   of myth
With the exaggerated child's-head among pillars
   and palings,
Holding in his grip the balloons of innumerable
   windows
And chased by the flowing malevolent army of the
   ceilings?

It is the dwarf, the yellow dwarf, with the minted
   cheeks,
With the roots of the fingers, with the wafer-thin
   cry,
In a maze of walls, lost in the nurseries of definition,
While shadows dance on shins of trumpets in a
   waning sky.

Voices are wired in the walls and rats are gnawing
   rumors,
The throat of music is bursting with the leadpipes
   of lust,
And the giant's face on the dwarf's shoulders is
   frightened
As the battle sounds strike the panes from the
   near-by past.

The pillars in the palace are reclining about like
   pistons
And the horses of parenthesis have run away into
   the woods:
The king is caught on the vast flypaper of the
   people:
There are holes as big as hovels in the wall of
   platitude.

The queen is ill from planting the garden with
   progeny
And her eyes are crossed off by vicious marks from
   her face:

She telephones the dwarf who puts his head in the
    instrument
To find his features come out in glacial coal bins
    of space.

The orgasms of distant guns attack at the lustful
    curtains
And soldiers are standing about in historical knots
    of lies
Warming the frozen tag-ends of lives around the
    spontaneous
Combustion of bosses who are stoking hollows of
    hired eyes.

The swine bulge in the snake bellies of the tele-
    graph wires
And bellow under flat clouds of ceilings in the
    interior;
Communication swallows the quicksilver swords
    of distance;
Headlines perform, in squadrons of plumes, on
    the warriors.

But the draughty palace of fable is full of feeble
    splendor,
And the yellow dwarf now in possession of know-
    ing documents
Runs after the newspapers cackling on the edge of
    freedom
While the golden cupboards tremble for the ageing
    sentiments.

The music of battlefields exhilarates the hidden
    overhead
And injects into the air a breakdown sense of
    release,
And the numerals wriggle off the lock boxes of the
    world
Unloosing a swarm of the venomous vultures of
    the peace.

But the dwarf, the yellow dwarf, with the sunspots
    for eyes
Is hunting in the archives in the moth holes in
    the palace,

And he tightens the torture boot around the spinal
　　column,
The steel twilight gleaming with the sweat of his
　　malice.

II

Now that the battle is on, keep off the palace
　　grounds,
You can hear the dwarf rummaging in the ele-
　　phant inside:
It's better to draw a curtain of birds around your
　　eyes,
Or fall into the picture book under the thumb of
　　a landslide—

Than to come upon spiders eating the iris of the
　　eyeball,
Or glimpse the yellow dwarf digesting the mem-
　　bers of princes.
Or see famous paintings loll, like tongues, from
　　their frames
Into a roomful of heroes pretending to harass
　　pretenses.

The sagging structure is propped between thought
　　and thinker,
The gilded lawns flow on under the smokescreen
　　of the laws:
The allover attack of a decaying body infiltrates
　　to the atom,
Even the beast in the violin hangs out with lopped-
　　off paws.

So run into the first thicket of verbs, the nest of
　　deeds,
Place a skyline between yourself and the grandiose
　　emblem,
For the inquisition wears the hypocritical jowls of
　　a palace,
There's nothing here to salvage, and yours is
　　another problem.

R. P. BLACKMUR
1904-

The Dead Ride Fast

Nobody ever galloped on this road
without probable cause. Nobody wants
false wind in the face at a dead end.
Nobody wants, this day, his hair to grow.
No one would disagree about that, unless
to cover up deeper agreement, hide
the robber's sense, the pounding, the vertigo,
the confusion under expert discernment:
all we leave out to make of faith a hope.

And if you think I am not talking about anything
it is because you have not looked out the window
where I wash and shave and sometimes trim my hair,
and have not seen the inviolable standstill
everything comes to, people, horses, cars,
beyond the little rise above the culvert.
It is that standstill finds all coming things
between the woods they come from and the rise
where, recognised, they seem already here.
With me it is no longer a matter of not looking
or whether this day everything comes at once;
because of that eddying standstill I am,
expectant, reverent, or suddenly degenerate,
always deliberately unprepared.

Perhaps you don't catch what I mean. Look here.
There have been bats in this house, variously
crawling and flitting, not easy to get out,
but always bats whether you knew them or not;
there have been seabirds beat against the window,
bill on, some die, but mostly only stun;
ducks in the marsh, with their known unknowable voices;
also telegrams delivered at night;
all these are wholesome until you stiffen to meet them.

You understand: I will not make of politics
a superstition, of religion a distrust,
of thought a mania. I will not look under beds

with stiffened eyes, knowing what I shall see.
I will look at horses, people, cars, look up
from shaving, and the hurried dead, look up
through the light-sodden, reverberating air—

until that day, hopeful, thoroughly prepared,
in my own glass I trim my snakey locks.

RICHARD EBERHART

1904-

"Mysticism Has Not the Patience to Wait for God's Revelation"

KIERKEGAARD

But to reach the archimedean point
Was all my steadfastness;
The disjointed times to teach
Courage from what is dreadful.

It was the glimpses in the lightning
Made me a sage, but made me say
No word to make another fight,
My own fighting heart full of dismay.

Spirit, soul, and fire are reached!
And springs of the mind, like springs of the feet
Tell all, all know, nothing wavers there!
All the flowers of my heart turned to ice-flowers,

Heaviness of the world prevailing,
("The higher we go the more terrible it is,")
Duplicity of man, heart-hate,
The hypocrite, the vain, the whipper, the cheat,

The eternal ape on the leash,
Drawing us down to faith,
Which the Greeks call divine folly,
The tug of laughter and of irony.

"The Goal of Intellectual Man"

The goal of intellectual man
Striving to do what he can
To bring down out of uncreated light
Illumination to our night

Is not possession of the fire
Annihilation of his own desire
To the source a secret soaring
And all his self outpouring

Nor is it an imageless place
Wherein there is no human face
Nor laws, nor hierarchies, nor dooms
And only the cold weight of the tomb

But it is human love, love
Concrete, specific, in a natural move
Gathering goodness, it is free
In the blood as in the mind's harmony,

It is love discoverable here
Difficult, dangerous, pure, clear,
The truth of the positive hour
Composing all of human power.

"I Walked Out to the Graveyard To See the Dead"

I walked out to the graveyard to see the dead
The iron gates were locked, I couldn't get in,
A golden pheasant on the dark fir boughs
Looked with fearful method at the sunset,

Said I, Sir bird, wink no more at me
I have had enough of my dark eye-smarting.
I cannot adore you, nor do I praise you,
But assign you to the rafters of Montaigne.

Who talks with the Absolute salutes a Shadow,
Who seeks himself shall lose himself;
And the golden pheasants are no help
And action must be learned from love of man.

The Groundhog

In June, amid the golden fields,
I saw a groundhog lying dead.
Dead lay he; my senses shook,
And mind outshot our naked frailty.
There lowly in the vigorous summer
His form began its senseless change,
And made my senses waver dim
Seeing nature ferocious in him.
Inspecting close his maggots' might
And seething cauldron of his being,
Half with loathing, half with a strange love,
I poked him with an angry stick.
The fever arose, became a flame
And Vigour circumscribed the skies,
Immense energy in the sun,
And through my frame a sunless trembling.
My stick had done nor good nor harm.
Then stood I silent in the day
Watching the object, as before;
And kept my reverence for knowledge
Trying for control, to be still,
To quell the passion of the blood;
Until I had bent down on my knees
Praying for joy in the sight of decay.
And so I left; and I returned
In Autumn strict of eye, to see
The sap gone out of the groundhog,
But the bony sodden hulk remained.
But the year had lost its meaning,
And in intellectual chains
I lost both love and loathing,
Mured up in the wall of wisdom.
Another summer took the fields again
Massive and burning, full of life,
But when I chanced upon the spot
There was only a little hair left,
And bones bleaching in the sunlight
Beautiful as architecture;
I watched them like a geometer,
And cut a walking stick from a birch.
It has been three years, now.
There is no sign of the groundhog.
I stood there in the whirling summer,

My hand capped a withered heart,
And thought of China and of Greece,
Of Alexander in his tent;
Of Montaigne in his tower,
Of Saint Theresa in her wild lament.

C. DAY LEWIS

1904-

O Dreams, O Destinations

I

For infants time is like a humming shell
Heard between sleep and sleep, wherein the shores
Foam-fringed, wind-fluted of the strange earth dwell
And the sea's cavernous hunger faintly roars.
It is the humming pole of summer lanes
Whose sound quivers like heat-haze endlessly
Over the corn, over the poppied plains—
An emanation from the earth or sky.
Faintly they hear, through the womb's lingering haze,
A rumour of that sea to which they are born:
They hear the ringing pole of summer days,
But need not know what hungers for the corn.
They are the lisping rushes in a stream—
Grace-notes of a profound, legato dream.

II

Children look down upon the morning-grey
Tissue of mist that veils a valley's lap:
Their fingers itch to tear it and unwrap
The flags, the roundabouts, the gala day.
They watch the spring rise inexhaustibly—
A breathing thread out of the eddied sand,
Sufficient to their day: but half their mind
Is on the sailed and glittering estuary.
Fondly we wish their mist might never break,
Knowing it hides so much that best were hidden:
We'd chain them by the spring, lest it should broaden
For them into a quicksand and a wreck.

But they slip through our fingers like the source,
Like mist, like time that has flagged out their course.

III

That was the fatal move, the ruination
Of innocence so innocently begun,
When in the lawless orchard of creation
The child left this fruit for that rosier one.
Reaching towards the far thing, we begin it;
Looking beyond, or backward, more and more
We grow unfaithful to the unique minute
Till, from neglect, its features stale and blur.
Fish, bird or beast was never thus unfaithful—
Man only casts the image of his joys
Beyond his senses' reach; and by this fateful
Act, he confirms the ambiguous power of choice.
Innocence made that first choice. It is she
Who weeps, a child chained to the outraged tree.

IV

Our youthtime passes down a colonnade
Shafted with alternating light and shade.
All's dark or dazzle there. Half in a dream
Rapturously we move, yet half afraid
Never to wake. That diamond-point, extreme
Brilliance engraved on us a classic theme:
The shaft of darkness had its lustre too,
Rising where earth's concentric mysteries gleam.
Oh youth-charmed hours, that made an avenue
Of fountains playing us on to love's full view,
A cypress walk to some romantic grave—
Waking, how false in outline and in hue
We find the dreams that flickered on our cave:
Only your fire, which cast them, still seems true.

V

All that time there was thunder in the air:
Our nerves branched and flickered with summer lightning.
The taut crab-apple, the pampas quivering, the glare
On the roses seemed irrelevant, or a heightening
At most of the sealed-up hour wherein we awaited
What?—some explosive oracle to abash
The platitudes on the lawn? heaven's delegated

Angel—the golden rod, our burning bush?
No storm broke. Yet in retrospect the rose
Mounting vermilion, fading, glowing again
Like a fire's heart, that breathless inspiration
Of pampas grass, crab-tree's attentive pose
Never were so divinely charged as then—
The veiled Word's flesh, a near annunciation.

VI

Symbols of gross experience!—our grief
Flowed, like a sacred river, underground:
Desire bred fierce abstractions on the mind,
Then like an eagle soared beyond belief.
Often we tried our breast against the thorn,
Our paces on the turf: whither we flew,
Why we should agonize, we hardly knew—
Nor what ached in us, asking to be born.
Ennui of youth!—thin air above the clouds,
Vain divination of the sunless stream
Mirror that impotence, till we redeem
Our birthright, and the shadowplay concludes.
Ah, not in dreams, but when our souls engage
With the common mesh and moil, we come of age.

VII

Older, we build a road where once our active
Heat threw up mountains and the deep dales veined:
We're glad to gain the limited objective,
Knowing the war we fight in has no end.
The road must needs follow each contour moulded
By that fire in its losing fight with earth:
We march over our past, we may behold it
Dreaming a slave's dream on our bivouac hearth.
Lost the archaic dawn wherein we started,
The appetite for wholeness: now we prize
Half-loaves, half-truths—enough for the half-hearted,
The gleam snatched from corruption satisfies.
Dead youth, forgive us if, all but defeated,
We raise a trophy where your honour lies.

VIII

But look, the old illusion still returns,
Walking a field-path where the succory burns

Like summer's eye, blue lustre-drops of noon,
And the heart follows it and freshly yearns:
Yearns to the sighing distances beyond
Each height of happiness, the vista drowned
In gold-dust haze, and dreams itself immune
From change and night to which all else is bound.
Love, we have caught perfection for a day
As succory holds a gem of halcyon ray:
Summer burns out, its flower will tarnish soon—
Deathless illusion, that could so relay
The truth of flesh and spirit, sun and clay
Singing for once together all in tune!

IX

To travel like a bird, lightly to view
Deserts where stone gods founder in the sand,
Ocean embraced in a white sleep with land;
To escape time, always to start anew.
To settle like a bird, make one devoted
Gesture of permanence upon the spray
Of shaken stars and autumns; in a bay
Beyond the crestfallen surges to have floated.
Each is our wish. Alas, the bird flies blind,
Hooded by a dark sense of destination:
Her weight on the glass calm leaves no impression,
Her home is soon a basketful of wind.
Travellers, we're fabric of the road we go;
We settle, but like feathers on time's flow.

Departure in the Dark

Nothing so sharply reminds a man he is mortal
As leaving a place
In a winter morning's dark, the air on his face
Unkind as the touch of sweating metal:
Simple goodbyes to children or friends become
A felon's numb
Farewell, and love that was a warm, a meeting place—
Love is the suicide's grave under the nettles.

Gloomed and clemmed as if by an imminent ice-age
Lies the dear world
Of your street-strolling, field-faring. The senses, curled
At the dead end of a shrinking passage,

Care not if close the inveterate hunters creep,
And memories sleep
Like mammoths in lost caves. Drear, extinct is the world,
And has no voice for consolation or presage.

There is always something at such times of the passover,
When the dazed heart
Beats for it knows not what, whether you part
From home or prison, acquaintance or lover—
Something wrong with the time-table, something unreal
In the scrambled meal
And the bag ready packed by the door, as though the heart
Has gone ahead, or is staying here for ever.

No doubt for the Israelites that early morning
It was hard to be sure
If home were prison or prison home: the desire
Going forth meets the desire returning.
This land, that had cut their pride down to the bone
Was now their own
By ancient deeds of sorrow. Beyond, there was nothing sure
But a desert of freedom to quench their fugitive yearnings.

At this blind hour the heart is informed of nature's
Ruling that man
Should be nowhere a more tenacious settler than
Among wry thorns and ruins, yet nurture
A seed of discontent in his ripest ease.
There's a kind of release
And a kind of torment in every goodbye for every man—
And will be, even to the last of his dark departures.

In the Heart of Contemplation

In the heart of contemplation—
Admiring, say, the frost-flowers of the white lilac,
Or lark's song busily sifting like sand-crystals
Through the pleased hourglass an afternoon of summer,
Or your beauty, dearer to me than these—
Discreetly a whisper in the ear,
The glance of one passing my window recall me
From lark, lilac, you, grown suddenly strangers.

In the plump and pastoral valley
Of a leisure time, among the trees like seabirds

Asleep on a glass calm, one shadow moves—
The sly reminder of the forgotten appointment.
All the shining pleasures, born to be innocent,
Grow dark with a truant's guilt:
The day's high heart falls flat, the oaks tremble,
And the shadow sliding over your face divides us.

In the act of decision only,
In the hearts cleared for action like lovers naked
For love, this shadow vanishes: there alone
There is nothing between our lives for it to thrive on.
You and I with lilac, lark and oak-leafed
Valley are bound together
As in the astounded clarity before death.
Nothing is innocent now but to act for life's sake.

"In Heaven, I Suppose, Lie Down Together"

In heaven, I suppose, lie down together
Agonised Pilate and the boa-constrictor
That swallows anything: but we must seize
One horn or the other of our antitheses.
When I consider each independent star
Wearing its world of darkness like a fur
And rubbing shoulders with infinity,
I am content experience should be
More discontinuous than the points pricked
Out by the mazy course of a derelict,
Iceberg, or Flying Dutchman, and the heart
Stationary and passive as a chart.
In such star-frenzy I could boast, betwixt
My yester and my morrow self are fixed
All the birds carolling and all the seas
Groaning from Greenwich to the Antipodes.

But an eccentric hour may come, when systems
Not stars divide the dark; and then life's pistons
Pounding into their secret cylinder
Begin to tickle the most anchorite ear
With hints of mechanisms that include
The man. And once that rhythm arrests the blood,
Who would be satisfied his mind is no
Continent but an archipelago?
They are preposterous paladins and prance
From myth to myth, who take an Agag stance

Upon the needle points of here and now,
Where only angels ought to tread. Allow
One jointure feasible to man, one state
Squared with another—then he can integrate
A million selves and where disorder ruled
Straddle a chaos and beget a world.

Peals of the New Year once for me came tumbling
Out of the narrow night like clusters of humming-
Birds loosed from a black bag, and rose again
Irresponsibly to silence: but now I strain
To follow them and see for miles around
Men square or shrug their shoulders at the sound.
Then I remember the pure and granite hills
Where first I caught an ideal tone that stills,
Like the beloved's breath asleep, all din
Of earth at traffic: silence's first-born,
Carrying over each sensual ravine
To inform the seer and uniform the seen.
So from this ark, this closet of the brain,
The dove emerges and flies back again
With a Messiah sprig of certitude—
Promise of ground below the sprawling flood.

ROBERT PENN WARREN

1905-

Revelation

Because he had spoken harshly to his mother,
The day became astonishingly bright,
The enormity of distance crept to him like a dog now,
And earth's own luminescence seemed to repel the night.

Roof was rent like loud paper tearing to admit
Sun-sulphurous splendor where had been before
But the submarine glimmer by kindly countenances lit.
As slow, phosphorescent dignities light the ocean floor.

By walls, by walks, chrysanthemum and aster,
All hairy, fat-petalled species, lean, confer,

And his ears, and heart, should burn at that insidious whisper
Which concerns him so, he knows; but he cannot make out the
    words.

The peacock screamed, and his feathered fury made
Legend shake, all day, while the sky ran pale as milk;
That night, all night, the buck rabbit stamped in the moonlit glade,
And the owl's brain glowed like a coal in the grove's combustible
    dark.

When Sulla smote and Rome was rent, Augustine
Recalled how Nature, shuddering, tore her gown,
And kind changed kind, and the blunt herbivorous tooth dripped
    blood;
At Duncan's death, at Dunsinane, chimneys blew down.

But, oh! his mother was kinder than ever Rome,
Dearer than Duncan—no wonder, then, Nature's frame
Thrilled in voluptuous hemispheres far off from his home;
But not in terror: only as the bride, as the bride.

In separateness only does love learn definition,
Though Brahma smiles beneath the dappled shade,
Though tears, that night, wet the pillow where the boy's head was
    laid
Dreamless of splendid antipodal agitation;

And though across what tide and tooth Time is,
He was to lean back toward that recalcitrant face,
He would think, than Sulla more fortunate, how once he had
    learned
Something important above love, and about love's grace.

Pursuit

The hunchback on the corner, with gum and shoelaces,
Has his own wisdom and pleasures, and may not be lured
To divulge them to you, for he has merely endured
Your appeal for his sympathy and your kind purchases;
And wears infirmity but as the general who turns
Apart, in his famous old greatcoat there on the hill
At dusk when the rapture and cannonade are still,
To muse withdrawn from the dead, from his gorgeous subalterns;
Or stares from the thicket of his familiar pain, like a fawn
That meets you a moment, wheels, in imperious innocence is gone.

Go to the clinic. Wait in the outer room
Where like an old possum the snag-nailed hand will hump
On its knee in murderous patience, and the pomp
Of pain swells like the Indies, or a plum.
And there you will stand, as on the Roman hill,
Stunned by each withdrawn gaze and severe shape,
The first barbarian victor stood to gape
At the sacrificial fathers, white-robed, still;
And even the feverish old Jew stares stern with authority
Till you feel like one who has come too late, or improperly clothed,
   to a party.

The doctor will take you now. He is burly and clean;
Listening, like lover or worshiper, bends at your heart;
But cannot make out just what it tries to impart;
So smiles; says you simply need a change of scene.
Of scene, of solace: therefore Florida,
Where Ponce de Leon clanked among the lilies,
Where white sails skit on blue and cavort like fillies,
And the shoulder gleams in the moonlit corridor.
A change of love: if love is a groping Godward, though blind,
No matter what crevice, cranny, chink, bright in dark, the pale
   tentacle find.

In Florida consider the flamingo
Its color passion but its neck a question;
Consider even that girl the other guests shun
On beach, at bar, in bed, for she may know
The secret you are seeking, after all;
Or the child you humbly sit by, excited and curly,
That screams on the shore at the sea's sunlit hurlyburly,
Till the mother calls its name, toward nightfall.
Till you sit alone: in the dire meridians, off Ireland, in fury
Of spume-tooth and dawnless sea-heave, salt rimes the lookout's
   devout eye.

Till you sit alone—which is the beginning of error—
Behind you the music and lights of the great hotel:
Solution, perhaps, is public, despair personal,
But history held to your breath clouds like a mirror.
There are many states, and towns in them, and faces,
But meanwhile, the little old lady in black, by the wall,
Who admires all the dancers, and tells you how just last fall
Her husband died in Ohio, and damp mists her glasses;
She blinks and croaks, like a toad or a Norn, in the horrible light,
And rattles her crutch, which may put forth a small bloom, perhaps
   white.

Terror

I Volontari Americani Presso Eserciti Stranieri Non Perdono La
Cittadinanza. IL MESSAGGERO, Roma, Sabato, 27 Gennaio, 1940.

Not picnics or pageants or the improbable
Powers of air whose tongues exclaim dominion
And gull the great man to follow his terrible
Star, suffice; not the window-box, or the bird on
The ledge, which mean so much to the invalid,
Nor the joy you leaned after, as by the tracks the grass
In the emptiness after the lighted Pullmans fled,
Suffices; nor faces, which, like distraction, pass
Under the street-lamps, teasing to faith or pleasure,
Suffice you, born to no adequate definition of terror.

For yours, like a puppy, is darling and inept,
Though his cold nose brush your hand while you laugh at his
    clowning;
Or the kitten you sleep with, though once or twice while you slept
It tried to suck your breath, and you dreamed of drowning,
Perjured like Clarence, sluiced from the perilous hatches;
But never of lunar wolf-waste or the arboreal
Malignancy, with the privy breath, which watches
And humps in the dark; but only a dream, after all.
At the worst, you think, with a little twinge of distress,
That contagion may nook in the comforting fur you love to caress.

Though some, unsatisfied and sick, have sought
That immitigable face, whose smile is ice,
And fired their hearts like pitch-pine, for they thought
Rather flame than the damp worm-tooth of compromise:
So Harry L. I knew, whose whores and gin
Had dwindled to a slick smile in the drug store
But for the absurd contraption of a plane,
Which flung on air the unformulable endeavor
While heart bled speed to lave the applauded name.
The crash was in an old cornfield; not even flame.

So some, whose passionate emptiness and tidal
Lust swayed toward the debris of Madrid,
And left New York to loll in their fierce idyll
Among the olives, where the snipers hid;
And now the North, to seek that visioned face
And polarize their iron of despair,
Who praise no beauty like the boreal grace

Which greens the dead eye under the rocket's flare.
They fight old friends, for their obsession knows
Only the immaculate itch, not human friends or foes.

They sought a secret which fat Franco's Moor,
Hieratic, white-robed, pitiless, might teach,
Who duped and dying but for pride, therefore
Hugged truth which cause or conscience scarcely reach.
As Jacob all night with the angelic foe,
They wrestled him who did not speak, but died,
And wrestle now, by frozen fen and floe,
New Courier, in fury sanctified;
And seek that face which, greasy, frost-breathed, in furs,
Bends to the bomb-sight over bitter Helsingfors.

Blood splashed on the terrorless intellect creates
Corrosive fizzle like the spattered lime,
And its enseamed stew but satiates
Itself, in that lewd and faceless pantomime.
You know, by radio, how hotly the world repeats,
When the brute crowd roars or the blunt boot-heels resound
In the Piazza or the Wilhelmplatz,
The crime of Onan, spilled upon the ground;
You know, whose dear hope Alexis Carrel kept
Alive in a test tube, where it monstrously grew, and slept.

But it is dead, and you now, guiltless, sink
To rest in lobbies, or pace gardens where
The slow god crumbles and the fountains prink,
Nor heed the criminal king, who paints the air
With discoursed madness and protruding eye,
Nor give the alarm, nor ask tonight where sleeps
That head which hooped the jewel Fidelity,
But like an old melon now, in the dank ditch, seeps;
But you crack nuts, while the conscience-stricken stare
Kisses the terror; for you see an empty chair.

VERNON WATKINS
1906-

The Sunbather

Inert he lies on the saltgold sand
And sees through his lids the scarlet sky.
The sea will run back if he breathes a sigh.
He can hide the sun with a roselit hand.

Loitering, he crossed the shingle-shore
Where his eyes looked back at the glint of shells.
With a quoit of stone he startled the bells
That sleep in the rocks' vibrating core.

Thought-blind to the chosen place he passed.
The seagulls rose, and circled, and dropped;
And there, throwing down his coat, he stopped.
He, touching the mould of the world, lies fast.

The noon-sun dodges around his knee.
The sand at his head now trembles pale.
The wind at his temples carries a tale
And before him flies the bewildered sea.

The sun, the sea and the wind are three
But he narrows them down with a dreaming eye.
With his hands at rest and his drawn-up thigh
He can imagine the sacred tree.

For a point of light has seeded all
And the beautiful seed has come to rest
For a sunblown moment in his breast,
A tree where the leaves will never fall.

"Come back. You were with us ages ago.
We have thrown your bones to the carrion gull.
To the dripping cave we have sold your skull,
And the delicate flower which was born to blow

Is lost in the flow of the marble sea.
We have made seaweeds out of your locks,

And your star-white bones in the vaulted rocks
Lie broken and cold, like shells in the scree."

So shades converse, and the world's dumb thud
Muffles their argument, Man, more strong,
Gives, to console their frightened song,
The beat that consoles them most, his blood.

The Mummy

His eyes are closed. They are closed. His eyes are closed.
His hands are clenched. They are clenched. His hands are clenched.
The messenger comes. The letters are disciplined; they are disposed.
The black light quivers. Earth on Earth is avenged.

What has left music fast in the sockets of bone?
Had all been pattern, images sight had seen,
Blood would lie quiet, but something strokes the light, and a groan
Of great-rooted calm repels those images: nothing they mean.

Nothing here lives but the music in the eyes.
Hunting-scene, warriors, chariot, palm and wing
Bid the blood rest, thought perch where the time-bird sings or flies,
Year chasing year, following and following.

But tears wash these bones where parchments whisper to sand.
Here a laid vase offers the flying stream.
Sand darkening wakes a harp-string hidden, plucked by a blind hand,
Crying this theme to the world, this world-surrounding theme:

Valiant, alive, his voice pursued the lands,
Ruled the white sea, held mountains in his keep.
Leave him with delicate instruments formed for delicate hands;
In this locked room of treasures let him who chose them sleep.

I lean down, crying: "Touch me, lay hold on my Spring,
Reach up, for I have loosened, tearing your skies,
Fountains of light, ages of listening!"
But the bound hands are folded, the fold its word denies.

What shudder of music unfulfilled vibrates?
What draws to a dust-grain's fall most distant stars?
In the last taper's light what shadow meditates?
What single, athletic shape never cast on wall or vase?

What shudder of birth and death? What shakes me most?
Job his Maker answering, the Stricken exclaiming "Rejoice!"
Gripping late in the shifting moment giant Earth, making Earth a
    ghost,
Who heard a great friend's death without a change of voice.

WILLIAM EMPSON
1906-

Flighting for Duck

Egyptian banks, an avenue of clay,
Define the drain between constructed marshes
(Two silted lakes, silver and brown, with grass,
Without background, far from hills, at evening).
Its pomp makes a high road between their sheets
(Mud shoals, a new alluvium, dabbled water,
Shallow, and specked with thistles, not yet mastered)
At the subdued triumph of whose end
Two transept banks, the castle guard, meet it,
Screening the deeper water they surround
With even line of low but commanding pinetrees
Dark but distinguished as a row of peacocks.
The darker silhouette is where a barn
Straddling two banks over a lesser channel
Stands pillared upon treetrunks like a guildhall
Empty, mudheaped, through which the alluvial scheme
Flows temporary as the modern world.
The mud's tough glue is drying our still feet.
A mild but powerful flow moves through the flats
Laden with soil to feed the further warping.

"What was that drumming in the sky? What cry
Squawked from the rustled rushes a reply?
Was it near? Are they coming?
Could you hear?" Sound travels a good way by night.
That farm dog barking's half a mile away.

But when the swarms gathering for food repay us
This hint of anti-aircraft is disarmed
And as the fleets at a shot reascend
The eye orders their unreachable chaos

(The stars are moving like these duck, but slower,
Sublime, their tails absurd, their voices harsh)
And analyses into groups the crowds.
Two surfaces of birds, higher and lower,
Rise up and cross each other and distend
As one flight to the river turns, alarmed.
They are out of shot, and like the turning clouds
From meditative cigarettes amuse,
Manure in smoke over the fructuant marsh,
Curled vapour, incense from the cult of Ouse.

Bang. Bang. Two duck blur 'mid the social crew;
For man created, to man's larder due.
With plump or splash on the new-nurtured field
To Reason's arm they proper homage yield.
The well-taught dogs wait but the voice to run,
Eager, and conscious of the murd'ring gun.

Starlit, mistcircled, one whole pearl embrowned,
An even dusked silver of earth and sky
Held me, dazzled with cobwebs, staring round.
The black band of my hat lept to my eye.
Alone in sight not coloured like the ground
It lit, like a struck match, everything by.

Four Legs, Two Legs, Three Legs

Delphic and Theban and Corinthian,
Three lines, by the odd chance, met at a point,
The delta zero, the case trivial.

A young man's cross-road but a shady one.
Killing a mistaken black cat in the dark
He had no other metaphysical trait.

God walks in a mysterious way
Neither delighteth he in any man's legs.

The wrecked girl, still raddled with Napoleon's paint,
Nose eaten by a less clear conqueror,
Still orientated to the average dawn,
Behind, Sahara, before, Nile and man
A toy abandoned, sure, after so many,
That the next sun will take her for a walk,
Still lifts a touching dog's face eager for a sign.

Not one for generalising his solutions
Oedipus placed the riddle with a name.
Another triumph for the commonplace.
While too much to pretend she fell and burst
It is a comfort that the Sphinx took such an answer.

Missing Dates

Slowly the poison the whole blood stream fills.
It is not the effort nor the failure tires.
The waste remains, the waste remains and kills.

It is not your system or clear sight that mills
Down small to the consequence a life requires;
Slowly the poison the whole blood stream fills.

They bled an old dog dry yet the exchange rills
Of young dog blood gave but a month's desires;
The waste remains, the waste remains and kills.

It is the Chinese tombs and the slag hills
Usurp the soil, and not the soil retires.
Slowly the poison the whole blood stream fills.

Not to have fire is to be a skin that shrills.
The complete fire is death. From partial fires
The waste remains, the waste remains and kills.

It is the poems you have lost, the ills
From missing dates, at which the heart expires.
Slowly the poison the whole blood stream fills.
The waste remains, the waste remains and kills.

BYRON VAZAKAS

1906-

All the Farewells

This is not the classic torso
　　pompous with its death, but
　　the obscene disorder of the
　　dying who cannot accept . . .

In the railroad station, the
    crowd is assembled, lugubrious
    as umbrellas expecting rain.
    The terminus tall windows arch

With requiem glow above the mausoleum
    marble floors; and groups that
    at the gates will be the mass
    that weeps and prays, are

Buttressed by bags, each life
    resolved to neat necessities.
    Young men in uniform half listen,
    in awkward attitudes, to words

That are a dyke restraining tears.
    The ticket clerk cannot return
    the cash, nor wish redeem the
    past that brought them here.

Yet their hearts search out the
    distances traversed, as though
    memory were a melody perpetuating
    pain. At the stationmaster's cue,

All move toward the platform's last,
    decisive theme. River-like,
    they flow between the bottle-neck
    of doors, and smooth and urgent

As a waterfall, descend to the final
    turbulence of tears. Mixed with
    the storm of locomotives anxious
    for release is this weeping and

Saying the amazingly simple things . . .
    The relationship at last is clear.
    All bid goodbye as the future
    vanishes with the tail-light around

The fatal curve, but repeat in endless
    farewells the pain of parting, and in
    that pain find undiscovered love, find
    interdependence in the flux of things.

The Progress of Photography

Slowly I mount the stairs to have
    my picture taken. And in the
    slightly dusty room, a shabby
    modern chair celebrates the

Funereal ceremony with artificial
    cheer. The occasion is a New
    Year, uncertain, melancholy,
    but hoping for a better than

The last. It is medieval. It is a
    world mad with carving, where
    times confers pain like a fungus
    on the face. Reflectors are

Arranged, the lights focussed for
    the most auspicious view.
    Disturbingly, my face repeats
    the past. It should not have

Been there, or was only, as air imagines
    sound. Now I am ready, and the
    camera makes what is seen seem
    what I feel. In the dark-room,

My features gradually emerge, less
    indistinct, and slowly I
    perceive familiar things take
    unfamiliar shapes: my portrait

Becomes the likeness of another.
    Quiet and persistent as pain,
    time's lens records its fatal
    photograph, enlarged and

Cancerous; and I am the terrible
    invalid, trapped within its
    unframed space by the strength of
    an illusion the will cannot destroy.

W. H. AUDEN

1907-

At the Grave of Henry James

The snow, less intransigeant than their marble,
Has left the defense of whiteness to these tombs;
 For all the pools at my feet
Accommodate blue now, and echo such clouds as occur
To the sky, and whatever bird or mourner the passing
 Moment remarks they repeat.

While the rocks, named after singular spaces
Within which images wandered once that caused
 All to tremble and offend,
Stand here in an innocent stillness, each marking the spot
Where one more series of errors lost its uniqueness
 And novelty came to an end.

To whose real advantage were such transactions
When words of reflection were exchanged for trees?
 What living occasion can
Be just to the absent? O noon but reflects on itself,
And the small taciturn stone that is the only witness
 To a great and talkative man

Has no more judgement than my ignorant shadow
Of odious comparisons or distant clocks
 Which challenge and interfere
With the heart's instantaneous reading of time, time that is
A warm enigma no longer in you for whom I
 Surrender my private cheer

Startling the awkward footsteps of my apprehension,
The flushed assault of your recognition is
 The *donnée* of this doubtful hour:
O stern proconsul of intractable provinces,
O poet of the difficult, dear addicted artist,
 Assent to my soil and flower.

As I stand awake on our solar fabric,
That primary machine, the earth, which gendarmes, banks,
 And aspirin pre-suppose.

On which the clumsy and sad may all sit down, and any who will
Say their a-ha to the beautiful, the common locus
    Of the master and the rose.

Our theatre, scaffold, and erotic city
Where all the infirm species are partners in the act
    Of encroachment bodies crave,
Though solitude in death is *de rigueur* for their flesh
And the self-denying hermit flies as it approaches
    Like the carnivore to a cave.

That its plural numbers may unite in meaning,
Its vulgar tongues unravel the knotted mass
    Of the improperly conjunct,
Open my eyes now to all its hinted significant forms,
Sharpen my ears to detect amid its brilliant uproar
    The low thud of the defunct.

O dwell, ironic at my living centre,
Half ancestor, half child; because the actual self
    Round whom time revolves so fast
Is so afraid of what its motions might possibly do
That the actor is never there when his really important
    Acts happen. Only the past

Is present, no one about but the dead as,
Equipped with a few inherited odds and ends,
    One after another we are
Fired into life to seek that unseen target where all
Our equivocal judgments are judged and resolved in
    One whole Alas or Hurrah.

And only the unborn remark the disaster
When, though it makes no difference to the pretty airs
    The bird of Appetite sings,
And Amour Propre is his usual amusing self,
Out from the jungle of an undistinguished moment
    The flexible shadow springs.

Now more than ever, when torches and snare-drums
Excite the squat women of the saurian brain
    Till a milling mob of fears
Breaks in insultingly on anywhere, when in our dreams
Pigs play on the organs and the blue sky runs shrieking
    As the Crack of Doom appears,

Are the good ghosts needed with the white magic
Of their subtle loves. War has no ambiguities
    Like a marriage; the result
Required of its *affaire fatale* is simple and sad,
The physical removal of all human objects
    That conceal the Difficult.

Then remember me that I may remember
The test we have to learn to shudder for is not
    An historical event,
That neither the low democracy of a nightmare nor
An army's primitive tidiness may deceive me
    About our predicament.

That catastrophic situation which neither
Victory nor defeat can annul; to be
    Deaf yet determined to sing,
To be lame and blind yet burning for the Great Good Place,
To be radically corrupt yet mournfully attracted
    By the Real Distinguished Thing.

And shall I not specially bless you as, vexed with
My little inferior questions, today I stand
    Beside the bed where you rest
Who opened such passionate arms to your *Bon* when It ran
Toward you with its overwhelming reasons pleading
    All beautifully in Its breast?

O with what innocence your hand submitted
To these formal rules that help a child to play,
    While your heart, fastidious as
A delicate nun, remained true to the rare noblesse
Of your lucid gift and, for its own sake, ignored the
    Resentful muttering Mass.

Whose ruminant hatred of all which cannot
Be simplified or stolen is still at large;
    No death can assuage its lust
To vilify the landscape of Distinction and see
The heart of the Personal brought to a systolic standstill,
    The Tall to diminished dust.

Preserve me, Master, from its vague incitement;
Yours be the disciplinary image that holds
    Me back from agreeable wrong.

And the clutch of eddying muddle, lest Proportion shed
The alpine chill of her shrugging editorial shoulder
　　　On my loose impromptu song.

Suggest; so may I segregate my disorder
Into districts of prospective value: approve;
　　　Lightly, lightly, then, may I dance
Over the frontier of the obvious and fumble no more
In the old limp pocket of the minor exhibition,
　　　Nor riot with irrelevance.

And no longer shoe geese or water stakes, but
Bolt in my day my grain of truth to the barn
　　　Where tribulations may leap
With their long-lost brothers at last in the festival
Of which not one had a dissenting image, and the
　　　Flushed immediacy sleep.

Into this city from the shining lowlands
Blows a wind that whispers of uncovered skulls
　　　And fresh ruins under the moon,
Of hopes that will not survive the *secousse* of this spring
Of blood and flames, of the terror that walks by night and
　　　The sickness that strikes at noon.

All will be judged. Master of nuance and scruple,
Pray for me and for all writers living or dead;
　　　Because there are many whose works
Are in better taste than their lives; because there is no end
To the vanity of our calling: make intercession
　　　For the treason of all clerks.

Because the darkness is never so distant,
And there is never much time for the arrogant
　　　Spirit to flutter its wings,
Or the broken bone to rejoice, or the cruel to cry
For Him whose property is always to have mercy, the author
　　　And giver of all good things.

Alonso to Ferdinand

　　　Dear Son, when the warm multitudes cry,
　　　Ascend your throne majestically,
　　　But keep in mind the waters where fish
　　　See sceptres descending with no wish

To touch them; sit regal and erect,
But imagine the sands where a crown
Has the status of a broken-down
Sofa or mutilated statue:
Remember as bells and cannon boom
The cold deep that does not envy you,
The sunburnt superficial kingdom
Where a king is an object.

Expect no help from others, for who
Talk sense to princes or refer to
The scorpion in official speeches
As they unveil some granite Progress
Leading a child and holding a bunch
Of lilies? In their Royal Zoos the
Shark and the octopus are tactfully
Omitted; synchronised clocks march on
Within their powers: without, remain
The ocean flats where no subscription
Concerts are given, the desert plain
Where there is nothing for lunch.

Only your darkness can tell you what
A prince's ornate mirror dare not,
Which you should fear more—the sea in which
A tyrant sinks entangled in rich
Robes while a mistress turns a white back
Upon his splutter, or the desert
Where an emperor stands in his shirt
While his diary is read by sneering
Beggars, and far off he notices
A lean horror flapping and hopping
Toward him with inhuman swiftness:
Learn from your dreams what you lack,

For as your fears are, so must you hope.
The Way of Justice is a tightrope
Where no prince is safe for one instant
Unless he trust his embarrassment,
As in his left ear the siren sings
Meltingly of water and a night
Where all flesh had peace, and on his right
The efreet offers a brilliant void
Where his mind could be perfectly clear
And all his limitations destroyed:

Many young princes soon disappear
To join all the unjust kings.

So, if you prosper, suspect those bright
Mornings when you whistle with a light
Heart. You are loved; you have never seen
The harbour so still, the park so green,
So many well-fed pigeons upon
Cupolas and triumphal arches,
So many stags and slender ladies
Beside the canals. Remember when
Your climate seems a permanent home
For marvellous creatures and great men,
What griefs and convulsions startled Rome,
Ecbatana, Babylon.

How narrow the space, how slight the chance
For civil pattern and importance
Between the watery vagueness and
The triviality of the sand,
How soon the lively trip is over
From loose craving to sharp aversion,
Aimless jelly to paralysed bone:
At the end of each successful day
Remember that the fire and the ice
Are never more than one step away
From the temperate city; it is
But a moment to either.

But should you fail to keep your kingdom
And, like your father before you, come
Where thought accuses and feeling mocks,
Believe your pain: praise the scorching rocks
For their desiccation of your lust,
Thank the bitter treatment of the tide
For its dissolution of your pride,
That the whirlwind may arrange your will
And the deluge release it to find
The spring in the desert, the fruitful
Island in the sea, where flesh and mind
Are delivered from mistrust.

Blue the sky beyond her humming sail
As I sit today by our ship's rail
Watching exuberant porpoises
Escort us homeward and writing this

For you to open when I am gone:
Read it, Ferdinand, with the blessing
Of Alonso, your father, once King
Of Naples, now ready to welcome
Death, but rejoicing in a new love,
A new peace, having heard the solemn
Music strike and seen the statue move
To forgive our illusion.

Musée Des Beaux Arts

About suffering they were never wrong,
The Old Masters: how well they understood
Its human position; how it takes place
While someone else is eating or opening a window or just walking
      dully along;
How, when the aged are reverently, passionately waiting
For the miraculous birth, there always must be
Children who did not specially want it to happen, skating
On a pond at the edge of the wood:
They never forgot
That even the dreadful martyrdom must run its course
Anyhow in a corner, some untidy spot
Where the dogs go on with their doggy life and the torturer's horse
Scratches its innocent behind on a tree.

In Breughel's *Icarus*, for instance: how everything turns away
Quite leisurely from the disaster; the ploughman may
Have heard the splash, the forsaken cry,
But for him it was not an important failure; the sun shone
As it had to on the white legs disappearing into the green
Water; and the expensive delicate ship that must have seen
Something amazing, a boy falling out of the sky,
Had somewhere to get to and sailed calmly on.

Petition

Sir, no man's enemy, forgiving all
But will his negative inversion, be prodigal:
Send to us power and light, a sovereign touch
Curing the intolerable neural itch,
The exhaustion of weaning, the liar's quinsy,
And the distortions of ingrown virginity.
Prohibit sharply the rehearsed response

And gradually correct the coward's stance;
Cover in time with beams those in retreat
That, spotted, they turn though the reverse were great;
Publish each healer that in city lives
Or country houses at the end of drives;
Harrow the house of the dead; look shining at
New styles of architecture, a change of heart.

"Lay Your Sleeping Head, My Love"

Lay your sleeping head, my love,
Human on my faithless arm;
Time and fevers burn away
Individual beauty from
Thoughtful children, and the grave
Proves the child ephemeral:
But in my arms till break of day
Let the living creature lie,
Mortal, guilty, but to me
The entirely beautiful.

Soul and body have no bounds:
To lovers as they lie upon
Her tolerant enchanted slope
In their ordinary swoon,
Grave the vision Venus sends
Of supernatural sympathy,
Universal love and hope;
While an abstract insight wakes
Among the glaciers and the rocks
The hermit's sensual ecstasy.

Certainty, fidelity
On the stroke of midnight pass
Like vibrations of a bell,
And fashionable madmen raise
Their pedantic boring cry:
Every farthing of the cost,
All the dreaded cards foretell,
Shall be paid, but from this night
Not a whisper, not a thought,
Not a kiss nor look be lost.

Beauty, midnight, vision dies:
Let the winds of dawn that blow

Softly round your dreaming head
Such a day of sweetness show
Eye and knocking heart may bless,
Find the mortal world enough;
Noons of dryness see you fed
By the involuntary powers,
Nights of insult let you pass
Watched by every human love.

As He Is

Wrapped in a yielding air, beside
  The flower's soundless hunger,
Close to the tree's clandestine tide,
  Close to the bird's high fever,
  Loud in his hope and anger,
Erect about his skeleton,
  Stands the expressive lover,
  Stands the deliberate man.

Beneath the hot incurious sun,
  Past stronger beasts and fairer
He picks his way, a living gun,
  With gun and lens and bible,
  A militant enquirer,
The friend, the rash, the enemy,
  The essayist, the able,
  Able at times to cry.

The friendless and unhated stone
  Lies everywhere about him,
The Brothered-One, the Not-Alone,
  The brothered and the hated
  Whose family have taught him
To set against the large and dumb,
  The timeless and the rooted,
  His money and his time.

For mother's fading hopes become
  Dull wives to his dull spirits
Soon dulled by nurse's moral thumb,
  That dullard fond betrayer,
  And, childish, he inherits
So soon by legal father tricked,
  The tall and gorgeous tower,
  Gorgeous but locked, but locked.

And ruled by dead men never met,
    By pious guess deluded,
Upon the stool of madness set
    Or stool of desolation,
    Sits murderous and clear-headed;
Enormous beauties round him move,
    For grandiose is his vision
    And grandiose his love.

Determined on Time's honest shield
    The lamb must face the tigress,
Their faithful quarrel never healed
    Though, faithless, he consider
    His dream of vaguer ages,
Hunter and victim reconciled,
    The lion and the adder,
    The adder and the child.

Fresh loves betray him, every day
    Over his green horizon
A fresh deserter rides away,
    And miles away birds mutter
    Of ambush and of treason;
To fresh defeats he still must move,
    To further griefs and greater,
    And the defeat of grief.

from

Commentary

Some of our dead are famous, but they would not care:
Evil is always personal and spectacular,
But goodness needs the evidence of all our lives,

And, even to exist, it must be shared as truth,
As freedom or as happiness. (For what is happiness
If not to witness joy upon the features of another?)

They did not live to be remembered specially as noble,
Like those who cultivated only cucumbers and melons
To prove that they were rich; and when we praise their names,

They shake their heads in warning, chiding us to give
Our gratitude to the Invisible College of the Humble,
Who through the ages have accomplished everything essential.

And stretch around our struggle as the normal landscape,
And mingle, fluent with our living, like the winds and waters,
The dust of all the dead that reddens every sunset;

Giving us courage to confront our enemies,
Not only on the Grand Canal, or in Madrid,
Across the campus of a university city,

But aid us everywhere, that in the lovers' bedroom,
The white laboratory, the school, the public meeting,
The enemies of life may be more passionately attacked.

And, if we care to listen, we can always hear them:
'Men are not innocent as beasts and never can be,
Man can improve but never will himself be perfect,

Only the free have disposition to be truthful,
Only the truthful have the interest to be just,
Only the just possess the will-power to be free.

For common justice can determine private freedom,
As a clear sky can tempt men to astronomy,
Or a peninsula persuade them to be sailors.

You talked of Liberty, but were not just; and now
Your enemies have called your bluff; for in your city,
Only the man behind the rifle had free-will.

One wish is common to you both, the wish to build
A world united as that Europe was in which
The flint-faced exile wrote his three-act comedy.

Lament not its decay; that shell was too constricting:
The years of private isolation had their lesson,
And in the interest of intelligence were necessary.

Now in the clutch of crisis and the bloody hour
You must defeat your enemies or perish, but remember,
Only by those who reverence it can life be mastered;

Only a whole and happy conscience can stand up
And answer their bleak lie; among the just,
And only there, is Unity compatible with Freedom.'

Night falls on China; the great arc of travelling shadow
Moves over land and ocean, altering life:
Thibet already silent, the packed Indias cooling,

Inert in the paralysis of caste. And though in Africa
The vegetation still grows fiercely like the young,
And in the cities that receive the slanting radiations

The lucky are at work, and most still know they suffer,
The dark will touch them soon: night's tiny noises
Will echo vivid in the owl's developed ear,

Vague in the anxious sentry's; and the moon look down
On battlefields and dead men lying, heaped like treasure,
On lovers ruined in a brief embrace, on ships

Where exiles watch the sea: and in the silence
The cry that streams out into the indifferent spaces,
And never stops or slackens, may be heard more clearly,

Above the everlasting murmur of the woods and rivers,
And more insistent than the lulling answer of the waltzes,
Or hum of printing-presses turning forests into lies;

As now I hear it, rising round me from Shanghai,
And mingling with the distant mutter of guerrilla fighting,
The voice of Man: 'O teach us to outgrow our madness.

Ruffle the perfect manners of the frozen heart,
And once again compel it to be awkward and alive,
To all it suffered once a weeping witness.

Clear from the head the masses of impressive rubbish;
Rally the lost and trembling forces of the will,
Gather them up and let them loose upon the earth,

Till, as the contribution of our star, we follow
The clear instructions of that Justice, in the shadow
Of Whose uplifting, loving, and constraining power
All human reasons do rejoice and operate.'

"Let the Florid Music Praise"

Let the florid music praise,
   The flute and the trumpet,
Beauty's conquest of your face:
In that land of flesh and bone,
Where from citadels on high

Her imperial standards fly,
Let the hot sun
Shine on, shine on.

O but the unloved have had power,
The weeping and striking,
Always: time will bring their hour;
Their secretive children walk
Through your vigilance of breath
To unpardonable death,
And my vows break
Before his look.

Casino

Only the hands are living; to the wheel attracted,
Are moved as deer trek desperately towards a creek
Through the dust and scrub of the desert, or gently
As sunflowers turn to the light.

And, as the night takes up the cries of feverish children,
The cravings of lions in dens, the loves of dons,
Gathers them all and remains the night, the
Great room is full of their prayers.

To the last feast of isolation self-invited
They flock, and in the rite of disbelief are joined;
From numbers all their stars are recreated,
The enchanted, the world, the sad.

Without, the rivers flow among the wholly living,
Quite near their trysts; and the mountains part them; and the bird
Deep in the greens and moistures of summer
Sings towards their work.

But here no nymph comes naked to the youngest shepherd;
The fountain is deserted; the laurel will not grow;
The labyrinth is safe but endless, and broken
As Ariadne's thread.

As deeper in these hands is grooved their fortune: 'Lucky
Were few, and it is possible that none was loved;
And what was godlike in this generation
Was never to be born.'

Perhaps

O Love, the interest itself in thoughtless Heaven,
Make simpler daily the beating of man's heart; within,
There in the ring where name and image meet,

Inspire them with such a longing as will make his thought
Alive like patterns a murmuration of starlings,
Rising in joy over wolds, unwittingly weave.

Here too on our little reef display your power,
This fortress perched on the edge of the Atlantic scarp,
The mote between all Europe and the exile-crowded sea;

And make us as *Newton* was who, in his garden watching
The apple falling towards *England,* became aware
Between himself and her of an eternal tie.

For now that dream which so long had contented our will,
I mean, of uniting the dead into a splendid empire,
Under whose fertilising flood the Lancashire moss

Sprouted up chimneys, and *Glamorgan* hid a life
Grim as a tidal rock-pool's in its glove-shaped valleys,
Is already retreating into her maternal shadow;

Leaving the furnaces gasping in the impossible air,
That flotsam at which *Dumbarton* gapes and hungers;
While upon wind-loved *Rowley* no hammer shakes

The cluster of mounds like a midget golf-course, graves
Of some who created these intelligible dangerous marvels,
Affectionate people, but crude their sense of glory.

Far-sighted as falcons, they looked down another future;
For the seed in their loins were hostile though afraid of their pride,
And, tall with a shadow now, inertly wait.

In bar, in netted chicken-farm, in lighthouse,
Standing on these impoverished constricted acres,
The ladies and gentlemen apart, too much alone,

Consider the years of the measured world begun,
The barren virtuous marriage of stone and water.
Yet, O, at this very moment of a hopeless sigh,

When, inland, they are thinking their thoughts but watching these
    islands
As children in *Chester* look to *Moel Fammau* to decide
On picnics by the clearness or withdrawal of her treeless crown.

Some possible dream, long coiled in the ammonite's slumber
Is uncurling, prepared to lay on our talk and reflection
Its military silence, its surgeon's idea of pain;

And out of the future into actual history,
As when *Merlin,* tamer of horses, and his lords to whom
Stonehenge was still a thought, the *Pillars* passed

And into the undared ocean swung north their prow,
Drives through the night and star-concealing dawn
For the virgin roadsteads of our hearts an unwavering keel.

LOUIS MacNEICE

1907-

Stylite

The saint on the pillar stands,
The pillar is alone,
He has stood so long
That he himself is stone;
Only his eyes
Range across the sand
Where no one ever comes
And the world is banned.

Then his eyes close,
He stands in his sleep,
Round his neck there comes
The conscience of a rope,
And the hangman counting
Counting to ten—
At nine he finds
He has eyes again.

The saint on the pillar stands,
The pillars are two,

A young man opposite
Stands in the blue,
A white Greek god,
Confident, with curled
Hair above the groin
And his eyes on the world.

March, 1940

June Thunder

The Junes were free and full, driving through tiny
Roads, the mudguards brushing the cowparsley,
Through fields of mustard and under boldly embattled
    Mays and chestnuts

Or between beeches verdurous and voluptuous
Or where broom and gorse beflagged the chalkland—
All the flare and gusto of the unenduring
    Joys of a season

Now returned but I note as more appropriate
To the maturer mood impending thunder
With an indigo sky and the garden hushed except for
    The treetops moving.

Then the curtains in my room blow suddenly inward,
The shrubbery rustles, birds fly heavily homeward,
The white flowers fade to nothing on the trees and rain comes
    Down like a dropscene.

Now there comes the catharsis, the cleansing downpour
Breaking the blossoms of our overdated fancies
Our old sentimentality and whimsicality
    Loves of the morning.

Blackness at half-past eight, the night's precursor,
Clouds like falling masonry and lightning's lavish
Annunciation, the sword of the mad archangel
    Flashed from the scabbard.

If only you would come and dare the crystal
Rampart of rain and the bottomless moat of thunder,
If only now you would come I should be happy
    Now if now only.

1937

The Sunlight on the Garden

The sunlight on the garden
Hardens and grows cold,
We cannot cage the minute
Within its nets of gold,
When all is told
We cannot beg for pardon.

Our freedom as free lances
Advances towards its end;
The earth compels, upon it
Sonnets and birds descend;
And soon, my friend,
We shall have no time for dances.

The sky was good for flying
Defying the church bells
And every evil iron
Siren and what it tells:
The earth compels,
We are dying, Egypt, dying

And not expecting pardon,
Hardened in heart anew,
But glad to have sat under
Thunder and rain with you,
And grateful too
For sunlight on the garden.

1937

An Eclogue for Christmas

A. I meet you in an evil time.
B.   The evil bells
Put out of our heads, I think, the thought of everything else.
A. The jaded calendar revolves,
    Its nuts need oil, carbon chokes the valves,
    The excess sugar of a diabetic culture
    Rotting the nerve of life and literature;
    Therefore when we bring out the old tinsel and frills
    To announce that Christ is born among the barbarous hills
    I turn to you whom a morose routine
    Saves from the mad vertigo of being what has been.

B. Analogue of me, you are wrong to turn to me,
    My country will not yield you any sanctuary,
    There is no pinpoint in any of the ordnance maps
    To save you when your towns and town-bred thoughts collapse,
    It is better to die *in situ* as I shall,
    One place is as bad as another. Go back where your instincts call
    And listen to the crying of the town-cats and the taxis again,
    Or wind your gramophone and eavesdrop on great men.

A. Jazz-weary of years of drums and Hawaiian guitar,
    Pivoting on the parquet I seem to have moved far
    From bombs and mud and gas, have stuttered on my feet
    Clinched to the streamlined and butter-smooth trulls of the élite,
    The lights irritating and gyrating and rotating in gauze—
    Pomade-dazzle, a slick beauty of gewgaws—
    I who was Harlequin in the childhood of the century,
    Posed by Picasso beside an endless opaque sea,
    Have seen myself sifted and splintered in broken facets,
    Tentative pencillings, endless liabilities, no assets,
    Abstractions scalpelled with a palette-knife
    Without reference to this particular life.
    And so it has gone on; I have not been allowed to be
    Myself in flesh or face, but abstracting and dissecting me
    They have made of me pure form, a symbol or a pastiche,
    Stylised profile, anything but soul and flesh:
    And that is why I turn this jaded music on
    To forswear thought and become an automaton.

B. There are in the country also of whom I am afraid—
    Men who put beer into a belly that is dead,
    Women in the forties with terrier and setter who whistle and
        swank
    Over down and plough and Roman road and daisied bank,
    Half-conscious that these barriers over which they stride
    Are nothing to the barbed wire that has grown round their pride.

A. And two there are, as I drive in the city, who suddenly perturb—
    The one sirening me to draw up by the kerb
    The other, as I lean back, my right leg stretched creating speed,
    Making me catch and stamp, the brakes shrieking, pull up dead:
    She wears silk stockings taunting the winter wind,
    He carries a white stick to mark that he is blind.

B. In the country they are still hunting, in the heavy shires
    Greyness is on the fields and sunset like a line of pyres
    Of barbarous heroes smoulders through the ancient air
    Hazed with factory dust and, orange opposite, the moon's glare,
    Goggling yokel-stubborn through the iron trees,
    Jeers at the end of us, our bland ancestral ease;

We shall go down like palaeolithic man
Before some new Ice Age or Genghiz Khan.

A. It is time for some new coinage, people have got so old,
   Hacked and handled and shiny from pocketing they have made
      bold
   To think that each is himself through these accidents, being
      blind
   To the fact that they are merely the counters of an unknown
      Mind.

B. A Mind that does not think, if such a thing can be,
   Mechanical Reason, capricious Identity.
   That I could be able to face this domination nor flinch—

A. The tin toys of the hawker move on the pavement inch by inch
   Not knowing that they are wound up; it is better to be so
   Than to be, like us, wound up and while running down to
      know—

B. But everywhere the pretence of individuality recurs—

A. Old faces frosted with powder and choked in furs.

B. The jutlipped farmer gazing over the humpbacked wall.

A. The commercial traveller joking in the urinal.—

B. I think things draw to an end, the soil is stale.

A. And over-elaboration will nothing now avail,
   The street is up again, gas, electricity or drains,
   Ever-changing conveniences, nothing comfortable remains
   Unimproved, as flagging Rome improved villa and sewer
   (A sound-proof library and a stable temperature).
   Our street is up, red lights sullenly mark
   The long trench of pipes, iron guts in the dark,
   And not till the Goths again come swarming down the hill
   Will cease the clangour of the pneumatic drill.
   But yet there is beauty narcotic and deciduous
   In this vast organism grown out of us:
   On all the traffic-islands stand white globes like moons,
   The city's haze is clouded amber that purrs and croons,
   And tilting by the noble curve bus after tall bus comes
   With an osculation of yellow light, with a glory like
      chrysanthemums.

B. The country gentry cannot change, they will die in their shoes
   From angry circumstance and moral self-abuse,
   Dying with a paltry fizzle they will prove their lives to be
   An ever-diluted drug, a spiritual tautology.
   They cannot live once their idols are turned out,
   None of them can endure, for how could they, possibly, without
   The flotsam of private property, pekinese and polyanthus,
   The good things which in the end turn to poison and pus,
   Without the bandy chairs and the sugar in the silver tongs

And the inter-ripple and resonance of years of dinner-gongs?
Or if they could find no more that cumulative proof
In the rain dripping off the conservatory roof?
What will happen when the only sanction the country-dweller
     has—

A. What will happen to us, planked and panelled with jazz?
    Who go to the theatre where a black man dances like an eel,
    Where pink thighs flash like the spokes of a wheel, where we
     feel
    That we know in advance all the jogtrot and the cake-walk jokes,
    All the bumfun and the gags of the comedians in boaters and
     toques,
    All the tricks of the virtuosos who invert the usual—

B. What will happen to us when the State takes down the manor
     wall,
    When there is no more private shooting or fishing, when the
     trees are all cut down,
    When faces are all dials and cannot smile or frown—

A. What will happen when the sniggering machine-guns in the
     hands of the young men
    Are trained on every flat and club and beauty parlour and
     Father's den?
    What will happen when our civilisation like a long pent
     balloon—

B. What will happen will happen; the whore and the buffoon
    Will come off best; no dreamers, they cannot lose their dream
    And are at least likely to be reinstated in the new régime.
    But one thing is not likely—

A.   Do not gloat over yourself
    Do not be your own vulture, high on some mountain shelf
    Huddle the pitiless abstractions bald about the neck
    Who will descend when you crumple in the plains a wreck.
    Over the randy of the theatre and cinema I hear songs
    Unlike anything—

B.   The lady of the house poises the silver tongs
    And picks a lump of sugar, 'ne plus ultra' she says
    'I cannot do otherwise, even to prolong my days'—

A. I cannot do otherwise either, to-night I will book my seat—

B. I will walk about the farm-yard which is replete
    As with the smell of dung so with memories—

A. I will gorge myself to satiety with the oddities
    Of every artiste, official or amateur,
    Who has pleased me in my rôle of hero-worshipper
    Who has pleased me in my rôle of individual man—

B. Let us lie once more, say 'What we think, we can'
    The old idealist lie—

A.   And for me before I die
    Let me go the round of the garish glare—
B.   And one the bare and high
    Places of England, the Wiltshire Downs and the Long Mynd
    Let the balls of my feet bounce on the turf, my face burn in
        the wind
    My eyelashes stinging in the wind, and the sheep like grey
        stones
    Humble my human pretensions—
A.   Let the saxophones and the xylophones
    And the cult of every technical excellence, the miles of canvas
        in the galleries
    And the canvas of the rich man's yacht snapping and tacking
        on the seas
    And the perfection of a grilled steak—
B.   Let all these so ephemeral things
    Be somehow permanent like the swallow's tangent wings:
    Good-bye to you, this day remember is Christmas, this morn
    They say, interpret it your own way, Christ is born.

                                                    1933

THEODORE ROETHKE

1908-

The Lost Son

I. THE FLIGHT

At Woodlawn I heard the dead cry:
I was lulled by the slamming of iron,
A slow drip over stones,
Toads brooding in wells.
All the leaves stuck out their tongues;
I shook the softening chalk of my bones,
Saying,
Snail, snail, glister me forward,
Bird, soft-sigh me home,
Worm, be with me.
This is my hard time.

Fished in an old wound,
The soft pond of repose;

Nothing nibbled my line,
Not even the minnows came.

Sat in an empty house
Watching shadows crawl,
Scratching.
There was one fly.

Voice, come out of the silence.
Say something.
Appear in the form of a spider
Or a moth beating the curtain.

Tell me:
Which is the way I take,
Out of what door do I go,
Where and to whom?

      Dark hollows said, lee to the wind,
      The moon said, back of an eel,
      The salt said, look by the sea,
      Your tears are not enough praise,
      You will find no comfort here,
In the kingdom of bang and blab.

Running lightly over spongy ground,
Past the pasture of flat stones,
The three elms,
The sheep strewn on a field,
Over a rickety bridge
Toward the quick-water, wrinkling and rippling.

Hunting along the river,
Down among the rubbish, the bug-riddled foliage,
By the muddy pond-edge, by bog-holes,
By the shrunken lake, hunting, in the heat of summer.

The shape of a rat?

      It's bigger than that.
      It's less than a leg
      And more than a nose,
      Just under the water
      It usually goes.

Is it soft like a mouse?
Can it wrinkle its nose?

Could it come in the house
On the tips of its toes?

Take the skin of a cat
And the back of an eel,
Then roll them in grease,
That's the way it would feel.

It's sleek as an otter
With wide webby toes,
Just under the water
It usually goes.

II. THE PIT

Where do the roots go?
    Look down under the leaves.
Who put the moss there?
    These stones have been here too long.
Who stunned the dirt into noise?
    Ask the mole, he knows.
I feel the slime of a wet nest.
    Beware Mother Mildew.
Nibble again, fish nerves.

III. THE GIBBER

At the wood's mouth,
By the cave's door,
I listened to something
I had heard before.

Dogs of the groin
Barked and howled,
The sun was against me,
The moon would not have me.

The weeds whined,
The snakes cried,
The cows and briars
Said to me: Die.

What a small song. What slow clouds. What dark water.
Hath the raine a father? All the caves are ice. Only the snow's
   here.

I'm cold. I'm cold all over. Rub me in father and mother.
Fear was my father, Father Fear.
His look drained the stones.

> What gliding shape
> Beckoning through halls,
> Stood poised on the stair,
> Fell dreamily down?

> From the mouths of jugs
> Perched on many shelves.
> I saw substance flowing
> That cold morning.

> Like a slither of eels
> That watery cheek
> As my own tongue kissed
> My lips awake.

Is this the storm's heart? The ground is unstilling itself.
My veins are running nowhere. Do the bones cast out their fire?
Is the seed leaving the old bed? These buds are live as birds.
Where, where are the tears of the world?
Let the kisses resound, flat like a butcher's palm;
Let the gestures freeze; our doom is already decided.
All the windows are burning! What's left of my life?
I want the old rage, the lash of primordial milk!
Good-bye, good-bye, old stones, the time-order is going.
I have married my hands to perpetual agitation,
I run, I run to the whistle of money.

> Money money money
> Water water water

How cool the grass is.
Has the bird left?
The stalk still sways.

Has the worm a shadow?
What do the clouds say?
These sweeps of light undo me.
Look, look, the ditch is running white!
I've more veins than a tree!
Kiss me, ashes, I'm falling through a dark swirl.

IV. THE RETURN

The way to the boiler was dark,
Dark all the way,
Over slippery cinders,
Through the long greenhouse.

The roses kept breathing in the dark.
They had many mouths to breathe with.
My knees made little winds underneath
Where the weeds slept.

There was always a single light
Swinging by the fire-pit
Where the fireman pulled out roses,
The big roses, the bloody clinkers.

      Once I stayed all night.
      The light in the morning came slowly over the white
      Snow.
      There were many kinds of cool
      Air.
      Then came
      Steam.
      Pipe-knock.

Scurry of warm over small plants.
Ordnung! ordnung!
Papa is coming!

      A fine haze moved off the leaves;
      Frost melted on far panes;
      The rose, the chrysanthemum turned toward the light.
      Even the hushed forms, the bent yellowy weeds
      Moved in a slow up-sway.

V.

It was beginning winter,
An in-between time,
The landscape still partly brown:
The bones of weeds kept swinging in the wind,
Above the blue snow.

It was beginning winter,
The light moved slowly over the frozen field,

Over the dry seed-crowns,
The beautiful surviving bones
Swinging in the wind.

Light traveled over the wide field;
Stayed.
The weeds stopped swinging.
The mind moved, not alone,
Through the clear air, in silence.

Was it light?
Was it light within?
Was it light within light?
Stillness becoming alive,
Yet still?

A lively understandable spirit
Once entertained you.
It will come again.
Be still.
Wait.

KATHLEEN RAINE

1908-

Love Poem

Yours is the face that the earth turns to me.
Continuous beyond its human features lie
The mountain forms that rest against the sky.
With your eyes, the reflecting rainbow, the sun's light
Sees me; forest and flowers, bird and beast
Know and hold me forever in the world's thought,
Creation's deep untroubled retrospect.

When your hand touches mine, it is the earth
That takes me—the deep grass,
And rocks and rivers; the green graves,
And children still unborn, and ancestors,
In love passed down from hand to hand from God.
Your love comes from the creation of the world,

From those paternal fingers, streaming through the clouds
That break with light the surface of the sea.

Here, where I trace your body with my hand,
Loves' presence has no end;
For these, your arms that hold me, are the world's.
In us, the continents, clouds and oceans meet
Our arbitrary selves, extensive with the night,
Lost, in the heart's worship, and the body's sleep.

Desire

I did not make the conditions of my life whereby
the laws of stars will never change, though I
say "Give me to a god, or I will die."

I am not wise, why must I know so much
that teaches me what I can never learn,
that I can put my trust in house or home.

The solid earth and the extensive sky
are flimsy and impermanent as I—
my earth, my love, my thought will die with me.

Oh lovely earth, with richer life than mine,
whose teeming seas and blooming fields decline
slowly toward stillness, yet remain!

For animals shall fly the secret plains,
and human greatness suffer greater pangs
while engines dance beneath revolving suns.

Your shrinking form, broken forgetful face,
your bursting entrails, and your cooling heart
shall all lie lifeless, cold and motionless.

The hot blood and the conscious grief shall cool,
and forests burn in their own funeral.

The Fall

It is the fall, the eternal fall of water,
of rock, of wounded birds, and the wounded heart,
the waterfall of freedom. Angels fall

like lovers from the azure, separate,
and die by that same death that ends us all.

Falling ten million years, we fling ourselves
again into the inviting arms of time;
our nuptial flight must end again in death
that serves for freedom time and time again
while the hard labouring mystic holds his breath.

The watching surface of the living sea
ever intact, smiles with the face of love,
where living blood drowns in its ecstasy,
impelled by nature that can mountains move,
feeling most freedom when it least is free.

Shall we go down, shall we go down together?
here on the mountain top, the wind and snow
urge us to fall, and go the way they go.
The way is clear, the end we shall not know,
the sea will carry us where tides run and currents flow.

STEPHEN SPENDER

1909-

Winter and Summer

Within my head, aches the perpetual winter
Of this violent time, where pleasures freeze.
My inner eye anticipates for ever
Looking through naked trees and running wheels
Onto a blank transparent sky
Leading to nothing; as though, through iron aims,
It was stared back at by the filmy surface
Of a lid covering its own despair.
Thus, when the summer breaks upon my face
With the outward shock of a green wave
Crested with leaves and creamy foam of flowers,
I think the luxurious lazy meadows
Are a deceiving canvas covering
With a balmy paint of leafy billows,
The furious volleys of charioteering power
Behind the sun, racing to destroy.

When under light lawns, heavy in their soil,
I hear the groaning of the wasted lives
Of those who revolve unreflecting wheels,
    Alas, I prove that I am right,
For if my shadowed mind affirmed the light
It would return to those green, foolish years
When to live seemed to stand knee-deep in flowers:
There, winter was an indoor accident,
Where, with head pressed against the glass, I watched
The garden, falsified by snow,
Waiting to melt, and become real again.

Port Bou

As a child holds a pet
Arms clutching but with hands that do not join
And the coiled animal watches the gap
To outer freedom in animal air,
So the earth-and-rock flesh arms of this harbour
Embrace but do not enclose the sea
Which, through a gap, vibrates to the open sea
Where ships and dolphins swim and above is the sun.
In the bright winter sunlight I sit on the stone parapet
Of a bridge; my circling arms rest on a newspaper
Empty in my mind as the glittering stone
Because I search for an image
And seeing an image I count out the coined words
To remember the childish headlands of this harbour.
A lorry halts beside me with creaking brakes
And I look up at warm waving flag-like faces
Of militiamen staring down at my French newspaper.
'How do they speak of our struggle, over the frontier?'
I hold out the paper, but they refuse,
They did not ask for anything so precious
But only for friendly words and to offer me cigarettes.
In their smiling faces the war finds peace, the famished mouths
Of the rusty carbines brush against their trousers
Almost as fragilely as reeds;
And wrapped in a cloth—old mother in a shawl—
The terrible machine-gun rests.
They shout, salute back as the truck jerks forward
Over the vigorous hill, beyond the headland.
An old man passes, his running mouth,
With three teeth like bullets, spits out 'pom-pom-pom.'
The children run after; and, more slowly, the women

Clutching their clothes, follow over the hill;
Till the village is empty, for the firing practice,
And I am left alone on the bridge at the exact centre
Where the cleaving river trickles like saliva.
At the exact centre, solitary as a target,
Where nothing moves against a background of cardboard houses
Except the disgraceful skirring dogs; and the firing begins,
Across the harbour mouth from headland to headland,
White flecks of foam gashed by lead in the sea;
And the echo trails over its iron lash
Whipping the flanks of the surrounding hills.
My circling arms rest on the newspaper,
My mind seems paper where dust and ink fall,
I tell myself the shooting is only for practice,
And my body seems a cloth which the machine-gun stitches
Like a sewing machine, neatly, with cotton from a reel;
And the solitary, irregular, thin 'paffs' from the carbines
Draw on long needles white threads through my navel.

An Elementary School Class Room in a Slum

Far far from gusty waves, these children's faces.
Like rootless weeds the torn hair round their paleness.
The tall girl with her weighed-down head. The paper-
seeming boy with rat's eyes. The stunted unlucky heir
Of twisted bones, reciting a father's gnarled disease,
His lesson from his desk. At back of the dim class,
One unnoted, sweet and young: his eyes live in a dream
Of squirrels' game, in tree room, other than this.

On sour cream walls, donations. Shakespeare's head
Cloudless at dawn, civilized dome riding all cities.
Belled, flowery, Tyrolese valley. Open-handed map
Awarding the world its world. And yet, for these
Children, these windows, not this world, are world,
Where all their future's painted with a fog,
A narrow street sealed in with a lead sky,
Far far from rivers, capes, and stars of words.

Surely Shakespeare is wicked, the map a bad example
With ships and sun and love tempting them to steal—
For lives that slyly turn in their cramped holes
From fog to endless night? On their slag heap, these children
Wear skins peeped through by bones and spectacles of steel
With mended glass, like bottle bits on stones.

All of their time and space are foggy slum
So blot their maps with slums as big as doom.

Unless, governor, teacher, inspector, visitor,
This map becomes their window and these windows
That open on their lives like crouching tombs
Break, O break open, till they break the town
And show the children to the fields and all their world
Azure on their sands, to let their tongues
Run naked into books, the white and green leaves open
The history theirs whose language is the sun.

Polar Exploration

Our single purpose was to walk through snow
With faces swung to their prodigious North
Like compass iron. As clerks in whited banks
With bird-claw pens column virgin paper,
To snow we added foot-prints.
Extensive whiteness drowned
All sense of space. We tramped through
Static, glaring days, Time's suspended blank.
That was in Spring and Autumn. Summer struck
Water over rocks, and half the world
Became a ship with a deep keel, the booming floes
And icebergs with their little birds:
Twittering Snow Bunting, Greenland Wheatear,
Red-throated Divers; imagine butterflies
Sulphurous cloudy yellow; glory of bees
That suck from saxifrage; crowberry,
Bilberry, cranberry, *Pyrola Uniflora.*
There followed Winter in a frozen hut
Warm enough at the kernel, but dare to sleep
With head against the wall—ice gummed my hair!
Hate Culver's loud breathing, despise Freeman's
Fidget for washing; love only the dogs
That whine for scraps, and scratch. Notice
How they run better (on short journeys) with a bitch.
In that, different from us.
Return, return, you warn. We do. There is
A network of railways, money, words, words, words.
Meals, papers, exchanges, debates,
Cinema, wireless: the worst, is Marriage.
We cannot sleep. At night we watch
A speaking clearness through cloudy paranoia.

These questions are white rifts:—Was
Ice our anger transformed? The raw, the motionless
Skies, were these the Spirit's hunger?
The continual and hypnotized march through snow,
The dropping nights of precious extinction, were these
Only the wide inventions of the will,
The frozen will's evasion? If this exists
In us as madness here, as coldness
In these summer, civilized sheets: Is the North,
Over there, a tangible, real madness,
A glittering simpleton, one without towns,
Only with bears and fish, a staring eye,
A new and singular sex?

"What I Expected Was"

What I expected was
Thunder, fighting,
Long struggles with men
And climbing.
After continual straining
I should grow strong;
Then the rocks would shake
And I should rest long.

What I had not foreseen
Was the gradual day
Weakening the will
Leaking the brightness away,
The lack of good to touch
The fading of body and soul
Like smoke before wind
Corrupt, unsubstantial.

The wearing of Time,
And the watching of cripples pass
With limbs shaped like questions
In their odd twist,
The pulverous grief
Melting the bones with pity,
The sick falling from earth—
These, I could not foresee.

For I had expected always
Some brightness to hold in trust,

Some final innocence
To save from dust;
That, hanging solid,
Would dangle through all
Like the created poem
Or the dazzling crystal.

MARGUERITE YOUNG

1910-

The White Rat

How now could body-soul's symbol be this
By love, or calculation, this white rat enraged
Caged in a theatre of emptiness,
His, a snowfall of footsteps and glittering eyes?

Nor moon, a compound of the unseen events,
Nor earth, as principle of tear or dew on flowers
Rounding, he considers now. By him are we clarified.

Who could have nurtured his body on penurious dew
Is caged, is caught like a tyrannical dragonfly
And made to actualize, O, mute actuality

In void denuded now of all but blank him
And cleaned of all but the white rat's space
And eyes like diamonds in his empty head.

Who could have walked transparent fretted on wind and waves,
Now he runs upon a branched track abstract
And is mechanical in every wintry act

And is body-soul, is the most distant hope!
Here, in this cage, Platonic double moons,
Here, in this cage, St. Augustine
Crying, O, my God, art Thou without or within?

For this rat's sensorium is his true knowledge
Nor star will shine beyond his death for him,
Nor wild rock goose be shy and wild in the dusk of foliage,
Afraid of foxes in the light of day,
Nor hoary owls like flowers skim lost in leaves.

Does God with diamond eyes look down on these
For the purposes of what intrinsic studies?

Noah's Ark

When world is water and all is flood, God said,
And the ark is wavering on rising seas,
Windowed on waters, a prison of purple wood
Like to Noah, the ark of soul and body,

Then salvaged from corruption by flood, in mated blisses
Are the twin foxes, the ravens, the three pacific doves,
And are zebras in a golden cage,
The ram, the ewe, the paired gazelles of love,

And in union blessed, are saved for future time
The meek sparrows, and all things of their kind,
Both male and female: yet have I ever aged,
It is the corrupt world of the mind.

For though in the dark hold are harmonies
As the antelope moon-spotted, the ostriches light-eyed,
The dual lions sleeping, and copulating butterflies,
And arch-angel flare on this sensual tide,

And though do rabbits breed and multiply
In this dark cavern of this estranged dream,
And there do adders coil in marriage, spiders weave,
And all is the assurance of one scheme,

Yet God is the impotent old man, and withered,
And the imaginings of His heart, as that vain Noah
Whose limbs extend in a sterile brood
And heart is the hive of all imaginings now

Or tree where do cling the mimic moths like bark;
For God is loneliest, He is creation's flaw
And celibate, nor passenger of this uniting ark.
Unmated were the beautiful He knew

And loneliest, as His voice speaking from the clouds
When water covers over the waste of all
And idea of lilies implicit with the crowd
And dust implicit with lilies of His skull.

ROBERT FITZGERALD
1910-

Colorado

Now the plains come to adore the mountain wall,
Their yellow fields running and bowing like waves
To celebrate in such serene order the fire
And love that bore these stony things. Now fragile
Air, sweet health of a superficial season
Garland a while the majesty of winter.

And I, not long nor with profit hereabouts,
Note merely the blue, the watercolor blue
A descriptive man would like; the rare
And rifted shadowline of trees, the smooth
Peaks too cold for the warm west to redden,
Much, or gild them. They remain sharply vague.

It is so, too, I think, with the remote
Populations of memory: they stand above
Our imperceptible journeys and indulgence,
Easily unseen by a simple turn of the head,
Impossible to grasp in contour, always a little
Shifting, and the same. Death has engraved them
Lovely and lofty, and my metaphysic
Smiles to align them here, the shadowy ones
Tinted so faint, yet luminous as gems.

A property of distance. And distance?
A requisite of the just, which is proportion,
Or holy measure, that the sages loved,
Being so fond of stringed instruments and so
Mild: they liked puppies as well as you;
And saw fit, being profound, not to reflect
Chaos unbounded, but to extract therefrom
Numerous order and magnificence.

So at least I interpret the very thin hostile azure
Wherein these stones are dipt, and I imagine
Of time and the great dead, they too
Correctly make a tune with me; let me
Behold by their grave light my miniscule
Part in the swaying and tranquil grandeur here.

Souls Lake

The evergreen shadow and the pale magnolia
Stripping slowly to the air of May
Stood still in the night of the honey trees.
At rest above a star pool with my friends,
Beside that grove most fit for elegies,
I made my phrase to out-enchant the night.

The epithalamion, the hush were due,
For I had fasted and gone blind to see
What night might be beyond our passages;
Those stars so chevalier in fearful heaven
Could not but lay their steel aside and come
With a grave glitter into my low room.

Vague though the population of the earth
Lay stretched and dry below the cypresses,
It was not round-about but in my night,
Bone of my bone, as an old man would say;
And all its stone weighed my mortality;
The pool would be my body and my eyes,

The air my garment and material
Whereof that wateriness and mirror lived—
The colorable, meek and limpid world.
Though I had sworn my element alien
To the pure mind of night, the cold princes,
Behold them there, and both worlds were the same.

The heart's planet seemed not so lonely then,
Seeing what kin it found in that reclining.
And ah, though sweet the catch of your chorales,
I heard no singing there among my friends;
But still were the great waves, the lions shining,
And infinite still the discourse of the night.

ELIZABETH BISHOP
1911-

The Monument

Now can you see the monument? It is of wood
built somewhat like a box. No. Built
like several boxes in descending sizes
one above the other.
Each is turned half-way round so that
its corners point toward the sides
of the one below and the angles alternate.
Then on the topmost cube is set
a sort of fleur-de-lys of weathered wood,
long petals of board, pierced with odd holes,
four-sided, stiff, ecclesiastical.
From it four thin, warped poles spring out,
(slanted like fishing-poles or flag-poles)
and from them jig-saw work hangs down,
four lines of vaguely whittled ornament
over the edges of the boxes
to the ground.
The monument is one-third set against
a sea; two-thirds against a sky.
The view is geared
(that is, the view's perspective)
so low there is no 'far away,'
and we are far away within the view.
A sea of narrow, horizontal boards
lies out behind our lonely monument,
its long grains alternating right and left
like floor-boards—spotted, swarming-still,
and motionless. A sky runs parallel,
and it is palings, coarser than the sea's:
splintery sunlight and long-fibred clouds.
'Why does that strange sea make no sound?
Is it because we're far away?
Where are we? Are we in Asia Minor,
or in Mongolia?'
                    An ancient promontory,
an ancient principality whose artist-prince
might have wanted to build a monument
to mark a tomb or boundary, or make

a melancholy or romantic scene of it . . .
'But that queer sea looks made of wood,
half-shining, like a driftwood sea.
And the sky looks wooden, grained with cloud.
It's like a stage-set; it is all so flat!
Those clouds are full of glistening splinters!
What is that?'
                    It is the monument.
'It's piled-up boxes,
outlined with shoddy fret-work, half-fallen off,
cracked and unpainted. It looks old.'
—The strong sunlight, the wind from the sea,
all the conditions of its existence,
may have flaked off the paint, if ever it was painted,
and made it homelier than it was.
'Why did you bring me here to see it?
A temple of crates in cramped and crated scenery,
what can it prove?
I am tired of breathing this eroded air,
this dryness in which the monument is cracking.'

It is an artifact
of wood. Wood holds together better
than sea or cloud or sand could by itself,
much better than real sea or sand or cloud.
It chose that way to grow and not to move.
The monument's an object, yet those decorations,
carelessly nailed, looking like nothing at all,
give it away as having life, and wishing;
wanting to be a monument, to cherish something.
The crudest scroll-work says 'commemorate,'
while once each day the light goes around it
like a prowling animal,
or the rain falls on it, or the wind blows into it.
It may be solid, may be hollow.
The bones of the artist-prince may be inside
or far away on even dryer soil.
But roughly but adequately it can shelter
what is within (which after all
cannot have been intended to be seen).
It is the beginning of a painting,
a piece of sculpture, or poem, or monument,
and all of wood. Watch it closely.

The Weed

I dreamed that dead, and meditating,
I lay upon a grave, or bed,
(at least, some cold and close-built bower).
In the cold heart, its final thought
stood frozen, drawn immense and clear,
stiff and idle as I was there;
and we remained unchanged together
for a year, a minute, an hour.
Suddenly there was a motion,
as startling, there, to every sense
as an explosion. Then it dropped
to insistent, cautious creeping
in the region of the heart,
prodding me from desperate sleep.
I raised my head. A slight young weed
had pushed up through the heart and its
green head was nodding on the breast.
(All this was in the dark.)
It grew an inch like a blade of grass;
next, one leaf shot out of its side
a twisting, waving flag, and then
two leaves moved like a semaphore.
The stem grew thick. The nervous roots
reached to each side; the graceful head
changed its position mysteriously,
since there was neither sun nor moon
to catch its young attention.
The rooted heart began to change
(not beat) and then it split apart
and from it broke a flood of water.
Two rivers glanced off from the sides,
one to the right, one to the left,
two rushing, half-clear streams,
(the ribs made of them two cascades)
which assuredly, smooth as glass,
went off through the fine black grains of earth.
The weed was almost swept away;
it struggled with its leaves,
lifting them fringed with heavy drops.
A few drops fell upon my face
and in my eyes, so I could see
(or, in that black place, thought I saw)
that each drop contained a light,

a small, illuminated scene;
the weed-deflected stream was made
itself, of racing images.
(As if a river should carry all
the scenes that it had once reflected
shut in its waters, and not floating
on momentary surfaces.)
The weed stood in the severed heart.
"What are you doing there?" I asked.
It lifted its head all dripping wet
(with my own thoughts?)
and answered then: 'I grow it,' it said,
'but to divide your heart again.'

ROBERT BHAIN CAMPBELL

1911-1940

Final Poem

Bed-ridden, laid by an age's malady
    In the island of a room,
Made private by my purse, I'm priced to lie
Amid the system of the walls, to look
Past pillow, water-jar, dark basin, book,
    Fret, stare, stop, and resume,
At sill and frame, that great bright windowpane
Between me and a tree, an avenue, and man.

My contract gave me to the doctor's will,
    The anaesthesia of ease,
Here in the doctrine of this hospital
That by some further wounds my wounds could cure,
Yet travel is from wound to wound, to fear,
    Discussions of disease,
And I am given up to Latin terms
Which translate me into a dream's alarms.

Beyond, boughs dimly on an iron rail ring;
    Beyond, men, women walk.
Where do they walk? whence come? what bring?
Their traffic moves from right to left—to where—

Filling with incomprehensible sound the air,
  Like bird cries, horns, their talk.
Automobiles and men beyond the pane
Exist beyond this state, our rules, our reign.

Men may not ail, nor words, outside these halls—
  Yet what if I signal, shout?
So bright the light is where on them it falls
The pane is dark upon this company,
And though I see, they never will see me.
  But if dark come without,
If dark come, dark, then might I light this light
That they could see me here, come, let me out.

Yet, dark may to them be enemy, attack,
  And fled the avenue,
Or, else, my bright framed self seem maniac.
By dark and light that pane divides me, then,
The surgeon that shall cut my tongue from men—
  Unless my blood renew,
Rise up, stand tall, and bid the nurse go tell:
My will goes, surgeon, toward that windowsill.

The Task

Tales and talismans I have chronicled
And worn, willing that one should tell us out,
The other charm some dragon of disbelief;
That one should build in the marketplace
A monumental grief, historic only,
Hub for the trade of life, and the other,
Metalled of the last element, close
The system, against questions of the sky be proof.

Yet when the last borne rock is wept, and when
The journeyman's work in the lands is done,
Now with the master's scaffold up, I fear:
What if the mind is honest, the eye as sure?—
Perhaps the impersonal hand in the act
Will make personal marble of grecian air,
Historically aspire, hypnotic, leap,
Embrace the posture in the fountained square.

And the Future's ray and redstar faith,
Composite of continents and that hope

That man is, love is, life is, the world is worth
The fighting for, may be a dream, no Star
Confounding suns; and intellect may be,
And all our engines, pride's brief technique
To ride the circuit of a vain orbit:
Derailed, a locket in extinction's wreck.

Yet, Ahab had his whale, and Lear his kingdom,
The one to pursue, the other to divide:
If death the end is, or that blind aged
Folly, yet there is voyage, the crew, some
Possible virtue in a tragic succession.
We get, we give: such respiration has breath
For a great body, may fan that Star,
May give us life before it gives us death.

ANNE RIDLER

1912-

For a Christening

MEDITATION AND INVOCATION

I

In June the early signs,
And after, the steady labour of subcutaneous growth:
Past the danger of dissolution in the third month,
And in the fifth, quickens.
But hidden while the leaves thicken, through the season when
    smooth corn
Grows bearded, through the peeling of the summer's gold fleece;
Hidden but with heart throbbing, while stars sharpen and throb in
    the skies,
While sunsets grow cold and orange, while winter airs are whirled
    and torn;
And at Candlemas with pain is born.
Lying with a right occipital position, what prompts it we may
    never know,
But at the appointed time dives down, down into the light—
Blinding snow-light, piercing the darkest corner with white,
Brightness of prick-eared cyclamen pink against the snow—
So long hidden, so sudden into sight.

II

You are our darling and our foreign guest;
We know all your origins, and this is to know nothing.
Distinguished stranger to whom we offer food and rest;
Yet made of our own natures; yet looked for with such longing.
Helpless wandering hands, the miniature of mine,
Fine skin and furious look and little raging voice—
Your looks are full human, your qualities all hidden:
It is your mere existence we have by heart, and rejoice.
The wide waters of wonder and comprehension pour
Through this narrow weir, and irresistible their power.
The rainbow multiple glory of our humanity cannot pierce
As does the single white beam of your being.
This makes your presence so shattering a grace,
Unsheathed suddenly from the womb: it was none of our intending
To set in train a miracle; and yet it is merely
Made palpable in you, missed elsewhere by diffusion.
Therefore we adore God-in-our-flesh as a baby:
Whose Being is His Essence, and outside It, illusion.
Later, the fulfilment, the example, death, misprision—
Here the extraordinary fact of Being, which we see
Stripped and simple as the speechless stranger on my knee.

III

Blessing, sleep and grow taller in sleeping.
Lie ever in kind keeping.
Infants curl in a cowrie of peace
And should lie lazy. After this ease,
When the soul out of its safe shell goes,
Stretched as you stretch those knees and toes,
What should I wish you? Intelligence first,
In a credulous age by instruction cursed.
Take from us both what immunity
We have from the germ of the printed lie.
Your father's calm temper I wish you, and
The shaping power of his confident hand.
Much, too, that is different and your own;
And may we learn to leave you alone.
For your part, forgive us the pain of living,
Grow in that harsh sun great-hearted and loving.

Sleep, little honey, then; sleep while the powers
Of the Nine Bright Shiners and the Seven Stars
Harmless, encircle: the natural world

Lifegiving, neutral, unless despoiled
By our greed or scorn. And wherever you sleep—
My arms outgrown—or waking weep,
Life is your lot: you lie in God's hand,
In His terrible mercy, world without end.

A Mile from Eden

With buds embalmed alive in ice,
Flies in amber, the wood lies:
On snow even the shadows are white,
And we walk tipsy with too much light.
In slanting rays, like the damned
Our footsteps flame but make no sound.
While in this waste we wander
I tell him again of the godlike Flounder,
The garish desires of the fisherman's wife
(Desires we saw from the first unsafe,
For the same sin, though tropical,
Is in the Garden and the Fall).
But as I describe the granted glories,
The crowns, candles, golden floors,
I see his longing in his eyes:
Eyes of the humble hoping for Heaven,
Eyes of Adam a mile from Eden.
I see him a child with his joys round him,
One foot still on the coral strand,
The sun like a locket hung from his hand,
Now a man with his griefs about him.

If his hunger is holy, where hers was greed,
Can he always avoid the wish to be God?
Heaven revolves, distant, perfect,
Placid and impregnable as in a Collect;
And we walk in a waste of snows,
Yet see that power before our eyes
Which if we learn its usage can
Break up the amber, reverse the sun,
The bird's-eye glory to full sight
Bring, and outcasts into delight.

ROY FULLER

1912-

The Plains

The only blossoms of the plains are black
And rubbery, the spiked spheres of the thorn,
And stuffed with ants. It is before the rains:
The stream is parched to pools, occasional
And green, where tortoise flop; the birds are songless;
Towers of whirling dust glide past like ghosts.
But in the brilliant sun, against the sky,
The river course is vivid and the grass
Flaxen: the strong striped haunches of the zebra,
The white fawn black, like flags, of the gazelles,
Move as emotions or as kindly actions.
The world is nothing but a fairy tale
Where everything is beautiful and good.

At night the stars were faint, the plateau chill;
The great herds gathered, were invisible,
And coughed and made inarticulate noises
Of fear and yearning: sounds of their many hooves
Came thudding quietly. The headlines caught
Eyes and the pallid racing forms. I thought
Of nothing but the word *humanity*:
And I was there outside the square of warmth,
In darkness, in the crowds and padding, crying.
Suddenly the creamy shafts of light
Revealed the lion. Slowly it swung its great
Maned head, then—loose, suede, yellow—loped away.
O purposeful and unapproachable!
Then later his repugnant hangers-on:
A pair of squint hyenas limping past.
This awful ceremony of the doomed, unknown
And innocent victim has its replicas
Embedded in our memories and in
Our history. The archetypal myths
Stirred in my mind.
                The next day over all
The sun was flooding and the sky rose tall.
Where rock had weathered through the soil I saw
A jackal running, barking, turning his head.

Four vultures sat upon the rock and pecked,
And when I neared them flew away on wings
Like hair. They left a purple scrap of skin.
Have I discovered all the plains can show me?
The animals gallop, spring, are beautiful,
And at the end of every day is night.

November, 1941

The objects are disposed: the sky is suitable.
Where the coast curves the waves' blown smoke
Blurs with the city's and the pencilled ships
Lumber like toys. The searchers for coal and driftwood
Bend; and the beach is littered with stones and leaves,
Antlers of seaweed, round gulls, to the belt
Of sand, like macadam, watered by the sea.

Well then? It is here one asks the question.
Here, under such a sky, with such that menace of purple,
One confronts the varieties of death and of people
With a certain sense of their inadequacy;
And the grandeur of historical conceptions,
The wheeling empires, appearance of lusty classes,
The alimentary organizations, the clever
Extrications from doom, seize the imagination
As though these forms, like gods, existed cruel,
Aloof, but eventually for our salvation.
And, as the shapes themselves of nature or
The inexorable patterns of nightmare, days
And the sequence of days pull our untidy acts
Into the formidable expression of time and destiny.
The tumbling ocean humps itself to Europe—
There the machines, the armies and the skies,
The stains of movement and the burning regions,
Have all the echoes of a myth and in
My blood reside inhuman power and guilt,
Whose fathers made both myth and progeny.

LAWRENCE DURRELL
1912-

Conon in Alexandria

I

Ash-heap of four cultures,
Bounded by Mareotis, a salt lake,
On which the winter rain rings and whitens,
In the waters, stiffens like eyes.

I have been four years bound here:
A time for sentences by the tripod:
Prophecies by those who were born dead,
Or who lost their character but kept their taste.

A solitary presumed quite happy,
Writing those interminable whining letters,
On the long beaches dimpled by the rain,
Tasting the island wind

Blown against wet lips and shutters out of Rhodes.
I say "presumed," but would not have it otherwise.

      *   *   *

Steps go down to the port
Beyond the Pharos. O my friends,
Surely these nightly visitations
Of islands in one's sleep must soon be over?

I have watched beside the others,
But always the more attentive, the more exacting:
The familiar papers on a table by the bed,
The plate of olives and the glass of wine.

You would think that thoughts so long rehearsed
Like the dry friction of ropes in the mind
Would cease to lead me where in Greece
The almond-candles and the statues burn.

The moon's cold seething fires over this white city,
Through four Februaries have not forgotten.

      *   *   *

Tonight the stars press idly on the nerves
As in a cobweb, heavy with dispersal:
Points of dew in a universe too large
Too formal to be more than terrible.

"There are sides of the self
One can seldom show. They live on and on
In an emergency of anguish always,
Waiting for parents in another."

Would you say that later, reading
Such simple propositions, the historian
Might be found to say: "The critic
In him made a humour of this passion.

The equations of a mind too conscious of ideas,
Fictions, not kisses, crossed the water between them"?

*　　　*　　　*

II

And later, Spring, which compels these separations
Will but define you further as she dies
In flowers downless and pure as Portia's cheek,
Interrupting perhaps the conversations of friends
On terraces where the fountains plane at time,

To leave this small acid precipitate to memory,
Of something small, screwed-up, and thrown aside.
"Partings like these are lucky. At least they wound."

And later by the hearthstone of a philosophy
You might have added: "The desert, yes, for exiles.
But its immensity only confines one further.
Its end seems always in oneself."

A gown stained at the arm-pits by a woman's body.
A letter unfinished because the ink gave out.

*　　　*　　　*

The lovers you describe as *"separating each other*
Further with every kiss": and your portrait
Of a man *"engaged in bitterly waiting*
For the day when art should become unnecessary,"

Were in the style and order, as when you say
"Freedom alone confines"; but do they show a love,

Fragmented everywhere by conscience and deceit,
Ending on this coast of torn-out lighthouses?

Or that neglected and unmerited Habit,
The structure that so long informed our growth?
Questions for a nursery wall! But are they true to these?

I have passed all this day in what they would call patience,
Not writing, alone in my window, with my flute,
Having read in a letter that last immortal February
That *"Music is only love, looking for words."*

At Epidaurus

The islands which whisper to the ambitious,
Washed all winter by the surviving stars
Are here hardly recalled: or only as
Stone choirs for the sea-bird,
Stone chairs for the statues of fishermen.
This civilized valley was dedicated to
The cult of the circle, the contemplation
And correction of famous maladies
Which the repeating flesh has bred in us also
By a continuous babyhood, like the worm in meat.

The only disorder is in what we bring here:
Cars drifting like leaves over the glades,
The penetration of clocks striking in London,
The composure of dolls and fanatics,
Financed migrations to the oldest sources:
A theatre where redemption was enacted,
Repentance won, the stones heavy with dew.
The olive signs the hill, signifying revival,
And the swallow's cot in the ruin seems how
Small yet defiant an exaggeration of love!

Here we can carry our own small deaths
With the resignation of place and identity;
A temple set severely like a dice
In the vale's Vergilian shade; once apparently
Ruled from the whitest light of the summer:
A formula for marble when the clouds
Troubled the architect, and the hill spoke
Volumes of thunder, the sibyllic god wept.

Here we are safe from everything but ourselves,
The dying leaves and the reports of love.

The land's lie, held safe from the sea,
Encourages the austerity of the grass chambers,
Provides a context understandably natural
For men who could divulge the forms of gods.
Here the mathematician entered his own problem,
A house built round his identity,
Round the fond yet mysterious seasons
Of green grass, the teaching of summer-astronomy.
Here the lover made his calculations by ferns,
And the hum of the chorus enchanted.

We, like the winter, are only visitors,
To prosper here the breathing grass,
Encouraging petals on a terrace, disturbing
Nothing, enduring the sun like girls
In a town window. The earth's flower
Blows here original with every spring,
Shines in the rising of a man's age
Into cold texts and precedents for time.
Everything is a slave to the ancestor, the order
Of old captains who sleep in the hill.

Then smile, my dear, above the holy wands,
Make the indefinite gesture of the hands,
Unlocking this world which is not our world.
The somnambulists walk again in the north
With the long black rifles, to bring us answers.
Useless a morality for slaves: useless
The shouting at echoes to silence them.
Most useless inhabitants of the kind blue air,
Four ragged travellers in Homer.
All causes end within the great Because.

To Argos

The roads lead southward, blue
Along a circumference of snow,
Identified now by the scholars
As a home for the cyclops, a habitation
For nymphs and ancient appearances.
Only the shepherd in his cowl
Who walks upon them really knows

The natural history in a sacred place;
Takes like a text of stone
A familiar cloud-shape or fortress,
Pointing at what is mutually seen,
His dark eyes wearing the crowsfoot.

Our idols have been betrayed
Not by the measurement of the dead ones
Who are lying under these mountains,
As under England our own fastidious
Heroes lie awake but do not judge.
Winter rubs at the ice like a hair,
Dividing time; and a single tree
Reflects here a mythical river.
Water limps on ice, or scribbles
On doors of sand its syllables,
All alone, in an empty land, alone.
This is what breaks the heart.

We say that the blood of Virgil
Grew again in the scarlet pompion,
Ever afterwards reserving the old poet
Memorials in his air, his water: so
In this land one encounters always
Agamemnon, Agamemnon; the voice
Of water falling on hair in caves,
The stonebreaker's hammer on walls,
A name held closer in the circles
Of bald granite than even these cyclamen,
Like children's ears attentive here,
Blown like glass from the floors of snow.

Truly, we the endowed who pass here
With the assurance of visitors in rugs
Can raise from the menhir no ghost
By the cold sound of English idioms.
Our true parenthood rests with the eagle,
We recognise him turning over his vaults.
Bones have no mouths to smile with
From the beds of companionable rivers dry.
The modern girls pose on a tomb smiling;
Night watches us on the western horn;
The hyssop and the vinegar have lost their meaning,
And this is what breaks the heart.

GEORGE BARKER
1913-

First Cycle of Love Poems

I

This morning take a holiday from unhappiness because
It is the greatest day there ever was
When he stepped down out of the nuptial arch
With the cross in his face and he shall search
For ever for the wreath and not even at his death
Really regret this day that gave him birth.

O history be kind and Time be short to him
Where he is anonymous and let him come to no harm
From the hammer of the diurnal, or the drum,
The sweatbox and the wheel where the dog's dream
Turns and is interminable. O be near always
You whom from far I shall not the less praise!

Let the gentle solstice, like the Fierral Bay
Where the Eleven Thousand Virgins keep
The fishes quiet in their arms, keep him asleep
All his life long in a long summer's day:
With the empty hourglass, the four-leafed clover,
The rock for the resurrection, and much love.

II

Here at my hand here at my heart lie still.
Will then the prince of index finger, your caduceus,
Alight on my lip like a dove on a window sill
Delivering in its claw the symbolic oleander?

Here at my heart here at my hand lie still
Till the dog-rose springs off its beds of bush
To run in circles leaping at your heel,
And nature, happy, curls up at your kiss.

Lie still, lie still, here at my heart lie still
Sleeping like thunderheads. Be over me dominant
So I shall sleep as the river sleeps under the hill
Kissing the foot and giving back the element.

Here at my hand lie still; lie still at my heart.
Sesame is on his tongue and the unicorn rages
Round the abdominal amphitheatre. I hear
His double engines drumming up the passages

O till his cumulus, over the angry bed
Arching, is rainbows. Volplane my bomber
Shuttling silver through the night I bride;
He spins his disc of kisses in my slumber.

And I lie still in heart and hand lie still,
All the streamers of welcome flaunting in my marrow
And flares I lift my arms are, because he will
Come down alighting on my bed like a meadow.

Then here in my heart he lies as dark as pillage
Where in my arms I hold
The murderer who, Samsoning up my five pillars,
Lies quiet now, for here at my heart I fold him.

III

The kiss is maypole where my seven
Happiest sins truss me to the rod:
The lightning cracks my face of heaven
When he leans down, when he leans down like a diver
Out of his breast's cloud.

The flammenwerfer and the fish
And also I acknowledge him creator.
Between his horizon of arms measures my wish,
My mirage of marriage that, one moment later,
Comes true in a flash.

O at your work you patient hundred thousand
With the hammer, the hour and the pen,
His harder labour is love. He has emblazoned
Everything, overnight everything has blossomed
With Love again.

IV

Then like the ship at rest in the bay
    I drop my sails and come home
To harbour in his arms and stay
    For ever harboured from harm.

On his foot's beach my combers ride
  The vaulted coral where he stands,
And spray against his rock of side
  Showers that fill his hands.

O whirlwinds catching up the sea
  And folding islands in your shawls,
Give him to me, give him to me,
  And I will wrap him in my shallows.

O the Red Sea parted long ago
  When the angel went whistling through,
My seas rise up in pride also
  To let his chariots through.

The masculine cliff-face gazes out
  At the smile of the horizon,
And disregards the sea that flaunts
  Her beauties by the dozen.

So he looks out over my subjugation
  Where the combers coil at his feet,
And sees, the far side of adulation,
  My Hesperides rise singing, one moment, from the ocean,
  And the next, sinking, weep.

But from the altitude of his domination
  O sometimes, like waterfalls,
His hand comes down through a gravity of anticipation
  And a constellation of nuptials.

Nightly to his archipelagoes where
  Apples adorn the pillar,
My kiss of fishes moves in schools and bears
  The body to him on a silver platter.

The syzygies, over our Balkan bed,
  Shed silver on the peninsula,
Against whose shores my waters beat their head
  Like rain on a red star.

The narwhal with a spike on its brow
  Spins thrashing through the wave:
His love is mine, who lashes now
  In the sweat of seas I gave.

Then morning, like a monument
   Glittering in a tree,
Reminds me of a former moment
When the first star was immanent
And the mountain, dominant,
   Leaned down and kissed me.

V

My joy, my jockey, my Gabriel
Who bares his horns above my sleep
Is sleeping now. And I shall keep him
In valley and on pinnacle
And marvellous in my tabernacle.

My peace is where his shoulder holds
My clouds among his skies of face;
His plenty is my peace, my peace.
And like a serpent by a boulder
His shade I rest in glory coiled.

Time will divide us, and the sea
Wring its sad hands all day between;
The autumn bring a change of scene.
But always and for ever he
At night will sleep and keep by me.

Sacred Elegy V

I

These errors loved no less than the saint loves arrows
Repeat, Love has left the world. He is not here.
O God, like Love revealing yourself in absence
So that, though farther than stars, like Love that sorrows
In separation, the desire in the heart of hearts
To come home to you makes you most manifest.
The booming zero spins as his halo where
Ashes of pride on all the tongues of sense
Crown us with negatives. O deal us in our deserts
The crumb of falling vanity. It is eucharist.

II

Everyone walking everywhere goes in a glow
Of geometrical progression, all meteors, in praise:

Hosannas on the tongues of the dumb shall raise
Roads for the gangs in chains to return to
God. They go hugging the traumas like halleluias
To the bodies that earn this beatitude. The Seven
Seas they crowd like the great sailing clippers,
Those homing migrants that, with their swallow-like sails set,
Swayed forward along the loneliness that opposed,
For nothing more than a meeting in heaven.

III

Therefore all things, in all three tenses,
Alone like the statue in an alcove of love,
Moving in obedient machinery, sleeping
Happy in impossible achievements, keeping
Close to each other because the night is dark;
The great man dreaming on the stones of circumstances,
The small wringing hands because rocks will not move:
The beast in its red kingdom, the star in its arc:
O all things, therefore, in shapes or in senses,
Know that they exist in the kiss of his Love.

IV

Incubus. Anæsthetist with glory in a bag,
Foreman with a sweatbox and a whip. Asphyxiator
Of the ecstatic. Sergeant with a grudge
Against the lost lovers in the park of creation,
Fiend behind the fiend behind the fiend behind the
Friend. Mastodon with mastery, monster with an ache
At the tooth of the ego, the dead drunk judge:
Wheresoever Thou art our agony will find Thee
Enthroned on the darkest altar of our heartbreak
Perfect. Beast, brute, bastard. O dog my God!

Summer Idyll

Sometimes in summer months, the matrix earth
Loaded to gold, the boughs arching downward
Burdened, the shallow and glucose streams
Teeming, flowers out, all gold camouflage
Of the collusive summer; but under the streams
Winter lies coldly, and coldly embedded in
The corn hunger lies germinally, want under

The abundance, poverty pulling down
The tautened boughs, and need is the seed.

Robe them in superb summer, at angles
Their bones penetrate, or with a principality
Of Spring possess them, under the breast
Space of a vacancy spreads like a foul
Ghost flower, want; and the pressure upon
The eyeball of their spirits, upon the organs
Of their spare bodies, the pressure upon
Their movement and their merriment, loving and
Living, the pressure upon their lives like deep
Seas, becomes insufferable.

Sometimes the summer lessens a moment the pressure.
Large as the summer rose some rise
Bathing in rivers or at evening harrying rabbits,
Indulging in games in meadows—and some are idle, strewn
Over the parks like soiled paper like summer
Insects, bathed in sweat or at evening harried
By watchmen, park-keepers, policemen—indulge in games
Dreaming as I dream of rest and cleanliness and cash.

And the gardens exhibit the regalia of the season
Like debutante queans, between which they wander
Blown with vague odours, seduced by the pure
Beauty, like drowned men floating in bright coral.
Summer, denuding young women, also denudes
Them, removes jackets, exposing backs—
Summer moves many up the river in boats

Trailing their fingers in the shadowed water; they
Too move by the river, and in the water shadows
Trail a hand, which need not find a bank,
Face downward, like bad fruit. Cathedrals and Building
Societies, as they appear, disappear; and Beethoven
Is played more loudly to deafen the Welsh echoes,
And Summer, blowing over the Mediterranean
Like swans, like perfect swans.

Holy Poems

C.B. IN MEMORIAM. JUNE, MCMXXXIX

I

I am Saint John on Patmos of my heart
Towered and tabernacled with illusion;
Black Michaels and gold Satans stand at hand
Gulling me with their gestures of temptation
To bring me down from the marvelous mountains
Where in Babylonian gardens I find
Spinoza's face hanging from every tree
Murmuring love of all our kith and kind:
Or I feel, cold as a draught on my arm,
The spiralling universe like a worm
Coiling for comfort; and in my mind
The three-winged dove among my dreams
Moaning for its apocalyptic home.

II

I bleed Sebastian's brother on the ground,
No good it does me: or I hang my hand
My harp-hand on the Haman tree, but no—
My blood smiles from the ground in pride,
My hand makes music when winds blow.
There is no martyrdom worse than a life,
Nor can it be bought off with a sacrifice.
I cannot cut my body to St. Peter's key,
Or, nipping off the hip-rose with a knife
Make me archangel, nor with a kiss
Claim thirty shillings, for no one will buy
The plaster Jesus that my master is,
Crossed on my pain and crucified in my eye.

III

The monarch who wears a shrieking crown
Is us. All whipping tongues and words
Flash at our head and doom us down:
The sex of our cherubim is swords.
When we step down out of our beds or doors
The burning bush springs up between our feet;
Our smile is bright with tiger, and the days
Turn us like dogs in their drums. Then comes

Spinning and shining among us like wheels,
Throwing off visions to lead us home,
God—snatches me up in finger and thumb,
Douses me like a glimmer. And I see
Cruel to be kind to all his kind is he.

KARL SHAPIRO

1913-

Elegy Written on a Frontporch

The sun burns on its sultry wick;
Stratus and cumulus unite.
I who am neither well nor sick
Sit in a wicker chair and write.

A hot wind presses at my lips.
I peel. Am totally undressed.
Pinkish, as though a part-eclipse,
Heat licks upon my naked breast.

Angles in quick succession rise.
Eyesight is stereopticon
As roof and roof geometrize
Perspective deviously drawn.

I face a heaven half-destroyed,
A skyscape alabaster, dead.
One living shadow on the void,
A Flying Fortress drones ahead.

Motion and fixity take shape;
The fallow rays intensify
Distinctness. Nothing can escape
The clean hard focus of the eye.

Noise into humming noise constricts;
The traffic mumbles deeper down.
Only a trolley contradicts,
Ticks by neurotically to town.

Stretched taut upon the light I scorch,
Writhe in my sweat and smoke and sun.

The evening paper hits the porch;
My honeymoon of peace is done.

Unmasticated pulp of life. . .
Decision finds me blind and deaf.
I do not finger for the strife
Of Delano and Mutt and Jeff,

Or bend upon my nudity's
Umbilicus, the fact of facts,
As one who drowns in light and sees
The newsreel of his private acts.

I do not hug my feet with glee
And smile into my cul-de-sac
Enamoured of the dignity
Of facing forward moving back.

But set my wired sight, reclaim
The rotted friendship and the fresh;
Tune in on him who changed his name
And her who stultified the flesh.

I see who came to marriage raw
With poverty and self-abuse;
Defendants to the general law,
Their ignorance was no excuse.

Instructors, graduates I see,
Scholars who sneered into their books,
The female doctors pouring tea,
Hundreds of victims of their looks.

The money-poise of some, the pride
Of those who whored on easy checks,
Sons of The Business, dressy, snide,
Disfigured in expensive wrecks.

Believers in the songhit, thin
With pounding to the hebroid jazz;
The studious drinkers feeding in
The cloaca of the middle-class.

I see too many who romanced
Defeat, unmasculine, debased;
The striptease puritans who danced
The long lewd ritual of waste.

All these I bury out of sight
Sans benefit of epitaph.
I turn my legs into the light,
Punch out a cigaret and laugh.

For one, the best against that rout,
Deserted, obdurate to see
Their weakly literate wear out
The old Horatian fallacy;

Spoke of the beauty-to-obey,
The life-expectancy of bone,
She turned her back upon the day
But will not lie at night alone.

Haircut

O wonderful nonsense of lotions of Lucky Tiger,
Of savory soaps and oils of bottle-bright green,
The gold of liqueurs, the unguents of Newark and Niger,
Powders and balms and waters washing me clean,

In mirrors of marble and silver I see us forever
Increasing, decreasing the puzzles of luminous spaces
As I turn, am revolved and pumped in the air on a lever,
With the backs of my heads in chorus with all of my faces.

Scissors and comb are mowing my hair into neatness,
Now pruning my ears, now smoothing my neck like a pain;
In the harvest of hair and the chaff of powdery sweetness
My snow-covered slopes grow dark with the wooly rain.

And the little boy cries, for it hurts to sever the curl,
And we too are quietly bleating to part with our coat.
Does the barber want blood in a dish? I am weak as a girl,
I desire my pendants, the fatherly chin of a goat.

I desire the pants of a bear, the nap of a monkey
Which trousers of friction have blighted down to my skin.
I am bare as a tusk, as jacketed up as a flunkey,
With the chest of a moth-eaten camel growing within.

But in death we shall flourish, you summer-dark leaves of my head.
While the flesh of the jaw ebbs away from the shores of my teeth;
You shall cover my sockets and soften the boards of my bed
And lie on the flat of my temples as proud as a wreath.

The Dome of Sunday

With focus sharp as Flemish-painted face
In film of varnish brightly fixed
And through a polished hand-lens deeply seen,
Sunday at noon through hyaline thin air
Sees down the street,
And in the camera of my eye depicts
Row-houses and row-lives:
Glass after glass, door after door the same,
Face after face the same, the same,
The brutal visibility the same;

As if one life emerging from one house
Would pause, a single image caught between
Two facing mirrors where vision multiplies
Beyond perspective,
A silent clatter in the high-speed eye
Spinning out photo-circulars of sight.

I see slip to the curb the long machines
Out of whose warm and windowed rooms pirouette
Shellacked with silk and light
The hard legs of our women.
Our women are one woman, dressed in black,
The carmine printed mouth
And cheeks as soft as muslin-glass belong
Outright to one dark dressy man,
Merely a swagger at her curvy side.

This is their visit to themselves:
All day from porch to porch they weave
A nonsense pattern through the even glare,
Stealing in surfaces
Cold vulgar glances at themselves.

And high up in the heated room all day
I wait behind the plate glass pane for one,
Hot as a voyeur for a glimpse of one,
The vision to blot out this woman's sheen;
All day my sight records expensively
Row-houses and row-lives.

But nothing happens; no diagonal
With melting shadow falls across the curb:

Neither the blinded negress lurching through fatigue,
Nor exiles bleeding from their pores.
Nor that bright bomb slipped lightly from its rack
To splinter every silvered glass and crystal prism,
Witch-bowl and perfume bottle
And billion candle-power dressing-bulb,
No direct hit to smash the shatter-proof
And lodge at last the quivering needle
Clean in the eye of one who stands transfixed
In fascination of her brightness.

DELMORE SCHWARTZ

1913-

"The Starlight's Intuitions Pierced the Twelve"

The starlight's intuitions pierced the twelve,
The brittle night sky sparkled like a tune
Tinkled and tapped out on the xylophone.
Empty and vain, a glittering dune, the moon
Arose too big, and, in the mood which ruled,
Seemed like a useless beauty in a pit;
And then one said, after he carefully spat:
"No matter what we do, he looks at it!

"I cannot see a child or find a girl
Beyond his smile which glows like that spring moon."
"—Nothing no more the same," the second said,
"Though all may be forgiven, never quite healed
The wound I bear as witness, standing by;
No ceremony surely appropriate,
Nor secret love, escape or sleep because
No matter what I do, he looks at it—"

"Now," said the third, "no thing will be the same:
I am as one who never shuts his eyes,
The sea and sky no more are marvellous,
I know no more true freshness or surprise!"
"Now," said the fourth, "nothing will be enough,
—I heard his voice accomplishing all wit:
No word can be unsaid, no deed withdrawn,
—No matter what is said, he measures it!"

"Vision, imagination, hope or dream
Believed, denied, the scene we wished to see?
It does not matter in the least: for what
Is altered if it is not true? That we
Saw goodness, as it is—*this* is the awe
And the abyss which we will not forget,
His story now the skull which holds all thought:
No matter what I think, I think of it!"

"And I will never be what once I was,"
Said one for long as single as a knife,
"And we will never be as once we were;
We have died once, this is a second life."
"My mind is spilled in moral chaos," one
Righteous as Job exclaimed, "now infinite
Suspicion of my heart stems what I will,
—No matter what I choose, he stares at it!"

"I am as one native in summer places,
—Ten weeks' excitement paid for by the rich;
Debauched by that, and then all winter bored,"
The sixth declared, "his peak left us a ditch."
"He came to make this life more difficult,"
The seventh said, "No one will ever fit
His measures' heights, all is inadequate:
No matter what we have, what good is it?"

"He gave forgiveness to us: what a gift!"
The eighth chimed in. "But now we know *how much*
Must be forgiven. But if forgiven, what?
The crime which was will be; and the least touch
Revives the memory: what is forgiveness worth?"
The ninth spoke thus: "Who now will ever sit
At ease in Zion at the Easter feast?
No matter what the place, he touches it!"

"And I will always stammer, since he spoke,"
One, who had been most eloquent, said, stammering,
"I looked too long at the sun; like too much light,
Too much of goodness is a boomerang,"
Laughed the eleventh of the troop, "I must
Try what he tried: I saw the infinite
Who walked the lake and raised the hopeless dead:
No matter what the feat, he first accomplished it!"

So spoke the twelfth; and then the twelve in chorus:
"Unspeakable unnatural goodness is

Risen and shines, and never will ignore us;
He glows forever in all consciousness;
Forgiveness, love, and hope possess the pit,
And bring our endless guilt, like shadow's bars:
No matter what we do, he stares at it!
What pity can each deny? what debt defer?
We know he looks at us like all the stars,
And we shall never be as once we were,
This life will never be what once it was!"

"The Heavy Bear Who Goes with Me"

"the withness of the body"
WHITEHEAD

The heavy bear who goes with me,
A manifold honey to smear his face,
Clumsy and lumbering here and there,
The central ton of every place,
The hungry beating brutish one
In love with candy, anger, and sleep,
Crazy factotum, dishevelling all,
Climbs the building, kicks the football,
Boxes his brother in the hate-ridden city.

Breathing at my side, that heavy animal,
That heavy bear who sleeps with me,
Howls in his sleep for a world of sugar,
A sweetness intimate as the water's clasp,
Howls in his sleep because the tight-rope
Trembles and shows the darkness beneath.
—The strutting show-off is terrified,
Dressed in his dress-suit, bulging his pants,
Trembles to think that his quivering meat
Must finally wince to nothing at all.

That inescapable animal walks with me,
Has followed me since the black womb held,
Moves where I move, distorting my gesture,
A caricature, a swollen shadow,
A stupid clown of the spirit's motive,
Perplexes and affronts with his own darkness,
The secret life of belly and bone,
Opaque, too near, my private, yet unknown,
Stretches to embrace the very dear

With whom I would walk without him near,
Touches her grossly, although a word
Would bare my heart and make me clear,
Stumbles, flounders, and strives to be fed ·
Dragging me with him in his mouthing care,
Amid the hundred million of his kind,
The scrimmage of appetite everywhere.

JEAN GARRIGUE

1913-

The Clovers

For the heart, willing and not willing,
Is glassed under as clover in a stand of storm water:
In the downy sink of the ground
Rain is an inch deep over the heads of those four-leaves
And the sides turn silver, in the embossed
Pond-meadow. Think of a whole army of clover
Hidden under, lace all, green as an apple!

For the heart, willing and not willing,
Stands in a rain-settle too, transparent
To all in a vale, where the firm skin of wish
Dapples and lines it with ill, ill,
And its veins are exposed, pale
To the tremble of world's rage, ail,
But not sky is reflected, not sun from the grey stench of heaven,
Not seed whistling by nor bird dipping.

Transparency has its savior, visible and invisible!
For, as the clover stem bears no relation
To its top parent, and under that water
Leaves stay in a stitching, sewn like a cobbled silk,
So the heart, as obscurely rooted,
Is as rooted, though with a pretty way
It lies in the film of flesh, a marrow of constancy.

But nor sun purifies nor strengthens by air
That warped delicacy!
And the dwarf hidden roots, apparent to none,
Obstruct the dark muscle, oh a clarity upside

But a dark land thereunder,
Willing, unwilling, ignorant and imitator,
In the source of that woodland, the improvident flood.

The Circle

The wood, swollen with mushrooms,
Those rotting like excrement,
Those blooming in monkey scarlet,
Branch-brown and butter yellow,
The wood, swollen with voices,
Those high-blood, tortured sexual cries,
The penitential voice singing,
The wood, branch-brown, branched with weeping:

Who am I, am I,
Where the mirror has splashed its bloodless blood,
Who am I in the bloodless wood?
I said: eternity is this:
The formless past within the glass,
The flesh deprived of its true lust,
The inward virtue of the flesh
Corroded by the formless past,
I said: damnation is this eternity,
The mind divorced at last from act,
Distracted senses caged now judged,
Those thumping ranters damned who drag
The battered actor through such mire,
The act full-judged but not altered
(The crooked blood cannot run straight)
Perversity steals the old color
And red runs white in secret ill.

I said: eternity is this travel
Around and round the center of the wood,
Beset by cries, the sullied pool,
The light of mushrooms, moths running
As large as mice on the forest floor,
The flesh, that battered animal,
Asserting its ample sty has dignity.
I said: eternity devours the mind,
Devours and cannot change by its devouring.
The outward terror remains the same,
And the wood, swollen with mushrooms, the dark wood.

MURIEL RUKEYSER

1913-

Reading Time: 1 Minute 26 Seconds

The fear of poetry is the
fear: mystery and fury of a midnight street
of windows whose low voluptuous voice
issues, and after that there is no peace.

That round waiting moment in the
theatre: curtain rises, dies into the ceiling
and here is played the scene with the mother
bandaging a revealed son's head. The bandage is torn off.
Curtain goes down. And here is the moment of proof.

That climax when the brain acknowledges the world,
all values extended into the blood awake.
Moment of proof. And as they say Brancusi did,
building his bird to extend through soaring air,
as Kafka planned stories that draw to eternity
through time extended. And the climax strikes.

Love touches so, that months after the look of
blue stare of love, the footbeat on the heart
is translated into the pure cry of birds
following air-cries, or poems, the new scene.
Moment of proof. That strikes long after act.

They fear it. They turn away, hand up palm out
fending off moment of proof, the straight look, poem.
The prolonged wound-consciousness after the bullet's shot.
The prolonged love after the look is dead,
the yellow joy after the song of the sun,
aftermath proof, extended radiance.

Rotten Lake Elegy

As I went down to Rotten Lake I remembered
the wrecked season, haunted by plans of salvage,
snow, the closed door, footsteps and resurrections,
    machinery of sorrow.

The warm grass gave to the feet and the stilltide water
was floor of evening and magnetic light and
reflection of wish, the black-haired beast with my eyes
        walking beside me.

The green and yellow lights, the street of water standing
point to the image of that house whose destruction
I weep when I weep you. My door (no), poems, rest,
        (don't say it!) untamable need.

                        *

When you have left the river you are a little way
nearer the lake; but I leave many times.
Parents parried my past; the present was poverty,
the future depended on my unfinished spirit.
There were no misgivings because there was no choice,
only regret for waste, and the wild knowledge:
growth and sorrow and discovery.

When you have left the river you proceed alone;
all love is likely to be illicit; and few
friends to command the soul; they are too feeble.
Rejecting the subtle and contemplative minds
as being too thin in the bone; and the gross thighs
and unevocative hands fail also. But the poet
and his wife, those who say Survive, remain;
and those two who were with me on the ship
leading me to the sum of the years, in Spain.

When you have left the river you will hear the war.
In the mountains, with tourists, in the insanest groves
the sound of kill, the precious face of peace.
And the sad frightened child, continual minor,
returns, nearer whole circle, O and nearer
all that was loved, the lake, the naked river,
what must be crossed and cut out of your heart,
what must be stood beside and straightly seen.

                        *

As I went down to Rotten Lake I remembered
how the one crime is need. The man lifting the loaf
with hunger as motive can offer no alibi, is
        always condemned.

These are the lines at the employment bureau
and the tense students at their examinations;

needing makes clumsy and robs them of their wish,
    in one fast gesture

plants on them failure of the imagination;
and lovers who lower their bodies into the chair
gently and sternly as if the flesh had been wounded,
    never can conquer.

Their need is too great, their vulnerable bodies
rigidly joined will snap, turn love away,
fear parts them, they lose their hands and voices, never
    get used to the world.

Walking at night, they are asked Are you your best friend's
best friend? and must say No, not yet, they are
love's vulnerable, and they go down to Rotten Lake
    hoping for wonders.

Dare it arrive, the day when weakness ends ?
When the insistence is strong, the wish converted?
I prophesy the meeting by the water
    of these desires.

I know what this, I have known the waking
when every night ended in one cliff-dream
of faces drowned beneath the porous rock
    brushed by the sea;

suffered the change: deprived erotic dreams
to images of that small house where peace
walked room to room and always with one face
    telling her stories,

and needed that, past loss, past fever, and the
attractive enemy who in my bed
touches all night the body of my sleep,
    improves my summer

with madness, impossible loss, and the dead music
of altered promise, a room torn up by the roots,
the desert that crosses from the door to the wall,
    continual bleeding,

and all the time that will which cancels enmity,
seeks its own Easter, arrives at the water-barrier;
must face it now, biting the lakeside ground;
    looks for its double,

the twin that must be met again, changeling need,
blazing in color somewhere, flying yellow
into the forest with its lucid edict:
    take to the world,

this is the honor of your flesh, the offering
of strangers, the faces of cities, honor of all your wish.
Immortal undoing! I say in my own voice. These prophecies
    may all come true,

out of the beaten season. I look in Rotten Lake
wait for the flame reflection, seeing only
the free beast flickering black along my side
    animal of my need,

and cry I want! I want! rising among the world
to gain my converted wish, the amazing desire
that keeps me alive, though the face be still, be still,
the slow dilated heart know nothing but lack,
now I begin again the private rising,
the ride to survival of that consuming bird
beating, up from dead lakes, ascents of fire.

DYLAN THOMAS

1914-

A Refusal to Mourn the Death, by Fire, of a Child in London

    Never until the mankind making
    Bird beast and flower
    Fathering and all humbling darkness
    Tells with silence the last light breaking
    And the still hour
    Is come of the sea tumbling in harness

    And I must enter again the round
    Zion of the water bead
    And the synagogue of the ear of corn
    Shall I let pray the shadow of a sound
    Or sow my salt seed
    In the least valley of sackcloth to mourn

The majesty and burning of the child's death.
I shall not murder
The mankind of her going with a grave truth
Nor blaspheme down the stations of the breath
With any further
Elegy of innocence and youth.

Deep with the first dead lies London's daughter,
Robed in the long friends,
The grains beyond age, the dark veins of her mother,
Secret by the unmourning water
Of the riding Thames.
After the first death, there is no other.

Fern Hill

Now as I was young and easy under the apple boughs
About the lilting house and happy as the grass was green,
   The night above the dingle starry,
     Time let me hail and climb
   Golden in the heydays of his eyes,
And honoured among wagons I was prince of the apple towns
And once below a time I lordly had the trees and leaves
     Trail with daisies and barley
   Down the rivers of the windfall light.

And as I was green and carefree, famous among the barns
About the happy yard and singing as the farm was home,
   In the sun that is young once only,
     Time let me play and be
   Golden in the mercy of his means,
And green and golden I was huntsman and herdsman, the calves
Sang to my horn, the foxes on the hills barked clear and cold,
     And the sabbath rang slowly
   In the pebbles of the holy streams.

All the sun long it was running, it was lovely, the hay-
Fields high as the house, the tunes from the chimneys, it was air
   And playing, lovely and watery
     And fire green as grass.
   And nightly under the simple stars
As I rode to sleep the owls were bearing the farm away,
All the moon long I heard, blessed among stables, the night-jars
   Flying with the ricks, and the horses
     Flashing into the dark.

And then to awake, and the farm, like a wanderer white
With the dew, come back, the cock on his shoulder: it was all
   Shining, it was Adam and maiden,
       The sky gathered again
   And the sun grew round that very day.
So it must have been after the birth of the simple light
In the first, spinning place, the spellbound horses walking warm
   Out of the whinnying green stable
   On to the fields of praise.

And honoured among foxes and pheasants by the gay house
Under the new made clouds and happy as the heart was long,
   In the sun born over and over,
       I ran my heedless ways,
   My wishes raced through the house-high hay
And nothing I cared, at my sky blue trades, that time allows
In all his tuneful turning so few and such morning songs
   Before the children green and golden
       Follow him out of grace,

Nothing I cared, in the lamb white days, that time would take me
Up to the swallow thronged loft by the shadow of my hand,
   In the moon that is always rising,
       Nor that riding to sleep
   I should hear him fly with the high fields
And wake to the farm forever fled from the childless land.
Oh as I was young and easy in the mercy of his means,
       Time held me green and dying
   Though I sang in my chains like the sea.

Vision and Prayer

Who
Are you
Who is born
In the next room
So loud to my own
That I can hear the womb
Opening and the dark run
Over the ghost and the dropped son
Behind the wall thin as a wren's bone?
In the birth bloody room unknown
To the burn and turn of time
And the heart print of man
Bows no baptism
But dark alone
Blessing on
The wild
Child.

I
Must lie
Still as stone
By the wren bone
Wall hearing the moan
Of the mother hidden
And the shadowed head of pain
Casting tomorrow like a thorn
And the midwives of miracles sing
Until the turbulent new born
Burns me his name and his flame
And the winged wall is torn
By his torrid crown
And the dark throne
From his loin
To bright
Light.

When
The wren
Bone writhes down
And the first dawn
Furied by his stream
Swarms on the kingdom come
Of the dazzler of heaven
And the splashed mothering maiden
Who bore him with a bonfire in
His mouth and rocked him like a storm
I shall run lost in sudden
Terror and shining from
The once hooded room
Crying in vain
In the caldron
Of his
Kiss

In
The spin
Of the sun
In the spuming
Cyclone of his wing
For I lost was who am
Crying at the man drenched throne
In the first fury of his stream
And the lightnings of adoration
Back to black silence melt and mourn
For I was lost who have come
To dumbfounding haven
And the finding one
And the high noon
Of his wound
Blinds my
Cry

There
Crouched bare
In the shrine
Of his blazing
Breast I shall waken
To the judge blown bedlam
Of the uncaged sea bottom
The cloud climb of the exhaling tomb
And the bidden dust upsailing
With his flame in every grain
O spiral of ascension
From the vultured urn
Of the morning
Of man when
The land
And

The
Born Sea
Praised the sun
The finding one
And upright Adam
Sang upon origin!
O the wings of the children!
The woundward flight of the ancient
Young from the canyons of oblivion!
The sky stride of the always slain
In battle! the happening
Of saints to their vision!
The world winding home!
And the whole pain
Flows open
And I
Die.

II

In the name of the lost who glory in
The swinish plains of carrion
Under the burial song
Of the birds of burden
Heavy with the drowned
And the green dust
And bearing
The ghost
From
The ground
Like pollen
On the black plume
And the beak of slime
I pray though I belong
Not wholly to that lamenting
Brethren for joy has moved within
The inmost marrow of my heart bone

That he who learns now the sun and moon
Of his mother's milk may return
Before the lips blaze and bloom
To the birth bloody room
Behind the wall's wren
Bone and be dumb
And the womb
That bore
For
All men
The adored
Infant light or
The dazzling prison
Yawn to his upcoming.
In the name of the wanton
Lost on the unchristened mountain
In the centre of dark I pray him

That he let the dead lie though they moan
For his briared hands to hoist them
To the shrine of his world's wound
And the blood drop's garden
Endure the stone
Blind host to sleep
In the dark
And deep
Rock
Awake
No heart bone
But let it break
On the mountain crown
Unsummoned by the sun
And the beating dust be blown
Down to the river rooting plain
Under the night forever falling.

Forever falling night is a known
Star and country to the legion
Of sleepers whose tongue I toll
To mourn his deluging
Light through sea and soil
And we have come
To know all
Places
Ways
Mazes
Passages
Quarters and graves
Of the endless fall.
Now common lazarus
Of the charting sleepers prays
Never to awake and arise
For the country of death is the heart's size

And the star of the lost the shape of the eyes.
In the name of the fatherless
In the name of the unborn
And the undesirers
Of midwiving morning's
Hands or instruments
O in the name
Of no one
Now or
No
One to
Be I pray
May the Crimson
Sun spin a grave grey
And the colour of clay
Stream upon his martyrdom
In the interpreted evening
And the known dark of the earth amen.

I turn the corner of prayer and burn
In a blessing of the sudden
Sun. In the name of the damned
I would turn back and run
To the hidden land
But the loud sun
Christens down
The sky.
I
Am found.
O let him
Scald me and drown
Me in his world's wound.
His lightning answers my
Cry. My voice burns in his hand.
Now I am lost in the blinding
One. The sun roars at the prayer's end.

Ceremony After a Fire Raid

I

Myselves
The grievers
Grieve
Among the street burned to tireless death
A child of a few hours
With its kneading mouth
Charred on the black breast of the grave
The mother dug, and its arms full of fires.

Begin
With singing
Sing
Darkness kindled back into beginning
When the caught tongue nodded blind,
A star was broken
Into the centuries of the child
Myselves grieve now, and miracles cannot atone.

Forgive
Us forgive
Us your death that myselves the believers
May hold it in a great flood
Till the blood shall spurt,
And the dust shall sing like a bird
As the grains blow, as your death grows, through our heart.

Crying
Your dying
Cry,
Child beyond cockcrow, by the fire-dwarfed
Street we chant the flying sea
In the body bereft.
Love is the last light spoken. Oh
Seed of sons in the loin of the black husk left.

II

I know not whether
Adam or Eve, the adorned holy bullock
Or the white ewe lamb
Or the chosen virgin
Laid in her snow
On the altar of London,

Was the first to die
In the cinder of the little skull,
O bride and bride groom
O Adam and Eve together
Lying in the lull
Under the sad breast of the head stone
White as the skeleton
Of the garden of Eden.

I know the legend
Of Adam and Eve is never for a second
Silent in my service
Over the dead infants
Over the one
Child who was priest and servants,
Word, singers, and tongue
In the cinder of the little skull,
Who was the serpent's
Nightfall and the fruit like a sun,
Man and woman undone,
Beginning crumbled back to darkness
Bare as the nurseries
Of the garden of wilderness.

III

Into the organpipes and steeples
Of the luminous cathedrals,
Into the weathercocks' molten mouths
Rippling in twelve-winded circles,
Into the dead clock burning the hour
Over the urn of sabbaths
Over the whirling ditch of daybreak
Over the sun's hovel and the slum of fire
And the golden pavements laid in requiems,
Into the bread in a wheatfield of flames,
Into the wine burning like brandy,
The masses of the sea
The masses of the sea under
The masses of the infant-bearing sea
Erupt, fountain, and enter to utter for ever
Glory glory glory
The sundering ultimate kingdom of genesis' thunder.

Among Those Killed in the Dawn Raid Was a Man Aged One Hundred

When the morning was waking over the war
He put on his clothes and stepped out and he died,
The locks yawned loose and a blast blew them wide,
He dropped where he loved on the burst pavement stone
And the funeral grains of the slaughtered floor.
Tell his street on its back he stopped a sun
And the craters of his eyes grew springshoots and fire
When all the keys shot from the locks, and rang.

Dig no more for the chains of his grey haired heart.
The heavenly ambulance drawn by a wound
Assembling waits for the spade's ring on the cage.
O keep his bones away from that common cart,
The morning is flying on the wings of his age
And a hundred storks perch on the sun's right hand.

"The Hand That Signed the Paper Felled a City"

The hand that signed the paper felled a city;
Five sovereign fingers taxed the breath,
Doubled the globe of dead and halved a country;
These five kings did a king to death.

The mighty hand leads to a sloping shoulder,
The finger joints are cramped with chalk;
A goose's quill has put an end to murder
That put an end to talk.

The hand that signed the treaty bred a fever,
And famine grew, and locusts came;
Great is the hand that holds dominion over
Man by a scribbled name.

The five kings count the dead but do not soften
The crusted wound nor pat the brow;
A hand rules pity as a hand rules heaven;
Hands have no tears to flow.

In Memory of Ann Jones

After the funeral, mule praises, brays,
Windshake of sailshaped ears, muffle-toed tap
Tap happily of one peg in the thick
Grave's foot, blinds down the lids, the teeth in black,
The spittled eyes, the salt ponds in the sleeves,
Morning smack of the spade that wakes up sleep,
Shakes a desolate boy who slits his throat
In the dark of the coffin and sheds dry leaves,
That breaks one bone to light with a judgment clout,
After the feast of tear-stuffed time and thistles
In a room with a stuffed fox and a stale fern,
I stand, for this memorial's sake, alone
In the snivelling hours with dead, humped Ann
Whose hooded, fountain heart once fell in puddles
Round the parched worlds of Wales and drowned each sun
(Though this for her is a monstrous image blindly
Magnified out of praise; her death was a still drop;
She would not have me sinking in the holy
Flood of her heart's fame; she would lie dumb and deep
And need no druid of her broken body).
But I, Ann's bard on a raised hearth, call all
The seas to service that her wood-tongued virtue
Babble like a bellbuoy over the hymning heads,
Bow down the walls of the ferned and foxy woods
That her love sing and swing through a brown chapel,
Bless her bent spirit with four, crossing birds.
Her flesh was meek as milk, but this skyward statue
With the wild breast and blessed and giant skull
Is carved from her in a room with a wet window
In a fiercely mourning house in a crooked year.
I know her scrubbed and sour humble hands
Lie with religion in their cramp, her threadbare
Whisper in a damp word, her wits drilled hollow,
Her fist of a face died clenched on a round pain;
And sculptured Ann is seventy years of stone.
These cloud-sopped, marble hands, this monumental
Argument of the hewn voice, gesture and psalm
Storm me forever over her grave until
The stuffed lung of the fox twitch and cry Love
And the strutting fern lay seeds on the black sill.

"The Force that through the Green Fuse Drives the Flower"

The force that through the green fuse drives the flower
Drives my green age; that blasts the roots of trees
Is my destroyer.
And I am dumb to tell the crooked rose
My youth is bent by the same wintry fever.

The force that drives the water through the rocks
Drives my red blood; that dries the mouthing streams
Turns mine to wax.
And I am dumb to mouth unto my veins
How at the mountain spring the same mouth sucks.

The hand that whirls the water in the pool
Stirs the quicksand; that ropes the blowing wind
Hauls my shroud sail.
And I am dumb to tell the hanging man
How of my clay is made the hangman's lime.

The lips of time leech to the fountain head;
Love drips and gathers, but the fallen blood
Shall calm her sores.
And I am dumb to tell a weather's wind
How time has ticked a heaven round the stars.

And I am dumb to tell the lover's tomb
How at my sheet goes the same crooked worm.

RANDALL JARRELL

1914-

The Snow-Leopard

His pads furring the scarp's rime,
Weightless in greys and ecru, gliding
Invisibly, incuriously
As the crystals of the cirri wandering
A mile below his absent eyes,
The leopard gazes at the caravan.

The yaks groaning with tea, the burlaps
Lapping and lapping each stunned universe
That gasps like a kettle for its thinning life
Are pools in the interminable abyss
That ranges up through ice, through air, to night.
Raiders of the unminding element,
The last cold capillaries of their kind,
They move so slowly they are motionless
To any eye less stubborn than a man's. . . .
From the implacable jumble of the blocks
The grains dance icily, a scouring plume,
Into the breath, sustaining, unsustainable,
They trade to that last stillness for their death.
They sense with misunderstanding horror, with desire
Behind the world their blood sets up in mist
The brute and geometrical necessity:
The leopard waving with a grating purr
His six-foot tail: the leopard, who looks sleepily—
Cold, fugitive, secure—at all he knows,
At all that he is: the heart of heartlessness.

A Pilot from the Carrier

Strapped at the center of the blazing wheel,
His flesh ice-white against the shattered mask,
He tears at the easy clasp, his sobbing breaths
Misting the fresh blood lightening to flame,
Darkening to smoke; trapped there in pain
And fire and breathlessness, he struggles free
Into the sunlight of the upper sky—
And falls, a quiet bundle in the sky,
The miles to warmth, to air, to waking:
To the great flowering of his life, the hemisphere
That holds his dangling years. In its long slow sway
The world steadies and is almost still. . . .
He is alone; and hangs in knowledge
Slight, separate, estranged: a lonely eye
Reading a child's first scrawl, the carrier's wake—
The travelling milk-like circle of a miss
Beside the plant-like genius of the smoke
That shades, on the little deck, the little blaze
Toy-like as the glitter of the wing-guns,
Shining as the fragile sun-marked plane
That grows to him, rubbed silver tipped with flame.

90 North

At home, in my flannel gown, like a bear to its floe,
I clambered to bed; up the globe's impossible sides
I sailed all night—till at last, with my black beard,
My furs and my dogs, I stood at the northern pole.

There in the childish night my companions lay frozen,
The stiff furs knocked at my starveling throat,
And I gave my great sigh—the flakes came huddling;
Were they really my end? In the darkness I turned to my rest.

Here, the flag snaps in the glare and silence
Of the unbroken ice. And I stand here,
The dogs bark, my beard is black, and I stare
At the North Pole. And now what? Why, go back.

Turn as I please, my step is to the south.
The world—my world spins on this final point
Of cold and wretchedness: all lines, all winds
End in this whirlpool I at last discover.

And it is meaningless. In the child's bed
After the night's voyage, in that warm world
Where people work and suffer till the death
That crowns the pain—in that Cloud-Cuckoo-Land

I reached my North and it had meaning.
Here at the actual pole of my existence,
Where all that I have done is meaningless,
Where I die or live by accident alone—

Where, living or dying, I am still alone;
Here where North, the night, the berg of death
Crowd to me out of the ignorant darkness,
I see at last that all the knowledge

I wrung from the darkness—that the darkness flung me—
Is worthless as ignorance: nothing comes from nothing,
The darkness from the darkness. Pain comes from the darkness
And we call it wisdom. It is pain.

JOHN BERRYMAN
1914-

The Song of the Demented Priest

I put those things there.—See them burn.
The emerald the azure and the gold
Hiss and crack, the blues and greens of the world
As if I were tired. Someone interferes
Everywhere with me. The clouds the clouds are torn
In ways I do not understand or love.

Licking my long lips, I looked upon God
And he flamed and was friendlier
Than you were, and he was small. Showing me—
Serpents and thin flowers; these were cold.
Dominion waved and glittered like the flare
From ice under a small sun. I wonder.

Afterward the violent and formal dancers
Came out, shaking their pithless heads.
I would instruct them but I cannot now,—
Because of the elements. They rise and move,
I nod a dance and they dance in the rain
In my red coat. I am the king of the dead.

Canto Amor

Dream in a dream the heavy soul somewhere
struck suddenly & dark down to its knees.
A griffin sighs off in the orphic air.

If (Unknown Majesty) I not confess
praise for the rack the rock the live sailor
under the blue sea,—yet I may You bless

always for hér, in fear & joy for hér
whose gesture summons ever when I grieve
me back and is my mage and minister.

—Muses, whose worship I may never leave
but for this pensive woman, now I dare,
teach me her praise! with her my praise receive.—

Three years already of the round world's war
had rolled by stoned & disappointed eyes
when she and I came where we were made for.

Pale as a star lost in returning skies,
more beautiful than midnight stars more frail
she moved towards me like chords, a sacrifice;

entombed in body trembling through the veil
arm upon arm, learning our ancient wound,
we see our one soul heal, recovering pale.

Then priestly sanction, then the drop of sound.
Quickly part to the cavern ever warm
deep from the march, body to body bound,

descend (my soul) out of dismantling storm
into the darkness where the world is made.
Come back to the bright air. Love is multiform.

Heartmating hesitating unafraid
although incredulous, she seemed to fill
the lilac shadow with light wherein she played,

whom sorry childhood had made sit quite still,
an orphan silence, unregarded sheen,
listening for any small soft note, not hopeful:

caricature: as once a maiden Queen,
flowering power comeliness kindness grace,
shattered her mirror, wept, would not be seen.

These pities moved. Also above her face
serious or flushed, swayed her fire-gold
not earthly hair, now moonless to unlace,

resistless flame, now in a sun more cold
great shells to whorl about each secret ear,
mysterious histories, strange shores, unfold.

New musics! One the music that we hear
this is the music which the masters make
out of their minds, profound solemn & clear.

And then the other music, in whose sake
all men perceive a gladness but we are drawn
less for that joy than utterly to take

our trial, naked in the music's vision,
the flowing ceremony of trouble and light,
all Loves becoming, none to rest upon.

Such Mozart made,—an ear so delicate
he fainted at a trumpet-call, a child
so delicate. So merciful that sight,

so stern, we follow rapt who ran awild.
Marriage is the second music, and thereof
we hear what we can bear, faithful & mild.

Therefore the streaming torches in the grove
through dark or bright, swiftly & now more near
cherish a festival of anxious love.

Dance for this music, Mistress to music dear,
more, that full storm through the disordered wood
ravens at midnight of my thirtieth year

and only the trial of our music should
still this irresolute air, only your voice
spelling the tempest may compel our good:

Sing then beyond my song: whirl & rejoice!

ALUN LEWIS

1915-1944

The Jungle

I

In mole-blue indolence the sun
Plays idly on the stagnant pool
In whose grey bed black swollen leaf
Holds Autumn rotting like an unfrocked priest.
The crocodile slides from the ochre sand
And drives the great translucent fish
Under the boughs across the running gravel.
Windfalls of brittle mast crunch as we come
To quench more than our thirst—our selves—

Beneath this bamboo bridge, the mantled pool
Where sleep exudes a sinister content
As though all strength of mind and limb must pass
And all fidelities and doubts dissolve,
The weighted world a bubble in each head,
The warm pacts of the flesh betrayed
By the nonchalance of a laugh,
The green indifference of this sleep.

II

Wandering and fortuitous the paths
We followed to this rendezvous today
Out of the mines and offices and dives,
The sidestreets of anxiety and want,
Huge cities known and distant as the stars,
Wheeling beyond our destiny and hope.
We did not notice how the accent changed
As shadows ride from precipice to plain
Closing the parks and cordoning the roads,
Clouding the humming cultures of the West—
The weekly bribe we paid the man in black,
The day shift sinking from the sun,
The blinding arc of rivets blown through steel,
The patient queues, headlines and slogans flung
Across a frightened continent, the town
Sullen and out of work, the little home
Semi-detached, suburban, transient
As fever or the anger of the old,
The best ones on some specious pretext gone.

But we who dream beside this jungle pool
Prefer the instinctive rightness of the poised
Pied kingfisher deep darting for a fish
To all the banal rectitude of states,
The dew-bright diamonds on a viper's back
To the slow poison of a meaning lost
And the vituperations of the just.

III

The banyan's branching clerestories close
The noon's harsh splendour to a head of light.
The black spot in the focus grows and grows:
The vagueness of the child, the lover's deep
And inarticulate bewilderment,

The willingness to please that made a wound,
The kneeling darkness and the hungry prayer;
Cargoes of anguish in the holds of joy,
The smooth deceitful stranger in the heart,
The tangled wrack of motives drifting down
An oceanic tide of Wrong.
And though the state has enemies we know
The greater enmity within ourselves.

Some things we cleaned like knives in earth,
Kept from the dew and rust of Time
Instinctive truths and elemental love,
Knowing the force that brings the teal and quail
From Turkestan across Himalayan snows
To Kashmir and the South alone can guide
That winging wildness home again.

Oh you who want us for ourselves,
Whose love can start the snow-rush in the woods
And melt the glacier in the dark coulisse,
Forgive this strange inconstancy of soul,
The face distorted in the jungle pool
That drowns its image in a mort of leaves.

IV

Gray monkeys gibber, ignorant and wise.
We are the ghosts, and they the denizens;
We are like them anonymous, unknown,
Avoiding what is human, near,
Skirting the villages, the paddy fields
Where boys sit timelessly to scare the crows
On bamboo platforms raised above their lives.

A trackless wilderness divides
Joy from its cause, the motive from the act:
The killing arm uncurls, strokes the soft moss;
The distant world is an obituary,
We do not hear the tappings of its dread.
The act sustains; there is no consequence.
Only aloneness, swinging slowly
Down the cold orbit of an older world
Than any they predicted in the schools,
Stirs the cold forest with a starry wind,
And sudden as the flashing of a sword
The dream exalts the bowed and golden head

And time is swept with a great turbulence,
The old temptation to remold the world.

The bamboos creak like an uneasy house;
The night is shrill with crickets, cold with space.
And if the mute pads on the sand should lift
Annihilating paws and strike us down
Then would some unimportant death resound
With the imprisoned music of the soul?
And we become the world we could not change?
Or does the will's long struggle end
With the last kindness of a foe or friend?

DAVID GASCOYNE
1916-

An Autumn Park

Dark suffocates the world; but such
Ubiquity of shadow is unequal. Here
At the spiked gates which crown the hill begins
A reign as of suspense within suspense:
Outside our area of sand-bagged mansions and of tense
But inarticulate expectancy of roars,
The unhistoric park
Extends indifference through all its air.

During these present days
None but the lonely and reflective care to walk
Through the unworldly and concealed preserves
Of vegetable integrity (where trees
Though murmurous at least are without words . . .)
For such unsocial ones the park negates
With its consistently non-human peace
All the loud mind-polluted world outside its gates.

When sudden sunrays break the brooding haze
Which makes monotonous these grounds,
Livid the little wind-flaked lakes appear,
Vivid the fever-mottled leaves still bound
By mouldering stalks to idly shaken boughs;
Brief light and breath intensify the scene

With glitter drifting across wet grass wastes
And odour of crushed bracken and raw sand . . .

These acres bordering on plains of brick
And brain and coin and newspaper and noise,
Still store for townsmen such as seek
Remembrance of the simpler earth that was
Our dwelling and contentment once, a chance
Of re-beholding that lost innocence; may show
To those that walk to-day there to forget, the true
And imminent glory breaking through Man's circumstance.

October, 1939

Jardin Du Palais Royal

TO B. VON M.

The sky's a faded blue and taut-stretched flag
Tenting the quadrangle. On three
Sides the arcade (tenebrous lanes
Down which at times patchouli'd ghosts flit by,—
Furtive reflections on the filmy panes
Of shops which seem to store only the dusts
And atmospheres of antiquated years,—
Intent on fusty vice), restricts the garden-
Statues' timeless gaze. Here inside this
Shut-off and bygone place, brown urchin birds
Play tag and twitter, jittering around
The central fountain's dance; while children chase
Their ragged shadows round about
The palinged trees, with screams; and iron chairs
With pattern-perforated seats drop their design
Like black lace on the gravel. There we sat
And watched that liquid trembling spire the wind
Made sway and break and spatter a thin spray
Like tears upon our hair and tight-clenched hands. . .
How long? I have forgotten. But you rocked
Backwards and forwards, scraping up small stones,
And never spoke. The day was in July,
Full of a whitish and exhausting glare. And I
Could only stare in silence, trying to see
Into the constantly disintegrating core
Round which the fountain ever climbed again;
Hearing the clack of feet that died away
Down the dim passage, and the unnerving din

Child-voices made behind us. O but then
You turned, and asked me with inconsolable eyes
The meaning of the pain that kept us dumb;
And then we both knew that our pact had been betrayed;
And that cold moment made the garden seem
Too like our lives, abandoned in a wilderness of Time,
Boxed-in by the frustrating and decayed
Walls of the haunted Memory's arcade.

JOHN MALCOLM BRINNIN

1916-

The Worm in the Whirling Cross

No further, fathering logos, withering son,
Shall I my sense for want of grace confess,
But vouch this matter of decaying green
That with a shark's tooth grin
Hinges the rooftree of my dwelling place.
Anguish I caught when I walked apple-wise
Shows me forever the first sun I mourn:
Wild Tigris at full spring, giraffes and O,
That water-logged, fell swoop of genesis.
What excellent ray divines it now? to learn
How leaf's mould burns, I would cross grain with you.
When your all-hallowed dome's dove-tailing brows
Fall to, by inscape clearing manscape new,
My groundswelled pride shall greet hailstorm and stress.

I'd east, I'd west, O dark idea of sleep
If from this dark idlesse and chrysalis
You'd spread your birdwise fan of shut third eyes
And on the cryptic idioms of snow
And tumid greensward show
The idols of your night to my idyllic day.
O toward identity
Be witness angel and dark partisan.

Upthrust down trodden bedrock's mighty main,
My slow bones stretched on tide-ledge, bog, and dune;
Time's tanglefoot, blood's vein that gags and blinds
Twin to his hungry intertwining twin,

I brushed big fish and fisted my curled hands
At brute Tyrannosaurus and tit-wren,
Honing the spirit flesh would eat alive,
Until, touched with the phosphor of self-love,
The forebrain glowed and light knew it was light.
Around that influence the flying fox,
Flanked by the archaeopteryx,
Sailed through the gloom, and restless under it
The little eohippus cropped his field;
One weather told the world how it grew old.

    Begot in, ah, God's ego we go well
Till, ill begun, O, sight be gone, we die.
Glow, blind worm, seed of that worm-eaten oak
Whose scattered marrow lines my wailing wall,
Yet from my death-beds, fly:
For I with ice-capped bee in outcropped lime
Am etched into hard time
Like diamonds trailing shucks of common coal:—
God's chemical to lesser dust withdraws,
His basilisk dissolves, chimerical
Light lacing light, while through frankincensed air's
Pin-pointless more or less,
Downcast, trumped up, the bored archangel blares.

    How is it ghost, that fin by fur I fare
Your Christ-crossed voyage yet arrive still born?
Packed in my brain your spade and sepulchre
Mark the dim stations of the way I come
Toward my lost other father, my lost home,
Yet wake to find a curling embryo:
But O, perhaps we know—
More than we know. . . . How does the mantis pray?
Does he not fix his dark Silurian eye,
Stark ebony, on the revolving day,
His mechanism pulleyed and well-strung,
And with precise antennae cautiously
Tuned all a-twitch to his licentious wing,
Sweep the charged space with vast humility?

    How else, but by the mind that breeds on bone
And of cross-bone finds issue do we prove
As tall toward heaven as the thought of it?
So minded may we not, spare heads of wit,
By foul means brought to these dead ends alive,
From double meanings strike the singleton?

God is the verb by whither out of whence
(Heigh-ho hosanna on Nirvana's couch)
Intransitive, yet active past pretense.
This nothing infinitely out of touch,
Spontaneous mote that kindled waters once,
Spies on the guilt-flecked whites of inner eyes
And drops a saint's-bait hook. "Deliverance,"
My ancient cries, and shakes the astonished trees:
"I found this notion in a lily-pond,
And with a rib-like wand
Divined it mine, umbilicus and crown:
Then on the stagnant pond the pregnant sun
Showed one preponderant lily and I knew;
Wherefor my knucklebones cracked in His praise,
And like to like my face looked in His face."

Old adamantine clay, dearly though I hold
Your myth and office, and your fall reflect,
Your matter's seasoned well but not well-told.
Before God's creature walked
His foetus somersaulting like a clown
Arrived here upside down;
His question was not, Shall I be foreborne?
But, How may I forebear what I am born?
Through the wet nurseries of the fig leaf one
Sweet wind distributed his song and story;
No sooner sung than sorry;
In speaking bush and philosophic stone,
He cut a finite figure twice his size;
The grave stone spoke, a little whittled wood
Grew out of hand and into Paradise;
He thought there were two sides to every grave
Mark of his design, and overweighed with love,
Put out his vessels of propitious blood.

Time-honored, O false fathered, dreaming you,
I fell through swells, ripped tide and undertow,
Ebb following on flow, the blind crab's house
Of furbelow that holds him far below:
"See! Sea-changed one," I said, "how the light goes!"
Alas, a sea-horse blue
As silence floating by was all his word;
So we become each other after all
(In time or late, as time alone will tell);
All ways my only now, I said or heard:
"Because I fell what me befalls, I will,

And will withal, in fly-blown amber guard
My yard of bones from senseless pyramids!
My word it was crowned the concentric Word
Combustible ditch-water simmered toward,
My fate it was unwound love's foetal cord.
Whirled word! and syllabus of all that hides
Manslaughter, the dog and go and do God
Might from his mill's almighty grindstone free.
Yet I am one. One moves me. None may die;
For all I know, horizons crossing me
My course at three crossroads pike vertical;
O when that cross is twirled, whereon I lie,
My hair and hide bound on the brain-racked wheel
Illusion spins, may fly wherefor and why;
As painted figures on a rolling ball
Show in their turns as one, I shall be whole;
—Yet still this bloodshot globe's an eyeball by
Mind's dead-eye dark blacked out, unless I say."

    Goodbye, god-father; sons go on their own
In the long run; farewell, old potentate,
Old lion-heart; though I know woebegone
And prophetless travail avail me nought.
Cast-off of dust, I bolt your five-barred gate
Once more, and clapped anew, through avenues
Of sand-stormed hours spilled time-counterwise,
Fall backwards back to the embalming lake
Where the cold moon's infertile eye keeps one
Twin cradle with the whole soft seed of man.
O bridegroom floating in the white bride's wake,
O mirror-pealing, moon-appalling face,
Your fire falls, locked antlers in the bough,
As over cowls of snow,
Arising, haloed with hot sapphire and ice,
First-born offspring of metamorphosis,
I ride my beast-king Christ through Paradise;
Yet will taboos their cutthroat totems raise,
And soon in bloodsoaked sorrow Sophocles
Will publish my dead issue and its name.
O fatal apple of your father's eye,
At this core of the matter lies your dream.
Ah well, ill-webbed or well this net plots my
Hell-bent heydey,—coiled from the eggshell skull,
Foundering truth of that profound doom's day
Dumbfounding all, boomeranged bone again,
Whistling fissions howl through God's cracked bowl;

Who loves his life leaves well enough alone,
Holding his tongue at Pentecost of death,
While somewhere shuttling slowly something weaves
For saw-toothed worms his rag bag mummy cloth,
—Sleep soundly, doom's man, sleep, and be dream's child:
—For, when all's twice told, all told we lie cold.

Stone rolling, cocksure morning, show my son,
And eastering, westering, with white windspread sail,
Touch these cold stones with specular design;
Toward my lean amplitude be bountiful,
With cockerel quill entablature such rule
As will prevail, and fill with blowing grain
The horn that bids the rakish wedding guest;
When worst comes to the worst, at your behest
Let wine-and-water's sons and daughters mix;
Bless, with good-natured artifice and wit,
Hands that would tend minds all mismarriage breaks,
And over guilt-edged beds long overwrought
Hang emblems from your seamless canopy.
Pull the reluctant water-coddled boy
Up by his roots, and shape his fungus foot
This way, and that way, so long as he may
Find his way forward by his afterthought.
Shine, androgyne, old soloist of dawn;
Your forelocked heirs arise, and on death's bane
Their life-spans overarch, where in the world
Inhuman nature bears one human child.

Host to the worm who'll entertain my clay,
I face my love's child with an untoward peace;
His eye's all sea as I remember sea
Where swordfish minnows shred God's images;
His song, swan song, pealed from the stripling tree
Fills my last breath whereon his mouth must close;
As the bough burns, the seed explodes in air:
Wherever I walk now, I wake not here.

ROBERT LOWELL
1917-

Mr. Edwards and the Spider

I saw the spiders marching through the air,
Swimming from tree to tree that mildewed day
  In latter August when the hay
   Came creaking to the barn. But where
    The wind is westerly,
Where gnarled November makes the spiders fly
Into the apparitions of the sky,
They purpose nothing but their ease and die
Urgently beating east to sunrise and the sea;

What are we in the hands of the great God?
It was in vain you set up thorn and briar
  In battle array against the fire
   And treason crackling in your blood;
    For the wild thorns grow tame
And will do nothing to oppose the flame;
Your lacerations tell the losing game
You play against a sickness past your cure.
How will the hands be strong? How will the heart endure?

A very little thing, a little worm,
Or hourglass-blazoned spider, it is said,
  Can kill a tiger. Will the dead
   Hold up his mirror and affirm
    To the four winds the smell
And flash of his authority? It's well
If God who holds you to the pit of hell,
Much as one holds a spider, will destroy,
Baffle and dissipate your soul. As a small boy

On Windsor Marsh, I saw the spider die
When thrown into the bowels of fierce fire:
  There's no long struggle, no desire
   To get up on its feet and fly—
    It stretches out its feet
And dies. This is the sinner's last retreat;
Yes, and no strength exerted on the heat
Then sinews the abolished will, when sick
And full of burning, it will whistle on a brick.

But who can plumb the sinking of that soul?
Josiah Hawley, picture yourself cast
  Into a brick-kiln where the blast
  Fans your quick vitals to a coal—
    If measured by a glass,
How long would it seem burning! Let there pass
A minute, ten, ten trillion; but the blaze
Is infinite, eternal: this is death,
To die and know it. This is the Black Widow, death.

The Drunken Fisherman

Wallowing in this bloody sty,
I cast for fish that pleased my eye
(Truly Jehovah's bow suspends
No pots of gold to weight its ends);
Only the blood-mouthed rainbow trout
Rose to my bait. They flopped about
My canvas creel until the moth
Corrupted its unstable cloth.

A calendar to tell the day;
A handkerchief to wave away
The gnats; a couch unstuffed with storm
Pouching a bottle in one arm;
A whiskey bottle full of worms;
And bedroom slacks: are these fit terms
To mete the worm whose molten rage
Boils in the belly of old age?

Once fishing was a rabbit's foot—
O wind blow cold, O wind blow hot,
Let suns stay in or suns step out:
Life danced a jig on the sperm-whale's spout—
The fisher's fluent and obscene
Catches kept his conscience clean.
Children, the raging memory drools
Over the glory of past pools.

Now the hot river, ebbing, hauls
Its bloody waters into holes;
A grain of sand inside my shoe
Mimics the moon that might undo
Man and Creation too; remorse,
Stinking, has puddled up its source;

Here tantrums thrash to a whale's rage.
This is the pot-hole of old age.

Is there no way to cast my hook
Out of this dynamited brook?
The Fisher's sons must cast about
When shallow waters peter out.
I will catch Christ with a greased worm,
And when the Prince of Darkness stalks
My bloodstream to its Stygian term . . .
On water the Man-Fisher walks.

The Quaker Graveyard in Nantucket

FOR WARREN WINSLOW, DEAD AT SEA

*Let man have dominion over the fishes of the sea and
the fowls of the air and the beasts and the whole
earth, and every creeping creature that moveth upon
the earth.*

I

A brackish reach of shoal off Madaket,—
The sea was still breaking violently and night
Had steamed into our North Atlantic Fleet,
When the drowned sailor clutched the drag-net. Light
Flashed from his matted head and marble feet,
He grappled at the net
With the coiled, hurdling muscles of his thighs:
The corpse was bloodless, a botch of reds and whites,
Its open, staring eyes
Were lustreless dead-lights
Or cabin-windows on a stranded hulk
Heavy with sand. We weight the body, close
Its eyes and heave it seaward whence it came,
Where the heel-headed dogfish barks its nose
On Ahab's void and forehead; and the name
Is blocked in yellow chalk.
Sailors, who pitch this portent at the sea
Where dreadnaughts shall confess
Its hell-bent deity,
When you are powerless
To sand-bag this Atlantic bulwark, faced
By the earth-shaker, green, unwearied, chaste
In his steel scales: ask for no Orphean lute

To pluck life back. The guns of the steeled fleet
Recoil and then repeat
The hoarse salute.

II

Whenever winds are moving and their breath
Heaves at the roped-in bulwarks of this pier,
The terns and sea-gulls tremble at your death
In these home waters. Sailor, can you hear
The Pequod's sea wings, beating landward, fall
Headlong and break on our Atlantic wall
Off 'Sconset, where the yawing S-boats splash
The bellbuoy, with ballooning spinnakers,
As the entangled, screeching mainsheet clears
The blocks: off Madaket, where lubbers lash
The heavy surf and throw their long lead squids
For blue-fish? Sea-gulls blink their heavy lids
Seaward. The winds' wings beat upon the stones,
Cousin, and scream for you and the claws rush
At the sea's throat and wring it in the slush
Of this old Quaker graveyard where the bones
Cry out in the long night for the hurt beast
Bobbing by Ahab's whaleboats in the East.

III

All you recovered from Poseidon died
With you, my cousin, and the harrowed brine
Is fruitless on the blue beard of the god,
Stretching beyond us to the castles in Spain,
Nantucket's westward haven. To Cape Cod
Guns, cradled on the tide,
Blast the eelgrass about a waterclock
Of bilge and backwash, roil the salt and sand
Lashing earth's scaffold, rock
Our warships in the hand
Of the great God, where time's contrition blues
Whatever it was these Quaker sailors lost
In the mad scramble of their lives. They died
When time was open-eyed,
Wooden and childish; only bones abide
There, in the nowhere, where their boats were tossed
Sky-high, where mariners had fabled news
Of Is, the swashing castle. What it cost
Them is their secret. In the monster's slick

I see the Quakers drown and hear their cry:
"If God himself had not been on our side,
If God himself had not been on our side,
When the Atlantic rose against us, why,
Then it had swallowed us up quick."

IV

This is the end of the whaleroad and the whale
Who spewed Nantucket bones on the thrashed swell
And stirred the troubled waters to whirlpools
To send the Pequod packing off to hell:
This is the end of them, three-quarters fools,
Snatching at straws to sail
Seaward and seaward on the turntail whale,
Spouting out blood and water as it rolls,
Sick as a dog to these Atlantic shoals:
Clamavimus, O depths. Let the sea-gulls wail

For water, for the deep where the high tide
Mutters to its hurt self, mutters and ebbs.
Waves wallow in their wash, go out and out,
Leave only the death-rattle of the crabs,
The beach increasing, it enormous snout
Sucking the ocean's side.
This is the end of running on the waves;
We are poured out like water. Who will dance
The mast-lashed master of Leviathans
Up from this field of Quakers in their unstoned graves?

V

When the whale's viscera go and the roll
Of its corruption overruns this world
Beyond tree-swept Nantucket and Wood's Hole
And Martha's Vineyard, Sailor, will your sword
Whistle and fall and sink into the fat?
In the great ash-pit of Jehoshaphat
The bones cry for the blood of the white whale,
The fat flukes arch and whack about its ears,
The death-lance churns into the sanctuary, tears
The gun-blue swingle, heaving like a flail,
And hacks the coiling life out: it works and drags
And rips the sperm-whale's midriff into rags,
Gobbets of blubber spill to wind and weather,
Sailor, and gulls go round the stoven timbers

Where the morning stars sing out together
And thunder shakes the white surf and dismembers
The red flag hammered in the mast-head. Hide,
Our steel, Jonas Messias, in Thy side.

VI

OUR LADY OF WALSINGHAM

There once the penitents took off their shoes
And then walked barefoot the remaining mile;
And the small trees, a stream and hedgerows file
Slowly along the munching English lane,
Like cows to the old shrine, until you lose
Track of your dragging pain.
The stream flows down under the druid tree,
Shiloah's whirlpools gurgle and make glad
The castle of God. Sailor, you were glad
And whistled Sion by that stream. But see:

Our Lady, too small for her canopy,
Sits near the altar. There's no comeliness
At all or charm in that expressionless
Face with its heavy eyelids. As before,
This face, for centuries a memory,
Non est species, neque decor,
Expressionless, expresses God: it goes
Past castled Sion. She knows what God knows,
Not Calvary's Cross nor crib at Bethlehem
Now, and the world shall come to Walsingham.

VII

The empty winds are creaking and the oak
Splatters and splatters on the cenotaph,
The boughs are trembling and a gaff
Bobs on the untimely stroke
Of the greased wash exploding on a shoal-bell
In the old mouth of the Atlantic. It's well;
Atlantic, you are fouled with the blue sailors,
Sea-monsters, upward angel, downward fish:
Unmarried and corroding, spare of flesh
Mart once of supercilious, wing'd clippers,
Atlantic, where your bell-trap guts its spoil
You could cut the brackish winds with a knife
Here in Nantucket, and cast up the time
When the Lord God formed man from the sea's slime

And breathed into his face the breath of life,
And blue-lung'd combers lumbered to the kill.
The Lord survives the rainbow of His will.

DUNSTAN THOMPSON

1918-

Largo

FOR WILLIAM ABRAHAMS

Of those whom I have known, the few and fatal friends,
All were ambiguous, deceitful, not to trust:
But like attracts its like, no doubt; and mirrors must
Be faithful to the image that they see. Light bends
   Only the spectrum in the glass:
   Prime colors are the ones which pass
   The less distorted. Friendship ends
In hatred or in love, ambivalence of lust:
Either, like Hamlet, haunted, doting on the least
Reflection of remorse; or else, like Richard, lost
   In vanity. The frozen hands
   That hold the mirror make demands;
And flexing fingers clutch the vision in a vise.
Each one betrays himself: the ghostly glazer understands
     Why he must work in ice.

All friends are false but you are true: the paradox
Is perfect tense in present time, whose parallel
Extends to meeting point; where, more than friends, we fell
Together on the other side of love; where clocks
   And mirrors were reversed to show
   Ourselves as only we could know;
   Where all the doors had secret locks
With double keys; and where the sliding panel, well
Concealed, gave us our exit through the palace wall.
There we have come and gone: twin kings, who roam at will
   Behind the court, behind the backs
   Of consort queens, behind the racks
On which their favorites lie who told them what to do.
For every cupid with a garland round the throne still lacks
     The look I give to you.

The goddess who presided at our birth was first
Of those in fancy clothes fate made us hate to fight:
The Greeks with gifts, good looks, so clever, so polite,
Like lovers quick to charm, disarming, too well versed
    In violence to wear weapons while
    They take a city for a smile.
    By doomed ancestral voices cursed
To wander from the womb, their claws plucked out our sight,
Who nighttime thinking we are followed down the street
By blind men like ourselves, turn round again, and wait,
    Only to hear the steps go past
    Us standing lonely there, at last
Aware how we have failed; are now the Trojan fool
For all the arty Hellenistic tarts in plaster cast:
    The ones who always rule.

We are alone with every sailor lost at sea
Whose drowning is repeated day by day. The sound
Of bells from buoys mourning sunken ships rings round
Us, warning away the launch that journeys you and me
    On last Cytherean trips in spring.
    There the rocks are where sirens sing
    Like nightingales of death. But we,
Hearing excitements, music for the ear, have bound
Our voyage to find its ending where the sterile sand
Spends pearls and coral on a skull. The sailing wind
    Is with us now and then: blows high
    As halcyon clouds across the sky:
Falls fast to doldrums while the moon is also young,
Untided, half to harvest whole. See how our sirens die
    Before their song is sung.

What we have always wanted, never had, the ease,
The fame of athletes, such happy heroes at a game,
Beloved by every likely lad, is not the same
As what we have: these measured methods how to please
    An indolent and doubtful boy,
    Who plays at darts, breaks for a toy
    The sometime valued heart. Why seize
The moment in the garden, on the stair, to blame
Our nameless Eros for his daring? Too little time
Is left for love. When we come back, what welcome home
    Will he award our wounded eyes?
    What uniform be his disguise

In dreams, when sleeping sentries always march away
Once more to war? Now is our novelty: we may surprise
    The faun at end of day.

Make no mistake, my soldier. Listen: bugle calls
Revoke your leisure like a leave, invade your peace
With orders on the run, and, loud as bombs, police
Your life for death. The poet's blood-brick tower falls:
    Even his vanity is gone,
    Which leaves the loser all alone.
    Not private poems, but public brawls
Demand his drumbeat history, the pulse that must increase
Until his heart is ransomed from its jewel. Revise
Your verse. Consider what king's killer did to those
    Who wrote their way between the shells
    That last delusive time. Farewells
Are folly to our serpent queen. She will not sign
Discharge of conscience for a masterpiece, but, hissing, tells
    Failure in every line.

We are the mountaineers who perish on the slopes
Of heaven high and perfect Himalayan peak:
Exhausted by the cold, we can no longer speak
To one another—only signal by the ropes.
    Those best before us have, alas,
    Plunged through a gentian-blue crevasse:
    The snow-blind flaw. Their glacial hopes
Shine as a stream of desperate stars, icebound, and bleak,
That mock their nimbused glory from a frigid lake.
Where we stand now, they stood much farther: climbing like
    Legendary guides. But traps
    Were waiting for their last collapse:
Inviting visions from the moon world air—misplace
A step to follow, dance to death. They fell, so we, perhaps
    May do as well with grace.

Now noble guests depart for good, wearing our loss
Like flowers. O Damon, decked with asphodel, who moves
Among the shadow dwellers. But he shall hear the hooves
Of unicorns at gallop, see them, coursing, toss
    Their fluted horns above the cool
    Unpoisoned waters in love's pool,
    And, kneeling, lay their heads across
A beatific virgin's breast. The day approves
His passage: sunlight on the secret river gives

Bright benediction to his boat. Elysian waves
  Bear him, the hero, far from us
  To join the gods. Illustrious!
No words may worship him. The laurel is not all
That withers at the roots, since we, lamenting him, are thus
    Autumnal for his fall.

Armed, say you? Armed, my lord. So, likewise, you and I,
Who with the butchered ghost must stalk the battlements,
Shall watch—cold-comfort guards—how lonely lie the tents
Where strangers sleep together just before they die.
  Look where their banners in the air
  Are half-staff hung. The cockcrow dare
  Of dawn is mourning in the sky.
Our thought like bayonets blood time. What precedents
Of passion shall we use to brave the coward? Once
Bombs are as roses, will he kiss the black-heart prince?
  Honor, more heavy than the sea,
  May overwhelm both you and me
To give no quarter choice at all: gay boys, whom war
Won janizary; youths, who flung away their shields. So we
    Are *mort à Singapore*.

Narcissus, doubled in the melting mirror, smiles
To see himself outfaced by tears, and, sorrowing, hands
His ace of love to harlequin of hearts, who stands
The distant edge of laughter. Time's joker still compiles
  Trick score of triumph, trumps the queen
  To play his knave of emeralds. Green
  Gamester reflects the water guiles
Of palming, reads the gambled cards, and then demands
Another pack to shuffle. But the glass partner bends
The fate five fingers round a saint's stigmata, wounds
  By dealing diamonds from his nails.
  No marveled metaphor avails
To vantage this beloved impersonator twin,
Whose coronet, crown crystal, qualifies a peer. My voice fails.
    In your name poems begin.

RICHARD WILBUR

1921-

Still, Citizen Sparrow

Still, citizen sparrow, this vulture which you call
Unnatural, let him but lumber again to air
Over the rotten office, let him bear
The carrion ballast up, and at the tall

Tip of the sky lie cruising. Then you'll see
That no more beautiful bird is in heaven's height,
No wider more placid wings, no watchfuller flight;
He shoulders nature there, the frightfully free,

The naked-headed one. Pardon him, you
Who dart in the orchard aisles, for it is he
Devours death, mocks mutability,
Has heart to make an end, keeps nature new.

Thinking of Noah, childheart, try to forget
How for so many bedlam hours his saw
Soured the song of birds with its wheezy gnaw,
And the slam of his hammer all the day beset

The people's ears. Forget that he could bear
To see the towns like coral under the keel,
And the fields so dismal deep. Try rather to feel
How high and weary it was, on the waters where

He rocked his only world, and everyone's.
Forgive the hero, you who would have died
Gladly with all you knew; he rode that tide
To Ararat; all men are Noah's sons.

O

The idle dayseye, the laborious wheel,
The osprey's tours, the pointblank matin sun
Sanctified first the circle; thence for fun
Doctors deduced a shape, which some called real
(So all games spoil), a shape of spare appeal,

Cryptic and clean, and endlessly spinning unspun.
Now I go backward, filling by one and one
Circles with hickory spokes and rich soft shields
Of petalled dayseyes, with herehastening steel
Volleys of daylight, writhing white looks of sun;
And I toss circles skyward to be undone
By actual wings, for wanting this repeal
I should go whirling a thin Euclidean reel,
No hawk or hickory to true my run.

HOWARD MOSS

1922-

Waterwall Blues

I gnarled me where the spinster tree
Unwound its green hosanna
And built its sorrow leaf by knee,
A lachrymal cabana.

The selfsame night I cracked my cowl,
Unwound myself with Anna:
Speech by speech and howl by howl
O don't you cry Susanna.

I left my childhood sadness near
The winder of blue water,
Walking in the windmill year
With his summer daughter.

That very night I spoke my piece,
Unwound my heigh-ho merry;
Started my newfangledness
Across her downtown ferry.

But when my halfway laughing gulls
Despair the death of her,
Dumb sorrow rides the same old hulls
With his mad mariner.

Around the Fish:
After Paul Klee

I

The mind from nature, divorced by love,
Stunned into being by the running wave,
Swims backward always. Around the fish,
Unreasoning sensation made a wish:
Parsley, persevering in a tree,
Maturely withers in the alchemy
Of elms and willows. So with us,
The elementary is most serious.

II

Wishing, the Fisher King sat down
(Bait was his body, but his catch, a crown!)
Incarnate fish food rose again,
Hooked to the level of his flawless line;
The sea stirred; sunlight's mica hurled
Aroma of the fish around the world;
Darwin breathed it on another shore,
Gasping the less than liquid air.

III

Swimmers, crying in the undertow,
A water blinds us where we go;
The whirlpool of the inner eye
Has wet ambitions, casts its fly
On sightless water; baited, fed,
Its fishing pole hangs by a thread.
But Christ lies on the blue plate, still.
The spawnless salmon strike to kill!

SIDNEY KEYES

1922-1943

"Were I To Mount Beyond the Field"

Were I to mount beyond the field
Of battle and the lovers' wood to that high-pillared house
Where the great sit, in stone unmoved yet knowing
The world's minute catastrophes;
Judged yet unjudging, presences of fame
And still perfection; were I to speak out clear
In that high house, a voice of light might answer.
Once a man cried and the great Orders heard him:
Pacing upon a windy wall at night
A pale unlearned poet out of Europe's
Erratic heart cried and was filled with speech.
Were I to cry, who in that proud hierarchy
Of the illustrious would pity me?
What should I cry, how should I learn their language?
The cold wind takes my words.
                                    What broad-winged eagle
Could bear me through this night, whose thoughts are pinioned?
No eagle now, for man's mind is divided
And the straight ways are shut, the singing
Voices are broken, there is only noise.
Yet knowing this, I will salute the presences,
Mounting a coward's stair.
                              The walls are harsh
To groping hands, under ascending feet
The smooth stairs twitter. Battle-noises mount
Behind me, and the grinning smoke
Hangs nooses in the air.
                            Pardon my coming
Who am not stone and have no final voice
To conquer chaos, neither sword nor laurel.
The gates are filled with mist; slow-turning pillars
Of cloud surround them. And beyond
Live death's great enemies, the undefeated.
These are a stronger nation. Death tried many
Ways to invade their citadel of mind,
Always in vain; until the mortal hour
When they at last let down the bridge and flung
The gates apart, but left no easy plunder.

A greater victory lay in that surrender,
They knew their enemy. His ambushes
Could not surprise them. Even separation
Meant nothing to their eyes, or changed their speech.
Maimed fingers, ebbing blood, the quarrelling of nerves
Could never frighten them; and broken armies
Were their continual triumph.

                Always came
The meeting in the myrtle-wood, escape
Between the slender trees, the rising
Of loved and lover into a clear sky;
Their images remaining in the lake
Like written words, the grateful air retaining
Their impress, like a dancer's or a bird's.

Wrestling with angels, they found out in time
Only the coward will resist that fall;
And so, embracing bravely the white limbs,
Engulfed in the long shining hair, they learnt
Humility and triumph.

                Some stretched out
Their hands to fire and calumny. Some ran
Upon the spikes of fear. Some lived for years
Alone with panic in a stuffy room
Until they grew good neighbours. Some were mad
Talking with flies and worms; and died for love
A double suicide without despair.

                These are the presences
Who sit beyond the gates, their heads as high
As towers in a dream, their silent faces
Unbitten by the frost, by rain unbeaten;
Their eyes like mirrors reinterpreting
The moon's distracted gaze, their strong hands folded.
Look in those eyes and learn the speech of pain;
Regard those hands, whose touch was clearer sight;
The stone lips curve, whose words were mountainous.
O my head I veil and turn my face to the wall
And pass from the place of wisdom's quiet children.
Their presence is a scroll of peace
Unrolled before the shattered face
Of the dead soldier and the straying lover.
I pass the shining gate
Into the unknown light
Of a low sun, knowing that death is conquered:

For the great have come home, whom all the clamour of history
Will never deafen or decrease their glory.

February-March, 1942

The Anti-Symbolist

If one could only be certain beyond all question
That nature revolves through a zodiac of symbols
Upon an axis of creative mind:
Then one might plan in expectation
Of enlightenment, a perfect revolution
Or at least repetition, and escape suspense.
But nothing seems related, incident or vision,
To any but an arbitrary thought:
The wind moving between the cypresses
Stirs only single leaf, stale wreath. To them
Fighting the roots and drowned beyond memory
Under the cypresses, there is no word for Wind,
And the wind never dies. The tall old woman
Eating her sandwiches on a pompous vault
And her dog who loves to play tag with tombstones,
Need never recur, yet link me with the drowned ones
Of earth, quite unforgettably.

We should not work that way. Anticipation
Is crooked thinking, for nature unobserved
Revolving never, remains its own reflection.
And time flows through us from its sources
Toward the unguessed waterfall, the desert
Of dry eternity; as old men in Greece
Saw dimly its current and our black Niagara.
Forward is not our business; but the higher
Reaches may at least be mapped
With some small boast of skill and application—
And enough science to arrive at morning
Without undue surprise or any fear
Before the estuary lashed with pain, the sharp
Lift of the bar, and feel the tide making westward.
Then only in that drowned man's paradise
Of Hy Brasil or currentless Sargasso,
May the dead and the wind and the old woman
And her dog and my over-curious mind
Meet neighbourly and mingle without question.

23rd May, 1941

JAMES MERRILL
1926-

Foliage of Vision

As landscapes richen after rain, the eye
Atones, turns fresh after a fit of tears.
When all the foliage of vision stirs
I glimpse the plump fruit hanging, falling, fallen
Where wasps are sputtering. In the full sky
Time, a lean wasp, sucks at the afternoon.

The tiny black and yellow agent of rot
Assaults the plum, stinging and singing. What
A marvel is the machinery of decay!
How rare the day's wrack! What fine violence
Went to inject its gall in the glad eye!
The plum lies all brocaded with corruption.

There is no wit in weeping, yet I wept
To hear the insect wrath and rhythm of time
Surround the plum that fell like a leper's thumb.
The hours, my friend, are felicitous imagery,
Yet I became their image to watch the sun
Dragging with it a scarlet palace down.

The eye attunes, pastoral warbler, always.
Joy in the cradle of calamity
Wakes though dim voices work at lullaby.
Triumph of vision: the act by which we see
Is both the landscape-gardening of dream
And the root's long revel under the clipped lawn.

I think of saints with hands pierced and wrenched eyes
Sensational beyond the art of sense,
As though whatever they saw was about to be
While feeling alters in its imminence
To palpable joy; of Dante's ascent in hell
To greet with a cleansed gaze the petaled spheres;

Of Darwin's articulate ecstasy as he stood
Before a tangled bank and watched the creatures
Of air and earth noble among much leafage

Dancing an order rooted not only in him
But in themselves, bird, fruit, wasp, limber vine,
Time and disaster and the limping blood.

The Black Swan

Black on flat water past the jonquil lawns
    Riding, the black swan draws
A private chaos warbling in its wake,
Assuming like a fourth dimension splendor
That calls the child with white ideas of swans
    Nearer to that green lake
  Where every paradox means wonder.

Though the black swan's arched neck is like
    A question-mark on the lake,
The swan outlaws all possible questioning,
A thing in itself, like love, like submarine
Disaster, or the first sound when we wake;
    And the swan-song it sings
  Is the huge silence of the swan.

Illusion: the black swan knows how to break
    Through expectation, beak
Aimed now at its own breast, now at its image,
And move across our lives, if the lake if life,
And by the gentlest turning of its neck
    Transform, in time, time's damage;
  To less than a black plume, time's grief.

Enchanter: the black swan has learned to enter
    Sorrow's lost secret center
Where like a maypole separate tragedies
Are wound about a tower of ribbons, and where
The central hollowness is that pure winter
    That does not change but is
  Always brilliant ice and air.

Always the black swan moves on the lake; always
    The blond child stands to gaze
As the tall emblem pivots and rides out
To the opposite side, always. The child upon
The bank, hands full of difficult marvels, stays
    Forever to cry aloud
  In anguish: I love the black swan.

APPENDIX

Preface

•

Myth and Metaphysics:
An Introduction to Modern Poetry

•

Notes

By KIMON FRIAR

PREFACE TO THE APPENDIX

DURING many years of lecturing in colleges, universities and at The Poetry Center in New York City, it became increasingly evident to this editor that only lack of proper orientation and the unavailability of definite information prevented a wide public from coming to a better understanding of modern poetry. The introduction which follows, *Myth and Metaphysics*, is meant to provide such an orientation; and the notes to the poems are meant to make available such material as may bring the reader into a closer and deeper relationship with the poems themselves. Information readily available in dictionaries or standard books of reference has been omitted.

Different methods have been employed that might destroy certain superficial obstructions to the poem and bring the reader cleanly before it for his own interpretation. Sometimes paraphrase has been attempted, as in Dylan Thomas' "In Memory of Ann Jones," or in Yeats' "Byzantium," and in such cases the reader is not to confuse paraphrase for poem; nor is the paraphrase meant to make sense in itself, but is to be read in close connection with the poem, for the paraphrase is of necessity awkward, incomplete, and even misleading. Often only one of several possible levels of meaning is noted, that which insures a logical continuity, and the reader is left to supply the alternatives. Most often, however, the notes are simply explanatory, such as may save the reader much drudgery and give him certain information which he may lack. At times, as in Eliot's *Ash Wednesday*, both paraphrase and explanatory notes have been supplied. Sometimes the poets themselves have sent material, and this has always been included and the source indicated. In some cases, as in Emily Dickinson's "Wonder Is Not Precisely Knowing," and in the eighth stanza of Hart Crane's "Atlantis," precise textual analysis has been attempted in order to give the reader some indication of modern idiom and trope, and of what might be done with a closer reading of the text.

In every case, however, it must be stressed that the reader is never to confuse any of the notes with the poems themselves; they are aids and nothing more. Inevitably an attempt at explanation at times becomes an attempt at interpretation, and when this happens the reader is free to accept or reject; it makes little difference, provided that he is himself brought into closer familiarity with the poem and elucidates his own understanding of it. The best compliment that may be given these notes is that they be found useful, and ultimately discarded. To students and teachers acquainted with many of the poems, it may often seem that the familiar has been explained and the obvious obscured, but this is in the nature of the case. Many poems which need explication have not been supplied with notes; this would have been impossible, and it is hoped that the reader has been given a method by which to overcome whatever other difficulties remain.

The editor is first of all indebted to the many workers in the field, too numerous and too well known to mention, who have published their analyses in books and periodicals. He is especially grateful to those poets who have supplied him with comments on their poems as printed here, or who have checked the editor's own interpretations. All *Author's Notes* for which no other source is indicated were written especially for this volume. He would like to thank the staffs of the various institutions who, with patient diligence, have helped him to overcome many difficulties; those of the New York Public Library, of Amherst College, of Adelphi College, and the students of various courses of the editor in Contemporary Poetry at Adelphi College, the Mills School, and the Poetry Center in New York City. For particular information in Athens, Greece, he wishes to thank the staffs of the British Institute (and its present director, Mr. Louis MacNeice), of the British School of Archeology, of the American School of Classical Studies, and of the Gennadion Library. He is greatly indebted to John Hinsdale Thompson of Stephens College for the painstaking notes he has so kindly supplied for *Finnegans Wake,* to Hubert Creekmore for certain clues to Pound's *Cantos,* and to those who have granted him permission to quote from sources or analyses, for which due credit is given in the text of these notes. He wishes to thank Mrs. Mina Diamandopoulos for checking the manuscript and proof of the Appendix, and most of all he is grateful to Miss Agnes Eisenberger for her patience and devotion in research, in checking and rechecking copy, and in the typing of manuscript. Since a prolonged stay in Greece during the publication of this book has made it impossible to be certain of complete accuracy, the editor of these notes hopes he may be forgiven any possible errors or omissions.

K.F.

The Medusa
Poros, Troezen
Greece

Myth and Metaphysics

AN INTRODUCTION TO MODERN POETRY

❦

I. RELIGION AND MYTHOLOGY

MODERN British and American poetry is a complex product, the heir of many schools and traditions. There is general agreement, however, that the modern idiom in poetry depends primarily on two traditions—the metaphysical, stemming from John Donne and his period, and the symbolist, stemming from Mallarmé. The mental climate of our time is such that nearly all of its worthy poetry has been influenced to some degree, either directly or indirectly, by these two periods and their tributaries. An anthology such as this, composed of poets writing in the modern idiom, is therefore certain to be weighted by metaphysical and symbolist poetry in which is expressed the highest endeavor of our age—an endeavor, it should now be more generally admitted, which has produced poetry comparable to the best in our literary history. The use of metaphysical and symbolist devices has grown out of the modern poet's search for a mythology which might replace that of the disintegrating Christian culture, and which might offer him some concrete body of belief for metaphor and metaphysic. This is not to say that every modern poet has been deliberately concerned with the problem. Yet all have to some degree been touched by an urgent need which is basic to the great transitional age in which we live. An introduction to modern poetry can best aid the reader who is puzzled by the complexity and density of modern idiom by explaining how this is related to metaphysical and symbolist devices rising out of the modern poet's search for myth.

Myths are projected dreams of the deep subconscious of a race, expressing the needs, fears, wishes, and aspirations of a people. Although symbols differ, all myths are representations of the same basic compulsions. When they are most complete, myths define the relationship of man to himself and to God in such a way that there is no distinction between symbol and meaning. A poet may then use the mythology of his age to present, in concrete symbols embodying a metaphysic, the most complete expression of his time. As a civilization declines, the chasm between symbols and their meaning widens until symbols become decorative form and their meaning becomes abstracted into philosophy. Before the separation becomes too great, mythologies may be used by layman and artist alike to express their profoundest resolutions concerning man's place in the universe. In this sense, a mythology may serve as a guide, explaining conduct and regulating ethics on both material and spiritual planes.

The Iliad, the Odyssey

Homer could write of his culture as an integrity of heroes, demigods, and divinities whose communication with men expressed those actions and maxims of conduct which summarized his culture and became guides not only to the later Periclean Greeks, but also to the entire occidental civilization which followed. If we recall the various attributes which his gods symbolized, or rather which they *were*, we become familiar with the motivations of the Greek race and the ideals to which they aspired. These ideals and motivations were not abstractions but the dramatic characters of a struggle expressing the integration of the individual and society. The lack of such integrity, the dislocation between myth and religious metaphysic, and the consequent disparity of fact and spirit are the central problems of the modern artist, whether he try to gather all modern ideologies into an epical summation, or sing the briefest and most personal lyric. In Greek culture, Aeschylus, Sophocles, and Euripides progressively demonstrated what T. S. Eliot has termed the "disassociation of sensibility." Plato and Aristotle finally abstracted their national myths in dialectic and category; the very title of Lucretius' epical poem, *On the Nature of Things*, becomes indicative of the transformation.[1]

The Divine Comedy

Virgil, the natural heir of Hellenistic ideologies, created a hero, Aeneas, who, in contrast to the free vitality of Odysseus, carries with him the remoteness of a priest in quest of answers, and the detachment of a hero free from passions of love and war. Thus Virgil, whose Fourth Eclogue reread by Christian eyes is messianic, becomes the true transitional guide of Dante to the threshold of the Christian paradise. It will be recalled that Virgil represented for Dante the type of human *philosophy*. Dante occupies the same position in relation to Christian culture that Homer did to Greek culture. Thomas Aquinas had already synthesized the Platonic and Aristotelian usages of the Christian Fathers into a theology which gave hierarchical position to all material and spiritual properties of

---

[1] An example, in modern times, is Robert Bridges' *The Testament of Beauty*.

the medieval cosmos. Thus Dante was freed by the belief of his society and the genius of Aquinas from any necessity of diverting his genius into the creation of critical or philosophical systems, and could therefore use and transform given symbols and systems of his culture into the concrete embodiment of a poem, the *Divine Comedy*, within whose aesthetic structure he could create his own world yet make it the unique but multiple blossom of medieval vision. In no poem before or since have aesthetic and ethical orders been so identical, have quantitative and qualitative rhythms been so simultaneously orchestrated. The complex mathematical ordering of the Inferno, Purgatory, and Paradise shows the close correlation of medieval science, philosophy, theology, and even a personal and political bias. Characters are derived from historical, mythological (both classical and Christian), and personal sources, yet so strong and permeating is the central thesis and corollary dogmas of the work that what in another poem may have seemed eccentric intrusion is here transformed and made relevant. Such organization of minute subdivisions in aesthetic and moral ordering makes possible a style and diction which is lucid yet profound, a clarity which can be distilled only from such resolved complexity. There is no tension between conflicting tendencies in such a style, for all is resolved, a crystal medium through transparencies of which the reader may gaze as far as his own vision permits. Since the *Divine Comedy*, we have known several poems perhaps as great, but none in which the affairs of man and his relation to God have been so ordered, for since Dante's time neither the world nor the artist's expression of it have known a comparable integrity. Every poet has since, in despair, tried to become a Dante.

Paradise Lost

The belief of Milton, as that of most Christian poets who follow, was not the immediate faith of Dante, but an argumentative belief expounding the historic Catholic tradition as modified by Reformation thinkers. *Paradise Lost* and *Paradise Regained* are not the clear reflections of an ordered theocracy, but the embattled fields of celestial, demonic, and heretical wars. Although the characters, not excluding Adam and Eve, are all supernatural, they are as humanized as the doctrines which they embody. Christ, Satan, Michael, Belial, Death, Sin, and even God, are actively involved in the titanic struggles of the soul toward a lost harmony. Man is infected with the perfectability of God, and God with the imperfectibility of man. Predestination is made conditional to the will of man; original sin becomes not the complete depravity of Calvinistic doctrine, but is made a bias which leaves the will free to choose between faith and disbelief and thus make man responsible for his own destiny; sharp distinctions between spirit and matter are obliterated, for God creates not out of Nothing but out of Chaos. What is revealed is the drama, the passion of our relationship to God, and not our *participation* in Him. Since Dante's time, the crevice between myth and metaphysics had widened to such an extent that Milton found it necessary to "justify the ways of God to man," a concept unthinkable to such a mind as Dante's. Dislocation is everywhere evident, in texture and dogma; turbidities of content make purity of style impossible. Instead, the result is a highly contrapuntal and syncopated orchestration. The discords of modern harmonics begin to be heard.

Faust

When Goethe, as a man of the world, sought to sum up European culture, he used Christian mythology with sophisticated consciousness, more in terms of philosophical symbols than as sacraments of faith. As the heir of Voltaire seeking the enfranchisement of the intellect, and as the heir of Rousseau seeking the enfranchisement of the heart, he wished to resolve both in the image of the completely civilized man: a humanistic and philosophical ideal. He sought to combine the inward and personal with the outward and general, romantic sensibility with classical intellectuality. The mysteries of Christian faith became for him the pragmatic devices for human betterment: the fall of Faust in eating of the apple of knowledge becomes *necessary* to his *rise,* for a humanistic interpretation of original sin now makes it seem that only through error and experiment is it possible for man to know himself and to fulfill his capacities. Man is seen to suffer still, not in atonement for original sin and as a prerequisite for grace, but because in striving to understand and to fulfill himself he discovers suffering to be the necessary consequence of the struggle by which he tests the validity of his beliefs and by which he forms his character. The Satan of Milton, so godlike in attribute that he might have defeated God, becomes Mephistopheles, the metaphysical spirit of negation, and Faust himself is not so much a hero as a temperament. During the same era, Keats was writing in *Hyperion* of the dethronement of gods; the half-divine protagonist of Shelley's *Prometheus Unbound* was giving place to the tortured introversion of Byron's *Manfred*; the heavenly host was being driven from the temple as if to usher in, upon the churning crest of some Walpurgis Night, the Industrial Revolution and its spiritual chaos. The eyes of men were turning inward, not upon the contemplation of some heroic image of belief, but on the reflection of themselves. Myth, now no longer an embodiment of cultural ideals, was becoming a cracked and individual mirror.

Faust was perhaps the last great epic in which the mythology of Christianity could be used with structural validity. Since Goethe,

the severance between the metaphysics and myth of Christianity has become so great that artists have been unable to use its myth alone as an "objective correlative" with which to systematize the diversity of the modern world. For most modern poets the Christian myth is no longer consubstantial with its ideals, although some have attempted to invoke through it what no longer breathes in it. For others, the Christian way of life has become a philosophic mode of conduct. To many more, both the ethos and myth of Christianity are illusions to be destroyed. Almost all find themselves and their world without some unifying way of life under which may be harmonized the conflicting interpretations brought on by religious, scientific, industrial, and, more recently, political revolutions. Life is nowhere seen steadily and whole, but under a number of perspectives relative to nothing central. Never has the interpenetration of cultures been so world-wide, or disintegration so universal.

II. T. S. ELIOT

It was inevitable that a compilation of all myths, such as Sir George Frazer's *The Golden Bough* (1890) should appear to give poets hope, for a time, of extracting a composite myth and metaphysic, but the book soon became not a bible of belief but rather a museum to be pilfered. Mythology had become anthropology.

The Waste Land

The most successful and extensive use of such anthropological structure was made by T. S. Eliot in *The Waste Land* (1922) in which he also made parallel use of the body of world literature as mythology. At that time Eliot wrote a review of Joyce's *Ulysses* in which the central problem of the modern poet and the thesis of this Introduction is succinctly announced:

In using the myth, in manipulating a continuous parallel between contemporaneity and antiquity, Mr. Joyce is pursuing a method which others must pursue after him. They will not be imitators, any more than the scientist who uses the discoveries of an Einstein in pursuing his own, independent, and further investigations. It is a simple way of controlling, of ordering, of giving a shape and a significance to the immense panorama of futility and anarchy which is contemporary history. It is a method already adumbrated by Mr. Yeats, and the need for which I believe Mr. Yeats to have been the first contemporary to be conscious. It is, I seriously believe, a step toward making the modern world possible in art.

Although *The Waste Land* is a poem of only 434 lines, it is a true epic in that its theme concerns man's relationship to himself and to God. Unlike Dante, whose stress is on the salvation granted man because of the passion of Christ's crucifixion, Eliot, like Milton in *Paradise Regained,* as mindful of heresies as of original sin, stresses the freedom which ensues from choice, a state which he further dramatized in *Murder in the Cathedral.* As a deliberate Man of Letters, he turned primarily to the body of world literature and sought to make it a world mythology correlated and directed by a Christian sensibility. This adroit juxtaposition of many literatures creates a richness of texture and reference. As in photomontage of the cinema where events of different times are shown occurring at the same moment, so time and space in this poem are devoid of sequence or place, and all history is telescoped in a simultaneous exposure wherein all cities, persons, motifs, and cultures are involved in an intricate and ironic counterpoint. Such juxtaposition in a simultaneous and timeless space becomes characteristic of modern craft, since the modern sensibility, although aware of many sources and comparisons, lacks the focus of a central myth. Although, as Eliot has pointed out, such a poem may be read on many levels, it communicates to a great extent on a first and intuitive level. Nevertheless, the deepest level on which the poem demands to be understood is not so much obscured from the general reader as it is removed from his convictions as a citizen of his nation and the world. Such aesthetic and anthropological structures serve more to order the poet's own sensibility and give form to his craft than to place in order similar confusions which the reader shares in common with the poet as a member of the same disintegrating age. Neither world literature nor anthropology are the heirs of our disenthroned mythologies.

Four Quartets

In *Ash Wednesday,* and in *Four Quartets,* Eliot has depended less on anthropological themes and on objective correlatives taken from *belles lettres* but has elaborated his aesthetic forms and has centralized his references to traditional church ritual and dogma. He still derives sustenance from private reading, but all four of the *Quartets* are unified by the main concern of Christian mystics: the quest for an illumination in time and through time of a timeless union with God, for the still center where all paradoxes are dissolved in God's love. Unable to identify the myths and precepts of Christianity with an integral faith, Eliot, like many whom he has influenced, has submitted himself to Christian dogma and ideology, as if by humility and patient dedication to faiths and myths no longer consubstantial, he might invoke a lost unity and receive, if only for a brief moment, the grace of revelation. Indeed, expert embalming does preserve, for memory if not for love, much of the grace and wisdom with which a beloved was animated. Many who have found no other unity in the world to replace their lost religious faith have turned with nostalgia to what Wallace Stevens has called "Profundum, physical thunder, dimensions in which/We believe without belief, beyond belief." Such dedication has given Eliot a strong center of evaluation from which he has formulated a craft and a diction, especially in *Four Quartets*, which for all its allusions approaches that lucidity which he has admired in Dante. Such simplicity, however, is a product of deliberate exclusions, not of multiplicities resolved into a whole by communal vision, and often results in an attenuation of personal vision. Eliot seems not so much to *express* the direct experience of mystical revelation as to *report* his contemplation of it as formed in a reading of mystical, primarily Christian, literature.

III. HART CRANE

Eliot may be the last important poet writing in English (not excepting Auden) who may with some success rehabilitate Christian mythology and metaphysic in an evaluation of modern culture. "It is a terrific problem that faces the poet of today—" Hart Crane wrote in 1925, "a world that is so in transition from a decayed culture toward a reorganization of human evaluations that there are few common terms, general denominators of speech that are solid enough or that ring with any vibration of spiritual conviction. The great mythologies of the past (including the Church) are deprived of enough façade to even launch good raillery against." Partly in revolt against what he considered to be the nihilism of *The Waste Land* and of Joyce's *Ulysses*, Crane sought to find materials and myths which would sustain his mystical faith in the destiny of mankind as exemplified in American tradition.

The Bridge

"What I am really handling, you see," he wrote Otto Kahn in exposition of *The Bridge* (1930), "is the Myth of America." In another letter he calls the poem "a synthesis of America and its structural identity," and later writes of his search for materials which might be "organic and active factors in the experience and perceptions of our common race, time, and belief. The very idea of a bridge, of course, is a form peculiarly dependent on spiritual convictions. It is an act of faith beside being a communication." Deeply religious yet lacking a religion, Crane sought to span the duality between man and nature by putting "positive and glowing spiritual content into Machinery," and, as he concludes in the proem of his epic, "of the curveship lend a myth to God." A bridge, however, is not a myth, but one symbol of a possible mythology. It may symbolize unity, oneness, resolution between dualities, but it still remains a static mathematical curve and not a series of personifications which embody the ego-ideals of a culture. Crane made an important contribution when he turned for further embodiments of his vision to the green beginnings of an American cultural tradition, to Columbus, Pocahantas, Rip Van Winkle, and Whitman, yet turned to them not as Eliot might, for literary reference, but for historical figures representative of cultural ideals. He planned to make each section of *The Bridge* a different vista of the historical and cultural past of America, but all to be seen with the eye of the present, vitalized by the spirit of the poet himself as actor and evaluator. The Inferno of the subway, the Paradiso of the bridge, the Dante-like peregrinations of the poet, however, are informed by no mature vision of life, but by a revivalist mysticism fed by no doctrine of knowledgeable values, and eventually starved by personal maladjustments. To study the parallel disintegrations of Hart Crane's life and the fabric of his poem is to see, as in few other poems of modern times, how inextricably mingled are an artist's private life, his craft, and his milieu.

IV. JAMES JOYCE

Instead of seeking for objective correlatives in the masterpieces of many literatures, some poets have tried to use some one literary masterpiece as myth.

Ulysses

This method was brought to epical proportions by Joyce in *Ulysses* (1922) by overlaying the activities of a single day in Dublin (June 16, 1904) on the single literary unity of Homer's *Odyssey*, a clever and remarkable idea, for the *Odyssey*, through centuries of study, is not only the cultural embodiment of the classical world, but part of the modern consciousness as well; its narrative has become universal folklore, and its characters have become typical personifications. Joyce thus hoped to found his epic of a day firmly on a literary colossus which has straddled almost three thousand years of civilization. The technical and historical unity between *Ulysses* and the *Odyssey*, nonetheless, is primarily one of implication, and Joyce sought further embodiments in other ancient myths, in symbols derived from the Catholic church, from Freudian analysis, and particularly from an aesthetic structure of his own. The principal theme is that which has concerned all epic poets, and which is prophetically announced by Stephen Dedalus in the conclusion of *A Portrait of the Artist as a Young Man:* "Welcome, O life! I go to encounter for the millionth time the reality of experience, and to forge in the smithy of my soul the uncreated conscience of my race." Joyce might as well have written that he intended to forge the chaotic subconscious of his culture, for the themes of other epics: those of original sin, immaculate conception, consubstantiability of father and son, predestination and free will, are, for the first time to an important degree in literature, given psychological as well as theological or anthropological motivations. Joyce's perspectives are naturalist in terms of narrative, Freudian in motivation and stream of consciousness, and Jesuitic in moral orientation. Aesthetic, thematic, and symbolistic structures are interwoven so adroitly that the reader is almost convinced that the dualities of the modern world have been resolved into an organic and not a mechanic integrity. Yet the book lacks that which is more than the sum of its parts, the *pneuma*, the breathing spirit which only a cultural unity may instill.

Finnegans Wake

If in *Ulysses* the hero is the common man, in *Finnegans Wake* the hero is all mankind, and part of nature, too. Humphrey Chimpden Earwicker is Adam, Here Comes Everybody who Haveth Childers Everywhere, he is a tavern keeper, Tristram, Napoleon, Prometheus, Christ, Osiris, Humpty Dumpty, Swift, Orestes, the Hill of Howth, Dublin, all cities and everything urban. Maggie, his wife, is Eve, Iseult, both Stella and Vanessa, Isis, Anna Livia Plurabella, the river Liffey, all rivers (including the eight in heaven and hell), and everything fluid, the clouds and the rain. Their twin sons, Shem and Shaun, are the dualities, thesis and antithesis in constant opposition. Shaun is the extrovert, the successful, the Postman who delivers other people's *belles lettres,* the bestseller, the senses, the Word made flesh; Shem is the introvert, the unsuccessful, the Penman who writes in blood on the parchment of his body, the unknown and disinherited, the seeker after the Word. They are also each other, their mother and father, and all of androgynous mankind. These dualities are further enlarged in battles between life and death, Satan and St. Michael, Cain and Abel, the Onat and the Cracehopper, the Mookse and the Gripes, the stone and the elm. In the night of his subconscious, Earwicker is haunted by the main paradoxes of theological disputation, now subsumed under overpowering feelings of guilt and anxiety. Like Stephen Dedalus who must seek his father and reconcile himself to his mother, Earwicker is also torn with "agenbite of inwit," remorse of conscience. Like the heroes of Kafka, feeling himself accused of an undetermined crime, he tosses in a nightmare of accusation in which every movement he makes is suspect and every motivation guilty. When the befuddled policeman arrests Earwicker for disturbing the peace and testifies against him, the policeman discovers in confusion that somehow he is also testifying against himself, for Earwicker is Here Comes Everybody, and the accuser and accused are one. The tail of the serpent is in his mouth again.

The structural ideology of *Finnegans Wake,* under which all other ideologies are subordinated, is a theory of history set forth by the eighteenth-century Italian philosopher, Giambattista Vico, in which civilizations are seen to pass through four cyclical movements: a theocracy when people imagine gods, an aristocracy when they create myths about their heroes, a democracy when they see themselves in terms of materiality, and a chaotic period in which democracy disintegrates in thunder and a new theocracy is formed. The progression of *Finnegans Wake* from images of darkness to those of light, from those of deepening guilt as the night deepens to those of affirmation as the peace (a word repeated in twenty-nine languages) of Sunday morning dawns, are further cyclical extensions in a spiralling progress. Dawn, of course, is only preparatory to another dark night of the soul, as the last sentence of *Finne gans Wake* continues into the first. In this envelopment exist the timeless and spaceless occurrences (they can hardly be called an action) which are simultaneously the dreams of Earwicker during one Saturday summer night and the dreams of all mankind during an infinite moment. Further, all objective correlatives and their themes are assimilated into a diction reconstructed from many languages, but only as alphabet, sound, and meaning are related in any single word basically English, until finally there is no referent between symbol and thought and each *is* the other by *presentation,* not invoked by *representation.* Everything is metamorphosed into the Word which is reality. "In the beginning," says St. John, "was the Word, and the Word was with God, and the Word was God." Thus all materialities of the cosmos are purified of substance into an aesthetically created World and Word enfolded in its own and only reality, and whose single tenuous relation to outer phenomena are the eyes which might, but need not, read it.

All of *Finnegans Wake* itself is one such Word, enfolded in itself as its last sentence enfolds itself in its first—a Word which Joyce demands that a reader spend a lifetime in interpreting. For Joyce this is equivalent to saying that we must necessarily spend our lifetime in trying to fathom the mystery which indeed we are, to read in frustration an obscure letter of dubious authorship in which we feel that all our questions must surely be answered. Such a letter appears and reappears in the larger Letter which is *Finnegans Wake* and which it reflects, as if Joyce stood between two facing mirrors and saw himself multiplied on all sides into infinity. Scratched up by a hen on a dunghill belonging to Earwicker's neighbor, said to be written by some female relative, it seems to be composed of chatty and irrelevant gossip about the marriages, children, deaths, and food habits of various friends. Throughout the hallucinations of his dream, Earwicker tries to read it, but cannot. At times it seems to be nothing but a smutty letter (it was sent from Boston); but then again it seems to be the art of *belles lettres* itself or perhaps the alphabet from alpha to omega, the handwriting on the wall. It is "that letter self-penned to one's other, that never perfect ever-planned" which Joyce wrote as his "letter to the world," *Finnegans Wake*, but in which he tried not so much to address a world as to create one.

V. WILLIAM BUTLER YEATS

A myth through which might be expressed a personal vision related to communal culture was a more conscious preoccupation for Yeats than for any of the poets thus far discussed.

A Vision

It drove him from one attempt to another—from attempts to formulate systems of mythological reference out of the literature of French symbolists, from magical, caballistic and theosophical rituals, from Celtic mythology—until he combined most of these in the aesthetic which he expounds in *A Vision,* first published in 1925, then revised and republished in 1937. As early as 1897, when the necessity for such structure became apparent to him, he wrote a commentary on Blake which expressed his own need: "he spoke confusedly and obscurely because he spoke of things for whose speaking he could find no models in the world about him. He was a symbolist who was trying to invent his symbols. . . . He was a man crying out for mythology, and trying to make one because he could not find one to his hand." Better than Blake[2] or any of his own contemporaries, Yeats has succeeded in keeping a balance between private symbolism and public communication, and those who have the courage to read his "celestial geometry," as Æ called it, may see the unity and continuity of his thought. Because no other poet of modern times has presented the metaphysical basis of his private use of myth so systematically, we have the unique opportunity in *A Vision* of watching a poet of major scope at work in formulating a system which he hoped might give him the integrity which his age lacked. In the dedication to the 1925 edition he wrote:

I wished for a system of thought that would leave my imagination free to create as it chose and yet make all that it created, or could create, part of one history, and that the soul's. The Greeks certainly had such a system, and Dante . . . and I think no man since. . . . I am the first to substitute for Biblical or mythological figures, historical movements

[2] See Mark Shorer's *William Blake, The Politics of Vision* (Henry Holt, New York, 1946) for a superb analysis of Blake's poetry in relation to myth, metaphysics, and politics, an analysis bearing directly on the central thesis of this Introduction.

and actual men and women . . . and I am longing to put it [*A Vision*] out of reach that I may write the poetry it seems to have made possible. I can now, if I have the energy, find the simplicity I have sought in vain.

When in early youth Yeats lost his Christian faith, he suffered his greatest loss. Driven by the necessity of finding some other body of belief, he traced each sensuous thought or philosophic idea "back to its earliest use, believing that there must be a tradition of belief older than any European Church, and founded upon the experience of a world before the modern bias." It is essential to notice that Yeats thought an impassioned and dramatic myth such as that of the Christian was no longer possible. Unity of Being, he felt, is impossible in an age like ours which does not possess Unity of Culture. He could only construct a Mask instead of a Myth and try to make it simple and intense. For all its seeming complexity, the basic psychology of *A Vision* is simple, and there can be no doubt of its intensity. Yeats was forced to seek symbols which necessarily invoked a personal vision, since he could find no universal agreement in his civilization. The split which occurs between symbol and ideology may not be true for the creator of the system or of the poems which depend on it, but it is true for the reader. This is the chief criticism to be offered *A Vision,* but such criticism merely defines a common problem; it would be truer to point out that Yeats succeeded better than any of his contemporaries in bridging the abyss between private symbol and public communication. *A Vision* makes a metaphysic and its symbols available in an orderly and cohesive fashion, and is, furthermore, a provocative contribution to modern aesthetics. Because of it Yeats was able to write some poems of brilliant simplicity and others of weighted and concentrated intensity which are among the best in all of English literature. For a time, when he first published his system, some of us hoped that he might be able to write an epic poem of which *A Vision* was the skeletal structure, for the book was an ordered exposition of man's personal, historical, and supernatural destiny. But no better example can be found of how a poet's creative powers are expended and sublimated in the effort to create a systematic mythology which only an age may grant. Unlike Dante's, the age of Yeats had no such mythology. The poetry of Yeats, and all modern poetry, are splendid fragments of a civilization never known and never built.[3]

VI. EZRA POUND

Of all modern poets who have sought for some system of evaluation to replace the dying religious mythology of Christianity, it is

[3] See *Commentary,* pp. 546-50, for an analysis of the human, historical, and supernatural phases of *A Vision.*

ironic that the poet who comes closest to solution [4] is one who has been indicted by the United States Government for treason: Ezra Pound. Since an epic poet is concerned to interpret a nation's destiny (and in modern times the destiny of one world) it is inevitable by the very nature of his task that he become personally involved in political thought and action, and bring to proof George Sorel's statement that political ideologies are the modern variants of myth.

The Cantos

"An epic," Pound has written, "is a poem containing history," and in the Cantos he has tried to show in what way the natural and not the supernatural history of mankind has conditioned its present political and spiritual dilemmas. He has tried to make judgments and to postulate the form of a new society. The objective correlative of his mythology is the body of world history and its flesh-and-blood heroes and villains; his ideology is based on an economic interpretation of history, and his ethics are derived from such economic evaluation. In the Cantos already published may be discerned a Dante-esque division into Inferno, Purgatory, and Paradise, but not the narrative or the progressive ascensions with which the Divine Comedy proceeds in time. These, according to Louis Zokovsky, are not so much physical places as mental states of "hate, comprehension and worship," simultaneously present and spatially juxtaposed under the economic determinism with which Pound brings them toward an ethical evaluation. The protagonist of the Cantos is not concerned, like Dante, to journey toward God and to evaluate the cosmos, nor like Milton to "justify the ways of God to man," but has substituted for the understanding of godhead an understanding of the use and misuse of Money. Those who misuse money—the usurers, bankers, politicians, financiers, munitions makers—are scorched by Pound with an infernal hatred. The gradual comprehension of the nature of money is the purgatorial fire man must suffer before he may make of his world a terrestrial Paradise: thus Pound traces the history of money from the origin and rise of banking and credit in fourteenth- and fifteenth-century Italy, inquires into the financing of the Napoleonic wars, sets forth the struggles of Jefferson and Van Buren to reform the monetary system of the United States, exposes the intrigues of munitions makers during the First World War, and draws historical parallels with certain Chinese dynasties. Pound's private purgatorial comprehension has led him to envision a terrestrial paradise and to praise it as it may be formulated according to the theories of Major C. H. Douglas on Social Credit, of Silvio Gesseli

---

[4] The Dynasts of Thomas Hardy, were it not so deficient as poetry, might have been considered.

on stamp script, of certain Canonist writers on economics, and of Mussolini on the Italian Corporate State. The titanic struggle on interplanetary fields between Man, God, and the Devil is transported to the economic battlefields of earth. Evil comes from the private control of money which foments war, and which by uneven distribution creates cycles of depression. Good comes from the state control of money which through issuance of certificates for work produced may regulate production for use and not for profit, may ensure the right to work, bring about shorter working hours, and by other material adjustments such as these lead mankind to cultural leisure and consequent spiritual unfolding—an ideal which makes Pound the natural heir of Goethe's humanitarianism. This ethical economy of Pound's is buttressed by the teachings of Confucius whose central thesis is that social order is a consequence of individual order. In the *Cantos,* religion and mythology have completed their long journey from the supernatural heavens into the political thought and history of man's development. We can find no better example of our thesis, nor a worse perversion of it. Ezra Pound, perhaps because during all of his life he has been deficient not so much in what he has hated as in what he has loved, has done the wrong thing for the right reason.

Theoretically, there is much in this program of which a supporter of socially planned economy for democratic ends will approve. It must be remembered that Mussolini once called himself a Socialist, and that Hitler's organization was deliberately named the National Socialist Party. Both fascism and nazism, with the cynical boldness characteristic of them, have consistently baited the masses with certain socialist aims, and then boldly perverted them to serve specially privileged minorities. They stood socialism on its head, and in a world as inverted as ours, it has seemed to many that mankind had finally been righted and stood on its feet. Undoubtedly various factors contributed to Pound's distorted vision: his bitterness against what he considered to be his own country's indifference to his talents, his exile, his political nearsightedness caused by long immersion in the Italian social scene, the flattering attention bestowed upon him by the fascist regime and Mussolini personally, and finally his *faith* in the spiritual and economic destiny of fascism as formulated by an inspired leader. Mussolini, he thought, was the heir of that Jefferson who wrote: "The best government is that which governs least." "Any thorough judgment of Mussolini," he wrote in *Jefferson and/or Mussolini,* "will be in a measure an act of faith, it will depend on what you *believe* the man means, what you believe he wants to accomplish." He believed in Mussolini as an inspired artist in social planning: "Treat him as anything save the artist and you will get muddled with contradictions." In this manner Pound evidently disposed of the many contradictions which he must have noted in the fascist regime. Finally, it seemed to him that Mussolini represented the Confucian ideal whose inner order would impart order to his nation: "Toward which I assert again my own firm belief that the Duce will stand not with despots and the lovers of power but with the lovers of ORDER, to kalon."

Pound's economic ordering of history and its ethical counterpart in the good and evil use of money seems to have no comparable aesthetic architecture. When but twenty-seven of the *Cantos* were published, Yeats wrote of a conversation in which Pound explained that when the hundreth canto is finished the entire poem will

display a structure like that of a Bach fugue. There will be no plot, no chronicle of events, no logic of discourse, but two themes, the Descent into Hades from Homer, a Metamorphosis from Ovid, and, mixed with these, mediaeval or modern historical characters. He has tried to produce that picture . . . where everything rounds or thrusts itself without edges, without contours—conventions of the intellect—from a splash of tints and shades; to achieve a work as characteristic of the art of our time as the paintings of Cézanne.

If the completed hundred *Cantos* will reveal a musical mathematics but remotely approximating the alphabetical notations with which Yeats goes on to supply for the "Bach fugue," poetry in structure and in orchestration can approach no closer to that abstract condition of music which Pater and the symbolist poets have desired. Such a musical structure is not even now apparent. If, on the other hand, we are meant to look upon the entire poem as upon a painting and see all at one time the anecdotal and historical motifs related to one another in space, as colors are harmonized upon a canvas, we find that the poem extends too far in time to be spatially apprehended as a unit. We are finally forced to wonder why the epic poetry of a man who almost makes a fetish of personal integrity and national order should seem so paradoxically disordered.

Perhaps the answer lies partly in certain theories of imagery which Pound derived from his study of Chinese poetry, and more particularly in a temperament as disordered as the world which it reflects. In diction, rhetoric, and syntax Pound is not only clear but idiomatic, relaxed, conversational, and has been as influential in our time as Wordsworth in his toward deflating the inflationary language of poetry and stripping it to the lean speed which is one of its characteristics today. With ironic incisiveness he has said that "poetry should be as well written as prose"; and as well spoken, he might have added, as the "conversation between intelligent men." By assimilating in his poetry not only the diction of contemporary conversation but also its cadences, yet by retaining that heightening of speech and tone which distinguishes poetry from reportage, Pound has elaborated a measure of phrasal rhythm which has been of major influence in contemporary metrics. His imagery as well as his rhythmical language, both outgrowths of his experiments in the free verse imagistic movement of the twenties, is clear, hard, and precise, but he places one image or anecdotal image against another in such a way that there seems to be little syntactical and no logical relationship between them. This method is much like that of Chinese ideography. Ideograms are both images and ideas of what they represent, and are set side by side, somewhat like a series of mural paintings that tell a story, or like sections of a comic strip, without the logical connectives necessary in English syntax but which the Chinese language lacks. Chinese ideograms, however, are concrete units of traditional meaning, whereas in English each image is a newly invented cluster of symbols and meanings between which the reader is accustomed to find a syntactical if not a logical relationship. To confuse two methods so semantically unrelated is perhaps to use neither English nor Chinese well. In modern metaphysical and symbolist poetry such ellipsis between single images or tropes is responsible for a concentrated power of great explosive suggestiveness,[5] but a similar ellipsis between anecdotal images and clusters of images produces a contrary effect of unravelment and dispersion. Pound's familiarity with Chinese ideography gave him materials, but the obscure use to which he put them comes from a compulsion basic to his temperament and directly related to his ideological, and even political, deviations. One has only to read his prose essays, and especially his treatises on economics and politics, to realize that he is temperamentally incapable of logical thought or sequence. Perhaps it may be said of Ezra Pound that he sees better than he thinks. His perceptions are again and again provocative, illuminating, brilliant, but his thinking is illogical and disorderly. This is why it has often been remarked that his translations are his own best poetry, for the original poet supplied him with an aesthetic and logical structure on which he could creatively improvise. "Homage to Sextus Propertius" may, for that reason, be his greatest work.

VII. FROM RELIGIOUS TO SOCIAL MYTHOLOGY

Ezra Pound must in reality face a jury of his peers and be judged by community standards like any other responsible citizen. In his dilemma we see a paradoxical and inevitably tragic conclusion. The very causes which brought him to treason also made it possible for him to see that political ideologies are the modern variants of myth. Neither anthropology, the physical and social sciences, comparative religions, world or national literatures may become the heirs of religious mythologies, because none of these are the vehicles of a

[5] For an example see O Thou . . . helm, p. 454.

way of life for the people. In our modern world it seems that only a political faith, like a religious faith, is a force powerful enough to permeate every stratum of society and bind the lowest with the highest, to reach into its deepest spiritual aspirations and its least economic needs. Neither the abstract theories behind any economic or political appraisal, nor any other abstract philosophical system may become persuasive forces unless they are directly embodied in political action as part of the constitutional law and environment of a people, much as the Platonic, Aristotelian, and Hebraic tenets of Christianity were embodied in church ritual. Practical fascism, nazism, and the political religion of Shinto are examples of secular faiths to whose myth and metaphysics peoples have dedicated themselves with a zeal and unity of purpose usually bestowed upon sacred belief.

The underlying motif of mankind has been the search for God, for the Father, for something or someone who is omniscient and omnipresent and in whose infinite perfectibility the dualities of mankind might be resolved. Out of its evolving historical nightmare, out of its suffering and consequent wishfulfillments, mankind has dreamt of a Being who would be able to solve the dualities of good and evil, of matter and spirit as posed in the theories of consubstantiation and the immaculate conception, of choice as indicated in the relationship between predestination and freedom of the will, in the guilt and anxiety complexes of original sin. Psychoanalysis has revealed that the image of the Father is later transferred to Society itself, and to its Authority, to the possibilities for good and evil which it extends to its subjects. The son's search for the spiritual father, then, may find its final rest in the identification of the individual with a society which offers him an economic and spiritual order. In such a society man need not direct his actions and his spirit toward a predestined and religious goal, but may create his own destiny out of given conditions and projected ideals. The dreams which he may then conceive out of his natural and spiritual development are limitless, more miraculous, and more mysterious than any which he has hitherto conceived for himself in religious mythologies. In such a society the poet may truly be the "maker," a creating god.

The poets we have discussed, in short, have all been trying to construct a metaphysic and a mythology denied them by their world, and have made abortive seizures of what can only be the product of a culture. This is not to blame them, but rather to explain their common problem, and indeed to praise them. All have been nothing less than heroic in their attempts to found order and integrity. If they have erred in identifying some aspects of their ordering with reactionary political thought, they are the natural products of environments whose degradation from democratic sources they are bound to reflect. The very complexity and profundity of their insight comes from their almost total immersion in the impurities of their cultures; if they have been incapable of the lucid simplicity of Dante, neither have they been capable of the simplicity of sentimentalization or wishfulfillment. In all cases they have been forced by their era to divert much of their creative energy to the critical construction of systems. In direct proportion to their efforts, a reader is also forced to give of his critical understanding in reading their works before he can come to full participation, but this is simply to explain a common problem in which the reader is as involved and responsible as the artist, for the obscurities of reference, the ambiguities of vision are the inevitable result of a lack of a communal spiritual language. To say that a reader must expend much critical effort in the decoding of a private language, of which *Finnegans Wake* is the supreme example, is but to name a situation and a fact which is inevitable, and not to expose a forgery or a perjury. If indeed these poets are to be read by a jury of their peers to judge whether they have forsworn their sacred prerogatives as poet-prophets, they will be found to have seen deeply and tragically, to have been oracular; and the jury, as the befuddled policeman who tried to testify against Earwicker, must find itself equally involved in whatever guilt might be exposed. If they are judged with Homer and Dante, they will be seen to lack, as our entire thesis has demonstrated, the simplicity of ordered wisdom, especially that which looks upon finalities as in the light of God; but on the other hand they will be seen to reveal a multiple insight, especially that which searches out motivation as in the light of guilt. Finally, they may be adjudged to be Great Minor Poets, to be Magnificent Failures, but such judgment and such failure is relative, and in their magnificent minority they have created some of the greatest poetry of our literature. Watching themselves in multiple mirrors, aware of every motivation and its reverse, they are the highly sophisticated masters of irony on whom irony must not be spared.

VIII. THE SEPARATION OF MAN FROM GOD

Now that two opposing ways of life are "dying each other's life, living each other's death," such words as "God," "religion," and "mythology" have little referential value to anything real, for they have been so amended by historical debate that they have lost almost all of their constitutional meaning. The younger poets, from W. H. Auden, George Barker, Dylan Thomas, David Gascoyne to Robert Lowell (only the latter is an American) must use such words and the concepts they signify in a vague, ironic, even torturous manner. Sometimes they are probed with such metaphysical nicety, as in Auden's *The Double Man* and *Christmas Oratoria*, that they

are attenuated and abstracted beyond belief. Sometimes, as Allen
Tate expresses it in his introduction to Lowell's poetry, "the Christian
symbolism is intellectualized and frequently given a savage satirical
direction; it points to the disappearance of Christian experience from
the modern world, and stands, perhaps, for the poet's own effort
to recover it." In the poetry of George Barker, and especially in the
"Sacred and Secular Elegies," the need to believe in the "dimension
in which / We believe without belief" becomes an agony of need
almost flagellant. The poet is forced to invoke godhead by inverse
and paradoxical images of evil. He is propelled to use excessively
violent symbols in order to shock himself, and his readers, into
awareness. The climax of this occurs in "Sacred Elegy V: Separation
of Man from God," and especially in the last stanza where God is
equated in a final frenzy with bestiality as well as with good, where
He becomes the God of the Apocalypse who kills because he loves,
and is thus described and invoked:

> Incubus. Anæsthetist with glory in a bag,
> Foreman with a sweatbox and a whip. Asphyxiator
> Of the ecstatic. Sergeant with a grudge
> Against the lost lovers in the park of creation,
> Fiend behind the fiend behind the fiend behind the
> Friend. Mastodon with mastery, monster with an ache
> At the tooth of the ego, the dead drunk judge:
> Whosoever Thou art our agony will find Thee
> Enthroned on the darkest altar of our heartbreak
> Perfect. Beast, brute, bastard. O dog my God!

It is inevitable that the poet's separation from God should now
be expressed with a remorseless, introspective agony. There is little
of moderation, but moments of extreme triumph and of extreme
lamentation. This separation, as we first noticed in Milton, is also
responsible for the sudden transitions and contrasts in imagery, the
series of crevised visions which seem to follow sometimes because
of a subconscious compulsive drive and sometimes because of the suggestions caused by the alliterative diction. This dualism invokes more
than it discloses, suggests more than it defines, and is the cause of
a severe dislocation between image and thought, rhythm and intellectual meaning, theme and tone, which is characteristic of modern
symbolist and metaphysical poetry. Fascinated by the Vision of Evil
because he so ardently desires the Vision of the Good (or God), such
a poet is helpless to separate charlatanism from integrity in the spiritual chaos of his age. His major themes necessarily become those of
"the expense of spirit in a waste of shame" for, as William Empson
has written, "The waste remains, the waste remains and kills." The
clown, the saint, the fool become his composite image. He is in
danger of becoming so victimized by his images and his suffering that

he may try to find an answer by confronting various psychological and even physical aspects of death, as if final revelation may be granted him during the split moment before complete renunciation. Robbed by his age of the purity of religious belief, such a poet is driven to vituperate what he most loves, is driven, according to Yeats, "to the greatest obstacle he may confront without suicidal despair." In a final semantic and ethical confusion, in a savagely paradoxical anagram, he is driven to equate God with dog, and to reveal the "Separation of Man from God" in its death agony.

Conflicting perspectives, the search for the Father, affect every modern poet's need for that "integrity of life" which John Webster sought after the breakdown of Elizabethan cohesion had ushered in the age of the "metaphysical" poets and our own similar problems. Unity of Being, as Yeats would say, is impossible without Unity of Culture, and the lack of it must lead to a dislocation in personality and artistry as well as to upheavals in civilization. The suicide of Hart Crane, the derangement of Baudelaire and Rimbaud, the refinements of Mallarmé, the obscurity of modern symbolist and metaphysical poets are directly related to this quest for an integrity which seems to be impossible of attainment in our day, yet the search for which is the only possible function of a serious poet. The various forceful, often heroic attempts which modern poets have made to fuse the fragmentations of their lives into a personal yet communal vision have produced an intensity in the modern poet's work which is related to integrity as mirage is to reality.

IX. METAPHYSICAL, SURREALIST, AND SYMBOLIST POETRY

Hitherto the term "metaphysical" has been used primarily to denote the ideologies of religions as embodied in myths, but it shall now be used primarily to denote a certain attitude in modern poetry related to symbolism and the problem of myth. Etymologically, "metaphysical" means "beyond the physical." In early historical usage it was synonymous with "supernatural," but became more ambiguous in meaning, as applied to poetry. According to John Dryden, it meant the "nice speculation of philosophy," to Samuel Johnson it was the "language of men of learning." It came to connote subtlety, refinement, abstraction, contemplation, transcendence, the witty, the fanciful, the imaginative. Since both symbolist poets and metaphysical poets lack unity of being and culture, and are unable to sum up in simplicity the multiples of the modern world, they have evolved highly complex orders by which to invoke or create the "formal and Final Causes," as Bacon has it, the Absolute, the mystical marriage with God. "The myths," as John Crowe Ransom has pointed out, "are conceits, born of metaphors. Religions are periodically produced by poets and destroyed by naturalists. . . . The metaphysical poets . . . recognize myth, as they recognized conceits, as a device of expression, its sanctity as the consequence of its public or social importance." Symbols, metaphors, conceits are the component parts of myth, as myth is an enlarged social metaphor. "Symbolism," according to C. M. Bowra in *The Heritage of Symbolism,* "was in origin a mystical kind of poetry whose technique depended on its metaphysics"; and again, "The essence of symbolism is in its insistence on a world of ideal beauty, and its conviction that this is realized through art . . . in certain characteristics aesthetic rapture may resemble religious devotion." The symbolist poet, by attaching special meanings to particular objects, words, or sounds tries to represent ideas and emotions by indirect rather than direct expression and thus to invoke a lost unity; the metaphysical poet elaborates an attitude by which he tries to yoke together the eclecticism of our culture.

The metaphysical poet pursues integrity by analysis, the symbolist poet invokes it by intuition. Disillusioned with the hypocrisy, sham, and unreality of the commonsense world, the symbolists (their predecessors the Dadaists and their followers the Surrealists) tried to hasten the disintegration of the modern world by a further "derangement of the senses" in order that, by recombining the exploded elements with little or no relation to their former structures and references, they might construct a truer world of inner reality. Since grammar and syntax are also logical structures related to the semantics of their culture, the symbolists discarded or concentrated traditional usage in order that their symbols might not be related by and to a dispirited order. "We must take rhetoric," Verlaine wrote to Rimbaud, "and wring its neck." For some symbolist poets words become so disassociated from what they originally represented that they are used less for what they denote than for what they connote; they come to take on a complete *phonetic* reality of their own almost devoid of semantic reference, and to compose a pure poetry of absolute musical abstraction. They are no longer *representations* of anything, but are in themselves *presentations* of their own self-contained, self-creating universe. To a great extent originated and refined by Mallarmé, this method was brought to its severest abstraction in English by Gertrude Stein, in whose poetry every word is disassociated from its meaning: each is a separate chord of sound invoking some entity which is never named, for to name it would be to falsify it with all the banalities of commonsense usage. This symbolist approach is the exact opposite of the metaphysical method of Joyce. Instead of isolating each word from its meanings, Joyce disintegrates a word into many meanings, grafts upon it many phonetic and semantic elements of other words from many languages, and produces a pun of pyrotechnical brilliance. The method of Stein is that of impressionism, much like the pointillesque technique of Seurat who decomposed the complex colors of nature into their primary elements and then juxtaposed them on the canvas in order to invoke a mental and physical fusion in the retina of the eye. The method of Joyce is that of metamorphosis, as in the paintings of Dali or Techelitchew, where parts of several already complex images combine by rearrangement to form parts of other images simultaneously in a visual pun which has the complexity of concurrent dreams.

Both symbolist and metaphysical poets depend upon subconscious sources, especially upon techniques of presenting subconscious imagery as originated by surrealism. Gertrude Stein developed her disassociative method by her early studies in automatic writing, and in *Finnegans Wake* Joyce perfected a verbal technique to present the subconscious dream-fantasies of mankind. In its purest form, surrealism is an automatic setting down of manifest dream-contents, whether of day or night, without rational order except that which may be privately known to the poet, or which might be revealed to the psychoanalyst as universal latent dream-thoughts. As such, surrealist poetry is as exciting as irrational fantasy and fairy tales, but its foremost contribution has been to extend the range of metaphor. It is related to symbolism in its dependence on intuitive suggestion, and to metaphysical poetry in its exploitation of the "conceit." Both symbolist and metaphysical poets have made use of surrealism to extend the range of the imagination and to amalgamate more disparate experiences by reconciling more discordant elements. The surrealist simile of Lautreamont: "beautiful as the chance encounter on a dissecting table of a sewing machine and an umbrella," the metaphysical simile of Eliot's "evening like a patient etherized upon a table," and the symbolist vision in "The Second Coming" of Yeats' rough beast with body of a lion and head of a man slouching toward Bethlehem to be born arise from similar subconscious sources, present similar violent dislocations, and quest for similar unities. The surrealist poet is related to the symbolist and metaphysical poet in his need for a cohesive mythological structure and an inner integrity founded upon it. According to Georges Lemaitre in *From Cubism to Surrealism in French Painting*, "Surrealism is not, properly speaking, an artistic or literary school. It is primarily a metaphysical attitude toward the whole of human existence. Art and literature are considered merely as means designed to help us reach a superior, ideal state."

In *A Dialogue on Modern Poetry* Miss Ruth Bailey sums up the attitude of the metaphysical poet succinctly, and thus also outlines similar concerns which a symbolist poet approaches more intuitively. The metaphysical poet, she writes, has

the power of practically being and doing many things at once. It is this power that is indicated in the phrases "sensuous thought," "unification of sensibility," "amalgamating disparate experience," and Coleridge's "balance or reconciliation of discordant qualities." The poet who has this power can make use of any kind of experience; in any one kind of experience he will show himself aware of the possibility of its opposite: thus his sentiment is always aware of the possibility of satire; his lyrical enthusiasm, of reason; his seriousness, of mockery; his admiration, of disgust. He can feel his thought: he can feel and think many discordant things at once; and he can fuse all these and make them into a whole.

Such a poet, the modern poet represented in an anthology such as this, must therefore use all his intellectual as well as his intuitive resources to bring congruity to discordant ideas and images; he must correlate whatever his subconscious offers him, but with superconscious awareness; his habitual mask is that of irony since he is always aware of contrary claims and possibilities; he is witty and fantastical, but with serious almost tragic purpose; he is rarely sentimental, for he is incapable of presenting any one view of life which is not complex or excludes the possibility of its opposite, and by the same token he prizes and is incapable of the sentiment and integrity of a man who sees life steadily and sees it whole. Miss Bailey is perhaps too sanguine when she says that the modern poet can fuse many discordant things at once and make them into a whole, for the chief characteristic of the modern poet is the intensity with which he invokes, pursues, and rarely attains such integrity. Most of the poems in this book are records of this pursuit, and if they do not often contain the clarity and serenity of realized vision, they are in their density and concentration closer to such vision than the easier solutions of our age which attain a spurious and superficial clarity chiefly by omission and avoidance.

Notes

ADAMS, LÉONIE. Brooklyn, N. Y., Dec. 9, 1899.

AIKEN, CONRAD. Savannah, Ga., Aug. 15, 1889.

AUDEN, W. H. York, England, Feb. 21, 1907.

AT THE GRAVE OF HENRY JAMES. *donnée*: "that which is given." *de rigueur*: "indispensable." *Amour Propre*: "self-love." *affaire fatale*: "fatal affair." *Bon*: "the Good." *secousse*: "agitation."

ALONSO. From *The Sea and the Mirror,* a poetic commentary on Shakespeare's *The Tempest.*

MUSÉE DES BEAUX ARTS: The Museum of Fine Arts in Brussels where is hung *The Fall of Icarus* by Pieter Brueghel. See reproduction in color opposite p. 222 in Thomas Craven's *A Treasury of Modern Art,* and Mr. Craven's comment: "It is the greatest conception of indifference in painting—an indifference which seems to flood the landscape, reducing the whole notion of classical mythology to a couple of lower extremities."

COMMENTARY. In its original version in *Journey to a War,* the prayer of Man began "O teach me to outgrow my madness," continued with the following stanza, now omitted: "It's better to be sane than mad, or liked than dreaded;/ It's better to sit down to nice meals than to nasty;/ It's better to sleep two than single; it's better to be happy." And concluded: "Till they construct at last a human justice,/ The contribution of our star, within the shadow/ Of which uplifting, loving, and constraining power/ All other reasons may rejoice and operate."

BARKER, GEORGE. Loughton, Essex, England, Feb. 26, 1913.

Author's Note: "You ask me for a Note on Poetry setting forth my attitude to the craft. I can tell you quite simply. It is an amorous attitude."

FIRST CYCLE OF LOVE POEMS. *Fierral Bay*: of the Eleven Thousand Virgins in the Falkland Islands, where prodigious quantities of fish are caught. *Flammenwerfer*: a flame thrower.

HOLY POEM, IV. See Revelations, I: 9. *Haman tree*: See Esther, III-VII. *St. Peter's Key*: See Matthew, XVI: 19.

SACRED ELEGY V. *Dog, god*: spell both words backwards.

BARNES, DJUNA. Cornwall-on-Hudson, N. Y., June 12, 1892.

NIGHTWOOD. The selections are from the fifth, sixth, and seventh chapters of the novel. The action takes place sometime in the 1920's, primarily in Paris. All the important characters, but for Felix, are American. Robin Vote marries Baron Felix Volkbein, whose title is fictitious, bears him a child, and leaves him. She is found at the circus by Nora Flood, who becomes attached to her and brings her home, but Robin, like a somnambulist, drifts away from the momentary security she has gained, and loses herself in the night among many loves and many identities. She is taken away to America by Jenny Petherbridge. The selections open with a visit Nora pays to Doctor Matthew O'Connor, a gynecologist of unorthodox ways, to find from him some understanding of what has happened. After a fruitless search for Robin, Nora returns to her home in America, and there one evening, in the decayed chapel on her estate, finds Robin on her knees before a contrived altar to the Madonna, turning to animal, crying and barking like a dog.

The main theme of the book is the distracted immersion of human beings in the dark grain of night and sleep, symbols of our bestial and primeval origins that drive us by suffering in search of our identities. Robin is the symbol of man's original nature, still more animal than human, completely amoral, destroyed by the ethical expectations of civilization; she is without conscious memory because her memory is the subconscious memory of the race. Felix is the dispossessed and wandering Jew who accepts the fake baronetcy his father before him had invented and, having no roots himself, is drawn to Robin as to one whose roots are fathomless. Nora is the woman of ethical consciousness, of normal memory, drawn to her opposite, who is Robin, and whom she does not understand. They are mutually destructive of one another: Nora awakens Robin from her animal torpor in which her acts were innocent because free of ethical judgment, and thus destroys her innocence so that Robin turns like a primitive to the Church, and finally and literally turns animal, "goes to the dogs." Nora's ethical universe in turn is corroded by the dark stirrings of Robin's amoral nature; she begins to understand and to feel its primitive compulsions, and is destroyed. Jenny has no identity whatsoever; her memory and her character are constructed bit by bit with whatever she can snatch from other memories, other personalities; her greatest gain is to snatch Robin away from Nora: Robin and Jenny are attracted to one another in recoil. The Doctor is the Greek chorus of the tragedy, one who feels and under-

stands all the inevitable agony which human beings undergo caught between their animal and ethical natures, between the night and the day,
and he is moved by pity and compassion, no less himself the victim
of a great betrayal. When Nora asks him the direct and naïve questions
about life and suffering eternally asked by all victims, he has compassion
for her simplicity and audacity, and knows that he cannot answer but
by irony and indirection, by weaving out of the suffering of the human
animal a lyrical threnody the theme of which is, as the Doctor concludes,
"nothing but wrath and weeping."

WATCHMAN, WHAT OF THE NIGHT. See Isaiah, XXI: 11-12. *Ah,
mon dieu . . .* : "Ah, my God! The fearful night! The night, which is
an immense plain, and the heart which is a small extremity!" *Notre
Dame-de-bonne-Garde*: Our Lady-of-Good-Care. *savon*: "soap." *bretelle*:
"suspender." *cantiques*: "canticles." *charter mortalis*: "mortal charter."
cardia: "heart."

BERRYMAN, JOHN. McAlester, Okla., Oct. 25, 1914.

CANTO AMOR. The accents point to where the poet wants the emphasis to fall.

BISHOP, ELIZABETH. Worcester, Mass., Feb. 8, 1911.

BISHOP, JOHN PEALE. Born, Charlestown, W. Va., May 21, 1892;
died, April 4, 1944.

THE RETURN: The fall of Rome and, by implication, that of modern
civilization.

BLACKMUR, RICHARD PALMER. Springfield, Mass., Jan. 21, 1904.

THE DEAD RIDE FAST. As he shaves and looks out of the window
the poet has a vision of the sudden standstill behind all movement and
phenomena, of the Medusa paralysis, of death. Although in his life
there are constant reminders of death, he acts as if he knows nothing
of that still center, acts in a deliberately unprepared manner—until the
day when, thoroughly prepared, he can meet death and deal with it.

BOGAN. LOUISE. Livermore Falls, Me., Aug. 11, 1897.

BRIDGES, ROBERT SEYMOUR. Born, Walmer, Kent, England, Oct. 23, 1844; died, April 21, 1930.

POOR POLL. φωνᾶντα συνετοῖσιν: "that speak to the intelligent." —Pindar, Second Olympian Ode, 85. κτῆμα ἐς αἰεί: "an everlasting possession."—Thucydides, I, 22. After speaking of the great care and difficulty with which he had ascertained his facts, Thucydides concludes: "My history is an everlasting possession, not a prize composition which is heard and forgotten." ἡ γλῶσσ' . . .:—Euripides, *Hypolitus*, 612. In reference to an oath which he felt forced to give, Hypolitus says: "It was my tongue and not my mind that swore." *'Tis . . . keep*: See Milton's "On the Morning of Christ's Nativity," line 92. *Wie . . .*: "How many days and nights have you stayed!"—from a poem of Goethe which Eckermann quotes in his *Conversations with Goethe*, April 5, 1829. *La possa . . .*: "The power of the legs put in truce."—*Purgatorio*, XVII, 75. *C'est . . .*: "It's the only difference, but it's important."—Francis Jammes, "Les Paturges," ("The Pastures") in *De l'Angelus de l'aube à l'Angelus du soir*, 1888-97 (Paris, *Mercure de France*, MCMXXI). (For additional notes see *Addenda*, p. 560).

BRINNIN, JOHN MALCOLM. Halifax, Nova Scotia, Sept. 13, 1916.

THE WORM IN THE WHIRLING CROSS. The editors are indebted for the following part analyses to John Frederick Nims, *A Critical Supplement to Poetry*, Nov., 1947. First stanza: "The *logos* is the Logos or 'Word' of the Gospel according to St. John: 'In the beginning was the Word. . .' It equals, in Webster's untechnical summary 'the actively expressed, creative, and revelatory thought and will of God'—identified, as St. John uses it, with Christ, seen as God made flesh (this poem is partly about a flesh-spirit relationship). But though the logos is the Son, it is also *fathering* in the sense that Christ is the father of men; it is *withering* (punningly applied to *son* instead of to 'sun') not only in that it is destructive of every antagonistic principle but in that adherence to the Logos demands suppression of the excesses of selfhood.

"The first two lines mean that the poet will no longer confess, as graceless and sinful, the activities of his flesh or 'sense.' 'Confess my sins' is the usual phrase; the poet, punningly and concisely, writes *confess my sense*. This is a kind of portmanteau syntax analogous to Lewis Carroll's portmanteau words: 'slithy' = 'lithe' + 'slimy.' In this poem the frequent use of puns may have functional value beyond the richness and ambivalence of meaning they achieve: just as the poem is concerned. . . with identity, so the poet uses puns, semantic devices of identity and nonidentity, to emphasize this aspect of his complex investigation. A somewhat similar purpose is served by the 'further' 'father' 'wither' sounds of the first line: the half-rhymes are not only ornamental but help convey a sense of the incantation, complexity, and riddle appropriate to the theme.

"*Vouch* means 'to attest, as a statement or its truth or accuracy; bear witness to; also, to answer or stand sponsor for.' The *matter of decaying green* is the *sense* of the preceding line; it means flesh in distinction to spirit: it is called *green* because (1) green is the color of decay, and all flesh is ephemeral, on the verge of decay; (2) green is a vegetation color, and the life of mere flesh, without spirit, is akin to the life of vegetation; (3) green has other relevant connotations: ignorance, envy, illness, and so on. *Matter* is a pun; it means not only 'affair' but 'purulent substance.' *The rooftree of my dwelling place* is apparently the highest part of the human structure, the skull. The *shark's tooth grin,* a fresh but appropriate symbol for the leer of a fleshless skull, is fastened, or *hinged,* to the *rooftree* by the *decaying green* of the flesh. Flesh, then, is an ambiguous principle; it covers, in both a benignant and a sinister sense, the grinning skull; decadent itself, it makes whole and secure the dwelling place of the human spirit. In summary, the first five lines of the poem express an acceptance of the life of flesh and sense as indispensable in spite of their imminent corruption.

"The apple (line 6) is the fruit, traditionally an apple, the eating of which led to Adam and Eve's expulsion from the garden of innocence. *Apple-wise* suggests three meanings: (1) like an apple, i.e., possessing only unconscious vegetable life; (2) wise (partially in an ironic sense, as in 'wise guy') in the way of apples, i.e., knowing about the apple of Eden and capable of making an independent decision about it; (3) wise with the sad wisdom that came from eating the forbidden apple on the Tree of Knowledge of Good and Evil. The line means that man learned anguish in Eden, ... a mythological way of saying in a primal state of innocence or unselfconsciousness (*the first sun*—which may also mean the *son* of line 1). The next two lines are an analysis or further explanation of the change and the consequent mourning: the giraffes perhaps symbolic of the ungainly but interesting barbaric *élan* of pre-conscious life; the Tigris a recollection (of course anachronistic) of a center of man's early activity, but, as *spring* indicates, there is also intended a pun on tiger, which has a powerful symbolic force in itself and is immeasurably reinforced by recollections of two of the great tigers of literature: Blake's beautiful terror in the forests of the night and Eliot's tiger in 'Gerontion': "In the juvescence of the year/ Came Christ the tiger. . ."

"The ninth line, given vehemence by the exclamatory *O* which precedes it, identifies more precisely, in tracing more accurately, the source of the anguish. It is not only the double disaster (Fall and Flood) of Genesis; it is, more profoundly, the event of individual genesis, of personal birth. When the human being, at a fell swoop, leaves the prenatal lake he is born to anguish: *genesis* repeats the pattern of 'Genesis.' Here Brinnin seems to infuse his Christian symbolism with the notion of happy pre-existence (cf. Wordsworth's 'Intimations'). At any rate, man's innocence and wholeness (or 'identity') have been lost at an early stage of his history.

"The tenth line wonders how they can be rediscovered in our time. *Ray* no longer means what it meant for Milton; a ray (X-ray, etc.) is a modern method of discovery for healing. It is possible that 'excellent' here affords an ironic comment on the inadequacy of science to deal with spirit.

"In line eleven, the *you* refers most probably to the *logos* of the beginning. To learn how *leaf mould burns*, that is, how the vestiges or last survivals of vegetative life achieve (1) splendor; (2) a proper and natural termination, one must *cross grain with* be grafted to, coöperate with (in spite of the dissonant hints of the adjective 'cross-grained') the logos or Christ, the highest embodiment of knowledge in a human form. The *dome's dove-tailing brows* again describes the skull with its beautiful articulations: when Christ was killed, it seems to say, his personal vision or *inscape* revealed new human vistas, new possibilities of human existence. As large waves (groundswells) are stirred up by earthquakes or other undersea disasters, so the individual is excited, by the example of the logos, to welcome the violences of the life of flesh, which the logos had also undergone."

CAMPBELL, ROBERT BHAIN. Born, Royal Oak, Mich., Oct. 29, 1911; died, Dec. 3, 1940.

CRANE, HAROLD HART. Born, Garrettsville, Ohio, July 21, 1899; died, April 26, 1932.

THE BROKEN TOWER. As the ringing bells shatter the tower, so do the emotions of a poet seeking to ring out his vision shatter the body. After the poet has rung the bells and has been taken up into their ecstasy, he is dropped into the hell, pit, and crucifixion of his daily life. The ringing, shadowed bells before dawn are for him the symbol of the ineffable Word which, as poet, he must try to utter. Sexton slave of the bells, he must ring them even though they break his being, so long as they give utterance through him. Then his impasse is broken with singing, with divine messages, *encyclicals*; then all the towers of song ring out, though wounded. The poet tries to interpret the voice of love in this broken world, though inconsequently and briefly. He sings, but is his song related at all to God's Word that brings both hope and despair? (The tower is also Christ, God made into man the poet; the Word made into the word, into the song of the poet; eternal joy and hope dashed into the despair of this world). The turmoil of his emotions allows him no answer; it is questionable whether truth can be found through the medium of man's flesh and emotions; yet perhaps the mortality of blood and emotion in memory and strife can build a spiritual tower, healed and pure, which may, inwardly and in silence, plumb the womb of the heart (purify the vision), see the divinity of nature and thus exalt love. For the genesis of this poem, see *Hart Crane* by Philip Horton, (New York, W. W. Norton, 1937) p. 292.

O CARIB ISLE! Nothing mourns the dead buried in the sands of a Caribbean island, only poisonous spiders and crabs frequent them.

Against this tropic death in the desert, the poet invokes the fertility of flowers and trees, and asks who the Master (the cruel God) of this island may be, responsible for the aridity, the mildew of the senses, the webbed and baked eyes. He envisages an ascension in terms of a flowering tree in which he is greeted by the heavenly host in the blue domain of God the ironic comedian (the Divine Comedy). This is a vision of acceptable death—not the helpless death in the desert like a turtle on its back waiting to be disemboweled. Cast like dross or cinder on the hurricane, congealed in the hot, smooth, and empty afternoon, he waits on the dried up (*sere*) shell of an island which is a burnt-out amulet, the Devil's gift. *doubloon . . . turnstile*: the medieval piratical isles contrasted to the machine age.

To Brooklyn Bridge. (See pp. 427-28).* The poem is a dedication, and invokes the bridge in winter. It opens with the image of a gull rising from the wintry waters of the East River, pivoting over the series of bays which comprise New York harbor, flying beyond the Statue of Liberty, and then disappearing like an apparition of sails which some clerk may in longing see as he works at his routine job of filing, until the day's work is ended and he descends in the elevator homeward. The contrast is between the freedom of seagull and bridge, and the mechanized life of modern man. The poet therefore thinks of the myth-starved modern man hurrying to the magic sleight-of-hand tricks of the cinema where he hopes to find some answer to his problems disclosed at any moment as, he thinks, it surely must have been disclosed to others. In contrast, the poet turns to the Bridge which, like God, symbolizes the unity of all discords, the integrity and wholeness which modern man lacks and seeks, which unites motion and stillness, and which finds its freedom in its necessity. From this serene and detached symbol, ironically, a member of the bedlam which is modern civilization scuttles out of the inferno of the subway, the confinement of apartment cell, the loft of skyscraper, and hurls himself to death before the speechless and passing crowd. Noon, like the jagged tooth of an acetylene torch, leaks down between the canyoned buildings of Wall Street, the financial center near Brooklyn Bridge; the tall derricks on the wharfs are busy all afternoon with loading and unloading cargo, and throughout all of this the Bridge sways gently and serenely in the North Atlantic breeze. The religious reward which it offers is as obscurely known as the heaven envisaged by the Jews. The blessing it gives to mankind is the anonymity by which the modern industrial worker built it (comparable to the anonymous builders of Gothic cathedrals) and which time cannot (1) raise to greater heights, (2) destroy. It is a harp (the breathing cables are like *choiring strings*) and an altar fused together by an ecstasy of scientific faith, the threshold to a messianic future, the prayer of the outcast, the cry of the lover. Seen at night in the light of traffic and stars, it seems, in the immaculate wholeness by which it declares itself (like the ineffable Word which is God) to be a condensation and symbol of eternity, and to cradle the night. Such vision is granted the poet in the actual darkness of its shadow and, by inference, in the spirit-

---

* Page references, unless otherwise stated, are to this book.

ual dark night of the soul in which the mystic sees clearest. The lights are now all out in the city's skyscrapers, the snow covers the sufferings of a year. The poet then prays to the Bridge to give man a mythological embodiment of God again to take the place of his lost religious mythologies, out of its grace and unity, its *curveship* (as one says "lordship").

AVE MARIA. (See *pray for us*, p. 467). Columbus's flagship was named *Santa Maria. Venient . . .*: "There will come an age in the far-off years when Ocean shall unloose the bonds of things, when the whole broad earth shall be revealed, when Tethys shall disclose new worlds and Thule not be the limit of the lands."—Seneca, *Medea*, 375-79. *Tethys*: a goddess of the sea; therefore, the sea. *Thule*: name given by the ancients to the farthest known land. Seneca prophesied the discovery of a new world, and Crane cites this as witness that Columbus had fulfilled an ancient destiny. He transforms the search of Columbus for the riches of Cathay into the quest of the mystic for the terrestrial paradise by means of a conquest of space and chaos. The poem is a monologue of Columbus as he is returning from his first voyage; he has just left Lisbon where he has been fêted by the King of Portugal, and is nearing the port of Palos in Huelva province, Spain, from which he had set out. *Be with me . . . Cathay*: After many years of delay, Columbus received the support of Queen Isabella of Spain primarily through the intercession of Luis de Santangel, receiver of the ecclesiastical revenues of the crown of Aragon; and of Juan Perez, former confessor of the Queen and guardian of a monastery near Palos. He planned to find a route to Japan, but also to set up intercourse with the grand Khan of China, or of Cathay as it was then called. Crane wrote: "The theme of 'Cathay' (its riches, etc.) ultimately is transmuted into a symbol of consciousness, knowledge, spiritual unity. A rather religious motivation. . . ."—Horton, *ibid.*, p. 198. *mail, valves, tendons*: medieval and industrial imagery to describe the waves in sunset. *caravel*: the setting sun on the horizon is likened to a vessel. *Indian*: Columbus thought he had reached China or India. *Yet lost . . .*: Yet all we have discovered may be lost if we give up our quest even for a moment. *I thought . . .*: Columbus recalls his anxious watch from night till dawn, hoping for a sight of land. *Genoa*: his birthplace where his dream was derided. *first seen*: At ten o'clock on the night of October 11, 1492, Columbus saw and pointed out a light, and at two in the morning a sailor on the accompanying ship *Nina* announced land. Columbus named it San Salvador, generally identified with Watlings Island in the Bahamas. *they*: the native Indians. *Madre Maria*: "Mother Mary". The *Santa Maria* had been abandoned; the *Nina*, the new flagship, and the *Pinta* had become separated. *mantle*: the sea; blue is also Mary's color. *cask*: Crane originally wrote "casque," mistaking the archaic word for "helmet" for a more poetic spelling of "cask." He describes here the recounting in Columbus's *Journal* of how a wooden cask containing records of the voyage was heaved overboard in case none of the ships should return safely but become the *pawn* of hurricanes. *two worlds*: the Old and the New. *tests the word*: the third world, that of water, becomes one of ordeal which tests the faith and belief of the pilgrims. *mutiny*: disbelieving and fearful, Columbus's crew often threatened to mutiny and turn back. *Moor*: Spain's natural and heathen enemy. *more than flesh*: found faith to cut into. *Yet under . . . fire*: the inmost prayer is heard, the storms subside, and the eyes, long starved for sight of land, finally concentrate on land, upon this turning world, bright in the early morning sun. *Like pearls . . . lee*: the New World is described in terms of gems because it is beautiful, and because it was hoped to be the source of riches. Columbus then warns King Ferdinand of Spain to take sparingly and religiously from this new treasure or its fullness may turn into famine, and reminds him of Isaiah's prophecies to the greedy children of Israel. *An herb . . .*: Columbus's reminiscence is ended, and we are again returned to the approach of the Spanish coast. *Saltes Bar*: near Palos. Crane wrote: "Observe the water-swell rhythm that persists until the Palos reference. Then the absolute and naked intimations of the great *Te Deum* of the court, later held,—here in terms of C's own cosmography."—Horton, *ibid.*, p. 208. *O Thou . . .*: Columbus's invocation to God as the Sea which tries the faith of man. *Utter . . .*: Each man must sail on his quest in utter loneliness. *who grindest . . . span*: the terror and love with which God tests us. *arguing*: shakes (1) with storm, (2) with doubt. *Teneriffe*: volcano of the Canary Islands off the northwest coast of Africa which erupted during Columbus's voyage. The flame of the corposant and the clouds of Teneriffe are signs that God shall lead Columbus to the New World as He had led Moses to the Promised Land: "And the Lord went before them by day in a pillar of cloud, to lead them the way; and by night in a pillar of fire, to give them light; to go by day and night."—Exodus, XIII: 21. *Te Deum Laudamus*: "We Praise Thee Lord," the hymn of thanksgiving sung on occasions of public rejoicing. *Of all . . . heel*: "O God, You yield us Your divine dispensation (*disposition*) amidst Your wheeling blue universe as we travel in time exploring Your amplitude, moving toward the true appointment we have with You through trial and error, avoiding shipwreck on hidden shoals. In the wake of our ship, O God, we hear Your whirling feet accompanying us." The syntax is ambiguous, so that phrase is related to phrase in many ways, but on this general theme. This is typical of much of Crane's poetry. *White toil . . . Fire*: Accompanied by a halo of sentinel stars, the ships sail toward the promised and fertile land, which is the full knowledge of God who suffered and died for our salvation (*the kindled Crown*), and toward which the meridians, aided by the poles and the sails, direct man in order to fulfill His purpose, which is to instill in man, through trial and suffering, a longing for the final shore of His kingdom beyond any shore of this world.

THE HARBOR DAWN. This follows "Ave Maria" in sequence and is the first of five sections which constitute *Powhatan's Daughter*, who is Pocahantas, the mythological body of America to be explored and known. On a snowing winter morning before dawn, in his room near Brooklyn Bridge and New York harbor, the poet awakens beside his sleeping lover and listens to the muffled sounds of the harbor as the city slowly awakens and the morning light makes blond the window, revealing room and lover. Crane wrote: "Here the movement of the verse is in considerable contrast to that of the Ave Maria, with its sea-swell crescendo and the climacteric [sic] vision of Columbus. This legato, in which images blur as objects only half apprehended on the border of sleep and consciousness, makes an admirable transition between the intervening centuries. The love motif (in italics) carries along a symbolism of the life and ages of man (here the sowing of the seed) which is further developed in each of the subsequent sections of Powhatan's daughter. . ."—Horton, *ibid.*, pp. 336-37. *400 years*: the "intervening centuries" between Columbus and today. *sometimes*: ambiguously used (1) "if they take away your sleep *sometimes*," (2) "*sometimes* they give it back again." *pillowed*: by snow and in sleep. *woman*: Pocahontas.

ATLANTIS. A mythological lost continent said to have sunk west of Gibraltar and which has traditionally symbolized the lost Golden Age of Man, the Promised Land. Crane refers to the "Atlantis theme, Eternity or the Absolute . . . it is into this Absolute that the finale to the whole poem (Atlantis) projects at the close of the book." He thought of this finale as "A sweeping dithyramb in which the Bridge becomes the symbol of consciousness spanning time and space." Elaborately in the first three stanzas, intermittently throughout the poem, the glittering Bridge in moonlight is invoked in musical terms as the *harp and altar* the *choiring strings* of the proem. *index*: night is the index of the universe. *staves*: (1) cables of the bridge, (2) staffs of music. *And through . . . dream*: The meshes and cables thread the arc of the bridge which in its divine *curveship* is the synopsis (the word has also a religious significance as in the "Synoptic" Gospels) of all the labyrinthine tides of man and his history as he drifts on the Eternal Sea, plying towards God and asking for His love. *Third and fourth stanzas*: The Bridge, silhouetted against the stars, is seen from below. *bars*: (1) cables, (2) of music. *New . . . sleep*: Between the two uprights, the *monoliths* of the bridge, the cables are woven in trestle formation like octaves. Beyond the ends of each upright the moon is seen shedding sleep to the sky and the earth. *aisle*: the Milky Way. *ring*: (1) encircle, (2) ring out. *palladium*: The Bridge is like a silver-white vessel of stars. *Tomorrow . . . spear*: The Bridge links past and future and the entire history of man which is a mysterious cipher he tries to read in martyrships of loving and dying as he inquires into the timeless, ironic, and indifferent unconcern of a quest (the *Divine Comedy*) in which he is being constantly wounded (much as were certain Christian mystics with the darts of divine love). *Like . . . Troy*: The glittering stars speak as with musical hammers (also the destructive blows of time) of ancient Tyre; on the anvil of time Troy has been riveted into silence with definite yet serene unconcern. The poet then envisages Jason, symbol of questing mankind, whose search for the Golden Fleece symbolizes the search for Atlantis: he is giving his orders, trying to net the air, to conquer space (symbolically, and with his sails). The wake of his ship beams, arches, and moves with the storming winds, and finally is squandered in the straits (Jason had to pass through the Dardanelles and the Hellespont.). After many terrors the longed-for Vision appears: the Bridge which lifts man from darkness into that light which is the Absolute. *Verb*: the Absolute is the Word, the Unmoved Mover which resolves all multiples and actions of time into perfect stillness, but is known and recast to mankind in multiple words. (See *Part V* and

Word, p. 471). *Paradigm*: the Absolute is a paradigm in that it is the Pattern of all, the word from which all words are conjugated, inflected, and declined. *We left . . . strings*: The return back into life from the heavenly vision; the bright lights of the haven retreat as the ship moves into dust and steel. But always the vision remains of the all-embracing choiring bridge to which all pray. *O Thou . . . helm*: This stanza may serve as an example of the extremely condensed use of metaphor and diction typical of modern poetry. The terms of comparison in a metaphor or trope are often omitted so that one thing is not so much compared to another as each is concretely and simultaneously *identified* with the other, a kind of tropic immediacy in which a new concept or image is created. Allen Tate has aptly named this the "fused metaphor." Single words are employed not on one level of meaning but exploited in all of their meanings, even in their contradictions. Thus the bridge here is more often *identified* with rather than *compared* to God, as the Absolute and the All-Knowing (*Cognizance*), as a creature of athletic prowess (*leaps*), a judge (*commits*), a cowboy (*lariat*), a chrysalis, a tailor (*stitch*), a horse, an organ, and a guide who leads mankind by love from time into eternal space where both time and space are one. A *steeled* Cognizance is, in terms of the actual bridge, not only made of steel but is also an indestructible Absolute which in harmonizing the multiple dualities of mankind (the *many twain*), must steel itself to do so, yet which in its imperturbable ordering of the universe seems to steel Itself against man's suffering (Job and the problem of evil). In its leap this Cognizance *commits the agile precincts of the lark's return*, that is, it includes within the sweep of its curveship not only the farthest reaches to which a lark may ascend but also all the spiritual and lyrical reach which *lark* implies. In addition, in *agile precincts*, the agility of the lark is, as if by empathy, transferred to the regions in which it flies, and *return* is at once the going forth as it is the coming back, appropriate in an apostrophe of that in which, as Christian mystics have often written, the way up and the way down, the beginning and the end, are one and the same. *Commits* means much more than (1) to "include," for it also means (2) to give in trust, (3) to preserve, as in the phrase to "commit to memory," (4) to imprison, as "commit to jail," and (5) to pledge, as to commit oneself to some cause, and all these meanings are indeed attributes of the paradox which is God. *Single chrysalis* not only means the original womb in which the many are subsumed, but also, by reminding us of the worm that turns into the butterfly, implies the hope of resurrection and transformation into the beautiful; the womb and tomb become interchangeable. Chrysalis, in whose sweep are girdled (*encinctured*) the singing many twain, is also the firmament of God's pluriverse, and, by a phonetic equivalence, the crystalline spheres and their music. *Thou art the stitch and stallion glow* is an image of the interwoven cables of the bridge reflecting the starlight in many glittering, sharp stitches, implying that God is the One who sews all rent things together again. The steel cables glow in starlight like a stallion, suggesting the stallion's sleek coat, the rippling flow of its muscles, the pulse of its masculine energy, and ultimately correlating its fecundity with the procreativity of God. This does not exhaust the possibilities of suggestion and invocation, but will serve to indicate the concentrated density of much modern poetry. It must further be kept in mind that each word and trope is not simply the sum of its constituent meanings, but in relation to sound and other imaginative and rhythmical factors within the stanza, becomes a recreation of language and vision. *Myth . . .*: the bridge and its attributes is mankind's new religious mythology, a symbol of God in whose awesome (*fell*, in the sense of "awful": "terrible" and "full of awe") light and resurrection death is conquered. *Sustained . . . torment*: As they revolve in birth, fulfillment and death, the cities and plains are symbols of the world's cyclical movement toward God in joy and sorrow, yet endowed and finally justified. *chemistry*: the scientific and other attributes which the bridge symbolizes are summed up in Crane's statement: "The initial impulses of our people will have to be gathered up toward the climax of the bridge, symbol of our constructive future, our unique identity, in which is also included our scientific hopes and achievements of the future."—Horton, *ibid.*, p. 142. *Forever . . . Love*: the new God, the new mythology, is implicit in the symbol of the bridge. *white*: religious and starlight image. The vibrant, glittering, singing bridge is symbolic of the new God, the new mythology in ascension, migration, and creation. *So to . . . Fire*: a highly compressed image in which the bridge represents the immaculate Eternity of God and the ensanguined suffering of man and Christ. *rainbows*: a celestial transformation of the bridge in its curveship; the rainbow was the covenant between Himself and man which God set in the heavens after the Flood. See Genesis, IX: 13. *serpent*: symbol of (1) time, (2) evil. *Eagle*: symbol of (1) space, (2) good.

VOYAGES. These poems were so entitled because they were to a great degree inspired by the person and travels of a sailor whom Crane knew. As a whole, they invoke the sea as the womb and tomb of life, as the source and end of love and passion, as an eternal imperturbability in which man finds his visions, yet in which he is wrecked and drowned. It will be remembered that Crane committed suicide by drowning.

I. The poet addresses his lover as if they were adrift on the winking, rimless and unfettered sea of eternity which in sensuous unconcern laughs at their loves, yet which, though it rends all in its tolling and sway of terror, spares the pieties that belong to love. So adrift in starlight in the slow adagio movement of the sea among its bright poinsettia-like islands, the poet asks his lover to hasten and fulfill for him in love those mysteries which the sea is confessing in terms of sleep, death, and desire. He then prays to the seasons and to time not to cast them ashore or bring them to their graves untimely, before they can have understood and seen that vision of paradise which the sea invokes. *undinal*: from "undine," a female water spirit who can obtain a human soul by marrying a mortal; symbol of the procreative sea. *wrapt*: (1) embraced, and (2) rapt. *inflections*: (1) speech, (2) enfolding. *sentences*: (1) moonlight tracings on the water, (2) utterances, (3) judgments which the sea as a judge in session passes. This word and *superscription* also refer to the "confessions" which the sea is uttering. *bells off San Salvador*: There is a legend of a city sunken off this island in the Bahamas; the poet hears the tolling of its underwater bells. *Adagio of islands*: Crane wrote: "The reference is to the motion of a boat through islands clustered thickly, the rhythm of the motion, etc. And it seems a much more direct and creative statement than any more logical employment of words such as 'coasting slowly through the islands,' besides ushering in a whole world of music."—Horton, *ibid.*, p. 327. *Prodigal*: the lover who, like a sailor on voyages, comes and goes. *Seal*: symbol of the sea. *spindrift*: the blown spray of the sea.

II. As they swim or float in the sea, side by side, the lover tells his beloved that he is kin (*consanguinity*) to the play of light, sea, and sky; that the sea lifts and laves him in holy gestures; that his rocking body is being admitted, past the whirl of sea and starlight, into the black swollen gates of the sea opening on a death which is not an annihilation (*carnage*) but a sea-change into song and love. He then asks to be admitted to such a voyage. *tendered*: (1) "proffered," and (2), by phonetic equivalence, "tender." *reliquary*: the sea is a casket for the holy body of the beloved. *transmemberment*: resurrection and transformation.

IV. Emerging from sleep after midnight, the lover and voyager watch the moonlit estuaries of the bay. In sleep, at least, the voyager belonged to the lover, but now the lover fears the tyranny of the moonlight and the sea which are deaf to his desire and draw the voyager toward a quest appealing because of its strange beauty and mystery. To the lover this is a godless image bringing death to his love; it is an anonymous piracy that steals away his beloved. He begs his beloved to turn from the drifting foam and its ghosts and to come home. *home*: (1) on earth, (2) in death together.

❧

CUMMINGS, EDWARD ESTLIN. Cambridge, Mass., Oct. 14, 1894.

❧

De La MARE, WALTER JOHN. Charlton, Kent, England, April 25, 1873.

❧

DICKINSON, EMILY. Born, Amherst, Mass., Dec. 10, 1830; died, May 15, 1886.

WONDER IS NOT PRECISELY KNOWING. The first two lines may be read in two different ways so as to describe either what wonder *is* or what it is *not*. The primary reading defines what wonder *is*; that is, it comes about when something is neither precisely known nor precisely unknown. The secondary reading states what wonder is *not*: that is, it is not either precisely to know or precisely to know not. The primary reading is the stronger and is supported by the syntax of the rest of the sentence, yet the secondary reading is strongly implied and echoed throughout the poem as part of the equivocal nature of what *wonder* is. In other words, the ambiguity of "wonder," ambiguously stated, is the very essence of the poem both as meaning and as syntax or technique. This double reading is continued: in the fourth line which states, primarily, that he who has not felt this condition has not *lived*, that is, has not "experienced" it; yet the line has a secondary meaning that he who has not felt this condition has not known what it is to live. In the fifth line, *suspense* is declared to be *his* maturer sister, in which "his" primarily refers to *wonder* and secondarily to the protagonist. The ambiguity of the next two lines lies not in the shifting meaning of any one word, nor in the grammar, but in the very nature of the statement made. The question is raised whether adult delight, composed of so much imprecision, bleakness, and suspense is to be acknowledged and accepted as a compound of pain, or whether such a "mature" resolution is not false— whether a *misgiving* does not then arise as to whether, after all, delight or unhappiness is not such a complex and paradoxical compound but (it is implied) is something simpler, more innocent, more unadulterated. All other ambiguities of life were misgivings, but now when we are ready to accept life as a painful delight, we find that this resolution may be a new misgiving. In the last line the entire situation is summed up by an audacious pun, for *gnat* is both the insect and the negation "not." The word *mangles* enlarges the small, irritating sting of the insect into the destructive blow of the Great Negation.

DOOLITTLE, HILDA. Bethlehem, Pa., Sept. 10, 1886.

DURRELL, LAWRENCE. Julundur, India, Feb. 27, 1912.

Author's Note: "Why do I write? In writing I can be most intimately myself for myself; poetry refines tastes, like a magnifying glass enlarges objects; when you are thoroughly refined away you understand more about the world and its penalties than you would if you just hoed beans all day and slept all night. Also, people just don't write poetry unless they hate being here in this ugly, trivial and common set-up which we call reality and which is a fabrication, intended to shut out the Really Real. I also write because apart from making love there isn't any occupation left which helps one to *be* more. Also if you think it isn't connected with vanity, desire for fame, and a taste for easy social victories in a world which absolutely overvalues poets, you are dead wrong. It is. When you feel utterly hopeless and helpless, then you decide to bite a piece out of your own immortality instead of waiting for it to come up in its natural time on the Wheel. And Presto! You have a dirty little ten-line piece with a market value of five cents a word to hang on your watch-chain."

To Argos and At Epidaurus. *Argos* was the country of Agamemnon who led the Greek forces against Troy. He was betrayed by his wife Clytemnestra and murdered by her in his bath on his return. *Epidaurus* is a town in Argolis and the chief seat of worship of Aesculapius, the god of medicine, whose temple and grove a few miles out of town was a shrine for pilgrims. *Author's Note*: "They are travel poems, reflections on ancient Greece compared to us modern Europeans: simple line drawings of Greek scenery from the lonely eye-piece of the contemporary traveller who has no spiritual baggage. Consequently, the ache and pain . . . The second stanza of "Argos": our heroes, idealists, poets, have been betrayed as the Greek ones were, but not by their dying; that is, *they* didn't betray us, but we them. *Our* death (spiritual) was the betrayal . . . Virgil's blood is said to have sprung up in some flower or other; *pompion* is the Elizabethan word for 'campion,' a flower. As Virgil lives again, so Agamemnon in this landscape, etc. . . . *Hyssop* and *vinegar* refer to Christ, to the religious attitude, to the world which is dead in us."

CONON IN ALEXANDRIA. *Author's Note*: "*Conon* is an imaginary Greek philosopher who visited me twice in my dreams, and with whom I occasionally identify myself; he is one of my masks, Melissa is another; I want my total poetic work to add up as a kind of tapestry of people, some real, some imaginary. Conon is real."

EBERHART, RICHARD. Austin, Minn., April 5, 1904.

Author's Note: "My poems are: (1) Individualistic in a non-individualistic world. (2) Biased and canted toward the spiritual. (3) Continuously changing integers around an integral wish and quest polarized in time. (4) Thrusts of imagination. (5) Sometimes instantaneous crystallizations of sublingual memories seated in childhood, but throned in disparate mature experience. (6) Fictions against loss. (7) Provisory suppositions, against a background of realization of our death, our fallacy of duration, of the supremacy of intellect against the flesh, all works of blood. (8) Rushes of blood, flesh and mortality to state the human condition, against the proposition of the value of mind. (9) Attempts to give pleasure in spite of pain—i.e., a condition of art. (10) To win the spirit and to lose the spirit, to capture the spirit, to know reality—but all definitions are themselves poetic, approximating poetry but less valuable than poetry. (11) Laughter and irony at all suppositions; the comic in precarious balance with the tragic. Life as sea-saw. (12) Search perturbed by its futility—limitation as extension. (13) Speech as a gift of nature, beyond learning. Twenty years of learning are overcome in an instant of Recognition: reading the spirit. Insight is honesty. Truth is a parable of contemplation. Poems are phases of understanding."

MYSTICISM HAS NOT THE PATIENCE TO WAIT FOR GOD'S REVELATION. The title and *The higher we go* . . .: are both from Kierkegaard.

I WALKED OUT TO THE GRAVEYARD TO SEE THE DEAD. *Author's Note*: "While I was a graduate student at Harvard (1932-33) I walked out to Mt. Auburn cemetery to see the graves of William and Henry James. The *golden pheasant* may or may not be the phoenix of Herodotus. His account is found in the Second Book, Chapter 73. The phoenix is an

Absolute, and therefore, like God, reasonably improbable. We accept God, as an Absolute, in faith, beyond reason. But we live in a world of apparent reason. Therefore the impossible (which the spirit is always trying to accomplish) is enjoined with the assignment of this fabulous bird to the *rafters of Montaigne,* who is employed as a symbol of reason. You will recall that Montaigne's rafters were decorated with some of his propositions. The poem is trying to humanize the Absolute. You only seek yourself when you try to look through the iron gates of death. The *sunset* suggests death, but also something splendid. This absolute phoenix-pheasant could only have a *fearful method,* as being far beyond our logic. He is the guardian of ultimate secrets. To him is imputed method, or so it would seem to man. It is the fearful method of an immortal, alien ability. There would be no objection to reading it, in addition to the notion of guardianship of something unknown, however suspected by reason to be fearful in the sense of death as negation and extinction, as a fearful method, contrary to the idea of sunset, by which the phoenix is magically resurrected; this offends us in our poor, human, unresurrected powers, so the dazzling bird is adjured against 'winking' at us, perplexing us continuously with a smarting of the sight, without anything being resolved. The pheasant might be a symbolic bird, might be an ornament of metal (cf. 'Sailing to Byzantium' [p. 32]). The word *Absolute* has references other than those to God or Immortality. The final quatrain attempts to resolve the poem, uses plain statements, locating men among his fellows, whose action must be learned from love. The dazzlement of immortality blinds and obfuscates man. Since the mystery is never resolved, this poem leans in humility on man himself, not as master, but against whom a greater power has closed the gates of ultimate knowledge. It admits the human condition."

ELIOT, THOMAS STEARNS. St. Louis, Mo., Sept. 26, 1888.

BURNT NORTON. *Mystical Union:* This poem, "The Dry Salvages," "East Coker," and "Little Gidding," each divided into five sections, comprise the poem *Four Quartets.* The central theme of all poems is the desire of the penitent to merge his soul into a mystical union with God, and is derived primarily from the Spanish mystic, St. John of the Cross, 1542-1591, whose *The Ascent of Mt. Carmel* and *The Dark Night of the Soul* are theological and psychological analyses of the mystical union, and were originally written to explain the full implications of his poetry. He was educated at a Jesuit school and at the University of Salamanca, then joined St. Teresa in the reformation of the Carmelites toward a more primitive and contemplative existence. He was persecuted all his life by the conservative Carmelites, often exiled, and early in his career jailed and tormented. It was in prison that he began to write his two most important poems, "The Spiritual Canticle," and "The Dark Night," of which his prose is later exegetical. Religious mysticism is concerned with a direct knowledge of God's presence in which the soul has, as a great reality, a sense of actual contact with Him, and the "mystical union" is such a union of the soul with God in contemplation. Its chief characteristic is that the presence of God is felt, without images, as direct experiences of illuminating and exalting infusion, known as spiritual touches, but which are obscure and partly incomprehensible. Its effect is a large increase in the penitent of charity, humility, and self-sacrificing devotion, accompanied, not infrequently, by the perfecting of the natural powers of contemplation. There are several grades of mystic union, such as the prayer of quiet, the full union in which the soul is more conscious and more certain of God's presence within it, ecstatic union, and finally the spiritual marriage and mergence with God. According to St. John, the penitent must purify his senses and his soul through dark nights of trial, contemplation, and suffering in a gradual ascent through ten degrees on the mystical ladder which is to bring him to divine love. This is the penitent's purgatory on earth and may shorten or dismiss a purgatory after death. In the Active Night, the beginner pursues salvation by aggressively stripping himself of all affections of the senses and spirit, and by seeking God actively through *meditation*; but the proficient enters into a Passive Night where he submits himself passively to the will of God in *contemplation*, knowing that salvation lies only in the power of God to bestow through His grace. In this state, writes St. John, "The desires of the sense and spirit are lulled to sleep and mortified, unable to relish anything either human or divine; the affections of the soul are thwarted and brought low, become helpless and have nothing to rest upon; the imagination is fettered, and unable to make any profitable reflections, the memory is gone, and the will, too, is dry and afflicted, and all the faculties are empty and useless, and, moreover, a dense and heavy cloud overshadows the soul, distresses it and holds it as if it were far away from God. . . . The truth is, that the nearer the soul comes to Him it perceives that darkness as greater and deeper because of its own weakness; thus the nearer the sun the greater the darkness and distress wrought by its great brightness, because our eyes are weak, imperfect, and defective. Hence it is that the spiritual light of God is so immeasurable, so far above the understanding, that when it comes near to it, it dims and blinds it. If a man wishes to be sure of the road he travels on, he must close his eyes and walk in the dark."

Structure: The structure of each poem in *Four Quartets*, and the relationship of one poem to another is, as the title implies, a musical one. In *The Music of Poetry* Eliot writes that the properties of music which most concern a poet are the sense of rhythm and the sense of structure, and that "The use of recurrent themes is as natural to poetry as to music. There are possibilities for verse which bear some analogy to the development of a theme by different groups of instruments; there are possibilities of transitions in a poem comparable to the different movements of a symphony or a quartet; there are possibilities of contrapuntal arrangement in subject matter." These devices are deliberately used not only throughout *Four Quartets*, but much earlier in *The Waste Land* where they were first elaborated in a structure in all ways identical with that of *Four Quartets*. They bear comparison with the sonata arrangement of a string quartet, especially with the late quartets of Beethoven, which often depart from the usual arrangement in four movements, ranging from five to seven; both of Eliot's poems and *The Quartet in A Minor, Opus 132,* are in five movements. The first movement, usually in fugue form, states the theme and countertheme of the subject and usually represents an antithesis or conflict of some kind; the second and slower movement extends and develops the conflicting themes with the addition of new materials, restatements and alterations; the third movement is composed of further exposition and variations with a deepening of subject matter, the mood is slow, meditative and often sad in a key of a relative minor which modulates back to the major key; the fourth movement is often a trio movement, a short interlude of rest, a lyrical plateau of suspension; the fifth movement is a vigorous resolution of all themes in an elaborate counterpoint climaxing to final synthesis and statement. This description holds true for all four of Eliot's *Quartets,* and for the five movements of each. The themes in words, phrases, images, and rhythms are progressively elaborated from quartet to quartet, until the ending section of the entire poem, Section V of "Little Gidding" is composed almost entirely of statements made throughout the other *Quartets* and brought to a resolved climax. The comparison between Eliot's *Quartets* and those of Beethoven, both in technique and subject matter, is an exact one, as is shown in the following summary of Beethoven's quartets by J. W. N. Sullivan in *Beethoven, His Spiritual Development* (Alfred A. Knopf, New York, 1927): "In these quartets the movements radiate, as it were, from a central experience. They do not represent stages in a journey, each stage being independent and existing in its own right. They represent separate experiences, but the meaning they take on in the quartet is derived from their relationship to a dominating, central experience. This is characteristic of the mystic vision to which everything in the world appears unified in the light of one fundamental experience. In these quartets, then, Beethoven is not describing to us a spiritual history; he is presenting us a vision of life. In each of the quartets many elements are surveyed, but from one central point of view. They are presented as apprehended by a special kind of awareness, they are seen in the light of one fundamental experience. It is not any kinship between the experiences described in the separate movements themselves, but the light in which they are seen, that gives to the works their profound homogeneity. . . . Beethoven had come to realize that his creative energy, which he at one time opposed to his destiny, in reality owed its very life to that destiny. It is not merely that he believed that the price was worth paying; he came to see it as necessary that a price should be paid. [In "Little Gidding" Eliot says "Costing not less than everything."] To be willing to suffer in order to create is one thing; to realize that one's creation necessitates one's suffering, that suffering is one of the greatest of God's gifts, is almost to reach a mystical solution to the problem of evil." Every line of *Four Quartets* revolves with almost monotonous and musical reiteration about the central vision of the mystical union with God. Eliot's concern with the problems of evil and suffering, and his resolution of them, are identical with this analysis of Beethoven.

Burnt Norton: a manor in Gloucestershire, England, near which Eliot lived for a while, and the formal garden of which may have suggested much of the imagery of the poem. Eliot has said that he was unacquainted with the history of the place. τοῦ λόγου. . .: "Although the word is in common use for all, most men live as if they had each a private wisdom of his own." "The way up and the way down are one and the same." E. M. Stephenson in *T. S. Eliot and the Lay Reader* (Fortune Press, London, 1947) quotes from a letter of Eliot: "Hermann Diels' *Fragmente der Vorsokratiker* is, I believe, still considered the standard text of the pre-Socratic philosophers . . . I should say that Herakleitos meant a great deal more than simply 'the word is in common use.' I think that he meant rather that the reason, the Logos, or the rational understanding of the nature of things is common or available to all men. '*Most people live as if they had a peculiar and individual insight.*' No one translation, however, can be considered as anything more than a limited interpretation since the meaning of key words in Greek philosophy can never be completely rendered in a modern language. That is my reason for my putting the Greek text instead of an English translation of it."

The theme of "Burnt Norton" is the immediate apprehension of a timeless reality felt in time and remembered in time.

Part I. The theme and countertheme is the conflict between time and the timeless, between flux and impermanence in the actual world of time, and the stillness and permanent simultaneity in a timeless and real world of eternity. In the blur of the present, past, and future of this world we are nonetheless conscious of a timelessness in which they are identical. Eliot is meditating on the words of Ecclesiastes: "That which hath been is now; and that which is to be hath already been; and God requireth that which is past."—III:15. Then comes the first of many thematic passages throughout his poetry and the *Quartets* of the spiritual presence of reality, of divine touches, of illuminations, of mystical union. These are strongly experienced in early childhood, are associated with sexual awakening, and are localized in a rose-garden; it is an experience which cuts through temporal time in which rose-leaves decay, the thrush is deceptive, and leaves die, and it gives access to a world of timeless reality. Among these unseen presences and unheard music there is a vision of fulfillment, of spiritual refreshment, of the rising of the waters in the waste land. Mankind, however, cannot bear the vision of such reality for long: the final consummation with God in the mystical union can only be found in death. (See second part of *to care* . . . *sit still*, p. 466). *unredeemable*: See *redeem the time*, p. 470. *rose-garden*: See 38-42, p. 477; also *rose*, p. 469. *gate*: (1) into the garden, (2) through the womb into the world of childhood. *Unheard music*: See *still is . . . unheard*, p. 471. *box circle*: This, the pool, and the lotus rising in it are, on one level, sexual imagery. *heart of light*: See Dante's, "from out the heart of one of the new lights there moved a voice."—*Paradiso*, XII 28-29. Suggestive also of Joseph Conrad's *Heart of Darkness*.

Part II. The theme is the partial apprehension in time and through time of the still-moving center which is God. All second movements of the *Quartets* are divided into two parts: the first states the theme and is always written in some formal and traditional meter, here unevenly rimed iambic-trochaic tetrameter; the second expands and comments on the theme, and is written in a relaxed and free medium which sometimes hovers about blank verse, and sometimes approximates the measure of sprung rhythm—only in "Little Gidding" does this section become formalized into a variant of terza rima, as a kind of formal technical resolution. *First Section*: The sensory (*garlic*) and beautiful (*sapphires*) things of this world clot our vision of the still center which is God (symbolized by the axle-tree of the wheel which is also the axis of the earth). The conflicting rhythms of this life, such as the pulsation of our blood and the pattern in which the pursued and the pursuer are involved, are in a gradual ascension finally resolved in the final and single rhythm and pattern which is God. *Garlic . . .*: According to Eliot this was suggested by a line of Mallarmé's sonnet *"M'introduire dans ton histoire,"* ("To fit myself into your story"): *"Tonnerre et rubis aux moyeux,"* ("Thunder and rubies at the axles"). Also compare with Ezra Pound's "plunging jewels in mud," *Canto XIV*, p. 115. *figured*: a suggestion as if the entire scene were figured upon a tapestry. *Second Section*: God is the Unmoved Mover in whose still center all paradoxes are resolved, and in Whom is release from the suffering which action inevitably brings; in Him partial ecstasies of heaven and the horrors of damnations are made one, but we cannot wholly know nor endure their fullness. Such complete spiritual consciousness, which may take us out of time, may only be known and conquered in time. *still point*: See *"Still is . . . unheard,* p. 471. *Erhebung*: "Elevation."

Part III. The quotation from St. John on page 460 is applicable to this entire section. We live in a dim flickering limbo, neither in the light of eternal salvation nor in the darkness of suffering and purification. The poet bids us seek our salvation by descending into the dark night of the soul and by stripping ourselves of all desire. This is one of two possible ways, that of the Dark Night of passive contemplation: (see *to care . . . sit still,* p. 466). St. John says, "Communications which are indeed of God have this property, that they humble the soul and at the same time exalt it. For upon this road to go down is to go up, and to go up to go down; for he that humbles himself is exalted and he that exalts himself is humbled." *distracted*: We are distracted from spiritual distraction by the distraction of worldly things.

Part IV. Every fourth section is a lyrical stasis written in rimed and formal stanzas. The penitent passively waits in the dark and sunless night, hoping and yet not daring to hope for signs of grace. The *sunflower* is a symbol of light; the *clematis* is also known as the Virgin's Bower; the *yew* is symbolic of release in death and immortality: (see *yews,* p. 471). The brief flash of light on the *kingfisher's wing* is symbolic of a glimpse into the central and still light of eternity which is God; the kingfisher is also Christ: (see p. 474). *light is still*: (1) is yet, (2) is quiet; (see *Still is . . . unheard,* p. 471).

Part V. All contradictions, dualities, and paradoxes found in time are now united and resolved in the timeless eternity of God, in the Platonic Form or Pattern which He is; the imprecise words of human speech are merged into His Word or Logos. All opposites coexist in a simultaneity in which they retain their identity yet are each other: the end and the beginning, movement and stillness are identical. The tempting voices of this world are dying ones and can no longer assail the Word of God. We may know the eternal and unmoving Pattern of God, which is Love, only through imitations and limitations of it in man's world of movement. To act, to move, is to depart from perfection and to become involved in man's world of desire and suffering. There is a sudden recapitulated vision of the symbols of revelation, the divine touches; in the light of the eternally present the poet is reminded how ridiculous, wasteful, and sad is our life in time as we know it, in the past and the future. Words, phrases, images, and concepts of the fifth movement are recapitulated from previous sections and resolved under the concept of the mystic union. *chimera*: we hear not only the actual cry of the fabulous beast killed by Bellerephon, but also the death of all things chimerical or illusionary. *figure of the ten stairs*: Miss Stephenson paraphrases a discussion she had with Eliot on November 24, 1943: "'The figure of the ten stairs' refers to the 'Bride' which is used symbolically of the Soul in its upward movement towards God. The 'ladder' or 'step' to which St. John of the Cross refers and which Mr. Eliot uses in poetry, with greater euphony as 'stairs' signifies Divine Love and Faith." St. John's description of The Ten Degrees of the Mystical Ladder of Divine Love is as follows: "The first degree of love makes the soul languish to its great profit . . . As a sick man loses the desire for, and the taste of all food . . . so the soul in this degree of love loses all pleasure of earthly things, and all desire of them, and changes its colour, that is, the conditions of the past life. It finds no comfort, pleasure, nor support anywhere. Second: So anxious is the soul now that it seeks the Beloved in all things; all its thought, words, and works are referred to Him; in eating, sleeping, and waking, all its anxieties are about Him. The third step of the ladder of love renders the soul active and fervent, so that it faints not. The soul, because of the great love it has for God, is in great pain and suffering because of the scantiness of its service . . . It looks upon itself therefore as unprofitable in all it does, and its life as worthless. Another most wonderful effect is that it looks upon itself as being in truth the very worst of souls. On this third step the very soul is far from giving way to vainglory or presumption, or from condemning others. When the soul is on the fourth step of the ladder of love, it falls into a state of suffering, but without weariness . . . It seeks not for consolations or sweetness either in God or elsewhere, neither does it pray for God's gifts, seeing clearly how many it has already received. For all it cares for now is how it shall please God, and serve Him, in some measure in return for His goodness, and for the graces it has received, and this at any end and every cost. This degree of love is exceedingly high. On the fifth step of the ladder the soul longs after God, and desires Him with impatience. Great is the eagerness of the soul on this step to embrace and be united to the Beloved. When the soul has ascended to the sixth step, it runs swiftly to God from Whom it receives many touches; and hope too runs without fainting, for love has made it strong and makes it fly rapidly. On the seventh step the soul becomes vehemently bold; in this intense and loving exaltation, no prudence can withhold it, no counsel control it, no shame restrain it; for the favour which God hath shown it has made it vehemently bold. On the eighth step the soul embraces the Beloved and holds Him fast . . . On this step of union the desires of the soul are satisfied, but not without interruption. Some souls ascend to this step and at once fall back; if they did not, and remained there, they would have attained to a certain state of blessedness in this life, and thus the soul tarries but briefly on this step of the ladder. On the ninth step the soul is on fire sweetly. This step is that of the perfect who burn away sweetly in God, for this sweet and delicious burning is the work of the Holy Ghost because of the union of the soul with God. St. Gregory says of the Apostles, that they burned interiorly with love sweetly, when the Holy Ghost descended upon them. On the tenth step of the ladder the soul becomes wholly assimilated into God in the beatific vision which it then immediately enjoys; for having ascended in this life to the ninth, it goeth forth out of the body. For these—they are few—being perfectly purified by love, do not pass through purgatory."

Ash Wednesday. A prayer in which the poet, ascending the purgatorial mount in penance and humility, struggles to purge himself of the world's temptations in order to focus his mind upon God, and prays for the merciful intercession of Our Lady.

Part I. Because the penitent in his advanced years neither hopes nor wishes to turn again to the ambitions, the vanished powers and infirm glories of worldly things, nor can hope to know again the true fleeting vision of God, nor to drink at sensory or spiritual sources, he rejoices that, though caught in a relativistic world, he can renounce even the blessèd face of hope or the voice of guidance, and in such penitence, stripped of both worldly and spiritual comfort, can wait in stillness, passively, caring for salvation yet not deeming himself sufficiently worthy of care, waiting for whatever grace God might care to bestow upon him. *Because I . . .*: First line of Guido Cavalcanti's *ballata* "In Exile at Sarzana," (*"Perch'io non spero di tornar già mai"*). The translation by Dante Gabriel Rossetti begins: "Because I think not ever to return,/ Ballad, to Tuscany,—/ Go therefore thou for me/ Straight to my lady's face,/ Who, of her noble grace,/ Shall show thee courtesy." The exiled Italian poet, in the place of his soul, sends his ballad to his lady (in the temporal sense) with "Tears and fresh agony" to tell her how death assails him, of his "body being now so nearly dead," of his "dead mind," of how he "served Love painfully," and bids it to worship that "calm and bright" lady "still in her purity." So does the penitent of *Ash Wednesday* speak of his withdrawal from the world, of his failing powers, and look to his Lady for succor. The penitent soul in St. John, when the purgative contemplation is most severe, "feels very keenly the shadow of death and the lamentations of death and the pains of hell, which consist in its feeling itself to be without God, and chastised and cast out, and unworthy of Him." The reference to "turning," the cyclical movement of the cadence, and the repetition of word and theme throughout the poem recall the spiraling circles which Dante ascends around the mountain of Purgatory leading to the Garden of Eden and thence to God, and also to the ten degrees of the mystical ladder of

Divine Love which St. John outlines in the penitent's progress to God.
(See p. 464). Compare also with a sermon by Lancelot Andrewes on
the opening words of the Epistle for Ash Wednesday, "Turn ye even
unto me, saith the Lord": "Now at this time is the turning of the year.
. . . Everything now turning that we also would make it our time to
turn to God in. . . . Upon this turning . . . the hinge turns, of our
well or evil doing for ever. . . . Repentance itself is nothing but a kind
of circling. . . . Which circle consists of two turnings. . . . First a turn
wherein we look forward to God and with our whole heart resolve to
turn to Him. Then a turn again wherein we look backward to our sins
wherein we have turned from God. . . . The wheel turns apace, and if we
turn not the rather these turnings may overtake us." *Desiring* . . .: But
for the alteration of one word, this is the seventh line of Shakespeare's
twenty-ninth sonnet: "Desiring this man's art and that man's scope."
Like the penitent, Shakespeare speaks of his "outcast state," of "troubling
deaf heaven with my bootless cries," of wishing himself "like one more
rich in hope," confessing that "With what I most enjoy contented least."
Eliot transfers Cavalcanti's and Shakespeare's symbols of profane to that
of sacred love. *agèd eagle*: St. John tells how God despoils the Old Man
and denudes him of "the faculties, the affections, spiritual and sensual,
interior and exterior, leaving the understanding in darkness, the will dry,
the memory empty." "God makes it to die of all that is not naturally God,
so that, once it is stripped and denuded of its former skin, He may begin
to clothe it anew. And thus its youth is renewed like the eagle's and
it is clothed with the new man, which, as the Apostle says, is according
to God." *transitory*: The moments of illumination which unite us to the
eternal are ironically spoken of as *transitory,* and the infirm glories of
this world as *positive.* Also this world and time are spoken of as
actual in contrast to the *real,* the *veritable* existence of God and
eternity. *renounce*: St. John says that in the purification of his will the
penitent must not only give up all temporal, natural, and sensory goods,
but also moral and spiritual goods. *forget*: St. John says that "The
memory must be stripped and emptied of all [sensory] knowledge. . . .
As God is without form or image, on which the memory may dwell,
so when the memory is united with God . . . it remains without form or
figure, with the imagination suppressed, and itself absorbed in supreme
felicity, in profound oblivion, remembering nothing." *dryer than the
will*: See *eagle* and *renounce,* above. The three signs which St. John
gives of the passive night of the senses are (1) "when we find no comfort in the things of God, and none also in created things," (2) "the soul
thinks that it is not serving God, but going backwards, because it is no
longer conscious of any sweetness in the things of God. . . . The cause
of this dryness is that God is transferring to the spirit the goods and
energies of the senses, which, being now unable to assimilate them, become dry, parched up, and empty"; (3) "inability to meditate and make
reflections, and to excite the imagination as before." *to care . . . sit still*:
In explaining the entry into the night of the senses, St. John says:
"Ordinarily the soul enters this night in two ways; one is the active way,
the other is the passive. The active way is that by which the soul is
able to make, and does make, efforts of its own to enter in, assisted by

divine grace. . . . The passive way is that in which the soul does nothing as of itself, neither does it make therein any efforts of its own; but it is God who works in it, giving special aids, and the soul is, as it were, freely consenting thereto." In this passive state the soul may perhaps be visited by unexpected divine touches and illuminations, by momentary revelations of what the final mystical union with God may be, the eternal moments for which man on earth waits, and the only reward of his living. Since these illuminations are the goal toward which the penitent in *Ash Wednesday* strives, and the only subject matter of all *Four Quartets,* we quote in full: "Sometimes, when the soul least thinks of it, and when it least desires it, God touches it divinely, causing certain recollections of Himself. Sometimes, too, the divine touches are sudden, occurring even while the soul is occupied with something else, and that occasionally of trifling moment. They are also so sensible and efficacious, that at times they make not only the soul, but the body also, to tremble. At other times they come gently, without any agitation whatever, accompanied by a deep sense of delight and spiritual refreshing. As this knowledge is communicated suddenly and independently of the will, the soul must not strive to receive it, but be humble and resigned; for God will do His work, how and when He will. . . . The means by which God effects this great work must be humility and patient suffering for love of Him, with resignation, and indifference as to all reward. These graces are not bestowed on the soul which cleaves to anything of its own . . . [but] which . . . loves Him in perfect detachment and disinterestedness." *pray for us . . .*: from the *Ave Maria,* "Hail, Mary, full of grace, the Lord is with thee, blessed art thou among women and blessed is the fruit of thy womb, Jesus. Holy Mary, mother of God, pray for us sinners now and at the hour of our death." First sentence is from Luke, 1: 28, 42; second sentence has been added by the Church.

Part II. In a continuation of his prayer from the *Ave Maria,* the penitent now addresses the Lady in a more personal manner to tell her that three leopards, which represent the powers and temptations of this world, have now denuded him of all sensory or mental being or attachments. There remain now only the pure dry bones of faith which through God's mercy, and especially through the intercession of the Lady, may perhaps live again by salvation and in resurrection. This recovery of both bodily and spiritual attributes rejected by the world can only come about by a complete denial by the penitent of all works, love and attachment, and is achieved only by a complete aridity of body and soul. God tells the bones to speak of these matters to the wind as if with divine inspiration, for the world will not listen. The bones, singing to themselves in faith, address God through the Lady who, like Christ in the role of man, was distressed, torn, exhausted, and worried, but who, like God Himself, is calm, whole, without temporal memory in His eternity, life-giving, reposeful, and single. In love of the singleness, peace and stillness of God, all inadequacies of temporal love must terminate; God is the conclusion of all that seems inconclusible; He is the ineffable Word. Thus do the bones, shining with faith, sing, knowing now that the Promised Land is not to be found in this world but in Paradise, the true inheritance where neither division nor unity matters, reached only by a pilgrimage through the desert of purgation and death. *Lady*: She is some idealized beautiful woman, such as Beatrice was to Dante, who in her loveliness and goodness may lead the penitent to God; she also symbolizes the Virgin Mary. In the "clear visual images" of the Lady, the leopards, and many other images and symbols, Eliot attains what Matthiessen, the American critic, calls a "paradoxical precision in vagueness" which allows the poet "to make as accurate a description of the objects as he can and let its indefinite associations unfold variously in different readers' minds." It is quite clear that the Lady, with all her associations, is an archetype of "merciful intercession," though she seems withdrawn and silent. *three white leopards*: the leopards may symbolize the hunger for worldly things which consumes us, they may also be the symbolical condensation of the leopard, the lion, and the she-wolf whom Dante met in the beginning of the *Inferno* when he was lost "in the middle of the journey of our life," and which symbolize worldly pleasure, ambition, and avarice. Among other attributes, *three* may remind us of the three main circles of the *Inferno*: those of Incontinence, Brutishness, and Fraud; or of the three kinds of defective love under which the sinners in the *Purgatorio* suffer: Excessive, Defective, and Perverted. White is the liturgical color used on all feasts of our Lord, our Lady, and of all women not martyrs. In their terrible feast, the leopards (the world, that is) have consumed and purged us of sin so that through suffering we might find salvation; like the devil used for good ends, they have performed a religious function and may well be vested with the whiteness of the bones and the Lady. In the choice of color there is also delicately implied a forgiveness. *juniper-tree*: See I Kings, XIX: 1-12. See also Jacob Grimm's *The Juniper Tree*, story of a boy murdered by his stepmother, baked into a black-pudding, and fed to his father. His bones are buried by his step-sister under a juniper-tree, and he is resurrected in the form of a singing bird. We are reminded of the Lady by the step-sister's benevolence, of the Christian Communion in the eating of the body, and of the Resurrection by the boy's rebirth. *cool of the day*: See Genesis III: 8. A reminder of the tree of Good and Evil. *fed to satiety . . . my legs my heart my liver*: In the article on "Animism" in the *Encyclopedia of Religion and Ethics,* I, 520, the section on leopards contains this sentence: "In South Africa a man who has killed a leopard remains in his hut three days; he practices continence and is *fed to satiety.*" In the same article we are told: "In many cases where the heart or liver or marrow is said to be eaten, or the blood drunk for the sake of obtaining its owner's strength, it is probable that the assimilation of the owner's soul or life is intended, since it is so commonly believed that the life of the soul is in one of these parts." All this has reference to Holy Communion in which the sinner eats of the body and drinks of the blood of Christ in order to receive strength and salvation. (See *99-103*, p. 484) *Shall these bones live*: See Ezekiel, XXXVII: 1-14. The Lord set Ezekiel down in the midst of a valley of dry bones. "And he said unto me, Son of man, can these bones live? [Note Eliot's change from "can" to "shall."] And I answered, O Lord God, thou knowest." The Lord then directs Ezekiel to prophesy to the bones that they may be covered with flesh and thus know His might. Ezekiel prophesies, the bones come together and are clothed, but have no breath in them. "Then said he unto me, Prophesy unto the wind, prophesy, son of man, and say to the wind, Thus saith the Lord God; Come from the four winds, O breath, and breathe upon these slain, that they may live." *bones . . . dry*: St. John: "The yearnings for God become so great in the soul that the very bones seem to be dried up by this thirst." *fruit of the gourd*: See Jonah, IV. The gourd is not only a symbol of the desert, but also a reminder that what God gives that can he also take away. *recovers*: (1) to cover anew as with flesh, (2) to bring back to health, (3) to redeem from sin. *burden of the grasshopper*: See Ecclesiastes, XII: 5. (See 23, p. 477). The entire Biblical chapter is relevant; notice also "he shall rise up at the voice of the bird," "desire shall fail," "because man goeth to his long home," "then shall the dust return to the earth as it was." *Burden* has two meanings: (1) the refrain or chorus of a song, (2) care, responsibility. *Rose*: Throughout his poetry Eliot uses the rose and the garden with secular, spiritual, and sexual-religious significance. (For full elucidation see Leonard Unger's "T. S. Eliot's Rose Garden: A Persistent Theme," *Southern Review*, Spring, 1942). The Rose Garden is always associated with the scene of the sexual-religious ecstasy which often occurs in childhood and is later recalled as the waning "Intimations of Immortality in Early Childhood" of which Wordsworth wrote, revelations of God which the older man tries to recapture, for "we had the experience and missed the meaning." The rose is also the personal symbol of the Virgin Mary; in many Renaissance paintings she is depicted within a walled rose garden, the gate of which is closed to symbolize her virginity. It is the rose of Christ when it is five-petalled with the five wounds of his crucifixion. And finally, it is the Mystical and Divine White Rose described by Dante in the last three cantos of the *Paradiso*, the petals of which are composed, rank upon rank, of the redeemed, and the center of which is God's blinding light. When Mary grants him final grace, Dante sees: "ingathered, bound by love in one volume, the scattered leaves of all the universe; substance and accidents and their relations, as though together fused, after such fashion that what I tell of its one simple flame."—*Paradiso*, XXXIII, 85-90. All of the last canto of the *Paradiso* throws light upon this passage, especially the opening prayer of St. Bernard to the Virgin. *memory*: As Dante looks upon God, he says, "Thenceforth was my vision mightier than our discourse, which faileth at such sight, and faileth memory at so great outrage."—*Ibid.*, XXXIII, 55-57. *This is . . . inheritance*: God gives directions to Ezekiel: "This is the land which ye shall divide by lot unto the tribes of Israel for inheritance, and these are their portions."—Ezekiel, XLVIII: 29.

Part III. Wrestling with himself and climbing Dante's purgatorial mount, the penitent sees a vision of himself struggling with the devil, followed by a nostalgic vision of the distractions of the flesh and the loveliness of the world: a pastoral figure in maytime, music, flowers, and memories of love. In humility and shame he cries out to God that he is unworthy. *stair*: When Eliot first published this section by itself, he entitled it *"Som de l'Escalina,"* "The Summit of the Stairway." (See *428*,

p. 495). We are reminded that in the purgatorial mount the penitents suffer in three cycles of Perverted, Defective, and Excessive Love comprised of the seven circles of the seven deadly sins, in the last summit of which, that of Carnality, Arnaut Daniel burns in a refining fire. (See also *figure of the ten stairs*, p. 464). *fetid*: the air is foul with the issue of purgation. *devil*: St. John lists seven spiritual imperfections of the beginning penitent, the third of which is the Tendency toward Sensuality: "Very often, in the midst of their spiritual exercises, and when they cannot help themselves, the impure movements and disturbances of sensuality are felt; and sometimes even when the mind is absorbed in prayer, or when they are receiving the sacraments of penance and the eucharist. . . . Some souls are so sensitive that they never experience spiritual fervour or consolation in prayer without the spirit of luxury intruding." (See *Rose*, p. 469). *hope and of despair*: See *to care . . . sit still*, p. 466. *old man's*: See *agèd eagle*, p. 466. *slotted . . . fig's fruit*: symbol of female genitalia. The fig has been traditionally associated with lust. *Lord I am not worthy*: During Mass and before the penitent consumes the body and blood of Christ, he says, "Lord, I am not worthy that thou shouldst enter under my roof. But speak the word only, and my soul shall be healed."

Part IV. In a series of statements which can be either declaratory or interrogative (and therefore echo the hesitancy and turning of the sinner) the penitent asks the Lady to be mindful of his pain and to intercede for him. Like Dante's Beatrice she is seen walking with others talking of trivial things, but as the type of the Virgin Mary she has made the Waste Land bearable by bringing him to spiritual fountains. Moving in a realm between two worlds, between sleep and waking, life and death, time and eternity, the twilit world between the violet and the violet where the three dreams of past, present, and future cross, she speaks no word, but acknowledges his distress, and signs to him encouragingly. He prays to her to redeem the sinful times and restore to them the vision of death and heaven now no longer visible, and to bring him to Jesus. *violet*: not only the twilit realm between dualities, but also the liturgical color used for both blessing and Mass on Ash Wednesday. *eternal dolour*: See 63, p. 480. *Sovegna vos*: "be mindful." The penitent asks the Lady to remember him in his pain, as Arnaut Daniel had begged of Dante; (see 428, p. 495). *the years*: These are the new years of purgation near death and between two worlds in which the Lady has helped the penitent to put behind him the distractions of the garden god, the *broadbacked figure*, its fiddles and now breathless flute. *Redeem the time*: "Awake thou that sleepest, and arise from the dead, and Christ shall give thee light. See that ye walk circumspectly, not as fools, but as wise, Redeeming the time, because the days are evil." —Ephesians, v:14-16. Also: "Walk in wisdom toward them that are without, redeeming the time."—Colossians, iv:5. In *Thoughts after Lambeth*, Eliot writes: "The World is trying the experiment of attempting to form a civilized but non-Christian mentality. The experiment will fail; but we must be very patient in awaiting its collapse; meanwhile redeeming the time: so that the Faith may be preserved alive through the dark ages before us; to renew and rebuild civilization, and save the

World from suicide." *higher dream*: In discussing the "pageantry" of the *Paradiso* in his essay on Dante, Eliot observes: "It belongs to the world of what I call the *high dream*, and the modern world seems capable only of the *low dream*." *While jewelled unicorns* . . .: A vision of death in beatitude. According to legend, the unicorn could only be captured by a Virgin, to whom it would come meekly and place its head upon her lap. *yews*: "The churchyard yew is an ancient symbol of the tree of life. . . . The tree of life has the promise of immortality and bliss."—"Trees and Plants," *Encyclopedia of Religion and Ethics*, p. 455. Thus, the Lady walks between life and eternity. *Redeem* . . . *the yew*: "Bring back the vision of God until death." *And after this our exile*: from one of the "Prayers after Low Mass": "Turn then, most gracious advocate, thine eyes of mercy toward us. And after this our exile, show unto us the blessed fruit of thy womb Jesus."

Part V. As in the distinction which Eliot makes between the capitalized *Rose* and the uncapitalized *rose*, he here distinguishes between the *Word* which is God Himself and the *word* which is the things of this world which God has created and by which he has made himself manifest and through which we apprehend Him darkly. The penitent says that even if men have turned from God, even if the ineffable Word is no longer heard or spoken, nevertheless God still exists within the world and for it. The world revolves about the still center of God who is its Unmoved Mover; His immobility is that in the center of greatest speed. The penitent recalls God's concern to know why mankind has turned from Him, and knows that He still abides with us; yet amid the darkness, desert, powers, oppositions and confusions of this world, and even in the right time, in light and among believers, He seems nowhere to be found. The penitent again calls upon the merciful Lady to intercede for all those who are terrified, who cannot surrender their will to God, who are in an agony of affirmation and denial, in the last stages of purgatory. *Word*: "In the beginning was the Word, and the Word was with God, and the Word was God. . . . All things were made by him. . . . And the light shineth in darkness; and the darkness comprehended it not."—John, I, 1-5. *Still is* . . . *unheard*: *Still* is used ambiguously and paradoxically to denote both the presence and absence of God: (1) "The unheard Word is still with us," and (2) "The unheard Word is silent." See a similar use of this word in Keats' "Ode to the Grecian Urn"; other lines of that poem are echoed in this passage and in *Four Quartets*: "Thou *still* unravished bride of quietness,/ Thou foster child of *silence* and slow *time*,/ . . . *Heard* melodies are sweet, but those *unheard*/ Are sweeter, therefore, ye soft pipes, play on, /Not to the sensual ear but more endeared/ Pipe to the *spirit ditties of no tone*." *O my people* . . .: God pleads with Israel: "O my people, what have I done unto thee? and wherein have I wearied thee? testify against me."—Micah, VI: 3. Eliot's use of the period instead of the question mark turns the statement from one of interrogation to one of dismay. The words also occur in a penitential ritual for Good Friday, "The Adoration of the Cross." *surrender*: See l. 404, of *The Waste Land*. *last blue rocks*: *last* and *blue* because these are in the purgatorial desert and are not the *dry, red* rocks of *The Waste Land*. Blue is also *Mary's colour*. *desert in the garden*: The dualities are involved in one another, as the word within the Word, or the wilderness in the Garden of Eden which is also the Garden of Gethsemane where Christ, like Adam, faced agony and doubt. *withered apple-seed*: reference to the apple eaten by Adam and Eve, and thus to the casting out of Original Sin by salvation through suffering.

Part VI. In spite of the fact that the penitent does not want to turn to the things of this world but to keep his mind upon God, he finds to his dismay that he still wavers between the profit and the loss, that the world still offers him a wide window from which stretches an unbearably beautiful vista, even though he knows that what he sees are empty forms sent to tempt him through the blind eye of the senses. In this intersection of time, caught between past, present, and future, and longing for the eternity of God, he prays for the many voices to drift away that he may hear the one voice of immortality. And finally, he cries to the Lady to help him that he may not deceive himself with the falsity of empty forms, with the "deceitful faces of hope and of despair," that he may resist no longer nor actively strive to reach God, but humbly abandon himself passively to the mercy and grace of God, to care and not to care, to sit still, finding whatever peace he can among the rocks by giving up his will completely to the will of God. *although*: The contrast between this *although* and the *because* which opens the poem is between "in spite of the fact that" and "for the reason that." *profit and loss*: See l. 314 of *The Waste Land*. *Bless me father*: A Catholic usually begins his confession with "Bless me father: I confess to almighty God and to you, father, that I have sinned." *ivory gates*: In Hades, Aeneas and the Sibyl are told: "Two gates of Sleep there are, whereof the one is said to be of horn, and thereby an easy outlet is given to true shades; the other gleaming with the sheen of polished ivory, but false are the dreams sent by spirits to the world above."—Virgil, *Aeneid*, VI. *Our peace in His will*: In the *Paradiso* a spirit tells Dante that all rejoice to be in no higher sphere than that to which Divine Love assigns them, for "His will is our peace."—III, 85. *Suffer me . . .*: From the Catholic Devotions of the Forty Hours, Visit IV: "Suffer me not to be separated from Thee." *And let my cry come unto Thee*: The response to the versicle "O Lord, hear my prayer."

THE WASTE LAND. (See pp. 425-26). *Author's Note*: "Not only the title, but the plan and a good deal of the incidental symbolism of the poem were suggested by Miss Jessie L. Weston's book on the Grail legend: *From Ritual to Romance* (Cambridge [Univ. Press, 1920]). Indeed, so deeply am I indebted, Miss Weston's book will elucidate the difficulties of the poem much better than my notes can do; and I recommend it (apart from the great interest of the book itself) to any who think such elucidation of the poem worth the trouble. To another work of anthropology I am indebted in general, one which has influenced our generation profoundly; I mean *The Golden Bough*; I have used especially the two volumes *Adonis, Attis, Osiris*. Anyone who is acquainted with these works will immediately recognise in the poem certain references to vegetation ceremonies."—*Collected Poems: 1909-1935*. (New York, Harcourt, Brace, 1936).

Miss Weston explains the significance and symbolism of certain Arthurian romances which tell of the Quest for the Holy Grail by tracing them to their origin in the ritual of such fertility gods as the Sumerian Tammuz, the Greek Adonis, the Egyptian Attis, and by showing how they persisted throughout the intervening centuries in folk legends, sword dances, and mummery plays. In the primary versions, the ruler of the land, known as the Fisher King, is dead and must be restored to life. In later versions he is said to suffer from the infirmities of old age, or to be disabled and ill from a wound on the thigh (indicating impotence) and must be made young or well again.

As a direct consequence of his disability, and in sympathetic reaction to it, war and poverty devastate the land, the rains cease to fall, the rivers dry up, vegetation withers, the animals cease to reproduce, the land becomes parched and waste awaiting his good health or resurrection. "The misfortunes of the land," writes Miss Weston, "have been treated rather as an accident, than as an essential, of the Grail story. . . . As a matter of fact I believe that the 'Waste Land' is really the very heart of our problem." A hero pure of heart must be found, such as Gawain, Galahad, or Perceval, to go in quest of the Holy Grail in order to ask of it certain mysterious questions. The Grail is to be found in the Grail Castle, or Chapel Perilous, in the very heart of the Waste Land, after the hero has undergone many physical hardships, temptations, and spiritual trials, the worse of which he suffers in the very grounds of the Chapel when nearest his fulfillment. If he remain pure in heart, he is granted a glimpse of the Grail and may then ask the mysterious questions concerning it or the Bleeding Lance. The king then revives or becomes well again, the rains fall, the rivers rise, the vegetation flourishes, the beasts are fertile, and the land becomes prosperous.

Miss Weston discusses the parallelism between the story and symbolism of this legend and those of the old fertility cults: "As Sir J. G. Frazer has before now pointed out, there are parallel and overlapping forms of this cult: the name of the god, and certain details of the ritual, may differ in different countries, but whether he hails from Babylon, Phrygia, or Phoenicia, whether he be called Tammuz, Attis, or Adonis, the main lines of the story are fixed, and invariable. Always he is young and beautiful, always the beloved of a great goddess; always he is the victim of a tragic and untimely death, a death which entails bitter loss and misfortune upon a mourning world, and which, for the salvation of that world, is followed by a resurrection, mourning and rejoicing. Death and Resurrection, mourning and rejoicing, present themselves in sharp antithesis in each and all of the forms." The fertility gods are, of course, anthropomorphic figures of certain Nature rituals: "The progress of the seasons, the birth of vegetation in spring, or its revival after the autumn rains, its glorious fruition in early summer, its decline and death under the maleficent influence either of the scorching sun, or the bitter winter cold, symbolically represented the corresponding stages in the life of this anthropomorphically conceived Being, whose annual progress from birth to death, from death to a renewed life, was celebrated with a ritual of corresponding alternations of rejoicing and lamentation." Miss Weston finds the earliest existing literary evidence of certain parallels with the

Grail stories in the Hindu *Rig-Veda*. A disproportionate number of the hymns are addressed to Indra, a god of weather, and it is from him that "the much desired boon of rain and abundant water is besought, and that the feat which above all others resounded to his praise . . . is precisely the feat by which the Grail heroes, Gawain and Perceval, rejoiced the hearts of a suffering folk, *i.e.* the restoration of the rivers to their channels, the 'Freeing of the Waters.'"

Finally Miss Weston demonstrates the relationship of both the fertility cults and the Romance Grail legends to the person of Christ and to Christianity. In its esoteric "Mystery" form the Grail story was freely utilized "for the imparting of high spiritual teaching concerning the relation of Man to the Divine Source of his being, and the possibility of a sensible union between Man and God. . . . Christianity . . . did not hesitate to utilize the already existing medium of instruction, but boldly identified the Deity of Vegetation, regarded as Life Principle, with the God of the Christian Faith. Thus, to certain of the early Christians, Attis was an earlier manifestation of the Logos, whom they held identical with Christ."

The relationship between the symbols in the fertility rituals and those in the Romance legends reveals that they held a dual sexual and religious meaning, especially the Bleeding Lance, the Grail, and the name of the Fisher King himself. Of the latter Miss Weston writes: "He is not merely a deeply symbolic figure, but the essential centre of the whole cult, a being semi-divine, semi-human, standing between his people and land, and the unseen forces which control their destiny. If the Grail story be based upon a Life ritual the character of the Fisher King is of the very essence of the tale, and his title, so far from being meaningless, expresses, for those who are at pains to seek, the intention and object of the perplexing whole. The Fisher King is . . . the very heart and centre of the whole mystery." His "title is naturally connected with the use of Fish symbol in early Christianity: the *Icthys* anagram [*sic*], as applied to Christ, the title 'Fishers of Men,' bestowed upon the Apostles, the Papal ring of the Fisherman . . . We can state with certainty that the Fish is a Life symbol of immemorial antiquity, and that the title of Fisher has, from the earliest ages, been associated with Deities who were held to be specially connected with the origin and preservation of Life." Thus the Fisher King, as Eliot uses him, is identified with those divinities who were supposed to lead men back from the shadow of death into life and are identical with Christ, the Fisher of men's souls, who undergoes a crucifixion and resurrection common to the Fisher King and the Fertility gods. It is interesting to notice, however, that the Fisher King is never depicted as a young man, and that in the Grail legends the symbol of Christ has suffered a "decomposition," as psychologists term it, part of his role, that of the mangled and resurrected one, being transferred to the Fisher King, and part, that of the youthful Messiah and the tempted one, being transferred to the knightly Quester. It need only be added that the Fish has always been a phallic symbol.

"The Grail," writes Miss Weston, "was something secret, mysterious and awful, the exact knowledge of which was reserved to a select few . . . . But Lance and Cup (or Vase) . . . are sex symbols of immemorial antiquity and world-wide diffusion, the Lance, or Spear, representing the Male, the Cup, or Vase, the Female reproductive energy. Found in juxtaposition, the Spear, upright in the Vase . . . their signification is admitted by all familiar with 'Life' symbolism, and they are absolutely in place as forming part of a ritual with the processes of life and reproductive vitality." This explains why the meaning of Bleeding Lance and Grail in the Grail legends is shrouded with mysterious obscurity, and explains the nature of the knight's Quest and the questions he is to ask about the Cup and Lance. In the Gawain legend we are told that "so soon as Sir Gawain asked of the Lance . . . the waters flowed again thro' their channel, and all the woods were turned to verdure." The Quest together with the trial and temptations involved is really an initiation into the physical and spiritual mysteries of life and death.

The thematic pattern of *The Waste Land* is now clear: the poem depicts a land in devastation and drought, in physical and spiritual debilitation brought on by the loss of religious belief symbolized by the illness or death of the Fisher King, of Christ, of Christianity, of all men and all women affected, and instanced by many examples from the world literature of the past and present. The time depicted is comparable to those dark days between Good Friday and Easter when there seems to be no hope of resurrection, during which we follow the agonized Quest of the Knight for the Holy Grail. It is erroneous to think, however, that the poem paints only the despair and waste of the modern world, for as we follow the knight-saviour thematically in the course of the poem, and as the devastations and temptations about us seem the more terrible the closer we come to our goal, the Perilous Chapel is nonetheless found, the rains do at least begin to fall, and God speaks to us out of the thunder to give us precepts by which to live.

The poem has many dramatic scenes and lyric interludes, is allusive and elliptical in the use of imagery and trope, imitates many literary styles under its own idiom, but is primarily musical in structure, a "music of ideas," and has basically the same structure which Eliot later used in *Four Quartets*. (See *Structure*, pp. 460-61).

Nam Sibyllam . . .: From the *Satyricon* of Gaius Petronius. At a banquet, the host, Trimalchio, turns to one of his guests, Agamemnon, and says: "For I saw with my own eyes a celebrated Sibyl at Cumae, hanging in a bottle, and when the Acolytes said, 'What do you wish, O Sibyl?' she replied, 'I wish to die.'" Granted by Apollo the gift of prophecy, the Cumaean Sibyl was once the oracular guide of a nation, and the guide of Aeneas through the realms of Hades. Apollo also granted her as many years as she had grains of dust in her hand, but she forgot to ask for youth, and so gradually withered away. (See l. 30 of *The Waste Land*.) This is the first of many thematic references to poets and prophets of many ages and countries who have declined from their high positions as directors of their nations' destinies, and are no longer heeded or consulted, but are caged, reviled, and mocked at. Eliot, as poet and prophet himself in a godless world, may perhaps best be identified as wearing the masks of the poet-prophets whom he quotes, especially that of Tiresias. *il miglior fabbro*: "the better craftsman." —*Purgatorio*, XXVI, 117. Guinicelli's tribute to Arnaut Daniel is transferred by Eliot to Ezra Pound, the founder or precursor of a new idiom in modern poetry: "'this one whom I distinguish to thee with my finger' (and he pointed to a spirit in front) 'was a better craftsman of the mother tongue.'"

Part I. The Burial of the Dead. The first section announces themes repeated and amplified throughout the poem, and introduces us to the *dramatis personae.* In the first paragraph the scene is set in that part of April when Christ, the Vegetation God, is crucified, and when there seems to be no hope of resurrection. It is a cruel month because it stirs up the beginnings of life in a people and land who wish only to die. We overhear remarks in the cafés of Central Europe, of belligerent nationalism, nostalgic memories of childhood experience when simple things were real and intense, wishes for escape, rootlessness and insomnia, ennui. Suddenly the voice of the poet-prophet arises, warning us of our desolation, pointing out the sterility of our land and of our lives. The key phrases, the musical motifs of the actual and spiritual drought of the *dead land* are here announced: the stony rubbish, the broken images, the dead tree, the rasping sound of the cricket, the dry stone, the lack of water, the red rock, the handful of dust, all of which are amplified throughout the poem, stated and restated, counterpointed and finally climaxed in the last recapitulating section, "What the Thunder Said." In direct contrast to this theme of drought and despair rises the countertheme, much like the lyrical second motif in Beethoven's compositions, of the lyrical freshness of early love: in the song of the sailor about his girl, in the memory of the hyacinth girl with wet hair. All symbols of life and hope in the poem, such as the situations of early love, water, and flowers, are always seen in terms of *memory and desire,* memories of lost opportunities, of incapacity, of silence, until water itself, the source of life, becomes in the Waste Land but an irritant *stirring dull roots with spring rain,* is *waste and empty,* and finally becomes the tomb instead of the womb of life, as in "Death by Water." We are then introduced to *Madame Sosostris,* who, with her affected accent, in turn introduces us, with a pack of cards, to the particular *dramatis personae* of the poem. She is the vulgarization of the poet-prophet into the cheap fortune teller, using those cards which originally foretold the rise and fall of waters and of nations to cast the horoscope of such people as *dear Mrs. Equitone.* One of the characters she presents, the anonymous *crowd,* is now shown in the brown fog of a winter dawn, shuffling, without hope or moral direction, over London Bridge to work. Someone suddenly confronts one of the crowd, and in the first of several hallucinatory passages, climaxed by one describing the approach to the Chapel Perilous in Part V, he asks if the buried corpse has begun to sprout—in other words, if there is any hope that the Vegetation God, that Christ, may arise and bring with him fertility to the land and freshness to the spirit. The title of this section, "The Burial of the Dead," is derived from this passage, and the quest is thus announced for the Holy Grail, for the fertility symbol, for the questions and answers which might heal or bring back to life the Fisher King and revitalize his Waste Land. *8: Starnbergersee:* a small resort lake near Munich where there is bathing, boating, dancing, etc.

10: *Hofgarten*: a public park in Munich with a zoo and many sidewalk cafés. 11: See Eliot's poem, "The Love Song of J. Alfred Prufrock": "I have measured out my life with coffee spoons." 12: "I am not a Russian, I stem from Lithuania, a true German." 20: When Eliot in his notes refers the reader to a specific sentence from which he quotes, the entire text from which it is taken will be found to be relevant and applicable to the main themes of *The Waste Land*. Lack of space forbids us extensive quotation, but the following passage, where God speaks to Ezekiel, may serve as an example: *"Son of man, I send thee to the children of Israel, to a rebellious nation that hath rebelled against me*: they and their fathers have *transgressed* against me, even unto this very day. For they are *impudent* children and *stiff-hearted*. . . . And they . . . yet *shall know that there hath been a prophet among them*. . . . And thou *shalt speak my words unto them*, whether they will hear, or whether they will forbear. . . . And when I looked, behold, a hand was sent unto me; *and lo, a roll of a book was therein* . . . and there was written therein *lamentations, and mourning, and woe."*—Ezekiel, II: 3-10. The parallelism is not only between the peoples of the ancient and the modern world who have turned from God, but also between the duties of the ancient prophet and those of the modern religious poet like Eliot who through his "roll of a book," "shall speak God's word." 23: "Remember now thy Creator in the days of thy youth, while the evil days come not . . . . [when] *fears shall be in the way*, and the almond tree shall flourish, and the *grasshopper shall be a burden*, and *desire shall fail* . . . or the *wheel* broken at the cistern. *Then shall the dust return to the earth* as it was . . . . Vanity of vanity saith the preacher; all is vanity . . . yea, he gave good heed, and sought out, and *set in order many proverbs* [a phrase which might serve as a motto for *The Waste Land*]. *The preacher sought to find out acceptable words*. . . . Let us hear the conclusion of the whole matter: Fear God, and keep his commandments: for this is the whole duty of man."—Ecclesiastes, XII: 1-13. The specific reference here is to the *cricket*, symbol of devastation; (see *cicada*, 1. 354 of *The Waste Land*, and *burden of the grasshopper*, p. 469). 25: Isaiah tells of the blessing of Christ's kingdom after the desolation: "Behold, a king shall reign in righteousness, and princes shall rule in judgment. And a man shall be as an hiding place from the wind, and a covert from the tempest; as *rivers of water in a dry place, as the shadow of a great rock in a weary land.*—Isaiah, XXXII: 1-2. 28-29: These images of morning and evening shadows are evocative of the coolness and nostalgia of those parts of day, in contrast to *fear in a handful of dust*, but they are also the first indications of the hallucinatory distortions brought on by thirst. 31-34: "The wind blows freshly toward the homeland; my Irish child, where are you waiting?"—Wagner, *Tristan und Isolde*, I, 5-8. Sung at the opening of the opera by a sailor who recalls the girl he has left behind. It is symbolic of the yearning and innocence of adolescent love which no longer exists in the Waste Land, but the main reference is to the lovers of the legend, the first of many to guilty, tragic, and "unholy love," (see 307, p. 490). 38-42: Leonard Unger in "T. S. Eliot's Rose Garden: A Persistent Theme," (*Southern Review*, Spring, 1942) traces in Eliot's poetry references to a childhood experience in a flower garden, which is basically sexual yet symbolical of the revelations of spiritual ecstasy; the climax of such imagery occurs in the opening section of "Burnt Norton." In referring to Dante's first meeting with Beatrice, Eliot writes in his essay on Dante, "In the first place, the type of sexual experience which Dante describes as occurring to him at the age of nine years is by no means impossible or unique. . . . It is not, I believe, meant as a description of what he *consciously* felt on his meeting with Beatrice, but rather as a description of what that meant on mature reflection upon it. The final cause is the attraction to God." See particularly Eliot's poem, "Dans Le Restaurant." The entrapped yet inhibited young man of this passage is the same one we meet in Eliot's "La Figlia Che Piange," where the girl is described with "Her hair over her arms and her arms full of flowers"; the young man in "Portrait of a Lady" who loses his self-possession "With the smell of hyacinths across the garden/ Recalling things that other people have desired"; the one awaited by the neurasthenic lady in Part III of *The Waste Land;* the same who becomes J. Alfred Prufrock. Lilacs, hyacinths, and primroses are all spring flowers, those whose dull roots are stirred with spring rain, *mixing memory and desire;* but, as we were told in Ecclesiastes, "desire shall fail." 39-40: In the last circle of the *Inferno* Dante finds himself in the presence of Satan amid such tremendous cold that he says, "I was neither living nor dead."—XXXIV, 25. 41: See *heart of light*, p. 462. Eliot's echo of Dante's *Paradiso* here confirms the religious meaning of the experience in the hyacinth garden. 42: As Tristan lies dying in Brittany, the look-out is asked if he sees any sign of Isolde's ship on the horizon, and he replies: "Empty and barren is the sea."—*Tristan und Isolde*, III, 24. Eliot has adroitly placed the experience in the garden between two references to the opera, the first a song of youthful love, before anything tragic has occurred, and the last a symbol of waste and death: even the water, the origin of life, is barren and empty. 43: *Madame Sosostris* (accent on the second syllable). Her *bad cold* subtly suggests that as a cheap prophet she is a bad poet. 46: *Author's Note:* "I am not familiar with the exact constitution of the Tarot pack of cards, from which I have obviously departed to suit my convenience. The Hanged Man, a member of the traditional pack, fits my purpose in two ways: because he is associated in my mind with the Hanged God of Frazer, and because I associate him with the hooded figure in the passage of the disciples to Emmaus in Part V. The Phoenician sailor and the Merchant appear later; also the 'crowds of people,' and Death by Water is executed in Part IV. The Man with Three Staves (an authentic member of the Tarot pack) I associate, quite arbitrarily, with the Fisher King himself."—*Collected Poems*. Of the Tarot, Miss Jessie Weston writes: "It is the name given to a pack of cards, seventy-eight in number, of which twenty-two are designated as the 'keys.' These cards are divided into four suits, which correspond with those of ordinary cards; they are: [1] Cup (Chalice, or Goblet)—Hearts; [2] Lance (Wand, or Sceptre) —Diamonds; [3] Sword—Spades; [4] Dish (Circles, or Pentangles, the form varies)—Clubs. To-day the Tarot has fallen somewhat into disre-

pute, being principally used for purposes of divination." Parallel designs were found in an Egyptian calendar "supposed to have been connected with the periodic rise and fall of the waters of the Nile. The
Tarot has also been connected with an ancient Chinese monument, traditionally erected in commemoration of the drying up of the waters
of the Deluge by Yao." 47: See Part IV of *The Waste Land*. Phlebas,
the drowned Phoenician Sailor, is representative of both the mercantile
genius of materialistic civilizations to which Eliot thematically refers
throughout the poem, and of the fertility gods like Tammuz and Adonis
who were torn to pieces and thrown into the sea. The Phoenicians were
the successors of the Cretans, and supreme in trade (1100-1000 B.C.).
The words *currants* in line 210 and *current* in line 315 links Phlebas
and Eugenides, the Smyrna merchant. 48: Phlebas-Eugenides is
further associated with Ferdinand, Prince of Naples, in Shakespeare's
The Tempest. Ferdinand weeps for his father who he thinks has
been drowned, and thus is identified and merged with the fertility god, much as Perceval and the Fisher King, or Christ and God
are aspects of the same identity. Like Perceval or Galahad, Ferdinand
is the lover pure in heart, and he and Miranda represent that unworldly
and innocent love which is no longer possible in the Waste Land. The
entire passage from Shakespeare is echoed throughout the poem. When
Ferdinand hears Ariel singing, he follows and says: "It sounds no more
and, sure, it waits upon/ Some God o' the island. Sitting on a bank/
Weeping again the king my father's wrack,/ This music crept by me
upon the waters . . . . (*Ariel Sings*) Full fathom five thy father lies;/
Of his bones are coral made;/ Those are pearls that were his eyes./
Nothing of him that doth fade/ But doth suffer a sea-change/ Into
something rich and strange." Thus the death of Ferdinand-Naples,
Perceval-Fisher King, Christ-God are referred to in such a way as to
suggest a baptismal sea-change into something rich and strange, by
which bones become coral and eyes become pearls, symbols of hope and
of salvation through baptism, of ultimate resurrection. 49-50: The profane and sacred aspects of womanhood are also merged. *Belladonna*:
On the other hand, she is the *Madonna*, the Mother-Lady, the Virgin,
the Immaculate One, the Madonna of the Rocks (which symbolize the
Church) as Da Vinci depicts her with the Christ child and the
young St. John the Baptist. Belladonna is also used as a cosmetic
for the eyes. (See *Lady*, p. 468). 51: *man with three staves*: This
man, arbitrarily associated by Eliot with the Fisher King, and an authentic member of the Tarot, may refer to the card of Three Scepters,
or Three Wands. It depicts a calm, stately person standing on a cliff's
edge looking at his ships of merchandise passing over the sea; three
staves are planted in the ground behind him. He represents enterprise,
commerce, trade, strength; the end of trouble, the suspension of adversity.
E. M. Stephenson in *T. S. Eliot and the Lay Reader* refers us to The
Fifth Tarot: "An Egyptian relic having relation to the triple Phallus
which represents the recovery of Osiris. It corresponds to the Idea of
Life, of animation." 51: *Wheel*: The Tenth Tarot, the Wheel of For-

tune, depicts Anubis in the form of a jackal clambering on one side, and Typhon in the form of a serpent on the other; above the Wheel is a sphinx-like figure holding a sword in one hand and a crown in the other. Anubis is the Egyptian God who conducts the dead to the judgment seat; Typhon is the spirit of Evil; sometimes one and sometimes the other is in the ascendant. The Wheel symbolizes Eternity, the Will of the Gods, Good or Bad Fortune, and is to be equated with the whirlpool of Part IV. 52: Eugenides, the Smyrna merchant of line 209, whose one eye hints at both evil and the profile view of a card. The mysterious burden he carries upon his back suggests Wordsworth's famous phrases from "Tintern Abbey": "the burthen of the mystery," "the heavy and the weary weight/ Of all this unintelligible world." Frazer tells of the satyr or silenus, Marsyas, who was famous for his flute playing. In his vanity he challenged Apollo, who tied him to a pine tree, flayed him alive, and cut him limb by limb. He is another type of fertility god, like Attis. In the Tarot he is hung head downward by one foot from a T-cross. His other foot is bent at right angles to the other and forms a cross. His face is usually serene, and he symbolizes Self-sacrifice, Devotion, Hope. 57: As her name suggests, *Mrs. Equitone* is an equitably toned lady of the "cultured" classes who cannot live without her daily horoscope. 60: In introducing the *crowds of people walking round in a ring*, Eliot refers us to Baudelaire's poem, "The Seven Old Men," which opens: "City swarming with people, city full of dreams." The poet then sees seven old men in a yellow fog, a vision of evil; he is shaken and horrified. 61: A time sequence is developed from this brown fog of a *winter dawn* to that of a *winter noon* of line 208 to the *evening hour* of line 220. 63: Eliot is pointing out the similarity between the hell of large cities and Dante's *Inferno*. Before he enters the Inferno, Dante reads over the Gate of Hell: "Through me is the way into the doleful city; through me the way into the eternal dolour; through me the way among the people lost . . . leave all hope, ye that enter."—*Inferno*, III, 1-9. He then sees a vast crowd of spirits running behind a flag in haste and confusion, urged on by furious wasps and hornets. These are the unhappy people who were never truly alive—who never awakened to take any part either in good or evil, to care for anything but themselves: "Heaven chased them forth to keep its beauty from impair; and the deep Hell receives them not, for the wicked would have some glory over them"—*Ibid.*, 40-42. Dante weeps for pity and says: "I should never have believed that death had undone so many."—*Ibid.*, 56-57. 64: Dante is brought to the first circle of the Inferno where he sees those spirits who lived without baptism or Christianity. He says, "Here was no plaint, that could be heard, except of sighs, which caused the eternal air to tremble."—*Ibid.*, IV, 25-7. Virgil, one of these, explains that "without hope we live in desire" of seeing God. This is another reference to desire, to the lost, and to the baptismal water of life in contrast to death by water, the empty and barren sea. 60-68: The crowd is going to work from Southwark across *London Bridge* which opens directly into *King William Street* leading to the Bank of England and Moorgate. "The main features of the part of the city proper to the East of the Bank is its gigantic business activity, and some old churches.

The direct route from the Bank to *London Bridge* is via *King William Street*, a wide and well-built thoroughfare leading to the South East. To the left, at the angle formed by this street and Lombard St., stands the Church of *St. Mary Woolnoth,* a building of some originality, erected by Nicholas Hawksmoor, a pupil of Wren, 1716-1727. The interior has 12 Corinthian columns and contains some good woodwork and banners of the Goldsmith Company. It was the only City church to remain intact throughout the air raids of 1940-45."—Muirhead, *Guide to London.* 68: *Author's Note:* "A phenomenon that I have often noticed."—*Collected Poems.* Eliot makes of this actual peculiarity a part of the frightening and weird atmosphere that surrounds the Chapel Perilous, for all references to various churches throughout *The Waste Land* are to the Chapel Perilous, finally reached in Part V. 69: The name *Stetson,* famous in haberdashery for many generations, is another link to mercantilism. 70: At the battle of Mylae (260 B.C.) the Romans gained their first naval victory over the Carthaginians, and captured or destroyed fifty vessels. 71: Part I derives its title from this passage. The corpse referred to in this delirious manner is the fertility god; Stetson is asked if there is any hope of resurrection. 74-75: A reference to another "unholy love" which occurs in *The White Devil* by John Webster, dramatist and contemporary of Shakespeare. At Rome the Duke of Brachiano and Vittoria Corombona have caused their wife and husband, respectively, to be murdered in order that nothing may impede their lust for one another. Flamineo, Vittoria's brother, acts as both their pimp and accomplice; he curses his mother, Cornelia, and his brother, Marcello, when both protest. Vittoria is brought to trial before her own brother, Francisco, Duke of Florence, and Monticelso, a Cardinal. She is called a whore, a "white devil," and is sentenced to a "place of penitent whores." After a scene of mutual suspicion, jealousy and quarreling, Brachiano contrives her escape; they fly to Padua, and marry. When Cornelia and Marcello try to come between Flamineo and his mistress, Zanche, Vittoria's Moorish maid, Flamineo curses his mother and later kills his brother in her presence. Lodovico, who has secretly worshipped Isabella, the former wife of Brachiano, poisons the helmet of Brachiano, who dies in great agony. Flamineo then demands from his sister some of the money left her by Brachiano's death, but she refuses. He suggests a suicide pact, and Vittoria and Zanche pretend to agree; he gives them the pistols, they shoot him, and then instead of shooting themselves, rush on him and trample him. He had, however, filled the pistols with blank cartridges, and is about to kill them for their treachery when Lodovico enters with accomplices and kills all three. In this play of sultry passion in which hardly a character is untainted, the mad Cornelia sings the following dirge when she buries Marcello: "Call for the robin red breast and the wren,/ Since o'er shady groves they hover,/ And with leaves and flowers do cover/ The friendless bodies of unburied men./ Call unto his funeral dole/ The ant, the field-mouse, and the mole,/ To rear him hillocks that shall keep him warm,/ And (when gay tombs are robbed) sustain no harm:/ But keep the wolf far thence, that's foe to man,/ For with his nails he'll dig them up again."—V, iv, 89-98. It will be noticed that Eliot has substituted (and capitalized) *Dog* for "wolf" and *friend* for "foe." It seems likely that the word thus capitalized refers to Sirius, the Dog-Star, and to the "periodic rise and fall of the waters of the Nile" which "brought fertility to the land." In *Adonis, Attis, Osiris,* Frazer tells how "Sirius, the brightest of all fixed stars, appeared at dawn in the east just before sunrise about the time of the summer solstice, and when the Nile began to rise." The reference, then, is to the possible "sprouting" of the dead corn god, to the resurrection of the fertility god; we see in what way the "Dog" is a "friend" to man, and the reasons for Eliot's substitution. 76: The reader, who has kept his detachment, and thought of himself as in no way involved in the disintegrations and evil of the Waste Land, is now dramatically implicated by being directly addressed through the concluding line of Baudelaire's poem which acts as his preface to *The Flowers of Evil.* Man is described sunk in sin and evil, brought to such Hell by the Devil who is Boredom, and the poem concludes: "It is Boredom! The eye fills with tears involuntarily./ He dreams of the scaffold while smoking his pipe./ You know him reader, this delicate monster./ *Hypocrite of a reader, my likeness, my brother!"*

Part II. A Game of Chess. Part II is divided sharply and dramatically into two sections, the first depicting the Waste Land of spirit in the upper classes, the second a similar waste in the lower classes. In verse rivaling the richness of texture and imagery of the Elizabethan and Romantic periods, a neurasthenic woman is described sitting before her vanity table. The senses are assaulted by a dazzling intermingling of light, color, odor, and sound: the flames of the seven-branched candelabra are simultaneously doubled and reflected in the mirror and the marble table-top, and reinforced by the glitter of jewels, until the atmosphere and the eye are splintered with light and colors of golden cupidons, jewels, flames, colored glass, green and orange flames, and the colored stone of the fireplace; the senses are drowned (ironic) in odors of unstoppered perfumes which are enhanced by the air that freshens from the window; the atmosphere is hazed with the smoke of flames fattened on the inflammable perfumed moisture of the air until the ceiling seems to stir. In this *desert* of the spirit the inviolate voice of the nightingale sings and is parodied by the world. The shuffle of footsteps is heard; all the room and its paintings seems to sway as in a drunken mirage, until the lady's hair spreads out in fiery points and glows into words: another of the many hallucinatory atmospheres which are part of the delirium of the Waste Land. All mention of liquid or water of any sort points to sterility, for even the perfumes are a mechanized modern product, are *synthetic;* the senses are *drowned* in odors, the burning wood is *sea*-wood; the dolphin, a fish symbol, *swims* in the colored marble in a sad light. The dialogue which follows between the neurasthenic, testy, infinitely bored lady living upon her nerves, and the Prufrockian young man paralyzed with bitterness and horror, yet without will to act, is in many ways similar to the situation of Eliot's earlier poem "Portrait of a Lady." Before the complete vacuity of their lives, the young man almost breaks out into a mad and jangling Shakespe*he*rian Rag (notice the spelling: Shakespeare, all the classics, all of tradition, have been cheapened and "jazzed up"); but when she does think of rushing down the street with her hair down in an incoherent rebellion against the ennui of their lives, he reminds himself and her, tightlipped, of the sick symbols of their frustrating amenities and their routined lives: the *hot water,* the *closed car,* the *game of chess,* the sleepless *waiting* for something to happen. The knock upon the door thus becomes more than the symbol of a social visit; it becomes the terror of time and destiny, merging finally into the HURRY UP PLEASE ITS TIME of the following section, reminding us of the un-redeemable time in which we waste our lives. On a literal level, the sentence is the reiterated request of a bartender in a London pub that his customers leave because it is closing time. A cockney girl is telling some companion about Lil and Albert and herself, a vulgar tale of sexual appetite, abortion, and denial of life: *What you get married for if you don't want children?* The appetites other than sexual are satisfied with what a pub might have to offer, or with a *hot gammon,* the "very good dinner" of "The Dry Salvages." Although this scene is in direct surface contrast to the preceding scene of the upper-class lady, the Waste Land of spirit is exactly the same. The entire scene may be compared to Eliot's "Sweeney Agonistes" where Doris, in reply to Sweeney's invitation to join him on a paradise isle where there is nothing but "birth and copulation and death," replies: "I'd be bored."

The contrast in style between these two sections may be paralleled exactly by every second section of each second movement of *Four Quartets.* In every instance the first section is rich in texture, orchestration, and imagery, and the meter or stanza is formal (in this particular section, mainly blank verse), whereas the second section is always a counterstatement in verse of almost prosaic laxity (in this instance the realism of dialect. 77-96: An elaborate pastiche of Shakespeare's *Antony and Cleopatra,* II, ii, 199-226, where Enobarbus, Antony's general, describes Cleopatra and her barge on the river Nile. Eliot is making a direct contrast between the enervated Prufrockian young man and the swash-buckling soldier, between the neurasthenic lady and the Queen of Egypt. But he is also reminding us that the love of Antony and Cleopatra was one of excess, that it ended in suicide and defeat, that it was an "unholy love." From the passage on the barge, Eliot has taken many details of color, odor, and sound; it begins: "The barge she sat in,/ like a burnished throne,/ Burn'd on the water; the poop was beaten gold." 77: The constellation Cassiopeia, which crudely resembles a chair, was named after a woman famous in mythology for her vanity, and condemned to eternity to watch her face in a mirror. The adjoining constellation is that of the seven-starred Pleiades, which may be paralleled to the seven-branched candelabra of the poem. See also The Revelation of St. John the Divine, 1, 12-20. 92: Another reference to Carthage, Rome, and unholy love. On his way to Italy, after the sack of Troy, where he is destined to found the Roman race, Aeneas tarries at Carthage where he and Dido, the Queen, fall in love. Warned by Jove to depart secretly, for Dido in her passion plots to restrain him, Aeneas sails under cover of night, and Dido casts herself on a funeral pyre, stabs herself, and dies. Eliot's reference is to the banquet which Dido gives in Aeneas' honor: *"dependent lychni laquearibus aureis/ incensi, et noctem flammis funalia vincunt,"* ("lighted lamps hang down

from the *fretted roof* of gold, and flaming torches drive out the night").
—*Aeneid*, I, 726-27. *94:* Copper flakes are sold commercially to be
thrown on log fires to color the flames. *98:* Milton, *Paradise Lost*, IV,
140. Reference to the first unholy love, that of Adam and Eve. Satan
views the Garden of Eden for the first time: "So on he fares, and to the
border comes/ Of Eden, where delicious Paradise,/ Now nearer, crowns
with her enclosure green,/ As with a rural mound, the champaign head/
Of a steep wilderness, whose hairy sides/ With thicket overgrown, grotesque and wild,/ Access deni'd; and overhead up grew/ Insuperable
height of loftiest shade,/ cedar, and pine, and fir, and branching palm,/
A *sylvan scene*, and as the ranks ascend/ Shade above shade, a
woody Theatre/ Of stateliest view." *99-103:* See Ovid, *Metamorphoses*,
VI, 412-674. Above the mantle of the fireplace is a painting of the
change of Philomela into a nightingale. Tereus, King of Thrace, married to Procne, rapes his wife's sister, Philomela, then cuts off her tongue.
In revenge, the sisters slaughter Itys, the young son of Tereus and
Procne, and feed him to Tereus. As he pursues them, the gods transform him into a hoopoe, Procne into a swallow, and Philomela into a
nightingale. This is not only another reference to unholy love, but
also (1) to the transformation of suffering into beauty: Philomela, violated in body, now sings with *inviolable voice*, and (2) to the eating
of human flesh, symbol of the Communion. (See *fed to satiety*, p. 468).
100: See line 205 of *The Waste Land*. *103:* Many Elizabethan songs
and poems were written about Philomela in which *jug* and *tereu* (the
name of the ravisher) denote her pitiful song. See John Lyly's "Alexander and Campaspe": "What bird so sings, yet does so wail?/ Oh, 'tis
the ravished nightingale,/ Jug, jug, jug, jug, tereu, she cries,/ And still
her woes at midnight rise." Because *the world pursues 'Jug Jug' to dirty
ears*, we are probably referred to the psychological symbol for the womb,
and thence to the degradation of the Holy Grail into the Jug, from holy
to unholy love. *103:* See line 204 of *The Waste Land*. *104:* The
other paintings on the wall are called *withered stumps of time* since
they also depict some violation. Ovid's description of Philomela's severed
tongue is in the convulsive mood of the rest of this scene: "The *mangled
root quivers*, while the severed tongue lies *palpitating* on the dark earth,
faintly murmuring; and, as the severed tail of a mangled snake is wont
to writhe, it *twitches convulsively*, and with its last dying movement it
seeks its mistress's feet." *115:* See line 195 of *The Waste Land*. *118:* In
John Webster's *The Devil's Law Case*, a Neopolitan nobleman, Contarino, is grievously wounded in a duel and lies on his death bed. He
makes out his will to Jolenta. Her brother, Romelio, in order to be assured
of the legacy, disguises himself, bribes the surgeons, then visits Contarino,
and stabs him. The blow, however, opens the wound, frees it from pus, and
thus saves his life. When the surgeons find him still breathing, one of them
says, "Is the wind in that doore still?" meaning, "Is he still alive?"—III, ii,
162. *113-123:* See 74-75, p. 481. In *The White Devil*, when Flamineo is
bound and about to be killed, his murderer asks, "What dost think on?"
Flamineo answers, "Nothing; of nothing: leave thy idle questions./ I
am in the way to study a long silence:/ To prate were idle. *I remember
nothing*./ There's nothing of so infinite vexation/ As man's own

thoughts."—V, vi, 203-07. In the same play, Brachiano, poisoned and delirious, sees many hideous visions. Vittoria says to him: "My lord, here's nothing," and he answers, "Nothing! rare! nothing! when I want money,/ Our treasury is empty, there is nothing."—V, iii, 106-08. The same negative echo is often heard in Webster's other great play, *The Duchess of Malfi*, especially in that scene where the Duchess is surrounded by madmen and where, to the query of her servant, "What think you of, madam?" she replies, "Of nothing;/ When I muse thus, I sleep."—IV, ii, 17-19. 125: See 48, p. 479. 126: See lines 35-41 of *The Waste Land*. It is as if the neurasthenic lady were once the girl in the hyacinth garden who now reminds him of an earlier time when he was even then *neither living nor dead*. 137: The title of Part II is derived from the play *Women Beware Women*, II, ii, by Thomas Middleton, an Elizabethan dramatist, who is also the author of *A Game at Chesse*. A young and beautiful Venetian noblewoman, Bianca, has been married beneath her to a Florentine clerk, Leantio, who, when he has to leave Florence on business, entrusts his wife to his mother's care. The Duke of Florence spies Bianca, becomes enamoured of her, and arranges with a friend, Livia, to seduce her. Livia invites the mother and Bianca to her home, and while she engages the mother in a game of chess, Bianca is shown about the house by another accomplice who soon leads her to the Duke. Middleton wrings all innuendo and double meaning out of the situation by arranging to have two games, that of chess and that of seduction, played on the stage simultaneously, one on the main stage and the other on the balcony of the Elizabethan stage. As Livia checkmates the mother, the Duke seduces Bianca. In his essay on Middleton, Eliot calls Bianca the "type of woman who is purely moved by vanity." 172: There are two ironic echoes here, the first from the popular folksong, "Good-night, ladies, we're going to leave you now," and the second from that scene in *Hamlet*, IV, v, 67-74, where the mad Ophelia is strewing flowers and singing snatches of bawdy songs: "I hope all will be well. We must be patient; *But I cannot but weep, to think they should lay him in the cold ground*. My brother shall know of it; and so I thank you for your good counsel. Come, my coach! *Good-night, ladies; good-night, ladies; good-night sweet ladies; good-night, good-night*." Notice the oblique reference to Part I, "The Burial of the Dead."

Part III. The Fire Sermon. Whereas in Part II the sterile love of an upper-class man and woman was depicted against a background of the great heroes and heroines of love, and that of the cockney lower-class against the pitiful and tragic story of Hamlet and Ophelia, in Part III are recounted, one after another, a series of middle-class sexual vulgarities. The Thames river is first shown in late autumn when the tent of foliage overbending it has broken and its leaves sink and clutch into the water (like the bodies of the sacrificed gods). Whatever nymphs of the mythological and happy past once inhabited these waters are now gone. If we are told that now in the cold weather there is no evidence of the debris which the modern descendants of the nymphs, the stenographers and white-collar girls, have left scattered about, it is only to be reminded, in terms of a puerile nostalgia, of the summer nights when they had left such evidence. The cold blast of time is now heard in the land, there are images of bone and rat, of fishing to no end, of a canal (a mechanized waterway), horns, motors, and reminders of Philomela's rape. We are then told of the vulgar affair of Sweeney and Mrs. Porter, of the unshaven Smyrna merchant Mr. Eugenides proposing a weekend in a second-rate water-front hotel, of a seduction scene between a pimply house agent's clerk and a bored typist. The music of the record which the typist plays on the gramophone after the seduction is over fades into the music heard in the various fishermen's pubs in Lower Thames street, and finally into the song of Wagner's three Rhine maidens now transformed into three Thames maidens who one after the other tell their story of indifferent seduction, of the trampled emotions and faded dreams of the hopeless. Out of this cauldron of unholy loves rise the warning voices of St. Augustine, of Buddha, and of Zechariah to preach a sermon of fire, to tell us that we are all burning in the unholy fires of our senses, of hell and purgatory. *176:* The sordidness of the contemporary scene is sharpened by the insertion, several times, of this refrain from Edmund Spenser's poem, "Prothalamion," which celebrates a marriage and its progress down the Thames. Eliot is contrasting the Spenserian nymphs in their bridal array with the modern nymphs and their *testimony of summer nights.* *182:* Psalms cxxxvii, in which the Hebrews, uprooted from their homes in Palestine, tell of their exile in Babylon: *"By the rivers of Babylon, there we sat down, yea, we wept, when we remembered Zion . . . How shall we sing the Lord's song in a strange land?"* This is the plight of a poet-prophet such as Eliot. The substitution of *Leman,* the Swiss name for Lake Geneva, reminds us also of the League of Nations, of the international political scene. *185:* Andrew Marvell in "To His Coy Mistress" tells his mistress that if they were granted time enough he would adore every part of her for centuries: *"But at my back I always hear/ Time's winged chariot hurrying near,/ And yonder all before us lie/ Deserts of vast eternity."* The wit, fantasy, and vitality in this poem is in contrast to all the neurotic, cheap, or bored love affairs recounted in this section. *189-90:* There is no hope for good fishing, for life and salvation, in a land where the river has become a canal and the chapel a gashouse. *191-92:* See 48, p. 479. Although the word "father" from the phrase in *The Tempest,* "the king my father's wrack," has here been altered by Eliot to *brother* and may simply indicate that the Fisher-King's fate extends to all of humanity, it is interesting to note that Miss Weston quotes one version of the Perceval story which introduces a Dead Knight who is "brother of the King, whose death by treachery has plunged the land in misery, and been the direct cause of the self-wounding of the King." And of course, Antonio, the *brother* of Prospero in *The Tempest,* has usurped the land and exiled the true King. Throughout these passages we are reminded of the Fisher King's death or illness, the Waste Land itself, and the fruitless quest. *196-98:* In his masque, *The Parliament of Bees,* John Day (1574-1640?) satirizes the "humours" of his age in the characters of bees: the quack, the braggard, the spendthrift, the lover, etc. When Polygamus, the Plush Bee, hears about the new brightly-colored ceiling on his neighbor's hive, he proclaims that he will outdo it: "Overhead/ A roof of woods and forests I'll have spread,/ Trees growing downwards, full of fallow-deer;/ When of a sudden, listening, you shall hear/ *A noise of horns and hunting, which shall bring/ Actaeon to Diana in the spring,/ Where all shall see her naked skin.*" *198:* See Eliot's poems, "Sweeney Agonistes," "Sweeney Among the Nightingales," "Sweeney Erect," and "Mr. Eliot's Sunday Morning Service." See also George Dibdin Pitt's *Sweeney Todd, The Demon Barber of Fleet Street: A Legendary Drama in Five Acts,* (Gerald Howe, London, 1928). There is a copy in the New York Public Library. *199-201: Author's Note:* "I do not know the origin of the ballad from which these lines are taken: it was reported to me from Sydney, Australia."—*Collected Poems.* (1) An American ballad entitled "Little Red Wing" pathetically tells of an Indian maid who waits for her warrior to return from war (but he has been killed in battle). The chorus begins: "Oh, the moon shines bright on Pretty Red Wing." (2) During World War I there was a ballad sung by the Anzacs, and later brought to Australia, about a brothel in Cairo operated by a Mrs. Porter and which burned down. In the original ballad, the parts washed by Mrs. Porter and her daughter were private. (3) We are ironically reminded of the woman of sin who washed the feet of Jesus with her tears and wiped them with her hair: (see Luke, VIII: 36-38). (4) In Wagner's *Parsifal,* the seductress Kundry, who scorned Christ on the Cross, washes the feet of Parsifal that he may enter the castle clean and pure. *202:* Last line of the sonnet "Parsifal" by Paul Verlaine. This variant of the Grail Quest, and that of Wagner's opera, tells of the king, Amfortas, who has been appointed keeper of the Grail, the vessel which caught the blood of crucified Jesus. Contrary to his solemn obligation to refrain from the love of women, he succumbs to Kundry, and is wounded with his own lance by the enchanter Klingsor. (Tradition has it that the wound is on the thigh and symbolizes the King's impotence and his land's consequent infertility.) The lance is that which pierced the side of Christ on the Cross. Amfortas suffers but cannot die nor be healed until a "guile-less fool" brings back the lance and touches the wound with it. Klingsor creates a magic garden and peoples it with beautiful maidens that they may seduce the knights of the Grail, but Parsifal resists them. Klingsor hurls the holy lance at Parsifal, but it remains suspended above his head. Parsifal seizes the lance, makes the sign of the cross, and at once Klingsor and his magic gardens disappear. After his feet have been washed by Kundry, he enters the Grail castle where Amfortas unveils the Grail, and touches the wounds of the King with the point of the holy lance. The King is healed, Kundry dies redeemed, and a dove descends from heaven. A literal translation of Verlaine's sonnet follows: "Parsifal has overcome the Maidens, their pretty babble and distracting lust—and his virgin boy's desire for the Flesh which tempts him to love the delicate breasts and that pretty babble. He has overcome the beautiful Woman of subtle heart, displaying her cool arms and her seductive throat; he has overcome Hell, and returns beneath his tent with a heavy trophy on his youthful arm, bearing the lance that pierced the supreme Side! He has healed the king, now he himself is king and priest of the essential very holy Treasure. In a robe of gold he adores,

glory and symbol, the pure cup where the true blood is resplendent.—
And, O those children's voices chanting in the dome!" 203-06: See 99-
103 and 103, p. 484. 205: See l. 100 of *The Waste Land.* 207: See 60,
p. 480. 209: See 52, p. 480. 211: *Author's Note:* "The currants were
quoted at a price 'carriage and insurance free to London'; and the Bill
of Lading, etc. were to be handed to the buyer upon payment of the
slight draft."—*Collected Poems.* Eliot was once a bank clerk. 213: See
258, p. 489. 218: *Author's Note:* "Tiresias, although a mere spectator
and not indeed a 'character,' is yet the most important personage in the
poem, uniting all the rest. Just as the one-eyed merchant, seller of currants, melts into the Phoenician Sailor, and the latter is not wholly distinct from Ferdinand Prince of Naples, so all the women are one woman,
and the two sexes meet in Tiresias. What Tiresias *sees,* in fact, is the
substance of the poem. The whole passage from Ovid is of great anthropological interest."—*Ibid.* Eliot then quotes the Latin text (*Metamorphoses* III, 316-338), of which the following is a translation: "While these
events according to the laws of destiny occurred, and while the child, the
twice-born Bacchus, in his cradle lay, 'tis told that Jupiter, a careless
hour, indulged too freely in the nectar cup; and having laid aside all
weighty cares, jested with Juno as she idled by. Freely the God began:
'Who doubts the truth? The female pleasure is a great delight, much
greater than the pleasure of a male.' Juno denied it; wherefore it was
agreed to ask Tiresias to declare the truth, than whom none knew both
male and female joys: for wandering in a green wood he had seen two
serpents coupling; and he took his staff and sharply struck them, till
they broke and fled. 'Tis marvelous, that instant he became a woman
from a man, and so remained while seven autumns passed. When eight
were told, again he saw them in their former plight; and thus he spoke:
'Since such a power was wrought, by one stroke of a staff my sex was
changed—again I strike!' And even as he struck the same two snakes,
his former sex returned; his manhood was restored. As both agreed to
choose him umpire of the sportive strife, he gave decision in support of
Jove; from this the disappointment Juno felt surpassed all reason, and
enraged, decreed eternal night should seal Tiresias' eyes,—Immortal
deities may never turn decrees and deeds of other Gods to naught, but
Jove, to recompense his loss of sight, endowed him with the gift of
prophecy." Tiresias stands in the exact center of the poem like a lighthouse casting its penetrating beams in all directions and seeing everywhere exactly that sordid waste of life which the seduction of the typist
by the small house agent's clerk symbolizes. 221: *Author's Note:* "This
may not appear as exact as Sappho's lines, but I had in mind the 'long-
shore' or 'dory' fisherman who returns at nightfall."—*Collected Poems.*
Sappho's lines to Hesperus, the Evening Star, were probably composed for
the wedding feast which preceded the ritual of conducting the bride to the
bridal chamber, and are thus in ironic contrast with the affair of the typist
and clerk: "Thou, Hesper, bringest homeward all/ That radiant dawn sped
far and wide,/ The sheep to fold, the goat to stall,/ The children to
their mother's side."—Trans. by Sir Rennell Rodd. See also R. L. Steven-
son's "Requiem": "Home is the sailor, home from the sea,/ And the
hunter home from the hill." 224: The typist's drying underthings spread

perilously in the sunset out of the *window* suggest a parody of the lines from Keats' "Ode to The Nightingale" which have often been called the summation of Romantic imagery: "Charmed magic *casements* opening on the foam/ Of *perilous* seas in faery lands forlorn." *231: Carbuncular*: pimply. *234: Bradford*: A manufacturing city which produced many of the *nouveaux riches,* who suddenly had money but neither culture nor manners. *245-46*: Tiresias lived for many generations in Thebes where he was often consulted in the marketplace below the walls. He was killed when Thebes was destroyed by war, but still retained his prophetic power in Hades where he was visited by Ulysses. *253*: In Chapter XXIV, "Fresh Calamities," of Oliver Goldsmith's *The Vicar of Wakefield,* the Vicar and his family are picnicking on those same melancholy grounds where Olivia, his daughter, first met her vile seducer. "Her mother, too, upon this occasion, felt a pleasing distress, and wept, and loved her daughter as before. 'Do my pretty Olivia,' cried she, 'let us have that little melancholy air your papa was so fond of.' . . . She complied in a manner so exquisitely pathetic as moved us." Olivia sings: "*When lovely woman stoops to folly*/ And finds too late that men betray,/ What charm can soothe her melancholy,/ What art can wash her guilt away?/ The only art her guilt to cover,/ To hide her shame from every eye,/ To give repentance to her lover/ And wring his bosom— is to die." But the modern typist puts a record on the gramophone. *257*: See *48*, p. *479. 258*: The *Strand,* parallel to the Thames, flows into Fleet Street, up Ludgate Hill, beyond St. Paul's Cathedral and into *Cannon Street* which is traversed by *Queen Victoria Street* as it cuts up from the Victoria embankment along the river, and ends at the Bank of England above London Bridge. *260-65: Lower Thames Street,* along the riverbank, is narrow and congested, and redolent of fish from end to end. *264*: Near London Bridge, to the right, is the church of St. Magnus the Martyr, rebuilt by Wren in 1676. The steeple, 185 ft. high, with its lantern, cupola, and flèche, one of Wren's masterpieces, was not completed till 1705. *Author's Note*: "The interior of St. Magnus Martyr is to my mind one of the finest among Wren's interiors. See *The Proposed Demolition of Nineteen City Churches*: (P. S. King & Son, Ltd.)."—*Collected Poems. 266*: *Author's Note*: "The Song of the (three) Thames-daughters begins here. From line 292 to 306 inclusive they speak in turn. V. *Götterdämmerung,* III, i: the Rhine-daughters."—*Ibid.* In the third act of Wagner's *Twilight of the Gods,* the three Rhine-daughters bewail the loss of the beauty of the Rhine caused by the theft of their gold, and beseech Siegfried to return the golden ring to them. *275-76: Greenwich* is a borough of London on the South side of the Thames, opposite of which is the *Isle of Dogs,* a peninsula commonly supposed to derive its name from the kennels belonging to Greenwich Palace. *277*: The refrain sung by the Rhine-daughters in *Götterdämmerung. 279*: In *The Reign of Elizabeth,* I, iv, J. A. Froude quotes many letters from Bishop De Quadra, first ambassador of Philip of Spain to the court of Elizabeth, recounting the scandal of the Queen's affair with Lord Robert Leicester— who was later under suspicion of having caused the murder of his wife in order that nothing might stand in the way of his marriage to the Queen. In a letter of June 30, 1561, De Quadra wrote: "In the afternoon we were in a barge, watching the games on the river. She was alone with the Lord Robert and myself on the poop, when they began to talk nonsense and went so far that Lord Robert at last said, as I was on the spot there was no reason why they should not be married if the Queen pleased. She said that perhaps I did not understand sufficient English. I let them trifle in this way for a time and then I said gravely to them both, that if they would be guided by me they would shake off the tyranny of those men who were oppressing the realm and them; they would restore religion and good order; and they could then marry when they pleased—and gladly would I be the priest to unite them." Eliot implies that, beneath the glitter of court pomp, such an affair in a courtly barge (a reminder of Cleopatra) is no different from that of the girl from the middle classes who allows herself to be seduced on the floor of a narrow canoe or at Moorgate. 293-300: *Highbury* is a middle-class residential district in the new section of London near Hampstead Heath. The royal borough of *Richmond* is a residential suburb and boating center in the west environs of London with a park eight miles in circumference, and is a favorite summer resort. *Kew* is a village adjoining Richmond and famous for its Kew or Royal Botanical Gardens. *Moorgate* is a slum area of London above London Bridge and beyond the Bank of England. *Margate,* on the Thames estuary, is a popular seaside resort. 293-94: In the *Purgatorio*, Dante comes upon those who were violently slain, who repented and made their peace with God at the last moment. He promises to bear news of them to their friends on earth. Among these is La Pia: one of the legends concerning her says that she came of a Sienese family and was put to death by her husband, either for jealousy or love for another woman, in the Sienese Maremma. She thus addresses Dante: "Remember me, who am La Pia: Siena made me, Maremma unmade me: 'tis known to him who, first plighting troth, has wedded me with his gem."—V, 133-36. 307: Eliot quotes the opening sentence of St. Augustine's *Confessions*, III, i: "To Carthage then I came, where a cauldron of unholy loves sang about mine ears." The text continues: "I was not in love as yet, yet I loved to be in love and with a more secret kind of want. . . . security I hated and that way too that had no snares in it, and all because I had a famine within me, even of that inward food (thyself, O God). . . . I defiled therefore the spring of friendship with the filth of uncleanliness, and I besullied the purity of it with the hell of lustfulness. . . . I was with much joy bound with sorrow-bringing embracements, even that I might be scourged with the iron burning rods of jealousy, and suspicions, and fears, and angers, and brawls." These confessions of Augustine's profligate youth bring to a climax the "cauldron of unholy loves" which Eliot has depicted or referred to in Parts II and III. 308: *Author's Note*: "The complete text of Buddha's Fire Sermon (which corresponds in importance to the Sermon on the Mount) from which these words are taken, will be found translated in the late Henry Clarke Warren's *Buddhism in Translation* (Harvard Oriental Series [Vol. III]). Mr. Warren was one of the great pioneers of Buddhist studies in the Occident."—*Collected Poems*. Buddha addresses his disciples on Gayā Head: "All things, O priests, are on fire. And what, O priests, are all these things which are on fire? The eye, O priests, is on fire; forms are on fire; eye-consciousness is on fire; impressions received by the eye are on fire; and whatever sensation, pleasant, unpleasant, or indifferent, originates in dependence on impressions received by the eye, that also is on fire. And with what are these on fire? With the fire of passion, say I, with the fire of hatred, with the fire of infatuation; with birth, old age, death, sorrow, lamentation, misery, grief, and despair are they on fire. The ear is on fire; sounds are on fire; . . . the nose is on fire; odors are on fire; . . . the tongue is on fire; tastes are on fire; . . . the body is on fire; things tangible are on fire." The learned and noble disciple, Buddha concludes, perceives this and therefore conceives an aversion for everything known through the mind or the senses. "And in conceiving this aversion, he becomes divested of passion, and by the absence of passion he becomes free, and when he is free he becomes aware that he is free; and he knows that rebirth is exhausted, that he has lived the holy life, that he had done what it behooved him to do, and that he is no more for this world. Now while this exposition was being delivered, the minds of the thousand priests became free from attachment and delivered from the depravities." 307-08: *Author's Note*: "The collocation of these two representatives of eastern and western asceticism, as the culmination of this part of the poem is not an accident."—*Collected Poems. 309*: "And he showed me Joshua the high priest standing before the angel of the Lord, and Satan standing at his right hand to resist him. And the Lord said unto Satan, The Lord rebuke thee, O Satan; even the Lord that hath chosen Jerusalem rebuke thee: is not this *a brand plucked out of the fire?"*— Zechariah, III: 1-2. Joshua typifies the restoration of the church. Eliot has given many portrayals of humanity without ethical, aesthetic or religious standards burning in an Inferno of lust and the senses. We are reminded, however, that flame purifies as well as destroys, that the sinner may cry out of purgatorial fires to God for salvation. (See Amos IV).

Like the third movement of a quartet, this section has been an elaboration on the theme of unholy loves, reaching its climax in the vision of Tiresias and the warnings of St. Augustine, Buddha, and Zechariah. Notice how the metrical structure is varied to parallel the subject matter of each section; the wave-like undulation of the barges on the Thames is underlined by the short, mainly two-stressed lines, and the mechanically metered and rimed section of the typist's seduction is reminiscent of the movement and form of Augustan couplets.

Part IV. Death by Water. (See l. 55 of *The Waste Land.*) Death by fire and death by water are dramatically and symbolically juxtaposed. The womb of life has become its tomb: "Empty and barren is the sea." This elegy fulfills the need for the lyrical short fourth movement of the Beethoven quartet structure, the calm before the thunder. 312: See 47, p. 479. 315: *current*: (1) "water-current," (see *48*, p. 479); (2) "raisins," (see l. 210 of *The Waste Land*); (3) "current of exchange." 318, 320: *whirlpool, wheel*: See 51 *Wheel*, p. 479.

Part V. What the Thunder Said: Author's Note: "In the first part of Part V three themes are employed: the journey to Emmaus, the approach to the Chapel Perilous (see Miss Weston's book) and the present decay of eastern Europe."—*Collected Poems*. This section is composed of dramatic portrayals of the crucifixion of Christ, the delirium and hallucination contingent on the sterility of the land, the disbelief in any possible hope of resurrection and salvation when despair is deepest just before Christ's resurrection, the sight of the Holy Grail in the Chapel Perilous, the fall of rain, the voice of God speaking from the thunder, and a final reminder of our fragmentary lives. It begins with the mocking and betrayal of Christ by the mob, his agony before the silence of God in the Garden of Gethsemene, the imprecations of the mob before the prison and palace of Herod and Pilate, and the earthquake and thunder heard at his crucifixion on Mount Calvary. The sterility of the land is now extreme; hallucinations and distortions arise as to one stumbling and dying of thirst in the desert: this is invoked not only by the imagery but also by the winding repetition of such words as *rock,* and *water,* until the movement becomes highly concentrated and intensified, and is climaxed by the hallucination of the sound of water in the song of the thrush. We are now beset with the delirious mirage of always seeing a ghostly third person (Christ, who has arisen, but who is not recognized in a godless land), with the mirage of godless nations lamenting as their civilizations explode about them. Finally, as the delirious and tempted Knight approaches the Chapel Perilous, the mind almost gives way, there are scenes of fantastic madness in which the world is turned upside down, the graves are tumbled, and the chapel seems empty and abandoned. Suddenly the cock crows, dispelling fear and illusions, the rain *does* begin to fall, and God speaks out of the thunder to give us disciplines for living: Give, Sympathize, Control, (*"Datta, Dayadhvam, Damyata"*). The first injunction is to give of ourselves in self-surrender and self-sacrifice, but as Eliot says in "East Coker" we are filled with the "fear of possession,/ Of belonging to one another, or to others, or to God." If, in an awful moment, we do dare to give of ourselves, we spend the rest of our lives trying to retract this daring, erasing it from our obituaries, leaving no memento of it on our tombstones or record of it in our last will and testament. And how can we learn to "Sympathize," to forget ourselves by immersing ourselves in the problems of others, for always we are locked up in the prison of our own egos and personalities, unable to leave it except for those moments of aethereal illumination which may relieve even such an arch-individualist as Coriolanus. If we can learn to give of ourselves and to live in sympathetic identification with others, perhaps we may also learn the art of self-control and thereby prepare ourselves to take on the most difficult of responsibilities: that of giving directions ourselves, of controlling our destinies and perhaps those of others, as an expert helmsman controls a ship. This is the vision seen in the midst of the Waste Land by the pure in heart, by Parsifal; by which the Fisher King may be healed, and by which his land and people may be brought to prosperity. But we are reminded that the Waste Land is still about us, that the vision and its application are to be striven for time and again in a land which is falling apart in broken images, without tradition, a bundle of fragments. Amid all this catastrophe, *there is only the trying* ("East Coker"), the fishing in an arid land, the attempt to put land and life in order. The poet tries to use as props against the ruins of modern civilization such fragments from the past as may help him form a mythology by which to live, based on the three disciplines, Give, Sympathize, Control, so that he may seek that peace that passeth understanding. 322-330: See Luke, xxii-xxiii. 328-329: See ll. 39-40, 63 of *The Waste Land*. Also the words of the angels to the women who came to anoint the body of Christ in the sepulchre: "Why seek ye the living among the dead? He is not here, but is risen." —Luke, xxiv, 5-6. 354: See l. 23 of *The Waste Land*; also 23, p. 477. 357: *Author's Note*: "This is *Turdus aonalaschkae pallasii* the hermit-thrush which I have heard in Quebec County. Chapman says (*Handbook of Birds of Eastern North America*) 'it is most at home in secluded woodland and thickety retreats. . . . Its notes are not remarkable for variety or volume, but in purity and sweetness of tone and exquisite modulation they are unequalled.' Its 'water-dripping song' is justly celebrated."—*Collected Poems*. 360: *Author's Note*: "The following lines were stimulated by an account of one of the Antarctic expeditions (I forget which, but I think one of Shackleton's): it was related that the party of explorers, at the extremity of their strength, had the constant delusion that there was *one more member* than could actually be counted."—*Ibid*. The twenty-fourth chapter of Luke is also relevant, especially that account which tells how Jesus after his resurrection accompanies two of his disciples on the road to Emmaus; but since they did not truly believe in their hearts that he would arise, they did not recognize him. Eliot not only refers us to the resurrection of the fertility god, but also to the fact that this is not a reality for the people of the Waste Land until suffering and repentence brings them to true vision. (See Eliot's note, 46, p. 478). 367-77: Eliot quotes in German from *Blick ins Chaos* ("*A Glimpse into Chaos*") of Hermann Hesse, the 1946 recipient of the Nobel Prize for Literature. A translation by Agnes Eisenberger reads: "Already half of Europe, already at least half of Eastern Europe is on the way to Chaos, driving drunken in sacred folly along the edge of the abyss and, drunken, singing hymn-like songs as Dmitri Karamasoff sang [in Dostoevski's *The Brothers Karamasov*]. Offended by these songs the burgher laughs, while the saint and seer listen to them with tears." 373: *Reforms* is used ironically, for the city is formed and reformed architecturally and religiously in a cycle of rising and falling cultures. 377: See ll. 60 and 207 of *The Waste Land*; also 60, p. 480. 378-85: climax of the hallucinatory passages; see especially lines 104-10 of *The Waste Land*. 385: This strongly suggests the voice of St. John the Baptist, in Oscar Wilde's *Salome*, calling out of the empty cistern in which he had been imprisoned, foretelling the doom of Herodiade and the coming of Christ. 389: Many of the details surrounding the *empty chapel* and the approach to it are taken from the chapter entitled, "The Perilous Chapel," in Miss Weston's book. The Hero "meets with strange and terrifying adventures in a mysterious Chapel." Here we find the moonlight, the open door of the Chapel, strange and threatening noises, a great storm, struggles of the Hero with a Black Hand and the Devil, and finally reference to the Perilous Cemetery in which three thousand slain knights of the Grail Quest have been buried. Miss Weston interprets the symbolism thus (the italics are hers): "*For this is the story of an initiation* (or perhaps it would be better to say the test of fitness for an initiation) *carried out on the astral plane, and reacting with fatal results upon the physical.* . . . The Mystery ritual comprised a double initiation, the Lower, into the mysteries of generation *i.e.*, of physical life; the higher, into the Spiritual Divine Life, where man is made one with God. . . . The tradition of the Perilous Chapel . . . was a reminiscence of the test for this lower initiation." 392-93: According to legend all ghosts or evil spirits are forced to depart on the crowing of a cock; see *Hamlet*, I, i, 157-164. We are also reminded of the cock who crew on the third denial of Christ by Peter; see Luke, xxii: 31-62. 394-98: See Miss Weston's reference to the freeing of the waters in India, p. 474. 400: *Author's Note*: "'Datta, dayadhvam, damyata' (Give, sympathize, control). The fable of the meaning of the Thunder is found in the *Brihadaranyaka-Upanishad*, 5, i. A translation is found in Deussen's *Sechzig Upanishads des Veda*, p. 489."—*Collected Poems*. A translation from the German by Agnes Eisenberger is as follows: "Three types of the sons of Prajapati lived with their father as students of Brahmin: gods, men, and demons. After they had lived with him as students of Brahmin, the gods said: 'Speak to us, O Lord.' And he uttered the one syllable, 'DA.' 'Have you understood?' he asked. 'We have understood,' they replied. 'You have told us "Damyata," that we should control ourselves.' 'Yes,' he said, 'you have understood.' Then the men said to him: 'Speak to us, O Lord!' And he uttered the one syllable: 'DA.' 'Have you understood?' he said. 'We have understood,' they said. 'You told us "Datta," that we should give alms.' 'Yes,' he said, 'you have understood.' Then the demons spoke to him: 'Speak to us, O Lord.' Then he uttered for them also the one syllable: 'DA.' 'Have you understood?' he said. 'You have told us "Dayadhvam," that we should have compassion.' 'Yes,' he said, 'you have understood.' This is what the divine voice, The Thunder, repeats when he says: DA, DA, DA: 'Control yourselves. Give alms. Be Compassionate.' Therefore one should practice these three things: Self-control, Alms-giving, and Compassion." Alms-giving is transformed by Eliot to a subjective self-giving; and *Damyata* is used by him not only to mean the subduing or control of self, but also that of others. 408: See 74-75, p. 481. After both his sister and his mistress shoot at him with pistols which he had previously loaded with blanks, Flamineo rails against women (V, vi, 155-59): "O men/ That lie upon your death-beds, and are haunted/ With howling wives, ne'er trust them! they'll remarry/ Ere the worm pierce your winding-sheet, ere the spider/ Make a thin curtain for your epitaphs." 412: *Author's Note*: "[See] F. H. Bradley, *Appearance and Reality*, p. 346. 'My external sensations are no less private to myself than are my thoughts or feelings. In either case my experience falls within my own circle, a circle closed on the outside; and, with all its elements alike, every sphere is opaque to the others which surround it. . . In brief, regarded as an existence which appears in a soul, the whole world for each is peculiar and private to that soul.'"—*Collected Poems*. See also Dante's *Inferno*, XXXIII, 46-47: In the ninth and last circle of Hell, Dante finds Count Ugolino and Archbishop Ruggieri frozen in the ice together in one pit, Ugolino eternally doomed to gnaw in hunger upon the head of Ruggieri. A note to the Carlyle-Wicksteed translation explains: "In 1288 the Guelfs were paramount in Pisa, but they were divided into two parties, led by Ugolino della Gherardesca and his grandson, Nino de' Visconti, respectively. The head of the Ghibellines was the Archbishop of the city, Ruggieri degli Ubaldini. In order to obtain supreme authority, Ugolino intrigued with Ruggieri, and succeeded in expelling Nino. He was, however, in his turn betrayed by the Archbishop who, seeing that the Guelfs were weakened, had Ugolino and four of his sons and grandsons imprisoned. When Guido of Montefeltro took command of the Pisan forces in March of the following year, 1289, the keys of the prison were thrown into the river and the captives left to starve." Eliot is referring us to the lines spoken by Ugolino from which he has taken the symbolism of key and prison: "And now below I heard the outlet of the horrible tower locked up." *417:* The story of Coriolanus is that of pride and self-interest. Because of his pride, and the ingratitude of the citizens, he was exiled from Rome. In rage, he joined an enemy, the Volscians, and attacked Rome to her very gates, but finally spared the city on the persuasion of his wife and son. He was now a traitor both to the Volscians and to Rome. See Eliot's poem "Coriolan," Shakespeare's *Coriolanus,* or Plutarch's *Coriolanus.* The tale of Coriolanus and that of Ugolino are told under the directive "sympathize" to show how much we are caught in the prison of our ego and self-interest. *424-25:* See *189-90,* p. 486; on the Fisher King, p. 474. *427:* A child's nursery rhyme (notice also reference to key and prison): "London bridge is falling down, falling down, falling down,/ London bridge is falling down, my fair lady./ Take the key and lock her up, lock her up, lock her up,/ Take the key and lock her up, my fair lady." *428:* In the topmost circle of purgatory, Arnaut Daniel, master of the obscure style in poetry (*trobas clus*) addresses Dante from the refining flames in lines which Eliot has used many times in his poetry: "'I am Arnaut that weep and go a-singing; in thought I see my past madness, and I see with joy the day which I await before me. Now I pray you, by that Goodness which guideth you to the summit of the stairway, be mindful in due time of my pain.' Then he hid him in the fire which refines them."—*Purgatorio,* XXVI, 142-48. Daniel looks forward to that day when his sins shall be completely purged in the refining fires of purgatory. The stairway is composed of those purgatorial circles which encircle the mount of purgatory and which lead to the Garden of Eden at its summit from which begins the ascent through the heavenly spheres to the final Goodness, to God. The stairway may also be that greater one beginning with the lowest circle in the Inferno and terminating in the blinding light of God that Dante sees in the center of the mystical Rose. In Eliot's poetry this circling stairway becomes the torturous and winding way of the soul's journey to a mystical union with God. (See also *figure of the ten stairs,* p. 464; *stair,* p. 469; *Sovegna vos,* p. 470; *il miglior fabbro,* p. 475). *429:* (1) The "Pervigilium Veneris," ("The Eve of St. Venus") a medieval poem of uncertain date and authorship, tells how all nature rejoices on the night of Venus, even the nightingale. The last two stanzas read: "Now hoarse-mouthed swans crash trumpeting over the pools; the maid of Tereus makes descant under the poplar shade, that you would think tunes of love issued thrilling from her mouth, and not a sister's complaint of a barbarous lord. Tomorrow shall be love for the loveless and for the lover tomorrow shall be love. She sings, we are mute: when is my spring coming? *when shall I be as the swallow,* that I may cease to be voiceless? I have lost the Muse in silence, nor does Apollo regard me." Eliot is also referring us to the plight of the modern poet. (2) See Tennyson's love song in *The Princess* beginning: "O Swallow, Swallow, flying, flying South." (3) See Swinburne's "Itylus," which begins: "Swallow, my sister, O sister swallow." The references are to innocent and budding love in spring which seems no longer possible in the modern world or to the poet who is aware like Philomela, that he must sing out of tragedy and cannot, like the swallow, forget. (4) The swallow is also the bird in Christian tradition that hovered over the Cross crying: "Console! Console!" 430: The second line of Gerard de Nerval's sonnet entitled "El Desdichado" ("The Unfortunate One"), one of a group called *The Chimeras.* The reference is to another desolate cry of the poet, to the knight in the Chapel Perilous: "I am the one from the depths, the bereaved, the unconsoled, *the Prince of Acquitaine in the ruined tower;* my only star is dead—and my starry lute bears the black sun of melancholy. In the night of the tomb, O you who have consoled me, give me back Pausilippo and the Italian sea, the flower that so delighted my desolate heart, and the trellis where the rose mingles with the vine. Am I cupid or Phoebus, Lusignan or Byron? My brow is red still from the kiss of the queen: I have dreamed in the grotto where the siren swims. . . . And twice I have, as conqueror, crossed the Acheron: now and then combining on the lyre of Orpheus the sighs of the saint and the fairy's cries." There is a Tarot card entitled "The Tower Struck by Lightning." 431: The entire poem may very well be composed of fragments which the poet has put together as a prop on which he leans for comfort and support and which he shores against his ruins. These are the *broken images* of line 22; compare Eliot's line with the opening of Ezra Pound's eighth *Canto:* "These fragments you have shelved (shored)." 432: The subtitle of Thomas Kyd's (1558-1594) *The Spanish Tragedy,* is *Hieronymo's mad againe.* Hieronymo is counsellor to the King of Spain. His son, Horatio, and the King's daughter, Bellimperia, fall in love. The Prince of Portugal, however, Balthazar, is also in love with Bellimperia, and together with the King's nephew, Lorenzo, murders Horatio. Horatio's mother, mad with grief, kills herself; Hieronymo is driven into periods of insanity, but discovers who the murderers are. When he is asked by Balthazar to prepare a play for the entertainment of the visiting King of Portugal, Hieronymo replies: *"Why then, I'll fit you,* say no more./ When I was young, I gave my mind/ And plied myself to fruitless poetry;/ Which though it profit the professor naught,/ Yet is it passing pleasing to the world."—IV, i, 69-73. The sentence "I'll fit you" has a double edge: Hieronymo is saying that he will "fit out" something for entertainment, and also "I'll fix you." He writes and assigns the parts in such a way that during the playing he stabs Lorenzo, while Bellimperia stabs Balthazar and then herself. Hieronymo bites off his tongue to avoid confessing (we are reminded of Philomela's severed tongue), and then tricks his captors into giving him a knife with which he kills Lorenzo's father and then himself. Not only is this the last of a series of references to Elizabethan tragedies, but also the last reference to the role of the poet who in the Waste Land must apply himself to "fruitless poetry," whose tongue is symbolically severed, for works of art today are but "stumps of time": *Why then Ile fit you*, the poet cries, and his grief and wit are both ironic. *434: Author's Note*: "Shantih. Repeated as here, a formal ending to an Upanishad. 'The Peace which passeth understanding' is our equivalent to this word."—*Collected Poems*.

The reader may now trace for himself the very clear yet complex manner in which Eliot has stated many of his themes and symbols like a "music of ideas," how he has restated and counterstated them, enlarged and finally resolved them at the end of the poem, exactly as in the structure of a quartet.

GERONTION. from γέρων, γερόντις, old man; pertaining to old men. (See *agèd eagle*, p. 466). *Thou hast . . .*: Shakespeare, *Measure for Measure*, III, i, 32-34. The Duke of Vienna, disguised as Friar Lodowick, advises Claudio, who is in prison condemned to die, that life is not worth living. The rest of the passage is pertinent to Eliot's poem: "for all thy blessed youth/ Becomes as aged, and doth beg the alms/ Of palsied Eld; and when thou art old and rich,/ Thou hast neither heat, affection, limb, nor beauty,/ To make thy riches pleasant. What's yet in this/ That bears the name of life? Yet in this life/ Lie hid moe thousands deaths; yet death we fear,/ That makes these odds all even." The theme is similar to that of Ecclesiastes. An old man waits in the spiritual and physical aridities of the Waste Land for a redeeming rain which he knows will never fall. In his youth he had not experienced the passionate action of a man fighting for his beliefs, and now, an old man without belief or desire, he waits for death in a decayed house and civilization amid images of inconsequence. He thinks of all those in the springtime who, when the tiger-like vitality of Christ in resurrection informs the earth and men with a sexual and religious expectation, partake of communion without belief, involved in meaningless attitudes and gestures. History, he muses, has taught us nothing; we have been guided by selfishness; she confuses and confounds us with what she teaches, for she starves us, whenever she gives us anything, by giving it too late, or too soon, or into wrong hands; the consequences are not those we had expected; good comes out of evil, and evil out of good. He tells his beloved in retrospect how at the crucial moment "desire has failed," how he turned or was turned from a possible participation in beauty and passion to be lost in fear and questioning, in an adulteration of his senses. These thoughts prolong in him whatever profit may come from a delirium now cold; the dulled senses need spices to feel; a unified participation in life has been fragmented into a wilderness of multiple reflections of it. *hot gates*: literal translation from the Greek of "Thermopylae," the pass where the Greeks defeated the Persians. *The word . . .*: See first section of Part V, p. 471. *Christ the tiger*: reference to vitality and communion; see *three white leopards*, p. 468, and *fed to satiety*, p. 468. *depraved*: May is a season of evil and betrayal as well as of hope and resurrection; see opening lines of *The Waste Land*. *to be eaten*: the Communion. *Mr. Silvero*, etc.: invented names. According to Mr. Matthiessen, Eliot's design "is to give the *exact* perceived detail, without comment, and let that picture carry its own connotations. As he said once in conversation, the images here are 'consciously concrete'; they correspond as closely as possible to something he has actually seen and remembered. But he also believes that if they are clearly rendered, they will stand for something larger than themselves; they will not depend for their apprehension upon any private reference, but will become 'unconsciously general.'"—*The Achievement of T. S. Eliot* (Oxford University Press, London, 1935), pp. 61-62. *the giving . . .*: Compare with Enobarbus's description of Cleopatra: "other women cloy/ The appetites they feed, but she makes hungry/ Where most she satisfies."—Shakespeare, *Antony and Cleopatra*, II, ii, 243-46. *rented*: we do not own life but merely have a lease on it. *concitation*: excitation, agitation. *Gives too late . . .*: Compare with Parts II and V of "East Coker." *spider*: symbol of death; see *408*, p. 494.

EMPSON, WILLIAM. Howden, Yorkshire, England, Sept. 27, 1906.

Author's Note: "No doubt the more sorts of poetry one can enjoy the better, apart from simply bad poetry; but the sort I should want to write myself is of a fairly narrow kind. There seems no point in struggling with the verse form unless it is using its powers of concentration, and to make it do this requires I think a state of tension or conflict in the writer, usually a painful one. If the poetry is sincere, I feel, you are writing it to find your own balance, even to cure yourself. This sort of poetry cannot worry much about the convenience of the reader, because it has more pressing business in hand; but it aims of course at being a real 'expression,' an externalization of the conflict into public terms, otherwise it would not work for the writer. I do not think that such poetry has to be 'intellectual' in the sense that the writer could explain it all in notes, in fact I wish I could write magical poetry like Dylan Thomas, some of which (though much less I think than people often say) probably couldn't be explained in notes. But the sort I write is all I think explainable, and the reader is meant to feel that the point of it is clear. The shooting poem here does not fit the theory or attitude I have tried to describe. The magazine of my college at Cambridge asked me for a poem, and as this seemed a gentlemanly public I thought they would like a poem about shooting, so I turned one out. It might be said that the result is a better poem than the ones I take more seriously, but this wouldn't be a refutation of my position; I am not trying to describe the conditions for any sort of good poem but the sort I should want to write and have generally tried to write."

MISSING DATES. *Author's Note*: "It is true about the *old dog*, at least I saw it reported somewhere, but the legend that a fifth or some such part of the soil of China is given up to ancestral tombs is (by the way) not true. Otherwise the poem, I think, consists of true statements, but I suppose what they add up to is a mood rather than an assertion, anyway not something you can feel all the time. The last verse is supposed to return with an effect of less pomp to the comparatively trivial, if not absurd, personal muddles which excited the general reflections. The point of the poem goes on, and ideally one should be able to emphasize a different word at each repetition. I think I got near that point in this use of the form."

FOUR LEGS, TWO LEGS, THREE LEGS. The riddle of the Sphinx was: "What walks on four legs in the morning, on two at midday, and on three at night?" Oedipus answered: "Man: in his infancy he crawls on all fours, in his youth he walks upright on two, and in his old age he supports himself with a cane." *Author's Note:* "It struck me in passing through Cairo that the Sphinx has a look of pathetic and devoted public spirit (like a good deal of Egyptian work) which makes the popular idea of her as a sinister mystery seem off the point. This made me think about Oedipus, who destroyed an ogre-like Sphinx by answering its riddle, and therefore had bad luck—at least they made him king out of gratitude for this feat, and that was how he came to marry his mother. He killed his father at a crossroad between the three towns of my first line; they seem meant to symbolize three ways of life, rather as the legs in the riddle do. A *delta* is a mathematical expression for the area of the triangle, here *zero;* he short-circuited life by keeping it all in the family. A metaphysician (somebody said) is like a blind man looking for a *black cat* in the dark which isn't there, and black cats are for luck. As Oedipus was wholly unconscious of his crimes it is uncertain whether he had an Oedipus complex, and he answered the riddle merely by saying Man, not by telling us anything about him. Napoleon's romantic *paint* can just be seen on her face; it is denied that her nose was broken by a deliberate cannon-shot of his. I have never seen anything in print about how dramatically she is placed between the desert and the sown; it seems that she always was, but at one time the river ran close under her paws." —*The Gathering Storm* (London, Faber & Faber, 1940) pp. 63-64.

FLIGHTING FOR DUCK. *Author's Note:* "This poem is about shooting on my brother's land, where I was brought up, in Yorkshire. We call it *flighting* when you wait round the marshes in the evening for the ducks to come and settle there to feed; they come at dusk and you go on as long as you can see. This country lies on the river Ouse, which joins the Humber estuary a mile further down, and the marshes are human products made for the purpose of *warping,* that is, enriching the soil with the river mud; you let the tides in on the selected fields for one or two years and then drain them again. All the land is under hightide-level like coastal Holland, and indeed was drained by Dutch engineers in the seventeenth century, who are among my ancestors. The *Egyptian* diggings are of course the great drains, which may be up to forty feet deep and a mile or two long, ending with a lock gate at the river bank which shuts automatically as the tide comes in unless you are warping. I believe there has been no warping done there since the one I was writing about, but it will have to be done again some time if the value of the land is to be kept up; the effects only last for about a generation."

FITZGERALD, ROBERT. Geneva, N. Y., Oct. 12, 1910.

Author's Note: "A sense of life, a sense of language and a sense of form collaborate to make a superior clarification of experience. It is exacting, delighting, and confirming; at its best a revelation, at its least an elegance. In the composition it begins with concept, visualization, phrase, rhythm or amusement, accreting one or more of the others, and is a craft among crafts."

COLORADO. As a Spanish past participle "Colorado" means the state of being tinted.

SOULS LAKE. An imaginary body of water. *Author's Note*: "Biologists speak of the 'surround' of a cell or any organic life. Favorable surrounds contain moisture. Moreover, identification with the surround is the traditional rough description of the experience roughly called, in the West, mystic."

FROST, ROBERT. San Francisco, Cal., March 26, 1875.

FULLER, ROY. Oldham, Lancashire, England, Feb. 11, 1912.

GARRIGUE, JEAN. Evansville, Ind., Dec. 8, 1913.

GASCOYNE, DAVID. Harrow, Middlesex, England, Oct. 1916.

GRAVES, ROBERT. London, England, July 26, 1895.

TO JUAN AT THE WINTER SOLSTICE. *Author's Note*: "This was begun just before, and completed just after, the birth of my seventh child on December 21, 1945. The *winter solstice* is the traditional birthday of all the 'Solar Heroes' or 'Demons of the Year' of antiquity, such as the Greek gods Apollo, Dionysus, Zeus, Hermes, Syrian Tammuz, Hercules, the Irish demi-gods Lugh and Cuchulain, the Egyptian Horus, and the Welsh Merlin and Llew Llaw. In Celtic popular mythology they are sometimes represented as poetically gifted infants who confound the bards or magicians of the court where they first appear. Their fate is bound up with that of the Moon Goddess who appears to them in her different characters at different seasons of the year, that is to say at different years of their life, as successively mother, lover, and layer-out. This poem epitomizes the theme of the Solar Hero's invariable fate, with circumstances deduced from all the relevant mythologies. That this one story and one story only is the central infinitely variable theme of all poetry is the true, firm contention of my *The White Goddess: A Historical Grammar of Poetic Myth* (Creative Age Press, New York, 1948). *Boreal Crown* is Corona Borealis, alias the Cretan Crown, which in Thracean-Libyan mythology, carried to Bronze Age Britain, was the purgatory where Solar Heroes went after death: in Welsh it was called 'Caer Arianrhod (the castle of the goddess Arianrhod—mother of the hero Llew Llaw). The *log* is the Yule log, burned at the year's end. The *great boar* kills practically all the heroes (even Zeus, according to one account) at the fall of the year."

GREENBERG, SAMUEL. Born, Vienna, Austria, Nov. 3, 1893; died Aug. 17, 1917.

GREGORY, HORACE VICTOR. Milwaukee, Wis., April 10, 1898.

HARDY, THOMAS. Born, Bockhampton, England, June 2, 1840; died Jan. 11, 1928.

ΑΓΝΩΣΤΩι ΘΕΩι: "to an unknown god."

HOPKINS, GERARD MANLEY. Born, Stratford, Essex, England, June 11, 1844; died June 8, 1889.

THAT NATURE IS A HERACLITEAN FIRE AND OF THE COMFORT OF THE RESURRECTION. Sonnet with three codas. Heraclitus regarded all things as resulting from the ceaseless transmutation, or flux, of a single primitive essence to which he gave the name of "fire." From fire all come, to fire all return; but the processes of change are presided over by divine law and universal reason. The harmony of the world thus "rests upon the opposite tension like that of the lyre and the bow." The scene is after a storm. The clouds are shown tossing and scampering (*chevy*) in the air. Splinters of light and tackles of shadow lace, lance and pair in long lashes. The boisterous wind beats away all creases left by yesterday's tempests; it dries up the squandered water in pools and ditches until the earth is like *squeezed dough;* it staunches and starches the crowded marks and masks which the feet of men have fretted in the mire by their tread. The million-fuelèd bonfire thus burns on (changing, Hopkins suggests, from one element to another, as Heraclitus thought earth, water and air turned into the final element of fire and back again). But if man, Nature's most individualized creation, is quenched, how quickly does his fiery impression on mind vanish! Both he and Nature are ultimately drowned in a great darkness. The shape of man, sheer, unique, shining like a star, is blotted out by death and time. But enough of such despair! The promise of the Resurrection is a clarion call to the heart, an eternal beam to the shipwrecked self. Let flesh fade and fall to the worm, let the world's conflagration leave but ash, for at the trumpet's call on the Day of Judgment, each person becomes at once as immortal as Christ, since He was Himself a man once and suffered in man's flesh for man's ultimate salvation and resurrection, that this poor Everyman Jack, this joke of a thing, this poor bit of broken crockery, this patch, matchwood, immortal diamond may, in truth, become an immortal diamond. *treadmire*: formed like "treadmill." *residuary*: The worm is the heir to what remains of the estate of nature and man. *patch*: a paltry fellow, a fool. *immortal diamond* . . .: The immortality of man, even in this life, is obscured; he is not a mortal diamond become immortal, but an immortal diamond whose light was obscured in this world and truly shines after his resurrection.

THE TERRIBLE SONNETS. Editor's title. Hopkins called them the "terrible sonnets" in a letter, meaning what his friend Canon Dixon before him had meant in saying that Hopkins' poems contained a quality of "terrible pathos . . . a right temper which goes to the point of the terrible; the terrible crystal."

Sonnet I. God makes man suffer in despair that his impurities may be sieved away by purification. *why wouldst* . . .: "Why would you rudely rock your right foot against me, that foot which can wring a world?" *Rock* as noun also suggests the weight and force of the rocking. The *right* foot is the stronger. *coil*: turmoil. *since (seems)*. . . .: "since, it seems, I kissed the rod, or the hand, rather, then my heart, etc." *kissed the rod*: The rod that chastizes and the hand that uplifts are one and the same. See Ezekiel xx, 37. *hero*: God. *Heaven-handling*: in such a manner as to suffer and thus be led to salvation.

Sonnet II. more pangs. . . .: suffering becomes progressively worse because it is schooled on past suffering. *herds-long*: image of cries heaving like frightened sheep huddling together. *age-old anvil*: of suffering. *Fury had shrieked*: Fury (the Furies) shrieks against any lull in the suffering which she wants to be *fell* (cruel, fierce, ferocious) since, perforce, she has only the briefness of a lifetime in which to impose suffering. *Hold them cheap.* . . .: Only that man is not afraid of the cliffs of the mind who has never hung there. The little endurance which man has cannot deal with the steeps and depths of the cliffs of the mind. The only comfort and shelter man can creep into against the whirlwind is the thought that sleep gives respite to the day and death to life.

Sonnet III. fell: (1) deadliness, (2) the covering of day, (3) the preterite of "fall." *witness*: I speak of all this as one who has witnessed and experienced it. *dead letters*: useless, for they never seem to reach God. *God's most* . . .: It was God's decree that I should taste bitterness, and that this should come out of self-knowledge. We are all cursed by original sin in our tainted bones, flesh, and blood. Each individual self is entrapped in his body, and the fervor of the self does not raise and sweeten the body as yeast does bread, but sours it instead. The scourge of all of us, even the best, is to be and to know their sweating selves; but the suffering of the lost, the unbelievers, is worse.

Selfyeast also implies the puffing up of the ego, the reliance and dependence on self.

SPELT FROM SIBYL'S LEAVES. The title refers to that hour of final reckoning which the Cumaean Sibyl foretells to Aeneas. She then speaks to him of the hope and salvation to come after many disasters. —*Aeneid*, VI, 95-97. Evening strains into the vast womb and tomb of night. The crescent moon (*hornlight*) is tenderly (*fond*) sinking in the west, the cold stars (*hoarlight*) now appear hung in the wilderness of space, featuring the heavens with fire. For earth has now unraveled all that constitutes her individualized being; her dappled and variegated selves stray, swarm each through the other (*throughther*) and are so steeped and mashed into each other that they are dismembered, and lose their memories and identities. Heart, exclaims the poet, you were right in your foreboding: the final night, which is death, overwhelms and ends everything. Against the metal-smooth bleak light the boughs now make a black damask-work, silhouetted like dragons, their leaves like beaks. This is the story of our life, the doom which the oracle foretold. Let waning life then unravel the multiplicity of her individualized variety; in the obliterating night of death everything is stripped away to reveal an essential core of either good or evil: let life then part the good sheep from the bad, pack them into pens of black and white, of right and wrong; let her consider and be aware of the final world where only these two divisions exist, one against the other; let her *be aware* (and also let her *beware*) of that tortuous rack in the individual self where man's naked thoughts of good and evil are expressed and contend against each other, grinding against each other in groans. *west . . . waste; earliest . . . earl*: play on words. *earl-stars*: principal stars, play on words. *you round me right with*: as in "you are right around me with"; also, the heart follows the poet as in the "rounds" of music or ballads. *sheathe- . . .*: sheatheless and shelterless.

SPRING AND FALL. The last line shifts in meaning between "It is for this, Margaret, that you are weeping," and "It is for yourself, Margaret, that you are weeping."

FELIX RANDAL. A Liverpool parishoner to whom Hopkins gave the last rites. *farrier*: blacksmith. *till time*: until that time when. *reprieve and ransom*: the Eucharist. *God rest . . .*: However he offended throughout his road in life, may God now rest and forgive him. *How far . . .*: How far from your thoughts was sickness and death when at the height of your vigor you prepared (*fettle*) a horse's shoe. *random*: stones of irregular shapes and sizes fitted about the forge at random.

THE CAGED SKYLARK. As a skylark who once in freedom could dare a gale but is now confined in a cage, so is the spirit of man imprisoned in his body. The bird no longer remembers the moors (*fells*) where he was free, but man works out the drudgery of his life day by day. To both come bursts of joy or rage. Man's spirit will never be free from his flesh, not even—at best—in heaven, for the flesh as well as the spirit will be resurrected: but then the flesh will lie as lightly on the spirit as the rainbow on meadow-down. See John Webster's *Duchess of*

Malfi, IV, ii, 127-131: "Didst thou ever see a lark in a cage? Such is the soul in the body: this world is like her little turf of grass, and the Heaven o'er our heads, like her looking-glass only gives us a miserable knowledge of the small compass of our prison."

HURRAHING IN HARVEST. *stooks*: stocks of corn. *Down*: a verb. *what lips. . . .*: no human lips ever greeted you more rapturously, more truly, or more musically. *his*: the Saviour's. *stallion stalwart, very-violet-sweet*: the hills are as strong as muscled as a stallion, yet as sweet and tender as violets with which they are covered, and as ethereal as if under violet light. *The heart. . . .*: when the beholder once sees such beauty, his heart flies out in rapture, and the earth seems to be hurled out from under his feet.

THE WINDHOVER. The poem is about and addresses the windhover (a falcon) and Christ. It states that true greatness of character shines out in the self-mastery that ensues under stress and conflict with outward forces. The greater a man is the more is his true glory revealed under the greatest odds. Thus, the innate beauty of the windhover is revealed in its meeting with and mastering of the *big wind*, just as the true glory of Christ is revealed in His Passion and Crucifixion when He suffered and died for the salvation of mankind. The heart of the poet, his entire capacity and love, watches *in hiding*—that is, watches in secret, abashed, and even from the holy and withdrawn "retreat" of the Jesuit priest. The bird is the favorite (*minion*) of the morning, the prince of the kingdom of delight, and it rides the rolling yet steady air beneath it like a horse, sometimes striding on high, sometimes making a swinging circle like the heel of a skater rounding a bend. The poet's heart is stirred with admiration for the achievement and mastery of the bird, and he cries out that here, in this bird and in the world, outward things like plumes and action, and inward things like valor and pride, *buckle*—that is, under stress and strain they gather together, are enclosed and enclose (as in "buckle in"), are crumpled, broken, and sacrificed ("buckle under"), and grapple and engage in battle ("buckle to"). The beauty of the bird's mastery of the wind in joy, and the beauty of Christ's mastery of the world and flesh in sacrifice and death are one and the same thing. The poet (continuing the metaphor of the horse) addresses both the bird and Christ as his knight (*chevalier*), from whose gallant and dangerous action a glorious radiance shines. There is nothing to wonder in this, says the poet, for the opposition which the plough meets as it cuts through the furrow (*sillion*) is what makes it shine, just as an ember, which seems blue and bleak with ash on the outside, as it falls through and meets the resistance of the air, is "wounded" and breaks open, revealing in its gashes the fiery, golden and vermilion inward flame. The use of such words as *fall*, *gall* and *gash* in the last line suggests the wounds and suffering of Christ and His Glory, the fire and glory that shine in His sacrifice.

HOUSMAN, ALFRED EDWARD. Born near Bromsgrove, Worcestershire, England, March 26, 1859; died, April 30, 1936.

JARRELL, RANDALL. Nashville, Tenn., May 6, 1914.

JEFFERS, JOHN ROBINSON. Pittsburgh, Pa., Jan. 10, 1887.

JOYCE, JAMES AUGUSTINE ALOYSIUS. Born, Rathgar (Dublin suburb), Ireland, Feb. 2, 1882; died, Jan. 13, 1941.

Since a thorough exegesis of any single page in *Finnegans Wake* (see pp. 429-31) would demand at least several pages of annotation, the few suggestions presented here merely illustrate a method of reading. As an example, the first page of the section, entitled *Anna Livia Plurabelle,* has been annotated at considerable length; annotations on the remainder of the two sections represent but a sketch of possible depth-meanings. However, the method will be meaningful only if the reader will acquaint himself with central themes and over-all context, *dramatis personae,* etc. in *Finnegans Wake* itself. For an introduction to these, see: *James Joyce,* Harry Levin (Norwalk, Conn., New Directions, 1941) and *A Skeleton Key to Finnegans Wake,* Joseph Campbell and Henry Morton Robinson (New York, Harcourt, Brace, 1944). The editor is indebted for the following notes to John Hinsdale Thompson of Stephens College.

FINNEGANS WAKE. The simplest statement that can be made about *Finnegans Wake* is that it is a nightmare centered on one man who, in a single night and in 628 pages, dreams about everything that ever happened. Such a statement is a simplification that comes out of desperation, runs head-on into inaccuracy, and ends inevitably in many qualifications. The difficulty of saying what the work is "about" will be familiar to anyone who has tried to tell about the dream he had last night, a dream that is remembered as significant and revealing, but one for which the person involved finds, much to his surprise, no logical means of explanation. To be believed and appraised, the dream must be experienced. And that, ideally, is also true of *Finnegans Wake.*

There are a few matters in the shifty dialectics of this great dream that have the constancy of facts. The dreamer's name is Humphrey Chimpden Earwicker; he has at various times been made aware that his name is a laughing matter to the Dubliners that know it: it sounds foreign to them; it carries a suggestion of an absurd nocturnal insect, the earwig; so that he is often called "H. C. Earwigger." He is often called so many other names that it is finally convenient to identify him as "HCE," the initials which are always those of his name of the moment. He is the proprietor of the "Bristol," a tavern that borders on the River

Liffey and Phoenix Park, Dublin. He has a wife, by whose side he is dreaming this very night, a daughter Isobel, and twin boys, Jerry and Kevin.

He also has a feeling of guilt, brought on partly because he drank more than the customary amount of his own brew earlier this Saturday evening, and partly because, in every way a commonplace person, he is being made to suffer for his share of universal guilt. Besides, he is not sure that he hasn't at some time done some shameful thing under some compulsion and circumstance which he cannot for the life of him remember explicitly. However, his guilty insistence upon returning to the scene of his crime, whatever its exact nature, suggests it was committed in Phoenix Park and concerned a pair of young women and a man, sometimes the two and sometimes the one and occasionally all three. Sometimes, too, the dream-sin shows an incestuous nature. It is of no comfort to HCE, who in the thick of the dream cannot guess his way out of things as the reader can, that his sin is not original in himself but is the Original Sin of Everyman, that what seems his incestuous yearning is an impersonal representation of middle-age man's attitude toward youth generally, and not necessarily, as it is made to seem, toward his own daughter. The epical uneasiness of his sleep can be accounted for further by the defeat he suffered upon standing for election to some minor office; his rejection at the polls has grown into a complex of general rejection.

This is about all there is to the "plot." Common gossip, the Nightmare of History, the antagonist of the piece, is concerned only in bringing about HCE's downfall; it is a part of this process, however, that his wife and children be thoroughly investigated and exposed in turn.

And yet this is not by any means all there is to it. The reader soon finds that H. C. Earwicker is insignificant compared to his greater self, "Howth Castle and Environs"; the self in which he becomes symbolically responsible for all that has happened or will happen in and around Dublin. He finds that when such is the husband's case the wife has become the local Liffey river; and he reads on to learn that the ambitions of neither are content with local celebrity. The giant hero is very soon unmistakably Everyman to all men; in the same time Anna Livia Plurabelle has extended her course until it is that of all the rivers of the world and all the waters of Life. Just as doing battle and building city on city is second nature to him, so is outlasting life and an ever-readiness for life to her a first and only Nature.

What the work is about in this greatly extended sense can again, more comfortably, be stated simply. It is about Death and Resurrection. And the affirmation implied in this ordering of the theme is more than rhetoric. Instead of the pessimistic necessity put upon what goes up to fall, we are witnesses of a sequence in which everything that comes tumbling down will as surely rise again. So large a theme invites endless variations; they are all in the book, and a few suggested in the glossary.

Finnegans Wake is put into motion, as, in Vico's theory, man's godconsciousness was, with a thunder-clap of the first magnitude. It is then sustained throughout its four parts—divisions corresponding to the

Viconian phases of history—by the drive of Like and Unlike in conflict, a powerful synthesis of "Wills" and "Won'ts" based largely on the dialectic of the philosopher Bruno. The book is opened—it is thematically without start or finish—at the noisy instant of Tim Finnegan's Fall, the drunken collapse of the hod-carrier of comic-ballad fame. His wake is as noisy as his downfall; but once it is satisfactorily accomplished, he is supplanted by "Here Comes Everybody," the colonizing "Haveth Childer Everywhere," whose personal-universal history is related for several chapters, before he too falls, his ghost as stubborn as Finnegan's.

The last chapter of this section is the famous one belonging to "Anna Livia Plurabelle," the last three pages of which are printed in this anthology. Two washerwomen are at their work on the banks of the Liffey, gossiping the day through about the affairs of HCE and ALP, dwelling on Anna's unselfish services to her master and on her steadfastness when the rest of the world holds his name in infamy. They have washed all the private linen of the pair, at the point at which the present selection breaks in, and are now airing it in public. There is little left to be rumored, and what remains is communicated with difficulty across the widening river as darkness and silence falls. Part One closes with one washerwoman requesting the other to tell a tale of Shem and Shaun.

Part Two accordingly leaves the parents for a while in order to take up the story of the younger generation for two chapters. The rest of the section is concerned with the comic-heroic exploits of a British lieutenant and a Russian general during the Crimean War. Earwicker, whose name has a suspiciously Scandinavian sound, makes the mistake of defending the Russian's side in the affray during the post-mortem that follows. The chauvinists depart from his pub in disdain, leaving the innkeeper to drink to his dejection from their unfinished glasses. In a stupor he sees himself as the Mark of Cornwall whose Iseult runs off with Tristram; whereupon he sees himself as Tristram.

Part Three spends three of its chapters on Shaun the "successful" twin, its fourth and last on HCE and ALP, in the bed from which they are called forth by the dream-frightened cry of Shem the "creative" twin.

Part Four, the shortest because it is that Viconian stage in which things come full-circle, brings an end to the fault-ridden night and promises the fresh start of a new day's clarity. The woman, who has felt her husband turning from her, is the first to begin awakening. The final ten-page paragraph of *Finnegans Wake*—chosen for this anthology as a river passage equal in every way to the lyrical "Anna Livia Plurabelle"—is devoted to her flowing, and ebbing, stream of consciousness. For it is part of the exquisite sadness here that as her thoughts flow toward morning, the riverrun of her life nears it end. But the interrupted sentence with which the book closes is completed at the re-beginning.

Part I. 1: *kennet*: (1) "ken it," "know it"; (2) Kennet. R., Eng. 4: *cold cher's gone ashley*: possibly, because of the Phoenix theme (in *FW*), to be read, "culture's gone to ashes"; *cher* (1) Fr., "dear"; suggests, also, "cheer," "chair"; (2) Cher R., Fr.; Ashley R., USA. 4: *Fieluhr?*: "viel uhr?" G., what time is it? 4: *Filou!*: (1) Fr., "pickpocket"; see *FW*, p. 82; (2) Fr., "thief"; perhaps, here, as "Time the thief!" The pickpocket and the request for the time of day are allusions to HCE's experience in Phoenix Park, Dublin. *4: saon*: (1) "soon"; (2) Saône R., Fr. *5: senne*: (1) "since"; (2) Senne R., Belg. *5: erewone*: (1) e'er a one; (2) Eire-one; (3) Samuel Butler's *Erehwon*—"nowhere" when read backward. *6: clogh*: (1) Ir. for "clock"; (2) the name of an Ir. river. *6-7: asunder. . . . reassemble*: In order to see what makes it tick, one must first analyze and then synthesize the matter. *7: back*: Danish, "brook." *7: bach*: G., "brook." *8: Aches-les-Pains*: Aix-les-Bains, Fr. watering-place. *8: Sexaloitez*: The Angelus bell is rung at six-hour periods; "Sex," L., "six"; "Läute," G., "tolling"; see similar passages, *FW*, pp. 58, 268, 327. *9-10*: The bell here rings out the old, rings in the new. *10: Godavari*: the name of the Indian river is accented on the second syllable; however, Joyce's own reading of the word suggests "God of Eire." *13: Der went*: The wind and the Derwent R., Eng. are rising. *14-16: sheets. . . . apron*: represent (*FW*, p. 158) the Mookse and the Gripes, who in turn represent the Earwicker twins, Shaun and Shem. *17-18: Six . . . ten . . . twelve . . . one*: The laundry count is 29, the sum used throughout to indicate the presence of HCE's "Leap-year" daughter, who is usually accompanied by 28 schoolmates. *19: Jossiph*: "joss," Pidgin English for "god"; hence, from "god-sib" and "gossib" to "gossip"; see "mutther-goosip," line 227. *20: Deataceas!*: (1) "dea," L., goddess; "tace," L., be silent; (2) Dea Tacita in Roman mythology was the mistress (ALP?) of Hercules (HCE?) and the nurse of Romulus and Remus (Shaun and Shem). *20: Whar-now*: (1) German river; (2) "Where now." *21: Allalivial, allalluvial*: All the living off-spring of ever-living Anna Livia, who are born in rain (Sp., "La lluvia") and, at the end of the mother-river's course, spread out alluvially. Alleluia! *22: alla stranger*: "à l'étranger," Fr., "abroad." *24: Dunders de Dunnes*: "dunder," a noise like thunder; "duns," anc. Ir. strongholds or hills; De Dananns, legendary settlers and, later, gods of Ireland. *24: Markland*: (1) the land of King Mark (Cornwall) and of Mark the Evangelist, both of whom are archetypes in *FW*; (2) borderland, frontier; the land of money, *i.e.*, USA. *24: Vineland*: America. *25: Brendan*: an allusion to the fabulous voyage across the Atlantic of the sixth-century Irish saint. *25: herring pool*: humorous term for the Atlantic ocean. *25: yangsee*: (1) Yankee; (2) Yangtze R., China. The substance of the sentence (24-25) is that the blustering Dunnes, having overflowed into America, now have swollen heads. *26: Biddy's beads*: "Biddy," (1) dim. of Bridget (St. B., patroness of Ireland); (2) Irish servant; (3) hen: particularly the hen of *FW* that "pecked up" the "traumscrapt," lines 255-59; "bead," (1) prayer; (2) Bede the Venerable, English monk and historian; "Bidding the beads," asking for the prayers of the flock. Superficially, the sentence hints that one of Mother Ireland's children has wound up in the gutter. *26-27: lost histereve*: (1) "yester-eve," last evening; (2) lost eve-of-history; (3) Hester, or Esther Vanhomrigh, Jonathan Swift's "Vanessa," whom Joyce names many times. *27-28: side strain of a main drain*: The Irish church as a "side strain" of the Mother Church in Rome (*Cloaca Maxima*)? or, perhaps, Ireland as an off-shoot of the main stream of history.

31-32: Beyond their first-level significance, the following words have identity as rivers: Orara, Orbe, Las Animas, Ussa, Ulla, Umba, Mezha. 33: *ufer*: G., river-bank. 36: *Finnleader*: Finn MacCool, leader of the Fianna. 36: *joakimono*: (1) Joachim; (2) "joki," Finnish, "river"; (3) kimono. 37: *forehengist*: "before Hengist," leader of the Jutes in their invasion of England, c. 449. 37-38: *Father of Otters*: (1) "Father of Waters"; *i.e.*, the Mississippi; (2) Father of Orders," St. Patrick. 39: Philip Astley's Royal Amphitheatre, a London circus of the late 18th century. 40-41: *ghostwhite horse of the Peppers*: "Some of us remember that there was an act in a circus called *Pepper's Ghost*, and that there is an Irish play called *The White Horse of the Peppers*."—Padraic Colum, preface to *Anna Livia Plurabelle*, N.Y., 1928. A representation of the White Horse, reputedly the ensign of the invading Saxons, was cut centuries ago on the face of the chalk downs in Berkshire, England. 44: *I sonht zo!*: (1) "ich sann so," G., I thought so; (2) Izontzo R., Italy. 46-47: The sentence as a whole seems to repeat the idea of *wabblyhips*. "Your last brat ('get') is Greek or Roman" (or "creek or human"); "Your rear gait (and 'gate') has the rheumatic creaks"; "creach," Ir., "plunder." 53: *husky*: "usque," Ir., "whiskey," whose full designation means "waters of life." 53: *hussars*: orig., "corsairs"; hence, used here to name yet more of Eire's, and Anna's, early suitors. 55: *I sar*: (1) "I saw"; (2) Isar R., Germany. 56: *Zezere!*: (1) "See, there!" (2) R., Portugal. 57-61: The ubiquitous Four of *FW* are here the Four Evangelists, Luke, Mark, Matthew, and John. 58: *meanam*: (1) "meaning"; (2) Menam R., Siam. 59: *meyne*: (1) "mean"; (2) Mayne R., Queensland. 60: *draves*: (1) "drives"; (2) Drave R., Hungary. 61-62: *Poolbeg flasher beyant*: Poolbeg lighthouse beyond, on Dublin Bay. 62: *pharphar*: (1) "far, far"; (2) the biblical Damascus R.; (3) "lighthouse" (see "pharos," "faro," "phare"). 62: *nyar*: (1) "nigh," "near"; (2) Nyar R., India. 62: *Kishtna*: a compound of (1) "the Kish lightship" (see p. 45, *Ulysses* and see "fireboat," *FW* line 63); (2) Kistna R., India; and (3) Krishna, R. and Hindu deity. 68-71: the following are river-names and their locations: Evenlode, Eng.; Save, Fr.; Jurna, Brazil; Sow, Eng.; Moy, Ire.; Towy, Wales. Moyvalley and Rathmines are suburbs of Dublin. 74: *foostherfather*: (1) "foosterer," Ir., a fussy, flustered person; and (2) foster-fathers." 74: *fingalls*: (1) Finn-Galls; (2) "Fingal," a famous long poem ascribed to the Irish poet Ossian by James Macpherson; (3) Fingal R., Tasmania. 74: *dotthergills*: (1) daughter-Gaels; (2) "dother" and "dotter" as vars. of "dodder," together with "gill," brook. 75: *gangsters*: suggests gangling youngsters, somewhat incorrigible. 76: *seven . . . hues*: the seven colors of the rainbow—to be named in lines 82-3—to the tune of "As I was going to St. Ives, I met a man with seven wives." 77: *Sudds*: (1) "suds," Slang, "beer"; (2) "sudd," floating vegetable matter sometimes forming temporary dams. 78: *Bifur*: "Before the bifurcation," perhaps; *i.e.*, the course of the Liffey as it nears the fork. 81: *milkidmass*: Michaelmas, happily for Joyce's concern with the number 29 (see line 17), is observed on September 29; here, the feast day is celebrated with goat's milk, possibly in deference to "Hegoat," the First Citizen of Dublin, and his "buckgoat paps" (see line

87). 82: *Tys Elvenland!*: (1) " 'Tis the land of the Elves and the land of the salmon" ("alevin"); (2) Tys Elv, Norway. 83: *Ordovico*: (1) "Ordovices," the Roman name for the Celts; (2) "ordo," L., "order," of Vico, whose theory of history is made to support much of the super-strata of *FW*. 83: *viricordo*: "Man" and History repeat themselves; Vico's "recorso," the fourth phase; the word of Joyce here, recording in reverse order much of the word before it, is a literal demonstration of a return to the "same anew." 84-85: *Northmen's thing . . .*: "The gathering of the Normans made Suffolk place, but how many ancestors more have gone into the making of each one of us?" 86: *eure*: (1) "your"; (2) Eure R., Fr. 86: *sanscreed*: (1) "Sanskrit"; (2) "without creed." 86: *eryan*: the "Eire-an" language in the Aryan group. 87: Eblanensis: Eblana, ancient capital of Ireland. 91: *Ho*: Chinese for "river." 93: *foos won't moos*: "fuss," G., "foot"; "moos," G., "moss"; "moosey," var. of "mosey": the feet of the washwoman who is changing into an elm tree are rooted to the spot and refuse to move.

Part IV. 101: *Folty*: "thick," as of the hair of the head, Italian, "capelli folti"; see also Ir. for "hairy," and for "treacherous"; "faulty" is certainly suggested; and, possibly "forty." 103: *Lispn!*: "lisp," ME. & OHG., "lispen"; and "listen!" 104: see archaic meaning of the words "wood" and "fond." 105: "Robinson Crusoe." 107-8: *cape to pede*: "cap-a-pie," "de pied en cap": to Dubliners, the cape of Howth suggests the reclining figure of a giant (the sleeping Finnegan) whose head is the Hill of Howth and whose feet turn up as two mounds in Phoenix Park. 108: *Terce*: var. of "tierce"; the fiddler's share, here, compares favorably with the "Sudds for me" of line 77; however, the hidden sum of 28 is shy of the "29" of lines 17-19; the river Tersa, USSR. 108-9: the clan of MacMerrier is also the Concord river, Merrimack. 109: *aruse*: Finnegan can be "aroused" only by "a ruse"; ME., "aroos"; "arrouse," *Obs.* "to sprinkle"; Tim Finnegan, in the music-hall "Ballad of F.'s W.," is aroused to life by spilled whiskey; "Eriu" (a'ryu), O Ir. form of "Erin," Ireland. 112-13: *Stout Stokes would take you offly*: Whitley Stokes, Irish poet and editor, might possibly have been considered guilty by Joyce of having "taken off" other poets rather "awfully"; or, "Stoke's disease" and too much Dublin Stout will also "take you off," off-handedly; Offley, in Herts, England, is reputed to be the burial-place of Offa, King of Mercia, traditionally considered the builder of Offa's Dyke, an impediment capable of causing Anna Livia "to slump"; and, since one of the chores of a popular river is that of sewerage, there is a further "offal" possibility; Stokes Bay, King's Sound, Australia. 113: *bored me to slump*: secondarily, in the sense of the word "bore" as a tidal wave rushing up an estuary; here, that of the Liffey—causing ALP to collapse, temporarily, and then perhaps to overflow into a "slump," or bog. 114: "Tak," Dan., "thanks." 114: *Yawhawaw*: perhaps, a pirate's "Yaw-haw-haw!" for the bottle of "vin" that her "toddy" gave her; or the change of course that the nautical "yaw" would bring about; also, "Yahweh"; and Swift's "Yahoos." 114: *Helpunto*: "Help unto"; the Hellespont. 114: *min*: Scand., "my"; Ir., "meal"; Min R., China. 115: *helpas*: "hjälpa," Swed., "help"; the sentence as a whole, perhaps "Father, help us unto food and drink." 121:

cosh: "cash"; anc. Cush, the valley of the Nile; "cush" (kŏŏsh), Dial., "cow"; the latter, together with the possibility that *bulge* stands secondarily for the "bag spear" (gae bulga) of one of its heroes, suggests the Irish classic, "The Cattle-Raid of Cooley." *122: Alby*: Purse-proud Albion's exploitation of poor ("aroon," Anglo-Ir., "darling") little Eirean; "Ailbe," the famous hound of the Leinster king, MacDatho; "Albis," anc. name of the river Elbe; perhaps, also, the English jingle, "The Bilge (bulge) was Algy." *125*: Wellington, the "Iron (ME. "iren") Duke"; as well as Erin's duke; "ein Ire," G., "an Irishman." *127: Rathgreany*: "rath," encampment; for the ways of "Graine," or Grace O'Malley, see note to ll. 234-5; Lough Greine, Ire.; Greina Pass, Switzerland, *129: The Head*: the headmaster of the boys' school, and the head of the Earwicker family, HCE, the Head of Howth. *129-30*: "High Heels and Low Heels," the Lilliputian political parties in *Gulliver's Travels*; specifically, the twins pricking at the heels of the father whom they are to supersede. *130: Galliver*: Gulliver; "gall-liver"; ever the Gall, Invader-twin of the native Gael; Gällivare, Swedish town near Baltic coast. *Gellover*: "llover," Sp., "rain" for the native Gael; Jack-and-Jill, etc. *132: The sehm asnuh*: see note, line 83. *133: nors in soun*: also, "noise and sound." *135-6: Quickenough and Doddpebble*: the old cronies are suspiciously like the laundry-women of "ALP," as well as Time & Space and Tree & Stone; the quicken tree, or aspen; and contrast "quick water" with the doddering River Dodder near Dublin—from which, perhaps, John Eglinton drew his "Pebbles from a Brook." *138: Laundersdale Minssions*: "launder," *Obs.*, "washerwoman"; "dale," vale; also, share; "launde," ME., a clearing in a forest, to be used for a hunting-ground; the rivers Laune, Ire., and Drysdale, Australia; and "minion," "ladylove," or "servile creature"; and the Landers' mission in the early 19th century up the Niger River—since Joyce uses the similar expedition of Mungo Park to symbolize British imperialism; Minch strait, Scot., and the River Mincius. *138*: The *googling* twin is likely the Glugg (Shem) of FW pp. 219-59. *139: wetting his widdle*: "wetting his little whistle," if no more; "to whiddle," Cant for "to peach" on someone, from "whids," "to hesitate verbosely"—Grose's dictionary; the last is a very certain characteristic of HCE; the Weddell Sea. *140: pearse orations*: Persse O'Reilly, who plays the important and difficult part of HCE's alter-ego. *144: Eager*: "eagre," syn. "bored," line 113; Aegir, Scand. Myth., lord of the sea-giants; Eger R., Czecho-Slovakia. *146: Findling*: G., "foundling." *146-47*: "as merry as a grig: an allusion to the apparent liveliness of a grig, or young eel,"—Grose. *148: Is is*: Isis, Egyptian goddess of fertility; the upper Thames R. *149: Slops hospodch*: "slap-dash"; "slop," Shakespeare, in the sense of loose breeches; Grose also quotes Palsgrave's "Payre of sloppe hoses"; and "hopscotch," "hotchpotch"; "hospodar" for innkeeper Earwicker, whose breeches "slopped" in Phoenix Park. *149*: FW, p. 107: "Privates Earwicker and a Pair of Sloppy Sluts plainly Showing all the Unmentionability falsely Accusing about the Raincoats" (i.e. "redcoats," the 3 soldier-witnesses); FW, p. 508, "Silks apeel and sulks alusty"; Slutsk R., USSR. *150*: The Dogger Banks, Copenhagen. *153: besomes*: "brooms," make a clean sweep of bygones. *154: Phoenix*: symbolically and geographically of central importance to FW which, if it can be narrowed to a single theme, is all-inclusively devoted to Death and Regeneration. Dublin's Phoenix Park—whose name is a happy corruption of the Irish for "a spring of running water"—has been the scene of other infamies than that of the Park's tavernkeeper, HCE. A pillar of the fabulous bird rising out of the flames of its own destruction was erected by Chesterfield in the 18th century. "Phoenix," to Joyce, is a convenient and convincing word for both "finished" and "Finn, again wake!" *155-57:* sentimental journey to St. Michael's Mount, since Lucifer has lost and *The Book of the Dead* is closed. Humpty-Dumpty, the eternal Ego, suffered a fall as great as that of Lucifer, Adam, the leaves of Autumn, Napoleon, the Holy Roman Empire, rain, Solness the Master Builder, mountains and Mohammedans, Tim Finnegan, Niagara, and all the other "happy faults" which FW so optimistically celebrates. *158: Gustsofairy:* "gusts-of-air," the Four Winds of Eire (see note, lines 57-61); "Gust of Vaerë," one of the four Hill-Trolls in the Norse folktale of "Peer Gynt." Joyce's familiarity with the name-source of Ibsen's dramatic poem can very well be taken for granted. *159: dannymans:* the Danish invaders pursued a good thing when they saw it. *164: Finvara:* Finavarra on Galway Bay, near Kinvarra, Ire.; "Finvaragh," one of the old-time Irish kings of the demons. *165: roly polony:* also, the Frog that would a-wooing go "with a rowley, powley, gammon, and spinach." *168: cuppinjars:* popinjays, "a reverend gentleman of the name of Mr. Coppinger"; as well as the "cups and jars," in the likes of which, whiskey (the "waters of life") and the eternal Irish "tay" are served throughout the book; the cup that kills—the jar of Tim Finnegan's fall from the coping was laid to whiskey—is also the cup that revives Finnegan at his own wake; a cupping jar or glass, used in bringing blood to the surface of the skin, will also induce a flush; in any case, the cups and jars are served as reminders of Death and Resurrection. *170: girdle:* "By earth and the cloudy but I badly want a brandnew bankside," ALP, FW p. 201. *171: Norwall:* North Wall was constructed to control, girdle-wise, a hook-shaped bank, port of Dublin; Joyce here reduces it to a word that reminds us of Norway. *172: Isaacsen's:* the 12 patriarchs and Joyce's 12 patrons are sons of Isaac. *172: slooped its line:* Anna's girdle (riverbank) has lost its give-and-take, and some "sloop" of commerce has "slipped its line"; perhaps at Liffey's "Loopline bridge," or perhaps in the Line R., Eng. *172-3: Fy arthoul:* Old Windy MacCool has apparently relieved himself in his sleep, and is at the same time being chided by his wife; "fy," ON., "fie!"; "artou," ME., "art thou"; also, "farther, Father!"; "Fire, thou!" "fiat," etc. *173: padder avilky:* Father of All, and of Dublin; Father Michael; see the voc. case of the Irish for Michael; "padder," a highwayman. *173-4: fol a:* "Fodla" (foh'la), a poetic name for Ireland; Fola Cataract, Sudan; the falls, possibly, which the two are approaching—Anna perhaps asking the great big brute of a man padding along behind to "follow little me." *174: languo of flows:* the "language of flowers" is as private as the "little language" of Swift and his "Pipette"—see "pippup," line 268; a language, also, of the "languor of the flowing river," of the Llangua River, Africa. *175: Jorgen Jargonsen:* Jergen's Lotion speaks a jargon of its own; the Danish poet and novelist,

Jorgensen, might be implied here, because of his book, "Flowers and Fruits." *177: glave*: glove; and Irish for "sword." *177: hugon*: Huggin, the usual dim. of Hugh, with added endearment; perhaps also the Huguenot, who played an important part in Irish history. *178: Smoos as an infams*: the skin of his hand, partly because of Jergen's Lotion, is "smooth as an infant's," with "infamy" added. *180: lifeness*: "like-ness"; "license," in Man's age-old compulsion for the taking-of-life; other meanings are abortive. *180: hodd*: He also hangs his "head" for the shame of the "license he was taking" in the Park, when the hue-and-cry was raised (he was "Shamey!-called" and "Shem-called"); the "hod" that he carried as Tim Finnegan to the *scaffold*. *181: fell design*: ALP refers to old rumors that HCE fell to his destruction on purpose: "fell," in an earlier sense, means "mount." *182: florizel*: HCE as a youth "in flower," in his prime; and as "Florizel," the lover of Perdita in Shake-speare's *Winter's Tale*. *183: peeling a twig*: as a youth, Achilles peeled a spear from a tree cut on Pelion, mt. in Thessaly; Cheiron the centaur, whose home this was, may have been the "little white horse" which was HCE's, and which grew to become the great white horse of later legend; the "drawing back of the glave" is yet effective here, of course. *185-6: the weight of old fletch*: the theme of Samuel Butler's *The Way of All Flesh* is here so appropriate as to make punning-words seem inspired flesh. *187: the church by the hearseyard*: one of several instances of Joyce's, perhaps ironic, fondness for Sheridan Lefanu's novel, *The House by the Churchyard*. *192: The Kinsella woman's man*: "The cad with the pope's wife, Lily Kinsella," FW 618; Kinsale—Ir., "the headland in the sea"—Seaport on the Bandon R.; Croghan Kinshela, Wicklow mts. *198*: "Goody Two-Shoes," the nursery tale, thought to have been written by Goldsmith, whose *Vicar of Wakefield*, is antici-pated by the "Viker" (ME. for "vicar") two lines earlier. *199: possum-botts*: "Puss-in-(French)Boots"; FW 96, "by such playing possum (HCE) bestly saved his brush with his posterity." *200: Buahbuah*: the Ir. name "Buagh" derives fr. Ir. for "victory." *203-4: Afartodays, afear-tonights . . . thadark*: the apprehensive backward glance of Man over the distance he has come from the dark of the womb and of pre-history; "the dark"; "that ark." *208-9: Les go dutc to Danegreven*: "Let's go D.U.T.C." (Dublin United Tramway Co.). *210*: "Gilligan" (vale and Gael), "Halligan" (mountain and Gall), Hoolihan ("Ireland, Mother of hoodlums"), and "Sullygan eight" are, among other things, the 12 patriarchs, the 12 patrons of HCE's pub, and the 12 jury-men that sit in judgment of him; the present version of each one of their names is of course additionally loaded; see, for example, "gillie," "galloglaigh," "hool"-again and "hooly"-again; the *rest of the guns*—besides being "the rest of the -gans" and "the rest of the dead-and-gone hoodlums"—are probably the three "Gunas" of Hindu philosophy: Pas-sion, Dullness, Inertia; attributes that have been applied to the Irish, by the Irish; Güns R. *211-2: Olobobo, ye foxy theagues*: also, "Ali Baba and the Forty Thieves," the thieves were boiled in oil as they hid in the 40 oil-jars; see, too, "fax," "teague." *212: The moskors thought to ball you out*: secondly, "The Muscovites (and their General) thought to massacre you with cannon-ball"; thirdly, "The maskers thought to throw (Gr. "ball") you out of, or 'bawl' you out at, the masquerade ball"; all three readings are direct references to HCE's troubled career. *213: the Wald Unicorns Master*: Captain Buckley—promoted since, as a lieutenant, he shot the Russian General—has several responsibilities at the moment: he is Master Huntsman and "Waldmeister"; and he is the master of "The Wildwood Unicorn," the stout Norwegian ship in which, as the Baltic sailor of line 124, he invaded Anna Livia up to and into Bristol tavern; apparently he has also sailed the Moskva and Bug rivers, the Irish, Killenaule, and the cold Unicorn Sea, pursuing some Moby Dick of the Arctic, the "narwhale" with the unicorn-tusk. *214: the Honourable Whilp*: the whipper-in of the whelps is also the Hon. "party whip," M.P. *214-15: Poynter*: a pointer is both the hunter and the hunted, a gun dog and a stag with horns of a given number of points; it is also a whaling device, here at hand for the Bugley Captain; the entire party comprises the three soldiers and the two "sluts" of Phoenix Park fame, all incognito; but, as always, with HCE the Stag at bay. *215: Tallyhaugh*: "tallyho!"; Tallaght, environs of Dublin, near the scene of the Fenian risings; "o talho," Port. for "butcher's shop," probably belongs, too, since Joyce has several times named deity the Butcher, the god of destruction. *215: Ballyhuntus*: Ballyhaunis, Ire.; presumably a happy-hunting ground. *216: riddletight raiding hats*: the two Lady-patients of Sir James Paget in their redingotes are dressed for riddling and raiding, in the manner of Grace O'Malley. *217: host*: the word, used here as a verb, is one of HCE's most important qualities; he plays the host to his Lord, to all-comers to Ireland, to the 12 patrons of his last-supper table in the tavern; in the active word, he "hoists," "hastes," "hast," and stutters when excited (var. of "hoast," cough). *218: capapole*: "cap-apie" here becomes "cap-a-poll" because HCE has forgotten himself and the teachings of Wm. Carleton, the Irish dictator of decorum; Sancho was given a similar lesson in *Don Quixote*; Gilbert's *James Joyce's Ulysses*, p. 167: "to the Romans, Ibsen, when living in their city, was merely the *Cappelone*—the fellow with the big hat"; HCE's cap is the top-o'-mountain to us. *227*: "Little Jack Horner sat in a corner" gossiping about HCE with "Mother Goose." *229: moighty*: "moiety," and "mighty" with an Irish brogue. *230: promnentory*: Howth promontory. *234-5: graciast kertssey*: Grace O'Malley reveals her presence; she proposes to repay Howth's scant "courtesy" ("Kersse"—the same name as Persse—is the son of the tailor of FW who might, in turn, make use of "kertssey," homespun material) with her most graceful, thankful, and gracious curtsey, as well as with—one suspects, knowing her pranksome nature —her most characteristically disgraceful "curt-says" and curses. Her Pidgin English double-talk in the next sentence takes Mahomet to the mountain, for the inscrutable question she is about to ask. *237-8: to link to light a pike on porpoise*: Exposed to the full blast of the Prancquean's riddle, the reader and the Earl of Howth at first recognize only the customary rhythm of "Peter Piper picked a peck of pickled peppers"; and finally, too, though a temporary message can be decoded from its words-of-the-moment, the ultimate meaning is always as furtive as the Meaning of Life which one later looks for in the Letter

from Boston, Mass. (see ll. 252-9). 238: *Armor*: Sir Amoricus Tristram
from Armorica (Brittany), who founded the St. Lawrence family and
erected the castle walls of Howth, whose gates the Prancquean stormed.
239: Bartholomew, one of the apostles; his name as spelled by Joyce
seems to contain the names of several other apostles. 240: Vanhomrigh,
the surname of one of the two Esthers in Swift's life; his pet name for
her, "Vanessa," is made up of the first syllables of her last and first
name; her last name has here a "hungry" (G., "hungrig" plus Du.
"hongerig") and Hungarian look; the latter to accompany the "Magyer
chief" of the previous sentence; Humphrey's "earwig" is also indicated.
242: *My currant bread's full of sillymottocraft*: jumping from the
human ALP to the River, the sense is that the Liffey is cluttered with
the rejectamenta of civilization; specifically, the breadth of the current
is full of a craft of the herring-boat sort, both sail- and motor-boats. 242:
"A 'loaf' is enough; and so is 'love.'" 244: *Flura's way*: the "Flowery
(with a slight French accent) Path" is the way of "The Floras," the 28
schoolgirls of "St. Bride's Finishing Establishment," who serve as an
escort, if not as a model, for Isobel Earwicker; "fluor" is also the way of a
flowing stream and, every 28 days, of the menses. 248: *scand . . .*: the
horizon is particularly scanned for the *rising* tide of Scandinavians coming into Ireland on the crest of the wave. 249: *Evora*: anc. Ebora,
Portugal; "everyone" told ALP that she should. 251: "Ourselves, ourselves alone": Sinn Fein motto. 252: "The sight of Salvation on the site
of the roar of the surf." 256-7: *Hack an axe, etc.*: the reader who has
looked for *the* answer to the riddle of Life in the earlier manifestations
of ALP's "mamafesta," hopefully and hopelessly always, is bound to be
psychologically defeated before he tries for conclusions in the last of
them all, as alluded to, 623 pages along in FW; however, with a
philosopher's incitement and patience, together with a familiarity with
the Norse Niblung legends ("Heth," for example) and with a fondness
for selecting apt symbols from the Hebrew alphabet, he may in the
present esoteric example so readjust the arms of "the hardest crux ever"
that they will perhaps indicate the immediate way out. . . . Joyce, who
has gone to the trouble of packing single words with an unnatural
number of meanings, has with equal deliberation withheld the one
meaning that is unnatural and inexpressible. 258: *dealt*: as a verb, "to
part"; but "delta," which also brings about a parting of the ways, has an
especial symbolical usefulness throughout FW; see "delth," line 360.
258-9: *traumscrapt*: the inexpressible, sad, scrap of a thought in which
articulate man has inscribed his pains and longings; in FW it is variously from HCE, ALP, and the "cousin, who signs hers with crosses,"
from Boston, Mass., in the new world beyond; it is supposed to have
been unearthed on the kitchen-midden of civilization by Belinda the
Hen "in the storyaboot starting from scratch," (see Aesop's *The Cock
and the Jewel*); its possible significance was first estimated by Shem;
whereupon the credit for discovering its worth and for making a prac-
ticable application of its message was assumed by Shaun the "successful"
twin; to its credulous and indifferent readers the Word of the letter was
inspirational as a matter of course; to the sincerely curious and hopeful
investigator the difficult text ultimately disclosed the absolutely nothing

that it contained. *260-1: On his mugisstosst surface*: the face of H.M., of God moves over the surface of the tossing waters; and "the glass" (of line 218) that His Lordship "never starts to finish." *264: ruddery dunner*: "Rudra," the storm-god of Vedic mythology; "rudera," "ruins"; helmsman; Kilruddery, near Bray Head, co. Dublin; basically, the concept that the religious idea was first awakened by the Voice of Thunder. *265: kissmiss*: "till the coming of Christmas"; "till the Second Coming of Christ"; "till a little 'kiss-miss' comes to supplant ALP in HCE's affections." *265: Lss.*: "liss," *Obs.* for "release," "remission," "rest," seems to fit the context. *267*: also, an acute tower of Babel leading to the gate of God; also, "Pepette" and "Bo-Peep" and "Stella" ("star"), references to pet names of Swift's two Esthers. *277: sinfintins*: the "saint" of St. Fintan, whose chapel is on Howth peninsula, is often pronounced "sin"; also, "for the love of the children of the Sinn Fein and the "Tans"; Sinn and Finn, rivers in Germany and Ireland. *277*: Baily Lighthouse, Hill of Howth. *281: dowling*: "dowle," grief, and "darling." *281: Wordherfhull*: the "old bhoy" is not only "wonderful," but full of blarney: "worder," *Obs.* for a verbose person; and the Wurdha R., India. *283: marashy*: "maraschino" seems indicated, but not fitting; Marash is a city in Asia Minor; beneath it all, it is of course "marshy." *283: Alpine*: the name of the perfume is the family name to which the Celts belong, including Mt. "Hump." *284: Medeurscodeignus*: L., "worthy"; perhaps with "medeor," L., "to be good for"; "sdegno," It., "disdain"; the Italian word appears in "The Sirens" of *Ulysses*; since the "Scandinavians" also appears close to the surface of the word, perhaps the "scotti," Ir., "raiders," and the "Danes" are present; "meader," Ir., "drinking cup": see n., line 171. *285: Astale of astoun*: also, "a stale tale of a stone" (lines 94-6), and the "Estella" of the author of *A Tale of a Tub* which dealt with corruptions, whose smell reached "even to the nose of high heaven." *286-7: Finsen makes cumhulments*: "Finn's son MacCumhail"; the somewhat shady "compliments" of the man contain "cumulus" clouds piled mountain-high; the "Captain" of that "Ark from the air" is also Noah looking for the rainbow of God's covenant whose promise radiates throughout FW. *288*: "Yet is no body present here which was not there before. Only is order othered. Nought is nulled. *Fuifiat!*" FW, 613. *289: samples*: ALP soon (line 388) proves to have been a tailor's daughter; in the *Kalevala*, the "Sampo" is a mill of the gods and the cause of conflict between the Finns and the Lapps; "the man of samples" is concerned in the scene in which "the Cad" confronts HCE; he is also St. Paul. *289: tinger winged ting*: Although ALP vibrates at the core of her being with HCE's primary effectiveness, the "ting-a-ling" of his phone-call ringing in her ear is as thrilling as an ear-wig winging into the same "hear"-ing organ. *294: crushts of lobsters*: the "crusts," the "shells"; and a suiting of the sound of the action of HCE's feat; "lobster" was an epithet for the British soldier whose redcoat was the color of broiled lobster and who, in Cromwellian times, was covered with shiny iron shells; the "redcoats" in the present case are "the three soldiers" of Phoenix Park; although HCE's earlier heroics would include crushing the Roundheads wherever he found them in Ireland. *295*: "Marianne,"—personification of Republican France—

"cherie"; "sherry off" makes "sheer off," makes Marian the Maid of the tales of the "Sheer-off of Sherwood Forest"; Sheri R., Africa. *296: beardwig*: "some clerk's" brief-case contains a false beard which contains another "earwig" all but hidden in its wiggery. *300: Cadmillers-folly*: the Cad, FW 36, was "swift to mate errhors." *300: Wellcrom*: Cromwell; who was anything but *Bellevenue* to Ireland. *301: Quid Superabit*: the motto of the Order of Saint Patrick, *Quis separabit?* (Who shall separate us?), over-laid with "overcome." *301-2: murphies*: are Irish potatoes and the 12 patrons of the pub; the *next course* of Irishman will be the "recorso" of Vico; the Plate, La Plata, and other rivers, will run a new course. *302-3*: The extravagant Irish are still pugnacious (*the* "cannon" *going strong*), so that the custom of HCE the Undertaker (Claffey was actually a Dublin pawnbroker) endures, and the tenements of the parish are as full of life as a rabbit warrren. *305: barsalooner*: the Four "bar-flies" are Barcelona smugglers, maybe, and are, certainly, smugglers under the great Borsalino hat of HCE the saloon-keeper. *306: Finglas*: a Dublin suburb; "Fingal," derived from Finn MacCumhail (Mac Cool), is the "Ossianic" poem by James Macpherson. *307: work in progress*: the provisional but long-ranged title of FW during the pre-publication decade in which excerpts appeared. *309: Rasselas, the Prince of Abyssinia*, by Samuel Johnson; "rastle," dial. var. of "wrestle"; and "rustle." *313-4: agres of roofs in parshes*: "agrah," Ir., "sweetheart"; "ager," one that ages; and, in Rom. Hist., lands acquired by conquest—which would here be made a part of imperialistic Eng. Hist.; plus "parching, perishing, parcels and patches of marshy parishes"; secondarily, "ages of 'Work in Progress.'" Eger R., Czecho-Slovakia, and Acre R., S. Amer., *314: Dom on dam, dim in dym*: "judgment" of the Irish "race" and its "poetry"; "dim, damp, fog." *315: Cooloosus*: "Colossus- MacCool." *315: knock*: a castle in Phoenix Park cemetery. *316: dustbins*: the "has-beens" of a Dublin gone to dust. *316: A lintil pea*: is our "A. L. Pea," made up here of "lintel" and "lentil"; i.e., on the threshold of a new age, what has been will be again. *320: dumblynass*: "dumble-, dummel-ness," slowness and stupidity. *320: sitta*: site; city; It., "città"; Sita, in the Indian Rāmāyana, the hero's wife; and, from the sublime back to the earth again, "sitta," Swed. for "sit." *323: soffran, allbeleaved*: a compounding of words to the effect that after all the years of its sovranty and exploitation, "Albi(-on)" leaves only suffering in Ireland; ALP's more personal lament is that as she reaches Fall time, she is bereft of her leaves; as well as abandoned, "beleaved." *326: The nik of a nad*: just as the word "jiffey" preceding is the Liffey's jiffy, so "the nick of time" here is that of "river," the Indian "nad"; it is also "Old Nick" in the "Serpent," the dial. "nadder" for "adder"; ("Nick and Mick," Lucifer and Michael, are of course as contrary as the twins Shem and Shaun, and are used accordingly in all of FW); "nad" is also the *Obs.* "had not," a lack of privilege in one person causing a contemptuous "nique" or "nod" of the head on the part of another person; somewhat offsetting this is the inscription, over the entrance of the Dublin War Memorial, of "NIKH," Gr. for "victory." *326-7: I waked you*: she "waked" him as his widow, as his helpmate, and as the driving-force of Nature.

328: vagurin: points to the Dubliner Maturin and his "Gothic" novel, *Melmouth the Wanderer;* see Fr., "vaguer," and other Romance langs. for words for "wander"; "vagabond," "vague," etc. *331: bowldstrong*: "Strongbow," earl of Pembroke, 12th cent. invader of Ireland. *332-3: adamant evar*: "strong as ever" (stronger than "Strongbow," because "all earls are weak at times, just as 'girls' are"), and "ever Adam and Eve." *333: norewere*: "Strongbow's castle on the Nore,"—Stephen, in *Ulysses;* "Noor," Du., "Norwegian"; "Njördhr," in Scand. Myth., a god of the waters. *335: bogue*: a nautical term for "to fall off from the wind"; and American-Fr. from Choctaw "bok" for "creek, brook." *335: arrohs*: probably is made up of "errors," "arrahs" (Irish exclamation), and "arras"; since "arrrows" derives from words akin to "arc," and is substantiated by the "bogue" before it, there is little doubt that the promise of the rainbow is at hand again. *335: Ludegude of the Lashlanns*: "Lhudd," lewd god of the anc. Britons, evolved into the later King Lud and the even later Arthurian King Lot, or Loth; the midmost of the three probably gave his name to "Ludgate" in the old wall of London; the Scandinavian King of Lochlin, the crude Swaran, was opposed by Fingal when the former invaded Ireland; Stephen, in *Ulysses,* thinks of himself as one of the "noble race of Lochlanns"; "Lachs" is G. for "salmon," throughout Ir. literature and FW a symbol of wisdom: rivers Lud, Eng., and Lachlan, N.S.W. *340: Strutt*: Sir Joseph Strutt, 18th cent. author of *Dresses and Habits of the English People. 341: forkful of fat*: forks in the river and deltas are ever Anna Livia's fate, and for good reason; a "fork" was once a pickpocket (see *Filou,* line 4); it is useful as a phallic symbol; Phorcus, the sea god and sire of the Gorgons; Anna has in fact complained before (FW 618): "No widower whother (Howth the widower) soever followed us about with a fork . . . he always sits forenenst us." Fork R., Canada. *342: Scieoula!*: very similar in sound to the Ir. for "storyteller"; and to "skjōla," ON. "tub"; see It. "sciolo" and "sciolto," and Ir. "sciolla"; one of the effects of the word—helped by the "king of whistlers" before it—is that of the shrill of bagpipes. *346: Find Me Colours*: "Find," var. of "Finn" MacCool; it refers again to Macpherson's *Fingal;* ALP's search for two things, the rainbow and the reappearance of the cultural hero, is a search for one—a new Golden Age. *347: Tobecontinued's tale*: the epic *Fingal* was continued in a sequel, *Temora;* in the Viconian sense it is the History that repeats itself; the same, but new. *347-8: while blubles blows there'll still be sealskers*: "while bugles (Gabriel's?) blow"; "as long as there are blubber-whales spouting bubbles"; ". . . there'll still be Seekers, sailors, and sealers"; the last word is here made up of "Danskers," Danes, and "sealkies," Scot. & Ir. dim. of "seal." *351: bark and tan*: "barkentine"; "Black and Tan," a police force recruited by the British to suppress the Irish risings of 1919-21. *352: fan me coolly*: Finn MacCool's first name is often so pronounced. *moss*: "mouse"; "moss," a peat bog. *353*: "Roaring Boy," a riotous young blade, one of the "night-prowlers" of 17th cent. London; Roaring Water Bay, Ire. *354: sheeny*: the "sheen" of a lightning-flash; also Ir. for "storm." *perce me rawly*: the Pearse and the O'Rahilly, from whom Joyce derives his Persse O'Reilly, were victims of the massacre of Sinn Feiners on Easter day, 1916. *357: Thorror*:

"Thorr," ON., "thunder"; "Thorer," according to one of the Sagas, a half-pirate, half-trader Viking, whose voyages included a call at the port of Dublin. *359: keys of me heart*: becomes—thanks to the etymology of "key"—Peg O' My Heart. *361-2: duv herself div. Inn this linn*: "duv," var. of "dubh," and "linn," turns this into the Bristol Inn, Dubhlinn; Swed. "lynne" means "mood"; "div," Scot., "do"; plus Inn, the anc. Aenus river, and Lynn Canal, Alaska. *362: nnow fforvell*: "Farvel," Dan., "Goodbye"; "forwelk," to dry up; "forvay," *Obs.*, to go astray, to err; the River Liffey, in performing either or both of the latter meanings, would find that it was Now Farewell Forever. *362-3*: alternate reading: feeling eeirie and lonely (dial. "wisht"), she wishes she could see the Hill of Howth more clearly as the Light on Dublin Bay grows closer; i.e. her eyes are misting as she approaches the end. *364: acoolsha*: "acushla," Ir. for "darling," slightly garbled in order to accommodate MacCool. *367: Imlamaya*: the biblical "Imlah" stands for repletion and plenitude, and so does the Hindu "Maya." *375-6: fails . . . feel . . . fall*: "Fail," "Ireland"; "feel," fr. AS. "faéle," "faithful, good"; in legend, the Stone of Fal cried out whenever it was trodden on by the rightful kings of Ireland; the Irish and American Feale and Fall rivers. *391: wild din*: perhaps also "wilding." *394-5: weird . . . hair*: now reigning in the place of her mother, the New Moon removes the Crescent in order to wear it as a badge of office in her own hair; "Weird," "Fate"; considering her daughter as the River which she is most often to be, the mother may also be wondering what she will wear ("weir," bank, levee) as a girdle. *395: the stormies*: "The Stormy Billows" are the daughters of "Ran," who entices mariners down to her dwelling-place in the deep, and of Aegir—see "Eager," line *144. 395: Hang ho!*: Hoang Ho, the Yellow River, China. *402: feary father*: "Feary," the name of several Irish saints, the most famous of whom was St. Fiachra the Solitary; primarily here, "Aweful, Fear-inspiring Father." *403: moananoaning*: Mananan mac Lir of Tuatha De Danann was traditionally associated with sea-trade, and was supposed to have originated in the Isle of Man; "mac Lir" makes him a "son of the Sea": "Flow over them with your waves and with your waters, Mananaan, Mananaan MacLir,"—p. 181, *Ulysses. 405: therrble prongs!*: Trident ("three-terrible forks") of the God of the Sea; "thurible," Eccl., "a censer." *406: more*: Russ., "sea"; Ir., "Mor," ancient, great; "mort," from Fr., "dead"; Mor R., Bengal: Murman coast, Archangel, White Sea. *411*: even Humpty-Dumpty's final testament is softened. *413: gull*: Gull of the Flail, anc. Ir. hero.

KEYES, SIDNEY. Born, Hartford, Kent, England, May 27, 1922; died, April 29, 1943.

WERE I TO MOUNT BEYOND THE FIELD. Part V of "The Foreign Gate." *Were I to cry . . . pity me*: a translation of the first line and a half of Rilke's first *Duino* elegy. *embracing . . . shining hair*: based on Epstein's statue *Jacob and the Angel.*

LAWRENCE, D. H. Born, Eastwood, Nottinghamshire, England, Sept. 17, 1885; died, March 2, 1930.

LEWIS, ALUN. Born, Wales, July 1, 1915; died March, 1944.

LEWIS, CECIL DAY. Ballintogher, Ireland, April 27, 1904.

"In Heaven I Suppose Lie Down Together." *Agag stance*: See 1 Samuel, xv: 32-33. *Where . . . tread*: "For fools rush in where angels fear to tread."—Pope, *Essay on Criticism,* l. 625.

LINDSAY, VACHEL. Born, Springfield, Ill., Nov. 10, 1879; died, Dec. 5, 1931.

LOWELL, ROBERT. Boston, Mass., March 1, 1917.

Mr. Edwards and the Spider. Jonathan Edwards, 1703-1758, American theologian, metaphysician, and Calvinist apologist. As a boy of twelve he wrote a series of scientific observations on the spider. One of the greatest of colonial sermons was his "Sinners in the Hands of an Angry God." *Josiah Hawley*: an opponent of Edwards.

The Drunken Fisherman. See note on Fisher King, p. 474.

The Quaker Graveyard in Nantucket. *Warren Winslow*: a cousin of the poet's; his ship was lost in the Atlantic during World War II. *Let man . . .*: See Genesis, 1: 26. *Ahab*: In Herman Melville's *Moby Dick*, Ahab is the captain of the whaling ship, the *Pequod*, which sailed out of Nantucket in search of the white whale, Moby Dick, who in a previous pursuit had bitten off Ahab's left leg. Moby Dick symbolizes for Ahab all the inscrutable malice of the universe, and his pursuit of it becomes a grappling with what seem to be the unmotivated forces of evil in the world. *Clamavimus*: "We have cried." See "Out of the depths have I cried unto thee, O Lord," Psalms cxxx: 1. *Leviathan*: probably the whale, see Psalms civ: 26. *ash-pit of Jehoshaphat*: See II Kings, ix; II Chronicles, xvii-xx. *Author's Note*: "The valley of judgment. The world, according to some prophets and scientists, will end in fire." *red flag*: See last pages of *Moby Dick.* Rammed by Moby Dick, the *Pequod* sinks beneath the waves. As the last few inches of the mainstaff are going under, the red arm of the Indian, Tashtego, rises out of the water, nailing the flag to the mainstaff. Feeling the wing of a bird (a sky-hawk) caught between hammer and mast, "the submerged savage beneath, in his death-gasp, kept his hammer frozen there; and so the bird of heaven, with archangelic shrieks, and his imperial beak thrust upwards, and his whole captive form folded in the flag of Ahab, went down with his ship, which, like Satan, would not sink to hell till she had dragged a living part of heaven along with her, and helmeted herself with it." *Jonas Messias*: Jonah is called the Messiah because his three days in the whale's belly are comparable to the three days Christ remained in the tomb before his resurrection. See Douay Bible. *Lady of Walsingham*: Shrine of the Virgin at Walsingham, England. *Author's Note*: "Our Lady of Walsingham is an adaptation of several paragraphs from E. I. Watkin's *Catholic Art and Culture*. The Virgin is a symbol of contemplation." *Non est . . .*: Isaiah prophesies that when the Lord comes among men he will not be desired for "he hath no form nor comeliness."—Isaiah, LIII: 2. *rainbow*: See Genesis, IX: 13.

MacLEISH, ARCHIBALD. Glencoe, Ill., May 7, 1892.

EINSTEIN. *Author's Note*: "The named places are all imaginary but real. That is to say—*The Acacias* are well known to me as a café but it was not that particular café I had in mind but that kind of café. So of the *Grand Hotel du Nord* of which there is at least one everywhere. There was a family of very German *Paepkes* in Glencoe, Illinois, where I was born and if they didn't own a *Sommergarten* it was because they were too rich. The *Back Stair* is the back stair that goes up behind the back panelling of every destiny."

MacNEICE, FREDERICK LOUIS. Belfast, Ireland, Sept. 12, 1907.

Author's Note: "Like most poets, I don't write poetry according to any theory but am, *qua* poet, an empiricist. I have proceeded by trial and error—but trial of different things at different times. In my earlier poems I was attempting something analogous to what Wordsworth was getting at with his 'real language of men'—not only in diction but also in rhythms. As I was at that time more interested in the surface of things, my imagery was largely topical and visual as I didn't so much mind writing rather diffusely, letting one descriptive passage lead to another. Later I got bored with description for its own sake and began to write more poems that were in the old-fashioned sense 'lyrics,' *i.e.* the expression of some one strong personal feeling, and in these I was also experimenting with fairly regular but intricate verse patterns and rhyme schemes. In turn I got tired of this, finding my content getting too narrow and my rhythms getting too pat. So I began aiming at *structure* in a more basic sense. *i.e.* subordinating all the elements of a poem to the poem itself, giving *e.g.* the preference to three dull-looking inter-dependent images over three brilliant isolated images. Going with this I paid much more attention to brute 'syntax'—to the relation between sentence structure and verse pattern. Thus in my more recent work, with the exception of certain long discursive pieces, I have deliberately gone in for *economy*. This means a frequent use of what I call 'twists'—something which appears straight-forward but is really below the belt. In imagery, particularly, I am now aiming at a *multum in parvo*, a con-centration of reference, *e.g.* in the following two lines describing a tart: 'Down a long bar/ Mascara scrawls a gloss on a torn leaf.' "

THE SUNLIGHT ON THE GARDEN. *We are dying*: See *Antony and Cleopatra*, IV, xv, 18, 41.

🐚

MASEFIELD, JOHN EDWARD. Ledbury, Herefordshire, England, June 1, 1878.

🐚

MASTERS, EDGAR LEE. Born, Garnett, Kan., Aug. 23, 1869; died March 5, 1950.

🐚

MERRILL, JAMES INGRAM. New York City, March 3, 1926.

🐚

MILLAY, EDNA ST. VINCENT. Rockland, Me., Feb. 22, 1892; died Oct. 19, 1950.

🐚

MOORE, MARIANNE. St. Louis, Mo., Nov. 5, 1887.

Author's Note *: "I tend to write in a patterned arrangement, with rhymes; stanza as it follows stanza being identical in number of syllables and rhyme-plan, with the first stanza. (Regarding the stanza as a unit, rather than the line, I sometimes divide a word at the end of a line, relying on a general straightforwardness of treatment to counteract the mannered effect.) I have a liking for the long syllable followed by three (or more) short syllables, 'lying *on the* air *there is a* bird,' and for the inconspicuous or light rhyme,—'let' in flageolet, for instance, being rhymed with 'set' in the lines, '*Its leaps should be set/ to the flageolet.*' I try to secure an effect of flowing continuity and am more and more impressed by the many correspondences between verse and instrumental music. I am against the stock phrase and an easier use of words in verse than would be tolerated in prose. I feel that the form is the out-ward equivalent of a determining inner conviction, and that the rhythm is the person."

THE MIND IS AN ENCHANTING THING. *Author's Note*: "One of the winters between 1930 and 1940, Gieseking gave at the Brooklyn Academy, a program of Handel, Bach, and Scarlatti, the moral of this poem being that there is something more important than outward rightness. One doesn't get through with the fact that Herod beheaded John the Baptist, 'for his oath's sake'; as one doesn't, I feel, get through with the injustice of the deaths died in the war, and in the first world war."

WHAT ARE YEARS? *Author's Note*: [This poem was] "partly written in 1931 and finished in 1939. The desperation attendant on moral fallibility is mitigated for me by admitting that the most willed and resolute vigilance may lapse, as with the Apostle Peter's denial that he could be capable of denial; but that failure, disgrace, and even death have now and again been redeemed into inviolateness by a sufficiently transfigured courage."

A GRAVE. *Author's Note* *: "As for 'A Grave,' it has a significance apart from the literal origin, which was a man who placed himself between my mother and me, and surf we were watching from a middle ledge of rocks on Monhegan Island after a storm. ('Don't be annoyed,' my mother said. 'It is human nature to stand in the middle of a thing.')"

THE STEEPLE-JACK. *Author's Note*: "C. J. Poole was the name of the steeple-jack who removed the Lafayette Avenue Presbyterian Church steeple at the time the 8th Avenue Independent Subway on Lafayette Avenue was being completed, threatening the foundation and other stonework of the church."

THE JERBOA. *cone*: *Author's Note*: "'Perforated with holes, it served as a fountain. Its inscription states "P. Cincius P. I. Salvius fecit." See Duff's *Freedmen in the Early Roman Empire.' The Periodical*, Feb., 1929 (Oxford University Press)."—*Selected Poems* (New York, Macmillan, 1935), p. 109. Miss Moore is quoting the caption under a fine photograph of the "Colossal Fir-Cone of Bronze" on page 4 of *The Periodical*. The cone rises out of a huge sculptured urn; to the right is a sculptured peacock. *dog-cat*: the cheetah or hunting-leopard. *stone locusts*: *Author's Note*: 'Toilet-box dating from about the twenty-second Egyptian Dynasty. *Illustrated London News*. 26th July, 1930." —*Ibid*. On page 162 of the periodical will be found a photograph of a *wooden* locust sent by a reader who writes: "It is a carved wooden toilet-box which may have contained a preparation from the flesh of the locust which was supposed to have a medicinal or cosmetic value. The wings are movable and form the lid of the box." *king's cane*: *Author's Note*: "Description by J. D. S. Pendlebury. *Illustrated London News*, 19th March, 1932."—*Ibid*. On page 427 is a photograph of "two ivory walking-stick handles in the shape of hands" from the time of Akhenaten, the Heretic Pharaoh. *folding bedroom*: *Author's Note*: "The portable bed-chamber of Queen Hetepheres presented to her by her son, Cheops.

* These two notes are taken from *The Oxford Anthology of American Literature*, Vol. II by Benet and Pearson. Used by permission of the Oxford University Press.

Described by Dr. G. A. Reisner. *Illustrated London News,* 7th May, 1932."—*Ibid.* The title of the article is "The Golden Travelling-Bed of the Mother of Cheops: A Gem of Egyptian Craftsmanship Nearly 5000 Years Ago: The Only Complete Example of an Old Kingdom Bed-Canopy—A Gift to Queen Hetepheres from King Sneferuw." It will be seen that Miss Moore has erroneously attributed the gift to the son and not the husband, and like Keats with "Cortez" has stoutly embedded the error in her poem. *Africanus:* Probably Scipio. Roman conquerors were given the name of a conquered country as a tribute. *match-thin:* *Author's Note:* "'There are little rats called jerboas which run on long hind-legs as thin as a match. The forelimbs are mere tiny hands.' Dr. R. L. Ditmars: p. 274, *Strange Animals I Have Known.*"—*Ibid.*

MOSS, HOWARD. New York City, Jan. 22, 1922.

MUIR, EDWIN. Orkney, Scotland, May 15, 1887.

Author's Note: "There is a vast area of life which science leaves in its original mystery; and this is the area with which poetry deals, or should deal. Science tries to discover those things which can be defined; poetry deals with those things which cannot be defined. It deals with life where life is most itself, most individual, and most universal; and in doing so it becomes a bond uniting mankind in time and space, a symbolical image of the unity of human experience through history, and throughout the diverse civilizations which make up the world at any moment. . . . The remedy is not to write popular poetry, for that would only confirm an error which seems to be spreading—that life can be explained, that it is 'nothing but' this or the other thing; and that all true poetry denies that error. Perhaps poets are partly to blame for the contracting interest in poetry, insofar as they have become analytical like the scientists. But the evil is obviously a wider one, and is due to the fact that we are becoming a more and more mechanical civilization, and do not seem to know how to stop. The ideal poetry for our needs today (if we could attain it) would be a poetry that was both simple and unexpected; not merely simple; not merely unexpected; but both together, and without effort. But this can only be prayed for."

The Grove. *Author's Note:* "This was written between the two wars, and expresses the feeling that life is contracting to a fatal point and is becoming a sort of jungle filled with heraldic monsters."

The Recurrence. *Author's Note:* "In one of his later books (I can't remember which) Nietzsche elaborates the idea of the Eternal Recurrence. He derives it from the assumption that while Matter is finite Time is infinite; therefore every possible combination and permutation of Matter must recur in Time an endless number of times. For instance Nietzsche must return to the same Germany, the same world, again and again, and again and again re-affirm, among other things, his idea of the Eternal Recurrence. Although it was in conflict with most of his other ideas, he regarded the Eternal Recurrence as something on which to exercise his spiritual muscles, a thing he was fond of doing. In the poem I adopt the idea for purposes of illustration, and then reject it in the last verse."

OWEN, WILFRED. Born, Oswestry, Shropshire, England, March 18, 1893; died, Nov. 4, 1918.

POUND, EZRA. Hailey, Idaho, Oct. 30, 1885.

THE CANTOS.

Cantos XVI, XIV, XV. These are known as the "Hell Cantos" and have been here compressed and rearranged to form a unit.

Canto XVI. Blake: See his The Marriage of Heaven and Hell. Peire Cardinal: Provençal troubadour, 1216-1271; see Pound's The Spirit of Romance. Il Fiorentino: "The Florentine," Dante. lo Sordels: Sordello of Mantua, one of the most celebrated of Italian troubadours, 1200-1270, who wrote in the Provençal tongue, and whom Dante revered because he sang of the purity of love. Throughout Cantos VI-VIII of his Purgatorio, Dante made him his critical and political guide to those kings and princes who had deferred their repentence. See Browning's poem "Sordello." These persons, it will be noticed, are not in hell, but before hell's mouth; they are the prophets of hell. crimen . . .: "the crime lies in the act."— E. P.* Palux Laerna: the Lernaean Swamp in the Peloponnesus where Hercules slew the Hydra. aqua morta: "dead water."—E. P. patet terra: "the earth opens."—E. P. Sigismundo: Sigismundo Malatesta, 1417-1468, ruler of Rimini, Italy, one of the figures who appears frequently in the Cantos as an archetype. He was a man of culture, a patron of artists and scholars, a warrior who entangled his domain in many ferocious battles, an unloyal partisan who sold his valor, violated his treaties, and defied the Pope. He was accused of murdering his first two wives, of violating his daughter, and of attempting the chastity of his son. Malatesta Novello: Malatesta the Younger, Sigismundo's brother, who maintained a fine library in his town of Gesena. Napoléon Barbiche: "Napoleon (the III) of the Goatee." Gaudier: Henri Gaudier-Brzeska, a young French sculptor of genius whom Pound discovered in London and encouraged, and about whom he wrote.a book. Killed in the First World War, 1915, aged 24. T.E.H.: T. E. Hulme, English philosopher and classicist, original member of the Imagist movement, the tenets of which he did much to elucidate. Killed in France, 1917, aged 34. Larmann, Vanderberg, Corcoran, Bimmy, Hammerton: Pound wrote the editor that these are all pseudonyms.

* Pound sent some notes to the editor in June, 1947. Some of these, and whatever foreign phrases which Pound wrote the editor were not quotations but his own, are followed by his initials.

Canto XIV. *mysterium*: "mystery." ΕΙΚΩΝ ΓΗΣ: "Image of Earth."
—E. P. *invidia*: "Envy," one of the Seven Deadly Sins. *corruptio*:
"corruption." *Episcopus*: "Bishop."

Canto XV. *Andiamo*: "Let's go." "*Whether in Naishapur or Babylon*":
Fitzgerald's *The Rubaiyat of Omar Khayyam*, Stanza VIII. Naishapur,
in Persia, was the birthplace of Khayyam. Ἥέλιον τ᾽ Ἥέλιον: "Sun,
the Sun."

Canto XX. *Zoe*: Byzantine empress, wife of Roman II, Argyrus, whom
she poisoned. Enthroned by Michael, the Paphlagonian, whom she
married immediately after murdering her husband. Died, 1050.
Marozia: Roman lady notorious for her profligacy; daughter of Theodora
and Theophylactus, the wife of Alberic I, Prince of Rome and Duke of
Spoletis, and the mistress of Pope Sergius III. Imprisoned by her son,
she died in 945 A.D. *Ho Bios*: "Life Itself." *cosi Elena vedi*: "Thus I
saw Helen." Virgil points out to Dante the souls of carnal sinners, among
whom is Helen of Troy. His comment begins: *Elena vedi*, "Helen see,
for whom so long a time of ill revolved."—*Inferno*, V, 64-65. *Nel fuoco
. . .*: "In the fire of love am I sent."—St. Francis of Assisi—E.P. *croceo*:
"yellow." *Mi mise . . .*: "am I sent, my recently betrothed." *lotophagi*:
"lotus-eaters." *spilla*: "pin." *Voce-profondo*: "deep voice." *ear-wax*: See
unstoppered, p. 528. *neson amumona*: ἀμύμονα νῆσον, "the goodly island" of the Sun to which Odysseus comes after his escape from Scylla
and Charybdis.—*Odyssey*, XII, 261. *ligur' aoide*: a phrase from the
Odyssey where Circe warns Odysseus about what the Sirens do to those
who heed their song: ἀλλά τε Σειρῆνες λιγυρῇ θέλγουσιν ἀοιδῇ, "but
the Sirens beguile him with their clear-toned song."—XII, 44. *Salustio*:
a Malatesta, son of Sigismundo. *Ixotta*: or Isotta, third wife of Sigismundo. *ac ferae familiares*: "the familiar beasts." *Somnus*: Roman God
of Sleep, son of Night, brother of Death. *chiostri*: "cloisters." *le
donne . . .*: "the ladies and the knights." *cramoisi*: "crimson." *diaspre*:
"jasper." *Borso*: of Esti, later Duke of Ferrar, 1413?-1471, whose reign
was peaceful and prosperous.

Canto XXI. *Placidia*: daughter of Theodosius the Great and Galla.
For a time she was regent of the Western Empire until her son came of
age. She died in 450 A.D. Her mausoleum is the church of St. Nazario
Celso. *exarchate*: viceroy of a Byzantine emperor. *les gradins*: "the
steps." *nel tramonto*: "in the sunset." "*Wind . . . mountain*": Pound wrote
the editor that this is not a quotation. *Ginetei kalon*: "It is born beautiful." *Actium*: promontory and town of Greece off which the fleet of
Antony and Cleopatra was defeated in 31 B.C. "*Damned . . . Pan*": Pound
wrote the editor that this is not a quotation. *Pines of Ise*: a shrine in Japan. *Inopos*: a tributary of the Nile. *Phoibos*: Apollo. *turris eburnea*:
"bright, ivory tower."—E. P. *Pallas*: Athena. *Athame*: Probably Atha-
mas who, driven mad by the Furies at the instance of Juno, pursued his
wife and son over a cliff. *Phaethusa*: one of the sisters of Phaethon;
while mourning his death she was turned into a tree. *Dis . . .*: Roman
God of the underworld, who kidnapped Proserpine to be his wife. Her
absence or presence on earth determined the seasons, winter when she
lived in Hades, summer when she came back to earth. "He spide her:

lovde her: caught her up: and all at once well nere."—Ovid, *Metamorphoses*, translated by Arthur Golding, 1567.

Canto XXIX. Arnaut: See 428, p. 495. *nondum* . . .: "not yet risen to shine." After the editor's translation of this phrase, Pound wrote "Belengal Alba." *Helios*: the sun. *prore*: "prows."

Canto XLVII. phtheggometha thasson: ἢ θεὸς ἠὲ γυνή· ἀλλὰ φθεγγώμεθα θᾶσσον.—*Odyssey*, X, 228. Some of Odysseus's crew come upon the palace of Circe, and watch her while she sings before a great web which she is weaving. Polites says, "Some goddess it is, or some woman. Come, let us call to her quickly." Circe then enchants the men and turns them into swine. Τὺ Διώνα . . .:—Bion, Idyl 1, "The Lament for Adonis," lines 93-94. "You, Dione, and the Fates [for] Adonis [weep]." Adonis was a beautiful youth loved by Aphrodite and slain by a wild boar. Dione was the mother of Aphrodite. Pound's version seems to be a corrupt one. The standard Oxford text of Wilamowitz reads: 'αἰαῖ' δ' ὀξὺ λέγοντι πολὺ πλέον ἢ παιῶνα./ καὶ Μοῖραι τὸν ῎Αδωνιν ἀνακλαίοισιν ἐν ῎Αιδα. The Graces are lamenting: "they shrilly cry 'alas, alas' instead of a song of joy. And the Fates weep for Adonis in Hades." Wilamowitz has substituted παιῶνα (paeon, song of praise or joy; or, even, Apollo) for the τὺ διώνα of the manuscripts which he considers to be corrupt. *Molü*: μῶλυ, the "magic herb" which Hermes gave to Odysseus to protect him from the magic wiles of Circe. (See *Addenda*, p. 560, for notes to Canto XLV.)

HUGH SELWYN MAUBERLEY. These poems are Pound's farewell to England just before his retirement to Paris and finally to Rapallo, Italy. In part, they show his disillusion with England as an environment sympathetic to the arts. Mauberley is partly fictitious and partly autobiographical, a character by means of which Pound presents his portrait of the exiled artist with point and irony, much of which is directed against himself. He is an artist not in tune with his times, which demand the cheap imitations of a mercantile society and not the genuine products based on traditional dedication to craft. An idealist who believes in the slogans of a cynical world, he is murdered in its wars; his revolt leads to an extreme aesthetic dedication to the arts and to loss of equilibrium in personal life, best represented by the artists of the 90's, that "tragic generation." Like the Jews he is doomed to exile; honors go to the opportunists; he becomes entangled in dilettantism, is patronized and tolerated, dreams of a world in which beauty and love are equated with a fulfilled dedication to the arts. In the second section, Mauberley is shown withdrawn from a world of aggression and love into a passive aestheticism composed of delicate artistry, or into a dream of beauty centered about a lady, or to a hedonistic exile among islands. *Vocat.* . . .: "The summer calls us into the shade."—Nemesianus, *Eclogue* IV, Roman poet, c. 283 A.D., who wrote about fishing, hunting, aquatics. The note of exile.

Part I. Portrait of the artist out of tune with his time, trying to revive the dead art of poetry, reviled and baited, roaming in the real and visionary islands of exile, obstinately dedicated to his art, forgotten in his manhood, and finally adding nothing to the lustre of poetry. *E. P. Ode* . . . .: "Ezra Pound, Ode on the Choice of His Tomb." But for the

"*E.P.*" and the "*Pour*" this is the title of an Ode by Pierre de Ronsard (1534-1585).—*Odes*, Book IV. *Capaneus*: one of the Seven Heroes who marched from Argos against Thebes and whom Zeus destroyed by lightning because he dared to defy him. The poet, rebellious against authority, is in similar danger; like the trout, he bites at illusionary bait. "Ἴδμεν . . . .: *Odyssey*, XII, 189. In full the line reads: "For we know all the toils that in wide Troy the Argives and Trojans endured through the will of the gods, and we know all things that come to pass upon the fruitful earth." This is the song which the Sirens sing to Odysseus and his comrades in order to entice them to stay. *unstoppered*: Odysseus had put wax into the ears of his crew that they might not hear the song of the Sirens. The poet indicates that he *wishes* to hear and be exiled from civilization. *His true . . . sundials*: The poet's true wife and home is his obstinate dedication to his art in exile; he would rather live in waywardness and enchantment than by mottoes and rules. *l'an. . .*: opening line of Villon's *Grand Testament* altered to the third person: "In the thirtieth year of my life." Pound was thirty-four in 1919 when "Hugh Selwyn Mauberley" was written. *the case. . .*: The poet ironically says that the history of this poet adds nothing to the lustre of poetry.

Part II. His age demands of the artist a cheap imitation of the genuine.

Part III. The decline of our civilization from that of the Greek. *mousseline of Cos*: muslin from a Greek island of the Dodecanese, famous for this fabric. *barbitos*: a musical instrument something like the lyre. τὸ καλὸν: "the beautiful." τίν' ἄνδρα . . .: from Pindar's Second Olympian Ode, line 2. The correct reading is τίνα θεόν, τιν' ἤρωα, τίνα δ' ἄνδρα κελαδήσομεν, and means, "what god, what hero, what man shall we loudly praise?"

Part IV. The disillusion of those who died in World War I "to make the world safe for democracy." *pro domo*: "for the home." *pro patria . . .*: *Dulce et decorum est pro patria more* ("It is sweet and fitting to die for one's country.")—Horace, *Odes*, XII, ii, 13.

Part V. The sacrifice of talent for an already ruined civilization.

Part VI. Yeux Glauques: "glaucous eyes," a brilliant yellow-green; Pound wrote the editor that the phrase is not a quotation. This poem recreates some of the troubles and personal affairs of the Pre-Raphaelite poets and painters of the 90's. They took as their models the painters of the epoch before Raphael, and aimed at fidelity to nature, sincerity, and delicacy of finish. Abused by the critics of their day for their technique and subject matter, and accused of immorality in their life and art, they were championed by *John Ruskin. King's Treasuries* is the title of the first lecture of Ruskin's *Sesame and Lilies* (1865) discussing the treasures which are to be found hidden in books. Robert *Buchanan* attacked the school in a review, entitled "The Fleshly School of Poetry," (*The Contemporary Review*, Oct. 1871), of Dante Gabriel Rossetti's *Poems.* The attack centered primarily on "Jenny," a poem about a thoughtful worldly young man who goes with Jenny, a London harlot, to her room and soliloquizes on the lot of the Jennys of this world while she sleeps, sitting on the floor, her head on his knees. The head and eyes of Pound's poem are those of Elizabeth Siddell, a young seamstress who was discovered by one of the Pre-Raphaelite painters, and who immediately became their favorite model and later Gabriel Rossetti's wife. On her death he buried a sheaf of his unpublished poems (including "Jenny") in her grave but later had them exhumed for publication. She is to be seen in Roman Hunt's *Sylvia*, Millais' *Ophelia*, Rossetti's *Beatrice*, and, according to this poem, in Sir Edmund Burne-Jones' painting *Cophetua and the Beggar Maid* (1884) which now hangs in the *Tate* Gallery in London. (The ballad of Cophetua, an African king who falls in love with and marries a beggar maid, is to be found in Percy's *Reliques*, and is retold by Tennyson in "The Beggar Maid.") Siddell's *eyes* were described as "greenish-blue" by William Rossetti, and as "golden-brown, agate colour" by Burne-Jones. When Edward Fitzgerald published his translation of the *Rubaiyat* of Omar Khayyam in 1859 it was *still-born* and received no attention until Rossetti discovered and praised it in the following year. *maquero*: one who seduces girls to live on their earnings, or ruins them and commits them to brothels.

Part VII. Siena . . . Maremma: See 293-94, p. 490. M. Verog recalls the decadent, religious, aesthetic, dissipated period of the 90's symbolized by the *Rhymers' Club*, founded in 1891, among the members of which were Dowson, Johnson, Yeats and Symons. Gaston Alexander *Gallifet* was a French general of the Franco-Prussian war who led a memorable cavalry charge at Sedan. Pound wrote the editor that *M. Verog* is Victor Plarr, 1863-1929, biographer of Dowson, and author of a book of poetry, *The Dorian Mood*, 1896. *Johnson* was converted to Catholicism, hence the reference to Cardinal Newman. He was a solitary drinker, and died from a fall, though not in a pub. *Dowson* died at the age of thirty-three, of tuberculosis, alcoholism, dissipation and hashish. The R. Rev. Arthur C. *Headlam* was the Bishop of Gloucester. Selwyn *Image* was co-editor of *The Hobby Horse*, a periodical which was the link between the poets of the 90's and the Pre-Raphaelites, and in which Dowson's "Cynara" first appeared.

Part VIII. Brennbaum: Portrait of the Great Exile, the Wandering Jew. *memories*: of the Hebraic exodus, of the forty-year wandering in the wilderness, of how Moses made water gush out of the Rock of Mt. *Horeb* and received the Ten Commandments from God on top of Mt. *Sinai*.

Part IX. Mr. Nixon: Portrait of the literary opportunist and best-seller, contemptuous of those who dedicate their life to their art without compromise and who are symbolized for him by the artists of the 90's. *Nixon*: "fictitious name for a real person."—E. P. *Bloughram*: "reference to Browning's bishop, allegoric."—E. P.

Part X. Portrait of the artist who refines his style in country retirement, unknown, with a country girl for mistress, living in a leaking house, expending his artistry on cooking.

Part XI. The lady curator of Milesian ware living in Ealing, a London suburb, is not touched by past glory but lives within the confines of her class and station. Tradition cannot survive in mercantile England.

Part XII. Daphne . . .: Pound wrote the editor that this is a translation, but does not say from whom. Daphne was a nymph pursued by Apollo; she eluded him by being transformed into a laurel tree. Portrait of the lady-patron for whom poets and poetry are another of the amenities with which to kill time. The poet compares her to the Daphne of his dreams and of antiquity, and recalls that *Fleet Street,* the rendezvous in the eighteenth century of men of letters who cultivated the Muses, and who clustered about Dr. Samuel *Johnson,* is now a center of merchandise. *Pieria:* in Macedonia, Greece, seat of the worship of the Muses.

Part XIII. Envoi: The poet tells his Lady that if his songs have as their subject her beauty and glories they will attain longevity, like roses laid in amber, and be sung by other lovers when they themselves have died. The poem is a variant of "Go Lovely Rose!" by Edmund Waller (1606-1687). Henry *Lawes:* (1596-1662) English composer, especially of airs.

MAUBERLEY. *Vacuos . . .:* "He bites vacuously at the air."—Ovid, *Metamorphoses,* VII, 786. Pound has substituted *vacuos* for the original *vanos,* "vainly." After Oedipus had destroyed the power of the sphinx who was ravaging Thebes, a second monster was sent to terrorize the city. It eluded all hunters and dogs until Cephalus set his dog, Laelaps, after it, the gift of Artemis: "The dog presses him hard, follows step by step, and, while he seems to hold him, does not hold him, and snaps at the empty air." Cephalus turns aside a moment from the pursuit to adjust his javelin, but when he looks again he beholds both the monster and the dog turned to stone, one the perpetual pursuer, the other the perpetual pursued, and both unconquered.

Part I. Dedicated to his art and wishing to recapture some of its classical glory, the poet, like certain painters of the Italian Renaissance, has not the skill to evoke fully the glory that was Greece, but only to present it with firmness and in part, in profile. *eau-forte par:* "etching by." Jules *Jaquemart:* 1837-1880, Parisian water-colorist and etcher. *strait:* small, narrow, strict, rigorous. Valeria *Messalina:* c. 8 A.D., wife of the Roman Emperor Claudius; murdered when she was twenty-four. Pound writes the editor that he had in mind a particular portrait, but that he cannot now remember which. Piero della *Francesca:* (1416?-1492) Umbrian painter who, according to Reinach, was "cold and impersonal"; there was "something spectral and disquieting, together with a touch of melancholy disdain, in his pale, straight figures." *Pisanello:* Vittore Pisano (1397-1455) Veronese painter and medalist, best known for his medals and plaques. His earliest medal was probably that of the Greek emperor John VII Paeologos, dated 1438-1439. Hence the *forge Archaia,* for Archaia is an ancient district of Greece and, by metonymy, Greece itself.

Part II. Qu'est . . .: "What do they know of love, and what can they understand? If they don't understand poetry, if they don't feel music, what can they understand of this passion, compared to which the rose is gross and the perfume of violets a clap of thunder?" *Caid Ali:* Pound wrote the editor that this is a pseudonym of his own. After three years of heavenly love, the poet notices that it, like all things, is fated to pass away. In the period of uncertainty and drifting estrangement, where values good and bad are entangled and must be sifted and purified in art, the poet finds himself, in retrospect, to be empty and without feeling. *Diabolus*: "the devil." *Anangke*: "Necessity," "Fate." *nuktis âgalma*: "the ornament (or statue) of night." *Nuktis* is probably an error for *nuktos*. *to agathon*: "the Good." *irides*: plural for the flower, iris. *diastasis*: "separation." *anaesthesis*: "insensibility," "loss of feeling." *Mouths* . . .: See *Vacuos*, p. 530.

Part III. "The Age Demanded": Pound refers the reader to Poem II, (p. 127) from which he has taken the title of this poem to indicate that the poet portrayed here cannot supply the cheap imitations which the age demands. He is as unfit for this as are the doves of Aphrodite, who pull the chariot of love, to be harnessed for drudgery. The capturing of a woman's beauty in art makes the season more beautiful for him but does not suggest any social application. He is troubled by the imagery of islands. Amid aggressive resistances to current irritations, he reacts by becoming mild, by retreating gradually into an armour of isolation which protects him against the impermanence of change and chance, until finally he lives in Olympian impassivity among perceptions of his own choosing. He immerses himself in a vision of islands again, a dream world from which it is not necessary to emerge as an artist and thus to compose or emend or conserve or refine. He is withdrawn from the world to a world of maudlin confession and subjective praise. His exile is made final by his rejection of the esteemed writers of his day, and by their rejection of him. *Cytheraean*: surname of Aphrodite, derived from Cythia, Crete, or the island of Cythera where she is said to have first landed after her birth from the sea, and where she had a temple. Her chariot was drawn by doves and swans. *apathein*: "impassivity."

Part IV. Portrait of the exiled artist voyaging among the Pacific islands, drifting like a hedonist in a subjective and disjuncted dream. *Moluccas*: variant for Molukka Islands, a group of spice-producing islands in the Malay Archipelago.

Part V. Medallion. Portrait of the Lady, like a Luini in porcelain, accompanying herself on the piano. Bernardino *Luini*: (1475?-1532?), Italian painter of the Lombard School, known, according to Reinach, for the dignified serenity of his paintings and their refinement of form. *Anadyomene*: literally "birth foam," a title of Aphrodite, referring to her birth from the sea. Salomon *Reinach*: (1858-1932) French archeologist who made invaluable discoveries in various parts of the ancient Greek world, best known for his *Orpheus* and *Apollo*.

THE RETURN. Modeled on the introductory poem to Henri de Regnier's *Medailles d'Argile*. Both poems are in the same tempo, the lines are cut at the same intervals. See Taupin, *Symbolisme Français*, p. 114.

RAINE, KATHLEEN. London, England, June 14, 1908.

RANSOM, JOHN CROWE. Pulaski, Tenn., April 30, 1888.

PAINTED HEAD. The speaker, a man with an *unlovely head*, sees the painting of a beautiful head separated (*abstracted*) from its body, and moralizes: Such a head did not scorn the body and wish to be separated from it; it has never fathered a book or a government; this painted abstraction (a play on words) of the head from its body is ironic, since such a beautiful head never knew the treason of desiring to be bodiless. His own head is unlovely because he has defamed the body which in revenge has wrought this image. The body is not made to feed and serve the head in order to be tyrannized by it, but to receive, in turn, an increase of being. Beauty is of the body; the head needs the body's love in order that the acropolis of its imagination may have substance and color, that its suffering may be embodied and ennobled. *nightingales*: a multiple symbol, but primarily the transformation out of pain into song: see 99-103, p. 484.

THE EQUILIBRISTS. Because of Honor, two lovers have forsworn each other in a torturous equilibrium, yet their desire remains. The question is raised: is physical consummation and its attendant states of Hell to be preferred to bodiless and spiritual marriage?

JUDITH OF BETHULIA. See Book of Judith, the Apocrypha.

READ, HERBERT. Nuscoates, Kirbymoorside, Yorkshire, England, Dec. 4, 1893.

Author's Note: "Like most modern poets I have made a fairly extensive record of my attitude to the craft of poetry in the various volumes of criticism I have published—see especially *Form in Modern Poetry*. My own technique springs from the Imagist school of T. E. Hulme, Ezra Pound and H. D. I have tried to be clear and precise in my expression, to fuse emotion and intellect, to avoid sentimentality. The English poetry I admire most was written between 1580 and 1600, by Peele, Daniel, Drayton, Marlowe, Chapman, and, of course, Shakespeare. My modern affinities are, I hope, with Hölderlin, Stefan George, Apollinaire. I dislike French rhetoric and English sentimentality. Pasternak seems to be a poet very close to my ideal, but unfortunately I cannot read him in his own language. I think it is a hopeless task to attempt to write popular poetry in an age of mass values. Love, the main theme of poetry, has been debased by the novel and the film beneath poetic recognition. The love of God, another source of poetic inspiration in the past, does not now exist. Nobody wants to read epics, even if modern life were to provide the subject matter. The poet is in retreat, celebrating intellectual beauty in his private chapel. But he is not an escapist—on the contrary, he is keeping alive the vital flame of art and understanding in a world that is doomed by its insensitiveness, its folly, its materialistic greed. The modern poet cannot be popular because in an organic unitary sense there is no longer any people."

A WORLD WITHIN A WAR. *Author's Note*: "This poem was written during the last war (1942-43) at my house which is about twenty miles west of London. It was written, therefore, within sound of the guns, the bombs, the droning bombers. It was written while the outcome of the struggle was still uncertain. It tries to express the faith of a pacifist in that situation—not a political pacifist, but a natural pacifist: not the negative attitude of a man who does not believe in war, but the positive attitude of a man who believes in peace. The epigraph is one of the maxims of Luc de Clapiers, Marquis de Vauvenargues (1715-47), a French moralist for whom I have long had a particular sympathy (see my essay on him in *The Sense of Glory*). The poem is, like most of my long poems, divided into 'movements' on the analogy of the musical sonata. The first movement is a description of my peaceful environment. The second movement, a short scherzo, is a jaunty account of the ideal activities of the poet in a reasonable world. The third is a statement of my general philosophy of life. Then, in the fourth movement, we get the impact of a brutal reality. The passage beginning *Their feet upon the peat and sand* is a reference to the painting of *The Death of S. Peter Martyr* in the National Gallery (London) attributed to Giovanni Bellini, in which Giorgione might have had a hand. The final "coda" is a direct statement of how I hoped I should act if the impact of war which so ominously threatened me and my family were to become actual." *L'esperance . . .*: "Hope is the only thing that is respected by disgust." II. *Book of Hours*: in Catholic ritual, prayers to be repeated at stated times of the day; also, the time for these devotions, or the book containing them.

RIDLER, ANNE. Rugby, Warwickshire, England, July 30, 1912.

FOR A CHRISTENING. *Nine Bright Shiners*: *Author's Note*: "See 'Green Grow the Rashes O,' *English County Songs* ed. Lucy Broadwood; refers to the nine months preceding birth."—*The Nine Bright Shiners* (London, Faber & Faber, 1943), p. 50.

A MILE FROM EDEN. *Flounder*: *Author's Note*: a fairy story by Grimm, the incantation of which is "Flounder, Flounder in the sea."

ROBINSON, EDWIN ARLINGTON. Born, Head Tide, Me., Dec. 22, 1869; died, April 6, 1935.

Eros Turannos: "Love is a tyrant."

ROETHKE, THEODORE. Saginaw, Mich., May 25, 1908.

ROSENBERG, ISAAC. Born, Bristol, Ireland, Nov. 25, 1890; died, April 1, 1918.

RUKEYSER, MURIEL. New York City, Dec. 15, 1913.

SANDBURG, CARL. Galesburg, Ill., Jan. 6, 1878.

SCHWARTZ, DELMORE. Brooklyn, N. Y., Dec. 8, 1913.

SHAPIRO, KARL. Baltimore, Md., Nov. 10, 1913.

ELEGY. *Delano*: F. D. Roosevelt. *Horatian fallacy*: the golden mean.

SITWELL, EDITH. Scarborough, England, Sept. 7, 1887.

TEARS. *Author's Note*: "'. . . Methusalem, with all his hundreds of years, was but a mushroom of a night's growth, to this day; and all the fair monarchies, with all their thousands of years, and all the powerful Kings and the beautiful Queens of this world, were but as a bed of flowers, some gathered at six, some at seven, some at eight, all in one morning, in respect of this day.' John Donne, Sermon LXXIII."—*Street Song*. (London, Macmillan, 1943), p. 20.

STILL FALLS THE RAIN. *Dives*: The rich man in the parable of "the rich man and Lazarus" who went to Hell.—Luke, XVI: 19-31. *O Ile . . . firmament*: Christopher Marlowe's *Doctor Faustus*, lines 1430-31. From the last soliloquy of Faustus, as he frantically tries to avoid his eternal punishment in Hell for having sold his soul to the devil.

SPENDER, STEPHEN. London, England, Feb. 28, 1909.

STEIN, GERTRUDE. Born, Allegheny, Pa., Feb. 3, 1874; died, July 27, 1946.

STEVENS, WALLACE. Reading, Pa., Oct. 2, 1879.

NOTES TOWARD A SUPREME FICTION. A poem of thirty poems with prologue and epilogue, divided into three groups entitled, "It Must Be Abstract," "It Must Change," "It Must Give Pleasure," embodying Stevens' mature views of the relationship between poetry, philosophy, imagination, and reality. The direct line of argument is given in two essays, "The Figure of the Youth as Virile Poet" (*Sewanee Review*, Autumn, 1944) and "The Noble Rider and the Sound of Words" (Allen Tate, ed., *The Language of Poetry*, Princeton University Press, 1942), in which Stevens concludes: "There is, in fact, a world of poetry indistinguishable from the world in which we live, or, I ought to say, no doubt, from the world in which we shall come to live, since what makes the poet the potent figure that he is, or was, or ought to be, is that he creates the world to which we turn incessantly and without knowing it and that he gives to life the supreme fictions without which we are unable to conceive of it." Poetry is the supreme fiction of life created by the personality of the poet as it grows and changes in a "radiant and productive atmosphere" composed out of the interdependence of the worlds of reality and imagination. The poem is an amalgamation and transformation in which reality and imagination are one, an apotheosis in which the total personality of the poet shares, an inquiry into being and reality, an imaginative ontology, a phase of metaphysics, a "supreme fiction." Poetry is concerned with the abstract because poetry and philosophy are one: philosophy is an "official" and poetry an "unofficial" view of being. Philosophy attempts to approach truth through reason and logical knowledge, poetry through the imagination and empirical knowledge. The danger of abstraction is that it might go beyond the imagination into fancy and illusion, into images removed from basis in fact, into systems religious and illusionary. Stevens insists that the world of reality is not a Platonic reflection of abstract ideas, but that the abstract imagination is created by the poet from the world of reality through the medium of his own personality composed of both reason and sensibility, and thus distinguishes between the credible and the incredible imagination. Poet and philosopher constantly project ideals of man and nature, but these are humanistic and not supernatural or fantastic, and derive from the world of reality: the measure of the poet is "the measure of his power to abstract himself, and to withdraw with him into his abstraction the reality on which the lovers of truth insist. He must be able to abstract himself and also to abstract reality, which he does by placing it in his imagination." Priority is given to the fact that poetry "must give pleasure," that the poet and his abstract imagination are steeped and formed in a world of sensual reality, in "the pleasures of merely circulating": "The pleasure is the pleasure of powers that create a truth that cannot be arrived by reason alone, a truth that the poet recognizes by sensation. The morality of the poet's radiant and productive atmosphere is the morality of the right sensation." The poet must create his unreal out of the real, his invisible out of the visible. The final emphasis lies in the fact that poetry and life "must change," that things-in-themselves in the world of reality, concepts in the world of the imagination, and the poet himself are formed in an endless process of continuous change, only momentarily arrested by the poems which the poet creates, and which themselves undergo changes in time. The conclusion is implied that the only reality is a changing and creative one, that life and poetry are supreme fictions, "that the imagination never brings anything into the world but . . . on the contrary, *like the personality of the poet in the act of creating, it is no more than a process* [italics the editor's], and desiring with all the power of our desire not to write falsely, do we not begin to think of the possibility that poetry is the only reality, after all, and that poetic truth is an actual truth, seen, it may be, by those whose range in the perception of fact, that is, whose sensibility, is greater than our own?" Poetry is the imagination of life. (There is an interesting parallelism between Stevens' point of view and the three metaphysical laws—not the politics—of dialectical materialism: (1) the law of the permeation of opposites, (2) the law of the negation of the negation—especially the permeation of opposites as a process in time, (3) and the law of the transformation of quality into quantity and of quantity into quality.)

"It Is the Celestial. . . .": Man shuttles back and forth between extremities of the changing multiplicities of nature and the unity of the first and final idea, filled with ennui at either extremity. He wants what he does not have; only desire remains. *apartments*: truths as opposed to the truth, multiform ideas to the first idea, categories to the category. *quick*: the life. *invention*: this world. "The Lion Roars. . . .": The young man, in the agony and suffering of his imagination, is nevertheless to become a man-hero, one of the heroic children who face reality (symbolized by the lion, elephant, and bear) and bring it to heel. *ephebe*: a youth on the threshold of manhood. *glitter-goes*: the blaring of the elephant in darkness is like the glittering on ancient reservoirs in Ceylon. "It Feels Good. . . .": Participating in nature through the sensations alone without the intrusion of philosophy, the giant (that thinker of the first idea) is good, is truth. The equilibriums which we seek between reality and the imagination, such as those of love, are not consciously achieved. The abstract imagination rises out of nature as academies out of a mist. *Schwärmerei*: "seething." "Bethou Me. . . .": The many voices of the birds are like the many voices of the poets, all crying out for the one voice, the one identity, the sole face, seeking the permanent artifice of stone, of art; they are minstrels without minstrelsy, poets without mythology. And this desire of theirs is an illusion which, like others before it, will also end. *bethou*: "be thou me"; also, "give me identity." *episcopus*: bishop.

Mrs. Alfred Uruguay. The lady on the plodding donkey ascends through the moonlight of imagination seeking the peak of reality, of fact, of *to be;* the rider descends to the village seeking the sun and the land of imagination. The poem is about the cyclical similarity between the two realms.

The Sense of the Sleight-of-Hand Man. The pleasures of participating in the changing flights of nature divested of gods and myths.

Connoisseur of Chaos. The relation of opposites to their ideal unity. The eagle is a symbol of ideality. A general statement of Stevens' is applicable here: "In the fewest possible words since, as between re-semblances one is always a little more perfect than another, and since, from this, it is easy for perfectionism of a sort to evolve, it is not too extravagant to think of resemblances and of the repetitions of re-semblances as a source of the ideal. In short, metaphor has its aspect of the ideal. This aspect of it cannot be dismissed merely because we think we have long since outlived the ideal. The truth is that we are constantly outliving it and yet the ideal itself remains alive with enormous life."

THE POEMS OF OUR CLIMATE. The modern mind, a product of many corroding pressures, cannot rest in strict perfection of natural things but must find its delight in the bitter-sweet of flawed perfections. This is an image of contemporary poetry, the relation between the poet and his environment.

ACADEMIC DISCOURSE AT HAVANA. Life is like an old casino in a park in that it is now divested of its colorful and primitive mythologies; old symbols are no longer adequate because they were based on illusion; the gods, the swans, are dead, the goober khan of myth is in the twilight of Götterdämmerung, we are left with a peanut parody. Even the serener myths of poetry, of true imagination, passed like a circus, because ordinary man thinks all imagination is falsifying and sinful. Reality resides in fact and in nothing else, in grandmother, in the burgher's breast. The poet should now take the place of the myth-maker, for his words are of things that do not exist without words, and yet are related to reality; he may thus be able to bridge the gap between the two worlds and to reconcile them. *Rouge-Fatima*: *Author's Note*: "Fa-tima was one of the foremost beautiful women in the world and I suppose I put the Rouge on by way of touching her up a bit." *goober khan*: a fantastic little building where peanuts are sold.

EVENING WITHOUT ANGELS. The objects of nature are beautiful in themselves or as natural symbols of man's moods and should not become symbols of supernatural or theological beliefs. Nature without angels is best, bare earth, bare night is best. Sunrise may evoke life and death with-out theological associations. *Mario Rossi*: *Author's Note*: "A young Ital-ian philosopher who taught at Naples. I exchanged a few letters with him many years ago. He knows English. He made a trip to the west of Ireland and wrote a little book about the trip which was of particular interest to me as reflecting what a man brought up in the light and color of Naples would feel in the mist and general dimness of the west of Ireland."

THE IDEA OF ORDER IN KEY WEST. The woman singing by the sea is symbolic of the poet creating his poetry, of the world which exists and that which the poet makes, of imagination and reality, of what one takes from the other and is. The poet is driven to arrange the unmoti-vated voices of nature into an order that may reveal mankind and its origins. A general statement of Stevens is applicable here: "It is not only that the imagination adheres to reality, but, also, that reality adheres to the imagination and that the interdependence is essential." "A poet's words are of things that do not exist without words." *Ramon Fernandez*: *Author's Note*: "I used two every day names. As I might have expected, they turned out to be an actual name."

THE EMPEROR OF ICE CREAM. An ironic, grotesque contrast between the dead lady and preparations for her funeral. Death as a physical fact stripped of emotional coloring. The girls do not dress for the funeral; the boys bring flowers, but casually; the muscular man preparing the food and the emperor of ice-cream are symbols of materialistic reality. Everything is exactly shown in the cold light of the lamp. *Let be be finale of seem*: (1) take whatever seems to be, as really being, (2) let that which is put an end to that which seems. Stevens once wrote of this poem: "This wears a deliberately commonplace costume, and yet it seems to me to contain something of the essential gaudiness of poetry."

TATE, ALLEN. Winchester, Ky., Nov. 19, 1899.

SEASONS OF THE SOUL. *Allor . . .*: In the Seventh Circle of the Inferno, Dante finds himself among those who have committed suicide. They have become stunted trees yielding poison and not fruit. "Then I stretched my hand a little forward, and plucked a branchlet from a great thorn, and the trunk of it cried, 'Why dost thou rend me?'"—*Inferno*, XIII, 31-33.

ODE TO THE CONFEDERATE DEAD. *Author's Note*:* "The structure of the ode is simple. Figure to yourself a man stopping at the gate of a Confederate graveyard on a late autumn afternoon. The leaves are falling; his first impressions bring him the *rumor of mortality*; and the desolation barely allows him, at the beginning of the second stanza, the heroically conventional surmise that the dead will enrich the earth, *where these memories grow*. From those quoted words to the end of the passage he pauses for a baroque meditation on the ravages of time, concluding with the figure of the *blind crab*. This creature has mobility but no direction, energy but no purposeful world to use it in: in the entire poem there are only two explicit symbols for the locked-in ego; the crab is the first and less explicit symbol, a mere hint, a planting of the idea that will become overt in its second instance—the jaguar towards the end. The crab is the first intimation of the nature of the moral conflict upon which the drama of the poem develops: the cut-offness of the modern 'intellectual man' from the world. The next long passage or strope, beginning *You know who have waited by the wall*, states the other term of the conflict. It is the theme of heroism, but heroism in a grand style, elevating even death from mere physical dissolution into a formal ritual: this heroism is a formal ebullience of the human spirit in an entire society, not private, romantic illusion—something better than moral heroism, great as that may be, for moral heroism,

* From "Narcissus as Narcissus," *On the Limits of Poetry*, (New York, William Morrow, 1948).

being personal and individual, may be achieved by certain men in all ages, even ages of decadence. But the late Hart Crane's commentary is better than any I can make: 'The theme of chivalry, a tradition of excess (not literally excess, rather active faith) which cannot be perpetuated in the fragmentary cosmos of today—those desires that should be yours tomorrow, but which, you know, will not persist nor find any way into action.' The structure then is a tension between the two themes, 'active faith' which has decayed, and the 'fragmentary cosmos' which surrounds us . . . In contemplating the heroic theme the man at the gate never quite commits himself to the illusion of its availability to him. The most that he can allow himself is the fancy that the blowing leaves are charging soldiers, but he rigorously returns to the refrain: *Only the wind—*of the *leaves flying.* I suppose it is a commentary on our age that the man at the gate never quite achieves the illusion that the leaves are heroic men, so that he may identify himself with them, as Keats and Shelley easily and beautifully did with nightingale and west winds. More than this, he cautions himself, reminds himself repeatedly of his subjective prison, his solipsism, by breaking off the half-illusion and coming back to the refrain of wind and leaves—a refrain that, as Hart Crane said, is necessary to the 'subjective continuity.' These two themes struggle for mastery up to the passage *we shall say only the leaves whispering/ In the improbable mist of nightfall* which is the end. It will be observed that the passage begins with a phrase taken from the wind-leaves refrain—the signal that it has won. The refrain has been fused with the main stream of the man's reflections, eliminating them and he cannot return even to an ironic vision of the heroes. There is nothing but death, the mere naturalism of death at that. Autumn and the leaves are death; the men who exemplified in a grand style an 'active faith' are dead; they are only the leaves. Shall we then worship death? ' . . . *set up the grave/ In the house?* The *ravenous grave . . .* ' that will take us before our time? The question is not answered, although as a kind of romanticism it might, if answered affirmatively, provide an illusory solution to the solipsism of the man; but he cannot accept it. Nor has he been able to live in his immediate world, the fragmentary cosmos. There is no practical solution, no solution offered for the edification of moralists . . . . The closing image, that of the serpent, is the ancient symbol of time, and I have tried to give it all the credibility of the commonplace by placing it in a mulberry bush—with the faint hope that the silkworm would somehow be implicit . . . . The *setting sun* I tried to use as a triple image, for the decline of the heroic age and for the actual scene of late afternoon, the latter not only natural desolation but spiritual desolation as well . . . again for a moment he thinks he hears the battle shout, but only for a moment; then the silence reaches him . . . This figure of the jaguar is the only explicit rendering of the Narcissus motif in the poem, but instead of a youth gazing into a pool, a predatory beast stares at a jungle stream, and leaps to devour himself."

THOMAS, DYLAN. Swansea, Wales, Oct. 27, 1914.

VISION AND PRAYER. In pattern-poetry, the varying line-lengths form a picture or design. The form probably originated in Asia Minor, was brought into the Greek Empire with the invasion of Cyrus and with the infiltration of Oriental influences in the school of Alexandria. It was popularized in the Western World primarily by means of the egg, axe, and wing pattern poems of Simias of Rhodes (300 B.C.) as published in the Greek Anthology. The first English pattern poem was written by Stephen Hawes in *The Convercyon of Swerers* in 1509. Others followed him, notably William Browne, George Withers, Frances Quarles, George Herbert, Robert Herrick, Thomas Traherne. The first part of "Vision and Prayer" is in the form of a diamond. Although the lines have an even time-beat, the meter is purely syllabic, increasing from one to nine syllables, and decreasing to one again. There are a few exceptions, and stanza five lacks its first eight-syllable line. Each stanza opens and closes with a rhymed couplet, and all other line terminations, but for *wound* in stanza four and *ancient* in stanza six, end in nasal sounds, either *n*, *m*, or *ng*. Part II, the Prayer, is in the form of an hourglass, or imitates the form of George Herbert's prayer, "Easter Wings." But for the addition of an extra seven-syllable line in stanza five, and a few other exceptions, the lines diminish from nine syllables to one and increase to nine again. The nasal terminations are not consistent, and diminish as the poem progresses; the rhymes are vicarious. Note that the last half of a diamond and the first half of another make an hourglass, and that the last half of an hourglass and the first half of another make a diamond: thus one form is hidden in that of the other. See also George Wither's *Farewell, Sweet Groves.*

The poet sees and hears, as in a Vision, the birth of Christ in the womb of his mother, as if the womb were a room separated from his own by the thin partition of a *wren's bone*, (symbolic of the infinitesimal distance that continuously separates man from God). The birth of Christ, and the consequent salvation of man through Christ's suffering, tears down this partition; the poet is caught up in the storm and lightning of this event which, like the unsolicited Love of God, floods down to mankind in Charity to save and to redeem. The poet, caught up in the wounded breast of Christ, sees in a Vision the ascension of all the dead on the Day of Judgment, the winding home, the end of all suffering through the suffering of Christ, and the dying into eternal life. In the second part, the Prayer, the poet, aware that man is not worth the suffering which Christ must undergo, prays that the Christ-Child return to the womb that bore Him. He prays that Christ let the wanton and dead lie unchristened even though they pray to Him to be born and to be saved through His agony and crucifixion. Let them still lie in the dark, the poet says, and be blown down like dirt under the forever falling night of man's fall from grace, into the country of death to which man has become accustomed. In the name of all the unworthy, who now no longer desire salvation, the poet prays that the dazzling sun of forgiveness and resurrection be dimmed. He is answered by the sudden blind blaze of the sun (God) which, regardless of man's defection from his God, of Its own free will and love, finds the sinner and takes him up in a blaze of glory.

IN MEMORY OF ANN JONES. After the funeral, the insincere praises and weeping, the shaking of heads, the muffled pegging down of the coffin, the pulling down of blinds (actual, spiritual, and in death), after marks of excessive sorrow—the teeth, as it were, in black, the eyes clogged with weeping, the hypocritical crying (a reversal of "laughing up one's sleeve"); after the sound of the grave-digger's spade that awakens the sleepers (but not the dead) and shakes the desolate boy who in his mind had already died of grief, but who cannot cry; after a sound like that on the Day of Judgment which shall announce Ann's deserved resurrection; after the wake, the indulgence in tears and pain, the poet stands in Ann's room with its stuffed fox and stale fern, recalling her. She was a humble-hearted and withdrawing woman, says the poet, whose goodness like a fountain quenched the parching sun and nourished the waste lands of Wales, though she needs no poet to magnify her image disproportionately, out of desire to praise her. Nevertheless, he calls upon the seas to sing out the praises of her virtue (which speaks out with an ingrained and natural tongue) that her natural virtue may ring out over the hymning heads, the woods, the chapel, that her spirit may be blessed by crossing birds flying in cross formation. Though she was meek, the poet thus magnifies her, out of the ferocity of his grief (the house and window are actual, yet symbolic of his eyes and body). He envisions her dead, humble, religious, wordless, witless, centered in pain, stone dead and seventy years old, and this image, he says, shall storm him with grief until the dead (symbolized by the fox) shall rise again in love, and the dead fern drop seeds of life again on the windowsill (and the sill of the grave).

THOMPSON, DUNSTAN. New London, Conn., Aug. 30, 1918.

VAN DOREN, MARK. Hope, Ill., June 13, 1894.

VAZAKAS, BYRON. New York City, Sept. 20, 1906.

WARREN, ROBERT PENN. Guthrie, Ky., April 24, 1905.

REVELATION. Author's Note: "'Revelation' was written in the spring of 1942. You ask about Sulla. Augustine refers to him in the City of God, Chapter 24, Book II, as the conqueror of his fellow-citizens—who broke the unity of the state, etc., offended his mother Rome, etc. (not

Augustine's phrase)—who was assisted by 'demons'. As for the change of kind—*the blunt herbivorous tooth dripped blood*—the upset of Nature as the result of the offense against the whole, against the texture of things, against the order of the world, this is a reference to Chapter 23, Book III, of the *City of God*. Augustine does not here mention Sulla as the offender, and puts the occasion as the social wars of the Latins against Rome." *Duncan.* . . .: See *Macbeth*, II, iii, 60.

Pursuit. *Author's Note*: " 'Pursuit' is very similar to 'Terror.' It deals with the same basic theme, and the *you* is the same *you* who seeks the 'answer' in the various quarters enumerated in the poem. No luck. But the *you* doesn't know how to look for the answer or quite what he is looking for. If he did know, he might get an answer, or a hint of it, even from the little old widow, the past of the sufferers who seem to have some truth which the *you* has missed. The poem was begun in Gambier, Ohio (the seat of Kenyon College) in August 1940 and was finished in Baton Rouge, Louisiana, in October of that year." Those sick at heart in modern civilization, unable to expiate their guilt, go to the clinic for diagnosis and feel like barbarians or disbelievers before either pagan sacrificial fathers or the authority of Jewry. The doctor cannot diagnose the malady; he advises a change of scene or heart: Florida, where the sick man tries to involve himself with the scene, the girl, and child, the old lady—all of whom are equally involved and can teach him nothing. Personal despair is the shadow of social despair and one is incurable without the other. You pursue and are pursued.

Terror. *Author's Note*: " 'Terror' was written in the winter of 1939-40 in Rome. The idea for the poem came when I saw in the Rome paper *Il Messaggero* (Saturday, Jan. 27) a report that U. S. volunteers serving in foreign armies would not lose their citizenship—this applying at the moment to Americans serving with the Finnish forces against Russia; and in (I think) the same paper, though perhaps another paper on the same day, a report of the 'death' of the chicken heart which Alexis Carel had kept alive for a long time in his laboratory and which had for popular-science writers the promise of a mortal immortality. I hesitate to paraphrase my own poem but I don't mind making some remarks about the background ideas suggested by the two juxtaposed news reports. On one hand, the business about the chicken heart seemed to summarize a view current in our time—that science (as popularly conceived) will solve the problem of evil by reducing it merely to a matter of 'adjustment' in the physical, social, economic, and political spheres. That same day I recalled a remark made in some book by John Strachey that after science had brought 'adjustment' to society it would then solve the problem of evil by bringing man a mortal immortality, by abolishing disease and death. It struck me as somewhat strange that Strachey should equate physical death and evil on a point-to-point basis, and should thereby imply that good and physical survival are identical. As for the report about the volunteers, I was struck by the thought that the same impulse which had made them go to fight Franco had made them go to fight Russia, their recent ally in Spain. That impulse officially manifested itself as a political idea, a solution for the problem of meaning in life in terms of 'adjustment,' but, for the purposes of the poem at least, I take a large component of that impulse to be the *passionate emptiness and tidal lust* of the modern man who, because he cannot find long-range meaning, seeks meaning in mere violence, the violence being what he wants and needs without reference ultimately to the political or other justification he may appeal to. So the two reports set us a paradox: the yearning for mere survival as meaning, and the appetite for death as meaning. As for the poem itself, the *adequate definition of terror* (lacking to the *you* of the poem, the modern man) is that proper sense of the human lot, the sense of limitation and the sense of the necessity for responsible action within that limitation. I should call that sense, when it is applied inclusively, the religious sense—though I don't insist on this. The pageants, the pleasures, the lust for power, the appetite for violence, the devotion to isolated ideas or ideals (isolated because not related to some over-all conception of the human situation) do not suffice. Even blood splashed on the *terrorless intellect* just gives a fizzle—doesn't mean anything. The Moor may have a secret because he is primitive, has a complete vision of his role, his *pride*, which is enough for him—but not enough for us. (That is what the modern devotee of violence is seeking. But it can't help him. He is not a primitive. He has inherited the responsibility to define his role more broadly in a more complicated world.) The *criminal king* at the end of the poem is, of course, Macbeth, who can see Banquo's ghost because he still has the *adequate definition of terror* despite all of his attempts to 'reason' himself out of it. ('A little water clears us of this deed,' Lady Macbeth tells him.) Macbeth still sees meaning, and in a sense *kisses the terror*. But the *you* of the poem sees only an empty chair. *Clarence* is the Duke of Clarence, as he appears in Shakespeare's *Richard III*, the *perjured* Clarence. Our ordinary terrors give us hints of the deeper, fundamental *terror* and we have bad dreams—like Clarence, whose dream of being sluiced off the hatches of a ship prefigured his real death—death by a hole-in-a-corner murder, the body crammed down in the butt of wine and not thrown into the great sea. The *Harry L.* of the poem is a real person, a boy I used to know who tried to get out of his private box, little dissipations, job in drug store, etc. by taking up flying—he had the temperament of the 'volunteers'—but who got killed in a crash in a corn field. The *Piazza* is the Piazza Venezia in Rome, the center of official Rome, the *Wilhelmplatz* is the corresponding thing in Berlin (so I believe—I don't know Berlin). Nazism, Fascism, embody both of the elements of the paradox mentioned above—the glorification of violence and death, the offer of salvation through practical success, adjustment, etc., the 'rational' state. But the boot-heels beating the stones in the Piazza or Wilhelmplatz set up echoes of the same impulses and desires across the Atlantic—all part of the same world, the same modernity, at one level." *Jacob*: See Genesis, xxxii: 24-32. *Onan*: See Genesis, xxxviii: 9.

WATKINS, VERNON. Swansea, Wales, June 27, 1906.

Author's Note: "I feel a poet must develop always from his own work, from his last best, testing at each new moment the integrity of what he has written. I believe it is always a miracle that makes a poem permanent; the first process is to seize all the elements of a vision, the second is the laborious task of giving them their true order and a beautiful shape, and the third is the gift of this luck, or miracle, which makes the poem permanent in the memory."

WHEELWRIGHT, JOHN. Born, Milton, Mass., Sept. 9, 1897; died, Sept. 15, 1940.

Ave Eva. "Hail Eva," a variant of *Ave Maria*. *wheel*: a pun on the poet's name.

WILBUR, RICHARD. New York City, March 1, 1921.

WILLIAMS, OSCAR. New York City, Dec. 29, 1900.

Author's Note: "Most of what we may call 'educated' humanity, while imbued with respect for science, neglects poetry, considering it not compatible with, or, at least, not directed by reality. Now reason is worthy of all respect, and is nowhere more respected than among poets. But any one avenue of reason may well become a rut. No one is more reasonable than the scientist, yet is he not the man who travels an undeviating road with such intentness on his direction that he loses the faculty of turning his head about to see the countryside? The poet knows that life is a whole commingled of reason, instinct and the objective world of *all* phenomena. He keeps it knit together by a spiritual understanding which is above reason, which it supervises through virtue of its ability to comprehend all, rather than one segment or function of life. Reason is a tool and not an accomplishment, a tool that the poet can on occasion use as well as the scientist. Because he is aware of life as a totality, the poet is closer to truth than the scientist and, above all, does surely the right thing at the right time. The scientist discovers, reveals, invents, but is his invention ever produced at the right time in so far as humanity is concerned? If so, it is only by accident and not by insight of the scientist. Did radio appear at the exact moment when it would answer a need in the enrichment of the human mind? Or did atomic power? The one came before public taste was educated in the values of music, or was so trained in psychology to resist advertising, the other just in time to improve killing instead of leisure. No poet would so mistake his timing. The poet perceives, he has the right sensation for his hour and he articulates this sensation. Moreover, it is only when he is right for his time and communicates the essentials of his time that he is a true poet who will communicate to the ages. There is a relationship between the state of society and the poet's poem, there is a relationship between the contemporary poet and the contemporary reader, which is exactly right. If people had learned earlier to expose themselves to poetry, undoubtedly we should not now be accustomed to contemplating the end of the world as imminent. (Thanks to the atomic bomb, today's poets may end the tradition, so they had better be read now.) For the poet is always on the side of life; consistent readers of poetry are also on the side of life. When a poet promulgates the sensuous pleasures he is no less moral than when he paints the hope of heaven, or reveals the truth of tragedy. To be on the side of life is to be moral."

MILK AT THE BOTTOM OF THE SEA. The poem is a symbol of the individual caught in the machine, which is here the house-ship. The snow is a symbol of disunity.

DWARF OF DISINTEGRATION. The dwarf, reminiscent of the Yellow Dwarf of fairy tales, is a symbol of mechanized civilization. *minted*: the money system. *king, queen*: symbols of religion and art.

WILLIAMS, WILLIAM CARLOS. Rutherford, N. J., Sept. 17, 1883.

Author's Note: "Our language in the United States being somewhat anonymous, its designation as 'English' in common parlance but especially in our universities, is misleading. Poetry being purely a matter of form, it would be well formally to designate what language we are using for it here before attempting to make a poem. Having surmounted that difficulty we must next listen to the language in order to discover what formal elements in it are suitable to our purpose. Invention would seem to be the next step. Many attempts will be made before our inventions will be fruitful. Finally something worthy of our language, our history and ourselves may emerge. In the interim every available resource open to us must be investigated—even those elements, traditional to English, which in the past have most led us astray. American poems since Whitman have, generally speaking, retreated steadily from his advanced position. It is to be hoped that with a better understanding of our position and opportunities we may do better."

THE CLOUDS. *Author's Note*: "Part one was written first. At the suggestion of a friend the other parts followed in order. It is a question as between the mind and—those warm clouds which pass for mystery in our lives. The poet is constantly tossed about between one and the other—but in our day the mind claims supremacy, a minority, which seems to rule, from which the various priests peek grinning or thundering or using adding machines."

THE MONSTROUS MARRIAGE. *Author's Note*: "Flesh is weak but love is great—where there is daring. And the mind must sometimes resort to strange devices, guarding the too tender flesh, to protect love's advances. Obviously this is a romantic love story and only 'monstrous' in that all unions between mythological beasts and women were monstrous."

BURNING THE CHRISTMAS GREENS. *Author's Note*: "An occurrence in our home. Certainly no one can escape the conclusion that this poem envisages a rebirth of the 'state' perhaps but certainly of the mind following the destruction of the shibboleths of tradition which often comfort it."

ST. FRANCIS EINSTEIN OF THE DAFFODILS. *Author's Note*: "It is always spring time for the mind when great discoveries are made. Is not Einstein, at the same time, saintly in the purity of his scientific imagining? And if a saint it seems to me that the thorough logic which St. Francis saw as sparrows or donkeys, equally to be loved with whatever other living aspect of the world, would apply equally to Einstein's arrival in the United States a number of years ago to celebrate the event in the season's shapes and colors of that moment."

WYLIE, ELINOR. Born, Somerville, N. Y., Sept. 7, 1885; died, Dec. 16, 1928.

YEATS, WILLIAM BUTLER. Born, Sandymount, Dublin, Ireland, June 13, 1865; died, Jan. 28, 1939.

Commentary: (See pp. 431-32). *A Vision* (London, Macmillan, 1937) * is the prose work in which Yeats sets forth the "celestial geometry" of his human, supernatural, and historical mythology; knowledge of it is necessary for the full understanding of his later poetry. He believed that all men are predominantly objective or subjective in temperament, that their natures are formed by a continual warfare between these two aspects. By "subjective" and "objective" is meant that differentiation commonly made between artists and scientists, between those who refer to an inner validity and those who refer to empirical evidence. The terms Yeats uses, however—"antithetical" and "primary"—are further specialized in meaning. The antithetical man is subjective, introverted, aristocratic, physical, concrete, imagistic; the primary man is objective, extroverted, socialistic, spiritual, abstract, contemplative. "Know Thy Opposite" is the motto of the first; "Know Thyself" that of the second. The antithetical man seeks not himself but the opposite of himself or of his condition; he seeks his *personality*. The primary man seeks to find himself by losing himself in submission to some objective; he seeks himself in outward circumstance, and eradicates his personality to make this possible; he seeks his *character*. The antithetical man achieves and defends his fulfillment by continual conflict with his opposite; the primary man strives to unite himself with other men, to return to the mass.

* All page references, unless otherwise specified, are to this book and this edition.

Both develop by conflict, the antithetical man in constant struggle with the primary aspect of his being, and the primary man in as constant a struggle to escape that part of his nature which is antithetical. Neither development nor consciousness is possible unless a man is suspended between contraries, and the greater the conflict the more intense the consciousness "because only the greatest obstacle that can be contemplated without despair, rouses the will to full intensity." At other times Yeats wrote that "men cannot engender until they are split in two," and again, "We begin to live when we conceive of life as tragedy." As the antithetical part of a man gains in ascendency, the primary diminishes, and vice versa. Thus personality (antithetical) and character (primary) are in constant flux within a man; his temperament at any one point shows what proportions of primary or antithetical are in ascendency.

Both antithetical and primary men are constituted of Four Faculties known as (1) *Will,* (2) *Mask,* (3) *Creative Mind,* and (4) *Body of Fate.* These correspond roughly, (1) to will or drive, (2) to emotion or what is desired, (3) to intellect or innate universal ideas, (4) and to environment and events as apprehended by the bodily and spiritual conditioning of a person. *Will,* a man's normal ego, is closely related to unspecified desire or instinct. In Yeats's words, "When not affected by the other Faculties it has neither emotion, morality, nor intellectual interest, but knows how things are done, how windows open and shut, how roads are crossed, everything that we call utility. It seeks its own continuance." It can attain expression of self-knowledge only by seeking the object of its desire, which is the *Mask. Mask,* then, is the emotional antithesis of the *Will,* the *Will's* idea of good, or of what it ought to be. Both *Will* and *Mask* are antithetical qualities which hover between will and its object of desire, between the Is and the Ought. *Creative Mind* is knowledge of ideas or universals; we might think of it as intellect did not Yeats insist that these ideas are innate. *Body of Fate* is the series of events forced on a man from without; it is not environment outside the consciousness of man, but events or situations as that particular being knows them through all his Four Faculties, a synthesis of heritage and environment. Both *Creative Mind* and *Body of Fate* are primary qualities; together they form a relation between thought and its object of desire, between the Knower and the Known.

A man predominantly antithetical must seek to become what he desires to be, which is the opposite of himself or of his condition, by freeing an emotional image of himself from events by the aid of his creative intelligence (that is, he must seek to deliver his *Mask* from his *Body of Fate* by the help of his *Creative Mind*). If he is predominantly primary, he must seek to find passivity by freeing his intellect from emotional opposition with the aid of his environment: (that is, he must deliver his *Creative Mind* from his *Mask* by the help of his *Body of Fate*). Such development transpires in a continuous struggle, for the two contrasting aspects are always trying to subjugate each other; if the primary takes ascendency in an antithetical person, or the antithetical in a primary, the man is then at odds with his essential nature, ceases to fulfill himself or his aims, and wanders frustrated in *Hodos*

Chamileontos, in the Path of the Chameleon, lacking integrity or Unity of Being. Such a man is not living according to his true personality or character, but has become confused in trying to be and live as someone else; he is said to wear a False and not a True *Mask,* and to develop a False and not a True *Creative Mind.*

(A helpful parallel may be drawn between Yeats' theories and those of Dr. Karl Jung in *Psychological Types,* although publication dates make it impossible for either to have read the other. Antithetical and primary types correspond to Jung's introvert and extrovert types with their "special tendency towards compensation for the onesidedness" of a man's temperament; the Four Faculties to Jung's "fourfold classification corresponding to the functions of thinking, feeling, sensation, and intuition. Each of these functions varies according to the general attitude, and thus eight variants are produced correspondent to the variants of Opposition and Discord.")

Yeats chose the lunar wheel, depicting the progress of the moon from dark to full to dark again in its twenty-eight phases, as a symbol with which to embody and analyze specific types of men representing specific Faculties. The lunar wheel is used because moon and sun are themselves opposed examples of antithetical and primary: the sun, like some ultimate Idea of the Good, phaseless and whole; the "inconstant" moon, like humanity and its history, perpetually waxing and waning. Sunlight reveals the complexities of the world, but moonlight casts a veil, blurring outlines until everything turns in upon itself to seek some inward image and make all Revelation. (Although the moon in its phases of dark and light is a symbol of the interplay between objective and subjective, it will be noted that the moon is itself a subjective or antithetical image, and this indicates the bias of Yeats' system.) Men predominantly primary are found in phases where the dark of the moon is in ascendency, those predominantly antithetical where light is in ascendency. In the relationship between light and dark, antithetical and primary, and in the direction of change, whether toward the full or the dark of the moon, (that is, whether toward more subjectivity or more objectivity) a man's temperament, its vicissitudes, and progress may be known.

In Phase 15, however, that of the full moon and of complete subjectivity where a man and his dream are one, and in Phase 1, that of the dark moon and complete objectivity and the threshold to the supernatural world, no human incarnations are possible because man is an impurity, a complexity of both light and dark, of subjective and objective. As Yeats says, "At Phase 15 mind was completely absorbed by being, but now [Phase 1] body is completely absorbed in its supernatural environment. . . . mind and body take whatever shape, accept whatever image is imprinted upon them . . . are indeed the instruments of supernatural manifestation, the final link between the living and more powerful beings." When a man dies, he leaves the "terrestrial condition," where "the heterogeneous is, and evil, for evil is the strain one upon another of opposites," becomes a spirit, and enters into the realm of the dead, that "condition of air where images have a borrowed life, that of memory or that reflected upon them when they symbolize colours and intensities of fire: the place of shades who are 'in the whirl of those who are fading,' and who cry like those amorous shades in the Japanese play . . . . Awhile they live again those passionate moments, not knowing they are dead, and then they know and may awake or half awake to be our visitors. How is their dream changed as Time drops away and their senses multiply? Does their stature alter, do their eyes grow more brilliant? Certainly the dreams stay the longer, the greater their passion when alive: Helen may still open her chamber door to Paris or watch him from the wall, and know she is dreaming because the nights and days are poignant or the stars unreckonably bright." This is the *Anima Mundi*, the Great Memory, where the dead must relive their memories through six different stages until they are completely purified, reach the "condition of fire," (a progress which usually takes about three generations) and be reborn on earth in whatever form they choose. These dead, "living in their memories," are the instincts, dreams, thoughts, and images of the living, but may also visit man in more corporeal form as mediatorial shades. Memories are related to the dead as dreams are related to the living, and both are interlocked, for they are "living each other's life, dying each other's death." They are both a means of reliving the past and being purified from it: the dead relive their terrestrial condition and the living relive their supernatural condition until both (and they are one spirit) lose all memory and enter into the pure condition of fire. The spirit as a mediatorial shade brings man "again and again to the place of choice, heightening temptation that the choice may be as final as possible, imposing his own lucidity upon events, leading his victim to whatever among works not impossible is the most difficult."

Both the living and the dead undergo perpetual cycles of change, for the spiritual realm also has its admixtures of antithetical and primary, only there the primary and not the antithetical should be in ascendency. The spirits have Four Principles which are the more etherealized counterparts of the Four Faculties, and they are *Husk, Passionate Body, Spirit* and *Celestial Body*. These must be completely purified in six stages during which they become more and more rarified until they disappear and the spirit loses all memory of either his terrestrial or his aerial existences. The first state is called *The Vision of the Blood Kindred*, of short duration, during which the spirit has "a vision of all those bound to us" through more immediate bodily memories. The *second state* is the most extensive and has several interlinked phases called *Meditation, Dreaming Back, Return,* and *Phantasmagoria*. In *Meditation*, "If the *Husk* so persist, the *Spirit* still continues to feel pleasure and pain, remains a fading distortion of living man . . . . If there has been great animal egotism, heightened by some moment of tragedy, the *Husk* may persist for centuries, recalled into a sort of life." The *Spirit* may ultimately find its *Celestial Body* "only after long and perhaps painful dreams of the past, and it is because of such dreams that the second stage is sometimes called the *Dreaming Back*" where "the *Spirit* is compelled to live over and over again the events that had most moved it . . . according to the intensity of the passion that accompanied them. . . . It is from the *Dreaming Back* of the dead . . . that we get the imagery of ordinary sleep." The *Return* "has for its object the *Spirit's* separation from the *Passionate Body,* considered as Nature, and from the *Husk* considered as pleasure and pain." The *Phantasmagoria* "exists to exhaust, not nature, not pain and pleasure, but emotion" for it completes "not only life but imagination." In the third stage, *Shiftings,* the spirit is purified of good and evil; in the fourth, *Marriage* or *Beatitude,* it reaches complete equilibrium; in the fifth, *Purification,* it loses all memory, and finally enters the final state of perfection, *Foreknowledge,* where it "must substitute the next incarnation, as fate has decreed it." During its six stages, the spirit may take various forms. The *final state* of perfection, comparable to Dante's vision of God as a holy fire in the center of the white rose, is called the *Thirteenth Sphere* but cannot be known to man except through the dualities of antithetical and primary, of the twenty-eight lunar phases, or of the twelve signs of the Zodiac. "The *Thirteenth Cone* is a sphere because sufficient to itself, but seen by Man it is a cone. It becomes even conscious of itself as so seen, like some great dancer, the perfect flower of modern culture, dancing some primitive dance and conscious of his or her own life and of the dance." In that ultimate sphere, "all sequence comes to an end, time comes to an end, and the soul puts on the rhythmic or luminous body and contemplates all the events of its memory and every possible impulse in an eternal possession of itself in one single moment. That condition alone is animate, all the rest is phantasy." In his poetry Yeats often uses images of dance and flame to symbolize this condition.

The first shadow of this ultimate Reality, the closest approximation by which it may be symbolized by man, is the Greatest Wheel or Year, (much like the Platonic Wheel of 26,000 years) which revolves once every 26,000 years of modern astronomy associated with the precession of the equinoxes. These are divided into twelve celestial and zodiacal months of some 2,200 years, each of which is known as The Great Wheel or Year which determines in its revolution the rise and fall of civilizations. Every Great Year is further divided into the twenty-eight lunar phases covering various eras of a civilization and thus becomes the archetype of the twenty-eight phases which govern the destiny of human temperament. Primary and antithetical civilizations thus follow one another in cycles of about 2,200 years, "dying each other's death, living each other's life," and undergo the same conflicts and progressions that govern a human being. The primary Babylonian civilization gave way to the antithetical Greek civilization some 2000 years before the birth of Christ, which in turn announced the birth of the primary Christian civilization, now waning and preparing for the coming antithetical civilization. In Yeats' three poems, "Leda and the Swan," "Two Songs from a Play," and "The Second Coming" are announced, respectively, the birth of the Greek, the Christian, and the new civilization to come.

NEWS FOR THE DELPHIC ORACLE. Porphyry, a follower and friend of Plotinus, tells how Amelius, another devotee, consulted the Cumaean Sibyl, the oracle of Apollo at Delphi, in order to learn where Plotinus' soul had gone, and then wrote of what the oracle had said: "Come, Sacred Choir, let us with one breath pour forth the utmost of all song!

Celestial! Man at first, but nearing now the lot of the divine! The bonds of human fate are loosed for you, and, strong of heart, you beat your eager way from out the roaring tumult of this fleshly life to the shores of that wave-washed coast free from the thronging of the guilty, thence to take the grateful path of the sinless soul. Where glows the splendor of God, where Right is throned in the stainless place, far from the wrong that mocks at law, where all is unison and winning tenderness and guileless joy. Where dwell the just Aeacus, and Plato, consecrated power, and fair Pythagoras and all else that form the choir of Immortal Love; there where the heart is ever lifted in joyous festival. O Blessed One, you have fought your many fights, now, crowned with unfading life, your days are with the Ever-Holy!"—*The Essence of Plotinus,* compiled by Grace H. Turnbull, based on a translation by Stephen MacKenna (Copyright, 1934, by Oxford University Press, New York). See also Yeats' poem "The Delphic Oracle Upon Plotinus." In the realm of the spirits between temporal earth and eternal fire recline the uncouth, lecherous, and magnificent heroes, lovers, philosophers of antiquity sighing in memory of passionate, earthly love of which they must be purified. Pythagoras, who had longed for this realm and had once described it, is here; and Plotinus is brought to these shores and sighs like the rest, the salt flakes of the sea still upon his breast, for the spirits are each conducted here on the back of a dolphin. The waters, dancing in immemorial and eternal rhythms, laugh in a detached nonhuman ecstasy as the dolphins finally pitch their burdens off in a bay where the choir of love wades to crown them with sacred laurels. Thetis has stripped Peleus naked, and as he gazes at her, blinded with love and tears, she hears deep in her body the sensuously unbearable music of Pan, and is possessed by an ecstatic vision of bestial lust and copulation. *Niamh* (Nē av), *Oisin* (Ū shéen): Yeats tells their story in his early poem "The Wanderings of Oisin." Niamh is a Sidhe (one of the fairy folk) and the daughter of Aengus, god of youth, beauty, and poetry. Oisin is the hero and poet of the Fenians, a legendary warrior-band of Ireland said to have flourished about 300 A.D. Niamh, symbol of unappeasable desires, takes Oisin away on a journey of several centuries to fairyland, the Happy Otherworld of the ancient Irish. *relive their death*: See seventh and eighth paragraphs of *Commentary,* pp. 548-50. Also first note to "Byzantium," p. 552.

LAPIS LAZULI. On July 6, 1935, Yeats wrote to Dorothy Wellesley: "I notice you have much lapis lazuli; someone has sent me a present of a great piece carved by some Chinese sculptor into the semblance of a mountain with temple, trees, path and an ascetic pupil about to climb the mountain. Ascetic, pupil, hard stone, eternal theme of the sensual east. The heroic cry in the midst of despair. But no, I am wrong, the east has its solutions always and therefore knows nothing of tragedy. It is we, not the east, that must raise the heroic cry." And in a letter a few days later: "To me the supreme aim is an act of faith and reason to make one rejoice in the midst of tragedy." Exactly a year later, out of this gift and these sentiments, he wrote "Lapis Lazuli," on July 25, 1936, and called it "almost the best I have made of recent years."—*Letters On Poetry to Dorothy Wellesley* (Copyright, 1940, by Oxford University Press, Inc., New York). *It*: i.e., " Tragedy." *Callimachus*: Of this Greek artisan Yeats writes: "With Callimachus pure Ionic revives again, as Furtwängler has proved, and upon the only example of his work known to us, a marble chair, a Persian is represented, and may one not discover a Persian symbol in that bronze lamp, shaped like a palm, known to us by a description in Pausanias? But he was an archaistic workman, and those who set him to work brought back public life to an older form. One may see in masters and man a momentary dip into ebbing Asia."—*A Vision*, p. 270. *Every discolouration . . . climb towards*: amid every imagined disaster there are symbols of joy: plum or cherry-branch.

BYZANTIUM. In his Diary for April 30, 1930, Yeats wrote: "Subject for a poem . . . Describe Byzantium as it is in the system towards the end of the first Christian millennium. A walking mummy. Flames at the street corners where the soul is purified, birds of hammered gold singing in the golden trees, in the harbour [sic], offering their backs to the wailing dead that they may carry them to paradise." Yeats depicts the spirits of the dead purifying themselves from the impurities of the living. (Paragraphs seven and eight, pp. 548-50 of *Commentary* bear directly on this poem.) It is night in Byzantium. The impure and unpurged living have withdrawn. The sounds of night have receded, the songs of night-walkers and the sound of the cathedral gong, which is not only a symbol of religious ritual tolling out the living and tolling in the dead, but also of the sensual music of impurities which later torments the sea. A cathedral dome, as of Santa Sophia, is lit by the stars or the moon; that is, during Phase 1 at the dark of the moon, or during Phase 15 when the stars recede in the glare of the full moon. Both are supernatural phases where no human incarnation is possible, for Phase 1 "is a supernatural incarnation, like Phase 15, because there is complete objectivity, and human life cannot be completely objective. At Phase 15 mind was completely absorbed by being, but now body is completely absorbed in its supernatural environment . . . . mind and body take whatever shape, accept whatever image is imprinted upon them . . . are indeed the instruments of supernatural manifestation, the final link between the living and more powerful beings."—*A Vision*, p. 183. In this great silence, the starlit or moonlit dome disdains the fury and mire of human duality. The spirits now begin to float in from the realm of the dead.

Yeats describes various forms which the spirit may take during the second state: "In the *Meditation* it wears the form it had immediately before death; in the *Dreaming Back* and the *Phantasmagoria*, should it appear to the living, it has the form of the dream, in the *Return* the form worn during the event explored, in the *Shiftings* whatever form was most familiar to others during its life; in the *Purification* whatever form it fancies."—*A Vision*, p. 235. The spirits live in Hades; the bobbin, or spindle of Hades, symbolizes the revolving and gyrating motions of the dead undergoing their purifications, and the mummy-cloth is a symbol of their lives revolving on that spindle. Reliving their previous lives in memory, by *Dreaming Back* and in *Return*, they thus unwind a similar natural spindle or gyre of their lives upon earth called the "winding path" so that they may become freed of all natural attributes or memories. Caught in a limbo of air between the Condition of Fire and the terrestrial condition, they receive an inflowing from both directions and must continually shuttle between them. "The inflowing from their mirrored life, who themselves receive it from the Condition of Fire, falls upon the Winding Path called the Path of the Serpent, and that inflowing coming alike to men and to animals is called natural . . . . In so far as a man is like all other men, the inflow finds him upon the winding path, and in so far as he is a saint or sage, upon the straight path." The spirit's "descending power," however, "is neither the winding nor the straight line but zigzag . . . it is the sudden lightning, for all his acts of power are instantaneous. We perceive in the pulsation of the artery, and after slowly decline."—*Essays*, (New York, Macmillan, 1924) pp. 528-529. Spirit now calls to spirit, and the poet, himself a spirit having neither the moisture nor the breath of the living, calls upon the superhuman in whom the dualities of life and death are being simultaneously resolved. The poet then turns to images of hammered golden birds wrought by human hands to such artifice that they seem inhuman and miraculous, identical in symbol to the spirits. In starlight these birds can crow like the cocks of Hades, a suggestion that if the spirits of the dead must recede before the crowing of a terrestrial cock, as legend has it, then the unpurged images of the living must recede before the cocks of Hades or the singing artificial birds of Byzantium. They sing of their singleness and changelessness, and scorn the passing, decaying birds and flowers of nature, the evil and passion of human complexity. The poet then turns again to the spirits of flame who in an agony of fire and trance are trying to die out of the complexities of human fury in a flaming dance which symbolizes the underlining rhythmic, gyrating pulse of creation. Since these spirits are composed of spiritual and not physical fire, no faggot can feed them, no flint can ignite them, no storm can disturb them, and they in turn cannot singe anything. They were once begotten out of the complexities of human blood which they must now purge away; also, like the bird who came out of the fire, spirit can beget spirit, flame beget flame "as one candle takes light from another."

In discussing that aspect of the second stage called *Phantasmagoria*, Yeats writes of those spirits that appear under the impulse of moral and emotional suffering, and recounts the story of a Japanese girl whose ghost tells a priest of a slight sin, which seems great to her because of her exaggerated conscience: "She is surrounded by flames, and though the priest explains that if she but ceased to believe in those flames they would cease to exist, believe she must, and the play ends in an elaborate dance, the dance of her agony."—*A Vision*, p. 231. Yeats reports the following conversation between himself and a spirit from the fifth state, that of *Purification*: "'We have no power,' said an inhabitant of the state, 'except to purify our intention,' and when I asked of what, replied: 'Of complexity.'"—*A Vision*, p. 233. The poet finally turns to a vision of the spirits astraddle on the backs of dolphins plunging in an element of water and who carry them back and forth between the terrestrial condition of the living and the spiritual condition of fire and air. (According to Mrs. Arthur Strong's *Apotheosis and After-Life*, dolphins, in the art of the ancient world, were symbols of the soul and its transit.) The miraculous handiwork of the Byzantium goldsmiths, which are themselves now symbols of spirit, break in upon this spiritual flood, and also, in another sense of "break," transcend, overcome, or defeat the flood. The marble mosaics on the dancing floor of the Emperor's pavement (the Forum of Constantine known as "The Pavement" because of its marble floor), also break in upon and are involved in the dance. Thus the poem ends with a whirling dance broken into fragmented images, images begetting images of both symbol and spirit, and all tossed upon a dolphin-torn and gong-tormented sea of complexity, fury, and blood.

SAILING TO BYZANTIUM. Having come to Byzantium, that imaginary country of the soul's desire, the aged poet says that the natural world is no country for old men, for there sing the real but dying birds, there all is a seething animal world of spawning and passion and decay where all are caught in a sensual music and neglect the deathless artifacts which the soul raises against the failing passions of the body. There an aged man is only a scarecrow unless his soul transform in joy and song every bodily loss into a monument of the soul's magnificence. Therefore he has come to Byzantium and prays that the spirits who live in God may descend to teach him such song until all desires and passions of the dying body may be consumed and gathered up into the indestructible artifice of eternity. He vows never to return to earth as any natural thing, but to take a form of artifice such as that of a Byzantine bird made of gold, which as a symbol of the comparative immortality of art over the things of nature, may sing of passing time timelessly and carelessly. Yeats writes: "I think if I could be given a month of Antiquity and leave to spend it where I chose, I would spend it in Byzantium a little before Justinian opened St. Sophia and closed the Academy of Plato. I think I could find in some little wine-shop some philosophical worker in mosaic who could answer all my questions, the supernatural descending nearer to him than to Plotinus even, for the pride of his delicate skill would make what was an instrument of power to princes and clerics, a murderous madness in the mob, show as a lovely flexible presence like that of a perfect human body. I think that in early Byzantium, maybe never before or since in recorded history, religious, aesthetic and practical life were one, that architect and artificers—though not, it may be, poets, for language had been the instrument of controversy and must have grown abstract—spoke to the multitude and the few alike. The painter, the mosaic worker, the worker in gold and silver, the illuminator of sacred books, were almost impersonal, almost perhaps without the consciousness of individual design, absorbed in their subject-matter and that the vision of a whole people."—*A Vision*, pp. 279-80. *That is* . . .: Hone reports that in hearing the first line of this poem during a rehearsal for a BBC broadcast, Yeats exclaimed: " 'Stop! That is the worst bit of syntax I ever wrote,' and promptly changed it to: 'Old men should quit a country where the young.' "—Hone, *W. B. Yeats* (New York, Macmillan, 1943) p. 488. *Those dying generations* . . . *drowsy Emperor*: Compare these phrases and the relationship between birdsong and the *artifice of eternity* with similar symbols and theme in Keats's "Ode to the Nightingale." *sages*: The spirits of the Thirteenth Cone, who have reached ultimate purification and knowledge, are known as the "Teaching Spirits." *holy fire*: After Yeats had finished this poem, a medium referred him to "'Third book from right bottom shelf, page 48 or 84, study.' On his return to Dublin he sought out the place. The book in question was a complete set of Blake's designs for Dante with numbered plates. On plate 84 he found 'Dante entering the Holy Fire,' on plate 48, 'The Serpent attacking Vanni Fucci.' When he referred to Dante he read that the serpent's sting is burned to ashes and that this symbolizes the 'temporal fire.'"—Hone, *op. cit.*, p. 398. (See also *Rose*, p. 469). *mosaic*: Yeats saw such a mosaic of martyrs on the walls of S. Appolinare Nuovo in Ravenna. *perne*: (1) "to change," after Dr. Perne, Master of Peterhouse, Cambridge, 1554-80, who changed his opinions adroitly. (2) In a note to another poem, Yeats writes that he was told in Ireland that "*pern* was another name for the spool . . . on which thread was wound."—*Collected Poems*, (New York, Macmillan, 1933) p. 449. *gyre*: In describing the cycles of history and human temperament, Yeats uses as a symbol two gyres revolving within each other in opposite directions, one primary and one antithetical, the tip of one on the base of the other, one expanding as the other contracts. *artifice of eternity*: In Yeats' theory, Byzantine civilization flourished in Phase 15, that of the full moon: "Because the 15th Phase can never find direct human expression, being a supernatural incarnation, it impressed upon work and thought an element of strain and artifice, a desire to combine elements which may be incompatible, or which suggest by their combination something supernatural."—*A Vision*, p. 292. *singing masters*: "in the condition of fire is all music and rest."—*Essays*, p. 523. *Stanza IV*: In its third discarnate state, the *Spirit* may "renounce the form of a man and take some shape from the social or religious tradition of its past life, symbolic of its condition."—*A Vision*, p. 224. In the fifth discarnate state, *Purification*, it may take "whatever form it fancies."—*A Vision*, p. 236. Yeats wishes to take the form of a Byzantine bird of hammered gold. *Author's Note*: "I have read somewhere that in the emperor's palace at Byzantium was a tree made of gold and silver, and artificial birds that sang."—*Collected Poems*, p. 450. Yeats writes of a "fifth element," a supernatural one beyond and above the four natural and traditional elements, and calls it "a bird born out of the fire."—*Essays*, p. 512.

TWO SONGS FROM A PLAY. The Virgin Mary stands triumphant over the corpse of Dionysus, the dead Greek civilization, his heart in her hands, while the Muses sing of the coming of the new Christian civilization, which shall also rise and fall with its own wars and its own Quest. Pity and not love is now the ruling force of the new civilization as the coming of Christ in agony and blood destroys the harmony, discipline and tolerance by which the Greeks lived. All things are consumed by what fulfills them: civilizations, love, art, war, all are fed and consumed by man's inflammable heart. See Yeats' drama, *The Resurrection*, (*Collected Plays*, New York, Macmillan, 1935) for which the first two stanzas of this poem are epilogue and the last two prologue. In the play a Syrian, a Hebrew, and a Greek discuss the prob-

ability of Christ's resurrection. In the streets worshippers are crying out
the resurrection of their pagan fertility god, and the Greek sees no reason
why Christ should not arise, for he has long been familiar with such
ritual. Tammuz and Adonis were resurrected before Christ. The Greek
represents the satirical close of his own antithetical civilization, for whom
such resurrection had become part of the imaginative artistry of drama;
Christ will arise, but he will be a lifeless phantom, an image of a
civilized imagination, and no more. For the Hebrew, Christ was but a
good man, "the best who ever lived," who had conceived himself to be
the Saviour whom the prophets had announced. The Hebrew mind
dwelt little on immortality; god existed only for social ordering. The
Syrian, however, who represents the antithetical East, believes in the supernatural and the irrational: "What if there is always something that
lies outside knowledge, outside order? What if at the moment when
knowledge and order seem complete that something appears . . . . What
if the irrational return? What if the circle begin again?" When Christ
does appear, the Greek mocks as the Hebrew kneels, for this, he knows,
is a phantom without flesh or bone or heart. He places his hand over
the figure's side, and shrieks out to feel its heart beating. A new, sorrowful knowledge is born within him as he says: "O Athens, Alexandria, Rome, something has come to destroy you! The heart of a
phantom is beating! Man has begun to die!" *Magnus Annus*: The
Great Year. Its "transition from Pisces to Aries had for generations been
associated with the ornamental death and resurrection of Dionysus.
Near that transition the women wailed him, and night showed the full
moon separating from the constellation Virgo."—*A Vision*, 1st ed., (London, T. W. Laurie, 1926) p. 156. *Another . . . yet*: "A second Tithys
shall then arise, and a second Argo to carry heroes; a second warfare, too,
shall come about, and again a great Achilles be sent to Troy."—Virgil,
Eclogue IV, 31-36. *fabulous darkness*: "The world became Christian,
'that fabulous formless darkness' as it seemed to a philosopher of the fourteenth century, [blotting] out 'every beautiful thing.'"—*A Vision*, p.
278. "Meanwhile the irrational force that would create confusion and uproar as with the cry 'The Babe, the Babe is born'—the women speaking
unknown tongues, the barbers and weavers expounding Divine revelation
with all the vulgarity of their servitude, the tables that move or resound
with raps—but creates a negligible sect."—*A Vision*, p. 277. *pity*: "We
say of Him because His sacrifice was voluntary that He was love itself,
and yet that part of Him which made Christendom was not love but pity,
and not pity for intellectual despair, though the man in Him, being *antithetical* like His age, knew it in the Garden, but *primary* pity, that for
the common lot, man's death, seeing that He raised Lazarus, sickness,
seeing that He healed many, sin [sic], seeing that He died. Love is created and preserved by intellectual analysis, for we love only that which
is unique, and it belongs to contemplation, not to action, for we would
not change that which we love."—*A Vision*, p. 275. It may be remembered that Yeats omitted Wilfred Owen from *The Oxford Book
of Modern Verse* because "pity is not a subject for poetry." *Babylonian
starlight*: The dark of the moon reigns at the beginning of each new civilization. Starlight now takes the place of moonlight, that of the Star of

Bethlehem announcing the new primary civilization, and that of the previous primary Babylonian civilization which had been blotted out by the Greek ascendency and which now returns to domination. In speaking of "Leda and the Swan," the annunciation of Greek civilization, Yeats writes: "when . . . I try to imagine what older civilization that annunciation rejected I can but see bird and woman blotting out some corner of the Babylonian mathematical starlight."—*A Vision*, p. 268. *blood*: used as a primary symbol in many of Yeats' poems: the violence of the transition. *Made all . . . discipline*: "The mind that brought the change, if considered as man only, is a climax of whatever Greek and Roman thought was most a contradiction to its age; but considered as more than man He controlled what Neo-Pythagorean and Stoic could not—irrational force. He could announce the new age, all that had not been thought of, or touched, or seen, because He could substitute for reason, miracle."—*A Vision*, pp. 274-75. *Everything . . . has fed*: "Why are these strange souls born everywhere today with hearts that Christianity, as shaped by history, cannot satisfy? Our love letters wear out our love; no school of painting outlasts its founders, every stroke of the brush exhausts the impulse . . . Why should we believe that religion can never being round its antithesis?"—*Autobiographies*, (New York, Macmillan, 1927) p. 388.

THE TOWER. A Norman tower of the seventeenth century at Ballylee in County Galway, originally part of Lady Gregory's estate. When Yeats bought it a few years before his marriage, it had two attached cottages, one of which was in ruins, a tiny walled garden, a grove of trees across the road, and was encircled by a river. Its four great apartments were connected by a winding stair, the first converted into a study, the second into a bedroom, and the top was never made habitable, "Half dead at the top." Yeats named it Thoor-Ballylee; "Thoor" is Irish for "castle." (See Hone, *op. cit.*, p. 340, for a sepia reproduction). It came to symbolize for Yeats many things: tradition and memory, the Platonic isolation of the artist, intellectual and spiritual asceticism, aloofness, solitude, and finally old age.

Part I. Ben Bulben: mountain in County Sligo. *Muse go pack . . .*: From a young man Yeats had striven to exclude abstractions from his poetry, yet the infusion of philosophic thought in his later poetry strengthened his imagination and technique.

Part II. The poet recalls the many legends and traditions about the tower and its region, stories mainly of people who were daemon-driven, who led passionate, violent, imaginative lives, of those who followed unappeasable desires; he wonders what they may teach him in accepting the discrepancies of old age. *foundations of a house*: In "Dust Hath Closed Helen's Eye" Yeats tells how he visited Ballylee "because Mary Hynes, a beautiful woman whose name is still a wonder by turf fires, died there sixty years ago. . . . An old man brought me a little way from the mill and the castle . . . and he said, 'That is the little old foundation of the house, but most of it is taken for building wall. . . . They say she was the handsomest girl in Ireland.'"—*Early Poems and Stories*, (New York, Macmillan, 1925) p. 160. *Mrs. French: Author's Note*: "Mrs. French lived in Peterswell in the eighteenth century and was related to Sir Jonah Barrington, who described the incident of the ears and the trouble that came of it."—*Collected Poems*, p. 451. *Stanzas 3-5*: Mary Hynes, and Raftery, the blind rambling poet who sang her praises. An old weaver told Yeats: "'Mary Hynes was the most beautiful thing ever made. . . . There was a lot of men up beyond Kilbecanty one night sitting together drinking, and talking of her, and one of them got up there in the morning.'"—*Early Poems and Stories*, p. 169. Yeats thinks of Hynes and Raftery as "perfect symbols of the sorrow of beauty and the magnificence and penury of dreams." *moon and sunlight*: symbols respectively of imagination and reality, antithetical and primary. *if I triumph*: in the exclusive reality of the imagination. *Hanrahan*: a daemon-driven schoolmaster and poet of whom Yeats has written. One Samhain Eve, in a barn where village men are sitting and drinking, he receives a message from his sweetheart, Mary Lavelle, informing him that her mother has died and that he is to claim her and the property before a month goes by. At the door he is halted by a stranger, an old man who moves a pack of cards and murmurs "Spades and Diamonds, Courage and Power; Clubs and Hearts, Knowledge and Pleasure." Under the hypnotic spell of the stranger, he stays to play at cards, until the room seems to darken and the cards in the stranger's hands turn into a hare and a pursuing pack of hounds. Hanrahan runs after the pack, and after a long chase, loses it, falls to sleep, and on awakening finds himself near a house where he discovers a beautiful woman sleeping on a throne, surrounded by four grey women who carry a cauldron, a great stone, a long spear, and a sword, which they proclaim to be Pleasure, Power, Courage, and Knowledge. He knows that something is expected of him, but as he remains silent the women regretfully say that the beautiful lady must sleep because Hanrahan is afraid, weak, and does not want them. He falls asleep again, awakes, and begins a year's distracted wandering, memoriless. On Samhain Eve, as he is playing cards with another group of young men, he suddenly remembers the message his sweetheart sent him, but when he runs to her home, he finds it in ruins, and learns that she has married some laboring man and gone to the city. The hounds and hare symbolize not only sexual desire, but also the pursuit of unappeasable desire which drives the poet from true fulfillment of earth, from possessing his Mary Lavelle, and which brings him to a vision of the Sleeping Beauty although he does not have the courage, power, pleasure or knowledge to awaken and possess her. Once he has seen a vision of her, however, he is "touched" and goes out of his wits, for she belongs to the Sidhe, the faery folk.—*Ibid.*, p. 397-412. *bawn*: Irish for "barn." *Stanzas 8-9*: *Author's Note*: "The ghosts have been seen at their game of dice in what is now my bedroom, and the old bankrupt man lived about a hundred years ago. According to one legend he could only leave the Castle upon a Sunday because of his creditors, and according to another he hid in the secret passage."—*Collected Poems*, p. 451. *Great Memory*: the great storehouse of nature's memory where every thought and action ever conceived remains, and from which come dreams, images, instincts. *necessitous . . . man*: the "bankrupt master." *blind . . . celebrant*: Raftery. *red man*: Hanrahan. *wench*: Mary Hynes. *Old lecher*: Since he had lost both possible and impossible beauty and love, Hanrahan sought to console himself with many women. Yeats then declares that if a man in his imagination dwells most on the lost ideal, (the *woman lost*) he turns away from the great labyrinth of the world, but that if he ever remembers it, as Hanrahan finally remembered Mary Lavelle, he swoons with the weight of attainable desire. In another story, "The Twisting of the Rope," the faery folk say of Hanrahan: "It is a pity for him that he refuses the call of the daughters of the Sidhe, for he will find no comfort in the love of the women of the earth to the end of life and time, and the cold of the grave is in his heart forever." —*Early Poems and Stories*, p. 423.

Part III. the fountain leap: In describing Shelley's *Prometheus Unbound*, Yeats writes: "at the end of things Prometheus and Asia are to live amid a happy world in a cave where a fountain 'leaps with an awakening sound'"; the fountain symbolizes generation and the source of life. *drop their cast*: the fisherman at dawn became for Yeats a symbol of the poet who in old age has stripped away all superfluities and in the "study of the soul" can perhaps write "one/ Poem maybe as cold/ And passionate as the dawn." Henry *Grattan*: (1746-1820), Irish statesman and upholder of Irish Independence in the English Parliament. *swan*: Author's Note: "In the passage about the Swan in Part III I have unconsciously echoed one of the loveliest lyrics of our time—Mr. Sturge Moore's 'Dying Swan.' I often recited it during an American tour, which explains the theft."—*Collected Poems*, p. 451. *I mock…Paradise*: "Aristotle and Plato end creative system—to die into the truth is still to die—and formula begins."—*A Vision*, p. 271. The thought that man has created everything out of his own dreaming and is not simply a shadow of Platonic Forms is a recurrent theme in Yeats. In a note to this section he corrects his interpretation of the two philosophers: "When I wrote the lines about Plato and Plotinus I forgot that it is something in our own eyes that makes us see them as all transcendence. Has not Plotinus written: 'Let every soul recall, then, at the outset the truth that the soul is the author of all living things, that it has breathed the life into them all, whatever is nourished by earth and sea, all the creatures of the air, the divine stars in the sky; it is the maker of the sun; itself formed and ordered this vast heaven and conducts all that rhythmic motion—and it is a principle distinct from all these to which it gives law and movement and life, for they gather or dissolve as soul brings them life or abandons them, but soul, since it never can abandon itself, is of 'eternal being.'" —*Collected Poems*, p. 452. *As at … wild nest*: symbol of the instinctive life. The study of how birds build their nests instinctively, Yeats thought, could teach us something about the great storehouse of nature's memory from which all dream and instinct come; (see *A Vision*, pp. 45-49). *this sedentary trade*: all his life Yeats admired his opposites: predatory men of action. *make my soul*: See "Sailing to Byzantium," p. 32.

NINETEEN HUNDRED AND NINETEEN. Hone writes of "Yeats' appearance at the Oxford Union to denounce the exploits of the expert gunmen, Black and Tan Auxiliaries, whom the British government had let loose upon Ireland to trace down the militants of the Irish Republican Army and terrorize the civil population. The poem 'Nineteen Hundred and Nineteen' was suggested by Lady Gregory's account of some of the horrors at Gort."—Hone, *op. cit.*, p. 352. The poet sees in bitterness that all law and goodness which he and his friends had tried to bring about have crumbled in hatred and war. All, materialist and idealist alike, are whirled about in the Platonic Year. The poet is left communing with the cold snows of his own solitary dream. Even his works, which are also doomed to ultimate destruction, mar the perfecting of the soul in solitude.

Part I. circle of the moon: See *Commentary*, p. 548. *ivories*: the chryselphantine statues of Zeus and Athena plundered in time of war.

Part II. Loie Fuller: An American dancer from Chicago, famous in Paris as "La Loié" for "The Serpentine Dance" and "Ballet of Light." Her specialty was to swirl draperies, tulle or gauze, under colored lights, into the form of flame or flower. *Platonic Year*: See *Commentary*, p. 550.

Part III. moralist or mythological poet: Socrates in Plato's *Phaedo*: "Will you not allow that I have as much of the spirit of prophecy in me as the swans? For they, when they perceive that they must die, having sung all their life long, do then sing more lustily than ever, rejoicing in the thought that they are about to go away to the god whose ministers they are. But men, because they are themselves afraid of death, slanderously affirm to the swans that they sing a lament at the last. . . . But because they are sacred to Apollo, they have a gift of prophecy, and anticipate the good things of another world; wherefore they sing and rejoice on that day more than ever they did before." *ancient habit sticks*: See *Commentary*, pp. 548-50.

Part VI. Author's Note: "The country people see at times certain apparitions whom they name now 'fallen angels,' now 'ancient inhabitants of the country,' and describe as riding at whiles 'with flowers upon the heads of the horses.' I have assumed in the sixth poem that these horsemen, now that the times worsen, give way to worse. My last symbol, Robert Artisson, was an evil spirit much run after in Kelkenny at the start of the fourteenth century. Are not those who travel in the whirling dust also in the Platonic Year?"—*Collected Poems*, p. 453. Dame Alice Kyteler was accused of dealings in magic and brought before an Inquisition held in Kilkenny in 1324. Robert Artisson was her incubus. *Herodias' daughters*: See Arthur Symons' poem, "The Dance of the Daughters Herodias."

YOUNG, MARGUERITE. Ind., 1910.

Addenda

To Bridge's Poor Poll, p. 447. *in peace . . . understanding*: see 434, *Shantih*. Throughout his poem Bridges seems to be mocking the polylingual style of *The Waste Land*. *dans la . . .*: "In the profound terror of everlasting night."—A line from Saint-Amant which Racine altered to

"C'etait pendant l'horreur d'une profonde nuit" ("It was during the horror of a profound night") in his *Athalie*, II, v. εἴθ' ὤφελ' . . .: "Would that the ship Argos had never sailed."—Euripides, *Medea*, line 1. Prologue spoken by the aged nurse of Medea, expressing the wish that Medea and Jason had never met. *absolument* . . .: from Francis Jammes. *Tu, Polle* . . .: "You, Poll, know nothing of these things, and cannot know."—Martial, Epigrams, LVII. In the original, the proper name is "Sparsus." *piis* . . .: "A happy escape may be offered to the righteous, if my prophecy be heeded."—Horace, Odes, XVI, 66. The original reads *datur* for *detur*.

To Pound's CANTO XLV. *Usura*: "usury." *harpes et luthes*: "harps and flutes."—François Villon,—E. P. *Gonzaga*: Francesco, Marquis of Mantua, who married Isabella d'Este. *Pietro Lombardo*: 1445?-1530? Venetian sculptor and architect. *Duccio*: Duccio di Buoninsegna, 1255-1319, first great painter of the Sienese School. *Pier della Francesca*: 1415?-1492, Umbrian painter. *Zuan Bellin'*: Giovanni Bellini, 1426?-1516?, painter of the Venetian School. *'La Calunnia'*: "The Calumny." *Angelico*: Giovanni da Fiesole, 1387-1455, known as Fra Angelico, Florentine School. *Ambrogio Praedis*: Giovanni Ambrogio de Predis, Italian painter born in Milan, 1508. *Adamo me fecit*: "Adam created me." Adam was the architect and sculptor of Zeno Maggiore, a basilica in Verona of the 11-12th century. *St. Trophime*: cathedral in Arles, France, rebuilt in 1152-80. *Saint Hilaire*: abbey-church in Poitiers, France, founded before the 6th century. *Memling*: Hans, Flemish painter, 1430-1495. CONTRA NATURAM: "contrary to nature," a phrase common to all Catholic theologians of the Renaissance. *Eleusis*: center of ancient Greek religious rituals.

INDEX OF TITLES

INDEX OF FIRST LINES

Hopkins

421
424
428
441
442

Geo Barker